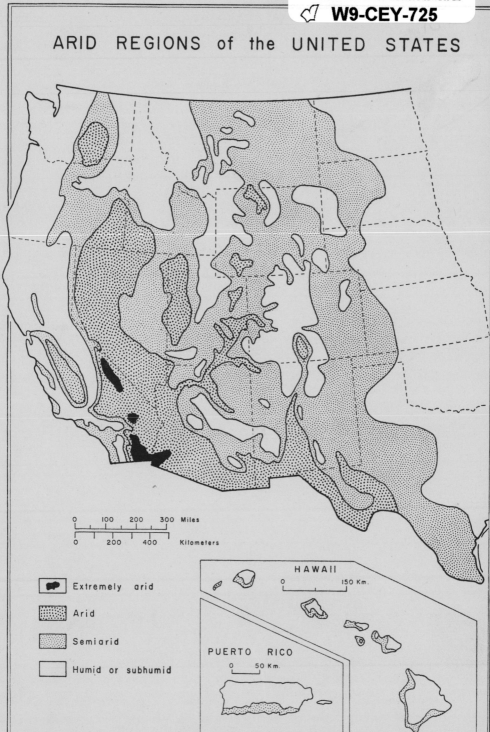

ARID REGIONS of the UNITED STATES

Scale:
0 100 200 300 Miles
0 200 400 Kilometers

Legend:
- ■ Extremely arid
- ▨ Arid
- ░ Semiarid
- □ Humid or subhumid

HAWAII
0 150 Km.

PUERTO RICO
0 50 Km.

Tumbling Russian thistles (*Salsola kali*) have piled up against this lonely barbed-wire fence near Winslow in northern Arizona. Behind the fence, the once rich rangeland now is overgrazed and badly wind eroded. The annual mean precipitation at Winslow, elevation 4850 feet (1478 meters) is a fraction more than 8 inches (200 millimeters). The Hopi Indians, whose reservation is nearby, call the troublesome *Salsola,* "the white man's plant." (Courtesy Robert R. Humphrey, University of Arizona)

Compiled by the Committee on
Desert and Arid Zones Research of the
American Association for the Advancement of Science

Cartography by ALBERT W. SMITH

CARLE HODGE, *Editor*

PETER C. DUISBERG, *Associate Editor*

ARIDITY and MAN

The Challenge of the Arid Lands in the United States

Publication No. 74

AMERICAN ASSOCIATION FOR THE ADVANCEMENT OF SCIENCE

WASHINGTON, D.C.   1963

Library of Congress Catalog Card Number 63-22003

Printed in the United States of America

The Horn-Shafer Company

Baltimore, Maryland

Foreword

A seed was planted in the arid southwestern soil at El Paso, Texas, in 1951: a symposium on the "Potentialities of Desert and Arid Lands," which was held during the annual meeting of the Southwestern and Rocky Mountain Division of the American Association for the Advancement of Science, in session that year at Texas Western College. At that time, renewed interest in arid-lands research was spreading around the world, and particularly in the places where water, always a limiting factor, has become a resource that is especially imperiled by the burgeoning of population. Less than a year earlier, the United Nations Educational, Scientific, and Cultural Organization (UNESCO) had formed its Advisory Committee on Arid Zone Research.

The El Paso program was a direct response to this interest, and from the symposium grew the division's Committee on Desert and Arid Zones Research (CODAZR). As Terah L. Smiley, the present committee chairman, has pointed out, the group was "fortunate in having been created prior to the last 10 years, which have seen unprecedented population growth in the Southwest. It is probably the only group to have had such an opportunity to observe closely the beginnings of the arid-lands technologic development from the point of view of actual residents as well as scientists."

With the cooperation of the national AAAS, UNESCO, and other organizations, the committee conceived and helped to carry through the historic interdisciplinary international meetings on the future of arid lands, held in 1955 in Albuquerque and Socorro, New Mexico. Six regional and two national symposiums also have been arranged since then by the committee. When UNESCO began to plan the first conference devoted to research on the Latin American arid lands, in Buenos Aires in September 1963, CODAZR was asked to serve as the conference coordinating unit in the United States and was expanded into a national committee for this purpose.

One contribution that CODAZR chose to make to the conference in Argentina was a book that, hopefully, would sum up the United States experience in the arid lands. *Aridity and Man* is the result.

The aim was to produce an interdisciplinary volume that would be of value, not only to researchers, but also to scientific administrators and governmental leaders. It was impossible, therefore, to consider any single subject as thoroughly as we would have liked to do. Both the English system and the metric system of weights and measures have been used in an effort to facilitate translation and, at the same time, make the publication widely comprehensible. For the same reasons, the scientific names of many plants and animals have been inserted in parentheses after the common names.

In order to have the Spanish copies available for the Buenos Aires meeting, it was necessary that the volume be planned, written, edited, translated, and printed in Spanish within a year. This was made possible by financial support from the Agency for International Development and a grant (NSF-G25199) from the National Science Foundation.

Obviously, this could not have been accomplished without the tremendous team effort that made the project unusual. *Aridity and Man* is the product of 74 scientists in 14 states and the District of Columbia, most of them writing under the handicap of a severe deadline. In one way or another, the assistance of many other people was needed. Regrettably, not all of them can be singled out for proper credit.

However, CODAZR is especially indebted to President Richard A. Harvill, of the University of Arizona, for making editorial office space and other facilities available at his institution. I wish to express my personal gratitude to William R. Mathews, editor and publisher of *The Arizona Daily Star,* for granting the leave of absence that allowed me to devote full time to this book.

Although their names do not appear in the table of contents, the contributions of several other persons were essential. At least once a day for more than a year, Smiley found himself heavily involved in the problems of the publication. The efforts on its behalf by Dael Wolfle, executive officer of the AAAS, were considerably beyond the call of duty.

In the Department of Geography at the University of Colorado,

a team of cartographers directed by Albert W. Smith worked tire-
lessly to complete the maps and charts on schedule.

Finally, there were two workers without whose wise and skilled
assistance *Aridity and Man* probably would not have met its deadline. They were Charlotte Meeting Phillips, general editor of the
AAAS symposium volumes, and Eileen B. Ferguson, whose value
to the project strongly belied her modest title of editorial secretary.

CARLE HODGE

Tucson, Arizona
July 1963

Preface

Lands of Little Water

"The soil is very fertile for maize, cotton, and for everything sown in it, as it is a temperate land. The natives cultivate sandy places without difficulty because they carefully guard the moisture from the snow.

"At this place this river is surrounded by an abundance of grape-vines, many walnut and other trees . . . . All this land is rather warm than cold . . . . We saw plants of natural flax similar to that of Spain and numerous prickly pears."*

These are words that could have been written any place, any time in an arid land. They are, in fact, the words of Diego Pérez de Luxán in his journal concerning the expedition into New Mexico led by Antonio de Espejo in 1582. There is nothing very remarkable about what Luxán wrote except perhaps the timelessness of the problem he recognized.

Again and again in the writings of explorers visiting for the first time peoples who have accommodated themselves to aridity, there appears the key idea that they have used with care the limited water supply. We in the machine age, so proud of what we call progress, either have yet to learn this lesson or, step by step and mistake by mistake, have to relearn what our ancient forebears once knew.

The distinguished naturalist, Joseph Wood Krutch, in his percep-

___
* D. Pérez de Luxán, *Expedition into New Mexico Made by Antonio de Espejo, 1582–1583, as Revealed in the Journal of Diego Pérez de Luxán, a Member of the Party,* G. P. Hammond and A. Rey, Translators (The Quivira Society, Los Angeles, Calif., 1929), pp. 100 and 106.

tive book, *The Voice of the Desert,* said that the biota of an arid land has three principal ways of meeting the water problem: by economizing, by storing, and by lying low. As he points out, the kangaroo rat (*Dipodomys* spp.) has even one more: it makes its own. With all these teachers before us, including the kangaroo rat, modern man is not yet studying the lessons with diligence. Indeed, the primitive cultures are teachers. In very practical terms, early man learned through eons of evolution. The native biota of an arid country can teach, for those who will learn to read, by what it has written on the landscape. With the tools of the ecologic and physiologic sciences available to us now, we should be able to read far more easily those lessons of the native biota than did our primitive forebears, but still we will not read.

Of the possibilities that Krutch learned from the plants and animals, modern civilization appears to know only storage. Storage to us has come to mean only surface storage in reservoirs, the engineering aspects of which we have developed to a high degree. But the more subtle ways of handling the water problem seem, for the most part, to be beyond us.

The second little sermon that is implied in Luxán's journal of 1582 is contained in the words, "similar to that of Spain." In addition to the arid lands of the southwestern United States, I have seen the arid plains of Mancha in New Castile, the Golodnaya Steppe of Uzbekistan, the dry hills of Peloponnesus, and the rocky crags of Baluchistan. I know, therefore, that I have seen in principle Chile, Libya, the Fertile Crescent, and many others. The characteristics displayed in one will be found, with minor variation, in the other arid lands of the world. This means, then, that the peoples in the arid zones, all over the world, have learned to make the kinds of adjustments that we in the United States at least are still trying to make, compatible with our particular type of civilization.

That some progress is being made, however, might be inferred from the fact that a group of studious and dedicated men, who know a variety of things about the problems of aridity, asked themselves what they could bring from the United States as a useful contribution to the UNESCO symposium on arid-zones research in Latin America in the fall of 1963. This book grew from their answer. Interestingly, the scientists judge that their best contribution might be to analyze the American experience in developing the arid portion of this country, with particular emphasis on places where the United States appears to have failed. There are, of course, successes to be reported also, but these scientists put particular emphasis on the places where we have failed to read well enough the lessons of our native biota and of our progenitors. The fact that this group of observant men can see the failures of our society in itself means progress.

This spirit of self-analysis and constructive criticism may not shine clearly through a book that, perforce, had to be written by a group of individuals rather than by a single author, but it certainly was the spirit in which this volume first was conceived and planned. It is the hope of the authors and of their interested colleagues that, being a review of our experience in the United States in developing and using our arid lands, others elsewhere in the world can profit by our example.

There is one further idea that will not, because of the nature of this volume, shine through as clearly as many of us would like to see it. Perhaps in the present context this idea would not appropriately be emphasized, but, being acquainted with most of the authors of these separate chapters, I know that it is important in the thinking of each one of them. Deserts, like all other natural habitats, have a variety of unique living and inanimate forms. Their very uniqueness makes them valuable. But the interrelationship between these forms and their environments is, because of the nature of aridity, poised in an even more delicate balance than that which characterizes other physiographic and climatic types. Many of these unique forms are as delicate as the equilibrium they maintain with the rest of the physical world. They can easily be lost, destroyed, or overlooked.

The unique parts of the physical world generally tend also to be scarce, and, partly because they are scarce, they are both valueless and invaluable. The development of resources that have potential monetary value needs no urging and will generally proceed in keeping with changes in the economic controls of supply and demand. But the features of any land that are monetarily valueless and are esthetically invaluable will soon enough be pushed over by the bulldozer of civilization, unless prior steps have been taken to recognize their worth and to protect them from either exploitation or ruination.

In the many lands where people still must fight for the very necessities of life, there is little room for protection of purely esthetic
values. But the time comes soon enough, with population expansion, when some at least will look back and wish that thought had
been given to the protection of rare species, unique history, and
exceptional scenery. This lesson, particularly, is one that is mani-
festly applicable to the arid zones.

LUNA B. LEOPOLD

Contributors

ARDEN A. BALTENSPERGER, Professor of Agronomy and Agronomist in the Agricultural Experiment Station, University of Arizona, Tucson [cultivated crops]

GORDON L. BENDER, Professor of Zoology, Arizona State University, Tempe [Chapter 11]

IVEN BENNETT, Chief, Desert and Tropical Section, Regional Environments Branch, Earth Sciences Division, Quartermaster Research and Engineering Center, U.S. Army, Natick, Massachusetts [insolation]

ROSHAN B. BHAPPU, Metallurgist, New Mexico Bureau of Mines and Mineral Resources, New Mexico Institute of Mining and Technology, Socorro [wet processing]

MELVIN L. BLANC, Southwest Area Climatologist, Weather Bureau, U.S. Department of Commerce, Tempe, Arizona [aridity causes]

THADIS W. BOX, Associate Professor of Range Management, Texas Technological College, Lubbock [range management]

MARX BROOK, Professor of Physics and Senior Physicist, New Mexico Institute of Mining and Technology, Socorro [thunderstorms]

KAY R. BROWER, Associate Professor of Chemistry, New Mexico Institute of Mining and Technology, Socorro [solar energy]

RUSSELL H. BROWN, Hydraulic Engineer (Research), Water Resources Division, Geological Survey, U.S. Department of the Interior, Phoenix, Arizona [Chapter 6]

HELEN L. CANNON, Geochemist, Branch of Geochemical Census, Geological Survey, U.S. Department of the Interior, Denver, Colorado [botanical prospecting]

IRA G. CLARK, Professor of History, New Mexico State University, University Park [Chapter 4]

The subject of each person's contribution is given in square brackets at the end of the entry.

MARION CLAWSON, Director, Land Use and Management Program, Resources for the Future, Inc., Washington, D.C. [Chapter 15]

BRUCE F. CURTIS, Professor of Geology and Chairman of the Department, University of Colorado, Boulder [petroleum; wind energy]

ARTHUR V. DODD, Meteorologist, Earth Sciences Division, Quartermaster Research and Engineering Center, U.S. Army, Natick, Massachusetts [Yuma microclimates]

EDWARD J. DORTIGNAC, Chief, Branch of Water Resource Management, Division of Watershed Management, Forest Service, U.S. Department of Agriculture, Washington, D.C. [Rio Puerco]

HAROLD E. DREGNE, Professor of Soils, New Mexico State University, University Park [Chapter 8]

PETER C. DUISBERG, Arid Lands Consultant, El Paso, Texas [associate editor; Chapter 16]

PAUL C. EKERN, Soil Physicist, Pineapple Research Institute of Hawaii, Honolulu [dew; fog drip; microclimate modification]

ALLEN F. FLANDERS, Hydrologic Services Division, Weather Bureau, U.S. Department of Commerce, Washington, D.C. [flash-flood warning]

JOEL E. FLETCHER, Research Investigations Leader, Watershed Engineering, Soil and Water Conservation Research Division, Agricultural Research Service, U.S. Department of Agriculture, Boise, Idaho [Chapter 10]

MAURICE C. FUERSTENAU, Associate Metallurgist, New Mexico Bureau of Mines and Mineral Resources, New Mexico Institute of Mining and Technology, Socorro [wet processing]

J. L. GARDNER, Botanist, Agricultural Research Service, U.S. Department of Agriculture, Tucson, Arizona [Chapter 9]

MORRIS E. GARNSEY, Professor of Economics and Chairman of the Department, University of Colorado, Boulder [Chapter 13]

HOWARD S. GENTRY, Botanist, New Crops Research Branch, Agricultural Research Service, U.S. Department of Agriculture, Beltsville, Maryland [new plant uses]

NORRIS W. GILBERT, Research Agronomist, Crops Research Division, Agricultural Research Service, U.S. Department of Agriculture, Mesa, Arizona [canaigre]

WARREN A. HALL, Associate Professor of Engineering and Director of the Water Resources Center (Statewide), University of California, Los Angeles [Los Angeles]

STAFFORD C. HAPP, Chief, Production Services Branch, Production Evaluation Division, U.S. Atomic Energy Commission, Grand Junction, Colorado [uranium]

JOHN W. HARSHBARGER, Professor of Geology and Head of the Department, University of Arizona, Tucson [Chapter 6]

JOHN HAY, Retired Water Engineer, Tucson, Arizona [upper Rio Grande]

DAVID M. HERSHFIELD, Research Meteorologist, Hydrograph Laboratory, Soil and Water Conservation Research Division, Agricultural Research Service, U.S. Department of Agriculture, Beltsville, Maryland [precipitation]

LESLIE HEWES, Professor of Geography and Chairman of the Department, University of Nebraska, Lincoln [short-grass Plains]

CARLE HODGE, Editor, *Arid Lands Research Newsletter* (CODAZR) ; and Science Editor, *The Arizona Daily Star* [editor; Chapter 1]

HAROLD A. HOFFMEISTER, Professor of Geography, University of Colorado, Boulder [Rocky Mountain and Sacramento Mountain region]

FRANK E. HOUGHTON, State Climatologist, Weather Bureau, U.S. Department of Commerce, Albuquerque, New Mexico [Weather Bureau records and research]

LYMAN C. HUFF, Geochemist, Branch of Geochemical Exploration, Geological Survey, U.S. Department of the Interior, Denver Colorado [geochemical exploration]

EDGAR A. IMHOFF, Resources Planner, State Planning Office, State of New Mexico, Santa Fe [Embudo]

QUENTIN A. JONES, Botanist, New Crops Research Branch, Crops Research Division, Agricultural Research Service, U.S. Department of Agriculture, Beltsville, Maryland [new plant uses]

PAUL R. JULIAN, High Altitude Observatory, Boulder, Colorado [long-range prediction]

HAROLD M. KAUTZ, Head, Engineering and Watershed Planning Unit, Soil Conservation Service, U.S. Department of Agriculture, Upper Darby, Pennsylvania [Sandstone Creek]

FRANK E. KOTTLOWSKI, Economic Geologist, New Mexico Bureau of Mines and Mineral Resources, New Mexico Institute of Mining and Technology, Socorro [coal; saline deposits]

CARL F. KRAENZEL, Professor of Rural Sociology, Montana State College, Bozeman [Great Plains]

FRITZ L. KRAMER, Associate Professor of Geography and Director of the College Museum, Colorado College, Colorado Springs [sagebrush zone]

C. W. LAURITZEN, Project Supervisor, Agricultural Research Service, U.S. Department of Agriculture, Logan, Utah [irrigation]

DOUGLAS H. K. LEE, Chief, Occupational Health Research and Training Facility, Public Health Service, U.S. Department of Health, Education and Welfare, Cincinnati, Ohio [Chapter 12]

LUNA B. LEOPOLD, Chief Hydraulic Engineer, Geological Survey, U.S. Department of the Interior, Washington, D.C. [Preface]

RICHARD F. LOGAN, Professor of Geography, University of California, Los Angeles [Pacific valleys; creosotebush zone]

JAMES A. McCLEARY, Professor of Botany, Orange State College, Fullerton, California [native plants]

ANDREW L. McCOMB, Professor of Watershed Management, Head of the Department, and Watershed Specialist in the Agricultural Experiment Station, University of Arizona, Tucson [Chapter 10]

RALPH M. McGEHEE, Associate Professor of Mathematics and Research Mathematician, Research and Development Division, New Mexico Institute of Mining and Technology, Socorro [Chapter 5]

WILLIAM G. McGINNIES, Professor of Dendrochronology and Director of the Laboratory of Tree-Ring Research, University of Arizona, Tucson [Chapter 10; dendrochronology]

JAMES R. McNITT, Assistant Mining Geologist, Division of Mines and Geology, The Resources Agency of California, Department of Conservation, San Francisco [geothermal energy]

DONALD D. MacPHAIL, Associate Professor of Geography and Chairman of the Department, University of Colorado, Boulder [Chapter 2]

DEAN E. MANN, Senior Staff, The Brookings Institution, Washington, D.C. [Chapter 14]

PAUL S. MARTIN, Associate Professor of Geochronology, University of Arizona, Tucson [palynology]

PEVERIL MEIGS, Chief, Earth Sciences Division, Quartermaster Research and Engineering Center, U.S. Army, Natick, Massachusetts [arid United States climates]

DAVID MITCHELL, Professor of Metallurgical and Mining Engineering, New Mexico Institute of Mining and Technology, Socorro [dry processing]

J. MURRAY MITCHELL, JR., Investigations Branch, Climatology, Weather Bureau, U.S. Department of Commerce, Washington, D.C. [microclimatology; prediction techniques]

GALE MONSON, Assistant Chief, Section of Public Use, Branch of Wildlife Refuges, Bureau of Sport Fisheries and Wildlife, U.S. Department of the Interior, Washington, D.C. [game research]

JEROME NAMIAS, Chief, Extended Forecast Branch, Weather Bureau, U.S. Department of Commerce, Washington, D.C. [long-range prediction]

TOR J. NORDENSON, Hydrologic Services Division, Weather Bureau, U.S. Department of Commerce, Washington, D.C. [flash-flood warning]

JOHN R. RITER, Chief Development Engineer, Bureau of Reclamation, U.S. Department of the Interior, Denver, Colorado [water power]

CARL B. ROUBICEK, Professor of Animal Science and Animal Scientist in the Agricultural Experiment Station, University of Arizona, Tucson [acclimatization of livestock]

JOSEPH A. SCHUFLE, Professor of Chemistry, New Mexico Institute of Mining and Technology, Socorro [Chapter 7]

WILLIAM D. SELLERS, Professor of Meteorology and Associate Meteorologist, Institute of Atmospheric Physics, University of Arizona, Tucson [Arizona climatology]

HERBERT E. SKIBITZKE, Research Mathematician, Water Resources Division, Geological Survey, U.S. Department of the Interior, and Lecturer in Hydrology, University of Arizona, Tucson [Chapter 6]

TERAH L. SMILEY, Professor of Geochronology and Director of the Geochronology Laboratories, University of Arizona, Tucson [chairman of editorial board]

ALBERT W. SMITH, Associate Professor of Geography, University of Colorado, Boulder [cartography]

EDWARD C. STONE, Associate Professor of Forestry, University of California, Berkeley [dew]

JOHN M. STREET, Assistant Professor of Geography, University of Hawaii, Honolulu [tropical arid lands]

HAROLD E. THOMAS, Geologist, Ground Water Branch, Geological Survey, U.S. Department of the Interior, Menlo Park, California [Central Valley]

ROBERT H. WEBER, Economic Geologist, New Mexico Bureau of Mines and Mineral Resources, New Mexico Institute of Mining and Technology, Socorro [miscellaneous minerals]

ANDREW W. WILSON, Professor of Geography and Area Development, University of Arizona, Tucson [Tucson]

NATHANIEL WOLLMAN, Professor of Economics and Chairman of the Department, University of New Mexico, Albuquerque [Chapter 13]

RICHARD B. WOODBURY, Associate Professor of Anthropology, University of Arizona, Tucson [Chapter 3]

Contents

Aridity and Man: An Interpretive Summary

CARLE HODGE

During the 1950's, a research team visited an Arizona ranch through which an intermittent river runs. The streambed, which is dry except during summer seasons of rain, was densely thicketed with saltcedar (*Tamarix pentandra*), a water-wasting plant considered by many range managers to be useless at best. The researchers wanted to determine the extent to which water yield might be enhanced by removing the growth, but the rancher was adamant. "Those are the only trees within miles," he told the surprised scientists. "Leave them alone."

The incident illustrates at least three social attitudes that are important to an understanding of the present-day civilization of the arid and semiarid West of the United States. These attitudes are toward resources, toward research findings, and toward the blind transfer of customs acquired in a humid environment. The attitudes toward resources are conditioned by time, place, and culture. For example, mesquite trees (*Prosopis* spp.) are being systematically eliminated from many rangelands, because they compete with grass. Once, however, the mesquite represented a real resource to the prehistoric Piman-speaking Indians, who relied on its beans for food, its bark for basketry, and its wood for fires and housing.

For all his prescience, John Wesley Powell, one of the first explorers of the western United States, could not have foreseen eight decades ago the potential of some western rivers as energy sources for hydroelectric power, just as the possibilities of power from nuclear energy are not fully understood at present. But Powell still personifies what man might have done in adapting to the dry lands. He insisted, first in 1878, that the political institutions and farming methods of the humid regions—from which the nation grew on the east coast—would have to be modified west of the 100th meridian. He devoted much of his life to campaigning for this principle, largely in vain.

It is only a little less true today that the scientists who are active in the field have a perspective of arid-lands problems that goes beyond what the politicians and the populace in general are willing to accept. This is the second factor symbolized by the Arizona rancher and his precious saltcedars (*Tamarix pentandra*), and it explains, in part, the third, and perhaps the most paradoxical, factor. In no other segment of the United States was the population multiplying more rapidly in the mid-20th century than in the semiarid and arid areas, nor did the economic future appear more promising; yet, nowhere else in the nation were the realities of a harsh physical environment so little comprehended.

The main cause of this lack of comprehension was, and continues to be, what Powell foresaw: the transfer westward of the customs and attitudes of the humid East. Had the United States first been colonized in California, and the pattern of settlement moved to the east, such an outlook might not have evolved. As it was, the settlers brought with them what Wallace Stegner has called "the agricultural *expectations* of people reared in a country of adequate rainfall" (*1*) .

Duststorms and Droughts

The people simply refused to believe that periods of little or no rainfall could last so long; but persist the droughts did. Some dramatic agricultural failures were a consequence. The most memorable, partly because they took place at a time of economic crisis everywhere, were those of the early 1930's on the semiarid Great Plains. Winds stripped the topsoil from vast areas and carried it halfway across the continent. In Pennsylvania, a professor of geology at Bryn Mawr College was able to calculate the western dustfall on his neighborhood by collecting the dust off his car, which, he reported, "fortunately had just previously been thoroughly cleaned" (*2*) .

Although major reforms in farming methods followed the great duststorms on the Plains, human attitudes are not easily changed. Twenty years later, Harvard University anthropologists studied a group of Texas farmers who, forced from their homeland by the drought of the 1930's, settled in New Mexico (3). The migrants began to raise there the same crop they had grown in Texas—beans—and with equally disastrous results. A local joke defined a bean farmer as "a man who is crazy enough to think he is going to make it next year."

None of this is to say that man, by and large, has failed in the West. He has irrigated the land, and he harvests rich products from what once was raw desert, and nearby he erects sprawling, prosperous cities. Much of his success, though, has been achieved at the expense of irreplaceable resources. To some extent, the *expectations* of the farmer have been transplanted to the city, where they are epitomized by that mark of the tidy North American homeowner, the well-watered lawn.

Bearing the brunt of the westward exodus of population are the arid regions that are afflicted by a combination of water problems—scarcity, sedimentation, and others (Fig. 1). A large number of the most explosively growing western cities depend on underground sources for municipal water, and many of these aquifers are being pumped out more rapidly than they can be recharged naturally (4).

In 1959, an examination of the Tucson, Arizona, area led scien-

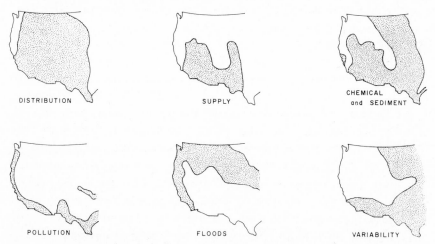

Fig. 1. The maps delineate the regions where six major water problems are the most likely to be found. Of the six, distribution of water is the most widespread worry in the West, but water is the scarcest in areas, such as the Southwest, where several of the problems overlap. (Courtesy U.S. Geological Survey)

tists of the University of Arizona and the U.S. Geological Survey to warn that the "local ground-water supplies will become depleted unless measures are taken to replenish the storage" (5). Although the study specifically suggested such measures, the city government refused to contribute financially to further investigations.

The citizens of some western cities where the water future is precarious pay no more for water than do those who live in humid regions and, therefore, are not encouraged to use any less. The irony of this "undervaluation of [an important] commodity" has been pointed out by geographer Gilbert F. White, who explains that, "in Chicago, with annual rainfall of 37 inches [940 millimeters] and a tremendous source [of water] within a mile [1.61 kilometers] of the shoreline, a middle-class family pays as much for its water as does a similar family in Boulder, Colorado, with an annual rainfall of 17 inches [432 millimeters] and a glacier source 20 miles [32 kilometers] away" (6, pp. 9–10).

White also refers to the irony of lawns in the oasis towns of the West: "Generally, the owner applies much more water than a water-budget analysis would show it [the lawn] needs. When in doubt he applies a little more. This is because the owner either doesn't know about or care about water-budgeting. He tends to use as much water as he is entitled to, and, indeed, the local water department hopes he will, so long as he doesn't exceed restrictions at times of peak demands. He resents any increase in rates as an infringement upon his inherited rights, and he thinks the more he uses, the less he should pay per gallon [liter]. An alternative would be to have no lawn at all and to cultivate a patio and border vegetation which gave him cooling relief with less water. He is slow to consider this or any other way of dealing with his arid climate. The house is unsuited to such a change because it was designed as though for a Connecticut seacoast village. His midwestern tradition tells him a neat lawn is a mark of respectable status. Moreover, watering, in either the homely tug-of-war methods of yesteryear or the missile-control-board method of tomorrow, has therapeutic value after a trying day. Here is the water user who thinks more water is the sure solution for a dry environment, consistently undervalues his commodity, and is reluctant to consider any alternatives to his heavy usage" (6, pp. 13–14).

This anomaly of inexpensive, often wasted water in the arid areas

This Resettlement Administration photograph, now considered a classic of the Dust Bowl days of the 1930's, shows an Oklahoma farmer and his sons as they walked against a dust-laden wind on their once productive cropland. (Courtesy Library of Congress)

can be carried a step further. As Table I indicates, westerners in general also use more water, relatively, than do easterners. The per-capita consumption of municipal water is twice as great in Arizona, and 3 times as great in Nevada, as it is in Arkansas or Vermont.

Terah L. Smiley, a geochronologist, has summed up the over-all problem: "We have learned that we can make the desert 'bloom,' changing it from an unproductive wasteland to a subtropic paradise by the application of water; but only now are we beginning to see the extreme price that we must pay for this activity in regard to our shrinking water supply.

"Few of us have actually learned to live in the desert; rather, we have brought with us our practices, ideas, economy, even our total lives from our former humid or subhumid climatic environments, and we have attempted to adapt the area to these ideas and practices. We are living in 'air-conditioned' oases environments, and this is costing us plenty in terms of resources" (7).

Table I.   Daily per-capita water use (in gallons[a]) from municipal water
systems in 1954, by selected states.

State	Water used	State	Water used
Western United States		Eastern United States	
Nevada	270	Michigan	213
Utah	223	New York	138
Arizona	170	Connecticut	137
New Mexico	150	Alabama	105
California	147	Arkansas	81
Total United States	147		

[a] One gallon (U.S.) equals 3.785 liters; 2.64 gallons equals 1 dekaliter.
   Source: U.S. Senate Select Committee on National Water Resources, *Future Water
Requirements for Muincipal Use,* Comm. Print 7 (Washington, D.C., 1960) , p. 8.

Geography of the West

If one knew the West only from fiction, one might visualize it as
a treeless, limitless land of sand dunes and the bleached bones of
cattle. In reality, very little of the country fits this picture. About
one-third of the 48 contiguous states is either arid or semiarid; this
third reaches west from the 100th meridian, or toward the Pacific
Ocean from western Texas and the Great Plains states. But in terrain, vegetation, and even in climate, it varies tremendously (see
Chapter 2) .

Westward from the Plains, the domain of the dry farmer and his
wheatfields, the tall grasses give way to shorter grasses and, eventually,
to desert. There are badlands laid bare by erosion and valleys turned
green by irrigation, and the relatively sparse population tends to
cluster in centers where water is available.

Big sagebrush (*Artemisia tridentata*) is the dominant vegetation
in the intermontane basins and plateaus, where winters can be cold
and the mean annual precipitation is likely to be between 6 and 20
inches (152 and 508 millimeters) . In the hot lowlands of southeastern California, by contrast, creosotebush (*Larrea divaricata*) is
a prevalent plant, and several seasons may pass without rainfall.
High, humid "islands" of forested mountains are scattered over
much of the West, giving rise to its rivers, providing the region with
recreation and timber, and greatly affecting its weather.

Despite these subregional differences, the semiarid and arid areas share at least one obvious environmental factor: a deficiency of moisture. Precipitation on the prairies and deserts not only is scarce but also, as Table II shows, is highly variable. "Average" years of rainfall mean little. According to a U.S. Geological Survey scientist, Harold E. Thomas, precipitation in every part of the Southwest was less than 85 percent of the record mean in at least 3 of the years from 1942 to 1956, "and in some areas as much as 13 of those years." He explains that "it is a general rule that dry years—when precipitation is less than average—are more frequent than wet years. In other words, the median rainfall—the amount that is exceeded in 50 percent of the years—is significantly less than the mean, or long-term average" (8). Statistics, then, certainly do not bolster the stubborn hope of homesteaders that "next year" may be better. The chances are that next year, or any one year, will be dry.

Moreover, the rate of evapotranspiration (which varies little from year to year) is great and exceeds precipitation in most of the West in 9 out of 10 years (9). Average annual evaporation from experimental pans at Las Cruces, New Mexico, where precipitation averages 8.5 inches (216 millimeters) yearly, was found to be more than 92 inches (2337 millimeters) (10), and geologist John W. Harshbarger has said that, of the precipitation that falls in Arizona, "less than 10 percent runs off as streamflow," and about half of that is lost to vapor (11).

The problems of adapting to such an environment were, of course,

Table II. Variation in precipitation in the western United States in inches[a].

Station	Median	Record mean	Observed maximum	Observed minimum	Standard deviation
Indio, Calif.	3.07	3.56	12.47	0.36	1.92
El Paso, Tex.	8.26	8.67	17.46	2.40	3.43
St. George, Utah	8.29	8.45	20.11	3.01	2.81
San Diego, Calif.	9.63	10.05	26.09	3.63	3.48
Tucson, Ariz.	10.80	11.19	20.90	4.73	3.26
Santa Fe, N. Mex.	13.73	14.18	26.75	7.31	4.25

[a] One inch equals 25.4 millimeters.

Source: H. E. Thomas, "The meteorologic phenomenon of drought in the Southwest," *U.S. Geol. Surv. Profess. Paper 372-A* (1962), p. A-15.

faced, even though on a comparatively limited scale, long before the
arrival of Europeans in the New World. Archeologic evidence suggests that man had started to spread across North America as early
as 10,000 years ago. The earliest inhabitants (Chapter 3) were hunters, however, and the climate probably was cooler and moister than
it is now. Wildlife, including large animals now extinct, was abundant. The Indians gradually learned to utilize native plants and,
as the continent became warmer and drier, there were the crude beginnings of agriculture.

Partly because the hunting and gathering people were widely dispersed, the diffusion of agricultural knowledge was not rapid. Maize,
beans, and squash, which were first cultivated farther to the south,
were introduced slowly into the present-day United States, perhaps
over several millenniums. But, by at least about 3500 B.C., some corn
was grown in western New Mexico, and, by around A.D. 800, the
prehistoric farmers had devised terraces to hold the soil in their
fields; those in southern Arizona irrigated their crops through an
elaborate network of canals and ditches.

Agriculture, nonetheless, provided an uncertain life in a region
where precipitation was so unpredictable. Whether or not changes
in climate, the most widely accepted theory, were to blame, a great
constriction occurred in the aboriginal agricultural areas, starting in
the 13th century. Three centuries later, the areas were only about
one-tenth as widespread as they once were.

If there is a lesson that modern men might learn from the successes and failures of the Indians, probably it is the need for balance
between social institutions and technology. The prehistoric populations simply were not large enough to afford any real comparison
between their adaptation to the land and the adaptations that are
required today; as advanced as Indian agricultural developments
were for their time, they were far too small in scale to affect the
environment materially. Thus, when Coronado marched into the
Southwest in 1540, the landscape was largely the product of nature
and had scarcely been disturbed by man.

Exploration and Settlement

The Spaniards and then the Mexicans who first colonized the
present western United States came from lands that also were arid

When W. H. Emory, of the Army Corps of Topographical Engineers, saw this part of central New Mexico near the Rio Grande in 1846, he found grass "in great abundance." Today, the same scene is dominated by creosotebush (*Larrea divaricata*) and tarbush (*Flourensia cernua*) and is all but bereft of grass. (Courtesy J. L. Gardner)

or semiarid, and they adjusted much more readily than the other Europeans who followed them. Although the northernmost settlements of New Spain were never, in present-day terms, extensive (Chapter 4), the political remnants of the Spanish empire, nevertheless, persisted in the West for 250 years.

Army explorers were the first United States citizens who penetrated and seriously studied the region. Their reports, which were less than encouraging, kindled the forbidding concept of the "great American desert." It was not until the California gold rush of 1849 that a westward migration of consequence took place, and not until 1853 that the United States acquired the last of its western territories. Then, after the Civil War, came the boom in railroad building (supported by government aid to the builders); the Homestead Act and other land acts, which made western ranges and farmlands available; and the growth of the industrial East, which created a market for the products of those lands.

A thread that is woven through *Aridity and Man* is the fact that the arid West would have developed in a very different manner, and certainly more slowly, had it not been an inseparable segment of a large, rich nation. This truth was especially apparent during and after World War II, when the region prospered more than ever before, chiefly because defense industries and military bases were established within it and tourists and retired people came to it in large numbers.

Owing in part to this economic infusion from the outside, the western United States is beginning, through industrialization, to shake off the shackles of the "extractive" economy—the exportation only of raw products—which has been one of its handicaps *(12)*. The potentialities of this continuing expansion may be virtually limitless. On the other hand, there remains the enigma of water supply.

Certainly water is available somewhere within reach, if the citizenry is willing to pay for diverting it. The key question is, On how grand a scale can the economy support the transportation of water at any given time? A proposed project, which would carry Colorado River water to central and southern Arizona, where three-fourths of the state's population lives, would cost $1.1 billion. Westerners always have held an abiding faith in science and engineering to solve their problems; usually their belief has been justified. But the average, uninformed westerner seems to be convinced today that, all else failing, scientists are on the verge of releasing rainfall from the clouds almost at will and of desalinizing unending quantities of sea water. Unfortunately, neither the attainment of the first of these accomplishments nor the practical application of the second is within the realm of immediate reality.

Weather, Water, and Energy

Indeed, recent research has shown not only that present-day techniques fail to increase precipitation appreciably—at least, on the arid flat lands—but also that a premise on which cloud seeding was based (the freezing of nuclei in clouds) may have been wrong (Chapter 5). As a result, meteorologists have taken a renewed interest in the basic physics and chemistry of clouds. Radar, which has been greatly improved since World War II, has become an important tool in this work. Other investigations have concentrated on the very small and the very large—on microclimatology and on global, large-scale atmospheric motions. The latter studies, particularly, are being furthered through the use of high-speed electronic computers.

Analog computers also have been programed, with considerable promise, to help hydrologists in understanding the complexities of ground water. Ground-water problems have been compounded by the expansion of population, by the cessation of surface streamflow in many places, and by the introduction of the centrifugal pump, a device that has profoundly affected the West (Chapter 6).

The centrifugal pump and modern drilling equipment have made possible deeper and deeper wells during the past half-century. As a result, irrigation has increased enormously. Ground water has been further depleted, and the challenge to water scientists has increased. One eventual answer may be the desalinization and demineralization of sea and brackish waters, and a number of pilot plants are already in operation. The costs at which they can produce potable water are approaching those paid by some municipalities but are too high, thus far, for agricultural use.

Water seldom is scarce, axiomatically, where there is enough energy to pump it from great depths. Therefore, it is ironic that the West, where the availability of water can be so crucial, is a major source of the raw materials of energy, particularly of petroleum, coal, and uranium (Chapter 7). Larger quantities of these are exported than are used within the region.

All of the nation's helium and most of its uranium are found in west Texas and the Mountain States. Indicator-plants—certain species that are affected by mineralization—have helped prospectors to discover deposits of uranium and other minerals. The region is also an important producer of metallic minerals, especially copper, and in some places dry processing of ores has been perfected as a means of saving water.

Although prospectors entered the then largely uncharted West long before farmers, and mining remains a potent economic and political force, mining has long been rivaled by agriculture as a producer of income. Agriculture, of course, had to abandon, immeasurably more so than mining, old methods and seek new ones in order to adapt to the aridity.

The necessity for managing the soils of the dry lands in ways different from those of the humid regions (Chapter 8) was a lesson that had to be learned slowly, and often painfully, by the pioneering farmers. Soil salinity, erosion, and waterlogging were severe and still are. The soils tend to be alkaline and calcareous. But by experience and experiments, farmers have found how to reclaim saline soils by leaching and have learned the ways in which water may be applied to do less harm and more good. They conserve soil moisture on the Great Plains by fallowing.

Apparently there is no reason why either dry farming or irrigation agriculture cannot continue and, possibly, because of research, with even greater future yields. Studies of soil-plant-water relationships and of soil classifications, among others, have been intensified. In another promising line of investigation, scientists in the U.S. Soil Conservation Service in southern New Mexico are analyzing the influence of landform and geologic conditions on soil development.

The most spectacular successes in western agriculture have taken place where there is irrigation: in Utah, on the high plains of west Texas, in the Salt and Colorado river valleys of Arizona, and, most of all, in California. As Table III illustrates, the trend toward additional areas of irrigation continues unabated. This, again, is most notably true in California (13). In that state's Imperial Valley—a great green patch against a backdrop of brown desert—vegetables are grown the year round with water diverted by gravitational flow

Table III. Irrigation development in 17 western states, by acres[a].

	Nonfederal land (1000's)	Federal land (1000's)	Total (1000's)	Cumulative total (1000's)
Before 1900	6,700	450	7,150	7,150
1900–1909	3,650	850	4,500	11,650
1910–1919	2,800	1,000	3,800	15,450
1920–1929	950	500	1,450	16,900
1930–1939	900	600	1,500	18,400
1940–1949	3,000	1,450	4,450	22,850
1950–1958	5,950	1,700	7,650	30,500
Total	23,950	6,550	30,500	30,500

[a] One acre equals 0.4047 hectare.
Source: U.S. Senate Select Committee on National Water Resources, *Future Needs for Reclamation in the Western States*, Comm. Print 14 (Washington, D.C., 1961), p. 5.

Cut through the sandy southern California desert, the All-American Canal carries Colorado River water 80 miles (129 kilometers) to the lush irrigated farms of the Imperial Valley. Six years were required for construction of the canal, which was completed in 1940. (Courtesy Imperial Irrigation District)

from the Colorado River. Sixty years ago, the valley was as parched and desolate as any to be found in the United States.

Problems are inherent in irrigation, of course, just as they are in the adaptation of plants and animals to an arid environment (Chapter 9). There are endless efforts to improve dams, ditches, and other structures, to reduce silting and evaporation, and to remove excess water from farmlands. Ditches are lined with concrete, and various chemicals are applied to the surface of reservoirs, in the hope of significantly reducing seepage and evaporation. The adaptation of animals and plants is more a matter of basic research.

Precisely how extreme heat affects livestock is not fully understood, but western ranges are extensively stocked with beef cattle that have been crossbred with the heat-tolerant Brahman (zebu) cattle of India. Range managers are seeking fuller use of their lands by removing brush, and low-value plants, such as the pricklypear cactus (*Opuntia* spp.), sometimes are utilized as emergency livestock feed.

In cultivated fields, plastic coverings and petroleum mulch have been applied to conserve moisture and raise the soil temperature around germinating seeds. Much research has been focused on the possibilities of drought-tolerant plants—those that require less moisture—or hybrids that might bring increased yields under the same climatic conditions. The development of an improved extra-long-staple cotton (*Gossypium barbadense*) brought considerably larger yields in the Southwest, where it must be irrigated. Irrigation, in fact, still is by far the largest user of water in the region (Fig. 2), despite the mushrooming of industry and urban population.

Watershed Problems

Almost always any discussion of the future of the West must begin with two questions. Where does the water come from? Can the supply be increased or even sustained? Irrigation, at least, often depends on surface flow. In the truly arid lands at low elevation, where this type of agriculture is concentrated, local runoff is undependable, if not all but nonexistent. The lifelines are the rivers that bring water down from the high, humid mountain chains.

So, oddly as it may strike persons who are oriented to humid environments, one cannot consider the fate of the North American deserts without considering snowfall. The maximizing of snowdrifts and the manipulation of higher-elevation watersheds are tasks to which numerous investigators have addressed themselves (Chapter 10). Among other approaches, they have set up snow fences to deepen drifts and have erased water-wasting plants from streambeds. In an effort to suppress transpiration, they have thinned watershed vegetation or replaced it with low moisture-using species. One difficulty is that not enough is known about the transpiration by certain plants; basic research along this line is being undertaken.

Although the forest products of the western mountains are not as vital as the water yielded, they are important assets to the arid areas below. Foresters and research scientists are especially concerned with forest regeneration and management and the control of insects and fires.

Native plants other than trees (Chapter 11) have proved so far to be of considerably less commercial worth. Wild stands of canaigre (*Rumex hymenosepalus*) have been harvested for their tannin content, and, to name another, the common creosotebush (*Larrea divari-cata*) has been turned into livestock feed. Laboratory screening has indicated that many other arid-lands plants are potentially valuable because they are rich in oil and protein. But, among other factors, the competition of synthetics and the lack of a real need for new crops have prevented extensive commercial development.

Lately, however, interest has risen in native plants and animals

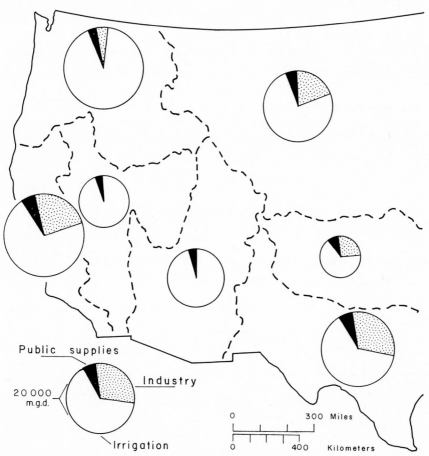

Public supplies

Industry

20 000
m.g.d.

Irrigation

0   300 Miles

0   400 Kilometers

Fig. 2. Irrigation agriculture uses more water in the West than is taken by public supplies and industry combined. The reverse is true, of course, in the humid East, where farming makes use of only a comparatively small portion of the available water. The graphs represent water use in millions of gallons (liters) per day (m.g.d.). (Courtesy U.S. Geological Survey)

simply for their esthetic value. Evidence of this belated appreciation is indicated by the interdisciplinary research in Arizona on the giant saguaro cactus (*Carnegiea gigantea*) and by the management by wildlife officials in the same state of the collared peccary, or javelina (*Pecari angulatus sonoriensis*), an animal once viewed as nothing more than a pest.

For the most part, man's admiration of the stark natural beauty, the generally mild climate, and the spaciousness of the arid lands is a quite recent phenomenon. Whether this attitude has developed too late to preserve much of the regional uniqueness against the encroachment of population is a matter that the present generation must decide.

Human Adaptation

Man himself, of course, lacks many of the endogenous adaptations that are naturally provided for the desert-dwelling plants and animals. But it is as true under arid conditions as elsewhere that man is among the most adaptive of creatures. Very little research has been done on the physiologic problems of man in the arid regions since the intense interest during World War II (Chapter 12). But enough had been performed previously to establish the fact that normal, healthy human beings should be scarcely limited by an arid environment, as long as they respect its extremes. However, much more work should be done toward practical application of the existing knowledge of how man should dress in such an environment and the sort of housing he should build.

Instead of designing buildings with the local climate in mind, people tend too often to rely entirely on air-conditioning machines to protect them from the heat of the summers in the arid lands. The air-conditioner has had a beneficial impact in the Southwest especially. Just as the windmill and the barbed-wire fence, in their time, helped to open the West to orderly occupation, the centrifugal pump and the air-conditioner have transformed the region into the sort of place it is today. Nevertheless, it is possible for planners and designers to take the environment into account without rejecting the amenities offered by technology.

Economically, the arid West poses a riddle (Chapter 13). It is poor in water, and yet it is rapidly growing in population, employment, and income. The answer appears to be that the lack of water has not been a barrier to this expansion, is not considered likely to be within the near future, but ultimately may become a serious deterrent, unless new sources of water are found or wiser use is made of existing supplies.

One possible alternative was proposed by a team of social scientists. It emerged from what well may have been the most significant arid-lands research in years. The researchers found in New Mexico (Chapter 13) that agriculture, traditionally one of the highest-priority users of water in the West, actually returns less to the total economy for the water it utilizes than do industry, cities, recreationists, and other users.

Presumably, the same ratio would apply in other arid states. Whether it would in other countries, with vastly different economies, is another matter, of course. But the diversion of more water to non-farm uses is likely to receive increasingly serious consideration in the western United States.

Such a change will not come easily. Although the political processes and the social values of the West were, in the main, superimposed from the East (Chapter 14), a number of institutions on the frontier were tailored to suit the exigencies of the period. Among them were western water laws. Although these laws became a bewildering, conflicting complex of statutes, compacts, and disputes, they were a step forward in that they recognized the priority of use. At the time this system of water rights took shape, though, the West was predominantly agricultural.

The durability in the West of certain other humid-regions attitudes becomes all the more remarkable when one considers them in context. For instance, the penchant for private ownership is as deeply ingrained here as anywhere else in the nation, in spite of the fact that much of the West is owned to this day by the federal government. But the attitude has asserted itself at various times; it was strongly felt during the early disposals of the public lands.

Like almost every other event or factor involved in the settlement of the West, the disposal of public lands was haphazard and often fraught with fraud and greed; yet, the action at least freed for farming vast areas that otherwise would have remained raw prairies.

This is the kind of paradox that makes difficult the judging of man's activities in the region (Chapter 15). Man has actuated the erosion of land, has denuded the forests, has reduced the grasslands to desert, and has polluted even the air he breathes. At the same time, he has brought huge areas under cultivation, constructed cities, and also built not only a materially rich region but a sound social structure. Where is the line to be drawn between plunder and progress? An answer is not easy but must be based on awareness that the dwindling natural resources must be husbanded more carefully in the West during the next century than they were during the century past.

Hope for the Future

If water that now evaporates or is otherwise lost could somehow be saved, a much larger population could be supported in the western United States; if even a portion of the water now used by agriculture could be diverted to industry, regional income could be increased manyfold. Before these things can be accomplished (Chapter 16), there must be planning and cooperation on a regionwide basis, rising above local and state jealousies and ambitions.

In other words, the over-all problem is largely a social one. The future of the arid West still hinges to an awesome extent on the answers that can be supplied by scientific research but, even more, it depends on public understanding of these answers and the public's willingness to act on this new knowledge in place of its old prejudices and traditions.

That the public may be ready for a better understanding of its arid environment was illustrated, with an ironic twist, in 1962 with the publication of a booklet in Phoenix, Arizona. The booklet, *Desert Survival* (14), was issued by local civil defense authorities and was designed for the obvious emergency. The citizens, most of them presumably city-dwellers, were cautioned by the publication that, to survive, they should walk in the desert only at night and that, if they are really hungry, rattlesnake (*Crotalus* spp.) meat provides a perfectly palatable meal. The present inhabitants of the arid lands, comfortable in their air-conditioned oases, may not be as far removed from their environment as most of them think they are.

Acknowledgments: Although all the authors in *Aridity and Man* contributed indirectly to this synthesis of the book, I wish to single out Peter C. Duisberg, J. L. Gardner, Terah L. Smiley, and Richard B. Woodbury for their specific suggestions.

REFERENCES

1. W. Stegner, "Editor's introduction" to J. W. Powell, *Report on the Lands of the Arid Regions of the United States* (Harvard Univ. Press, Belknap Div., Cambridge, Mass., 1962), p. x.
2. E. H. Watson, "Note on the duststorm of November 13, 1933," *Science* **79,** 320 (1934).
3. E. Z. Vogt, *Modern Homesteaders* (Harvard Univ. Press, Belknap Div., Cambridge, Mass., 1955), p. 201.
4. R. Z. Brown, "United States water supply versus population growth," *Population Bull.* **17,** 6 (1961).
5. University of Arizona Rillito Creek Hydrologic Commission and U.S. Geological Survey, *Capturing Additional Water in the Tucson Area* (U.S. Geological Survey, Dept. of the Interior, Tucson, Arizona, 1959), p. 1.
6. G. F. White, *The Changing Role of Water in Arid Lands,* Riecker lecture 6, November 1960 (Univ. of Arizona Press, Tucson, 1962).
7. T. L. Smiley, "Arid lands: the problem and a reply," unpublished paper presented before Am. Assoc. for the Advancement of Science, Philadelphia, Pa., 1962.
8. H. E. Thomas, "The meteorologic phenomenon of drought in the Southwest," *U.S. Geol. Surv. Profess. Paper 372-A* (1962), p. A-15.
9. G. Michel *et al.,* "Survey of methods for evaporation control," *J. Am. Water Works Assoc.* **55,** 157–168 (1963).
10. E. L. Hardy, J. C. Overpeck, and C. P. Wilson, *Precipitation and Evaporation in New Mexico* (New Mexico State Univ., University Park, 1939).
11. J. W. Harshbarger, "Capturing additional water for the increase of supplies," in *Land and Water Use,* W. Thorne, Ed. (Am. Assoc. for the Advancement of Science, Washington, D.C., 1963), p. 213.
12. A. W. Wilson, "The impact of an exploding population on a semi-developed state: the case of Arizona," *Arizona Rev.* **2** (5), 5–9 (1962).
13. H. F. Gregor, "Push to the desert," *Science* **129,** 1329–1339 (1959).
14. Maricopa County–City of Phoenix Civil Defense Joint Council, *Desert Survival* (Phoenix, Ariz., 1962).

Regional Setting

Donald D. MacPhail

Aridity is seasonal and annual; it accompanies heat and cold alike, and it varies in intensity. To understand this, one must know the attributes of the many regions that are called *arid* or *semiarid* and cover about one-third of the land area of the United States. But *aridity* is a term that cannot be described to everyone's satisfaction.

"The arid zone," said the late Homer L. Shantz, "has not been precisely defined. Probably in no zone on the earth are there greater swings in precipitation, temperature, and aridity" (*1*, p. 3). To define such a zone properly would probably not be possible, for if done, the definition would be bound largely to a single factor of the environment. A definition based on climatic data would not be the same as one based on soils, on vegetation, on animal distribution, or on land use. Since none of these aspects of the landscape is, by itself, satisfactory for delineating the exact boundary of the arid zone, it is necessary to consider each one in order to understand the many broad regional patterns of the physical landscape and the interrelationships of the arid environment.

The climatic expression of aridity is more difficult to ascertain than one might suppose. A statement of the amount of rainfall received by a given locality says nothing about the distribution of rainfall throughout the year or its over-all effectiveness. Aridity is an expression of water deficiency; and water deficiency is induced not only by lack of precipitation but also by conditions of soil moisture and permeability, evaporation, transpiration by plants, and the intensity and duration of sunlight, heat, humidity, and wind.

Many investigators have attempted to express the effects of these factors as quantitative indexes. Widely used in the United States is

---

Contributors to this chapter were Leslie Hewes, Harold A. Hoffmeister, Fritz L. Kramer, Richard F. Logan, and John M. Street.

C. W. Thornthwaite's index, which, stated simply, establishes a
ratio between water deficiency (or surplus) and water need expressed as potential evaporation and transpiration (2). Thornthwaite saw that potential evapotranspiration was a useful idea, and
he established moisture regions on the basis of water surplus or deficiency. A modified version of these regions was published in 1960
by Peveril Meigs and is adapted in generalized form as an end paper
of this book (3).

Characteristics of Aridity

Three stages of dry climate emerge—semiarid, arid, and extremely
arid. Semiarid lands occupy one-fourth of the United States, and
arid lands another 10 percent (4). Extremely arid conditions, where
there has been at least 1 year without rain, are confined to relatively
small areas in the Death and Imperial valleys of California.

Most of the semiarid and arid regions lie roughly between the
100th meridian and the Sierra Nevada and Cascade ranges. Offshore,
there are scattered arid and semiarid areas on the Hawaiian Islands
and Puerto Rico; these tropical dry zones follow narrow belts along
leeward coasts and generally are more semiarid than arid.

What is a semarid climate? If Thornthwaite's moisture index is
applied, a pronounced water deficit prevails in the coastal valleys of
southern California, the Colorado Plateau (s), most of the Wyoming
basins, in many intermontane basins of the Rocky Mountains, and
the entire extent of the short-grass Plains. The eastern margin of
these Plains is the conventional boundary between the dry and the
humid United States. In reality, however, this is a dynamic and
fluctuating border.

In a given year, semiaridity may extend as far east as western
Wisconsin, northwestern Iowa, and western Louisiana. What the
eastern boundary of the short-grass Plains does indicate is the prevalence of drought. West of this limit, semiarid conditions have occurred from one-half to three-fourths of the years of record. These
characteristics also are manifest in observable landscape conditions.
To the west, the natural grasses change from tall to short varieties,
and the percentage of land in crops drops significantly. Grazing is
the dominant land use, except where irrigation is possible or where
the land is too steep and rocky.

Arid conditions, where the moisture deficiency is severe, apply to parts of the Columbia Basin of Washington State, the San Joaquin Valley (which is the southern half of the Central Valley of California), parts of the Wyoming basins, and almost all of the Mohave, Sonoran, and Chihuahuan deserts.

In most of the West, there is moisture deficiency throughout the year. The western portions of the northern Rocky Mountains, the Blue Mountains of northeastern Oregon, the northern Willamette Valley of Oregon, and the most mountainous areas of California experience serious periods of moisture deficiency during the summer. There, the uneven seasonal distribution of precipitation accentuates the problem of dryness. Summer deficits of water are more moderate along the margins of the Puget Sound Lowland in Washington, in the middle Rockies of Wyoming and Utah, and along the high plateau border in Arizona. There is, in fact, along the entire length of the Rocky Mountains, a sharp east-west break in the seasonal pattern of precipitation. Where cold, dry Canadian air dominates the winters east of the Rockies, summer rainfall maximums are the rule.

Conversely, across the entire intermontane regions to the Pacific valleys, winter rainfall and summer drought are usual, since the mid-latitude, west-coast rainfall regime makes itself felt to a greater or lesser degree as far east as the continental divide.

Effects of Rainfall

In a land that lacks water, it is curious that running water is the most important sculptor of the landscape. When the rain comes, the scant vegetative cover does little to spare weak shale or clay outcrops from savage bombardment by the raindrops. Torrents of water rush outward and downward instead of soaking into the compacted earth. The shale, eroded deeply, becomes a dense barren mass of oversteepened valleys and razor-sharp ridges known as *badlands,* creating the desolate character of the Big Badlands of South Dakota and the Borrego Badlands of California.

Water works sporadically in the arid zones. Brief storms send rampaging waters down steep-walled drywashes, or *arroyos.* Debris and mud, carried along in the currents, soon drop on the floor of the arroyo or on the gentle slope of the adjacent basin, or *bolson,* as the force of the stream dissipates. Sediment-choked streams disgorge alluvial fans, which often coalesce into continuous, smooth slopes called *bajadas.*

Large quantities of alluvium frequently block the existing stream courses, then new channels cross the fans in different directions. The upper parts of the fans frequently are scarred by many of these dry, shallow watercourses that radiate from the mountain canyons. Farther downslope, the sandy or clayey flat, or *playa,* of the bolson usually is covered by encrusted salt, remnant of an ephemeral lake. Water, which usually is present just below the playa surface, often is saturated with brine and is high in mineral content. As the basins gradually fill with alluvium, salts, interbedded occasionally with clay, accumulate in layers hundreds of feet (meters) thick.

The short-run nature of desert streams confines most of the drainage to interior basins, such as those of western Wyoming or the Black Rock Desert in northwest Nevada. Only the main rivers, which have their sources in the high, humid "islands" of the Rocky Mountains, traverse the driest parts of the region to reach the sea. These are the Colorado, the Columbia, and the Rio Grande. Across the plains east of the Rockies, tributaries of the Missouri, Arkansas, and Red rivers flow into the humid basin of the Mississippi and ultimately to the Gulf of Mexico.

Other landscapes result from resistance to erosion by water. These possess either precipitous slopes or very low relief, with few examples between the extremes. Tough sandstones or basalts cap the surface of the Colorado and Columbia plateaus. Frequently, these are incised by steep-walled canyons a half-mile (approximately 1 kilometer) deep. The Black Canyon of the Gunnison River, and Grand, Marble, and Glen canyons of the Colorado River are examples. Flat-topped mesas, inclined cuestas, or solitary pinnacles and buttes often stand above the surrounding plain, stubbornly and slowly succumbing to the ravages of weathering.

Because of the great fluctuation of daily temperature, rapid expansion and contraction of the exposed rock surfaces help to crack and disintegrate them; large amounts of the detached debris accumulate and are gradually washed away.

Most of the arid United States has a classic type of desert landscape. Mountain ranges occur in echelon, fringed by smooth-sloping bedrock pediments. These massive fault-blocks, most of which are

Colorado River waters have cut 700 feet (213.4 meters) into the plateau surface on the Arizona-Utah border. Glen Canyon Dam, photographed in 1962 as it neared completion, was designed to provide electricity, stream control, and recreation. (Courtesy U.S. Bureau of Reclamation)

alined north and south, form the crests of ranges. Broad bolsons intervene between them. This "basin-and-range country" typifies the Great Basin and the entire region of creosotebush (*Larrea divaricata*).

Contrary to popular belief, winds have rather limited erosive effects in the truly arid parts of the mountain West. Some sand and dust, blown away from playas and lower alluvial fans, redeposit either as miniature dunes in the lee of bushes or as a veneer on the upper alluvial fans at the windward sides of bolsons, below the mountain rims.

Several large accumulations of sand (the Algodones Dunes west of Yuma, Arizona; the Devil's Playground near Baker, California; and the dunes in Death Valley) are associated with Pleistocene streams or lakes and apparently are not growing appreciably today. Other notable sand areas include the glistening, transverse dunes of white gypsum crystals in New Mexico's Tularosa Basin near Alamo-gordo, the Great Sand Dunes of Colorado's San Luis Valley, and the widespread Sand Hills of Nebraska, which occur on the eastward margin of the semiarid plains. Such areas, however, compose only a small fragment of the western United States.

Wind has a more vital role on the short-grass portions of the Great Plains and similar areas of low relief. During years of drought, when the Plains are denuded of protective vegetative cover, the wind has whipped clouds of fine, powdery, orange-yellow dust several thousand feet (meters) into the air. Some of the most severe dust-storms have deposited more than 30 tons of dust per square mile (12 metric tons per square kilometer) (5).

Zonal Soils

In general terms, the soils of the West have in common the soil-forming process of calcification and thus are called *Pedocals*. Their distribution is shown in Fig. 1. The dryness of climate permits the accumulation of lime in these soils; this is not the case in humid regions. The major groups of the Pedocals have a definite regional basis that consists of many local soils with similarities of profile. Over a long period of time, the effect of climatic and biotic factors on a great variety of geologic materials has brought about the de-velopment of the distinctive characters of the zonal soils.

In the semiarid short-grass Plains, the Chestnut, Reddish Chest-nut, Brown, and Reddish Brown soils predominate (6). The zonal soils become shallower with greater aridity. In the cooler parts of the intermountain regions, Sierozem or Gray Desert soils prevail. Many Sierozems are underlain with a hardpan layer. These desert soils are notably deficient in organic matter but have an abundance of soluble salts and minerals, which can make them highly produc-tive when they are irrigated. In some cases, however, excessive salinity or alkalinity makes this impossible.

Red Desert soils abound in the warm deserts of the Southwest and the Tropics. These reddish-brown and pinkish-gray crumbly soils overlie a heavier dull-red substratum, which, in turn, grades into the ever-present layer of lime carbonate. Like the Sierozems, these soils are quite productive when they are cultivated under irrigation. The

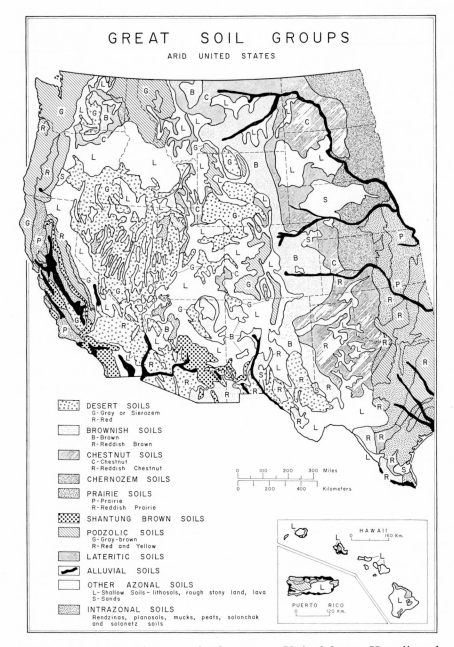

GREAT SOIL GROUPS
ARID UNITED STATES

DESERT SOILS
G- Gray or Sierozem
R- Red

BROWNISH SOILS
B- Brown
R- Reddish Brown

CHESTNUT SOILS
C- Chestnut
R- Reddish Chestnut

CHERNOZEM SOILS

PRAIRIE SOILS
P- Prairie
R- Reddish Prairie

SHANTUNG BROWN SOILS

PODZOLIC SOILS
G- Gray-brown
R- Red and Yellow

LATERITIC SOILS

ALLUVIAL SOILS

OTHER AZONAL SOILS
L- Shallow Soils - lithosols, rough stony land, lava
S- Sands

INTRAZONAL SOILS
Rendzinas, planosols, mucks, peats, solonchak
and solonetz soils

HAWAII

PUERTO RICO

Fig. 1. The great soil groups in the western United States, Hawaii, and
Puerto Rico. (Adapted from U.S. Department of Agriculture map)

Red Desert soils are bordered in many places by the nonlimy Shantung Brown soils that developed under a forested grassland and the
wet and dry subhumid climate.

In the humid mountain ranges of the West, a Gray-Brown Podzolic soil appears frequently; elsewhere in the mountains, thin, shallow, rocky soils, called *lithosols,* have evolved on the steepest slopes.
Sand dunes, river-bottom soils, bogs, swamps, and alkali flats, all are
of recent origin and develop from local, rather than regional, conditions.

Generally speaking, the Pedocals, with their variable horizons of
surface moisture and dry subsoil, extend beyond the geographic
limits that would satisfy arid conditions of climate and vegetation.
As Shantz points out, the estimated area of arid land in the world
is 43 percent, if the estimate is based on Pedocals; 36 percent, based
on climate; 35 percent, based on interior drainage; and 35 percent,
based on natural vegetation (*1*).

Western Vegetation

Vegetative cover can be one of the most effective indications of
aridity, because there is close correlation of plants with soil, climate,
and land use. Successful interpretation depends on recognition of
the regional vegetative patterns that result from plant associations,
not of single species. Some principal indicator-species are adjusted
to long periods of rest brought on by perennial or seasonal drought.

Creosotebush (*Larrea divaricata*) and sagebrush (*Artemisia* spp.)
are remarkably accurate in delineation of the arid intermountain regions. Creosotebush grows exclusively in the southern part of this
region, and sagebrush appears at higher elevations and farther north.
Where the low, monotonous silvery-brown cover of sagebrush spreads
across the landscape, winters are cold and Sierozem soils predominate. The distribution of sagebrush from the Columbia and Wyoming basins in the north to the southern limits of the Great Basin
and Colorado Plateau outlines a major subregion of the West.

In like manner, the olive-green hue of the creosotebush stretches
over the entire border with Mexico from California to the mouth
of the Rio Grande; its presence is evidence of a warm desert climate
with mild winters and a region of Red Desert soils. Although the
range of creosotebush has probably not been extended within his-

Creosotebush (*Larrea divaricata*) covers a desert slope in southern New Mexico. In the background, the dark-toned line is mesquite (*Prosopis juliflora*), originally seeded there as pack animals followed the historic Jornada del Muerto between Chihuahua in Mexico and Santa Fe. (Courtesy J. L. Gardner)

toric times, this plant has increased in prominence in some areas. Descriptions of the tablelands along the Rio Grande of 100 years ago indicate excellent stands of grass in places that are now completely dominated by creosotebush (*Larrea*) or mesquite (*Prosopis* spp.) (7).

Using physical landscape, vegetation, and landform, it is possible to recognize several phytogeomorphic, or natural, regions. Each region has its own characteristics and, thus, has its own potential for economic development.

But, transcending regional differences, the pressing problem of water availability is evident everywhere in the pattern of settlement. In contrast with the eastern United States, the population of the arid and semiarid regions is highly concentrated in nodes. A rather sparse rural population may be found everywhere, except where irrigation is well developed, in close proximity to rapidly growing cities.

The geographic outline of the Rocky Mountains and the Colorado Plateau can be readily discerned on a population map (see Fig. 1, Chapter 13). Where the mountains meet the eastern plains, there is a continuous north-to-south string of cities—Great Falls, Billings, Casper, Cheyenne, Denver, Pueblo, Santa Fe, Albuquerque, and El Paso.

The oases of Tucson, Phoenix, Provo, Salt Lake City, Boise, and Spokane line the western fringe of the mountainous moisture belt. Other clusters of population are found on the Staked Plains of the Texas Panhandle and in the valleys of the Pacific Coast. These are some of the fastest-growing areas in the United States.

It is significant that these densely populated areas reflect only in part the land-use patterns around them (see Fig. 2). Many of the largest cities now are important manufacturing centers, in addition to their normal regional service functions in commerce, finance, and government. Activities such as food processing and meatpacking reflect long-established practices in the various regions, and the commonest uses of the arid and semiarid lands still are sheep and cattle grazing. Extensive grazing is common to all but the extremely arid parts of the intermountain regions.

The main irrigated crops of the West are sugar beets, potatoes, vegetables, cotton, alfalfa, apples, grapes, and citrus fruits. The crops under cultivation without irrigation are drought-resistant grains— winter and spring wheat and sorghum—found on the subhumid margins of the short-grass Plains, the Columbia Basin, and the Central Valley of California.

When the available facts are analyzed, the physical and cultural landscapes are easily grouped into several regions, as may be seen in Fig. 3. The intrinsic character and potential of each are discussed here.

Pacific Valleys

In the geologic past, deformation of the earth's crust in the extreme western United States formed a broken line of north-to-south flat-bottomed valleys between the Sierra Nevada and Cascade ranges and the Pacific Coast. In this structural chain, the coastal lowlands of southern California and the Central Valley of California are significantly arid or semiarid.

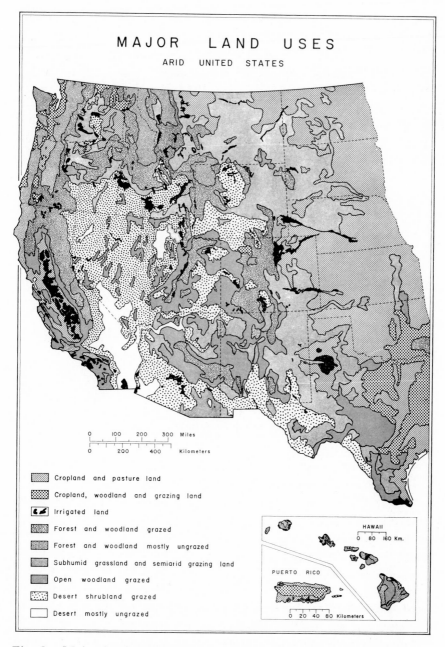

MAJOR LAND USES
ARID UNITED STATES

0   100   200   300 Miles
0   200   400   Kilometers

Cropland and pasture land

Cropland, woodland and grazing land

Irrigated land

Forest and woodland grazed

Forest and woodland mostly ungrazed

Subhumid grassland and semiarid grazing land

Open woodland grazed

Desert shrubland grazed

Desert mostly ungrazed

HAWAII
0   80 160 Km.

PUERTO RICO

0 20 40 80 Kilometers

Fig. 2. Major land uses by area in the arid West include dry farming
and forestry; the irrigated lands also are of great importance. (Courtesy
U.S. Department of Agriculture)

In coastal southern California, the climate, generally semiarid, changes markedly with the extremes in relief. Temperatures are moderate along the coast at all seasons, but inland areas are hot in summer and cool in winter, and the adjacent mountains are warm in summer and cold in winter (see Table I). Precipitation varies greatly with the local orographic situation. Rainless summers, generally speaking, persist in all of the Pacific valleys, although the extent and intensity of the summer drought diminish progressively northward.

Adapted to survive the long, dry summer, the vegetation of the southern California coast has most of its physiologic development during late winter and spring. Chaparral is the natural cover, except along the streams, where grass-carpeted valleys are dotted with oak (*Quercus* spp.).

Not all of the agriculture is irrigated, despite the rainless summer. Grain, planted early in the winter, matures in late spring and early summer; walnuts, almonds, apricots, and other tree crops fare well on winter rain with mulching to conserve water. Lima beans, tomatoes, and geraniums are cultivated in the foggy, frost-free coastal belt without supplemental water. The more lucrative crops of coastal southern California, however, are irrigated, chiefly with water from wells drilled into the alluvial fill of local basins. Some water also is available from supplies imported by the Los Angeles area. Frost-sensitive crops, such as lemons, oranges, and avocados, grow on upper alluvial fans and lower hill slopes, where the cold air freely drains away.

The San Joaquin-Sacramento valleys, generally referred to as the Central Valley, form a gigantic mountain-girt trough. The great width of the smooth valley floor gives the illusion of a flat, endless plain rather than an enclosed depression. Streams issuing from the Sierra Nevada (see end-paper map), and to a lesser degree from the Coast Range, have carried into the valley a great volume of alluvium, much of which is deposited as huge fans. In the southernmost third of the Central Valley, these have formed an area of interior drainage without a natural surface outlet to the sea.

The climate of the valley varies from dry, subhumid in the Sacramento Valley to arid in most of the San Joaquin. Summer rainfall is virtually nonexistent, just as it is along the southern coast, and

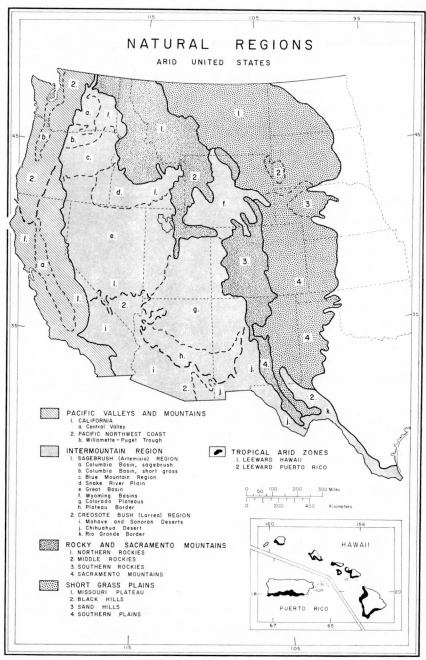

Fig. 3. The natural (phytogeomorphic) regions in the continental western United States can be divided into four major groups.

Table I. Climatic records.

Station	Mean annual precipitation	Summer precipitation, Apr.–Sept.	Winter precipitation, Oct.–Mar.	Mean maximum temperature, July	Mean minimum temperature, Jan.
Southern California					
Santa Monica (coast)	14.90 in. (378.5 mm)	1.04 in. (26.4 mm)	13.86 in. (352.0 mm)	75°F (23.9°C)	46°F (7.8°C)
Riverside (interior)	11.53 in. (292.9 mm)	1.71 in. (43.4 mm)	9.82 in. (249.4 mm)	94°F (34.4°C)	38°F (3.3°C)
Big Bear Lake (mountains)	36.35 in. (923.3 mm)	5.38 in. (136.7 mm)	30.97 in. (786.6 mm)	77°F (25°C)	15°F (−9.4°C)
Central Valley, Calif.					
Buttonwillow (southern valley)	5.5 in. (139.7 mm)	0.97 in. (24.6 mm)	4.53 in. (115.1 mm)	101°F (38.3°C)	33°F (0.6°C)
Red Bluff (northern valley)	23.1 in. (586.7 mm)	3.6 in. (91.4 mm)	19.5 in. (495.3 mm)	98°F (36.7°C)	36.9°F (2.7°C)
Larrea region					
Phoenix, Ariz. (Sonoran Desert)	7.20 in. (182.9 mm)	3.16 in. (80.3 mm)	4.04 in. (102.6 mm)	104.6°F (40.3°C)	37.3°F (2.9°C)
El Paso, Tex. (Chihuahuan Desert)	7.89 in. (200.4 mm)	5.00 in. (127.0 mm)	2.89 in. (73.4 mm)	93.9°F (34.4°C)	31.5°F (−0.3°C)

Source: U.S. Weather Bureau.

extreme heat and low relative humidity combine with low precipitation to raise evapotranspiration to very high rates.

The original vegetation was adjusted to this arduous climate. Now, however, weedy annuals replace the perennial grasses where the land remains in pasture. These annuals sprout after winter rains, carpeting the land with herbage and colorful flowers; maturing in late spring, the plants die in early summer, and the land turns a lifeless brown until winter.

Today, much of the valley is irrigated, and many different crops are grown. East of the San Joaquin River, farming is intensive; in size, the farms usually are not more than 20 to 40 acres (8 to 16 hectares). In contrast, on the drier, unirrigated western valley floor, a single field may be 320 acres (129.5 hectares), and the spacious, mechanized farms produce mainly dry-field barley and wheat (8).

Sagebrush Zone

In the intermountain regions, one is almost never out of sight of mountains but is *in* them only rarely. Because of the persistently clear air that is common to high elevations, the mountains are always visible. Great variations in climate follow the extremes of elevation from 282 feet (86 meters) below sea level in Death Valley to more than 14,000 feet (4267 meters) above sea level in the White Mountains nearby. The creosotebush zone (warm desert) and the sagebrush zone (cool desert) divide the regions into two main sectors. Within each, smaller and distinct subregions emerge.

Sagebrush (*Artemisia* spp.) carpets all of the basins of Wyoming west of the Bighorn and Rocky mountains, reaching southward over the lower parts of the Colorado Plateau and westward over the entire Great Basin and Snake River Plain. This ubiquitous shrub also covers the driest section of the Columbia Basin in the lee of the Cascade Mountains. Although these areas give the impression of flatness, they are high country. Few are less than 2000 feet (600 meters), and most of them exceed 5000 feet (1500 meters) above the sea. Elevation, in part, explains why the temperature ranges some 10 degrees cooler on the Fahrenheit scale (5 degrees cooler on the Celsius scale) than in the southern deserts of the creosotebush. Mean January temperatures fall below freezing, except in the southernmost edge of the zone. The bright sun glares over the entire sagebrush area 70 to 90 percent of the time during the summer. During winter, the average sunshine drops to about 60 percent. Daily extremes of temperatures, owing to elevation and to scant protective cloud cover, are great, particularly during the summer.

The dry northern subregion, the Columbia Basin, carries a mighty river that skirts around its northern and western margin. On its journey from the Canadian Rockies to the Pacific, the Columbia River occupies a steep-walled canyon 2000 to 3000 feet (600 to 900 meters) below the flat lava surface of the basin. Despite the depth of the canyon, the river and its tributaries have exposed only a small portion of the massive basalt flows that blanket the entire area.

Because the river lies so far below the plateau surface, little of the great volume of flowing water is readily available for agriculture. Water diverted from the Columbia at Grand Coulee Dam into the abandoned river channels and man-made canals now irrigates hundreds of thousands of acres (hectares). Skirting the arid core of the Columbia Basin is a semiarid belt that has been largely plowed up and planted to winter wheat.

The Blue Mountains, which form a spur of the Rocky Mountains south of the Columbia Basin, are clothed in ponderosa pine (*Pinus ponderosa*) and rise to 4000 feet (1219 meters) to become a moisture reservoir for their semiarid fringes. Man has made these highlands an area of seasonal grazing and forestry.

The Snake River Plain spreads in a crescent across 16,000 square miles (41,440 square kilometers) of southern Idaho. This monotonously rolling surface is deceptive, in both name and appearance; it is structural, not river-built. Occupying only a small portion of the plain, the river itself slips along, often hidden from view in a box canyon deeply entrenched in the lava surface. The gentle surface of the plain belies its hostile nature. It is built on the horizontal flows of lava, and cinder cones rise frequently from the plain.

Much of the basaltic surface is broken and rocky and is insufficiently weathered to form good, workable soil. Where soil has collected in pockets of the lava sheets or where wind-driven loess has piled up on upland benches and tablelands, man has settled. Sufficient to permit dry farming of grain, the annual precipitation averages 14 to 16 inches (356 to 406 millimeters) on the tablelands in the eastern Snake River Plain (*8*). Agriculture cannot succeed farther west on the plain without irrigation. Irrigation is centered

Potatoes are harvested in an irrigated field at the foot of the Wasatch Range near Ogden, Utah. Water here in the Weber Basin project is stored by a dam for use during the dry summer of the sagebrush (*Artemisia* spp.) zone. (Courtesy U.S. Bureau of Reclamation)

on Pocatello, Twin Falls, and Boise, which hold most of Idaho's population. The principal output includes the world-famous Idaho potato, sugar beets, and dairy products.

The easternmost extent of sagebrush (*Artemisia* spp.) lies in the Wyoming basins, which separate the southern and middle Rocky Mountains. These sparsely populated, level plateaus rise to elevations between 6500 and 7500 feet (1981 and 2286 meters). Aside from mining for fossil fuels, the sagebrush landscape is used seasonally for sheep grazing, with some cattle.

On the Colorado Plateau, which joins the Wyoming basins on the south and the southern Rockies on the west, a brilliant spectrum of colors is exposed in the flat-lying sedimentary beds. The colors and the deep and weirdly eroded canyons cut by the Colorado River and its tributaries combine to produce one of the most magnificently scenic regions on earth. The plateau, which comprises several separately named plateaus, covers an area of about 130,000 square miles (336,700 square kilometers) (9). The spectacular canyons are best developed in the heart of the plateau, where the change from the surface to canyon is abrupt and precipitous.

The forested, dissected plateau border has two precipitation maximums—summer and winter (see Table II). A supremely important water-catchment area is the belt of ponderosa pine (*Pinus ponderosa*) forest, 300 miles (approximately 485 kilometers) long, along the rim of the Mogollon Plateau in central Arizona and southwestern New Mexico.

Deeply entrenched canyons discourage irrigation farming, which is possible only in a few favored localities. In western Colorado, a lush, green oasis of small farms has developed in the Grand Valley along the Colorado River. In a few small valleys in eastern Utah, alfalfa is irrigated to supplement livestock feed. Yearlong grazing is widespread over all of the Colorado Plateau.

The Great Basin, which is centered on the state of Nevada, is classic "basin-and-range" country. Its ranges are uplifted and tilted blocks. Both flora and fauna may be entirely lacking in the lower sections of the bolsons, but in most of the lower elevations, sagebrush and other shrubs prevail.

The forested ranges serve as important local moisture reserves, especially during the dry season; some of the higher eastern ranges receive more than 15 inches (381 millimeters) of precipitation annually. The western Great Basin in the lee of the Sierra Nevada gets the least amount, on the average usually 5 inches (127 millimeters), or even less, each year. A small-scale repetition of this phenomenon occurs on the lee side of numerous pine-clad individual ranges, where less moisture occurs than on the windward side. Summer showers fall more frequently with increasing distance from the coast. The rainiest month shifts from winter to spring toward the east (January in Reno, Nevada; March in Salt Lake City, Utah) in this land of cold winters and warm summers. Settlement in the Great Basin, "the undisputed domain of cattle, sheep, and coyotes" (8, p. 189), is extremely sparse, and extensive seasonal grazing is the only land use. The carrying capacity of the range is so low that the land is not suited for individual homesteads. Rather, large ranching operations graze stock with permits on substantial tracts of public land.

Table II. Climatic records.

Station	Mean annual precipitation	Summer precipitation, Apr.–Sept.	Winter precipitation, Oct.–Mar.	Mean maximum temperature, July	Mean minimum temperature, Jan.
Colorado Plateau (s)					
Green River, Utah (northern plateau)	6.13 in. (155.7 mm)	3.42 in. (86.9 mm)	2.71 in. (68.6 mm)	100.4°F (38.0°C)	8.1°F (−13.3°C)
Crown Point, N. Mex. (central plateau)	11.28 in. (286.5 mm)	7.64 in. (194.1 mm)	3.65 in. (92.7 mm)	84.8°F (29.3°C)	19.6°F (−6.9°C)
Prescott, Ariz. (plateau border)	20.71 in. (526.0 mm)	9.99 in. (253.7 mm)	10.72 in. (272.3 mm)	90.4°F (32.4°C)	19.1°F (−7.2°C)
Great Basin					
Reno, Nev. (western basin)	7.15 in. (181.6 mm)	2.10 in. (53.3 mm)	5.05 in. (128.3 mm)	90.4°F (32.4°C)	17.2°F (−8.2°C)
Salt Lake City, Utah (eastern basin)	13.90 in. (353.1 mm)	6.12 in. (155.4 mm)	7.78 in. (197.6 mm)	92.1°F (33.4°C)	19.5°F (−6.9°C)
Short-grass Plains					
Great Falls, Mont. (northern plains)	14.1 in. (358.1 mm)	4.35 in. (110.5 mm)	9.72 in. (246.9 mm)	83.7°F (28.7°C)	13.5°F (−10.3°C)
Denver, Colo. (central plains)	14.8 in. (375.9 mm)	4.62 in. (117.4 mm)	10.19 in. (258.8 mm)	87.4°F (30.8°C)	16.8°F (−8.4°C)
Lubbock, Tex. (southern plains)	18.8 in. (477.5 mm)	5.58 in. (141.7 mm)	13.24 in. (336.3 mm)	93.9°F (34.4°C)	26.4°F (−3.1°C)

Source: U.S. Weather Bureau.

Apart from occasional ranch and mining camps, the population is concentrated in the oases on the periphery of the region. Salt Lake City and several other towns populate the Great Salt Lake oasis (10). At the western extreme of the Great Basin, at the foot of the Sierra Nevada, is the Reno–Carson City oasis. Farther east, irrigated lands border the Carson and Truckee rivers and stretch like a beaded string along the Humboldt before it disappears in the desert.

Creosotebush Zone

Creosotebush (*Larrea divaricata*) dominates the region that extends southward into Mexico (see Fig. 3). In southern Nevada, the plant gives way to its northern neighbor, the sagebrush (*Artemisia* spp.). Although there is disagreement on boundaries and even on names, the *Larrea* zone can conveniently be divided into four units. The moderately high Mohave Desert between 2000 and 5000 feet (600 and 1500 meters) lies west of the Colorado River and north of the 34th parallel, stretching northward into Death Valley and southern Nevada. The Sonoran Desert, reaching into southeastern California and southern Arizona from coastal Mexico, is relatively low, from sea level or below to somewhat above 2000 feet (600 meters). The higher Chihuahuan Desert includes a small portion of southeastern Arizona, much of the Rio Grande Valley and Tularosa Basin of New Mexico, and a small section of Texas west of the Guadalupe and Davis mountains. A change to the east in the flora and general landscape suggests the fourth unit, the Rio Grande border, which follows the Pecos River and lower Rio Grande to the Gulf of Mexico.

Like the Great Basin, this region is mostly built by large-scale block-faulting. Greatly elongated upthrust and downdropped masses are alined roughly north and south. Nearly the entire region is arid or extremely arid, yet a few mountains rise high enough to have semiarid or humid climates on their upper slopes.

The western Mohave Desert was once probably large mountain masses but now is worn low to almost undistinguishable relief. In some places, this virtually achieves the perfection of the *pediment dome,* the end-product of erosion under desert conditions. Occasional knobby or mountainous remnants remain, but in no way do they resemble the typical block-fault mountain of the basin-and-range type.

Water from the lower Colorado River flows through the Coachella Canal, foreground, to irrigate the Imperial Valley of California. This scene is a basin-and-range landscape of the Sonoran Desert. (Courtesy U.S. Bureau of Reclamation)

It is across basin-and-range landscape that the Rio Grande, after emerging from the southern Rocky Mountains, "picks its way across the disordered surface [of New Mexico] from basin to basin" until it reaches El Paso (11). In like manner, the Colorado, Salt, and Gila rivers find their courses across the drab *Larrea*-covered bolsons of Arizona and California.

The Colorado River, with a giant fan-shaped delta, has dammed completely the structural extension of the Gulf of California, denying entry to floodwaters from the gulf into the below-sea-level (235 feet or 71.6 meters) Salton trough. When it was first viewed by white men, the trough was dry, but in 1905 the river surged in through a canal that had been dug to irrigate the Imperial Valley. For 2 years the water flowed, creating a large shallow lake now called the Salton Sea. When the river was forced back into its previous course, the lake receded through evaporation. It would have dried up completely if it had not been renewed by large amounts of irrigation tail water from the Colorado River, brought to the farms of the Imperial Valley by the All-American and Coachella canals.

Very little rain and hot summers characterize all of the *Larrea* region. The amounts and seasonal distribution of precipitation, humidity, and winter temperatures differ in the several subregions. Soaking winter rains are characteristic of the western Mohave Desert. Winter brings snow regularly to the high Chihuahuan Desert and where altitudes exceed 3000 feet (900 meters). Summer rains pelt down in torrents from towering thunderheads, sometimes causing disastrous local floods. From New Mexico eastward, these convective thunderstorms are from tropical airmasses that originate over the Gulf of Mexico. At El Paso, 65 percent of the yearly precipitation occurs in the summer. However, not all of these showers there and elsewhere reach the ground, for some are only tantalizing phantoms evaporating in the hot, dry air.

Because prolonged drought is frequent and geographic distribution is variable, annual precipitation figures are misleading. Calculated averages represent a nonexisting midpoint between flood and drought. Bagdad, California, had no rain between 3 October 1912 and 8 November 1914, but in 1905, 9.9 inches (251.5 millimeters) fell. Nearby Death Valley, the driest place in the United States, received 0.15 inch (3.8 millimeters) in 1932, but in 1941, 4.62 inches (117.3 millimeters). The entire zone suffers from low humidity, except the part that is close to the Gulfs of California and Mexico.

The high summer temperatures diminish only with altitude. Death Valley holds one of the world's highest temperature records, 134° Fahrenheit (56.7° Celsius) on 10 July 1913. The mean daily maximum for July there is 116° Fahrenheit (46.7° Celsius). For comparative maximum daily temperatures in July, see Fig. 4.

The creosotebush, which emits a pungent, tarry aroma after a desert rain, is associated everywhere with a number of distinct plant communities. Each community is disposed to special conditions of climate, soil, drainage, and slope. The geography of these plants becomes a study in subtle environmental change. Like the domesticated orange trees, frost-sensitive desert plants could not survive subfreezing temperatures without warm "thermal belts." Strong air drainage on alluvial fans and low hills makes a "warm" environment for a broad belt of cactuses, yuccas, and agaves interspersed with a variety of low shrubs. On the other hand, the weirdly branched

Joshua tree (*Yucca brevifolia*) needs a period of dormancy in the comparative winter cold of the high western Mohave to survive.

Low, gray-domed bur-sage (*Franseria dumosa* in California; *F. deltoidea* in Arizona) and cactuses mix with creosotebush on the lower bajada slopes of the desert basins. Cactus reaches its most superb development in the Sonoran Desert of Arizona, especially on

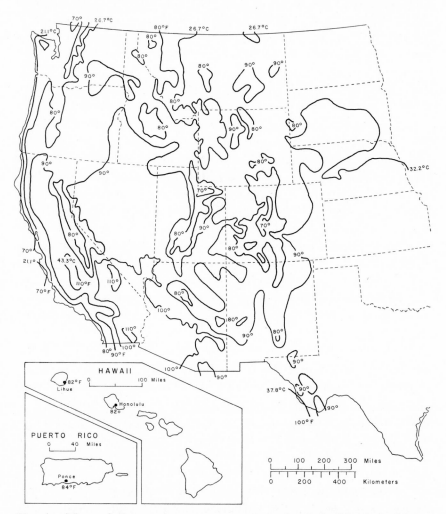

Fig. 4. Mean daily maximum temperatures for July hit their highest marks in the low desert valleys of southeastern California. Except where specifically identified as Celsius (C), all readings are Fahrenheit (F). (Adapted from a U.S. Weather Bureau map)

the coarser soils of the bajadas. The grasslands of the Chihuahuan Desert are adjusted to the summer rains from the east.

The mild winters and long, hot summers of the Sonoran Desert and the Rio Grande border give them a special advantage commercially. Frost-free seasons of not less than 300 days permit the growth of "off-season" winter food crops, frost-sensitive fruits, and a variety of subtropic industrial crops. Thus, the oases of the Imperial Valley, on the Gila and Colorado rivers at Phoenix and Yuma, and of the lower Rio Grande on the Gulf Coast are important to the national economy.

Rocky and Sacramento Mountain Regions

The Rocky Mountains play a powerful role in the life of the arid West. No discussion of aridity would be complete without due consideration of the contradictions and extremes that the mountains represent. The Rockies are responsible, to a large extent, for the aridity. They screen the adjacent plains and plateaus from rain-bearing airmasses. On the other hand, they serve as a huge rain-catcher and are the source of the streams whose waters are basic to much of the economy of the dry lands that spread out, apron-like, from their flanks. Latitude, altitude, and topography combine to create much diversity in local climate. In favored localities, the mountains provide rich resources that support thriving economic communities, but permanent settlement is sparse over large broken expanses.

The Rocky Mountain system, together with the Sacramento Mountain region (the Sacramento, Guadalupe, Davis, and Santiago mountains of southern New Mexico and west Texas), forms a long rampart from the Canadian border to the Rio Grande. The system is about 200 miles (322 kilometers) wide and trends along a sinuous axis from northwest to southeast for approximately 1500 miles (2414 kilometers). The Rockies, rising up between the plateaus, basins and ranges, and plains, have been carved out of a great structural arch. The Sacramento region, although it is geographically continuous, is not part of the Rockies geologically but is actually the easternmost part of the block-faulted ranges of the intermountain regions.

Variety and complexity typify the structure and landforms. Uncounted numbers of peaks rise 6000 to 8000 feet (1829 to 2438 meters) above the surrounding country. Some of the most ruggedly beautiful of the mountain masses result from deep erosion in extrusive and intrusive volcanics, such as the San Juan Mountains of Colorado and the Absaroka peaks of Yellowstone National Park. Many areas of subdued topography are scattered in the mountain complex, however. Extensive, elevated erosion surfaces, intermontane basins, parks, and broad valleys are dispersed widely throughout the region.

The Rocky Mountains are the birthplace of countless small streams, which combine and create the great rivers that support much of the agricultural, municipal, and industrial life of the dry plains. Fed by water from rains and melting snow and ice, these streams have eroded a maze of canyons and broad valleys through the uplands. The demand for their water exceeds the supply in many areas, as lowland populations continue to increase at an accelerated rate. A series of reservoirs on both slopes of the Rocky Mountains, in addition to transmountain diversion tunnels, control the flow of the water to areas of greatest need.

Even the dominant controls of climate—the mountain barrier, elevation, local relief, and latitude—are quite variable. Although the Rockies stand as a great climatic screen, their windward- and leeward-slope relationships are not fixed. As a result, the western slopes become the windward, wet slopes only when they are under the influence of Pacific airmasses and the passage of cyclonic cold fronts. The eastern slopes become the windward, wet slopes when gulf airmasses are dominant, and the western slopes then lie in the rain shadow of the mountains. However, more of the total precipitation occurs in winter, as snow, on the western side than on the eastern side of the barrier, and the snowpack remains longer on the ground on the western side. In contrast, many protected basins and valleys receive little moisture and remain as deserts.

The mountains also serve as uncluttered playgrounds for people seeking recreation. They are also the source of many valuable wood products. Except in the northern Rockies, the abrupt topographic break between plains and mountains is accompanied by an equally sharp change from grassland to narrow-leaved coniferous forests. At high altitudes, the timberline is boldly developed and marks the transition between the forest and the Alpine-tundra formations. The mountain forests occur in distinct zones; their character and ecology are discussed in detail in Chapter 10. Timberline, which decreases in altitude from about 12,000 feet (3658 meters) in southern New Mexico to 10,600 feet (3231 meters) in Montana, marks the lower limit of the Alpine tundra.

Transhumance, the movement of grazing livestock to high mountain pastures in summer and back to lower valleys and plains in winter, is almost universal throughout the region. The range for cattle is largely confined to the lower slopes of the forested zones and the grassy parklands. Sheep generally are grazed on drier ranges or on the rich, nutritive grasses and sedges in the Alpine tundra and subalpine Engelmann spruce-fir (*Picea engelmannii-Abies* spp.) zones.

Agriculture in the mountains, which is dependent on the markets in tourist and commercial centers, is widely dispersed. The occasional level or more gently sloping areas that will support either irrigation or dry farming are essentially the home base or center for the more important pastoral activities. Thin, lithosolic soils cover most of the mountains; but, in many of the dry basins, parks, and broad valleys, immature soils have developed in the alluvium and are quite productive when rain or irrigation water is available.

Tourism and recreation activities probably support more people in the Rocky Mountains than all other industries, and without tourism many of the populated areas would disappear. Tourism, which formerly was confined mainly to the summer season, now continues throughout the year, as more and more people are attracted by the opportunities to engage in winter sports.

Short-Grass Plains

The short-grass Plains form the nation's largest grassland in a long swath east of the Rocky Mountains. They extend across the Canadian border and south to the Pecos River. The eastern margin follows the limits of short grasses mapped by Homer Shantz (*12*). The wind-formed Sand Hills of Nebraska lie astride the semiarid climatic boundary and are included because the grassland economy that characterizes these hills is typical of the western Great Plains.

A sparse cover of *Yucca*, creosotebush (*Larrea divaricata*), and Joshua trees (*Yucca brevifolia*) typifies an arid, gravel slope in southern Nevada. In the distance, shales are being eroded into badlands. (Courtesy Robert R. Humphrey, University of Arizona)

Cultivation has been a precarious, marginal enterprise where it has been pushed westward into the short-grass country. Now, the already sparse rural population is declining, although numbers are increasing in the major cities. Crop failure and losses of livestock on a gigantic scale started the migration out of the Plains. However, dry farming continues to move into the still drier areas.

The broad, unifying expanses of grassland and plain are in part illusory, for the Black Hills, the Missouri Plateau, the Nebraska Sand Hills, the southern short-grass, or High, Plains, each has its unique character. The usual concept of the Great Plains as a flat, featureless expanse is realized only in the Staked Plains of the Texas Panhandle and eastern New Mexico. There, in every direction, flatness extends beyond the range of the eye. Other areas are, of course, broad and smooth, but not as extensive as in the Staked Plains. Flatness is indeed broken in the high, rough, lava-capped mesas of northern New Mexico and in the Sand Hills of Nebraska.

The dry climate, coupled with the short grass and a shortage of wood and water, usually is strange and unattractive to people who are accustomed to the humid woodlands of the East. In general, precipitation is the greatest along the eastern margin of the southern Plains. Except for a narrow belt that hugs the Rocky Mountains, precipitation in the region decreases westward and northward from the Gulf of Mexico, the primary source of moisture. Most of it falls as rain during the summer. During the winter, icy blasts of polar or Canadian air roll down the Plains unimpeded from the north. The summers are warm and somewhat more humid than the winters, when the sky is clear and the air is subfreezing for long periods (see Table II).

High wind and long hours of sunshine contribute to high rates of evaporation, making the effectiveness of precipitation low (10). Windbreaks are often required to reduce the force of destructive winds. Although unusually torrential and destructive rains do occur, typically, the rain comes to the Plains as showers. The amount of precipitation in a single shower and the time of year when it falls are of utmost importance to the plainsman. Light rains are of little value during hot weather, although they are beneficial at other times (13). Showers may fall too early or too late in a growing season to help the small grain in its early stage of development.

Retention of moisture is of basic importance to dry farming and stock raising in the drier sections of the short-grass Plains. The degree of slope and the texture of the soil at the surface can be critical. Excessive runoff is a problem, particularly on the thin, heavy, fine-textured soils that cover large areas of central and southeastern Montana, western South Dakota, and northeastern Wyoming. On the other hand, very sandy lands, such as those in the Nebraska Sand Hills and along many rivers in the central and southern Plains, are especially receptive to moisture. Unfortunately, they are limited in fertility and very susceptible to wind erosion, making them of little use except for pasture or hay. Rough lands of shale and sand can be used only for light, scattered grazing and rank high as demerit, or problem, areas (see Fig. 5); stock raising is decreasing. In contrast, soils of considerable fertility, fine, windblown dust or loess, are found widely in the central and southern Plains and along the northern glacial margin, which roughly parallels the Missouri River. In these fertile areas, the plainsmen practice dry farming.

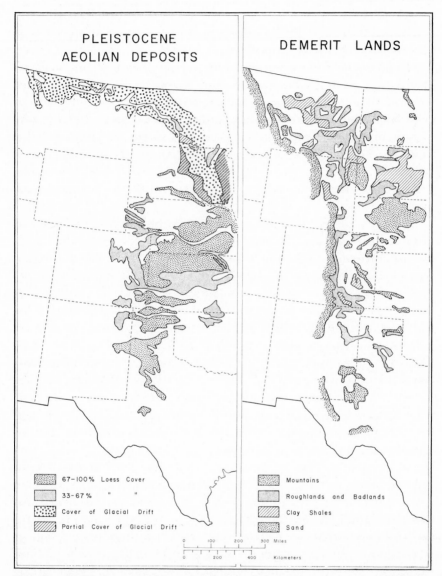

PLEISTOCENE
AEOLIAN DEPOSITS

DEMERIT LANDS

67-100% Loess Cover
33-67 %   "   "
Cover of Glacial Drift
Partial Cover of Glacial Drift

Mountains
Roughlands and Badlands
Clay Shales
Sand

0   100   200   300 Miles
0   200   400   Kilometers

Fig. 5. Demerit, or problem, lands are those that are too mountainous, rough, sandy, or clayey for full agricultural use. The loessal and glacial drift areas of the Plains tend to be fertile.

Wheat is planted in the northern Plains in great strips perpendicular to the direction of the prevailing wind; the alternating strips of cultivated and fallow land are set in rectangular blocks. To the drier west, this landscape is replaced by rolling range, whose monotonous expanse is broken only by the river valleys with their groves of cottonwoods (*Populus sargentii*).

The characteristic vegetation of the western Great Plains is short, native grass. Common species include the purple-spiked blue grama (*Bouteloua gracilis*), which does not grow during drought and occurs on loamy-clay uplands; buffalograss (*Buchloe dactyloides*), whose gray-green foliage also may be seen in the uplands; and the western wheatgrass (*Agropyron*). These short grasses may be invaded by taller species from the subhumid eastern prairies during wetter years; then the invaders retreat again in the face of prolonged drought.

Although grazing appears to dominate the area because of the broad expanse of land it occupies, the direct gross return per acre (hectare) from crops in much of the region exceeds that from pasture by more than 10 to 1. Even in the Sand Hills, for example, 80 percent of the area of most of the counties was devoted to pasture in 1935, 18 percent to permanent hay, and only 2 percent to crops. Yet the crops were more valuable than pasture (*14*).

Recurrent drought on the Plains has started the quest for water beneath the surface. From southwest Kansas to the Texas Panhandle, land under irrigation from well water has developed considerably. West Texas now outranks the South Platte Basin in irrigated area. The Llano Estacado around Lubbock, Texas, is the fastest-growing irrigated area in the United States and the largest outside of California (*15*). Here cotton is the primary crop, but, in the irrigated districts in Montana, alfalfa for winter livestock feed predominates. On the Colorado piedmont, alfalfa and sugar beets rule supreme. The highly mechanized dry-farm regions, which are stricken periodically by drought and crop failure, specialize in spring and winter wheat in the central part and grain sorghum and cotton in the south. In all these areas, much land is allowed to lie fallow to conserve moisture for the crop that follows, particularly wheat.

The towns and cities of the Plains grew in the oases where irrigation developed, where the transportation routes have by easy choice followed the valleys, and where there are attractive opportunities for business, service, processing, and manufacturing. The Denver metropolitan area (population 929,383 in 1960), with its sprawling, expanding suburbs, is the largest urban center of the region.

Wheat is alternated with fallow strips on the dry farms of Cascade County, near Great Falls, Montana. Shelterbelts and strips "across the wind" are characteristics of the Great Plains; they provide protection from high winds. (Courtesy U.S. Department of Agriculture, Soil Conservation Service)

Tropical Arid Zones

The environments of Hawaii and Puerto Rico deserve special consideration. These islands, separated by 5600 miles (9010 kilometers), have many common aspects: latitude, economic development, and dry coastal lowlands. Northeast trade winds prevail in both areas. They ascend mountainous slopes and bring copious amounts of rainfall as they cool. The air continues around the rugged backbones of the islands and, as it descends to the leeward slopes, warms under compression. In Hawaii, these zones occur on the western and southern margins of the large islands of Hawaii, Maui, Molokai, Oahu, and Kauai. The small islands of Kahoolawe and Niihau, which are completely arid, nestle in the lee of huge volcanoes. On Maui, Oahu, and Molokai, the dry areas push inland along protected saddle-shaped valleys (*16*). In the Commonwealth of Puerto Rico, an east-west semiarid belt along the southern coast parallels the main Cordillera Central.

Because of high rates of evaporation, high temperature, low relative humidity, and constant wind, precipitation effectiveness is roughly half that of the mid-latitudes of the mainland United States (*17*). Tropical stations that receive more or less than 40 inches (approximately 1000 millimeters) on the average each year could be considered as subhumid (or humid) and semiarid (or arid), respectively (*6*). But excessively drained, steep slopes and porous soils can produce drought well beyond this climatic limit. In fact, it is common to see cultivated crops under irrigation in localities that receive as much as 50 inches (1270 millimeters) of precipitation annually. The need for irrigating is heightened by well-defined dry seasons.

Scarcity of water for agricultural, industrial, and residential development mars the attractiveness of the leeward localities for settlement. Water is ample on the larger islands of Hawaii and on Puerto Rico. Problems exist, however, in collecting and transporting it from areas of surplus to areas of deficit. Farmers of southern Puerto Rico get supplemental water from wells, tapping in alluvial deposits along the coast.

Ground-water supplies in Hawaii are vital, since there is no chance to construct reservoirs where rock is usually porous and where streams plunge down steep gradients. Some Hawaiian ground water is perched at high levels above impermeable layers of rock or confined between lava dikes. Such water becomes available when tunnels are driven into the mountains. Trapped ground water is sometimes subject to artesian pressure near sea level and is tapped by skimming tunnels or drilling ordinary wells.

About half of the cultivated lands of the Hawaiian Islands are in semiarid or arid settings (*18*). The major land use of the arid lowlands is the grazing of beef cattle. Grazing forage is abundant in the winter rainy season, and mesquite (*Prosopis chilensis*) pods abound during the dry summer. Sugarcane predominates on irrigated land. Irrigated canefields occupy portions of the isthmus of Maui and the dry zones of Oahu and Kaui.

Acknowledgments: The cooperation and assistance of Peveril Meigs is gratefully acknowledged. Mary H. MacPhail and Genevieve A. Caldwell helped in compiling and preparing the manuscript.

REFERENCES

1. H. L. Shantz, "History and problems of arid lands development," in *The Future of Arid Lands,* G. F. White, Ed. (Am. Assoc. for the Advancement of Science, Washington, D.C., 1956), pp. 3–25.
2. C. W. Thornthwaite, "An approach toward a rational classification of climate," *Geograph. Rev.* **38**, 55–94 (1948).
3. P. Meigs, "World distribution of arid and semiarid homoclimes," *Rev. Res. Arid Zone Hydrol. (UNESCO),* Map 393, Rev. 1 (1953).
4. ———, "Arid and semiarid climatic types of the world," *Proc. Intern. Geograph. Union, 17th Congr., Washington, D.C.* (1957).
5. P. G. Worcester, *A Textbook of Geomorphology* (Van Nostrand, Princeton, N.J., 1948), p. 220.
6. U.S. Dept. of Agriculture, *Soils and Man, Yearbook Agr., U.S. Dept. Agr.* **1938** (1938).
7. J. L. Gardner, "Vegetation of the creosotebush area of the Rio Grande Valley in New Mexico," *Ecol. Monographs* **21**, 381–383 (1951).
8. F. J. Marschner, "Land use and its patterns in the United States," *U.S. Dept. Agr., Agr. Handbook 153* (1958).
9. W. W. Atwood, *The Physiographic Provinces of North America* (Ginn, Boston, 1940).
10. C. L. White and E. J. Foscue, *Regional Geography of Anglo-America* (Prentice-Hall, Englewood Cliffs, N.J., ed. 2, 1954), pp. 283, 347.
11. N. M. Fenneman, *Physiography of Western United States* (McGraw-Hill, New York, 1931), pp. 1–91, 390–392.
12. H. L. Shantz and R. Zon, "Natural vegetation," in *Atlas of American Agriculture* (U.S. Dept. of Agriculture, Washington, D.C., 1924).
13. J. B. Brandon and O. R. Mathews, "Dry land rotation and tillage experiments of the Akron (Colorado) field station," *U.S. Dept. Agr. Circ. 700* (1944), p. 8.
14. U.S. Congress, *The Western Range,* S. Doc. 199, 74th Congr., 2nd sess. (Washington, D.C., 1936), p. 299.
15. U.S. Bureau of the Census, "A graphic summary of land utilization," *U.S. Census of Agriculture, 1959* (1962), vol. 5, Spec. Repts., pt. 6, chap. 1, pp. 21–22.
16. M. G. Cline *et al., Soil Survey of the Territory of Hawaii* (U.S. Dept. of Agriculture, Washington, D.C., 1955).
17. R. C. Roberts, *Soil Survey of Puerto Rico* (U.S. Dept. of Agriculture, Washington, D.C., 1942).
18. H. Bartholomew and Associates, *An Inventory of Available Information on Land Use in Hawaii* (Economic Planning and Coordination Authority, Honolulu, 1957).

3

Indian Adaptations to
Arid Environments

RICHARD B. WOODBURY

Before the white man came to the New World, the areas we now classify as *arid* and *semiarid* were the scene of both simple and complex cultural developments. Such great advances as the domestication of plants, the development of skilled metallurgy, and the rise of urban centers took place in the arid regions of Central and South America. Within what is now the United States, no native culture reached the civilized stage that marked the cultures of the Mexican Plateau and the Andes. Yet for America north of Mexico the peaks in population density, which is one rough criterion of human success in exploitation of the environment, were on the Colorado Plateau and on the Pacific Coast just north of San Francisco Bay.

The aboriginal occupations of the arid western United States were varied, ranging from scattered hunters and gatherers with an extremely simple technology and social organization, in the Great Basin, to villages of skilled irrigators whose fields covered thousands of acres (hectares) along the Rio Grande, the Gila, and the Salt rivers. None of these groups depended on others outside their own arid homeland for consumption goods. Some produced agricultural surpluses that supported sizable numbers of craftsmen and priests, but the scarce and uncertain water supplies placed some limitations on population.

The Indian was not independent of his arid environment or oblivious of it. Instead, he used it with great skill, overcame many of its limitations, and worked out a great variety of adaptations to it. These were, of course, cultural, and not instinctive, behavior; they were learned by each individual from other members of the group, rather than by his own trials and errors. Through language, complex behavior systems are transmitted from one generation to another; and because cultural behavior can be learned quickly, new adaptations sometimes can be made with great rapidity. Yet cultures also change slowly at times, each person continuing the patterns of activity learned from early childhood, with no reexamination or readjustment of them in the light of changed external conditions.

Arrival of Man in the New World

There is good evidence that man had entered and spread widely throughout the New World by about 10,000 years ago (1). The route of entry was through northeastern Siberia to Alaska; hence, the first arrivals in what is now the western United States probably moved in slowly from the north in small groups and gradually learned to make use of the new food resources they encountered.

The climate and vegetation of the Pleistocene epoch were, at times, markedly different from the present, even far beyond the glacial borders. With cooler and moister conditions, areas now in grassland had coniferous forests. Some of the present-day deserts had heavy grass with tree-bordered streams. For example, pollen studies in southeastern Arizona indicate that what is now the upper part of the Sonoran Desert supported woodland in the past, with pine, oak, juniper, and sagebrush (2). Sites on the Llano Estacado of New Mexico and Texas, where mammoth and bison once were killed and butchered, show evidence of former ponds and marshes, although today there is no permanent surface water in the region. The earliest arrivals in the New World, then, did not necessarily face, and have to adjust to, an arid environment. If they came during or late in the Wisconsin glaciation, when sea levels were low enough to permit passage from Siberia to Alaska, they would have had many centuries of cool, moist conditions.

Food Gatherers

Two main kinds of subsistence economy were developed by the early inhabitants of North America: one was based on the collection of wild plant foods supplemented with the hunting of small game; the other was based primarily on the hunting of large game, including some of the now extinct large grazing animals. The utilization of plant resources was a new development, since the necessary plants would have been absent to the many generations of hunters who made the slow expansion eastward across Bering Strait and then southward. Essential to the collection and preparation of plant seeds by the food gatherers were baskets, tumplines for carrying them, sieves, grinding slabs or mortars, and many other artifacts (3). It is important to realize that the development of techniques and equipment represents a skilled specialization, and not a crude or casual exploitation of the environment. Intimate knowledge of the area and its plants (and of the small animals trapped, shot, or clubbed) was necessary. Many of the small seeds are indigestible by human beings unless the hard husks are broken by heat (parched with hot coals in basket trays) or crushed.

Once the potentialities of these abundant, widespread, but unspectacular resources were fully understood by the families or bands roaming the West, this way of life could continue as long as the natural resources were available. Indeed, the Shoshonean-speakers of Utah and Nevada were still living by these same techniques in the 19th century and were forced to change only when the invading white man introduced changes (cattle, fencing, dams, weeds, and so forth). If duration is an indication of the success of a pattern of existence, then these gathering people of the grasslands and deserts achieved an outstandingly successful subsistence adjustment.

Big-Game Hunters

A different type of skill and probably a considerable degree of cooperative effort within the small, frequently moving bands were needed for success in hunting the large grazing animals that were present in the West until 7000 or 8000 years ago. Much of the hunting was done at waterholes and streams, where bison, camels, horses, mammoths, and mastodons, as well as smaller animals, could be ambushed and killed at short range. Hunting was with spears or darts, propelled with a short throwing stick, or thrust, or hurled by hand. The distinctive lanceolate points with a thin, flaked channel on each side (Clovis and Folsom types) have proved to be helpful in correlating sites of these hunters, since only a few sites have radiocarbon dates.

The disappearance of most of the large grazing animals brought an end to this subsistence pattern, whereas the gathering pattern continued into times of greater aridity. The relative roles played by man and climate in the extinction of these late Pleistocene animals is still disputed, but if waterholes dwindled and herds were forced into more constricted ranges, even a few scattered bands of hunters eventually might have killed off one herd after another. The human population dependent on these animals did not, I believe, die with them but gradually increased its dependence on plant foods and small game. If the recent work of Paul S. Martin, palynologist at the University of Arizona, proves to be correct, no significant climatic change occurred to contribute to extinction of the animals. Man may deserve the entire credit or blame.

Introduction of Agriculture

The next major change in the ways in which the aborigines used the arid western portions of North America was extremely slow to come. The gathering and small-scale hunting pattern persisted with little change for many millenniums. But it provided a valuable basis for the eventual use of domestic plants, since the relationships of plants to moisture, temperature, and other conditions were already clearly understood, and the equipment used in gathering and preparing wild seeds was equally appropriate for domestic plant foods. Thus, the stage was set for the introduction of agriculture long before the event actually occurred. Initially, the only change required in basic subsistence patterns was a somewhat less mobile life, with at least part of the group staying with the crops from planting to harvesting.

The beginnings of New World agriculture were far to the south of the area considered here, and as in so many aspects of aboriginal culture, the peoples north of the Rio Grande were peripheral, the receivers, rather than the donors, of new ideas. Maize was the major domestic plant of the North American Indians, with beans and squash the most important supplemental crops. All three of these species seem to have been domesticated in Mexico beginning before 5000 B.C., with the changes from wild plant to cultigen proceeding over several thousand years. Recently Paul C. Mangelsdorf, Harvard University botanist, and his associates have crossed varieties of corn containing early, primitive characteristics, as is seen by dissection of archeologic specimens (4). They have demonstrated that the primitive cultivated maize was a pod-popcorn, having the valuable characteristic that, with no special preparation, the kernels could be heated and would "pop" into an edible starchy mass. The yield of these early corn plants was slight; only the remarkable later mutations and hybridizations resulted in a crop that could be depended on for the basis of Indian economy.

For the area that is now the southwestern United States, maize agriculture did not begin until about 3500 B.C., the radiocarbon date of tiny ears of corn from Bat Cave in west-central New Mexico. This suggests a 1000- to 2000-year interval during which knowledge and use of maize spread along the upland zone of the Sierra Madre and its Arizona-New Mexico continuation, a distance of some 1700 miles (2700 kilometers). Diffusion took this long because of the slowness with which maize became a high-yielding plant and the sparseness of the population through which it spread. Plant gatherers and small-animal hunters live in small groups, each roaming a sizable territory. Thus the opportunities for the transmission of new culture traits, such as maize cultivation, are reduced to a minimum. A band might add maize to its diet and grow small patches at suitable locations, and yet the seeds and the necessary knowledge of their use would not be acquired by another band 12 or 18 miles (20 or 30 kilometers) away. Contributing to this slowness of diffusion was probably the conservatism of groups who had worked out an effective scheme of exploiting wild food resources, a conservatism reflected in the persistence of the pattern for some 10 millenniums.

Village-Farming Life

Advantageous as the aboriginal pattern of agriculture may seem, based on maize and supplemented by squash, beans, and a few other plants, it nevertheless took millenniums to become established. It was a profound, though gradual, break with the past, since the sequence of preparing the ground, planting, cultivating, and harvesting precluded much of the former seasonal movement. Farming had the great advantage that stored food supplies usually could support the group through the winter. Although population density for most of the arid West probably did not increase markedly with the adoption of agriculture, concentrations in favored locations were possible on a scale that food collecting had never permitted.

Religious and artisan groups within the larger whole could develop, focusing their energies on many special activities that ultimately benefited the entire village. Individual specialization could develop advantageously; hence, the expert weaver, potter, housebuilder, jeweler, wood-carver, or other craftsman achieved and passed on skills far beyond what the "jack-of-all-trades" in a nomadic band ever could achieve. This pattern of village life is associated with farming, not only in parts of North America, but throughout the world.

Villages and Water Sources

Archeologic evidence indicates that the first farms in the Southwest were on the Colorado Plateau or the plateau border, where rainfall probably was ample for dry farming. The highest elevations would not have been suitable, because of the too-short growing season, even though water was abundant. Much of the terrain was rough and steep, and some of the soils were unproductive. At much lower elevations summer rainfall would have been scanty for successful germination and growth of crops. The oldest villages for which evidence of agriculture reasonably can be dated fall within the 4th to the 8th centuries A.D., and lie at elevations of 3500 to 6800 feet (1100 to 2100 meters) (5). The only exception is on the Gila River in Arizona at about 1200 feet (365 meters), where annual precipitation is about 10 inches (254 millimeters). Since this is insufficient for dry farming, the Indians simply may have planted in the wet margins of the river after the spring floods.

This, then, may indicate the beginning of a type of farming that was not wholly dependent on direct precipitation. But even with the development of this and more elaborate techniques to use surface water, farming was restricted. The spread of aboriginal farming was limited severely by environmental shortcomings that were beyond the technologic skills of the Indians to compensate for, with the partial exception of the water supply. The water supply was the "major variable" subject to human manipulation and, thus, became a major focus of effort.

The maximum spread of Indian agriculture, as is shown in Fig. 1, was achieved prior to the droughts of the 12th and 13th centuries. Farming spread to Texas, New Mexico, Colorado, Utah, Nevada, and Arizona, with its furthest reaches near Great Salt Lake in the north and along the Canadian River toward the east. On the Great Plains, agriculture spread westward from the Mississippi Valley and eastern woodlands, where it had reached from Mexico in an expansion separate from, but related to, that into the Southwest. Farming advanced along the major rivers, such as the Platte and the Missouri, avoiding the intervening grasslands.

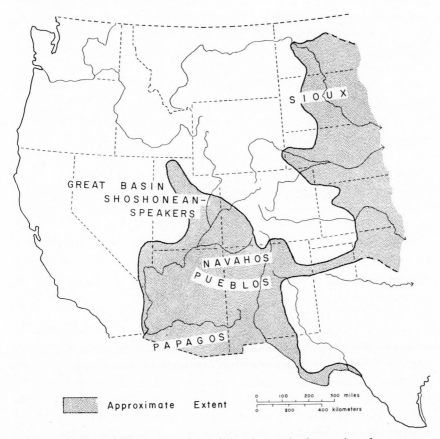

Fig. 1. Maximum extent of prehistoric agriculture in the western United States. All of this area was not farmed simultaneously, and by the 16th century agriculturists had abandoned much of it. Tribal names show the location in historical times of the Indian groups discussed in this chapter.

It is impossible to show the hundreds of small areas that never supported farming. The map should, ideally, show a myriad of tiny oases, each based on a fairly dependable water supply, separated by larger areas used for the hunting and collection of wild plant foods. But wherever Indians did establish farming villages, the pattern of subsistence seems to have been the optimum use of the environment, within the limitations posed by a simple technology. Fields could be prepared for planting with the digging stick or the stone or the buffalo scapula hoe. Planting was with a simple dibble. Women and children, as well as men, guarded ripening crops from birds, deer, and rodents, and the harvest was carried on human backs to carefully built storehouses, where each family hoped to have reserves to carry it through at least one or two poor years. Only in the manipulation of the water supply did Indian farmers effectively modify the environmental situation in order to improve significantly the acreage and yield of their farms.

Water-Control Techniques

Small terraces on steep, intermittent streams, ditches fed by springs and creeks, and the large-scale irrigation of the Gila-Salt and the Rio Grande drainages have long been recognized by archeologists and recently have received intensive study. Man's entire relationship with his environment currently is receiving new attention by anthropologists. Although the technology of the Indians was simple and their engineering knowledge elementary, in comparison with ours, they were more successful than has been realized in managing the water available for farming.

One of the most widely employed techniques was the building of small terraces of dry stone masonry across steep, intermittent streams. Soil rapidly accumulated behind each wall, and, during periods of streamflow, moisture was held in sufficient quantity to produce better crops than those in the surrounding area. At Mesa Verde National Park in southwestern Colorado, recent work by Arthur H. Rohn disclosed 40 series of terraces containing more than 900 individual terraces on the slopes of Chapin Mesa. In the Point of Pines area of east-central Arizona similar terraces have been carefully mapped and analyzed (6). The area that such locations added to farmland was probably not as important as the insurance they

Prehistoric stone terraces at Mesa Verde, Colorado, held back soil and accumulated moisture for the watering of crops. (Courtesy R. B. Woodbury)

provided for a crop in all but the most extreme droughts and the higher yields that they gave. These terraced fields are known in most of the area of prehistoric farming and undoubtedly contributed significantly to the success of many farming settlements.

Judged by the age of some nearby archeologically dated ruins, the terraces at Point of Pines probably were built from the 11th century onward. Those of Mesa Verde are of about the same age. All of these simple but efficient structures increased the agricultural potentiality of rugged, uncertainly watered land, using moisture that naturally concentrated in these locations but would otherwise have been lost.

On gentler slopes without well-defined drainage channels, and on some quite steep, rocky slopes, low walls or lines of boulders often

were built along the contour to serve a function similar to that of
the terraces. On nearly level ground, these lines of boulders were
sometimes laid out in irregular grids and probably had the additional purpose of protecting the soil from wind erosion and eliminating stones from the land to be farmed.

Another widely used farming technique is water spreading, the
planting of crops at the mouths of small canyons or arroyos, where
the gradient abruptly decreases and water tends to soak into the
ground. A little careful ditching and banking around plants at the
moment of runoff assures the optimum use of each small flow. As
with terraces, the area involved may be small, but it is far better
watered than the adjacent land. This type of farming has continued
in use by the Papagos and Hopis of southern and northeastern Arizona, respectively. It has been determined (7) that Hopi fields from
14 to 247 acres (6 to 100 hectares) in size each received runoff from
a watershed with 15 to 30 times its area. In arid areas with infrequent, intense local summer rains, this is excellent assurance of water
for a particular field location, resulting from the Indian farmers'
careful observation of natural conditions.

In contrast to these methods for making better use of water where
it occurred naturally, the Indian farmers of the Southwest also
brought water to their fields by means of ditches. These ranged in
size from 1.5 feet (0.5 meter) wide (as at Montezuma Castle National Monument in the Verde Valley of Arizona, where ditches are
preserved by a natural mineral deposit) to 33 feet (10 meters) or
more in width for the larger canals along the Gila and Salt rivers
in southern Arizona (8, 9). The large canals were as much as 10
to 12 miles (16 to 20 kilometers) long, and, although built without
engineering instruments, they followed a regular gradient successfully, allowing water to move from a place where it could not be
used or was overabundant to a place where it could irrigate crops.
The large canals of southern Arizona are of special interest because
of their number and size. Conservative estimates suggest more than
185 miles (300 kilometers) of main canals, and the total may have
been twice this. Canals irrigated areas as far as 7 or 7.5 miles (11 or
12 kilometers) from live water and watered many thousands of acres
(hectares) of intensively cultivated land. The oldest dated trace of
a major canal was built about A.D. 800. A long, slow development is
probable, starting from simple floodwater farming along the banks

of large rivers, with planting taking place as soon as spring floods subsided.

Decline of Village-Farming Life

The widely established farming villages of the Southwest and the considerable penetration of horticulture into the northern short-grass Plains rested on a highly successful exploitative pattern—maize, beans, and squash raised in sufficient quantities to provide reserves against occasional poor years, with villages, sometimes of several hundred people, maintaining themselves on the same farmlands for many generations. Nevertheless, this farming life was precarious, always threatened by the many aspects of the environment over which the Indians had little or no control. In both the Plains and the Southwest, it failed at innumerable locations. Beginning in the 13th century, one settlement after another was abandoned, and by the 16th century the area of village-farming life was about one-tenth of what it had been earlier. Among explanations for this eclipse, disease and raiding nomads can be dismissed for lack of convincing evidence. Climatic change of some sort is repeatedly invoked as an explanation and is almost certainly correct. But both the nature of the change and details of its effect on aboriginal farming are still far from clear.

There is evidence from tree-ring studies of a long and severe drought in the 13th century, undoubtedly sufficient to have resulted in crop failures year after year in some places. It may have set off a cycle of erosion, through the reduction of vegetative cover. Another climatic fluctuation, a shift toward lower temperatures and, therefore, a shorter growing season, also may have contributed importantly to the withdrawal of aboriginal farmers from many areas at higher elevations.

By the 16th century, in the Southwest, there were villages of farmers only on the Rio Grande in New Mexico and at a few locations westward to the Hopi villages of northeastern Arizona, along a short stretch of the Gila River, and in scattered locations in Chihuahua and Sonora in Mexico. On the short-grass Plains there were still farmers along the middle Missouri River, but nowhere to the south. Many of these villages remained during white settlement as enclaves where traditional Indian farming methods were practiced, and where

New World crops long adapted to arid conditions survived until white plant breeders and farmers became interested in them. Small, widely dispersed populations, relying on a large assortment of wild species, gave up their collecting economy only when the inroads of white hunters, ranchers, and farmers destroyed the plants and animals on which they had depended. One such group in the Southwest, the immigrant Navahos, had adopted a semidependence on agriculture from contact with native farmers they found in the Rio Grande drainage, before the coming of the whites.

Intrusion by Adaptable Athabascans

Although the Navahos and Apaches, speakers of closely related Athabascan languages, now are among the largest groups of Indians in the nation, they are recent arrivals from the Far North. Archeologic evidence is lacking to trace the movement of their ancestors southward, but small bands probably moved down the eastern side of the Rocky Mountains, occasionally wandering east as far as the outlying farming villages of the Plains; other bands may have moved south through the intermontane region onto the Colorado Plateau. By about the beginning of the 16th century, they had reached northwestern New Mexico. Extensive recent research has failed to support the long-held belief in a much earlier Athabascan arrival.

Although they came to the Southwest as hunters and plant collectors, they quickly acquired the farming skills of the Pueblo Indian villagers whose ancestral lands they were infiltrating. The rapidity of this fundamental economic change is evidence of a remarkable ability in cultural adaptation that marks the Navahos. "The Navahos show, on the one hand, a general lack of emotional resistance to learning new techniques and using foreign tools, and, on the other, a capacity for making alien techniques fit in with their preexistent design for living" (10, p. 28).

With the acquisition of farming, the Navaho population probably expanded, as did the area they occupied. They only partially adopted, however, the village pattern of life, most families preferring to live scattered along the valleys where their fields were. The source of their agricultural techniques and crops and also of their architecture, weaving, and pottery-making in the 16th and 17th centuries

Present-day Hopis in Arizona terrace their hillside gardens in much the
same manner as their forefathers did. (Courtesy U.S. Department of
Agriculture, Soil Conservation Service)

is, nevertheless, clearly Puebloan. But the Navahos maintained their
linguistic and political independence; and their basic outlook on
the world—their value system—altered hardly at all.

By the beginning of the 18th century, however, two other conspicuous elements in Navaho life were being adopted: sheepherding
and the use of horses. Although the Puebloans and possibly the
Navahos acquired a few sheep, cattle, and horses as early as 1540
from the Coronado expedition, the farming pattern really was not
changed. Sheepherding, when the Navahos later took it up, provided
a means of using large tracts of sparse grassland and replaced hunting
as a source of meat. Weaving was greatly stimulated by the increased
wool supply, and by the time that Arizona and New Mexico were
wrested from Mexico and added to the United States, herding and
weaving were well established as basic parts of Navaho life. When
the Navahos were released by the U.S. Army in 1868, after 4 years
of captivity (11), they were given 15,000 sheep and goats as a start

toward renewed self-sufficiency. An increase in numbers led to serious overgrazing of the range in later years and to the bitterly opposed stock-reduction program that was carried through by the Bureau of Indian Affairs in the 1930's.

In only about four centuries the Navahos transformed themselves from a handful of hunters and collectors into a settled, numerous folk, who depended on corn farming and on large flocks of sheep and goats for subsistence and on horses for transportation and wealth. Not only their economy was transformed, but also their dress and architecture, their handicrafts, and their religious rituals. Nevertheless, their adjustment to the arid lands they had made theirs was precarious. From their first arrival in the Southwest until the mid-19th century their numbers probably increased about tenfold; in 1864 the captives totaled 8354. In the last 100 years the population has increased tenfold again, and the total is now approximately 100,000 (12). Population increase has brought critical problems. In spite of its 16 million acres (6.5 million hectares), the reservation's resources have proved to be hopelessly inadequate for a farming and herding life.

Shift to Wagework

The next great economic change for the Navahos was learning to work for wages. This required new habits and points of view, the shift to a money economy instead of a subsistence economy. Decades of experience at stores in the Navaho country (Fig. 1) had only partly familiarized the tribe with money as a medium of exchange, since much of the business was for credit, and a Navaho's wool, rugs, silver jewelry, or other goods were credited against his account on the trader's books. It was not until after 1930 that wagework and cash became a crucial part of the income, at a time when erosion, overgrazing, and drought were causing extreme hardship. By 1940 about one-third of all Navaho income was from wages, mostly on the reservation and for the government (10). Off-reservation work has increased steadily as the Navahos have learned better the kinds of skills needed by white employers and the kind of life that depends on cash instead of subsistence from fields and flocks. This has been slow, however, compared with surrounding non-Indian areas. By 1960 about 70 percent of Navaho income came from wages, but per-capita income was about one-third of that of the nation as a whole.

Undoubtedly the least expected means that the Navahos have found for taking advantage of their resources, and their increasing skills, is in their capable management of the mineral wealth discovered on their land. Since the United States government holds title to reservation lands in trust for the tribe, any leases and royalties go to the tribal treasury. Not until 1947 did the tribe employ an attorney to assist in protecting its interests, and only in the last three decades has the tribal organization become truly effective (a tribal council with a popularly elected chairman; full-time expert employees in charge of such matters as public welfare, resources, and law enforcement; and a tribal judiciary). The result has been close scrutiny by the Navahos of the terms of mineral and other leases, and also substantial expenditures by the tribe for long-term developments to supplement the extensive federal program of range management, irrigation, public health, industrial development, resources appraisal, and so on.

Making this development possible has been the substantial income from helium, oil, natural gas, coal, vanadium, and uranium, all found on the reservation in significant quantities. For example, in 1960 there were 860 producing oil wells there with an annual output of 34 million barrels (5.5 million cubic meters). Tribal income on oil and gas leases has been about $110 million since 1935, and other minerals have added some $7 million more (*12*).

Through the efforts of the tribal council, royalty rates have been increased substantially over those originally specified by federal authorities. Oil companies have been forced to shut down wells until installations permitted the marketing of natural gas that was being wasted; employment of reasonable numbers of Navahos has been required in oil and other mineral activities; and several small industries have been attracted to the reservation.

The financial opportunities afforded the tribe by this flow of wealth have been important. In a 3-year period, 40 new chapter houses were built at a cost of $50,000 to $60,000 each, providing community centers and meeting places for the "chapters," which form the local means of partial self-government. An off-reservation ranch was purchased on which to maintain the tribal herd of breeding rams. A tribal public works program, to alleviate economic distress in selected areas, was begun in 1957, with tribal appropriations totaling $5 million for this purpose in 1960. In 1954 a tribal scholarship program was started, supported by a trust fund that now has an annual *income* of $400,000; by 1961 there were 130 Navahos with college degrees, a highly promising advance for a tribe determined to manage well its complex affairs.

The record is unique among Indian tribes, both in growth in numbers and wealth and in the Navahos' ability to remain self-respecting and forward-looking in spite of the hardships they have undergone and the forces that have tended to change every aspect of their culture. They are almost unique, too, in the unforeseen wealth that their reservation has brought them, although oil and timber have proved to be substantial assets to a few other Indian groups. The Navahos, then, are not an example of what any tribe might do, but they suggest the latent talents that may be brought to light by a special sequence of events. The current trend among the Navahos toward technologically complex uses of their reservation resources parallels the suggestion made repeatedly that arid areas, in general, hold more promise of supporting substantial populations through mining and manufacturing than through the traditional herding and farming economies.

Although each Indian group has gone through a somewhat different sequence of adjustments to white contact, a common pattern has been initial intermittent contacts with white explorers; then a sudden rush of miners, ranchers, or farmers whose efforts to preempt land and water for their own uses led to violence and raids by the Indians; eventual subjugation by military force and the confinement of the remnants of the Indian group on a reservation; unsuccessful efforts by government agents to convert the Indians to herding and farming; and finally partial adjustment of the Indians as marginal farmers, unskilled laborers, and relief recipients.

The Navahos conform in part to this generalized sequence but to a lesser degree than some other groups. The next few pages contain a brief discussion of three other "tribes," which followed somewhat different paths of adaptation to the new circumstances they found forced on them. They differed from the Navahos and from one another in their precontact cultures. The means by which white culture reached them also differed; hence, the diversity of their responses and acculturation is expectable *(13)*.

Collapse of Great Basin Culture

At the time of the first white explorations and settlement of the Great Basin (or intermontane region) the aboriginal population consisted of small, scattered groups of Shoshonean-speakers, the Utes, Shoshones, and Paiutes. Their culture in most details was a continuation of the millenniums-old pattern of dependence on wild plants with supplementary hunting. Because of the sparseness of natural resources, population density was low. Indian groups larger than a family were never more than temporary, seasonal gatherings, usually brought together by a rich crop of pine nuts (*Pinus monophylla* and *P. edulis*). These nuts were collected in great quantities and furnished the main food through the winter. Most of the year each family moved systematically over a poorly defined "territory" extending 22 miles (35 kilometers) or more in all directions from the winter camp. On the average, a family of five needed the natural products of 115 to 150 square miles (300 to 400 square kilometers) for subsistence (*14*).

Except for occasional multifamily rabbit drives and antelope hunts, families dug roots, collected seeds and insects, and hunted rodents independently. Since an area would support only a few people, families preferred to scatter widely. For this meager but usually sufficient existence, the traditional skills, equipment, and knowledge developed through the centuries had proved to be adequate. But the culture of these Indians of Utah and Nevada was not capable of easy adjustment to new circumstances; the balance was too delicate, and their adaptation to the Great Basin environment was too little suited for any other conditions.

Sporadic contacts by explorers and trappers from 1776 onward produced no serious ecologic or cultural disturbances, but in the 1840's large numbers of immigrants traveling with horses, cattle, and wagons, began to cross the area and occasionally clashed with the Indians, who were viewed with suspicion and hostility. Indians often raided the wagon trains for any animals that could be killed and eaten. This second phase of contact began to disturb the Indian way of living through the destruction of grass and game. With the discovery of gold in California in 1848 and in Nevada in 1849, miners and immigrants swarmed westward, and the depletion of plant, animal, and water resources increased rapidly. Although in

1850 the Shoshones of northern Nevada were still stealing horses only for food, 10 years later they, like other Great Basin groups, had formed mounted predatory bands, which raided white travelers and settlers with frequent success. This phase was brief, for white settlers with Army assistance quickly broke the strength of the raiders. In spite of serious efforts to settle Indians in agricultural communities, there was little success, partly because of the Indians' inexperience, and partly because the white settlers repeatedly dispossessed the Indians from fertile land (15). More and more, the Indians were reduced to living as hangers-on, beggars, scavengers, and pilferers in the growing white communities.

When reservations were established in the Great Basin, they were on lands less attractive to white settlers and often remote from the Indians' former homes. With meager funds from the federal government, Indian agents attempted to provide issues of rations that would prevent outright starvation, but Indian life continued to deteriorate; only a few Indians learned to farm successfully on the poor land with inadequate water supplies to which they were confined. They lacked tools, seed, and knowledge; also, they were unprepared, socially and psychologically, for a settled life with the rigorous scheduling of work that irrigation farming demanded.

One of the most catastrophic congressional acts, in terms of long-term effects on the Indians, was the Allotment Act of 1887, which permitted small parcels of reservation lands to be given to individual Indians. With no tradition of individual landholding, and under strong pressure from both Indian Service officials and the land-hungry public, much of the best land was leased or sold—not only from Utah and Nevada reservations, but throughout the West. As an Indian agent's report of 1905 pointed out, the Utes seemed to attach value only to money and not to land; they were selling land and horses, virtually their only valuables, for small sums that were spent quickly.

Today there are still Utes, Shoshones, and Paiutes in the Great Basin area, many on reservations and others scattered throughout the white man's settlements. They have preserved fragments of their traditional culture but rarely as an effectively functioning pattern of behavior. In spite of some increase in self-respect and consciousness of their own identity in the last few decades, the trend toward absorption, both physically and culturally, into the surrounding non-

Indian population continues. Economically the Indians now live by the same techniques as their white neighbors, perhaps with less recurrent hardship than in prehistoric days, but precariously and on an impoverished scale compared with the surrounding population.

Rise and Fall of the Sioux

For at least a century the "typical Indian" of popular imagination in both the Old World and the New has been the mounted warrior and buffalo hunter of the Plains. This figure is a product of the Europeanization of the New World, however, since his horse and gun both were foreign additions to his aboriginal cultural heritage. Moreover, some "Plains" tribes, such as the Teton-Dakota (the western Sioux), were not even occupants of the Plains until historic times (16).

The Dakotas began to move westward in the latter part of the 18th century as a result of pressure from other Indian groups to the east. By the time their movement had reached the Black Hills of western South Dakota, they had large herds of horses. Although the buffalo had been hunted on foot on the Plains for millenniums, groups on horseback could increase greatly their hunting effectiveness, in both the search for buffalo herds and the sudden attack.

The Dakotas successfully ousted one tribe after another from the fine buffalo lands of Nebraska, North and South Dakota, Wyoming, and Montana, and on this vast "sea of grass" they prospered and grew wealthy. Through the Chippewas and the French trappers and traders, they obtained guns, beads, knives, and other goods that they valued. But this Indian adaptation to life on the dry, windswept northern Plains was only a short-lived phase in a series of changes, a result of the welding of two important innovations, the horse and the gun, to an already existent mobile hunting culture. As buffalo hides succeeded beaver pelts in the fur trade, the slaughter of buffaloes began to reduce seriously the once "numberless herds." But a greater threat to the Dakotas appeared before the decimation of the buffalo became a problem.

Large-scale overland migration by settlers began in 1841, and the Dakotas and other Plains tribes sensed at once the threat to their lands and livelihood. There were countless attacks on wagon trains, and atrocities on both sides, but westward migration continued. In

1854 large-scale military campaigns began against the Sioux, with
the inevitable result that they finally capitulated and were confined
to reservations. By 1877 their power was broken, the buffalo as a
natural resource was wiped out, and an era of peaceful, settled, and
impoverished existence began (*17*).

The Dakotas' adaptation to Plains life had required vast, sparsely
occupied tracts of land and was based on the buffalo, which provided
not only food but clothing, shelter (the poles of the tipi were covered
with hide), essential equipment (sinew for sewing, bones for scrap-
ers, leather for containers), and finally fuel (sun-dried buffalo drop-
pings, which made a hot and nearly smokeless fire). With confinement on reservations and the buffalo gone, the reaction of the Indians was at first complete apathy or bitter despair. The erratic and
often ill-planned efforts of Indian agents and missionaries to turn
them into settled farmers and to educate them in the white man's
ways too often brought only opposition and failure. Most of their
land was unsuited for farming, even if they had had the necessary
skills and equipment. Gradually the Sioux have accepted the material culture of the white man, insofar as it has been available to
them. But many traditional beliefs and attitudes persist and make
their way of life a hybrid that is neither satisfying to them nor
successful in providing the necessities of existence.

Adjustment to Reservation Life

For briefly tracing the Indians' adjustment to their new circumstances and the development of the new patterns by which their semiarid Plains environment might be used, the Pine Ridge Reservation
of the Sioux in southwestern South Dakota can serve as an example
(*18*). Several features marked the early years of reservation life.
Schooling for children was enforced by every means the agent could
employ, including jailing of truants and their parents. Military discipline was employed in the boarding schools, and the use of the
Dakota language and the wearing of native clothing or Indian hair
styles were forbidden. Although methods today are less harsh, many
teachers in Indian schools still see as their main goal the creation of
individuals with the white man's attitudes and ambitions.

An equally profound influence in the changing of Dakota life was
the complete breakdown of the power and influence of the chiefs.

The chiefs could not now relieve the poverty and hunger of their people as could the Indian agents, who controlled the issuing of government rations. Thus the Sioux lapsed into a paternalism that made "Washington" the final source of authority and material assistance. Although some farming was practiced in early reservation days, monthly issues of rations were needed to alleviate even partly the acute hardships that most families faced. Nevertheless, a start was made toward self-sufficiency, but not through the farming that was initially seen as the essential concomitant of reservation life.

As early as the 1870's some Sioux began to raise cattle, the first stock being some of the animals regularly issued by the Army. By 1885 there were 10,000 head on the Pine Ridge Reservation, for example, and by 1912 about 40,000. This was, in many respects, ideal grazing land, and the growth of a cattle economy was hampered chiefly by the government policy of allotting reservation land to Indians individually, a perpetuation of the American myth of the self-sufficient farmer. Unfortunately, when beef prices were high in

Lines of stones mark the boundaries of farm plots that overlook the Gila River in Arizona. The fields probably were abandoned by A.D. 1400. (Courtesy R. B. Woodbury)

World War I, the Indians were encouraged to sell off their herds, partly by pressure from whites who wanted to lease the rangeland. By 1917 the Indian herds were gone and the range was in the hands of non-Indian lessees.

Briefly, the Indians enjoyed a splurge of spending from their new wealth. Then in 1921, the postwar depression resulted in defaulting on the leases, and the Indians' income ceased. The Bureau of Indian Affairs began to encourage the Indians to sell their allotments of farmland to the swarms of land speculators and wheat farmers who came into the northern Plains. Again, the Indians' profits were quickly gone, and the combination of severe drought beginning in 1924 and the great depression in 1929 left the entire area desperately eroded and poverty-stricken. In 1937 the government again began to encourage the growth of the cattle business, recognizing that the rangeland is the only major resource of the Indians. But even with supplementary wagework and federal aid in establishing a herd, few families have become self-sufficient.

There have been several scientific studies of the plight and prospects of the Sioux in the last three decades. The most recent of these (19) focused on the Lower Brulé Reservation of South Dakota, which lies along the Missouri River. Although originally it was nearly 247,000 acres (100,000 hectares) in extent, about 40 percent of the land has been sold to non-Indians by the Indians to whom it was allotted. The remainder is rangeland, except for about 6200 acres (2500 hectares) of cropland and woodland, and most of this is now flooded by the waters behind Fort Randall Dam.

Although the tribe has been compensated by money voted by Congress, and part of this sum has been used for tribal land acquisition, the Lower Brulé are still seriously lacking in land on which they can hope to become self-sufficient. Like many Indian groups, their economic condition reached a low point in the 1930's; in 1935 only 7 out of 102 families in the Lower Brulé community were self-supporting. Fifteen years later, the sale of livestock reached $166,000 a year, providing about half of the group's entire income (but much of it went to a few fairly prosperous Indian ranchers). By 1958 livestock sales had declined; welfare assistance made up one-fourth of the community's income; selling and leasing some of their allotted land, another one-fourth; and wages, one-fifth of the total income.

Most of the Lower Brulé land is suited only for cattle raising, which can support adequately but a fraction of the group. Their human resources are limited by lack of skills, poor health, and unfamiliarity with the planning and management that small independent businesses would require. The accumulation of capital or even material wealth beyond the level of the community is hampered by the Sioux tradition of hospitality and sharing and the persistence of strong kinship ties, which make every individual feel both the need and the desire to share widely and generously.

Many non-Indians in the United States have expected that the Indian population gradually would be absorbed as Indians left reservations for work in towns and cities, and that those remaining would become self-supporting; thus the nation's "Indian problem" would disappear. Only the fragmentation and dispersal into the very bottom of the white economic community of such groups as the Great Basin Shoshonean-speakers support this prediction. Recent Sioux history shows how unrealistic it is, even for economically depressed tribes. The Lower Brulé, for example, are slowly becoming more effective as a group, working through their tribal council on long-range economic and social plans, with vigorous help from the Bureau of Indian Affairs. They retain certain Indian ways, even though they have adopted many white customs, and can look forward to continuation as an Indian group with an increasing degree of self-government, economic self-sufficiency, and self-respect.

Papago Struggles in the Desert

When the Spanish missionaries and explorers pushed north into Sonora and what is now southern Arizona, they found the Papagos living in small, widely scattered villages in the desert region that today includes their reservation. The Papagos had worked out a life that took the best possible advantage of their extremely limited water supplies. They spent the winter months in "well villages" in the canyons of the many mountain ranges, where there were springs and small wells, and the summer months near their cornfields, located where intermittent streams from the mountains spread out on the desert, or in the broad valleys where water could be impounded by simple earth dams. But farming was precarious and gave only a part of their diet; wild plant foods, such as the mesquite (*Prosopis juliflora*) bean, the fruit of the saguaro cactus (*Carnegiea gigantea*);

and many small seeds and greens, were indispensable. Hunting contributed a small but important part of their food supply.

Contacts with the Spaniards, mainly through missions, changed Papago life only slightly, although systematic attempts were made to introduce domestic animals and new crops. When the Papago country became part of the United States in 1854, as a result of the Gadsden Purchase, the aboriginal way of life had changed relatively little (20).

With the invasion of their lands by white miners and ranchers from 1870 onward, changes came rapidly. Mining towns flourished briefly and collapsed, but some of their wells remained as permanent assets of the Papagos. The expanding cattle industry of the white settlers soon resulted in serious depletion of the natural vegetation; and, with the growth of Papago stock raising, competition for grass and water was strong. The Papago Reservation was not created until 1916, and by then much of its sparse natural vegetation was destroyed; erosion had made many farming areas unusable. It was impossible for the old life to continue. The Papagos managed to continue some farming, but on a decreasing scale, and their herds of cattle deteriorated, even though many new wells were drilled by the government.

By the 1920's and 1930's, the Papagos were close to destitution, with disease and malnutrition taking a serious toll. When the Papago development program was prepared by the tribe and the Bureau of Indian Affairs in 1949, it was determined that 56 percent of Papago income came from wagework, 27 percent from cattle, and only 7 percent from farming. This reflected a rapid change toward a cash economy, but average family income was only $1500 a year, about one-third of the average for Arizona farm families.

No substantial mineral resources have been found on the Papago Reservation, and the cattle business, in the hands of only a few families in each district, supports but a small proportion of the people, in spite of substantial efforts to upgrade stock, reduce erosion, improve water supplies, and introduce better marketing practices. To a greater degree than on most Indian reservations, the people themselves are the only major resource on which hopes for a better future can be based. Fortunately, the Papagos have a tradition of hard, steady, hand-labor—essential for either their precarious and

Terraced Navaho fields near Tuba City, Arizona, are irrigated from springs. The ditch at the left protects them against erosion. (Courtesy U.S. Department of Agriculture, Soil Conservation Service)

difficult farming or their gathering of substantial amounts of wild plant foods.

The Papago Reservation has rapidly growing commercial farming areas and industries close to its boundaries, so there are opportunities for off-reservation labor. Because of the handicaps of little education, poor English, and lack of training in needed skills, the Papagos qualified mainly for unskilled jobs in farm labor when they began to work for wages. Gradually they have developed the skills needed for better jobs, and employment not only has increased but has become more permanent and better paid.

Until recently, it has been assumed that Papago wagework would be largely seasonal, involving only a minority of the population. Recent investigations at the University of Arizona by R. A. Hackenberg and H. I. Padfield show clearly that these assumptions have been wrong; 45 percent of the Papago population was found to be living *off* the reservation, a proportion that has increased since this calcu-

lation was made in 1959. Many Papago children are born and
live off the reservation, but many older people shift residence to the
reservation. Although the reservation is not yet a "retirement home"
for the Papagos, there is a trend in this direction, since the economic
opportunities in surrounding areas are rapidly increasing and those
on the reservation are improving only slowly. Papago farm labor
is no longer mainly temporary and unskilled, and Papagos are preferred on many farms as equipment operators and are sometimes
permanent employees.

Even with the substantial cash income that this wagework is bringing, however, and with much of it being returned to relatives on the
reservation, most of the Papagos live at an economic level far below
that of the surrounding area. How far increased off-reservation employment will improve their standard of living is uncertain, but it
may prove to be more important than the limited progress possible
from on-reservation programs to aid cattle raisers and farmers. At
the present, possibilities are being explored by the tribe and the Indian Service for using the growing pool of skilled Papago labor to
attract small industries to the reservation itself.

Indian Adjustments and Prospects

Even from the small sample of Indian groups presented here it
should be apparent that there was great diversity in the adaptations
they made to their arid environments. Wild plants and animals contributed varying proportions of the diet—least for the Pueblo villages, most for the Shoshonean-speakers of the Great Basin and the
Sioux. The Pueblos depended mainly on farming, whereas Papago
farming was a valuable, but not a preponderant, contribution to
their livelihood. Besides the variety of subsistence patterns, there
was constant change, even before the acculturation of the past few
centuries. The Sioux shifted from a woodland life to the prairies
under only indirect influence from the white pressures much farther
east. The Navahos' farming was acquired from Puebloan neighbors
before contact with European culture. Not only were many successful patterns of adjustment developed by the Indians, but continued
modification took place as a result of contacts and conflicts between
different groups.

For many Indians the initial phase of white contact permitted useful additions to their technology and disrupted their traditional life very little. The Navaho acquisition of sheep and the securing of firearms by the Sioux illustrate changes that were mainly helpful, even though sometimes later they led to undesirable effects. The Indian's means of exploiting his harsh environment had been limited in precontact times by his simple technology, and at first the additions brought by the white man were welcomed. Later troubles came more, perhaps, from the displacement of Indians from their land or the destruction of its resources than from any other single result of contact with the white man.

White settlement in the United States was on lands formerly used by the Indians, and little or no provision was made for incorporating the natives into the new pattern of land use. Pushed aside, defeated when he fought back, and finally confined on reservations, the Indian found his traditional culture unsuited for the drastically changed circumstances that he was forced into. The learning of new means of supporting himself has been a slow and painful process, by no means yet completed. It should be realized that the plight of the Indian in the last century or so is not the result of environmental causes such as aridity. The causes are social, and the arid environment has simply added to the problem by making solutions more difficult and substitutes for the old economy few and often unpromising.

Another factor, not unique to the Indians of the arid West, has also aggravated their problems in recent decades. This is the substantial population increase that most tribes have experienced as a result of a continued high birth rate and gradually improving health conditions. In their rapid increase in numbers, often far ahead of the expansion of the economy, the Indians share the plight of the peoples of many "underdeveloped" areas throughout the world. In many ways, then, the problems that have arisen from the impact of the European world on the Indians of the western United States can be viewed, not as the special problem of our arid West, but as a small part of the worldwide problem of the nonliterate, nonindustrial world confronted by the technology, the political expansion, and the social and ethical systems of the Western world.

When one considers the factors that make the Indian groups of the western United States distinctive in their aboriginal adaptations and postcontact adjustments, the persistence of the culture of the Pueblo villagers is conspicuous. Subdued by military force and actively missionized for generations, they still have managed to maintain a strong core of traditional practices and attitudes. In spite of many vicissitudes, including serious famine and disease in the 17th and 18th centuries, they mostly have remained in their traditional homes, continuing their farming life with only small, gradual innovations. Today, however, changes are coming far more rapidly, and the Puebloans are finding their reservation resources inadequate to meet their rising expectations; for many, jobs in nearby or distant towns are essential to maintain the living standards they desire.

The Navahos and Papagos, like the Pueblo villagers, still live where the white man first encountered them. The Navahos, even though made prisoners by the Army and confined for 4 years, succeeded in returning and reestablishing themselves. The Papagos have never been entirely displaced. But the Navahos are also remarkable for the success they have shown in incorporating into their culture useful elements from the groups with which they have been in contact.

Among all of these groups there is a growing awareness of their own problems, and, since the Indian Reorganization Act, passed by Congress in 1934, Indian tribes have been encouraged to form tribal organizations that are capable of making decisions and handling some tribal affairs. Leadership has developed slowly, and factionalism (between conservatives and progressives, between those with and without allotted land, or between residents and nonresidents of a reservation) has not succeeded in crippling attempts at concerted action. Gradually, a measure of self-government has arisen, sometimes fostered and sometimes opposed by the vacillating policies of the federal Bureau of Indian Affairs. Nevertheless, the situation has changed profoundly in only a generation, and many tribes today have a far greater unity than they ever did in the past. Indian "self-government" is not always successful, and some of their planning has been impractical; but, as one Indian leader has said, after generations of governmental plans with as many failures as successes, the Indians now want the "freedom to make their own mistakes."

The "Indian problem" is not disappearing through the assimilation of Indians into the rest of the population. Instead, the Indians are forming a large number of cultural subgroups, each distinct but with much in common with the rest of the culture of the United

States. This is in accord with the nation's tradition of heterogeneity and of hospitality to ethnic and racial minorities, each maintaining some identity even after accommodating itself to the culture of the population that surrounds it.

In general, these minorities contribute mostly rather minor culture traits to the dominant culture—from the Indians of the United States such things as moccasins, hominy, and, more significantly, maize, tobacco, and other crop plants. But the long, successful adaptation of Indian groups to the arid West and their ability to support themselves with limited, though varied, resources make it advisable that we give more attention to any techniques that might deserve emulation in our current attempts to use this same region.

For example, the stone or adobe (dried mud) house with its thick earth-covered roof and small doors and windows is far better suited to conserve nighttime coolness and keep out daytime heat in the desert than are our poorly insulated houses with an excess of glass. The Indian's simple but effective systems to control erosion and conserve moisture have been copied, in principle, in the stone check-dams and boulder lines along contours built by the Soil Conservation Service. Indian farming made full use of even very small and localized supplies of water, with small, widely dispersed gardens to supplement larger fields on level and better-watered land; we have no generally acceptable means of making similar use of these numerous small water sources, many of them representing runoff that is largely lost through evaporation. In the hot summers that characterize much of the arid West, the Indian work pattern used the early morning hours of relative coolness and avoided the midday and afternoon heat as much as possible; much of our busy coming and going, even in desert areas, is concentrated in the hottest part of the day. Suggestions for "air-conditioning whole cities" seem to be a cumbersome substitute for better-adapted daily work schedules.

These and other contributions that Indian traditional adaptations to hot and arid surroundings might make may be minor, compared with the elaborate methods our technology offers for circumventing or compensating for environmental limitations. But these Indian adaptations should not be ignored, since they reveal a philosophy of working *with* the environment rather than *against* it, which made possible for the Indians a far longer use of these arid areas than their white successors have yet achieved. In the continuing effort to understand the dry lands of the nation and to use them effectively, this philosophy may be an indispensable ingredient for success.

Acknowledgments: I am grateful to the following for their helpful criticisms and suggestions: Gilbert D. Bartell, Edward P. Dozier, Robert A. Hackenberg, and Edward H. Spicer, University of Arizona, Tucson; John W. Bennett, Washington University, St. Louis; Ernest Schusky, Southern Illinois University, Carbondale; and Nathalie F. S. Woodbury, Arizona State Museum, Tucson.

REFERENCES

1. G. R. Willey, "New World prehistory," *Science* **131**, 73–86 (1960).
2. P. S. Martin and J. Gray, "Pollen analysis and the Cenozoic," *Science* **137**, 103–111 (1962).
3. J. D. Jennings, "Danger cave," *Mem. Soc. Am. Archaeol.* **14** (1957).
4. P. C. Mangelsdorf, "Ancestor of corn," *Science* **128**, 1313–1320 (1958).
5. E. W. Haury, "The greater American Southwest," in *Courses toward Urban Life*, R. J. Braidwood and G. R. Willey, Eds. *Viking Fund Publ. Anthropol.* **32** (Aldine, Chicago, 1962).
6. R. B. Woodbury, "Prehistoric agriculture at Point of Pines, Arizona," *Mem. Soc. Am. Archaeol.* **17** (1961).
7. J. T. Hack, "The changing physical environment of the Hopi Indians of Arizona," *Peabody Mus. Papers* **35** (1942).
8. R. B. Woodbury, "The Hohokam canals at Pueblo Grande, Arizona," *Am. Antiq.* **26**, 267–270 (1960).
9. ———, "A reappraisal of Hohokam irrigation," *Am. Anthropol.* **63**, 550–560 (1961).
10. C. Kluckhohn and D. Leighton, *The Navaho* (Harvard Univ. Press, Cambridge, Mass., 1946).
11. R. Underhill, *Here Come the Navaho!* Indian Life and Customs, 8, U.S. Indian Service (Haskell Inst., Lawrence, Kans., 1953).
12. R. W. Young, *The Navajo Yearbook, 1951–1961*, Rept. 8 (Navajo Agency, Window Rock, Ariz., 1961).
13. E. H. Spicer, Ed., *Perspectives in American Indian Culture Change* (Univ. of Chicago Press, Chicago, 1961).
14. J. H. Steward, in *Theory of Culture Change*, J. H. Steward, Ed. (Univ. of Illinois Press, Urbana, 1955).
15. J. S. Harris, in *Acculturation in Seven American Indian Tribes*, R. Linton, Ed. (Appleton-Century-Crofts, New York, 1940).
16. J. C. Ewers, *Teton-Dakota Ethnology and History* (U.S. National Park Service, Berkeley, Calif., 1937).
17. S. Mekeel, "A short history of the Teton-Dakota," *N. Dakota Hist. Quart.* **10**, 136–205 (1943).

18. G. MacGregor, *Warriors without Weapons, a Study of the Society and Personality Development of the Pine Ridge Sioux* (Univ. of Chicago Press, Chicago, 1946).
19. E. Schusky, *Politics and Planning in a Dakota Indian Community* (Inst. Indian Studies, Univ. of South Dakota, Vermillion, 1959).
20. A. Joseph, R. B. Spicer, and J. Chesky, *The Desert People, a Study of the Papago Indians of Southern Arizona* (Univ. of Chicago Press, Chicago, 1949).

4

Historical Framework

Ira G. Clark

Although the semiarid and arid regions of the West attracted one of the earliest European cultures in the present United States, they were the last to develop their resources. Spanish colonization of New Mexico antedated Jamestown, but the Anglo-American traders and trappers who arrived at that remote outpost early in the 19th century found the economic and social institutions virtually unchanged after 200 years. The first explorers sent out by the federal government to trace the courses of rivers feeding the Mississippi uniformly dismissed everything beyond the 98th meridian as a vast desert, incapable of sustaining an advanced society. Thus, the early history of the present western United States followed a pattern common to other dry zones: relatively static social institutions, with the reports on the region offering no encouragement for its future development.

The extreme desert concept was modified mildly by adventurers who entered the forbidding interior after the early unfavorable appraisals. Bit by bit, information accumulated: from mountain men and Santa Fe traders; from travelers attracted to the West by their own curiosity; from overland immigrants drawn to the Pacific Coast by glowing accounts of economic opportunity in Mexican California and the Oregon country. Mass migration to the West did not take place until the discovery of gold in California, an event that occurred almost simultaneously with one of even greater significance: the transfer to the United States of a vast area between the Great Plains and the Pacific Ocean.

Henceforth, the development of these semiarid and arid regions deviated considerably from that of comparable regions elsewhere. The annexation, coming as it did on the eve of tremendous urbanization and industrialization within the country, meant that the West would be integrated rapidly into a nation that was making demands for maximum productivity on all of its parts.

Spanish Period

Within 15 years after Hernán Cortés subjugated the Aztecs and laid the foundation for the viceroyalty of New Spain, there were rumors of rich cities far to the north. Francisco Vásquez de Coronado secured the coveted commission to determine the truth of these stories and, in 1540, began his epic-making journey, which disproved the legends and, in so doing, took his party across plateaus, mountains, and buffalo plains from the present Arizona to west Texas, and north into Kansas. His experience cooled the enthusiasm of others. Meanwhile, the frontier of New Spain was drawn northward rapidly by the discovery of rich mining districts.

It took a generation for gold seekers to forget what Coronado had learned about the rumored wealth still far in advance of the frontier, but brown-robed Franciscans had not forgotten the accounts of sedentary semicivilized Indians ready for conversion to "the true faith." Forty years after Coronado, new reports of riches encouraged the sons of wealthy ranchers and mineowners to add their petitions to those of the Franciscans for permission to lead parties north. The petitions bore fruit, and, as a result of a series of expeditions, a permanent Spanish colony came into being late in the 16th century. Disillusionment followed, but the stubbornness of the friars and early colonists kept the little settlement of Santa Fe (in the present New Mexico) alive, precariously tied to New Spain by a trail infested by Apache Indians. Coming from an arid area, these settlers accommodated themselves to their environment, engaging in subsistence agriculture and the sheep raising so characteristic of a Spanish economy.

The dynamic Spanish advance of the 16th century was already slowing down as this expansion took place. In the 17th century, however, Franciscans did press north on the great central plateau of Mexico, and Jesuit missionaries followed the Pacific slope from river valley to river valley. The indomitable Father Eusebio Kino laid the basis for the occupation of the Sonoran Desert as far north as his mission stations near the present Nogales and Tucson, Arizona. Upper California did not offer sufficient attractions to merit its occupation; 250 years elapsed between its discovery and its occupation. Not until 1767, when José de Gálvez, a visitor-general, recommended the occupation of California as a plan for frontier defense, was there a concerted effort to attract colonists to that remote area. Incidental to this movement, in 1769 an exploratory party discovered San Francisco Bay, which gave some immediacy to this last northern thrust of Spain. Once again, the chance for quick wealth appeared to be remote, and the California presidios, missions, and villages struggled along as a neglected part of the empire.

The northern provinces were buffers, of importance only as protection for the heart of New Spain. At the end of the Spanish period, scattered and isolated posts stretched from San Diego to San Francisco along the Pacific Coast, and from the tiny garrisons in the present Arizona's Santa Cruz Valley, by way of Santa Fe and the El Paso settlements, to San Antonio, Texas.

In spite of Spain's fear of foreign intrusion into the northern provinces, a few outsiders reached the remote Spanish outposts. Most of these were French-speaking visitors from Mississippi Valley posts, which, after 1763, were part of the Spanish domain. Although the United States acquired the vast, but undefined, Louisiana Territory in 1803, the danger from that source was not immediate, because the westward-moving frontier was just beginning to creep along the Missouri River and would slow down when it reached the big bend of that river, far short of the Spanish provinces. True, some traders and trappers did go beyond the frontier to compete with their own countrymen and British subjects for pelts far up the Missouri and its tributaries, but few risked imprisonment to trap on Spanish waters or to carry on an illicit trade with the jealously guarded Spanish frontier towns (1). This was the situation when, in 1819, the United States and Spain agreed on a boundary between their lands.

Great American Desert

Thomas Jefferson, with his unquenchable curiosity, was already organizing an expedition to the Pacific Coast before Napoleon's offer to sell Louisiana. This was the memorable Lewis and Clark expedition, which, in achieving its goal, brought back sketchy, but concrete, information about the interior. Jefferson's plans for extensive examination of the major rivers in Louisiana Territory were limited by the unwillingness of Congress to appropriate as much money as the President requested. He succeeded, however, in sending out a few parties. The most significant was led by Zebulon M. Pike, who was to explore the headwaters of the Red and Arkansas rivers. Pike and his men, entering a country whose ownership was still in doubt and wandering into what was undeniably Spanish territory, fell into the hands of Spaniards on the upper Rio Grande. They were taken to Santa Fe, then to Chihuahua, and finally across Texas, before being delivered to United States authorities at Natchitoches, Louisiana.

Although Pike's journal was taken from him, in 1810 he wrote an account of his expedition. He reported that he had passed through a hostile environment that offered no opportunities for development (2). The journals of the Lewis and Clark expedition were published in 1814. They did not specifically condemn the country through which the party passed, although certain entries in the journals certainly implied wasteland. These told of great areas that seemed to be destitute of vegetation except along streams (3).

Fourteen years after Pike's return, Stephen H. Long led a party into the Rocky Mountains by way of the Platte River. Although Long added little information, he not only verified Pike's adverse appraisal but extended it, thereby popularizing the concept of a "great American desert," which would remain forever the domain of nomadic tribesmen because it was unfit for an agrarian society (4).

The popular eastern notion of the nature of the trans-Mississippi West is nowhere better illustrated than in the attempt to create a "permanent Indian frontier." The central government had been under constant pressure from several states east of the Mississippi River to remove the Indians from within their borders, thus opening Indian lands to white settlers. Here, indeed, was a suitable use for the "great American desert": to serve as a home for all Indians, freeing the eastern part of the country from their presence and placing them safely beyond the deepest possible penetration by pioneer farmers.

Changing "Desert" Concept

The permanent Indian frontier actually was in a state of dissolution at the time it was being created, because the first faint cracks were beginning to appear in the widely held desert concept. Trappers and fur traders, penetrating in search of the one admitted resource of the Far West, were adding bits of information. Most of the early stories of the unlettered mountain men were carried by word of mouth through the great fur-trading center at St. Louis—accounts of thrilling adventure and unbelievable scenic wonders. Their tales were not detached, objective appraisals of the resources of the West, but from them emerged a modified concept: the West might be a savage, uninhabitable wilderness, but it was not a barren desert waste.

Santa Fe traders also contributed to the breaking of the barrier created by Pike, Long, and others. In 1821, a party of Indian traders under William Becknell met by chance a detachment of Mexican soldiers and were invited to trade at Santa Fe (5). This changed attitude was occasioned by the independence of Mexico from Spain and the adoption by Mexico of a policy of opening the trade of New Mexico but taxing it heavily. The trade developed rapidly after Becknell demonstrated the practicability of taking wagons to Santa Fe. Besides learning of the weakness of the bond between Mexico and its northern provinces, these early traders found that the possibilities were greater and the outlook for economic development more optimistic than had been indicated by earlier explorers.

Others, too, were learning something of the resources of the West. Sea-otter hunters had visited the Pacific Coast early in the 19th century, and the first major narrative about California came from one such hunter, William Shaler. Spanish restrictions discouraged the early trade, but it revived and flourished for a time as the result of Mexico's liberalized policies. Fur hunters were joined by traders. "Boston ships" rounded the Horn to reach California, and their buyers went inland to cattle-rich missions and *ranchos* to secure tallow for candlemakers and hides for the growing boot and shoe industry of New England.

Gradually the United States became aware of the Pacific Coast. To the exhortations of the expansionist senators from Missouri, Thomas

Hart Benton and Lewis F. Linn, were added the writings of early popularizers of Oregon and California: Hall J. Kelley, Thomas J. Farnham, Washington Irving, William Slacum, Zenas Leonard, and Richard Henry Dana, as well as numerous articles written by missionaries for church journals. All published by 1840, these were merely the prelude to an even more extensive outpouring through the following decade, including Charles Wilkes's narrative, Thomas O. Larkin's letters, Alfred Robinson's *Life in California,* and John Charles Fremont's reports.

Although California was a Mexican province, and Oregon was jointly occupied by England and the United States, the popularization of both areas led to organized expeditions to the Pacific. The Bidwell-Bartleson party was the pioneer. In 1841, it followed the route that would become famous as the Oregon-California Trail and would be traveled annually by one or more parties thereafter. Smaller, less publicized groups from Santa Fe and Taos also were going west by way of the old Spanish Trail or the Gila River.

The interior also had its chroniclers: James Ohio Pattie's *Personal Narrative,* accounts of the Texan Santa Fe expedition by George W. Kendall and Thomas Falconer, Joel Palmer's Rocky Mountain journals, Josiah Gregg's *Commerce of the Prairies,* Lewis H. Garrard's *Wah-to-yah,* George Frederick Ruxton's fascinating observations on life in the Rockies, and Frederick Wislizenus's account of his tour of northern Mexico. Of all the observers, John Charles Fremont was the most influential in modifying the desert concept. Endowed with intellectual curiosity, he acquired a substantial background in the techniques of scientific observation. He was also influenced by the views of his father-in-law, Senator Benton, who for years had been a staunch advocate of western expansion and the need for fast, certain transportation to the Pacific. Fremont did not verify; he questioned. He looked for the things that would invite, not repel, occupation. He described the interior areas that would sustain population, giving his reasons for so believing, and he gave a glowing report about the agricultural possibilities of California (6). This was the type of information the expansionist and the frontiersman wanted to hear.

The Pacific railroad project was an incentive for the accumulation of information about the West in the 1840's. Its earliest ardent advocate, Asa Whitney, was treated at first as a wild-eyed visionary, but his idea gained popularity, even though such a railroad would cross lands either belonging to Mexico or jointly occupied with England, depending on the route chosen.

Acquisition by the United States

With the exception of the western fringe of Louisiana Territory, the arid and semiarid lands came into the possession of the United States in the mid-19th century, as is shown in Fig. 1. The agreement with England in 1818 providing for joint occupancy of the

Fig. 1. The vast movement toward the Pacific Ocean by which the United States acquired its western lands began in 1803 with the then ill-defined Louisiana Purchase and was completed by the middle of the 19th century. The major routes followed by the settlers of the new frontiers are shown here.

Oregon country was made in anticipation of a future settlement that would result in the United States' acquiring a Pacific outlet. The Spanish treaty of 1819 apparently had established the limit of expansion to the Southwest, in spite of a minority group that contended that the Rio Grande should have been the western boundary of Louisiana. International boundaries never had operated as an insurmountable barrier to restless frontiersmen, but there appeared to be more effective deterrents to the breaching of this particular one: the distance from the westward-moving agricultural frontier, the absence of navigable streams, the apparent lack of economic opportunity, and the presence of wild Plains Indian tribes to block the way. These had furnished the northern Mexican states with their real protection from intrusion, but they lost much of their effectiveness in the quarter-century after the signing of the Louisiana boundary treaty.

An aggressive, highly mobile frontier had crossed the Mississippi River. Although it would not push into the semiarid lands for several decades, it had already served as a prime recruiting ground for *filibusterers* venturing into Spanish territory and soon would provide followers for *impresarios* settling Texas under Mexican colonization laws and for organizers of wagon trains to California and Oregon (7). Sparsely settled western lands offered the possibility of personal gain to ambitious frontiersmen. In time, however, their strong nationalism sublimated the materialistic drive into a supposedly divinely inspired mission to carry the enlightened institutions of their own nation to the less fortunate. This spirit was identified by the term *manifest destiny* (8).

The extension of the boundaries of the United States to the Pacific Ocean occurred almost simultaneously in both the Oregon country and the northern Mexican provinces. The annexation of the Republic of Texas by the United States came in the spring of 1845, after a bitterly contested battle in Congress. There was full realization that the action was an open threat of war with Mexico, which had refused to recognize the independence of that young republic. Meanwhile, expansionists to the Northwest were demanding abrogation of the agreement for joint occupancy of the Oregon country. Unwilling to risk the possibility of war on two fronts, President James K. Polk readily accepted the extension of the 49th parallel to the Pacific as the solution to the Oregon question.

War with Mexico did occur, and, in the treaty that followed (1848), Mexico not only recognized the annexation of Texas but also ceded lands to the west. In 1853 the Gadsden Purchase rounded out the contiguous continental limits of the United States. At the time of these acquisitions, it was fairly common knowledge that there were many primitive Indians in the new possessions, a picturesque but rudimentary Spanish-American culture in the valley of the Rio Grande, scattered fur-trading posts in the Rockies, and a potential agrarian society in the valleys of California and Oregon.

The fur trade, which had been the most productive source of knowledge about the Far West, was waning, but there were new sources of information. The exciting prospect of a railroad to the Pacific had taken on new life, now that it was possible to build wholly across lands belonging to the United States. The rivalry of budding Mississippi Valley cities and their ambitious political spokesmen, however, created sectional differences over the specific route and wrecked any possibility for immediate construction. In the meantime, the Pacific railroad surveys were completed and their voluminous findings published. Fremont's reports already were popular reading and soon were followed by those of William H. Emory, Philip St. George Cooke, James W. Abert, James H. Simpson, Howard Stansbury, and Joseph C. Ives, as well as the more personalized accounts of John Russell Bartlett and Gwinn Harris Heap. Gold seekers were flocking to California. The Mormons (Latter-Day Saints) were spreading over the Great Basin.

The discovery of gold at Sutter's Mill in January 1848 was certainly the most spectacular advertising that California could have received. Some gold seekers from the East went by sea, and others by southern routes; the great majority, however, waited impatiently at the bend of the Missouri River for the earliest spring grasses so that they could cross half a continent to reach the diggings by way of the California Trail. The unusually large amount of free gold in California, which could be taken through placer methods with a minimum of capital investment, gave to this mad rush an aura of excitement missing in the later rushes.

Meanwhile, the movement of the Latter-Day Saints, or Mormons, into the Great Basin suggested the hidden possibilities of the interior. Adherents of this tightly knit religious sect had moved as a body from state to state, but wherever they went they encountered

violent hostility. Their occupation of Utah, therefore, represented
the aspirations of a persecuted group seeking a location beyond the
reach of inimical neighbors.

While the Mexican War was still in progress, the vanguard of the
Mormons arrived at Salt Lake, in the present Utah, initiating the
most skillfully organized wholesale migration in United States history. Their simple objective was to establish a self-sufficient society
free from outside influence, but their historical significance was
more profound. They proved that a successful and prosperous society could flourish in the heart of the arid lands and demonstrated
how it could be accomplished: careful planning and selection of
sites, cooperative effort, and frugal husbanding of resources. The
Mormons moved into watered valleys in every direction from Salt
Lake City, following the same pattern of occupation that had been
successful in establishing the parent settlement.

Governmental Problems

The steady flow of emigrants to the West created problems that
required immediate attention in the nation's capital. The absorbing
question in the East—the controversy over extension of slavery into
the Mexican Cession—was overshadowed in the West by the immediate need for transportation facilities, government, and defense.

The establishment of speedy, regularly scheduled mail service and
more adequate means of travel between the Mississippi Valley and
the Pacific Coast was more than a matter of convenience; it was essential to control of the entire West and to protection of the Pacific
Coast from possible attack. By sea California was no closer to the
United States than to other maritime powers; in the absence of roads,
the great western landmass was actually an obstacle to military operations. There was also the problem of supplying remote inland settlements and wilderness garrisons, which had almost no contacts with
the outside world.

An obvious answer was the speedy completion of a Pacific railway, but sectional controversy blocked this action. Since there had
to be stopgap solutions, through the 1850's there were extensive surveys for wagon, as well as rail, routes, and toward the end of the
decade the subsidizing of overland mail by stage (9, 10). Until
secession made possible an agreement on a northern railroad route,

the West had to depend on slowly crawling wagon trains for supplies and on somewhat faster overland stages for passenger and mail service.

The creation of civil government for the new western states was a matter of urgency. Normal procedures were already well established, 12 public land areas having passed through territorial periods and emerged as states. The process had been one of simply transplanting existing Anglo-American institutions into newly occupied areas. Administration of the territories prior to statehood was carried on by political appointees, rather than through a permanent civil service. This provided considerable flexibility, because rigid precedents were lacking and the territorial officials were highly susceptible to local pressures (11). Territorial government, therefore, was one of traditional Anglo-American institutions as modified by local economic and political considerations. California, with a population that justified statehood and restive under a hybrid military government, clamored for admission to the Union; the Mormons submitted the constitution of "Deseret" (Utah) for consideration by Congress; New Mexico petitioned for some type of organized government.

A number of factors were operating in the mid-19th century that disrupted the more or less orderly processes of the past. The slavery controversy had delayed the organization of Oregon Territory for 2 years, and the debate over the extension of slavery into the Mexican Cession was threatening dissolution of the Union. Any attempt to satisfy the needs of the region for civil government would have to resolve this issue, and the admission of California would upset the delicate balance between slave and free states. Local problems added complications: general hostility toward the Mormons and their institution of polygamy, and mistrust of the Spanish-American inhabitants of New Mexico in matters of both loyalty and adaptability to local self-government. The shaky compromise in 1850 did provide statehood for California and territorial governments for Utah and New Mexico to account for the remainder of the cession.

At times, western innovations modified laws and practices of the more mature areas. With neither mining law nor precedent to guide them, California mining camps established their own local rules, a time-honored device for legalizing an extralegal position. California set the pattern for other mining districts, and in 1866 Congress recognized the legality of local mining law, establishing the principle of private exploitation of mineral resources on the public domain (*12*). The Mormons replaced the common-law doctrine of riparian rights with the more workable arid-lands doctrine of appropriation, which drastically modified the laws governing water rights in all semiarid and arid states (*13*). The extension of suffrage to women developed early in the West and was copied in the East.

Although defense against Indians was not a new experience in American history, the problems were somewhat different in the semi-arid and arid regions. Hardy tribesmen, with their knowledge of survival in an inhospitable land, could resist effectively any undesirable intruders. Since the primary concern in the 1850's was protection of the emigrant routes, rather than a contest for the Indian hunting grounds of the interior, the obvious solution was to establish friendly relations with the natives. The United States attempted by treaties to keep relations on the most pacific terms possible, but outbreaks became increasingly frequent later in the decade.

Railroads and the Mining Frontier

Economic developments during the Civil War years and the post-war period tied the West more closely to the East and resulted in further exploitation of the arid zones' resources. Basic to all else was the completion of a railroad to the Pacific Coast.

Local and sectional rivalries, as well as constitutional arguments, had delayed congressional action on the railroad project. The city chosen as the eastern terminus, and the areas it served, would be in a position to dominate the trade of the West. As a consequence, whenever Congress considered any bill providing for construction along a specific route, supporters of rival projects banded together to defeat the measure (*14*). Proponents of the various routes accused each other of acting for purely selfish motives. There was also a southern bloc that opposed, on constitutional principles, the granting of public lands to encourage railroad building. The secession of the southern states made possible the passage of the Pacific railroad bill by removing this bloc from Congress and by eliminating from consideration the southern routes.

The Central Pacific Railroad, building east from Sacramento, and the Union Pacific, building west from Omaha, crept slowly toward each other during the war years, then speeded up shortly thereafter to meet at Promontory Point, Utah, in May 1869. The long-awaited Pacific railroad was now a reality. Four more lines reached the Pacific Coast within the next 15 years, thus justifying the arguments used by proponents of all the routes.

The building of the transcontinental railroads is a classic example of the mixed economy that has been characteristic of much western development. That rail lines were needed to serve the interior settlements and reach the Pacific was unquestioned in the early 1850's, but it was evident that private capital, unassisted, would never undertake their construction. The idea of government assistance, therefore, was inherent in all proposals. As finally passed, the Pacific railroad measure provided for the granting of public lands to the Union Pacific and to the Central Pacific, a practice that was extended to all western railroads through the 1860's.

The West was peculiarly dependent on railroads, because it had no major navigable rivers and the cost of moving bulky commodities by wagon was prohibitive. Railroads made possible the occupation of the arid and semiarid regions by farmers, stockmen, and others whose activities could be profitable only if freight costs were low. Regular schedules and fast service, particularly after the advent of refrigeration, encouraged specialization, so that each region could produce the items for which it was best fitted. Cattle, wheat, cotton, vegetables, and citrus fruits now could be added to gold, silver, and furs in contributing to the economic development of the West. Railroads were the bond that tied together the increasingly interdependent sections of the nation.

The rapid development and subsequent decline of the California mining districts left in their wake the prospectors who would spend their lives following the will-o'-the-wisp of "the big strike." They rushed feverishly to each new diggings or wandered into the unexplored and forbidding wilderness in search of gold and silver. Unsuccessful on the western slope of the Sierra Nevada, some crossed the mountains and participated in the excitement created by the Comstock lode. Others, who had looked briefly at the Colorado Rockies en route to California, now returned to examine them more thoroughly and were successful enough to cause the first "Pikes Peak" rush in 1859.

Rich strikes followed in rapid order during the next 40 years: on the Clearwater and Salmon rivers, at Alder Gulch and Last Chance Gulch, and near Tucson and Gila City in the 1860's; at Butte, Leadville, Globe, Tombstone, and in the Black Hills in the 1870's; at Coeur d'Alene in the 1880's; at Cripple Creek in the 1890's; and at Tonopah, Goldfield, and Amargosa City early in the new century. In addition to gold and silver, copper became a major mineral resource scattered widely through the arid regions. Borax gave economic importance to Death Valley.

None of the later strikes followed the pattern of the California rush. Except for limited pockets, the mineral wealth was locked in quartz. Prospectors could hold rich "feet" but could not develop their claims, because they lacked the capital for crushing and processing. A combination of eastern capital and western resources developed an industry far different from that of California placer mining. As strikes drew thousands of adventurers to new sites, often remote from existing governments, new territories were carved out of the original ones, multiplying the total number. Of even more significance nationally was the predominance of silver production, which cheapened the price of that metal in relation to gold. This gave rise to the demand by cheap-money advocates for the free and unlimited coinage of silver at the ratio of 16 to 1, a major political issue toward the end of the century.

Cattle Barons, Explorers, and Indians

Shortly after the Civil War ended, the range-cattle industry spread over the Plains, and, for the first time, this area was viewed as something more than a major barrier to Pacific-bound immigrants. Grazing was not new to the semiarid and arid regions. Stock raising had been of primary importance on every Spanish frontier, and sheep raising had been the heart of the struggling economy of New Mexico from the inception of that province. The lack of available markets kept the value of sheep and cattle depressed in the northern Mexican provinces, and straying stock was not a matter of particular concern. Blessed with a natural breeding and feeding ground, straying cattle from Spanish herds had multiplied rapidly. Displaced Civil War veterans, particularly those from the South who had returned to find their homes in shambles, turned to the West to start anew. They joined with resident Texans to create an industry based on driving

this wild stock to market. The industry spread rapidly to the
northern Plains as cattle were driven along newly opened trails.

The cattle industry did not develop in a vacuum but was part
of a national development, without which it never could have occurred. Wild stock had grazed undisturbed for generations with only
isolated efforts to drive the animals to distant markets. The Plains
could be turned to their natural economic use only after city-dwellers
were demanding great quantities of food, railheads were pushing beyond occupied areas where towns and fencing blocked cattle drives,
and the meat-packing industry was organizing so that it could
slaughter and process thousands of head daily. The cattle industry
not only fed the people of the cities; it also fed some of the major
industries that created those cities.

After the spectacular collapse of the range-cattle industry in 1887,
barbed wire made possible the rise of ranching. Sheep raisers contested with cattlemen for grazing lands and, after a bitter struggle,
became entrenched in mountain and plateau areas, but cattle continued to dominate the Plains.

Reconnaissance and Politics

With miners, Mormons, and livestock raisers occupying limited
areas of the arid West, the time was ripe to collect more information
about its unknown portions. Californians had undertaken a notable
survey of the state's resources in the 1860's, but the mapping and detailed examination of the interior territories were projects that required action by the federal government. Four rival surveys were
in the field in the 1870's. They not only competed openly for funds
and publicity but also reflected a sharp jurisdictional conflict between the War Department and the Department of the Interior.

One military reconnaissance, under the command of George M.
Wheeler, ranged widely over the region west of the 100th meridian;
the other military survey, headed by Clarence King, surveyed a 100-
mile (160-kilometer) belt along the railroad route. Ferdinand V.
Hayden, in charge of the more ambitious of the Interior Department
parties, explored widely in the Rocky Mountains and Great Basin
during a 10-year period. The John Wesley Powell survey, more
modest in both numbers and appropriations than the others, was
more purely scientific. Generally speaking, the instructions under

which these parties operated called for an extensive examination of the potential resources of the country and a study of all factors that would affect settlement.

The leader of each party made his particular contributions. Wheeler's massive reports departed sharply from those of his military predecessors in emphasizing the character of the country rather than routes of travel across it. Hayden was largely responsible for the government's setting aside Yellowstone National Park, initiating the national park system. Clarence King became the first director of the U.S. Geological Survey when the various surveys were consolidated under the Department of the Interior in 1879. Powell's contributions were the most significant of all. His recommendations on land policy in the arid and semiarid zones (most of them highly unpopular at the time) were to help to shape the course of scientific land use and conservation activities in the 20th century. Among his proposals were the scientific classification of land in determining the size of homesteads, comprehensive planning for the use of natural resources with limited national controls, and, in embryonic form, multipurpose river-basin development (15).

Postwar developments in the semiarid and arid zones brought the government face to face with the problem of adopting a permanent Indian policy. It was no longer possible to resort to the temporary expedient of shoving the Indians ahead of the advancing frontier. There were no hunting grounds safe from intrusion by whites schooled in a tradition of complete disregard for Indian rights. There were additional complications. For years the Bureau of Indian Affairs had been charged with corruptness, and there was a bitter contest between the Interior and War departments for administrative control of Indian affairs (16). Congress was divided sharply on the matter of proper Indian policy. The Indian frontier was violent and chaotic. Quarrels between miners and the Indians of the Colorado area, culminating in the Sand Creek Massacre, had left the Cheyennes and Arapahos homeless and hostile. After their forced removal to Dakota, the Minnesota Sioux were sullen, and their kinsmen to the west were determined to resist further white penetration.

The Indian problem had to be solved before the lands from the Great Plains to the Sierra Nevada could be occupied with any degree of safety, and the answer was necessarily national rather than regional. Politically, the problem was solved by the adoption of a reservation policy in anticipation of the conversion of the Indians to an agrarian society. Simple in its conception, it was difficult in fulfillment. There was much vacillation in its administration, the Indians were generally hostile, the selection of some of the reservations was ill-advised, and the policy was carried out in an atmosphere of armed conflict. Resolution of the problem on the Plains came through neither force of arms nor governmental policy but rather through the destruction of the buffalo herds, which had been the heart of the Indian economy. Without these herds, the Plains Indians had to adopt a new way of life.

Agriculture and Statehood

A striking feature of the later 19th century was the encroachment of an agricultural society on the "cattle kingdom." Historically, the agrarian frontier had proceeded in fairly orderly fashion, following rivers and paths into the lands just beyond the line of established settlement. The pattern was broken at mid-century. From the western edge of the fertile prairies, ambitious land seekers undertook the arduous trek across the western interior to reach the valleys of the Pacific, convinced that the intervening plains and plateaus were barren of agricultural opportunity. Only a fortunate few, located near surface water and in the vicinity of such local markets as military posts, Indian reservations, or mining camps, attempted fulltime agricultural activities in the arid zones. But, finally, the interior West was all that was left for restless pioneer farmers, who always had accepted as a matter of course the existence of desirable unoccupied farmland just beyond the line of settlement.

The conversion of the arid lands to agricultural uses fitted neatly into a complex pattern that was reshaping American agriculture. Despite the importance of some commercial crops, farming had remained basically a subsistence occupation in which the small surpluses, vital though they might be, were incidental to taking a living directly from the soil. The requirements of an industrializing nation rendered this system obsolete. Now the American farmer not only had to supply food for the urban population but also had to furnish enormous quantities of basic raw materials to industry. To meet this demand, he had to sacrifice some of his self-sufficiency so that he could produce to capacity the things for which his land was best suited. This continuing and growing demand turned the attention of the agricultural frontier to the semiarid lands.

At this time, a number of new factors made the Plains more attractive than ever before. Railroads began to provide inspiration as well as transportation. The federal government liberalized the public-land laws and enacted legislation directed toward agricultural research. A more obscure, but highly significant, factor was the adaptability of the dry lands to the new commercial agriculture.

The railroads, which had pushed ahead of agricultural settlement to furnish shipping points for Plains cattle, carried with them the seeds of destruction of the grazing economy that they had helped to create. Eager to develop a more stable traffic than that furnished by seasonal cattle shipments, the railroads publicized the vacant public lands along their lines, disposed of their own lands at low prices, and carried on extensive colonizing campaigns both domestically and abroad, hoping to dot the Plains with agricultural marketing towns. They found allies in the sparsely settled western territories that were fighting desperately to attract population in spite of some local resistance by the range lords.

The proper disposition of public lands had been a highly controversial issue in American politics from the beginning of the nation. The general course of legislation was one of easing the requirements for securing title to land, and by the 1850's there was widespread support for a policy of giving homesteads to bona fide settlers. In 1862, President Lincoln signed the Homestead Act. This was the same year that a Department of Agriculture was created and public lands were given to the states to endow agricultural and mechanical colleges (the land-grant schools).

On its face productive of much good, the Homestead Act did not effectively prevent continued speculation in the public lands; furthermore, it was partially self-defeating because the quarter-section (65 hectares), which congressmen unacquainted with dry-land conditions accepted as the proper size for a homestead, was simply an uneconomic unit in regions where climatic conditions dictated extensive, rather than intensive, farming (*17, 18*). In spite of the shortcomings of the act, railroads and local immigration bureaus seized on "free lands in the West" as a powerful talking point to attract settlers.

The unpredictability of farming in semiarid country was not immediately apparent as farmers, hesitantly at first, then with increasing confidence, pushed onto the Plains, drawn west by a wet cycle in which conventional tillage methods proved to be adequate. Some adjustments had to be made. Windmills, recently adapted to Plains conditions, and cisterns supplemented the meager supply of water; dugouts and sodhouses replaced frame buildings; barbed wire, a new invention, substituted for the traditional rail and stone fences (*19*).

The return of a dry cycle in the late 1880's practically destroyed the budding Plains agriculture and all but depopulated the entire region. The spirit-breaking drought dramatically demonstrated that attempts to employ the methods used in humid areas had to fail. The answer, if there was an answer, lay in the development of techniques that could make maximum use of the scant rainfall and in the discovery of drought-resistant crops.

Both the government and the western railroads were major contributors to the method that became known as *dry farming*. The Department of Agriculture, western land-grant colleges, and, after 1887, agricultural experiment stations joined in their research efforts. They gradually developed methods for conserving what moisture was available, embodying such principles as contour plowing to prevent runoff. At the same time, they were carrying on a worldwide search for crops peculiarly suited for dry regions and developing drought-resistant strains of domestic crops. Realizing that they had to hold the new settlers they had attracted to the Plains, the railroads became the major popularizers of the new methods. They hired agricultural agents to act as advisers, to cooperate with individual farmers in demonstration plots using new techniques, to organize agricultural clubs among adults and youths, to distribute experiment station and agricultural college bulletins, and, on occasion, to write their own bulletins.

Despite the tribulations of dry farming, it basically fitted the pattern of commercial agriculture and gave added impetus to industrialization. Crop failures were frequent, and the yield per acre was consistently low. The answer was to cultivate more acres, and these would be planted to the few things that could be grown. This meant that the dry farmer would produce surpluses that he had to sell in order to buy the things he could not produce. Had he been able to diversify, he still would have been tied to cash crops, because the cultivation of extensive acreages under dry-farming methods was impossible without machinery (20). Although grain from the semiarid farmlands helped to build a great milling industry, the purchase of machinery necessary to cultivate these lands contributed to the boom in the manufacture of farm implements.

Politically, the evolution of the semiarid and arid zones in the later 19th century was generally quite similar to that which had been followed historically by other undeveloped areas. Smaller, organized territories split away from the great regional territories along lines determined by population movements. These, in turn, could anticipate statehood as political expediency or continued population growth dictated. In 1889 and 1890, Congress admitted six arid and semiarid states into the Union (21).

There were some exceptions to the normal development. For political reasons, Nevada achieved statehood in 1864 and Colorado in 1876. Because of popular prejudice against the Mormon institution of polygamy, Utah was denied statehood until 1896. New Mexico and Arizona did not become states until 1912. This delay had many causes, chief of which were the beliefs that the people of New Mexico, with deeply rooted Spanish backgrounds, were schooled in a different sort of political tradition, and that most of the inhabitants were non-English-speaking, illiterate, or both (22). Arizona, with less Spanish influence, nevertheless, lagged in acquiring statehood because its political aspirations were tied by history and geography to those of New Mexico.

Reclamation and Conservation

The activities of Powell and others, together with the realization that the "limitless" unoccupied agricultural lands in the West were rapidly becoming limited, led to a great interest in irrigation. The practice of irrigating land antedated by many generations the appearance of European cultures in the arid and semiarid zones and was carried on by the Spaniards after their arrival. From the inception of their Great Basin colonies, the Mormons depended on irrigation, and it had been attempted with varying degrees of success locally in such geographically diverse projects as the German cooperative at Anaheim, California; Jack Swilling's ditch at Wickenburg, Arizona; the E. N. Carter development on Black's Fork in

Wyoming; and the Union Colony at Greeley, Colorado. State legislatures also encouraged private projects. California took the lead with its act of 1875, which authorized the organization of an irrigation district with the power to bond itself.

Active federal intervention began in 1894 with the unsatisfactory Carey Land Act, which provided up to 1 million acres (404,700 hectares) of public lands to each of 10 states to promote irrigation. The basic law was the Reclamation Act of 1902, popularly called the Newlands Act because of the prominent role played by Representative Francis G. Newlands, of Nevada, in drafting the measure and securing its passage over bitter opposition led by Joseph G. Cannon, one of the most powerful figures in the Republican party. This act provided for direct governmental construction of projects from revenues received from the sale of public lands in the West. All costs ultimately would be borne by the water users, who would pay into a revolving fund to be used for new projects. Although the Reclamation Act did not always operate as anticipated, growing out of it were 25 early projects scattered through the dry states and including, among others, the Salt River in Arizona, Truckee-Carson in Nevada, Orland in California, Uncompahgre in Colorado, Elephant Butte in New Mexico, Minidoka in Idaho, Milk River in Montana, Yakima in Washington, and Belle Fourche in South Dakota.

Federal participation in irrigation development became entwined with the entire conservation movement as the early conservationists realized that the natural resources of the nation not only were exhaustible but were, in fact, becoming dangerously depleted. Although conservation was not peculiar to the western states, it was of particular importance to them because of the amount of public land and quantity of unexploited resources remaining within their boundaries and the opportunity to reclaim arid lands. The Forest Reserves Act of 1891 gave to the executive branch the power to withdraw forested areas from private entry, but, although President Harrison had created the Yellowstone Timberland Reserve in Wyoming, the active conservation movement is identified with the administration of Theodore Roosevelt. The President himself was its aggressive leader.

Leaders in the movement recognized the tight interrelationship of conservation in its various aspects: timbered watersheds, prevention of soil erosion, preservation of mineral resources, flood control, and protection of navigable streams. They were also conscious of the fundamental importance of damsites, now broadened to include the future development of hydroelectric power. Here, indeed, was an area in which there were fundamental conflicts of philosophy—state versus federal control and private exploitation as opposed to governmental intervention to protect natural resources. There was a sectional division of opinion *(23)*.

Westerners, in general, argued that the East had used its resources wastefully but in so doing had seized economic leadership and now was willing to husband carefully the resources of the West, thus preventing its rapid development. Conservationists answered that the prodigality of the 19th century no longer could be tolerated, because the government had an obligation to protect the interests of future generations.

The fight was bitter, and there was no clear-cut victory. Roosevelt defined the issues and determined the battlelines in a struggle that would continue far beyond his tenure in office. A powerful opposition, including the budding hydroelectric-power interests and significant segments of the mineral, timber, and livestock industries, fought back vigorously against what they termed "governmental landlordism." The President's greatest contribution was his success in mustering popular support. Other than the Reclamation Act, his immediate successes included extensive withdrawals of timber and coal land from private entry and the creation of various conservation commissions. Although Roosevelt's successor, William Howard Taft, was never able to live down an undeserved reputation of being unsympathetic toward conservation, his accomplishments were also impressive.

Conservation was overshadowed by other national issues during the Woodrow Wilson administration, but there were some advances, notably the creation of the Agricultural Extension Service in 1914 and the National Park Service in 1916. The major conservation measure of the 1920's was legislation authorizing the Boulder Canyon project. The bitter controversy that raged through the Harding and Coolidge administrations over Muscle Shoals, although immediately concerned with the Tennessee Valley, was of significance to the West because of the possible effect on the development of its own river basins.

The New Deal and the West

The depression that struck in 1929 and deepened early in the following decade led to the usual demands for a change of political administration and for a critical reexamination of the nation's economy, including a profound interest in the preservation of its resources. Within a month after Franklin D. Roosevelt took office, Congress created the Civilian Conservation Corps, which recruited young unemployed men for various types of work, such as fighting fires, seeding trees and native grasses, working on flood-control and wildlife projects, and building roads and firebreaks on public lands. Owing to the nature of the work, there was a heavy concentration of CCC camps in the West. In 1933, Congress also passed legislation that established a planning board (later to become the National Resources Planning Board), instituted a soil erosion service in the Department of the Interior, and resolved the controversy over Muscle Shoals by creating the Tennessee Valley Authority to administer the controlled development of that great river basin. At this time there was also a notable increase in the research activities of existing conservation agencies.

The terrible duststorms, or "black blizzards," which swept across the Texas and Oklahoma panhandles and adjacent areas in the spring of 1934, blowing away tons of topsoil and reducing much of the land to drifted sand, made the nation acutely aware of its soil resources. The government pushed the timber shelterbelt program on the Plains and enlarged the soil erosion service into the Soil Conservation Service, transferring it to the Department of Agriculture. The Taylor Grazing Act of 1934 had as its purpose the prevention of overgrazing and soil deterioration and the orderly use of the public range by the livestock industry. Construction by the Department of Agriculture of reservoirs, ponds, wells, and other water facilities in the arid zones was authorized in 1936.

Conservation programs were not limited to soil resources. Congress permitted the oil-producing states to enter into a compact to prorate the volume of production in this highly competitive field. Flood control also required regional cooperation. The Flood Control Act of 1936 encouraged states to enter into compacts for this purpose and extended federal financial assistance. Although some of the dams that resulted were strictly for flood control, most of them were designed for multiple functions. Two great projects on the Columbia River—Grand Coulee and Bonneville—were under construction before there was a flood-control act, but the Colorado–Big Thompson, the California Central Valley, and the Missouri River projects benefited from this law and subsequent amendatory legislation. Through the sometimes strained cooperation of many agencies, notably the Bureau of Reclamation and the Army Corps of Engineers, water power was harnessed for use in irrigation and for the production of hydroelectric power, the improvement of navigability of rivers, the restoration of ground and surface water, the protection of wildlife, the prevention of stream pollution, and the creation of recreational areas.

The contest over conservation in the 1930's was reminiscent of the days of Theodore Roosevelt. The same basic conflicts of philosophy were evident, and the arguments were largely a restatement of those from the earlier period. Powerful economic groups were again deeply involved. Newly created agencies were under constant attack, and some, such as the National Resources Planning Board, were destroyed (24).

Agencies associated with the preservation of the nation's resources inevitably overlapped in their activities, producing administrative and philosophic conflicts. The Agriculture and Interior departments each claimed a primacy of interest; the Grazing and Forest services supported the principle of multiple use, and the National Park Service insisted on reserving much of the primitive land in its natural state. The agencies disagreed among themselves on which of the competing public and private land uses would serve best the national interest. There was sharp conflict among the various agencies created to give advice and technical assistance to landowners in the economic use of their properties. As new agencies were created, they encountered resistance from existing ones, which jealously guarded their areas of interest from possible intrusion.

Conservation agencies have not been able to prevent all destruction of natural resources, of course. Shameful overgrazing destroyed the native grasses on millions of acres and permitted invasions by uneconomic plants. More spectacular because of the great destructiveness in a limited time-span, the Dust Bowl demonstrated the tragic consequences of attempts to convert grassland to cultivated crops in an area of scant rainfall and high winds. Ruthless competition led to criminally wasteful logging and oil-drilling operations.

Recent Resources Development

Awakened interest in the fate of the public domain tied in closely with the development of the West's most important economic resources. No other region possessed, in either variety or magnitude, its scenic and climatic attractions. Grand Canyon, Yosemite, Yellowstone, Rocky Mountain, Big Bend, and Carlsbad Caverns were a few of its many national parks. Winter attractions varied from mild, sunshiny weather to winter sports areas, in many instances in close proximity; summer offered crisp mountain temperatures and clear fishing streams. Furthermore, the arid Southwest had long enjoyed a reputation for its natural curative qualities. But climate and scenery were economically valueless unless large numbers of health seekers and pleasure seekers were willing to pay for enjoying such attractions.

The American tradition of mobility, combined with a high living standard and leisure time, furnished the tourists. Railroads were a partial answer to the problem of transportation, but the great flood followed the mass production of low-priced automobiles. The federal government played no small part when it embarked on a grant-in-aid policy to assist in building a nationwide network of hard-surfaced roads. The completion of highways to the west coast contributed greatly to the growth of the western states. Garages and filling stations, motels and restaurants, fresh juice and vegetable wayside stands, racetracks and casinos, pleasure resorts and medical clinics became major sources of revenue, as did the sale of Indian jewelry, blankets and rugs, and of ore specimens, petrified wood, and semiprecious stones.

Mining continued to play a major role in the dry-land economy. Most of the minerals were not peculiar to arid zones but were there by geologic accident; nonetheless, their influence was sometimes greater than that of resources more characteristic of arid regions. Although the precious metals and copper, petroleum, and uranium have attracted more attention, many prosaic minerals of great importance to an industrial nation have quietly contributed to the economy.

The development of the arid regions produced a disproportionate number of town-dwellers (25). Paradoxically, this distribution of population did not indicate heavy industrialization, because the West suffered from such limiting factors as inadequate water supplies, distance to markets, and unfavorable freight differentials. Certain industries that, by their nature, were not adversely affected by these factors, however, established themselves in the West. Pioneer moving-picture makers migrated to southern California to take advantage of the favorable climatic conditions and, in time, made Hollywood the film capital of the world. Some primary processors of raw materials, mineral and agricultural, greatly expanded their operations in the 20th century. In the 1920's, California began to experience significant industrial development in such fields as aircraft production (25). Some cities grew to commanding size and, in doing so, attracted new industries that were either adaptable to the prevailing natural limitations or capable of operating profitably because of local markets. As time went on, citrus groves were uprooted to make way for factories or urban subdivisions; lands previously dedicated to orchards and vineyards were appropriated for paved highways to serve the cities.

Cities created new problems, most notably their demands on the most precious of all western resources—water. Multiple-purpose dams, broadened in their scope to serve the urban need for electricity and for recreational areas, were unable to offer a solution for the millions of gallons of water required daily by the domestic and industrial users in the cities. In spite of their willingness to spend extravagant sums to bring water from great distances, the urban centers still find the quantity inadequate, and there can be no security for the future until as-yet-untapped sources become available.

One great western bonanza of the 20th century—defense activities of the federal government—was reserved for the days after World War II. It was a modern twist to an old theme of the arid West, where, from the earliest days of occupation, frontier military posts had called into existence villages to supply their immediate needs and had provided local markets for livestock raised on isolated ranches. With developments in rocketry and missiles, in the air arm of national defense, and in nuclear warfare, the military once more brought prosperity.

The ushering in of the atomic age with the blast at Trinity Site, in the New Mexico desert, had been preceded by experimentation under strictest secrecy in a remote mountain area of northern New Mexico. This was merely the prelude to the tremendous expansion that was to follow. The absence of economic resources became an economic resource in itself. Great barren expanses, with little or no population, and with favorable year-round weather, were ideal for testing missiles and aircraft. Great multiple-purpose dams had new users for electric energy and new visitors to their recreational areas. Nearby cities benefited because they became centers for the booming electronic, aerospace, and related industries, which made no excessive demands on the water supply, did not suffer too severely from freight rates, and now had available markets nearby. Research activities resulted in a steady flow of mathematicians, physicists, and engineers into the West and the birth of such rarefied scientific centers as Los Alamos. Specialized industrialization attracted technicians and a highly skilled labor force. Last of the nation to retain vestiges of the old frontier, the arid West was now the center of the new space-age frontier, which holds the key to the future.

Balance Sheet on the Arid West

Basic to all else in the development of the dry West was its membership in a larger state, geographically contiguous and enjoying the same political rights and institutions. There was complete freedom of movement—of people, of commodities, of capital, of ideas— within the borders of a nation notable for its tradition of extreme mobility. The rapid maturation of the American West resulted largely from the pressure of a dynamic economy making tremendous industrial strides, with the capacity to supply capital, railroads, and machinery and implements in return for the raw products of each raw-materials area. The federal government played a very important part by following a policy that encouraged both industrialization and the rapid opening of the West.

Westerners have not consistently applauded the results of sectional interdependence. Aware that the partnership was indispensable, nonetheless, they were critical of the manner in which it operated. They resented the dictation of policy from the East, as well as the draining away of what they considered a disproportionate share of the profits to their absentee associates.

The needs of the nation dictated a continuously changing image of the West. For more than 100 years this change has been one of gradual rejection of the concept of a great irreclaimable wasteland and of growing confidence in the ability of man to use more efficiently the known resources and to uncover additional ones. The results of this increasingly optimistic appraisal, however, have not been uniformly beneficial. This has been particularly true when the resources were developed too rapidly or were improperly used. The great promise of the grasslands was negated in part by overgrazing. The Dust Bowl of the 1930's illustrated the disastrous effects of pushing to an extreme the adaptation of a marginal agricultural area, which, viewed from the present, obviously had to fail. The economic base furnished by minerals ended with their exhaustion, as the numerous ghost towns of the West testify.

Walter Prescott Webb contends (26) that Pike and Long basically were correct in their appraisal of the West and views pessimistically its future. The 17 arid and semiarid states, he insists, are understandable only when they are studied in terms of the prevailing dryness, which has created oasis cultures, with population clustered where water is available. These states also comprise an area of depletable raw materials (particularly a meager water supply), which are being exhausted rapidly.

No one can deny that Webb accurately describes conditions that prevent the arid West from developing along the same lines as humid regions, and that he presents sound historical evidence to prove that it has stubbornly resisted change. He fails, however, to discuss the possibility of turning its characteristic features—notably dryness, heat, and wasteland—into assets. He discusses Nevada's creation of an "oasis of iniquity" to attract visitors but is silent about the winter resorts of the Southwest where warmth and sunshine are the attractions. He mentions that the first atomic explosion occurred in an unpopulated New Mexico wasteland but does not add that desert areas have become centers for aerospace research—a matter of more than transitory importance in a space-conscious age.

With full awareness of Webb's omission of some of its basic exploitable resources, the West, nevertheless, can profit from his realistic appraisal. In spite of the remarkable development of this great region in recent years, its people must take into consideration its limitations, as well as its promise, in plans for future growth.

They must determine what economic activities are of permanent value and must conserve carefully and use to the best advantage the exhaustible resources while they search for new ones.

Acknowledgments: I am indebted to John Porter Bloom, staff historian for the National Park Service, Washington, D.C., and to Sigurd Johansen, of New Mexico State University, for many helpful suggestions in the content and organization of this chapter.

REFERENCES

1. P. C. Phillips, *The Fur Trade* (Univ. of Oklahoma Press, Norman, 1961).
2. W. E. Hollon, *The Lost Pathfinder, Zebulon Montgomery Pike* (Univ. of Oklahoma Press, Norman, 1949).
3. E. W. Gilbert, *The Exploration of Western America, 1800–1850* (Cambridge Univ. Press, Cambridge, England, 1933).
4. J. R. Bell, *The Journal of Captain John R. Bell, Official Journalist for the Stephen H. Long Expedition to the Rocky Mountains, 1820,* L. Hafen, Ed. (Arthur H. Clark, Glendale, Calif., 1957).
5. R. L. Duffus, *The Santa Fe Trail* (Longmans, Green, London, 1930).
6. J. C. Fremont, *Narratives of Exploration and Adventure,* A. Nevins, Ed. (Longmans, Green, New York, 1956).
7. R. A. Billington, *Westward Expansion, a History of the American Frontier* (Macmillan, New York, ed. 2, 1960).
8. B. A. DeVoto, *The Year of Decision, 1846* (Little, Brown, Boston, 1943).
9. W. T. Jackson, *Wagon Roads West: A Study of Federal Road Construction in the Trans-Mississippi West, 1846–1869* (Univ. of California Press, Berkeley, 1952).
10. W. H. Goetzmann, *Army Explorations in the American West, 1803–1863* (Yale Univ. Press, New Haven, Conn., 1959).
11. E. S. Pomeroy, *The Territories and the United States, 1861–1890: Studies in Colonial Administration* (Univ. of Pennsylvania Press, Philadelphia, 1947).
12. M. Clawson, *Uncle Sam's Acres* (Dodd, Mead, New York, 1951).
13. R. E. Huffman, *Irrigation Development and Public Water Policy* (Ronald, New York, 1953).
14. R. R. Russel, *Improvement of Communication with the Pacific Coast as an Issue in American Politics, 1783–1864* (Torch, Cedar Rapids, Iowa, 1948).
15. W. E. Stegner, *Beyond the Hundredth Meridian: John Wesley Powell and the Second Opening of the West* (Houghton Mifflin, Boston, 1954).

16. F. L. Paxson, *The Last American Frontier* (Macmillan, New York, 1911).

17. P. W. Gates, "The Homestead Act in an incongruous land system," *Am. Hist. Rev.* **41**, 652–681 (1936).

18. F. W. Shannon, *The Farmer's Last Frontier: Agriculture, 1860–1897* (Farrar & Rinehart, New York, 1945).

19. W. P. Webb, *The Great Plains* (Ginn, Boston, 1931).

20. L. B. Schmitt, "The agricultural revolution in the prairies and Great Plains of the United States," *Agr. Hist.* **8**, 169–195 (1934).

21. F. H. Jonas, Ed., *Western Politics* (Univ. of Utah Press, Salt Lake City, 1961).

22. L. I. Perrigo, *Our Spanish Southwest* (Banks Upshaw, Dallas, Texas, 1960).

23. E. L. Peffer, *The Closing of the Public Domain: Disposal and Reservation Policies, 1900–1950* (Stanford Univ. Press, Stanford, Calif., 1951).

24. D. M. Coyle, *Conservation, an American Story of Conflict and Accomplishment* (Rutgers Univ. Press, New Brunswick, N.J., 1957).

25. C. M. Zierer, Ed., *California and the Southwest* (Wiley, New York, 1956).

26. W. P. Webb, "The American West: perpetual mirage," *Harper's Magazine* **214**, 25–31 (May 1957).

5

Weather: Complex Causes of Aridity

RALPH M. McGEHEE

Arid regions are characterized by precipitation that, most of the time, is insufficient to replenish losses of soil moisture by evaporation, transpiration, and other mechanisms. Many factors—including solar radiation, temperature, humidity, wind, topography, and vegetation—affect soil moisture losses.

Precipitation in arid regions usually is highly variable and, consequently, is unreliable. This characteristic is often as important as, or even more important than, the small average amounts; it introduces an element of chance in the use of arid lands that must be considered in realistic planning.

Conditions that decrease the amounts of precipitation or increase the need for precipitation, or both, cause increases in aridity. Two conditions are necessary to obtain precipitation. There must be a supply of moist air, and there must be a means for removing this moisture from the air. The principal sources of moisture in the atmosphere are the oceans, and the principal mechanism of condensation is the expansion cooling that occurs in rising air.

Moisture is carried from the oceans to the continents by the major wind systems of the earth. As one moves from the equator in either direction toward the poles, the first belt of winds encountered are the trade winds. These blow generally from the northeast in the northern latitudes and from the southeast in the southern latitudes.

Contributors to this chapter were IVEN BENNETT, MELVIN L. BLANC, MARX BROOK, ARTHUR V. DODD, PAUL C. EKERN, ALLEN F. FLANDERS, DAVID M. HERSHFIELD, FRANK E. HOUGHTON, PAUL R. JULIAN, PAUL S. MARTIN, PEVERIL MEIGS, J. MURRAY MITCHELL, JR., JEROME NAMIAS, TOR J. NORDENSON, WILLIAM D. SELLERS, and EDWARD C. STONE.

At about 30° latitude either north or south of the equator occurs a belt of light winds or calms. Here the air is generally descending and dry. Most of the great deserts of the world lie in these latitudes. In the broad middle belts from about 30° to 60° north and south latitude, cyclonic storms from the west dominate. Cold air currents from the polar regions meet warm, moist air from the tropical oceans, and the encounters spawn the great storms that provide most of the rainfall in the middle latitudes.

The principal causes of aridity are large scale and persistent. Climates are affected also by such factors as the locations and sizes of the continents. The wind belts control much of the climate, and determine the major wet and dry areas, of the world. Places in the belts of descending air, in the lee of mountain chains, and near cold ocean currents, all are likely to have arid conditions. Shown in Fig. 1 are the world's major arid and semiarid areas.

On the margins of many of these areas, considerable variation in the amount of precipitation occurs from year to year. There are wet periods and dry periods. These periods follow irregular changes in the atmospheric circulation of the earth. In some years, a marginal area will be favored with an unusually large share of moisture-laden winds. Rain will fall, and crops will thrive. In other years, the winds are dry, and crops perish.

The sparse cloudiness that is typical of arid regions allows nearly maximum solar radiation to reach the earth's surface. If moisture is available, the high radiant energy causes high evapotranspiration rates.

Aridity in the United States

In the United States, the semiarid and arid areas occur in a broad belt of mountain and desert land some 600 miles (965 kilometers) wide and nearly 1100 miles (1770 kilometers) long, lying generally between the western margins of the Great Plains and the crests of the Sierra Nevada–Cascade barrier (in the south, reaching westward to the Pacific Coast) and extending north-to-south from border to border (1). The region can be divided into two major climatic zones—a northern zone including, roughly, the area between the Canadian border and the Utah-Arizona line, and a southern zone comprising most of New Mexico, Arizona, and southern California.

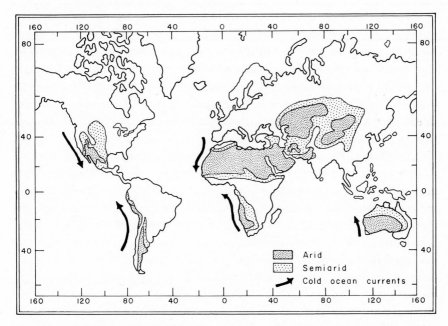

Fig. 1. More than a third of the earth's surface is either arid or semiarid, as is indicated by this map. Most of the regions in which water
limits activity occur along a wide belt at about 30° latitude north and
south of the equator, where the winds are descending and dry. (Adapted
from Tannehill, in "Climatology—reviews of research," *Arid Zone Research,* UNESCO, No. 10, p. 160, 1958)

Except when they are determined by topography, the boundaries of
climatic zones are seldom sharp.

The northern zone lies in the belt of westerly cyclonic storms.
A large part of the moisture in these storms is extracted by the
western mountains. These storms bring most of the annual precipitation during the winter and early spring months. Generally,
precipitation increases with elevation and is the greatest on the
windward slopes and crests of mountain ranges. Mean annual precipitation for the northern zone ranges from a low of about 4 inches
(102 millimeters) in the desert valleys west of the Great Salt Lake
to highs of more than 60 inches (1524 millimeters) in the mountains
of central Idaho and central Washington.

The southern zone has several climatic influences. In winter, it
is frequently penetrated by frontal systems of the cyclonic storms

from the west and north. Occasionally, centers of the storms pass through, or develop within, the zone. These fronts and storms produce a primary winter maximum of precipitation in mountains and high plateaus and a secondary winter peak at lower elevations. In summer, typical large-scale pressure patterns are such that southerly to southeasterly winds are common in the central and eastern areas of the zone, bringing in moisture from the Gulf of Mexico and producing a summer maximum of precipitation at lower elevations and a secondary summer peak at higher elevations.

Infrequently, there are surges of moisture from the Pacific. The subtropic zone of descending air (subsidence) is dominant in spring, summer, and fall, causing long periods of clear, dry weather, or droughts. Precipitation from the Gulf of Mexico seldom moves westward to the Arizona-California line; western Arizona and southern California tend to be dry in summer. The infrequent penetration of moisture into the areas of southern California and western Arizona that lie east of the Sierras leaves the lower elevations of these areas true deserts.

In the southern zone, the mean annual precipitation ranges from a low of about 2 inches (50.8 millimeters) in Death Valley of California to a high of more than 30 inches (762 millimeters) in the mountains of northern Arizona and New Mexico. In general, temperatures at lower elevations are high and humidities are low, a condition that causes rapid depletion of soil moisture. Day to night temperature differences are large. Average monthly precipitation for selected stations in the arid zones is shown in Fig. 2.

In both northern and southern zones, strong winds occur frequently in spring, and occasionally at other times, and contribute to the erosion features that are so characteristic of the region.

Within both zones, there is a great diversity of local climates, ranging between the extremes of humid, cold and torrid, dry. Wide local variations are caused primarily by topography but depend, too, on general air circulation, relative position in the region, and latitude. It is not uncommon to find some valleys receiving only 4 to 5 inches (102 to 127 millimeters) of precipitation, and mountain slopes less than 40 miles (64 kilometers) away receiving in excess of 40 inches (1016 millimeters). These large and abrupt differences form an important feature of the climate of the arid regions. High country, which itself may not be habitable, often receives snow and rain that provide the water resources that make possible the use of semiarid lands in the vicinity and sometimes at great distances.

The climate has not always been so dry. During the geologic past,

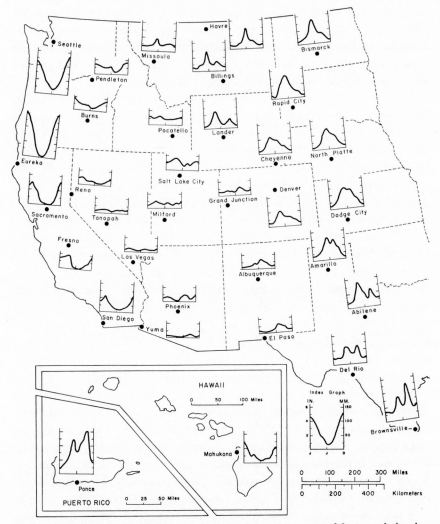

Fig. 2. Patterns of aridity are traced by mean monthly precipitation totals compiled by the U.S. Weather Bureau. Generally, precipitation increases with elevation. Death Valley in California, west of Las Vegas, Nevada, records the annual average low of about 2 inches (51 millimeters). (Adapted from U.S. Weather Bureau map, "Mean monthly total precipitation, inches, 1960")

beginning about 70 million years ago, a gradual cooling occurred. Early in this period, the temperate zone was, on an average, 10° to 15° of latitude north of its present position. Gradual, although fluctuating, cooling led to present-day conditions. About 20 million years ago, the Great Basin had an average rainfall of 35 to 45 inches (889 to 1143 millimeters); by 5 million years ago, the rainfall had dropped to 10 to 16 inches (254 to 406 millimeters) yearly. The climate in the past 1 million years is characterized by wet, cold periods alternating with dry, warm periods.

During wet, cold periods, there were glaciers on the higher mountains and lakes in the intermountain valleys. During dry, warm periods, the climate was much the same as it is at present. Traditionally, the last 10,000 years have been interpreted as representing three climatic episodes. The maximum in warmth and aridity (the Altithermal) was thought to have occurred in the middle, from 2500 to 5000 B.C., with cooler, wetter conditions in higher mountains. Recent pollen studies, though, failed to reveal an "Altithermal" drought and pointed instead to the possibility of increased monsoon precipitation at that time (2). Minor variations have taken place at 2- to 5-century intervals. A drought in the Southwest that began in 1921 has been interrupted in only a very few years since and appears to be more severe than any one since the late 1200's (3).

Research in Meteorology

The western United States was settled under conditions of individual freedom. Many early development projects failed because there was no foresight of the natural consequences that were predictable. As population density has continued to increase, limitations on the use of arid lands have been realized more frequently. Thus the need for knowing—and considering—the limitations imposed by nature cannot be avoided. Research must be relied on to provide criterions for the optimal future development of arid lands.

It should be emphasized that the prediction of the consequences of specific uses of arid lands will seldom be completely determinate. The variability of weather precludes exact predictions. Very useful predictions can be stated, however, in probability terms, and land uses that have little probability of success can be avoided.

Partly because of the small population in the arid regions of the

United States, the research effort there has been small until recent years. Thunderstorm studies were begun at the University of New Mexico in the 1930's and at the New Mexico Institute of Mining and Technology in the mid-1940's and have been continued with increasing effort to the present. The Institute of Atmospheric Physics at the University of Arizona, created in the mid-1950's, has expanding programs in arid-zones climatology, cloud physics, radar meteorology, atmospheric electricity, micrometeorology, and atmospheric dynamics. The Desert Research Institute of the University of Nevada and the National Center for Atmospheric Research, Boulder, Colorado, were established recently and also plan programs in arid-zones meteorology.

Micrometeorologic research is being done at several federal and state experiment stations in the arid regions. Smaller programs exist at other institutions. Some coordination of research efforts in the United States is being effected by the Committee on Desert and Arid Zones Research (CODAZR) of the American Association for the Advancement of Science, and internationally by the United Nations Educational, Scientific, and Cultural Organization (UNESCO). The research effort is increasing, as is the need for knowledge in the field.

Climatic History

Many sciences produce clues to the history of climate, among them geology, archeology, geomorphology, glacial geology, palynology, and dendrochronology. Emphasis here is given to palynology and dendrochronology, which provide some detail in the evidence they produce.

Fossil pollen grains are an imprint of past vegetation. Their potential in the stratigraphy of arid areas first was anticipated in 1944 by Edward S. Deevey, who sought to apply the method to archeologic trash in Mexico. Wide-scale application of palynology in arid regions, however, awaited the perfection of means of chemically extracting pollen from inorganic matrixes.

Now, the array of pollen-rich sediments under study includes the mud of dry lakes (2), flood-plain alluvium, and archeologic sites. Prehistoric man may be related to his environment by examination of his feces. Human dung found in dry caves of Glen Canyon in

Arizona contain abundant pollen of maize, squash, and other plants.

Knowledge of climatic history within the past several millenniums has been increased greatly by dendrochronology, or tree-ring science. Its techniques were developed by Andrew E. Douglass and his students at the University of Arizona, which now has a Laboratory of Tree-Ring Research. Relative widths of growth rings in trees are a measure of the total environmental factors that influence growth rates. In some places, growth rate is determined largely by climatologic conditions. Tree-ring data suggest that no substantial change has occurred in the climate of the southwestern United States within the past 1500 years (3), although fluctuations have occurred during that time. Such data can be used to date climatic occurrences to within 1 year.

Precipitation

Arid-zones-precipitation research in the United States has provided much useful information and at least partial solutions to some problems. A large part of the applied research has been performed by engineers and scientists of the federal government in connection with water-planning projects and the building of hydraulic structures. Other research, generally more basic in nature, has been performed by scientists at the universities.

Rainfall studies have been made in Arizona by James E. McDonald and William D. Sellers, of the Institute of Atmospheric Physics. They applied statistical techniques to determine and describe the rainfall characteristics (4, 5). By establishing primary factors in rainfall, such investigations provide fundamental knowledge that is useful for prediction of rainfall occurrence. Determination of the usual rainfall patterns is a prerequisite to measurement of the effects of weather-modification experiments. Comparisons between humid- and arid-precipitation patterns help to define the extent to which research in the one can be applied to the other.

Some recent observations of thunderstorm rainfall from several dense rain-gage networks set up by the U.S. Agricultural Research Service in Arizona, Idaho, and New Mexico indicate that as many as 12 storm centers may occur over an area of 100 square miles (259 square kilometers); but 80 percent of these storms may cover less

Ancient bristlecone pines (*Pinus aristata*) in the White Mountains of California contain clues to past climates. These trees, which grow under semiarid conditions at high elevations, reach an age of more than 4000 years and are said to be the world's oldest living things. They are the subject of continuing study by dendrochronologists—tree-ring researchers —with National Science Foundation support. (Courtesy University of Arizona, Laboratory of Tree-Ring Research)

than 4.5 square miles (11.7 square kilometers). Gage density varies
from 1 per 4 square miles (10.4 square kilometers) to 4 per square
mile (2.6 square kilometers).

Techniques have been developed for estimating the probable
maximum precipitation for a basin watershed (6). The purpose of
this estimate is to define the rainstorm that will produce the largest
runoff in a watershed. Flood-control systems ideally should be designed on the basis of the probable maximum precipitation. Rain-
fall-frequency studies (7) contribute to the design of hydraulic
structures when calculated risks are acceptable. Frequencies of rainy
and drought periods of given duration have been determined for
some stations; these are useful for planning purposes (8).

Maps of mean seasonal and annual rainfall are being refined by
the U.S. Weather Bureau; and interpolation procedures, which are
necessary because of the limited number of data stations, are being
improved to include the variations in slope, aspect, elevation, and
other environmental characteristics (9).

Since precipitation in arid regions is generally both small and out
of phase with the growing season, agriculture must depend largely
on irrigation. Water-supply forecasting techniques are being improved to include weighted rainfall data, snow accumulations, and
soil-moisture measurements.

Insolation

Direct solar radiation, or insolation, plays a large role in shaping
the natural and cultural environments of most arid lands, since a
high level of solar energy is closely linked to moisture deficiency.
Insolation has other important consequences for arid lands. A
prime concern is conservation of the limited water resources that
are available for irrigation, and for this purpose there is no more
important information than data on the daily and annual regimes of
insolation. One of the first acts of the U.S. Bureau of Reclamation
in the Glen Canyon project was to install an Eppley pyrheliometer
at the damsite at Page, Arizona, to collect insolation data to support
evaporation studies for the future reservoir. Of course, evaporation
of irrigation water is increased greatly by high insolation levels; and
the greater the intensity of insolation, the greater the tendency for
plants to transpire and require irrigation.

Protective building features, such as large overhanging eaves that shade windows during high sun but permit entrance of low sunlight, are an architectural response to insolation. Where air-conditioning is used, efficient systems cannot be designed without consideration of the solar-energy contribution to the heat environment of buildings. Finally, many arid regions have an extremely high potential for the use of insolation for home and industrial heating and for its application as a form of energy to convert brackish or sea water to fresh water.

Despite the importance of knowledge of insolation to the development of arid lands, systematic studies of its place in the natural environment of such areas are difficult to find. Only since 1950 have suitable networks of insolation stations been located in some of the major arid regions of the world (the United States, Australia, Union of South Africa, and Israel now have such networks). As yet, however, these networks are not sufficiently dense to serve alone as a base for an adequate description of the insolation in the areas they serve.

In a study completed in 1962 by Iven Bennett (10), daily values of insolation from 10 stations for the period 1950 to 1960 were used as a starting point to describe the distribution in space and time of solar radiation in the intermontane basin and plateau region of the western United States. The outstanding feature of the intermontane insolation climate was a strong north-to-south insolation gradient that existed most of the year but was the strongest in midwinter when the solar elevation was at its lowest point. For a short time in midsummer, the gradient broke down and high values were found throughout the region. During the warm half of the year, in fact, daily values of insolation in the arid West averaged higher than those for corresponding latitudes anywhere else on earth.

Wind and Thunderstorms

Both the Weather Bureau and the National Center for Atmospheric Research have continuing programs of research on large-scale atmospheric motions. Although these studies are not specifically concerned with winds in any single region, they are likely to contribute knowledge of particular benefit to the arid zones, especially improved prediction of precipitation and of droughts. To date, wind research on the arid zones has been focused mainly on the microclimate scale.

Windiness, especially in the spring, is characteristic of the arid United States, and erosion features, sculptured in part by wind and windblown sand, are typical. Sparse vegetation gives little surface protection. *Dust devils*—whirling columns of air, dust, and debris— are seen frequently on hot days. Rugged topography favors local wind effects. Aridity is increased by the drying effect of surface winds. Yet winds bring in the moisture that reaches the arid regions and influence precipitation there.

Virga (fallout) from cumulus clouds over New Mexico and Arizona is a common sight during the summer months. Indeed, it is much more common than the rain that reaches the earth below: long precipitation streamers falling earthward commonly disappear by evaporation before they reach the ground, a fact that emphasizes the nature of the dry-air environment of clouds in semiarid lands. Although cumulative rainfall at the ground is small, the incidence of summer thunderstorms over New Mexico and Arizona is exceeded only in such areas as Florida and the Gulf Coast. At Socorro, New Mexico, for example, thunderstorms during the months of July, August, and September contribute approximately 50 percent of the total annual rainfall. It is natural, therefore, that thunderstorm research in the southwestern United States is a vigorous and growing activity.

As early as 1936, E. J. Workman and Robert E. Holzer, then at the University of New Mexico, were examining the electric nature of lightning and thunderstorms (*11*). But it was not until 1946, after the advent of radar, that the electric values were related to the meteorologic environment. Research by Workman and Stephen E. Reynolds (*12*) at the New Mexico Institute of Mining and Technology stimulated interest in the relationships between electric activity and precipitation growth in thunderstorms.

Further efforts by Reynolds and Marx Brook at the same institute established relationships among electric activity, precipitation growth, and convection (*13*). Bernard Vonnegut and Charles B. Moore, of A. D. Little, Inc., also working in New Mexico, have continued these investigations. A better understanding of the role of electric fields in droplet growth is necessary to an evaluation of the many processes that compete in producing rain. Already, Moore

Dark precipitation streamers are pictured as they fall from a typically forming thunderstorm over the high, dry San Augustin Plain in western New Mexico. Most of this moisture evaporates before dampening the earth below. (Courtesy New Mexico Institute of Mining and Technology)

and Vonnegut have demonstrated that droplet-growth equations should be revised in order to account for apparent collection efficiencies of up to 400 percent.

The study of cloud-particle growth by radar has not been without its difficulties. An indirect probing technique, radar has been, at best, a rather blunt research tool plagued by a multitude of assumptions and uncertainties regarding the nature, population, and size of the scattering particles. Interpretation of radar echoes during various phases of a thunderstorm is an open subject of prime importance.

Recent research at the Institute of Atmospheric Physics by Louis J. Battan and Benjamin M. Herman has gone far in pointing up the difficulties in quantitative measurement of clouds by radar. Extensive calculations of the radar cross section were made for water, ice, and wet ice spheres; and, from these, the inherent ambiguity in conventional radar techniques is apparent. These results were verified experimentally by David Atlas, of the Air Force Cambridge Research Center, and Frank H. Ludlam, in the United Kingdom.

Radar techniques are being improved at a number of institutions. Battan, A. Richard Kassander, and John B. Theiss (*14*), in Arizona, and Roland J. Pilié, at Cornell Aeronautical Laboratories, have applied Doppler radar techniques to the study of the precipitation velocity (and, hence, size) spectrum. Preliminary reports are encouraging. The Doppler method may help to eliminate a major source of uncertainty in quantitative radar measurements. Scientists at the New Mexico Institute of Mining and Technology are trying to distinguish between spheric and nonspheric shapes of precipitation particles with a radar cross-polarization technique, an approach that should be useful, too, in distinguishing between precipitation and lightning-channel echoes.

Needed is a detailed description in both space and time of the air motion in and around cumulus congestus and cumulonimbus clouds. Pat Squires, at the National Center for Atmospheric Research, Boulder, Colorado, is attempting to formulate a mathematical model of the updraft. Recent measurements by both Soviet and American scientists show liquid water contents in excess of 0.6 gram per cubic foot (20 grams per cubic meter) in clouds at levels of 7.5 miles (12.1 kilometers), above sea level. This area of thunderstorm research must be expanded. Some measurements are emerging now as a result of the national severe-storms project.

Microclimatology

Man, animals, and plants live in microclimates. A microclimate may be defined loosely as the climate of any local area that differs from the prevailing large-scale climate. The area may be a hill slope, a valley, an arroyo bed, a city, an oasis, an irrigation ditch, the top of plant cover, or the soil surface beneath a plant cover.

It is typical of arid regions that most of the insolation energy goes into increasing the temperature of surface and air, rather than into latent heat of evaporation, because moisture is not available to evaporate. In comparison with humid areas, humidity blankets seldom impede radiation cooling at night. Large thermal and moisture gradients and rapid changes occur often in microclimates, because of their nearness to surfaces whose conditions vary with place and time.

In contrast to man's present inability to influence climates on a large scale, his influence on microclimates often is significant. Structures, cultivation, and irrigation, all change the temperature, humidity, and air movement. Air-conditioning and refrigeration make human habitation of arid regions more tolerable.

The complete statistical description of microclimates, to say nothing of their physical explanation, is a matter of profound complexity. Much of our knowledge is at best descriptive. Nevertheless, a few guiding physical principles can be recognized; they form the bedrock of the research now in progress and planned for the future.

Altitude, slope, surface albedo (reflectivity), soil moisture, soil heat capacity, plant structure, and evapotranspiration are factors that influence temperature and humidity. Prevailing winds and topography influence air movements. Modern theories of heat balance, turbulence, and atmospheric diffusion help in estimating the degree of influence of these factors, provided that field measurements of the physical values necessary to its application are available. These parameters include atmospheric stability and its diurnal variation.

Microclimatologic research in the arid United States has not received the emphasis it deserves. Energy partition and evapotranspiration have been studied and instrumentation has been developed, for example, at the Institute of Atmospheric Physics in Arizona (15). The Army Quartermaster Research and Engineering Center has reported on microclimates near Yuma, Arizona (16).

In Hawaii, the Pineapple Research Institute is conducting research in microclimate modification by the use of plants with low transpiration ratios. A real breakthrough in water economy for arid zones may take place with the selection of vegetation that has low transpiration rates. Of particular interest is the reduction in water use that occurs as the vegetation mat increases, shades the soil, and lowers soil temperatures. The use of such plants for both fiber and forage has been established. The Pineapple Research Institute also is looking into the use of mulches and self-mulching soils in micro-climate modification, radiation balance, and heat advection.

Microclimatology is interrelated with, and is an important facet of, other arid-lands research, including work in water conservation, agriculture, and forestry. Research in these areas by agencies of the federal government, universities, and state agricultural experiment stations is contributing to our knowledge.

Other Phenomenons

Certain phenomenons should be mentioned, which, though not important in all arid zones, are significant in some. For instance, dew may be significant to the water supply in certain of them. Dew forms on cold surfaces when the adjacent air cools below a critical temperature called the *dew point*. Surfaces on which it forms usually are cooled by radiation. High-radiation cooling favors, but low humidity restricts, dew in most arid lands. The source of the mois-ture of dew frequently is evapotranspiration rather than condensa-tion of airmass humidity. In this event, the water supply is not increased by the occurrence of dew but rather is conserved. Measure-ments of dew accumulation under natural conditions, and theoreti-cal estimates, are subject to inaccuracies. Little is known of the use made of dew by the flora and fauna in places where precipitation is scanty.

Because there is little cloud cover to impede radiation from the earth in arid zones, pronounced night cooling is often sufficient to result in frost. Drainage of cold air into low places also favors frost formation. Radiation frost shortens the growing seasons in cool zones; and in warm areas, the occasional occurrence of frost damages susceptible vegetation, notably citrus trees and vegetable crops. Wind machines (which mix air near the ground with warmer air above), sprinkling, and oil or other heaters sometimes prevent radiation frost. Meteorologists can forecast frost with considerable accuracy.

The Pineapple Research Institute of Hawaii has noted that, under certain circumstances, direct interception of water by vegetation from fog or cloud may supply more moisture than rainfall. Measure-ments on the dry island of Lanai showed 50 inches (1270 milli-meters) of annual fog drip, compared with an annual rainfall of 30

inches (762 millimeters). Several mist deserts of South America and
the dew ponds of England bear out the importance of this process.
Within arid lands, it may be effective in some coastal deserts and
in mountainous terrain with prevailing upslope winds.

Conditions that encourage air pollution appear often in subtropic
arid zones, where atmospheric subsidence commonly causes temperature inversions (atmospheric strata in which temperature increases
with elevation). These zones, moreover, lack the precipitation that,
in humid regions, washes pollutants from the air. Radiation cooling
at night sets up inversions near the ground, especially in valleys.
Temperature inversions inhibit vertical motion of air and usually
are accompanied by light surface winds. Topography also may re-
strict air movements. In the West, then, these conditions pose serious
air-pollution problems for Los Angeles, Phoenix, and other population centers.

Through research, meteorologists have learned to estimate pollution from single sources under given meteorologic conditions (17).
They can recognize, and frequently forecast, conditions favorable
to pollution.

Work of Weather Bureau

A discussion of climatology research anywhere in the United States
would not be complete without mention of the data-gathering facilities, records, and research of the Weather Bureau in the U.S.
Department of Commerce. By statute, the bureau is required to
"record the climatic conditions of the United States." Its networks
of observing stations yield weather information from more than
12,000 localities.

Weather records from the various stations are processed and filed
at the National Weather Records Center in Asheville, N.C., which
is maintained by the bureau as part of the National Archives. Information is disseminated by routine publications, and special climatologic data, tabulations, and analyses are available at cost to
other agencies, industry, private meteorologists, and research workers
(18). Recent contributions to meteorologic research by the bureau's
Office of Climatology in Washington, D.C., include summarization,
analysis, and publication of historical data for use as background
and reference material. A considerable number of new climatic

maps in the "National Atlas Series" and materials from the 1960 decennial census of climate have been published.

Methods for measuring soil temperature and moisture are being refined. In applied climatology, probabilities of snow loads and air-conditioning design factors have been prepared in cooperation with other agencies. The analysis of trends and oscillations in climate has continued, as have the interpolation and determination of normals.

Studies of the effects of urbanization on historical temperature trends and the climate of the environment, an analysis of worldwide temperature trends since 1880, and analyses of several series of observations for rhythms in long weather records also have been made. Cooperation with universities in the various states, through the state climatologists, has resulted in numerous contributions, particularly in the field of agricultural climatologic statistics.

Weather Prediction

Of primary importance in semiarid lands is the ability to predict when marginal areas will be dry, and when they will be wet enough to grow crops. One means of stating drought expectancy, which is realizable wherever there are comparatively long records of precipitation or soil moisture, or both, consists of suitably framed statements of climatologic probability. For example, the probability of receiving less than some significant threshold total of precipitation in periods of various lengths may be stated as a function of the time of year (8), as is illustrated in Fig. 3.

In the technical sense, statements of climatologic expectancy are not predictions or forecasts. *Predictions* (or *forecasts*) are definite statements or statistical estimates of the occurrence of a future event over and above the climatologically expected value of that event. The status of long-range prediction techniques was summarized in a statement published in 1962 by the American Meteorological Society (19). This statement, which reflects the overwhelming opinion of the meteorologic profession, says, in effect, that there is at present no known technique of weather prediction for periods greater than about 1 month that gives results better than would be expected by chance.

Research on the enigma of long-range forecasting is tied to research on the general circulation of the atmosphere—the movement of air and the behavior of the atmosphere on a global scale. The climate of a region is a result of this behavior in a time-integrated sense. Only by an understanding of the manner in which our atmosphere operates will it be possible to predict future behavior of the atmosphere. Research toward this goal has been of a basic nature, depending primarily on the development of mathematical models. Few of the obstacles that must be overcome to produce long-range forecasts have as yet yielded to investigation.

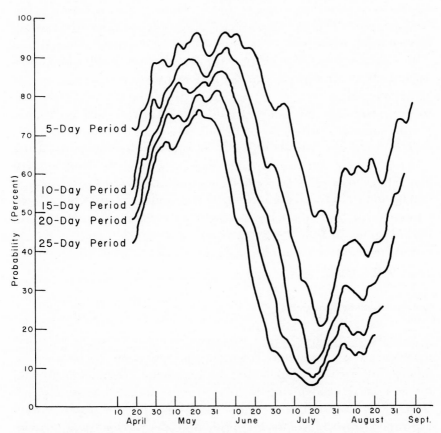

Fig. 3. Probabilities of drought periods at extremely arid Yuma, Arizona, are based on past records, indicating how the time of year affects the likelihood of precipitation. (Adapted from C. R. Green, in *Technical Reports on the Meteorology and Climatology of Arid Regions*, No. 8, University of Arizona, Institute of Atmospheric Physics, Tucson, 1960)

Because the atmosphere is a turbulent fluid, the mathematical equations describing the action of a fluid cannot be used in their classical form. The way in which the equations must be modified has evaded scientists for decades. Nor has the problem of incorporating water in its various phases into the equations of atmospheric motion been solved, although there has been substantial progress in understanding the development of storms and the motions of the upper-air currents.

High-speed electronic computers are making possible research studies that would have been hitherto impractical because of the large amounts of data and the detailed calculations involved. The complex models of the atmosphere are tractable only with the aid of such computers.

But because of the many physical processes involved and, among other factors, the virtual impossibility of observing the atmosphere at an adequate number of points in space, a precise description of future events cannot be anticipated as the ultimate result of weather-prediction research. The best promise of predictions beyond a month or so rests in probability statements achieved through a combination of the physical-dynamic approach, using a model of the general circulation, with a statistical description of possible events.

The joining of the dynamic and statistical techniques represents a new, fertile, and largely untouched field. The forecasts that result may be given in terms of probability, or they may be given with a confidence figure indicating the degree of uncertainty inherent in a particular forecast.

Severe-Weather Warnings

In most arid zones, severe weather, aside from intense heat and dryness, is not a frequently recurring problem. In some, however, hail causes extensive crop damage. Strong winds, frequently hot and dry and perhaps laden with blowing sand, temporarily impose severe stresses. One must cope with flash floods spawned of sudden torrential rains, which may spread considerable destruction along arroyos and mountain valleys.

To some extent, meteorologic services in arid regions may anticipate heavy rains by several hours. Experience in the United States indicates that a comparatively dense network of specially instrumented weather-reporting stations, on the order of a 30- by 40-mile (48.3- by 64.4-kilometer) grid, together with a means of rapid communication, would be required as a first step toward improvement of advance-warning capabilities.

Currently, the Weather Bureau has three operational programs that are of benefit to flash-flood warning services. The first is a special severe-storms unit, located in Kansas City, Missouri, which forecasts severe weather for the entire United States. The second program, the quantitative precipitation unit located in the National Meteorological Center in Suitland, Maryland, issues forecasts of the precipitation expected within 24 hours. By delineating the areas where heavy rainfall is expected, the local flash-flood warning networks can be alerted.

The third program is radar surveillance. The Weather Bureau has greatly expanded its radar program in recent years with the development of a specialized weather radar, the WSR-57. Considerable progress has been realized in hydrologic applications of the radar, which has proved to be very useful in defining areas of precipitation. This is particularly important for thunderstorm rainfall, which can be so spotty that existing rain-gage networks cannot provide an adequate sampling. In extreme instances, thunderstorm rains have occurred without any rainfall being recorded by the precipitation gages. Progress has been made in the analysis of radar echoes to determine the amount of rainfall. The radar has also proved to be extremely valuable in alerting flash-flood warning networks of an approaching severe storm.

Weather Modification

Spectacular changes in cloud forms were obtained in experiments begun late in the 1940's by Irving Langmuir, Vincent J. Schaefer, and Vonnegut, who used Dry Ice and silver iodide to modify clouds having ambient temperatures below freezing. The seeding induced ice phases in the clouds, replacing the supercooled water phases.

A notable experiment in Project Cirrus was the periodic seeding of December 1949 to July 1951, in which Langmuir dispensed silver iodide on a regular weekly schedule (regardless of weather conditions), using a single ground-based generator at Socorro, New Mexico. He presented statistical evidence (20) to correlate his seeding with widespread effects in rainfall, upper-air temperature, and other phenomenons in the Mississippi, Ohio, and Tennessee valleys. There was no evidence of increase in precipitation in New Mexico. In fact, in the vicinity of the generator, the seeding period may have been unusually dry.

Notwithstanding the strength of its statistical evidence, the Langmuir report did not receive general acceptance. Primarily, this was because he did not choose to give a physical (cause-and-effect) explanation of the correlated events—periodic seeding in New Mexico and dramatic "effects" elsewhere. Also natural 7-day resonances in the atmosphere and the operations of commercial cloud seeders, who spread much larger quantities of silver iodide in the same period in the Southwest, could not be ignored in any interpretation of the experiment.

The apparent pronounced results from the periodic seeding program of Project Cirrus have never been explained fully. If they were caused by seeding, the answer no doubt lies in a fundamental understanding of atmospheric and cloud physics that is yet to be attained. Workman has suggested (21) that seeding also affects the thermodynamic structure of the atmosphere, especially the vertical distributions of temperature and moisture. Seeding in the arid zones may inhibit the development of large convective systems, with consequent retention of potential energy in the atmosphere. Then this retained energy might later influence the weather.

After the early experiments on cloud modification, tremendous efforts were devoted to inducing rain by these techniques. Interest reached a peak about 1952, continued for 2 or 3 years, and then diminished rapidly as the "rainmakers" failed to cause, or increase, precipitation with any consistency.

It appears now that the fundamental assumption in the early attempts—that sublimation (freezing) nuclei are essential in the rainmaking process in supercooled clouds—is false (21). Natural shower precipitation can and does take place without the prior existence of an abundance of sublimation nuclei in a cloud. It has been suggested, in fact, that the absence of appreciable numbers of sublimation nuclei favors the development of thunderstorm precipitation in semiarid areas of the United States. Cloud seeding does influence the development of supercooled clouds but not always with the effect of increasing precipitation. Cloud seeding in Arizona, directed by

Battan and Kassander, has not indicated a significant increase in precipitation caused by the seeding of convective clouds from airplanes (22).

A great deal of cloud seeding still continues. Under some conditions, evidence indicates that it can increase local precipitation, but these conditions are not commonly found in arid lands. Although the widespread effects reported in Project Cirrus certainly suggest the possibility of some control with reasonable economy, the capabilities for significant climate modification, especially in arid zones, have not been demonstrated. It appears to be desirable to make an entirely new start as far as the arid lands are concerned. The development of realistic mathematical models of the atmosphere would permit the investigation of proposed weather-control measures without the risk of the serious consequences possible from tampering with the atmosphere.

The National Science Foundation now is responsible for the program in weather-modification research (23). The foundation supports much research in universities and by private concerns and coordinates research among government agencies. Current projects include cloud physics, precipitation processes, cloud electrification, cloud modification, and hail suppression.

Future Research

Researchers have just begun to delve into the many mysteries of meteorology. In arid regions, climate limits man's activities in ways that are understood only poorly. An understanding of these limitations will provide guidance for the wise use of the arid lands and their resources.

Lack of, and the high cost of, instrumentation have limited studies; instrumentation deserves high priority. A better method of making integrated measurements of the water content of the atmosphere would be especially useful in arid zones. Electronic data-processing techniques will allow greater exploitation of the vast stores of data from meteorologic investigations.

Weather stations in arid regions not only are sparse but also are located predominantly in valleys and on plains, where precipitation is small. Few stations exist in the high country, which collects the greater part of the water supply. More data are needed from higher elevations to permit realistic descriptions of climates and water supplies.

Techniques are needed to describe better the climate in places where local data are scarce. Climatic analog maps of the world, delineating areas that have similar climates, have been prepared for UNESCO by Peveril Meigs (24), but more information is needed on the crops and techniques that might be introduced from one part of the world into another.

An immediate need is for more precipitation observations from dense rain-gage networks. A great deal is known about the variability of a single station's annual, seasonal, and extreme rainfall. Practically no information is available, however, on variability in time of these three factors on an area-wide basis. Yet the areal distribution is required for hydrometeorologic purposes.

Many regions are relatively dry because they are situated on the leeward sides of high mountains, but very little attention has been paid to the precipitation that forms on windward slopes and drifts beyond the crest to the lee, even though this spillover is important in defining the rainfall pattern. Spillover has been investigated almost entirely from a theoretic point of view.

Water salinity is a problem in the arid United States. Whether or not, or how much, the chemicals in precipitation may contribute to this problem remains unknown.

Required for insolation research are adequate station networks. If the stations are carefully distributed, planned, and integrated with a larger network that collects general climatic information, the methods developed by Bennett (10) can be used, after 4 or 5 years of accumulation of data, to present a generalized description of the insolation climate. A need exists for frequency distributions of daily and hourly insolation totals for specific periods of time and specific weather conditions. All of this is essential if insolation data are to help to solve problems that arise from the development and use of arid lands.

Data also must be collected for conditions appropriate to different agricultural crops. Almost nothing is known, for instance, of the insolation that actually reaches the soil under a stand of cotton. Finally, the spectral nature (wavelength distribution) of insolation that reaches the earth's surface in arid lands is not adequately known. Many consequences of insolation are dependent not so much on the total energy in the solar spectrum as on the levels within certain narrow spectral bands.

In arid zones, knowledge is inadequate on the distributions of moisture and temperature in the lower atmosphere. Too, many problems in the microclimate realm are barely touched. Badly needed are adequate theories of heat balance, turbulence, and diffusion. Many questions related to microclimates remain to be answered: shelterbelts (trees or hedgerows that interrupt surface winds) modify microclimates, at least the wind factor; do they also conserve soil moisture to a significant degree? What are the criterions for control of nocturnal cold-air drainage to minimize frost? What are the optimum microclimates for certain flora and fauna or the retardant microclimates for others, and how may these be most easily obtained? What can be done to minimize the effects of air pollutants?

It would be important to know whether the recent drought in the Southwest is a definite trend or a short-range fluctuation, and whether its causes are related to those of the increased mean temperatures observed concurrently in North America. Although trends do occur, they are neither understood nor predictable. Because of the complexity of the atmosphere, direct analysis is difficult and usually impractical. Models may assist in interpreting the causes of atmospheric behavior—for example, its response to solar-radiation levels.

The dominant goal of most of the cloud-seeding efforts has been to produce precipitation. Perhaps enhancement of the snowpack in the highlands of the arid zones would be easier than increasing the precipitation on the lowlands, where success to the present has evaded the rainmakers. Severe storms (often thunderstorms) involve much convective activity and may be subject to modification. All modifications involve alteration of energy configurations. If a control operation is practical, an opportune time and place for effecting the control with reduced energy input probably exists. A knowledge of the phenomenons and processes involved, or an accurate model, is needed to determine the best time and place for modification operations.

Specific research plans of the U.S. Weather Bureau are outlined in a Weather Bureau publication (25). A goal of development of the arid zones is to provide a reasonable accord between use and resources on a long-term basis. This accord seldom will be static. As basic knowledge increases, further investigations will be conceived more soundly. For the benefit of all, some freedom in research might be sacrificed to coordination and to concentration on efforts of promise and of immediate need.

The nature of the atmosphere is such that a complete knowledge is not to be expected. Research will never find a stopping point.

Acknowledgments: The author expresses appreciation to F. E. Kottlowski and E. J. Workman, both of the New Mexico Institute of Mining and Technology; W. G. McGinnies, University of Arizona; and V. J. Schaefer, State University of New York, all of whom were helpful in the preparation of this chapter.

REFERENCES

1. R. W. Bailey, "Climate and settlement of the arid regions," and J. Leighly, "Settlement and cultivation in the summer-dry climates," in *Climate and Man, Yearbook Agr., U.S. Dept. Agr.* **1941** (1941).
2. P. S. Martin, Jr., *The Last 10,000 Years, a Pollen Analytic Investigation of the American Southwest* (Univ. of Arizona Press, Tucson, 1963).
3. E. Schulman, *Dendroclimatic Changes in Semiarid America* (Univ. of Arizona Press, Tucson, 1956).
4. J. E. McDonald, "Variability of precipitation in an arid region: a survey of characteristics for Arizona," *Univ. Ariz. Inst. Atmospheric Phys. Tech. Rept. 1* (1956).
5. W. D. Sellers, "Precipitation trends in Arizona and western New Mexico," *Proc. Western Snow Conf., Santa Fe, N. Mex.* (Fort Collins, Colo., 1960).
6. U.S. Weather Bureau, "Generalized estimates of probable maximum precipitation for the United States west of the 105th meridian," *U.S. Weather Bur. Tech. Paper 38* (1961).
7. D. M. Hershfield, "Rainfall frequency atlas of the United States for durations from 30 minutes to 24 hours and return periods from 1 to 100 years," *U.S. Weather Bur. Tech. Paper 40* (1961).
8. C. R. Green, "Probabilities of drought and rainy periods for selected points in the southwestern United States," *Univ. Ariz. Inst. Atmospheric Phys. Tech. Rept. 8* (1960).
9. W. E. Hiatt, "The analysis of precipitation data," *Phys. and Econ. Found. of Nat. Resources Ser. 4* (Interior and Insular Affairs Comm., U.S. House of Representatives, Washington, D.C., 1953), pp. 186–206.

10. I. Bennett, "Climatology of insolation in the intermontane basins and plateaus of the western United States," thesis submitted in partial fulfillment of the requirements for the Ph.D. degree at Boston University, 1962.
11. E. J. Workman, R. E. Holzer, and G. T. Pelsor, "The electrical structure of thunderstorms," *U.S. Natl. Advisory Comm. Aeron.* (now *Natl. Aeron. Space Admin.*) *Tech. Note 864* (1942).
12. E. J. Workman and S. E. Reynolds, "Electrical activity as related to thunderstorm cell growth," *Bull. Am. Meteorol. Soc.* **30**, 142 (1949).
13. S. E. Reynolds, *Compendium of Thunderstorm Electricity* (New Mexico Institute of Mining and Technology, Research and Development Div., Socorro, 1954).
14. L. J. Battan, A. R. Kassander, Jr., and J. B. Theiss, "Observations of convective clouds by means of pulsed-Doppler radar," *Univ. Ariz. Inst. Atmospheric Phys. Sci. Rept. 20* (1963).
15. W. D. Sellers and C. N. Hodges, "The energy balance of non-uniform soil surfaces," *J. Atmospheric Sci.* **19** (1962).
16. A. V. Dodd and H. M. McPhilimy, "Yuma summer microclimate," *U.S. Army Quartermaster Res. and Eng. Center Tech. Rept. EP-120* (1959).
17. H. Wexler, "The role of meteorology in air pollution," in *Air Pollution* (Columbia Univ. Press, New York, 1961), p. 49.
18. G. L. Barger and J. C. Nyhan, *Climatology at Work* (U.S. Weather Bureau, Washington, D.C., 1960).
19. Statement on weather forecasting, *Bull. Am. Meteorol. Soc.* **43**, 251 (1962).
20. I. Langmuir and V. J. Schaefer, "Final report, Project Cirrus," *General Electric Res. Lab. Rept. RL-785* (1953).
21. E. J. Workman, "The problem of weather modification," *Science* **138**, 407 (1962).
22. L. J. Battan and A. R. Kassander, Jr., "Evaluation of effects of airborne silver iodide seeding of convective clouds," *Univ. Ariz. Inst. Atmospheric Phys. Sci. Rept. 18* (1962).
23. National Science Foundation, *Weather Modification,* 3rd ann. rept., 1961 (Washington, D.C., 1962).
24. P. Meigs, "Distribution of arid homoclimates," *United Nations Maps,* No. 392, Eastern Hemisphere, and No. 393, Western Hemisphere (United Nations, New York, 1960).
25. U.S. Weather Bureau, *Research Progress and Plans of the U.S. Weather Bureau, Fiscal Year 1962* (Washington, D.C., 1962).

6

Water and Its Use

HERBERT E. SKIBITZKE

RUSSELL H. BROWN

JOHN W. HARSHBARGER

Technical advancement in man's ability to pump water has changed considerably the character and extent of the development of arid regions. As late as 1900, the difficulty of drilling wells and lifting water from subsurface reservoirs prevented large-scale utilization of most of these areas.

How water once was used in an arid region is typified to a certain extent by the prehistoric irrigation methods of Indian tribes in southern Arizona. Their brush dams diverted water into a widespread system of canals.

According to some archeologists, the canals were constructed with a gradient less than that of the stream, and, after several hundred years, the land became waterlogged. Consequently, the Indians moved and dug other canals with even flatter gradients, these prehistorians say; but because that soil also became waterlogged, the ancient agricultural efforts finally failed altogether.

By the time Europeans moved into the area, water levels had declined from drainage. But the new settlers installed an irrigation system similar to that of the Indians, and a similar sequence of events followed. By 1922, the land was waterlogged once more. By then, however, there were two new technologic developments that would change the hydrologic regimen: the centrifugal pump for deep pumping and drilling equipment for construction of deep wells.

Deep pumping introduced an economically efficient way to make ground water available. As a result, land was cultivated outside the waterlogged area, and agriculture spread into the surrounding desert. By the end of World War II, irrigation existed over a large part of central Arizona. Later, the growth took place at an even more ac-

celerated rate—extending to valleys where the water table was 400
feet (120 meters) or more deep—until the irrigated lands extended
from mountain slope to mountain slope. Because the ground water
is being depleted rapidly, the future of this irrigation empire can
only be surmised.

The technical factors involved in the study and control of water
resources must include the environmental change that has occurred.
At the turn of the century, the ground-water hydrologist was concerned largely with locating wells for efficient pumpage, and the engineering was resolved generally by the mapping of water levels in
the area. Wells were located, in most cases, where water levels were
shallow. As irrigation increased and the region grew in population,
and as improvements in pumping and well drilling continued,
deeper ground-water supplies were within reach. But the problem
still was mainly the location and pumping of water.

In recent years, however, water levels began to decline over a
broad area around each well; the result was a lowering of the levels
in neighboring wells. Nearby wells failed in some cases or, at least,
were reduced in efficiency. Accordingly, the mutual interference
effect of wells pumping close together became important to hydrologists. The economic significance of mutual interference required techniques to measure and predict the characteristics of
drawdown near a single well system. In time, these techniques also
included the mutual effects of the well and nearby streams or other
sources of potential recharge, and eventually the investigation of still
larger-scale water systems.

Paralleling the growth of scientific ground-water hydrology were
questions related directly to the construction of dams. Predictions
of available water at any given site along a river system were based,
at most, on 4- or 5-year studies. At first, the obvious choices for sites
were those that allowed the accumulation of the largest reservoir
volume. The reduction of evaporation by the choice of deep reservoirs was not considered at that time. But as the better sites were
utilized and a greater demand for storage of water became apparent,
a more careful analysis had to be made of the location and operation
of reservoirs.

Essentially, the effect of stream reservoir systems is to depress the
fluctuations in water supply and to shift the phase of the annual
variations in flow. As time went on, therefore, hydrologists became

more and more interested in the environmental control on water supply. As water supplies diminished, reservoir analyses focused on evaporation losses in the canals and reservoirs. Rivers, such as the Santa Cruz, Gila, and Salt in southern Arizona, dried up because of diversions and the pumping of ground water.

Interrelationships of Sources

Since World War II, the problem has become even more complex. Hydrologists have had to analyze the interrelated overdevelopment of ground water and surface water alike. In the western states (Fig. 1), the cessation of streamflow and the continuous lowering of the ground-water table has brought forth a new look at the hydrologic questions that confront the water scientist. Former methods of analysis required mathematical models, which, in turn, required idealization of the physical problem. The mathematical observations, thus, were dependent on small perturbations of a given system. These small-difference formulas were of little use in analyzing the depletion process. Large differences are exerted on the environment; the rivers are being greatly reduced in flow, and ground-water levels are being lowered.

The interrelationships among these factors become significant. An example of the change of emphasis can be seen in the application of historical streamflow records. These become much less useful as a region becomes developed, because the spread of civilization modifies the watersheds.

Millions of acre feet (cubic meters) of water are utilized in the arid regions of the United States, although a large amount of water evaporates to the atmosphere. Obviously, certain controls on the climate are sought. It may be possible in the future to modify the weather by changing the oceanic currents, or in some other manner. Thus man can conceivably exert control on the water supply in some of the arid regions of the world, and the hydrologists would then be faced with an even larger scale analysis, involving all the dynamics of water in its vapor, liquid, and solid forms over the surface of the earth.

Ultimately, as man's need for water becomes more urgent and as the utilization of his supplies becomes more complete, hydrology must become a complete systems analysis. The study will always tend toward a more complete synthesis of the environmental factors over a larger region. Two approaches have developed; one is a cause-and-effect concept; the other is a statistical analysis.

The latter consists of collecting information and sorting out the purely random relationships from the functional ones through the use of autocorrelation function or similar mathematical models. In the past, if long-term records were available, this technique usually would have been adequate. But the encroachment of environmental changes certainly prevents this today. Construction of surface-water reservoirs and the installation of ground-water pumping regimes alters the regional hydrology in such a way that the factors downstream also can be greatly affected. This inherent functional relationship has occurred in recent times over short periods; yet, a short-term statistical analysis will not yield the functional relationship.

The recent environmental changes that would vitiate the use of statistics go beyond the simple reservoir and ground-water effects. In the watersheds surrounding the desert areas, livestock tanks have been constructed on nearly every tributary to the major streams. These tanks, or ponds, cause large evaporation losses in the upper part of the watershed, thus preventing use of the water in the lower watershed.

River channels in the Southwest originally were choked with riparian vegetation. Because the surface flow has vanished and the water table has fallen, the vegetation is gone, and the river channels are now long expanses of sand. The sand in the dry riverbeds, in fact, has become a valuable mineral in some places. Mud moves down the channel in a transit environment that is different from the environment prevailing before the development of the river channel. If there were major floods, there would be tremendous damage; industrial sites in and along the channel would be destroyed, but the river flood itself might not be as high as it would have been 50 years ago, because the river-drained channel is free from vegetation. The flood plain has become a site of industrial and home development; in most cases this development takes place with the knowledge of the risk involved, but the rewards from speculation for industrial sites along the flood plains are quite adequate to pay off rapidly the large economic investment. It is necessary that hydrologists understand, and be able to analyze, this encroachment of man's public works upon the environment.

Nature of the Water Problem

In a way, the incidence of flooding typifies the manner in which the water problems of an arid region change with the incursions of civilization. Land development creates far-reaching effects in river-channel regimes. Cities tend to rise near rivers, because the first populations usually rely on an agricultural economy, which is partly dependent on streamflow. So, in their growing phases, the settlements are subjected to the larger floods on the main stream. As suburbs develop and the urban centers spread outward, the flood danger is aggravated by the many smaller ephemeral streams.

Fig. 1. The major drainage basins of the West are outlined on this map. Many tributaries, especially in the Southwest, have ceased to flow, except ephemerally, and ground-water tables are dropping in many places. (Courtesy U.S. Coast and Geodetic Survey)

Small ephemeral streams in the desert may have flash-flood flows that equal the average flow of some of the largest rivers in the United States. For a few hours, the streams may spread over the whole countryside. For example, the Bill Williams River, near Alamo, Arizona (1), which normally has a mean flow of less than 100 cubic feet (3 cubic meters) per second, flowed 46,000 cubic feet (1300 cubic meters) per second on 14 March 1941. Compare this rate with the Colorado River at Yuma, Arizona, where the mean annual flow before 1930 was less than 30,000 cubic feet (850 cubic meters) per second. Although extensive housing developments have highlighted the flood hazard, it obviously is not possible to guard against all possible floods. The only feasible approach is to state the probable hazard in terms of repetition rate and magnitude.

Nothing dramatizes the result of encroachment on the desert more than the ephemeral streams and their flood plains. Runoff sometimes increases, and sometimes it decreases. The extensive areas of grass that covered much of the arid United States in 1900 were depleted by grazing or by extended periods of drought. This substantial change in watershed cover is faithfully reflected by runoff data.

Surface-water supplies for the first settlers may seem plentiful. They simply must average or smooth out the annual flood and dry periods, a goal that can be achieved by the construction of reservoirs. During the development of surface-water resources, however, new problems may be created, such as the waterlogging of irrigated lands. An important distinction can be made between development of the surface-water resources and development of the ground-water resources. If no great watershed modification occurs, a certain identifiable surface-water supply is available perennially. Given infinite time, the supply is infinite. But this is not true of ground water. Regardless of time, there is only a finite supply.

Since a shortage of water is inevitable in any arid region, the possible additional sources of water become crucial. Throughout the world, in or bordering on these regions, there are many saline water deposits. These tremendous stored reserves of "contaminated" water are available if some economical way can be found to extract the salts. Interest in desalinization is growing in the United States, and a large desalinization plant has been constructed at Buckeye, Arizona, to furnish the town's municipal water supply. The plant has been in operation since October 1962 and now converts about

650,000 gallons (2,463,500 liters) per day of salty ground water, using an electrodialysis system perfected by a commercial company in Cambridge, Massachusetts.

Raw water travels a grid path between alternate anion and cation exchange resin membranes subjected to an electric current. The separated mineral content is flushed away as a brine, using about 25 percent of the water inflow. The inflow water, which contains 2140 parts per million of minerals (mostly calcium, sodium, magnesium, and other minor salts), is reduced to about 440 parts per million for delivery into the distribution system. The brine is piped to the sewer plant and mixed with sewage effluent. On 1 July 1963, a plant was dedicated for the conversion of salty ground water from wells near Roswell, New Mexico. This is one of the two demonstration plants operated in the semiarid United States by the Office of Saline Water, U.S. Department of the Interior.

Present-day desalinization techniques, however, have not advanced to the point of furnishing water for irrigation at feasible prices. They can provide water at costs low enough for home or industrial water supplies, and it is reasonable to expect that in time desalinization will find significant application in the arid regions.

Weather-modification ideas have been the subject of some speculation, but ways of implementing them remain to be found. If large-scale changes could be wrought in the oceans, these might affect the weather in arid regions. Nuclear reactors in the ocean could heat the sea water on a planet-wide scale. The magnitude of this heating process would be so large that it could modify some oceanic currents, thereby possibly changing the weather off the coast of some arid regions. Despite considerable skepticism, this idea, nevertheless, is being seriously examined as a possible remedy for water shortages.

In somewhat the same vein, attention is being given to changes caused in the earth's albedo (reflectivity) by nuclear detonations in the upper atmosphere. Large portions of the earth could be effectively "shaded" from some of the energy that emanates from the sun. A reduction in total energy would, in many ways, benefit the arid regions of the world but would debilitate the rest of the earth. The question of using such a technique, if it were feasible, would have to be agreed upon by the countries on both sides of the continental landmasses affected.

Sedimentation and Pollution

Hydrologists also are seeking a better understanding of the factors that control stream geometry and sedimentation (2). Investigations are in progress, notable among which are the U.S. Geological Survey field studies by Luna Leopold of the streams debauching from the Wind River Range near Riverton, Wyoming; by Thomas Maddock of the Rio Grande near El Paso, Texas; and theoretical analyses by Walter Langbein of data being gathered or made available for these and other streams throughout the United States.

The investigations will include attempts to analyze the erosional effects of streams. Long fingers of erosion already have been observed spreading up the alluvial cones, cutting into virgin areas, and leaving deep channels. These effects are, to a certain extent, controllable, but the precise description and prediction of their occurrence are not yet calculable.

Changes in sediment deposition in the inland river basins produce particular problems. Rivers that formerly flowed through the arid regions, effectively removing some sediments, have been dried up by the development of surface water. It follows, then, that these sediments now are deposited somewhere in the river basins. At Hoover (Boulder) Dam on the Colorado River, much of the reservoir has been occupied by sediment (3). In the first 14 years of operational records, about 2000 million tons (1800 million metric tons) of sediments were deposited. The estimated sediment capacity of the reservoir is about 75,000 million tons (68,000 million metric tons). Formerly this sediment would have been deposited by the river in the Gulf of California, but since the cessation of natural flow it is simply left to accumulate in the man-made reservoirs.

Sediment deposition is compounded by the small ephemeral streams that carry their own sediment loads into the larger river channels. Because natural flows no longer occur in the larger channels, the sediments accumulate as small alluvial cones at the mouths of the ephemeral streams. Such sediment collection in the old river channels could be a hazard in the event of future floods. What formerly was open channel would be congested.

Stream-pollution problems in arid regions differ somewhat from those found elsewhere. The streams that flow through the humid regions carry away pollutants. This is not true in arid regions, because streamflow is seldom sufficient to transport pollutants out of the area. Sewage-disposal plants in arid regions commonly discharge their effluent into the old, dry river channels with some subsequent infiltration to the ground-water system. In such populous places as Phoenix, Arizona, a city that now exceeds the half-million mark, the quantity of effluent from sewage-disposal plants may become a severe problem. The proper reprocessing of waste water will, evidently, be extremely important in arid regions and, thus, will be an economic factor to be considered when it is no longer feasible simply to let waste water seep into the ground.

Streams in arid regions often carry substantial amounts of dissolved salts or evaporation residues. In irrigation with surface water, some salt remains on, or in, the soil after water has been removed by evapotranspiration or seepage. The shortage and the expense of water are such that farmers tend to use as little water as possible. Thus the salts that are brought in by the surface water are not continuously flushed downward or carried out again (4). They may, in fact, accumulate in the first few inches (centimeters) of soil in the farmed areas, or may develop large alkali flats in some places. This concentration is accentuated by the extremely high evaporation potentials that are prevalent in arid regions. Although the problem is not yet widespread throughout the arid regions of the United States, the threat is ever present, and localized evidence of the phenomenon already appears at scattered sites. In the designing of irrigation projects on the lower Colorado River, for example, part of the design requirement includes provision of water for flushing out the salt accumulations.

A final group of problems related to ground water in arid lands deserves mention. Many well casings were perforated in such a way that air was allowed access to the zone of aeration above the water table. With the cyclic changes in atmospheric pressure, this, in effect, created a huge pump, which evaporates the water between the water table and the land surface. The resulting desiccation in the older irrigated areas of the Southwest has led to some land subsidence and the formation of huge earth cracks. To date, the damage has not been severe, since it is confined mostly to highways and railroads. However, earth cracks in some places, among them Pinal County, Arizona (5), have spread across farmland, completely upsetting the irrigation techniques. Wells and public works, including earth structures for flood-control projects, are endangered. This kind of problem undoubtedly will become more critical.

Role of the Water Scientist

The task of solving water problems depends on a particular viewpoint. Community goals usually are, first, to obtain water and, second, to cope with, or resist, the stresses of nature; they differ substantially from those of the scientist.

To the scientist, the problems consist of interpretations that relate cause and effect; that is, relate water need and the stress imposed by satisfying that need. A complex process, this often entails certain abstractions, of which the community has little understanding. For instance, geologists map the lithology in an area; this is a form of mapping that is usually accomplished in terms of some geologic dating phenomenon. Although defining the lithology is of little consequence to the community, it is the only means by which the hydrologist can interpret his data in the light of broader regional information.

Figure 2 illustrates the scientist's role in the community effort. The idealized planning group shown is established to study the relationship of water needs to stress. The sociologic relationships and economic elements are judged with the aid of experts in these fields. The hydrologist works with the planning group as an adviser, but this is not a desirable role from the standpoint of connecting the engineering problems with economic and sociologic considerations. The scientist should be concerned primarily with the physical controls that bear on the problem at hand. He should be able to ascertain the resultant influences or stresses on the cause toward which the community is working. When the planning group decides to act, he should be able to predict the physical results of that action. Economic and sociologic factors must be the concern of other people in the group.

The way in which hydrologic studies must examine the physical controls in the natural water system can be seen in Fig. 3. Evidently, the function that relates cause to effect is in the environmental controls. Examples of such controls, for a ground-water system, are rock permeability and storage coefficient. In a surface-water system, the controls are more complex and involve such things as evapotranspira-

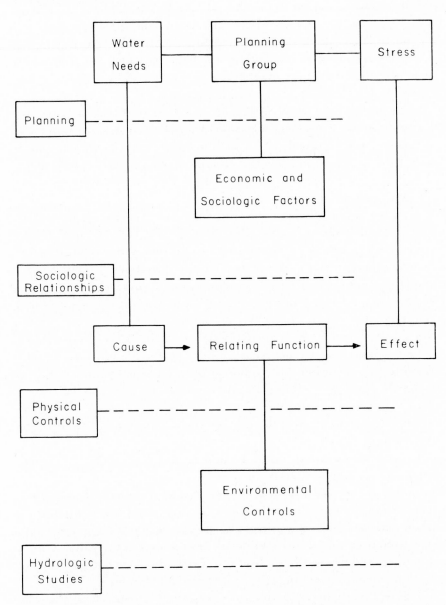

Fig. 2.   In an idealized community-planning organization that seeks to solve water problems, the role of the hydrologist should be as an adviser on the physical controls involved. The sociologic and economic elements should be judged with the advice of other experts. Usually, the goals of a community, which is more interested in obtaining water than in the stresses of nature, differ substantially from those of a scientist.

tion, shape of the drainage area, slope of the land surface, and length of the stream. All of these relationships should be well understood by planning groups. Too often, the way in which economic and sociologic decisions may involve the environmental controls are lost in attempts to simplify the planning process.

The study of environmental controls often rests with a large and complex agency. Almost all natural features pertinent to water use encompass such a broad region that an individual planner in a local area quickly discovers that the cost of investigation is prohibitive. Thus, the government must plan and collect the information over an area large enough to be significant.

It is interesting to note the difference between the surface-water and ground-water segments illustrated in Fig. 3. In the surface-water system, the cause generally is the rainfall; the relating function is inherent in the previously cited environmental factors; and the effect is the resulting runoff, commonly represented as a hydrograph that indicates the amount of water flowing at any selected point on the stream channel. An important point is that the influence of man, for a system involving primarily surface water, is directed against the environment itself. Evidences for this are the removal of vegetation cover, the rerouting and changing of stream channels, and the building of stock tanks. But man as yet exerts little control over the causative factor that initiates the impulses in the surface-water system—the occurrence of rainfall and all its related properties.

In sharp contrast is his influence on the ground-water system. Man now impinges directly on the causative factors that initiate the impulses in the system, rather than on the environment. In pumping water from, or injecting it into, the underground reservoir, the relating function is the aquifer—the porous water-bearing rock—and its boundaries; and these boundaries are unaffected by man's actions. The results of interest in ground water may include changes in water level, changes in water quality, or factors related to both.

It is well in hydrologic studies to keep in mind that changes in the runoff or in the water-level hydrographs, or in any similar displays of effect, usually contain economic, or possibly sociologic, implications. Before a long-range study begins, an attempt should be made to foresee these aspects and to consider how they might be modified. Physical considerations and physical measurements must be relating factors. One must analyze carefully this relationship before choosing the physical factors that will be involved.

Rainstorms and Runoff

An analysis of water development and management is predicated on a thorough understanding of the physical setting and the hydro-

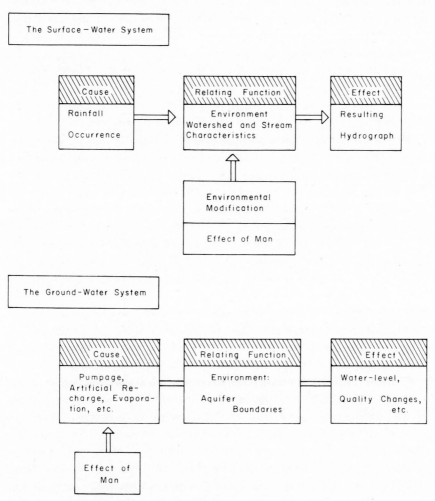

Fig. 3. This chart of cause-and-effect relationships shows that man is the cause in ground-water control; but, with surface water, his influence is directed against the environment itself.

logic parameters that are needed to show how some perturbing cause is related to an ensuing effect. Because the problems of surface water and ground water differ so greatly, it is appropriate to consider them separately, giving attention first to the surface-water system.

The nature of the runoff is among the first questions to be answered. In arid lands, runoff usually occurs only in separate parts of large drainage areas. The source usually is thunderstorms. These storms seldom are larger than 10 square miles (26 square kilometers) in area and generally are much smaller. Thus the contributing part of the drainage area may be only one-tenth, or even as little as one-hundredth, of the total (Fig. 4).

Several controls on runoff are readily recognized. These include the effects of topography, the nature of the rocks and soil, the retention and use of water by plants, and the soil storage capacity. Soil storage capacity is especially significant, because it concerns capillary and evaporation phenomenons. Virtually all the precipitation that reaches the land surface evaporates almost immediately and returns to the atmosphere as water vapor. Capillary forces draw the remainder into the soil, and most of it is recycled later back to the atmosphere. Most of the precipitation, then, affects neither surface water nor ground water.

The net effect of the influences on runoff is to delay its appearance. During the first few minutes of a rain, the surface soil (because of capillarity) can accommodate a tremendous rate of downward water movement. But the rate at which soil can admit water diminishes rapidly (Fig. 5), and runoff begins if the rain lasts long enough.

This delay is compounded by the initial buildup of a thin film of water on the land surface (Fig. 6). The film thickness increases until runoff occurs.

Considerable time elapses between the inception of runoff at an elemental drainage area and its observation at the site or area of interest. While one such delay is being generated, however, others are in various stages of formation as other runoff emerges from similar elemental parts of the basin. The summation of these delay periods at the desired downstream site comprises the hydrograph configuration that the hydrologist seeks to predict. The delay periods are important, therefore, and should be amenable to mathematical description.

Nevertheless, such periods are more complex than is generally conceded. W. B. Langbein has pointed out that some are, in essence, conservative fields of force; as the water moves down the channel a nearly constant waveform and peak height are maintained (6). Other delay periods typify dissipative force fields; they represent the combined effects of channel friction and storage, with the consequent change in waveform and decay in peak height. Examples of the two delay types are easily found in flood records. Low flood crests tend to be depressed, and their rate of movement diminished, as they progress downstream. For high flood crests, however, the channel is fuller and, from a percentage standpoint, friction and

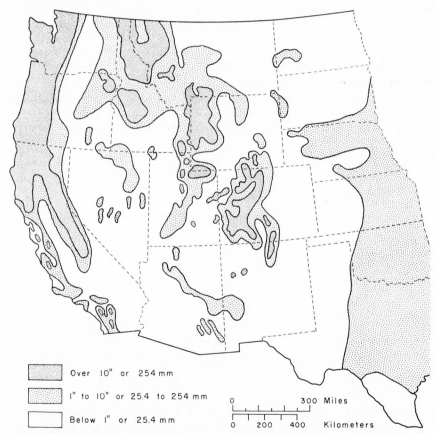

Over 10" or 254 mm

1" to 10" or 25.4 to 254 mm

Below 1" or 25.4 mm

0   300 Miles

0   200   400   Kilometers

Fig. 4. The average annual runoff totals 1 inch (25.4 millimeters) or less over most of the arid West. In individual drainages, as little as one-hundredth of the total area may contribute runoff. (Courtesy U.S. Coast and Geodetic Survey)

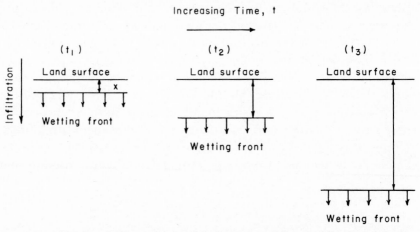

Fig. 5. Runoff is delayed as soil takes up water during the first few minutes of rainfall. The rate at which soil can admit water diminishes rapidly, however. The infiltration gradient equals capillary force/x. The capillary force, acting at the wetting front, remains nearly constant. As t increases, x increases and the infiltration gradient rapidly decreases. Thus, as t increases, the rate of infiltration rapidly decreases.

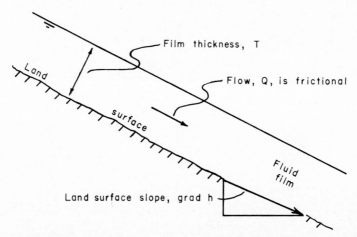

Fig. 6. During the onset of precipitation, a thin film of water builds up on the soil surface and delays runoff. The film thickens until runoff begins. Q equals TP grad h; P has the nature of a permeability coefficient and can be assumed to be constant; grad h is constant; thus, Q, contributing to runoff, changes as T changes. The storage component of the runoff-delay characteristic also changes with T.

storage are much less significant (Fig. 7) ; thus, the wave crest moves down the channel virtually undiminished in height and speed.

In the historical records for a stream, recognition of the floodflows for which the crest tends to dissipate, as well as those for which it maintains itself, is very important. To control stream systems, man might be better advised to increase the frictional and storage factors, deliberately creating a dissipative force field. Although this would reduce and delay flood crests, it also would require assured availability of channel storage to prevent the stream from leaving its banks.

The traditional method for analyzing the runoff characteristic of a given rainfall is to construct a unit hydrograph. If this can be ac-

DISSIPATIVE FORCE FIELD

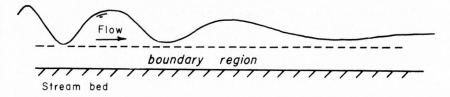

CONSERVATIVE FORCE FIELD

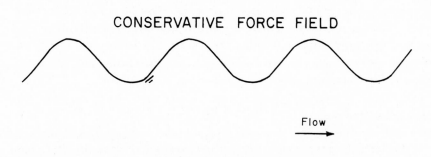

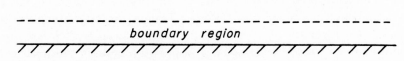

Fig. 7. Friction and storage factors slow the movement of low flood crests. When crests are high and channels are full, downstream flow is undiminished.

complished, the runoff hydrograph for any other rainfall amount is found simply by multiplying the unit hydrograph by a factor that reflects the ratio between that rainfall and the earlier given rainfall. The technique can be extended to longer rainfall periods or to the summation of a series of rainfall pulses.

The appearance of the hydrograph depends partly on where and how much rain has fallen. At best, a unit hydrograph can be applied only to the subbasins in a region whose physical features can be conveniently averaged or lumped together. The subbasin hydrographs, with suitable individual delay characteristics, can be added to establish the runoff for some desired downstream point. This summing process has been outlined by James Dooge (7), who considered the basin as a combined "storage" and "delay" device. The storage feature is the ability of the land surface to retain water for a short time; the delay feature is the time needed to move the water to the site for which the hydrograph is desired.

Until recently, the unit hydrograph appeared to be the only analytic hope. Now, however, electronic analog computers have practically assured a new and extremely versatile technique. Computer elements have been constructed that are capable of simulating the most involved hydrologic phenomenons. With such elements, the rainfall need no longer be idealized as a unit-impulse function but may instead be described as any appropriate complex input function. Present-day computer elements, or linkages, are only the first step in a larger program for developing techniques to analyze entire regions, constructing the whole from small individual elements and their delay characteristics.

Man-Made Changes

Purposefully delayed to this point is recognition of the fact that, in the southwestern United States, civilization is drastically changing watershed characteristics. These changes might reasonably be viewed as a foretaste of what may ultimately happen in other arid regions of the world. Phenomenal population growth, with all the construction activity this implies, has widely altered the topography. In particular, large highway embankments, stretching across the arid regions, act as dams that tend to spread or reroute local floods and the runoff in ephemeral streams. Probably the most important fu-

Electronic computers, such as this one in Phoenix, can be programed to simulate the physical environment of ground water. The use of computer elements has opened a whole new field of analysis to hydrologists. (Courtesy U.S. Department of the Interior, Geological Survey)

ture problems facing hydrologists in the Southwest are those that will concern the effects of watershed modification.

Although the foregoing observations have been restricted to runoff, obviously they are related to other significant parameters. The delays that may affect or characterize surface-water movement in a drainage area also affect evaporation. A delay in water movement—that is, an increase in the storage—means an increase in evaporation. Examples appear in the construction of dams, with consequent opportunities for some of the stored water to be converted to vapor and leave the area before it can be used beneficially farther downstream. It might be argued that in the relatively undeveloped upper parts of a watershed, nature's process of converting liquid water to vapor is nonbeneficial, whereas in the more developed lower parts, particularly in the agricultural areas, the evaporation process is important, and ways must be found to describe it quantitatively for both natural and man-inspired events.

The amount of water lost, or transpired, by vegetation is difficult to determine. Invariably in the arid lands the areas of riparian vegetation are in river channels. Because the channels are complex and heterogeneous geologic units, the permeability of any underlying water-bearing material cannot be expressed. It is impossible to calculate, by any scheme of water-table mapping or observation, how much water moves into the areas of plant transpiration. Techniques for approximating the amount of water lost by plants that grow in a river channel have been reported by J. S. Gatewood and others (8), but these methods remain inexact. Subsequent studies of vapor transport in the atmosphere, by direct observation and by energy-budget analysis, have been described by Earl Harbeck and his colleagues (9). By observation and measurement in the air of the amount of water vapor leaving an area (Fig. 8), such techniques could lead to the needed determination of evapotranspiration losses.

Ultimately, the hydrologist must know how much water falls on an area, and how much of it could cause runoff. He realizes that he must seek part of the answer in weather prediction. But often he is interested only in a relatively small area, perhaps of about 100 square miles (259 square kilometers), if data for the planning of, say, a bridge culvert are needed. The small area may in its own right contain features that affect the weather. Massive rock exposures may accumulate heat during the day, release it during late afternoon or early evening, and thereby produce the air instability that sets off thunderstorm generation. Meteorology, therefore, might be further developed along lines that are more directly useful to the hydrologist.

This need is further dramatized by the fact that runoff is produced by only a very few of the many small thunderstorms and light rains that occur in arid regions. Only a storm that is large in terms of rate or duration of rainfall causes runoff. Such a storm results from extreme conditions that heretofore have not been predictable in detail. In a small study area, decades may pass before enough rain falls to cause the flow of small ephemeral streams.

The surface-water problems of small watershed areas obviously demand a data-collection system that will minimize the wait for hydrologic events. Much interest is now developing in the southwestern United States in radar-tracking systems to detect the occurrence, extent in area, and movement of rainfall that is intense enough to bring runoff. This technique permits simultaneous accumulation of rainfall and runoff statistics over a broad region that embraces many adjacent small areas, materially shortening the waiting period. At present, research in this field is in progress at the Phoenix, Arizona, office of the U.S. Geological Survey, at U.S. Weather Bureau facilities in southern Nevada, and at the Desert Research Institute at the University of Nevada in Reno.

Runoff data gathered during the past 60 years or more for such major rivers as the Colorado, the Gila, and the Salt now are of questionable value. The watersheds have been so transformed by man during the past 10 to 20 years that one cannot justifiably extrapolate the historical records. Confronted by modern engineering demands

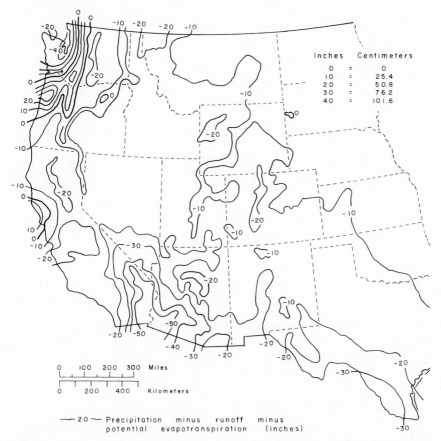

Fig. 8. A net moisture deficiency prevails in most of the West. This condition is calculated by subtracting runoff and potential evapotranspiration from precipitation.

in areas where there is much information, as well as in wide desert expanses where there is little, the hydrologist obviously can ill afford to launch the 60-year study that a statistical analysis might require. He must be able to single out quickly the significant causes and effects and to develop ways to assemble rapidly the supporting data.

Ground-Water Measurement

Ground-water development focuses primarily on the environmental characteristics (10). Generally these are less likely to change than those involved in surface-water problems, but measurement of them is difficult because they are hidden in aquifers below the land surface. At only the few points where wells are drilled can some physical parameters be measured. Between these points, interpolation is the only way to assess how an aquifer's flow may vary. Unfortunately, real accomplishments in this special field have been disappointingly few, and much important work remains to be done.

Particularly significant in the control of ground-water flow is the permeability coefficient. Permeability is a measure of the hydraulic gradient needed to keep water moving in an aquifer. This, in turn, controls the slope of the water table, which indicates the depth to water below the land surface. The depth, of course, suggests the cost of pumping and also forewarns against waterlogging or related drainage problems.

Through the past 30 years techniques have been developed for measuring permeability, but the results are still far from adequate. Field techniques commonly employ the discharge or recharge of wells and rely on an analysis of how the effects of operating the well spread out in the aquifer (11). That the results are not sufficiently reliable is attributable to complexities in the mathematical analysis and the natural departures from man's idealizations. The permeability function can vary over distances of a relatively few feet by a factor as high as 10^{23}. Although a field test using a well may yield a permeability value that represents an average or composite for a fair-sized area, it remains only a "point" sample as far as regional extent of the aquifer is concerned. The same reasoning underscores the difficulties in any attempt to obtain useful permeability data through laboratory measurements on core samples or drill cuttings.

A better appraisal can be given the regional variations in permeability by an analysis of the flow patterns that were to be found throughout the aquifer before man began to develop the water. This approach is more difficult and requires a more complex mathematical description of the flow regime.

Further complicating field determination is the fact that water moves through porous material in three dimensions, not just two. The sediments that comprise most aquifers are known to have been deposited in such a manner that the permeability differs with respect to all three principal coordinate axes. Vertical, as well as lateral, changes may be substantial. Yet the changes in vertical permeability are not easily measured. These changes may exercise considerable control on the ground-water flow. In the pumping of some shallow aquifers in the arid Southwest, a considerable amount of upward flow is thereby induced. The phenomenon is predictable, because, in the drilling of wells, the deeper the drill penetrates the water-bearing strata, the higher the water level rises in the well.

The storage coefficient of water-bearing material, or of an aquifer, is especially important in the analysis of ground-water problems in arid zones. This parameter represents the ability of the materials or aquifer to accept or release water only under gravitational force. Hydrologists recognize that the natural water movement in an aquifer is so slow that it can be ignored in most arid-zones water development. Its principal effect will be restricted to control of the shape of the localized cone of depression that forms around a pumped well. The real control on water development is the amount of ground water in storage. This constitutes a reservoir that can be exploited.

The nature of the storage coefficient is more complicated than its definition might imply, and further research is needed to enlarge the timeworn concepts. An approach toward ultimate fuller understanding continues to be found in its dual nature (12). For the water-table aquifer, the coefficient indicates water that can be recovered through gravity drainage; for the artesian aquifer, it indicates water that will emerge as hydraulic-gradient changes squeeze or compress the aquifer. The coefficient for an artesian aquifer is only about one-thousandth of that for a water-table aquifer. Actually, the dual nature applies, regardless of aquifer type, but the dominating feature for each type is as described. These properties of the storage coefficient remove it from the category of a simple coefficient and make it, instead, a functional relationship. The measurement problems are very similar to, and every bit as frustrating as, those pertaining to permeability determinations.

The compressive feature of the storage coefficient is imperfectly understood, although U.S. Geological Survey studies and measurements in the San Joaquin Valley, California, by J. F. Poland and his associates are describing the mechanics involved (*13*). Evidently most of the compressive effect takes place in the first few inches (centimeters) of the clay layers that confine an aquifer. Compression of the aquifer sands, or even of the aquifer as a whole, is almost insignificant by comparison.

The storage coefficient may not be the same for a water-table rise as it is for a subsequent decline. If the porous earth material is primarily sand but has many clay lenses scattered throughout, it will take more water into storage when it is first saturated than it will subsequently release by gravity drainage. This is because water is drawn into, and held in, the clays by capillary forces; ultimately it may leave if evaporation can occur over the clay surfaces.

An adequate analysis of the manner in which an aquifer responds to development hinges on more than improved determinations of the permeability and storage parameters. Equally important in arid regions are the boundary conditions that are created or brought about by man. A good example is seen in many irrigated areas in the Southwest where the water table has risen unchecked until direct evaporation equals the total amount of water available. Another example, also found in the southwestern United States, relates to the common practice of constructing wells with casing perforated through the entire thickness of the saturated water-yielding deposits. Under the protracted pumping of many wells, the water table lowers throughout a broad area. Sections of the perforated well casings become dewatered. These expose the aquifer to oscillatory influx and efflux of air, as the atmospheric pressure rises or falls. Evaporation accompanies the air movement; thus, again man has created a new discharge boundary condition. The amount of water lost in this manner can be considerable and may even exceed the amount that would have been lost if the water had been stored in a surface reservoir.

Somewhere in the task usually confronted by the hydrologist who seeks to analyze ground-water problems is the requirement to relate changes in water level or hydraulic gradient to the stresses imposed

on the system by man. A number of equations are available, some
borrowed from the literature on heat conduction in solids, for performing this mathematically. However, the idealizations and assumptions used in deriving the equations limit their application to
rather simple field situations. The equations are far from adequate
to solve the complex spatial relationships that are inherent in the
permeability and storage parameters, to say nothing of the added
complexities in the variety of new boundary conditions that are
continually being introduced by man.

Use of Computers

Electronic analog computers show great promise in allowing the
hydrologist to cope more effectively with ground-water problems.
Considerable development of, and experience in, this relatively new
analytic technique has been realized within the U.S. Geological
Survey, particularly through the efforts of H. E. Skibitzke and his
associates in Phoenix, Arizona. Analog computers can easily simulate all the complexities of the physical environment, as well as the
natural and man-induced boundary conditions, peculiar to ground-
water systems (14). If the hydrologist can satisfactorily observe and
describe the field environment, he can now be much better
equipped than ever before to assay the consequences of the water
development contemplated. Present-day analog computers, however,
give insight only into the hydraulic-gradient distribution throughout
the flow system. The companion need, often encountered, is to evaluate the flow-line patterns that are orthogonal to the hydraulic-
gradient patterns. This may be satisfied through future research on
computers whose design employs principles of transport phenomenons.

Some concluding remarks seem appropriate concerning water development in arid regions. The fact that man can choose the rate
at which he exploits ground water makes hydrologic analysis even
more difficult by drawing in sociologic and economic factors. That
arid-zones water supplies are being depleted attests to man's determination to master his environment.

The significance of recharge to underground reservoirs is greatly
misunderstood, especially in the arid zones. In general, recharge
is a constant characteristic on which man has little effect. In an

Investigations on the suppression of evaporation are conducted with evaporation pans and plastic-lined ponds by the Institute for Water Utilization at the University of Arizona. Chemical coverings are placed atop the water, and the water budget is carefully controlled. (Courtesy Sol Resnick)

area under study, recharge commonly is not known, but this does not necessarily hinder the hydrologic appraisal of cause-and-effect relationships. Because the recharge is constant, it would appear in any analysis only as a zero-change relationship. Despite this property, recharge continues to be the great illusion of the hydrologist. Much time, effort, and money are still poured into recharge studies, yet the data when finally assembled are not applied to the hydrologic analysis. The amount and distribution in space of recharge have very little importance to the regional hydrologic analysis.

In recent years, there have been investigations that look toward the possibility of increasing water supplies by means of artificial recharge. Dean Muckel (15) and Sol Resnick (16) have reported on some of their work in the Southwest that outlines the potential and problems encountered. Artificial-recharge methods are basically aimed at conserving floodwaters to supplement ground-water supplies, particularly where there may be serious overdraft of ground-water reserves. Recharging through wells offers some promise in areas where dams are not feasible because of the storage of surface water. Nevertheless, much more information is needed for each particular subsurface-reservoir environment to overcome certain difficulties encountered.

The prospects that artificial recharge might offset some discharge losses in an arid region may justify the expense. The ephemeral nature of water that might be available for recharge implies a need to maintain the necessary diversion or control works during many years in which no water would appear. When a flash flood does occur, it is a fleeting event and is limited in area in relation to the underground reservoir. Furthermore, to be successful, the recharge must reach the ground-water reservoir near the area where the water is to be used, because there is a long time delay in producing water-level rises at any great distance away.

Arid regions commonly lack not only water but also power. Strangely enough, if the energy can somehow be supplied, the water is promptly forthcoming by pumping from the usually present underlying reservoir. The tremendous amounts of energy needed to develop an arid region in this manner have prompted recent interest in the use of nuclear energy. If this becomes a reality, the hydrologist can anticipate even greater demands. There would be the added problem of safe disposal of radioactive masses in the arid-zones environment.

REFERENCES

1. U.S. Geological Survey, "Compilation of records of surface waters of the United States through September 1950," pt. 9, "Colorado River Basin," *U.S. Geol. Surv. Water Supply Paper 1313* (1954).
2. L. B. Leopold and T. Maddock, Jr., "The hydraulic geometry of stream channels and some physiographic implications," *U.S. Geol. Surv. Profess. Paper 252* (1953).
3. W. A. Smith, C. P. Wetter, G. B. Cummings, and others, "Comprehensive survey of sedimentation in Lake Mead, 1948–1949," *U.S. Geol. Surv. Profess. Paper 295* (1960).
4. S. K. Love, "Quality of surface waters for irrigation, western United States, 1957," *U.S. Geol. Surv. Water Supply Paper 1524* (1960).
5. G. M. Robinson and D. E. Peterson, "Notes on earth fissures in southern Arizona," *U.S. Geol. Surv. Circ. 466* (1962).
6. W. B. Langbein, *Storage in Relation to Flood Waves in Hydrology* (Dover, New York, 1949), pp. 561–571.

7. J. C. I. Dooge, "A general theory of the unit hydrograph," *J. Geophys. Res.* **64**, 241–256 (1959).

8. J. S. Gatewood, T. W. Robinson, B. R. Colby, J. D. Hem, and L. C. Halpenny, "Use of water by bottom-land vegetation in lower Safford Valley, Arizona," *U.S. Geol. Surv. Water Supply Paper 1103* (1950).

9. G. E. Harbeck, Jr., and others, "Water-loss investigations: Lake Hefner studies base data report," *U.S. Geol. Surv. Profess. Papers 269* and *270* (1954).

10. J. W. Harshbarger, "Techniques of ground-water development in the Navajo country: Arizona, New Mexico, and Utah, U.S.A.," *Intern. Assoc. Sci. Hydrol. (Athens) Publ. 57* (1961), pp. 657–679.

11. R. H. Brown, "Selected procedures for analyzing aquifer test data," *J. Am. Water Works Assoc.* **45**, 844–866 (1953).

12. J. G. Ferris, "Ground-water hydraulics, theory," pt. 1, *U.S. Geol. Surv. Water Supply Paper 1536-E* (1962).

13. J. F. Poland, "Land subsidence in the San Joaquin Valley, California, and its effect on estimates of ground-water reservoirs," *Intern. Assoc. Sci. Hydrol. Publ. 52* (1960), pp. 324–335.

14. H. E. Skibitzke, "Electronic computers as an aid to the analysis of hydrologic problems," *Intern. Assoc. Sci. Hydrol. Publ. 52* (1960), pp. 347–358.

15. D. C. Muckel, "Replenishment of ground-water supplies by artificial means," *U.S. Dept. Agr. Tech. Bull. 1195* (1961).

16. S. Resnick and G. M. Maddox, "Artificial ground-water recharge," *Proc. 5th Watershed Symp.* (Watershed Management Div., State Land Dept., Phoenix, Ariz., 1961).

7

Minerals and Energy Sources in the Arid West

Joseph A. Schufle

In addition to their obviously vast potential reserve of solar energy, the arid regions of the United States certainly contain their full share of fossil fuels, reserves of nuclear-energy minerals, and other energy sources. Many people are beginning to realize that the ultimate limitation on the supply of minerals in the world is actually a limit imposed by the supply of energy.

Technologic progress in the exploitation of mineral resources makes possible the use of lower- and lower-grade ores as better-grade deposits become exhausted. Reserves of ore that may originally have been uneconomical to process become economic reserves when the price of the mineral rises high enough.

The surface of the earth is composed largely of iron and aluminum silicates, and only the energy to crush and grind the rock and extract the iron is needed. Therefore, the real problem in the evaluation of mineral resources is whether there will be enough energy available at reasonable cost to do the job of extraction. Trends in energy consumption in the United States during the past few decades are shown in Fig. 1.

Except for water power, all of the sources of energy indicated in Fig. 1 are drawing on the fossil-fuel reserves. Many people think of these reserves as being inexhaustible, but Harrison Brown has shown a possible future pattern of world energy consumption from fossil fuels in which a peak fossil-fuel consumption is likely to be

Contributors to this chapter were Roshan B. Bhappu, Kay R. Brower, Helen L. Cannon, Bruce F. Curtis, Maurice C. Fuerstenau, Stafford C. Happ, Lyman C. Huff, Frank E. Kottlowski, James R. McNitt, David Mitchell, John R. Riter, and Robert H. Weber.

reached in the next century or so (*1*). Of course, it appears to be certain that nuclear energy soon will be supplying a considerable portion of our energy needs; and, if the disposal of waste products from reactors does not present an insurmountable problem, perhaps there is no reason to be unduly concerned about future energy resources.

If this development should not take place, however, man may have to fall back on the earth's last great source of energy, the sun itself, and this is not too dim a prospect. Eugene Ayres and Charles A. Scarlott, of the Stanford Research Institute in California, have estimated that as much energy reaches the earth in the form of solar radiation in 3 days as is stored in all its fossil-fuel reserves (*2*). If man ever must use this tremendous supply of energy, the arid lands would become one of the most logical areas in which to live, since they receive solar radiation in the greatest abundance.

What are the possible sources of energy that are readily available for man's use, and how are they distributed in the arid United States? Table I shows that water power is of relatively minor importance in the present over-all energy consumption of the nation. It is likely to be even less so in the arid regions, where water is

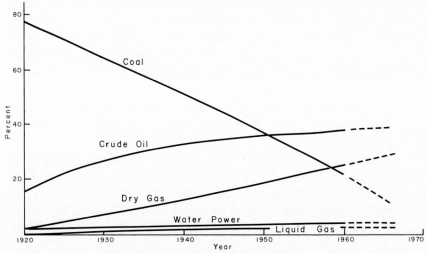

Fig. 1. This graph of percentages of total energy consumption provided in the United States by various fuels illustrates that the relative consumption of coal has dropped markedly and the use of crude oil and gas has risen.

Table. I.   Energy consumption in the United States, 1920–1960.

			Percentage of total energy consumption				
Year	Exports	Imports	Coal	Crude oil	Dry gas	Liquid gas	Water power
1920	2.0		78.4	15.3	4.2	0.2	3.9
1930	2.2		61.2	27.6	8.8	1.1	3.5
1940	0.7		52.4	32.1	11.4	1.0	3.8
1950		1.2	37.8	36.0	18.0	2.3	4.7
1960		3.2	23.2	38.2	28.3	3.2	3.9

Source: U.S. Bureau of Mines, *Minerals Yearbook, 1960.*

scarce. Wind energy and geothermal energy might be expected to be of even less importance. A quantitative examination of these energy sources will provide a good idea of the best direction to be taken in future development.

Minerals in the Arid Regions

Mineral resources are likely to be distributed as randomly in arid regions as they are elsewhere, and, except for saline deposits of recent origin, they probably occur no more frequently. Nonetheless, they may be easier to find in arid environments, and mining has usually assumed a major role in these regions of the United States, simply because, here, it has provided one of the best ways for men to make a living.

Some idea of the value of mineral resources to the economic development of the arid United States can be gathered from the reports on the income from federal lands that were made by Marion Clawson and Burnell Held in 1957 (3). Approximately 410 million acres (166 million hectares), or about 90 percent, of the 455 million acres (184 million hectares) of federally owned land are located in the arid regions, roughly in the area west of the 100th meridian. Therefore, a discussion of income from federal lands is largely a discussion of income from such lands in the arid United States. These lands, in turn, comprise about 46 percent of the total land area in the United States. In 1950, the government received $29 million from mineral leases on the federal land, or 77 percent of its income from such land. These receipts soared to $100 million (or 67 percent) in 1960. By 1980, they are expected to total $260 million (79 percent).

Some of the mineral resources in the arid United States are described in the following sections, and an attempt is made to evaluate some of the more important minerals. For the purpose of this report, mineral deposits are arbitrarily divided into three categories: (i) saline deposits, (ii) fuels, (iii) other metallic and nonmetallic ore deposits.

Saline Deposits

The minerals that are the most characteristic of arid regions are saline deposits, sometimes called *evaporites,* because their precipitation from concentrated solution is caused by evaporation. Rock salt $(NaCl)$, gypsum $(CaSO_4 \cdot 2H_2O)$, and anhydrite $(CaSO_4)$ are the most common. Limestone and dolomite are not considered to be evaporites, since they originate chiefly in a different process. Other evaporite minerals that form minor amounts of many saline deposits, but are economically important, are potassium and magnesium salts, such as sylvite (KCl), langbeinite $(K_2SO_4 \cdot 2MgSO_4)$, carnallite $(KCl \cdot MgCl_2 \cdot 6H_2O)$, and kainite $(KMgClSO_4 \cdot 3H_2O)$. Most of the saline deposits were formed by evaporation of sea water in shallow inland bays or inlets. Some of them, however, result from evaporation of salt lakes, examples of which are Great Salt Lake in Utah, Owens and Searles Lakes in California, and Laguna del Perro in the Estancia Valley of New Mexico.

The most spectacular of the American evaporites is the Ochoan series of rocks, late Permian in age, of the Delaware Basin in southeastern New Mexico and adjoining parts of Texas (4). The basic unit of the Ochoan is the Castile Anhydrite. It lies under an area roughly 200 miles (340 kilometers) in diameter, and about 95 percent of this formation is made up of salts evaporated from marine brine. The Castile is 1800 feet (600 meters) thick and is thinly banded with alternating layers of light-gray gypsum-anhydrite and dark-brown calcite $(CaCO_3)$.

The middle Ochoan unit, the Salado Salt, is about 2000 feet (700 meters) thick and is almost entirely composed of sodium chloride (halite). Important interbeds are of potassium-rich minerals: red sylvite; gray langbeinite; brownish, bitter-tasting carnallite; and pale-red polyhalite $(K_2Ca_2Mg(SO_4)_4 \cdot 2H_2O)$. Since all of these salts are highly soluble in water, the Salado Salt nowhere crops out at the surface of the ground. East of Carlsbad, New Mexico, the potash-rich beds are mined underground and supply about 90 percent of the national production of potash, which is used chiefly as fertilizer. In 1961, the potassium salts produced in New Mexico were valued at $83 million.

Salt lakes are interesting features that are found in arid lands throughout the world. When the waters that feed such lakes flow through sedimentary rocks, then the waters of the lake largely contain dissolved sodium chloride. Great Salt Lake in Utah is an example. Its waters contain a concentration of salt dissolved from sedimentary beds, which were, in turn, precipitated long ages ago in a marine environment. In contrast, lakes supplied with water from regions of igneous rocks are highly alkaline and contain relatively large amounts of carbonate salts as well as sodium chloride. Created in this manner were Owens Lake in California and Humboldt Lake, or Humboldt Sink, in Nevada. A particularly unusual example is Lake Lucero in New Mexico, which lies windward of the famous White Sands National Monument, the vast gypsum dunes in the Tularosa Basin. Rocks in the source areas of Lake Lucero contain much gypsum. This is leached from the bedrock, carried in solution to Lake Lucero, and there precipitated as gypsum upon evaporation.

Within the muds of the lake flat and in the silts along the shore, some of the gypsum crystals grow to blades 1 foot (30 centimeters) or more in length in a mineral form called *selenite*. However, most of the deposited gypsum has been broken up by restless desert winds and is driven into dunes of white "sand" that range from 10 to 50 feet (3 to 15 meters) in height. These dunes, part of which are set aside for permanent preservation in White Sands National Monument, cover more than 245 square miles (600 square kilometers) and contain almost 4 billion tons $(4 \times 10^9$ metric tons) of pure gypsum, which is approximately equal to a 350-year supply for the entire United States at the present rate of consumption (5).

Alkali flats and saltpans are common in the arid parts of the United States. During periods of heavy rain, these dry flats become temporary lakes. When the lakes dry up again, the dissolved salts are redeposited as evaporites, the most abundant being rock salt and the carbonates and sulfates of sodium. In time, thick deposits of interbedded crystalline salts, clays, and silts may accumulate. Laguna del Perro in New Mexico, which was visited on the field trip held during the International Arid Lands Conference in 1955, is one of several scores of salt basins alined along the lowest axis of the Estancia Basin in central New Mexico.

Great Salt Lake, Utah, is the shrunken remnant of the huge Pleistocene-age Lake Bonneville. Its size changes with climatic changes, but it is about 2000 square miles (5000 square kilometers) in area, which is only about one-tenth of the size of the original Lake Bonneville. Up to 28 percent of the water's weight consists of dissolved solids. By comparison, the average salinity of the Dead Sea, at the eastern end of the Mediterranean Sea, is about 25 percent. Great Salt Lake is about 7 times as salty as the ocean (6). The human body floats high in its waters, and rock salt is produced commercially from evaporating basins along the shore.

Searles Lake, California, is one of the largest exposed bodies of salt in the United States. Large tonnages of a great variety of salts are extracted from this lake. The surface is so hard and thick that it supports an entire extraction plant. This top layer of hard salt is 70 feet (23 meters) thick in the central area and about 30 feet (10 meters) thick beneath surface muds in a surrounding area. Below this surface layer is impervious mud, and then a second layer of salt. About 45 percent of these layers is pore space, which is filled with a heavy brine. The brine from both salt layers is drawn up in wells, and various products are produced by fractional crystallization of the brine. The chief products are potassium chloride, sodium sulfate, sodium carbonate, lithium carbonate, sodium borate, and bromine.

Reserves of salines in the arid western United States are enormous. Estimates of rock salt (sodium chloride) reserves made by W. G. Pierce and E. J. Rich, of the U.S. Geological Survey, in 1962 indicated that 1700 cubic miles (7000 cubic kilometers) of salt underlie just the western part of the state of North Dakota (7). The Salado Salt formation in southeastern New Mexico contains about the same volume of halite and other salts. It is believed that the United States has sufficient reserves of gypsum near markets to last for 2000 years at the present rate of use.

Petroleum Deposits

Petroleum reserves in the West constitute two-thirds of the United States total, yet only one-third of the petroleum produced in the West is consumed there. Thus, the West is a heavy supplier to the rest of the country. Petroleum occurs almost exclusively in sedimentary rocks. It is, therefore, relatively easy, once the general geologic features of the land are known, to classify an area roughly according to its potential for producing oil and gas. Such a classification for the arid West (Fig. 2) shows that much of the land falls into either the "productive" or the "favorable" class.

The eastern favorable area represents a very ancient continental border on which porous rocks and petroleum source-beds accumulated together, and the present western continental border is the site of recent accumulations of petroleum-rich beds. The intervening broad area of doubtful possibilities has been squeezed and shattered so thoroughly that beds suitably porous to contain petroleum may be expected only rarely. Certainly more than 0.25 million holes have been drilled in the 17-state area of the arid United States in the search for petroleum.

Thick deposits of rocks called *oil shale* also lie in these regions, particularly around the mutual corner of Colorado, Utah, and Wyoming (Fig. 3). The shale must be mined and then heated in a retort to convert the organic material (kerogen) into oil. Estimates vary on the oil potential of these deposits, but it is believed that all domestic fuel requirements for 6 years could be supplied by the readily accessible oil shale, and that at least 10 times this amount of fuel is available in potentially minable shale of good quality. Putting it another way, the easily available oil shale could supply about 14 times the annual current oil consumption of the United States. The known reserves of oil shale are about equal to the nation's proved reserves of liquid petroleum. It is a reassuring prospect to have these reserves of oil shale to draw upon, but it is worth noting that the total reserves of oil shale still represent only about a 21-year energy supply for the United States at the estimated demand rate for the year 2000.

Some work has been done on in-place combustion of shale, but results were not encouraging, mainly because of the difficulty of maintaining combustion in an impervious rock. Although suggested nuclear explosions in oil shales have not yet materialized, the limited success in Project Gnome, in which an atomic blast in a salt deposit in southeastern New Mexico in 1961 produced a fused cavity underground, may revive interest in such a test on oil shale.

Oil sometimes seeps upward through the rocks until it comes close to the surface, where it evaporates and leaves a sticky bitumen lodged in shallow formations called *tar sands*. They occur in two large deposits in eastern Utah, in six important areas in California, and in smaller amounts in Colorado, New Mexico, and Wyoming. Their total estimated proved oil potential is 2.5×10^9 barrels, of which nearly 90 percent is in the two Utah deposits. Since the current demand for petroleum in the United States is about 3.5×10^9 barrels annually, these tar sands could furnish only about two-thirds of a year's supply. Tar sands are not now produced for fuel purposes, and their use awaits improved market conditions.

At one place in eastern Utah, oil has been expressed toward the surface, filled the fractures in the rocks, and hardened. Veins of a brilliant black, solid hydrocarbon, *gilsonite*, resulted. About 1000 tons (907 metric tons) of gilsonite per day are now extracted, ground, and mixed in a water slurry, which is pumped through a pipeline to a refinery in western Colorado. There it is converted into petroleum products that are equivalent to about 2 million barrels of crude oil per year. Unfortunately, there is little chance of repeating this ingenious venture elsewhere in the United States. Virtually all the nation's known gilsonite occurs in this lonely part of Utah.

Petroleum exploration and petroleum production have provided a forceful economic stimulus. Of course, their importance in any one district depends on the size of the petroleum accumulations in relation to other parts of the economy. In west Texas and central Oklahoma, oil and gas are dominant. In such states as North Dakota, Utah, Colorado, and New Mexico, the smaller production occupies an important, but not commanding, commercial position. On the other hand, in California's Los Angeles basin, it is exceedingly large but has only a modest effect on the total economy, since southern California has so many other industries.

The petroleum industry in the United States has managed to meet swiftly rising demands and still maintain sizable reserves. Although 15 of the western states produce some petroleum, the amount is very small in four of them. A good estimate is that about 3×10^{14} kilowatt hours of oil and gas energy has been discovered in the 17-state area, of which nearly 60 percent has already been used, the remaining 40 percent being in proved reserves. This supply has required continuing discoveries, and many of the discoveries have resulted from careful examination of the earth's surface by geologists and other earth scientists.

In recent years, the studies of the earth's surface have been ac-

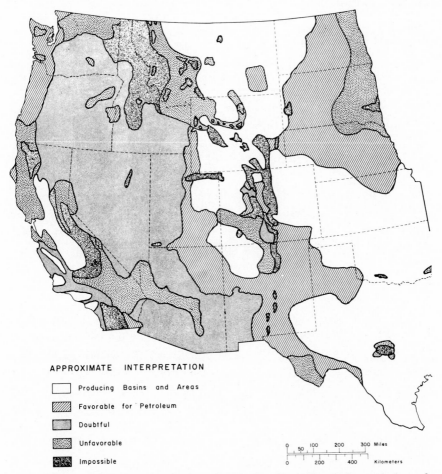

APPROXIMATE   INTERPRETATION

☐ Producing Basins and Areas

▨ Favorable for Petroleum

▨ Doubtful

▨ Unfavorable

▨ Impossible

0   50   100   200   300 Miles
0   200   400   Kilometers

Fig. 2.   Petroleum potential of land can be determined through knowledge of the general geologic features. Such a classification suggests that the occurrence of petroleum is likely in much of the West.

celerated by new techniques. One technique of particular use in the exploration for petroleum is aerial photography. Stereoscopic photographs can provide useful estimates of elevations of key formations and may quickly reveal important geologic structures. Arid lands lend themselves especially well to this technique. Because there is little soil cover and vegetation, rock exposures are usually excellent. The mountainous topography that contributes to the aridity also makes easier the examination of geologic formations in the basins; there the structures often are exposed to view on upturned edges along mountain flanks.

High Cost of Production

Drilling costs in arid lands often are several times higher than those elsewhere. The high costs are brought about by special housing needs; water-, fuel-, and equipment-supply problems; and communications difficulties. Substitution of compressed air for the usual drilling mud as a circulating fluid has become increasingly popular in drilling operations in dry areas, and the process often results in dramatic reduction of well costs.

A collateral benefit of exploratory drilling has been the discovery of deep supplies of fresh water. The drilling of deep wells for water alone would be prohibitively expensive, but often the boreholes that do not produce petroleum are converted by the oil companies into a water supply for the landholders. The discovery of valuable Permian salt beds in the Delaware Basin of southeastern New Mexico resulted from exploratory drilling in search of petroleum.

Petroleum production in arid regions also presents special problems. In addition to the readily apparent problems of maintaining and supplying expensive field installations in remote areas, the disposal of produced water, which is often rather saline, is costly, because the surface-drainage water is used extensively for irrigation and should not be polluted. Reinjection of formation water often becomes necessary. Water-injection methods for increasing oil recovery may become very expensive, unless subsurface water can be used.

Oil or gas in an arid region usually must be transported long distances to consumers. In recent years, large pipelines thousands of miles (kilometers) in length have been built to transport oil and gas that are produced in the arid regions to points on the east and west coasts where consumption is heavy. Small remote fields, however, may be costly to operate. Oil can be removed by truck or rail, but at the present time, natural gas can be transported only by pipeline.

Geologists are increasingly able to trace the processes of oil accumulation and to predict the location of porous reservoir rocks. But they need better methods to translate their measurements on the small pieces of rock that are extracted from drill holes into terms that better characterize the very large volumes of rock involved

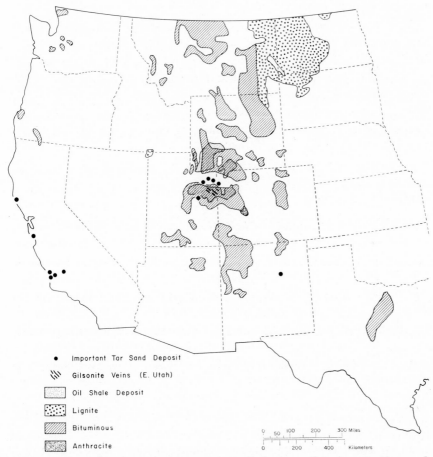

- ●   Important Tar Sand Deposit
- 〰   Gilsonite Veins (E. Utah)
- Oil Shale Deposit
- Lignite
- Bituminous
- Anthracite

Fig. 3.   Deposits of tar sand, gilsonite, oil shale, and coal underlie much of the arid United States, as is indicated on this map. Shale must be heated in a retort before oil can be recovered.

in the structure of the earth's surface. There is promise that recent studies of rock magnetism will provide a basis for deducing the conditions under which some ancient sandstone reservoir formations were deposited. A better understanding of underground circulation of fluids, however, is sorely needed, despite the recent marked advances in this field. Research on colored aerial photographs indicates that they can be especially useful in arid lands.

Some large areas of the central part of the arid United States remain only superficially explored. They are covered by layers of volcanic rocks, which so far have defied efforts to learn what lies beneath them.

The known reserves of petroleum in arid regions of the United States are sufficient to last the entire country for about 15 years. The efficiency of methods of finding and producing petroleum has improved markedly during the past few decades, but the arid West may be said to have reached a mature stage of petroleum development. The easy finds were made by less advanced methods, and the deeper, more obscure accumulations are now being uncovered by modern techniques. As a result, the percentage of wells in which oil is found has remained rather constant for some years.

Distribution of Coal

Extensive coal deposits underlie the arid western half of the United States. All were laid down, of course, under entirely different conditions of climate from those now prevailing—that is, in coastal marshes and swamps under warm, humid conditions in ancient geologic times. The production of bituminous coal and lignite in the West is summarized in Table II. Paul Averitt, of the U.S. Geological Survey, recently estimated the coal reserves of the United States

Table II. Production of bituminous coal and lignite, arid regions of the United States, 1960.

Number of mines	279
Annual production (thousands of tons[a])	16,203
Annual production (10^{12} kw hr)	0.12
Total production to end of 1960 (thousands of tons[a])	2,178,119
Total production to end of 1960 (10^{12} kw hr)	16

[a] One ton equals 0.907 metric ton.
Source: U.S. Bureau of Mines, *Minerals Yearbook, 1960.*

This open-pit copper mine at Santa Rita, New Mexico, is one of the largest in the world. The Spaniards first dug copper here, from an underground mine, in 1880. The present pit is more than 1 mile (1.6 kilometers) across and 800 feet (244 meters) deep. (Courtesy Kennecott Copper Corporation)

(8). Beds are found widely in New Mexico, Colorado, Utah, Wyoming, Montana, and North Dakota, and in smaller areas in South Dakota, Arizona, Idaho, California, Oregon, and Washington. Most of the coal is subbituminous and lignite, but large deposits of bituminous coal occur in Colorado, Utah, New Mexico, Wyoming, and Washington. Some moderate-sized reserves of anthracite occur in New Mexico, Colorado, and Washington. At our present rate of consumption of perhaps 500 million tons (450 million metric tons) per year, the coal reserves of the arid part of the United States may be sufficient to last for nearly 1000 years.

On the other hand, coal has supplied a smaller and smaller proportion of the nation's energy during the past 30 years. There is some indication that the trend may be reversed in the near future if the increasing use of coal in steam-generating plants materializes, as is expected. Nationally, the fast-growing electric utility industry is now the largest single user of coal. This use by utilities is particularly important in the West, since electric power plants can be built near coal deposits.

Metallic Minerals

During the first quarter of the present century, improved technology in the milling of metal-bearing ores and development of large-scale, low-cost mining methods contributed to a rapidly expanding mineral industry in the West. There was a shift in emphasis from precious to base metals. Gold and silver became increasingly the by-products from the refining of copper, lead, and zinc ores. Recently, the accelerated growth of urban populations, as well as the greater demands by modern industries, has created markets for a widening range of nonmetallic and industrial minerals and fuels.

Exploitation of these materials may be expected to assume even greater significance. Mineral resources currently are the principal economic element in large portions of the arid regions. The products are of incalculable value in placing the United States among the few largely self-sufficient nations in terms of mineral resources, and in supplying many of the needs of the free world. In most cases, available production figures (9) record the total output of entire states that lie within the arid regions; the yield from a few sub-humid areas within some of these states accordingly is included.

If the mineral productivity of the West can be characterized by one commodity, copper unquestionably merits this distinction, for the arid United States is the major copper producer of the world. The Spaniards mined copper in the Southwest long before it became United States territory. In common with many of the other base metals, early production of copper was from numerous relatively small, high-grade deposits. Technologic developments in mining and milling since the turn of the century have permitted marked reductions in the grade of profitable copper ores (average copper content of ores mined was 1.59 percent in 1924 and 0.73 percent in 1960). The acceptability of lower-grade ores has meant a tremendous increase in available reserves.

The bulk of current and projectable production is from large, low-grade disseminated deposits that have been categorized as *por-*

phyry coppers (*10*). Production from the region in 1960 was 1,002,026 short tons (909,038 metric tons) of copper, 75 percent of which was mined by open-pit methods; total production from the earliest records through 1960 was 39,126,177 short tons (35,495,267 metric tons). Current production is largely from Arizona, Utah, Montana, Nevada, and New Mexico, with Arizona alone contributing more than one-half of the total in 1960. By-product recovery of gold, silver, and molybdenum from the milling and refining of copper ores is a highly important source of these metals. Sulfuric acid is a by-product of some copper smelters.

Lead, zinc, gold, and silver, in that order, also are important products of the arid West. Production of these and other metallic minerals is given in Table III. Rising costs in the extraction of gold have not been balanced in recent years by increases in the market price, which was fixed at $35 per troy ounce (31.1 grams) by a government order issued in 1934.

Uranium, Iron, and Manganese

Spurred by military demands, the search for uranium ores has been eminently successful in the arid regions (Fig. 4). Modern tools

Table III. Metallic mineral production, arid United States.

Metal	Annual production (tons[a], unless otherwise specified)	Year	Percentage of U.S. total
Copper	1,002,026 (Cu content)	1960	88
Lead	199,688 (Pb content)	1951–1955 avg.	55
Zinc	319,601 (Zn content)	1951–1955 avg.	55
Gold	1,496,626 troy oz[b]	1960	90
Silver	30,398,259 troy oz[b]	1960	99
Uranium	7,931,954 (ore)	1960	99
Manganese	190,057 (ore)	1959	85
Iron	5,321,000 (ore)	1960	3
Molybdenum	11,700,000 (ore)	1960	100 approx.
Vanadium	4,971 (V content)	1960	100 approx.
Tungsten	6,669 (W content)	1960	100 approx.
Mercury	1,093 (Hg content)	1960	87

[a] One ton equals 0.907 metric ton.
[b] One troy ounce equals 31.103 grams.

of mineral exploration, involving geologic, geophysical, geochemical, geobotanic, and engineering techniques, have been used more extensively and intensively than in any other area and episode in history. The results are indicated by the extension of known reserves from about 1 million tons (907,200 metric tons) of ore in 1948 to 82 million tons (74,390,400 metric tons) in 1960. There has been significant production from at least 50 mining districts in 13 of the arid states, with the greatest concentrations of activity on the Colorado Plateau in northwestern New Mexico, southwestern Colorado, south-

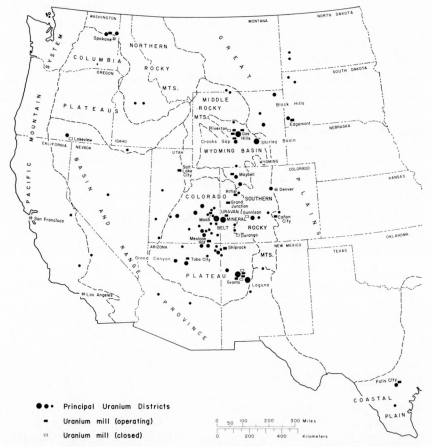

Fig. 4. The principal uranium districts are scattered through the Mountain and Pacific Coast states, although the most productive are in the Colorado Plateau area and in Wyoming. Uranium mills also are shown. (Courtesy U.S. Atomic Energy Commission)

eastern Utah, and northeastern Arizona and in the basins of central Wyoming.

The ores occur largely in sandstones of Mesozoic age and have been mined by both underground and open-pit methods. Leading producers are New Mexico, Wyoming, Colorado, and Utah. Vanadium is a by-product from uranium ores of the region, and selenium, molybdenum, and scandium are potential by-products.

Iron and manganese production has never been large. Regional production of iron ore constituted only 3 percent of the national production in 1960. Numerous known deposits are widely distributed, but their generally small size, the excessively high content of impurities, such as titanium, in some of the larger high-grade deposits, and the high costs of transportation of ore to smelters have inhibited their utilization.

Molybdenum is an increasingly important product. The Climax Mine in Colorado, one of the world's largest underground operations and the only major domestic mine operated chiefly for molybdenum in 1960, produced 11.7 million tons (10,614,240 metric tons) of ore in that year.

Vanadium production in ore and concentrates also showed a significant increase in 1960 of 34 percent over the previous year, as a result of export demands.

Clays of many types are being exploited at increasing rates to meet the growing demands, which are largely within the region but are also in other parts of the United States. The prevalence of lightweight aggregate materials of volcanic origin—pumice, perlite, and scoria—makes the arid areas an important source of these commodities. Ores of beryllium, chromium, tin, lithium minerals, mica, phosphate rock, and the rare earths are among the additional products of the region.

Helium Resources

A unique regional resource is helium, which is estimated to total about 1.6×10^{11} cubic feet (4.5×10^9 cubic meters) in reserve. More than 95 percent of this reserve is contained in four fields in Kansas, Oklahoma, and Texas. Consumption in the United States is growing at the rate of 8 to 10 percent each year. The gas is useful because of its inertness, lightness, rapid diffusion, and low temperature of liquefaction. Much of it is used by military agencies as a filler for missiles. It is pumped into liquid-oxygen tanks, where it expands and fills the space left when the oxygen is used up, thus lending strength and rigidity to the missile structure. Large amounts are used as a cooling fluid in gas-cooled nuclear reactors, as a leak detector, and as an inert shielding medium in arc welding.

Four private companies, under a program sponsored by the U.S. Department of the Interior, were constructing in 1962 five new extraction plants in Kansas and Texas, thus quadrupling the capacity of all plants in operation at that time.

Gas produced in these new plants is to be collected by pipeline and stored near Amarillo, Texas, in the government's underground area, which will contain more than 7×10^{10} cubic feet $(2 \times 10^9$ cubic meters). This is all part of the governmental program to conserve helium, large quantities of which were being wasted in the production of natural gas from helium-bearing gasfields. The Helium Act of 1925, as amended in 1961, authorizes the U.S. Department of the Interior to spend $47.5 million each year to buy and store helium for future needs. It is estimated that the planned extraction-plant capacity will meet all future needs until 1985, still leaving about 5.3×10^{10} cubic feet $(1.5 \times 10^9$ cubic meters) in storage at that time.

In November 1961, the nation's first privately owned plant was opened at Navajo, Arizona. Five other extraction facilities, all owned by the U.S. Department of the Interior, Bureau of Mines, are located in Texas, New Mexico, and Oklahoma. Research has been conducted by the Bureau of Mines, Amarillo Helium Activity, to improve the production and transportation of helium.

Aridity as a Factor

It should be noted that, with the exception of certain deposits of saline materials, the mineral resources of the western United States are not directly related in origin to the present arid environment. Rather, they stem from the complex, highly varied conditions of the geologic past. Processes of sedimentation during inundations by ancient seas and under continental conditions during periods of marine withdrawal, igneous intrusions and volcanic eruptions, with their associated mineral-bearing solutions, fracturing and folding of the crustal rocks by tectonic forces that provided channelways and traps, all these helped to form the varied and widely distributed minerals.

Aridity undoubtedly has aided man's discovery and exploitation of many of the mineral deposits by inhibiting the growth of obscuring vegetative cover and by causing deeply weathered soils. Large-scale mining by open-pit methods was thus facilitated, but, at the same time, the environment has impeded or blocked the exploitation of placers and other types of deposits that require large volumes of readily available water.

As known minerals near the earth's surface are mined out, discovery of new deposits becomes necessary. More sophisticated methods must then be devised for discovering deposits that are hidden at some depth. Some of these techniques have been developed in physics, chemistry, and biology and are termed variously *geophysical, geochemical, biogeochemical,* and *geobotanic prospecting.* Some of them are particularly applicable to use in arid regions.

Geobotanic Prospecting

Botanic methods of prospecting have proved to be more effective in the arid regions than in humid regions. This can be explained by the greater depth of root penetration that plants develop and by differences in ground-water conditions. All of these techniques depend on the capacity of the plants to absorb, and to be affected by, high concentrations of minerals. The upward migration of soluble salts in the soil is greater in some arid regions because of the greater loss of water at the earth's surface by evaporation.

Plants have been an aid to prospecting in arid regions in at least three ways. In the indicator-plant approach, researchers map the distribution of a particular species that is affected by the sought-for mineral. Or the appearance of plants growing in a mineralized area is studied for physiologic or morphologic changes that are caused by hidden concentrations; sometimes this is done by terrain analysis through aerial photography. A third method is chemical analysis to detect the differences in composition of plants that are caused by the mineral composition of soil water.

Species used as indicator-plants are those that are particularly abundant near ore deposits. Their distribution can be mapped to outline mineralized ground, without recourse to chemical analysis. The association of such plants with boron deposits has been noted by C. B. Hunt in Death Valley, California. There, desert holly of the goosefoot family (*Atriplex hymenelytra*) extensively covers soils that contain more than 1000 parts per million of boron, in which creosotebush (*Larrea*) and many other plants are unable to grow.

On the semiarid Colorado Plateau, selenium indicator-plants have been used to find uranium ores. Several species of milkvetch (*Astragalus* spp.) were effective in indicating such mineralized ground. It was noted that the plants were more useful in prospecting in the dry areas of the plateau than in the forested mountains. The distribution of California poppies (*Eschscholtzia* spp.) has been studied around copper deposits in Arizona, and this plant was shown to be associated with mineralized ground (11). It is suggested that the controlling factor in this case is not the ore itself but rather the increased acidity that is associated with the copper. The copper, in turn, increases the availability of phosphorus, which has been shown experimentally to be required by the poppy. This change would not be noticeable in a more humid area, where the distribution of poppies probably would not be affected by copper.

Various minerals in the soil affect the appearance of plants and provide a means of prospecting, as has been pointed out. Small amounts of boron in the soil, it was determined by Soviet investigators, stimulated plants to grow to 2 to 3 times their normal size; large concentrations, however, depressed growth. Thus, the increase in size of plants, a second blooming period, and the degree of stem deformity can be used in prospecting for oil. The increase in size of plants growing in bituminous soils may be accentuated in arid regions by the increased storage capacity for moisture possessed by such soils (12). Effects of radiation or uranium itself on plant growth are seen only on dumps around uranium mines or around highly oxidized deposits and have not proved to be useful.

Prospecting by plant analysis is effective where some plants develop extremely deep root systems. Of particular interest is the analysis of vegetation for molybdenum in prospecting for copper deposits. Although copper is comparatively immobile in alkaline waters, the molybdenum usually associated with copper is highly mobile and is readily taken up by vegetation. The most valuable genus for molybdenum analysis was found to be *Astragalus*. Anomalous values in the

Milkvetch (*Astragalus* spp.) has been used by geobotanic prospectors on the Colorado Plateau. The plant was found to be an effective indicator there of the presence of selenium and associated deposits of uranium.

molybdenum content of mesquite (*Prosopis* spp.) that grew over mineralized zones lying at depths of 150 feet (50 meters) have been reported in the Southwest (*13*). Plant analysis as a means of prospecting for copper deposits in filled alluvial basins shows great promise. Biogeochemistry also has been brought into the search for uranium on the Colorado Plateau; pinyon (*Pinus* spp.) and juniper (*Juniperus* spp.) were the plants most commonly used (*14*). Under arid conditions, the roots of these trees travel down fractures for long distances in their search for water. A perched water table may occur at the same level as the ore, and the plant roots penetrate the ore body itself. Roots of juniper and pinyon have been encountered in mines 90 to 180 feet (30 to 60 meters) and more beneath the surface.

All of these developments are in their infancy. Integrated research by botanists, chemists, and geologists should be encouraged, because many valuable deposits of minerals remain to be discovered under thick covers of alluvium and barren rock.

Geochemical Methods

Geochemical prospecting, a very useful tool in modern mineral exploration, has had some success in arid regions. Samples of soil, stream water, or ground water are analyzed for minute quantities of the valuable elements. The results may be plotted on a map with points of equal concentration connected by contour lines. Areas of high concentration will then be obvious and can be explored further. Or, in another type of exploration, the chemical element may be traced up a stream to the source of the metal. This is much like the time-honored method of the prospector who panned the streambed for gold and then traced the metal upstream.

Analytic methods that are sensitive to much smaller amounts of an element than the ordinary assay of an ore are required. Colorimetric tests have been found to be useful for this purpose and are sufficiently simple to be made in field laboratories. Tests are available for arsenic, antimony, beryllium, chromium, cobalt, copper, lead, mercury, molybdenum, nickel, tin, tungsten, vanadium, uranium, and zinc (15).

Copper is typical of the metals for which these methods have proved to be valuable. The porphyry-copper deposits of the arid United States are our major sources of that metal, and most of the porphyry-copper ore bodies contain copper and iron sulfides, which, upon weathering, yield acid sulfates. Where these deposits are exposed at the land surface, much of the copper may have been leached from the upper rocks and redeposited below as an enriched zone. Geologists usually examine the leached outcrops for evidence of the former presence of copper minerals. If such evidence is found, cores then are drilled to explore the enriched rock at depth. Geochemical methods have aided many such explorations in recent years. The surface rock and soil may be leached of all recognizable copper minerals and yet may contain 300 parts per million of copper, or more. More than 100 parts per million of copper in the soil is considered anomalous.

Under favorable conditions, anomalous amounts of copper can be detected many miles away from the ore deposit that is their source. Near Safford, Arizona, copper is detectable in the silt of the alluvium at the mouth of the desert wash that drains the copper-bearing San Juan quartz monzonite rock. Figure 5, a geochemi-

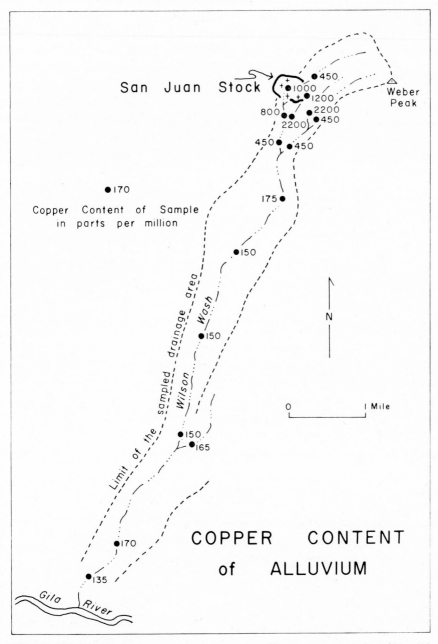

Fig. 5.   Copper content in alluvium was traced more than 7 miles (11 kilometers) down a desert wash from the San Juan porphyry rock where it originated near Safford, Arizona.

196   ARIDITY AND MAN

cal map, shows that the copper content of the alluvium becomes
lower downstream as it is progressively diluted with barren sediment,
yet it can be traced more than 7 miles (11 kilometers), far beyond
the limit of recognizable copper-ore minerals in the sediment. Since
most ore metals can be detected for long distances from their source
by such methods, it is possible to prospect large mountain ranges
for many different metal deposits simply by testing each major wash.

Sediments also may cover up and conceal a copper-bearing rock,
as was shown near Safford, Arizona (Fig. 6). A cross section of the
area indicates that, where the ore body is exposed, the soil has a
copper content of about 1500 to 2000 parts per million, readily dis-
tinguishable from the background level of 100 parts per million, or
less. However, where sediments 10 feet (3 meters) or more thick
cover the ore-bearing rock, relatively normal amounts of copper were
found in the soil. The evidence indicates that, in this case, the
copper has not yet had time to be diffused upward to the surface.

Near covered ore deposits, the ground water, particularly if it is
acidic, often will contain abnormal amounts of the elements from
the ore body. In arid regions, however, the ground water is usually
alkaline, and many metals will be precipitated from solution, rather
than be carried outward or upward through the soil. In such an environment, copper, for example, would not be diffused any great
distance from an ore body, and other elements present in the ore
body that are soluble in alkaline solutions may act as indicators of
the presence of the more valuable element. In the case of copper
deposits, molybdenum is nearly always present.

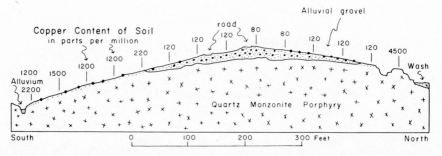

Fig. 6. A cross section shows how sediments—in this case, alluvial
gravel—can conceal an ore body. Copper content (parts per million)
of the soil is labeled in this diagram of a Safford, Arizona, study.

Molybdenum is quite soluble in ground water in arid regions and can be traced long distances. Recent studies in the Pima, Arizona, district disclose that molybdenum in abnormal concentrations can be detected in well water and in mesquite (*Prosopis* spp.), a deep-rooted plant, for more than 8 miles (13 kilometers) from concealed copper deposits (13). Copper anomalies, on the other hand, were detectable in the soil and ground water only about 3 miles (5 kilometers) from the deposit. Although geochemical methods by themselves have not led to the discovery of any important copper deposits in the arid United States, they have been helpful in finding many. As the methods of analysis and sampling are improved, and as the processes of the dispersion of ore are better understood, geochemistry should prove to be increasingly useful.

Geophysical Techniques

Geophysical methods have helped geologists to discover new petroleum deposits, particularly in interior basins. Here, sediments cover up the lower rocks, and surface work tells little about subsurface structure. In such places, the geophysicist can provide information on the architecture, if not the composition, of rocks at great depths beneath the sediments. The most successful among the geophysical techniques has been the seismic method, by which we record the time required for sonic waves to reflect from deeply buried surfaces of the bedrock. Charges of high explosives, detonated in shallow holes, usually are employed to generate sonic waves. Since a seismograph crew in the field costs from $25,000 to $40,000 per month to maintain, this work is justified only to obtain critical information in favorable areas. Other information on subsurface structure also may be provided by the measurements of gravity and magnetic force. Both gravitometers and magnetometers have been adapted for use in airplanes to make rapid surveys of an area.

One of the more interesting developments in geophysical exploration in arid regions has been the scientific "water witching" developed by Victor Vacquier (16). He introduces large voltages into the ground through two current electrodes. The potential between two other electrodes placed inside the two current electrodes is measured as it decreases after the current is shut off. The potential induced in the ground dies away slowly, its character varying with

the depth to water. Laboratory studies suggest that the effect may
be electrochemical in nature (*17*).

Processing of Ores

After an ore body is discovered, of course, it is still necessary to
extract the metal somehow. Because many of the processes for this
extraction require water, their use is somewhat limited in regions
where water is scarce. Therefore, the dry processing of minerals may
be necessary. Processes of this type require no water, although they
still use fluids to transport material and as a dispersion medium for
the separation of mineral particles.

Concentration requires breaking up of the mined ore into particles small enough to permit separation of the valuable mineral
from the surrounding waste material, or *gangue,* and water usually
is used in transporting the ore through the grinding mills. Furthermore, almost every grinding installation includes a classifier to
separate material that has been ground to finished size from over-
sized material that requires additional grinding. Classification is
always wet when the grinding is wet, but both may be performed
without water. Standard commercial equipment is sold widely for
this use. In dry grinding and classification, air replaces water as the
transporting fluid.

Separation of valuable mineral from gangue may be accomplished
by numerous methods. The flotation method is invariably wet, and
electrostatic methods are invariably dry. The other two general
methods, gravity concentration and electromagnetic separation, may
be either wet or dry, although dry gravity-separation methods are
comparatively rare.

Gravity-separation methods depend on buoyancy or inertia to
separate a mineral of one density from the gangue of a different
density. Dry gravity separation generally requires the substitution
of air for water as the lubricating fluid that permits the separating
forces to act. The buoyant force exerted by air on mineral particles,
however, is negligible; hence, the methods that use air for a separating fluid must depend largely on inertia forces. These methods,
thus, are usually ingenious modifications of the elementary principle
of winnowing, which was used by primitive people to separate kernels of grain from chaff. One such device is the "air table," which

separates the more dense from the less dense minerals by forcing a stream of air up though a slowly moving bed of mineral particles. The light minerals are separated by levitation on a moving quicksand of solid particles in air.

Electromagnetic separating devices are of two general kinds: those intended for concentrating strongly magnetic materials like magnetite and, perhaps, ilmenite from relatively nonmagnetic minerals, and those intended for separating relatively feebly magnetic materials on the basis of their paramagnetic properties. The latter separators are not useful for separating coarse ore, because of the difficulty of producing strong magnetic fields of large dimensions. The magnetic fields used are sharply convergent, and the shapes of the fields are achieved by sophisticated designs. Separation at very fine sizes is not very satisfactory, because concentrates may be impure, unless production rates are very low. Thus, close sizing of the material that is fed to dry magnetic separators is required for effective concentration.

Electrostatic concentration is the only exclusively dry method used for mineral separation. It functions by selectively establishing electric charges on mineral particles. Good conductors dissipate their charge rapidly and nonconductors very slowly. Suitable arrangements for selective grounding of the charged particles permit the charged and uncharged particles to report to different stations. As is the case with magnetic separators, very coarse and very fine particles are difficult to separate. Contrary to an opinion held by many, electrostatic concentration machines are not necessarily devices of low capacity. Recently, I. M. LeBaron and W. C. Knopf described the application of electrostatic methods to dry commercial treatment of feldspar ore and potentially to dry treatment of potash ore (18).

Perhaps one of the more interesting present-day developments is the effort of a British company to utilize low-cost tetrabromoethane for heavy-liquid separation of minerals (19). This company's recently developed method for producing this heavy liquid, specific gravity 2.9, at greatly reduced cost may permit commercial heavy-liquid separations of valuable minerals that are difficult by other methods.

Another dry method of ore concentration that was developed for processing salt deposits may become of more general interest for other minerals in areas where water is scarce. Crude salt is exposed to radiant heat, which raises the temperature of different minerals at different rates according to their thermal properties (20). The most easily heated minerals adhere to a heat-sensitive coating on a conveyor belt and are easily separated from other minerals.

Natural and induced radioactivity possibly may be used in the future to separate minerals (21). Natural radioactivity, or that induced by the bombardment of minerals with neutrons, might separate minerals, because of the kind and intensity of the radioactivity. The biggest problem appears to be a suitable inexpensive neutron source.

Dry-land placer-mining machines appear from time to time, particularly machines designed to recover gold from desert placers. The moisture content of the dust-sized mineral solids just below the desert surface has handicapped these machines, because it is difficult to free the fine gold from other fine solids unless the fines are nearly bone-dry. One company is using a 15-cubic-yard (11.5-cubic-meter) per hour portable dry-land gold dredge on the San Domingo placer mines near Wickenburg, Arizona (22).

Further processing of ores beyond the concentration stages may involve reduction of metals (smelting), roasting or calcining, expanding to achieve low-bulk density, and many other processes. Although it is possible to conduct most of these processes with little water if the economic incentive exists, water usually is used to cool refractories and critical metal parts.

Areas for profitable research in dry mineral processing are many. Perfection of the heavy-liquid method of concentration appears to be of great importance to mineral processing in arid regions. Electromagnetic and electrostatic methods of concentration suitable for use with particle sizes both larger and smaller than are now practical would be very valuable.

Wet processing of ores continues in the majority of cases, despite the attractiveness of dry-processing methods for arid regions. Usually considerable amounts of water are used even in the arid United States. Flotation methods are used in processing sulfide ores, such as the copper ores of the Southwest.

The most notable examples of systematic water conservation in the industry in the United States are found among the lead and zinc mills of southeast Missouri, which recover 80 to 90 percent of the mill water used. Copper-flotation plants and uranium-leaching mills

A dry-land gold dredge, designed for operations on arid sites, takes a cut at a placer mine near Wickenburg, Arizona, to determine the richness of the gravels. The generator mounted on the truck is the energy source. (Courtesy Hirsch Brothers Machinery Company)

in the Southwest also recover from 70 to 85 percent of the water they use. In general, the used water is collected in tailing ponds and is allowed to clarify by settling. Often the slimy portion of the effluent is discharged at the top of the pile of tailings, and the water is filtered as it seeps through the pile. Evaporation losses from storage ponds in arid regions may exceed 100 inches (2500 millimeters) per year. Such losses may be decreased by spraying a material such as dodecyl alcohol on the surface to form a monomolecular film, which acts as a vapor barrier.

Nuclear Energy

As demands for energy continue to rise, the reserves of fossil fuels will eventually disappear, or their use will have to be limited largely to production of chemicals or steel, for example. It is not yet certain that nuclear energy will be able to take over the energy demands of man. If present estimates of the reserves of nuclear energy prove to be realizable, however, man's energy demands can be satisfied for a long time to come.

It is difficult to estimate the potential for production in a field so newly developed, and there is little point in differentiating the arid lands from the rest of the United States in estimating the energy potential in such an uncertain field. Almost the entire present uranium-mining industry, however, is located in the arid United States.

If consumption of energy in the United States increases at the expected rate, the reserves of fossil fuels may be exhausted in a century or two. In addition, the nation may wish to reserve some of its fossil fuels for special uses, such as the production of chemicals from petroleum and the use of coke for steelmaking. However, according to estimates made by the U.S. Atomic Energy Commission, the reserves of nuclear fuel appear to be enough for an indefinite, but almost unlimited, future, if the reserves can be fully utilized.

Recent studies have led to the conclusion that large water-cooled nuclear power plants can now be built to generate electric energy initially at a cost competitive with conventional fuel plants in the highest-cost areas of the country. Six prototype civilian nuclear power plants, built with government assistance and in operation since 1962, have a combined capacity of about 850,000 kilowatts, or about 0.5 percent of the total installed United States capacity. Ten other plants under construction will increase the combined capacity by about one-half. All of these have been designed primarily to develop technical information and operating experience. Nuclear power plants become economically more competitive as the size of the plant increases, and the growing trend to very large installations thus favors nuclear energy.

Solar Energy

The availability of more than 1 kilowatt of energy per square meter from sunlight at the earth's surface has, for many years, encouraged efforts to replace energy from muscles or fuels with this seemingly free source. Extensive research has included space heating, water heating, refrigeration, water distillation, irrigation pumping, cooking, high-temperature research, power for space vehicles, and large-scale production of power by heat engines, thermoelectricity, photoelectricity, and photochemical reactions.

Yet, the only applications of economic importance thus far are the powering of space vehicles and the provision of low-cost heat for

A solar-energy multiple-effect humidification plant, shown here, was tested by the University of Arizona. A plane-surface evaporator is at the left, and asphalt and plastic collectors are at the right. A larger experimental desalinization plant has been set up by the university on the Mexican coast. (Courtesy University of Arizona)

houses and swimming pools. It should be pointed out, though, that unless a great amount of nuclear energy from breeder reactors or controlled fusion becomes economically available in the next century, it will be necessary to rely increasingly on the sun as a substitute for, or adjunct to, energy from fossil fuels.

Research on solar-heated houses began in 1939 at the Godfrey L. Cabot solar-energy-conversion research project at the Massachusetts Institute of Technology. The results were summarized by Maria Telkes in 1949 (23). The Telkes house stored solar energy in the form of the heat of fusion of glauber salt. A recent solar house incorporating earlier developmental work is that of Harry E. Thomason (24).

The solar-heating system built by George O. G. Löf in his own home in Colorado is of interest because of its location in the West at about 5000 feet (1600 meters) above sea level. A bed of gravel proved to be an effective and economical collector for the storage of heat, functioning both as a heat exchanger and as a storage medium

(25). Research also is being conducted at the Solar Energy Laboratory of the University of Arizona (26). According to most reports, the annual cost of solar heating is only slightly greater than the interest on the initial investment and is comparable to the cost of conventional heating.

The solar water heater is the first well-established commercial use of solar collectors. It was estimated in 1951 that there were 50,000 units in use in the Miami, Florida, area alone. H. C. Hottel, of the Massachusetts Institute of Technology, has estimated that the cost of a solar water-heating system in Florida would be repaid in cost of fuel saved in 4 to 8 years, depending on the other energy source (27).

Refrigeration and cooling by solar energy are especially interesting, since sunshine is the most abundant in areas where the need for cooling is the greatest. Absorption refrigeration permits direct use of the sun's heat without prior conversion to mechanical energy. A large solar-absorption refrigerator has been constructed at the University of Arizona, in which lithium bromide is used as the refrigerant and a 10-ton (9000-kilogram) steel-plate collector is used to absorb solar heat. A summary of solar cooling by Gerald T. Ward, of McGill University, reports that solar refrigerators can now be manufactured to sell for $25 (28).

In arid lands, there often is a considerable supply of saline water, from either the ground or the sea, and for many years attempts have been made to obtain fresh water in these regions by solar distillation. Since the thermodynamic efficiency of the purification of sea water by simple distillation is approximately 0.1 percent, it is tempting to explore multiple-effect systems. Work on such a system is being done by Carl N. Hodges at the University of Arizona. After completion of feasibility tests in Tucson, the university set up in July 1963 a multiple-effect humidification plant to desalinize sea water experimentally at Puerto Penasco, Sonora, Mexico.

Cost Factor

There remains the possibility of simple distillation without moving parts of concentrators, and many types of apparatus have been designed for this purpose. The Office of Saline Water of the U.S. Department of the Interior in 1952 set a cost goal of 40 cents per

1000 gallons (4000 liters) for municipal water, and therefore the capitalization of a solar still at 5-percent interest should not exceed $3 per square yard (1.2 square meters). Such a low construction cost seems unattainable at present.

There also have been serious efforts to use solar energy to pump irrigation water in arid lands. The two largest solar-energy power plants ever built, the Shuman-Boys 100-horsepower plant in Meadi, Egypt, and the Willsie-Boyle 20-horsepower plant in Needles, California, were used for this purpose. Both were abandoned after a few years of operation, in the early part of this century, because they were several times more expensive than conventional steam power plants. The real economic limitation, however, appears to lie in the cost of the collector.

The obvious wastefulness of cooking with wood fires in underdeveloped parts of the world has inspired a number of solar cookers and ovens. Parabolic reflectors of area up to 1 square yard (1.2 square meters) are commonly used to furnish about 0.5 kilowatt of energy. Maria Telkes has reviewed several designs (29). The most serious objection to solar cooking is that it can be done only out of doors while the sun is shining.

Although a fantastic variety of methods have been proposed for the large-scale economic utilization of solar energy, all founder on the rocks of capital outlay. In order to compete with conventional electric power, it is necessary to limit expenditures to less than $20 per square yard (1.2 square meters) of collector surface, exclusive of maintenance or provision for the storage of energy. Almost the only hope of attaining this figure awaits the development of thin-film photovoltaic materials (chemical substances that convert light energy directly into electric energy) that are capable of operating without attention for several years. The present solar cells cost approximately $100 per watt, and there is little hope of lowering the cost unless polycrystalline semiconductors can be developed.

Water Power

It can be estimated that perhaps one-third of the solar energy that falls on the earth's surface is converted into potential energy by evaporation of water from the surface into the atmosphere. We can calculate, then, from the solar constant that enough solar energy is converted into the potential energy of water in the atmosphere to lift 2.2×10^{12} tons (2×10^{12} metric tons) of water each day from the earth's surface. If this entire amount returned to earth as precipitation, it would equal about 57 inches (1440 millimeters) of rainfall.

Runoff from the rivers of the arid United States is erratic, as can be seen in Fig. 7. Over most of the arid West, hydroelectric power plays only a supporting role as a supplier of energy. As incoming population shrinks the empty spaces between them, more and more of the western waterways are being put to work. The hydroelectric energy generated in the 17 western states in 1959 was about 40 percent of the total electric energy generated. By states, the percentage varied from less than 1 percent in Kansas to about 95 percent in Idaho, Montana, Oregon, and Washington.

As of 1959, the estimated underdeveloped water power was about 64 million kilowatts, or approximately 3.5 times the hydroelectric power being produced in the area. Between 1959 and 1962, more of the water power has been developed, and both public and private agencies currently are developing still more. The extent to

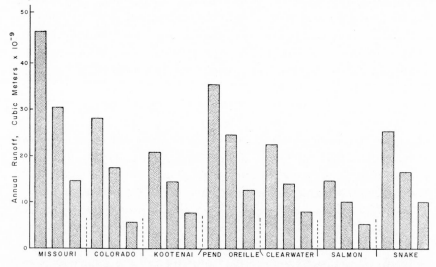

Fig. 7. Rivers flow erratically in arid lands. Shown here in cubic meters times 10^9 (1 cubic meter equals 35.31 cubic feet) is the variation in annual runoff—the maximum, average, and minimum on record—for seven streams in the western United States.

Table IV.   Comparison of annual energy potential produced in various forms, arid United States, 1959–1960.

Item	Annual production (10^{12} kw hr)	Percentage of total
Hydroelectric power plants	0.085	1.5
Bituminous coal produced	0.12	2.1
Petroleum produced	3.1	54.3
Natural gas produced	2.4	42.1
Total	5.7	100.0

which this will continue depends on practical considerations. Need, cost, and other functions to be served by multipurpose projects, including water storage for irrigation and recreation, must be weighed.

Hydroelectric energy is compared in Table IV with other forms of energy generated in the 17 states, suggesting that the former, even if fully developed, is unlikely to provide more than a minor part of the energy needed. But water power, like solar energy, is available for use indefinitely. Although the water-power potential of the arid United States has been developed to the extent of about one-fourth of the estimated maximum available, the potential of most of the rest of the world, except Europe, is relatively underdeveloped.

In 1959, the ownership of all power plants in the West was about as follows, in terms of capacity: private utility companies, 55 percent; municipal, 11 percent; national, 20 percent; other publicly owned plants, 6 percent; industrial, 8 percent. Where both hydroelectric and fuel plants are feeding energy into the same system, a recent tendency has been to use the fuel plants for the base load and hydroelectric power plants only for peak loads.

In the Pacific Northwest, where the runoff of the Columbia River basin averages nearly 10 times that of any other river in the arid United States, and fossil fuels have not been found to any extent, hydroelectric energy constitutes a major part of the present energy resources. There, the average plant-load factors are about 60 percent for hydroelectric power plants.

Federal development of power usually has been planned as part of multiple-purpose projects, which involve the regulation of stream-flow for flood control, irrigation, navigation, and recreation (see

Fig. 8). In planning hydroelectric developments in the arid West, for example, adequate allowances must be made for the depletion effects of irrigation on streamflow.

Wind Energy

The very feeling of the arid West emerges in a traditional cowboy song about the land "where the wind blows free." The energy of the wind always has been irritatingly obvious to settlers, and it is not surprising that they became interested in harnessing some of its energy. A traveler through the West still sees many a windmill pumping water into storage tanks, principally for use by cattle.

Large windmills had been operating in Europe and particularly in the Netherlands, of course, for at least 700 years before the first steel-vane windmills appeared in the United States at the end of the 19th century. The latter proved to be so adaptable to needs in rural areas before the advent of rural electrification that their use spread rapidly.

A few decades later, wind-driven fractional-kilowatt electric generators connected to storage batteries came into common use; many are still operating. But gasoline engines and rural electrification have largely displaced wind-driven machinery in the United States, and during recent years there has been very little research on wind power. The research that has been done has only emphasized the uneconomical character of wind engines in this country (30, 31). It remains possible, nonetheless, that wind power may still be practical in some sparsely settled arid lands.

Estimates of the world's wind energy are highly speculative, but it appears that the earth's atmosphere may develop something of the order of 10^{16} kilowatt hours of kinetic energy per year. Only a small part of this, possibly a few ten-thousandths, could be retrieved, because generators can be located only in the lowest layers of the atmosphere. Considering that the arid regions of the United States have an area equal to about 1 percent of the earth's surface, we may reasonably estimate that 1 percent of the total wind energy is available to this country. This gives a figure of about 10^{10} kilowatt hours of wind energy possibly retrievable in the region, or only about 0.05 percent of the total energy of all kinds produced in the area.

Another factor is the impracticality of building a machine of the great structural strength that would be necessary to make full use of winds of high speed, which occur only infrequently at best. A rather extensive survey of microclimatic conditions was made near

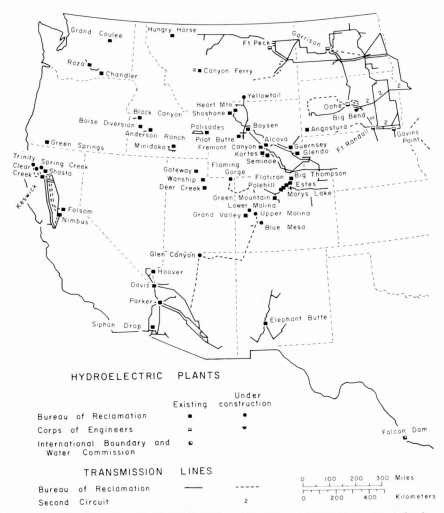

Fig. 8.   Major federal hydroelectric projects, reading from the left, include California's Central Valley project, the Columbia, Great Basin, and Colorado River developments, the Fryingpan-Arkansas in Colorado, and the Missouri River project.   (Courtesy U.S. Bureau of Reclamation)

Rutland, Vermont, in preparation for the large Smith-Putnam wind-driven electric generator that was erected there in 1941. It was found that a difference of 300 feet (100 meters) or so in location might alter average wind speed considerably and annual power output by as much as twofold. After its technical feasibility had been demonstrated, this generator was abandoned 5 years later; its economic value was questionable compared with a conventional generator of comparable output (1250 kilowatts).

As a source of intermittent power, windmills are highly satisfactory. There is little doubt that they will continue to be used for pumping water for many years. But where electric energy can be supplied from hydroelectric or fuel-operated electric power plants, wind-generated energy is rarely competitive in cost or convenience.

Geothermal Energy

All the areas throughout the world where natural steam and heat are being investigated and developed are located in regions of Cenozoic volcanism. It appears, therefore, that the source of such heat is hot, magmatic material intruded from the interior of the earth into the crust. The heat energy is then carried nearer to the surface by thermal fluids, such as ground water, which permeate the crust principally along steeply dipping faults. Both the Geysers and the Salton Sea thermal areas in California are associated with structural depressions in the earth's surface that are commonly connected with Tertiary and Quarternary volcanism.

The California and Nevada deserts, where neither fossil fuels nor hydroelectric energy are readily available, present the most favorable conditions in the United States for geothermal power. Power generated from natural steam has several economic advantages. There is, of course, no fuel cost in comparison with the more conventional steam-generating plants, and the capital investment needed to develop a natural steam field is, in most cases, smaller than that needed to construct either hydroelectric or fuel-operated steam-generating facilities of the same capacity.

As early as 1904, the potential of geothermal energy was recognized in Italy. The first steam well was drilled in 1904 in Larderello, Tuscany, in a field that, in 1961, would have a productive capacity in excess of 300,000 kilowatts (*32*). Development in the United States has come more slowly. Between 1958 and 1962, approximately 20 thermal areas were drilled, most of them in California and Nevada. Of these 20 areas, the Geysers, located in Sonoma County, California, is the only one operating; it is producing electric energy at a capacity of 12,500 kilowatts. In April 1962, construction began on a second generating unit that will double the capacity of the plant. Five other thermal areas in the West show considerable promise and have had some development: Casa Diablo hot springs and the Salton Sea thermal area in California and the Beowawe, Brady, and Steamboat hot springs areas in Nevada.

In fields that produce saturated steam, temperature and pressure can be expected to increase with depth. Where the conducting fissures intersect permeable strata, the thermal fluid spreads laterally into the permeable rocks. Because the area over which the fluid migrates in the permeable rocks is so much larger than the cross section of the fissure, the hot fluid in the permeable beds is easier to locate, but it probably exists at lower temperature and pressure than the fluid in the original fissure.

Investigation is needed on how to evaluate steam reserves in thermal areas. If data are collected at the same rate with which they have been gathered during the past 10 years, there will soon be a firm basis on which to assess the future economic importance of geothermal energy. At present, energy generated from the existing geothermal facilities is less than 0.5 percent of the total hydroelectric energy generated in the arid United States each year.

REFERENCES

1. H. Brown, *Challenge of Man's Future* (Secker and Warburg, London, 1954).
2. E. Ayres and C. A. Scarlott, *Energy Sources, the Wealth of the World* (McGraw-Hill, New York, 1952).
3. M. Clawson and B. Held, *The Federal Lands* (Johns Hopkins Press, Baltimore, Md., 1957).
4. H. J. Smith, "Potash in the Permian basin," *J. Ind. Eng. Chem.* **30**, 854 (1938).
5. R. H. Weber and F. E. Kottlowski, "Gypsum resources of New Mexico," *New Mexico Bur. Mines and Mineral Resources Bull. 68* (1959).

6. F. W. Clarke, "The data of geochemistry," *U.S. Geol. Surv. Bull.* *770* (1924).

7. W. G. Pierce and E. J. Rich, "Saline reserves," *U.S. Geol. Surv. Bull.* *1148* (1962).

8. P. Averitt, "Coal reserves in the U.S.," *U.S. Geol. Surv. Bull. 1136* (1961).

9. U.S. Bureau of Mines, *Minerals Yearbook, 1960* (U.S. Govt. Printing Office, Washington, 1961), vol. 1.

10. A. B. Parsons, *The Porphyry Coppers in 1956* (Am. Inst. of Mining, Metallurgical, and Petroleum Engineers, New York, 1957).

11. T. S. Lovering, L. C. Huff, and H. Almond, "Geobotanical prospecting for copper," *Econ. Geol.* **45**, 493–514 (1950).

12. E. A. Vostokova, D. D. Vyshivkin, S. M. Kasianova, N. G. Nesvetaylova, and A. M. Shvyrayeva, "Plant growth in arid regions," *Aerogeol. Tresta Trudy* **1**, 99–118 (1955).

13. L. C. Huff and A. P. Marranzino, "Geochemical prospecting for copper," *U.S. Geol. Surv. Profess. Paper 424-B* (1961), pp. B308–310.

14. H. L. Cannon, "Geobotanical prospecting," *U.S. Geol. Surv. Bull. 1030-M* (1957), pp. 399–516.

15. F. N. Ward, H. W. Lakin, and F. C. Canney, "Useful tests for geochemical prospecting," *U.S. Geol. Surv. Bull.* (in press).

16. V. Vacquier, C. R. Holmes, P. R. Kintzinger, and M. LaVergne, "Geophysical exploration for ground water by induced polarization," *Geophysics* **22**, 660–687 (1957).

17. J. A. Schufle, "Ion exchange and induced polarization," *Geophysics* **24**, 164–166 (1959).

18. I. M. LeBaron and W. C. Knopf, "Application of electrostatics to feldspar beneficiation," *Trans. Am. Inst. Mining, Met., Petrol. Engrs.* **211**, 1087 (1958).

19. Baker-Perkins, Ltd., "Heavy media separations," *TBE Bull.* (1960–1962), Nos. 1–10.

20. A. L. Wisner, "Differential adhesion for mineral separations," *Mining World* **23**, 46 (25 Apr. 1961).

21. A. M. Gaudin, F. E. Senffle, and W. L. Greyberger, "Mineral separations using radioactivity," *Eng. Mining J.* **153**, 95 (Nov. 1952).

22. "Portable dry land gold dredge," *Mining World* **23**, 45 (Jan. 1961).

23. M. Telkes, "A review of solar house heating," *Heating and Ventilating* **49**, 68–74 (1949).

24. H. E. Thomason, "The solar house," *Solar Energy* **4**, 11 (1960).

25. G. O. G. Löf, "Solar house heating," *Proc. World Symp. Appl. Solar Energy, Phoenix, Ariz., 1955* (1956).

26. R. W. Bliss, Jr., "Solar energy for house heating," *U.N. Conf. New Sources of Energy, Rome, Italy, 1961*.

27. H. C. Hottel, "Residential uses of solar energy," *Proc. World Symp. Appl. Solar Energy, Phoenix, Ariz., 1955* (1956).

28. G. T. Ward, "Utilization of solar energy," *Food Agr. Organ., U.N., Agr. Eng. Branch Bull. 16* (1961), pp. 51–57.
29. M. Telkes, "Solar cookers," *Solar Energy* **3**, 1 (1959).
30. P. C. Putnam, *Power from the Wind* (Van Nostrand, Princeton, N.J., 1948).
31. UNESCO, "Wind and solar energy," *Proc. New Delhi Symp.* (1956).
32. R. Burgassi, "Geothermal Energy," *U.N. Conf. New Sources of Energy, Rome Italy, 1961.*

8

Soils of the Arid West

Harold E. Dregne

Recognition that the soils of the arid regions must be managed differently from those of the humid regions came slowly and at great personal cost to the first settlers. Early attempts to cultivate land in the western United States utilized knowledge gained from farming in the humid East, since the pattern of migration was from east to west. Wholesale transfer of successful eastern practices often led to crop failures and soil destruction, particularly where dry farming was attempted. Wind erosion, soil salinity, and waterlogging, although not restricted to arid areas, have become major problems there and demand special attention. The destructive character of water erosion is accentuated where vegetative cover is sparse and rains are brief but torrential.

Pioneers in soils research in the West, such as E. W. Hilgard, in California, and J. A. Widtsoe, in Utah, realized that a departure from former practices was necessary if a successful agriculture was to be developed. Soils formed under an arid climate are typically alkaline and calcareous and, because of the absence of leaching, frequently are inherently fertile, even though low in organic matter. They lack water, so the conservation and judicious use of the available water supply becomes of paramount importance for rangelands, dry farming, or irrigation.

In their 1934 report of the soils along the 52°-Fahrenheit (11°-Celsius) isotherm across the Great Plains from Colorado to Missouri, Hans Jenny and C. D. Leonard (1) noted several of the differences that occur as precipitation decreases. They collected surface samples of virgin and cultivated fields that represented upland soils developed from wind-laid (loessal) deposits. They found that, with decreasing average annual precipitation, nitrogen, organic carbon (an index of organic matter), clay, and the depth to lime layers decrease regularly, but soil pH (alkalinity) increases. Later studies showed that the same relationships extend into the Desert great soil groups.

Coarse-textured sandy, gravelly, and stony soils dominate the upland areas in the arid regions because the soil formed so slowly. Fine-textured silts and clays are typically confined to river valleys and to closed drainage basins where runoff accumulates from higher areas. Although sandy soils introduce problems of wind erosion, their widespread occurrence in potential dry-farming areas is fortunate. John Wesley Powell, in his 1878 report on the arid lands, commented that in the Bear River Valley of northern Utah, as well as in all other localities where dry farming was successful, the soil was sandy, and this appeared to be an essential condition. For a man reared in the humid East, where sandy soils are frequently the poorest, this was a particularly astute observation. Subsequent studies have shown that the water relationships of sandy soils are the key to their superiority in the more arid sections of the dry-farming region, as well as on rangelands.

Early Dry Farming

Experiments with dry farming were started in Colorado in the 1890's but were interrupted soon afterward. The Utah Agricultural Experiment Station initiated research in 1901 in the dry-farming area of northern Utah. From these studies, Widtsoe laid the framework within which much of that peculiarly arid type of agriculture has been developed. His classic book, *Dry Farming* (2), points out that droughts and near-droughts are recurring phenomenons for which plans must be made. Among his recommendations was "always farm as if a year of drouth were coming."

In the selection of dry-farming sites, he underlined the need for choosing deep, uniform soils and avoiding those that have gravel or hardpan layers near the surface. Unless the soil was deep and fairly uniform, root growth would be restricted, and the soil could not hold the amount of moisture needed to carry a crop over between rains. Other points that Widtsoe emphasized included deeper-than-usual cultivation to open up the soil; fallowing every 1 to 4 years (depending on the amount of annual precipitation) ; removal of all weeds during the fallow period; cultivation after every rain to produce a mulch and thereby reduce evaporation losses; the saving of all crop residues; seeding only by drilling; planting deeply and at about one-half the rate used in the humid regions; and the choosing of adapted varieties of crops. He noted the need for good machinery for the special tillage necessary to conserve moisture.

A noteworthy contribution at this period was Widtsoe's conviction that dry farming could be successful if there was an understanding of the principles that governed soil-plant relationships in arid regions.

Hilgard, who went to California in 1875, directed much of his attention to finding solutions to the perpetual problem of soil salinity in irrigation agriculture. He learned, on his arrival at Berkeley, that salt accumulations had rendered unproductive many thousands of acres (hectares) of irrigated land near Tulare. Using chemical analyses and extensive field observations of soil conditions and plant growth, Hilgard proposed that reclamation of white alkali soils could be accomplished by washing the salts out of the soil. For sodium, or sodic, soils, he concluded that neutralization of the sodium carbonate with gypsum (hydrated calcium sulfate) was essential, after which the soils would be leached—for example, with white alkali.

Leaching still is the only practical way to reclaim saline soils, and application of gypsum is the most common technique used to reclaim sodium soils. Later, soil chemists proved that the adsorption of sodium on soil particles is the principal cause of the trouble associated with black alkali soils.

Hilgard emphasized that, with either kind of alkali, good soil drainage was necessary. Since poor drainage usually caused the trouble in the first place, reclamation was impossible without adequate drainage. This dictum is as good today as it was then.

During the late 19th century and early 20th century, agricultural research in the West experienced a considerable expansion. Almost all of the state agricultural experiment stations began investigations of salinity, waterlogging, fertility, water movement in soils, and erosion control in arid lands.

Soil Surveys

Recognition of the importance of soil-profile characteristics and soil constituents in determining where the good land lay, and what problems might be expected when their use was intensified, led to a soil-survey program by the U.S. Department of Agriculture. In 1899, the first three soil surveys conducted in the United States were made, and two of them were in the irrigated West, in New Mexico and Utah. Although admittedly crude, they were well received and marked the first step in the comprehensive soil-survey program that is in operation today.

The concept that climate determines soil characteristics was developed originally, or concurrently, in the semiarid regions of Russia by Dokuchaev and in the United States by Hilgard. Two conditions not found in humid regions contributed to this idea. One of these was the presence of extensive grassland plains (the Great Plains in the United States), where soil, climate, and vegetation varied in a gradual manner from the wet to the dry end. The other was the occurrence in the high mountains of arid regions of gradual transitions from Desert-type soils and vegetation at the base to Alpine-type soils and vegetation at the top (vertical zonation). C. F. Marbut, of the U.S. Department of Agriculture, introduced the climate concept into the soil-survey program in the 1920's.

Soil surveys in the arid regions, conducted cooperatively by the Department of Agriculture and the state agricultural experiment stations, were concentrated in the irrigated areas, although some were made in the dry-farming sections, particularly in the western Great Plains. During the years, the scale of mapping gradually increased until now it is not unusual to employ scales as large as 16 inches to 1 mile (25.2 centimeters to 1 kilometer), which is 256 times larger than the early maps. Even this scale sometimes is inadequate to show significant differences in stratified soils of alluvial valleys.

Extension of such surveys to dry-farming lands and rangelands became practical with the advent of aerial photography. The laborious, time-consuming system of planetabling to construct base maps in areas where roads were scarce, and where farms and ranches were measured in square miles instead of acres, would not have permitted the soils to be mapped in the foreseeable future.

With the establishment in 1935 of the Soil Conservation Service within the Department of Agriculture, soil surveys were given new impetus, since the basic premise of the Soil Conservation Service is "to use each soil according to its capability and to treat it according to its needs."

Research on fertility developed rather slowly in the arid regions, partly because the inherent fertility of the soils was generally high and crop yields were good when water was adequate. Another reason was that salinity, waterlogging, and wind erosion were more acute problems. Early work demonstrated the benefit of nitrogen after land had been cropped for a few years; rotations that included legumes were recommended to maintain fertility. In time, the benefit of phosphorus to legumes grown under irrigation was recognized, too, and commercial nitrogen and phosphorus fertilizers came into use.

Soils research in the arid regions today increasingly stresses the fundamental physics, chemistry, and biology of soils and the soil-plant-water relationships. Finding what often are only temporary solutions to immediate problems is frequently necessary, but real progress depends on learning why soils behave as they do. That considerable success has been achieved is attested by the bountiful crops raised in the dry-farming and irrigated areas of the West. There is no doubt, however, that the full potential has not been achieved, and much remains to be done.

Water Relationships

Efficient use of water is vital in the arid regions, both to conserve the limited supply and to avoid waterlogging. Ideally, the amount of water in the soil and its availability to plants should be measured continuously. No single device has been developed that will do this. Instead, calibration curves that relate amount to availability are constructed for individual soils. Once such curves are made, either condition can be calculated from the other.

L. A. Richards and Willard Gardner (3), in Utah, invented the tensiometer to measure the availability to plants of soil water, and George A. Bouyoucos and A. H. Mick (4), in Michigan, devised the gypsum block to determine the amount of water present in the soil. Either device can be placed in the soil and left there and then can be read at any time; it is not necessary to remove a soil sample for laboratory testing.

Commercial development of these devices has enabled farmers to use them in scheduling irrigation. Most of the evidence indicates that, under arid climatic conditions, soil moisture in the root zone must be maintained at a high level, usually at suctions of less than 1 atmosphere, for maximum growth of plants.

The neutron-scattering method (5) is another nondestructive way to record changes continuously in the amount of moisture, although the high cost of equipment has restricted its use to research.

Determination of the availability of water to plants can be complicated by appreciable quantities of soluble salts in the soil (6). Osmotic-pressure effects from the soluble salts must be added to the suction effects that soil particles exert on water. A soil having a moisture suction of 1 atmosphere and an osmotic pressure in the soil solution of 1 atmosphere would exert a 2-atmosphere pull, which the plant would have to overcome in order to take up water. The combined effect sometimes is called *soil-moisture stress* or *total suction*. A psychrometric technique conceived by L. A. Richards and Gen Ogata (7), at the U.S. Salinity Laboratory at Riverside, California, for determining water-vapor pressure holds promise as a means of simultaneously measuring soil-moisture suction and osmotic-pressure effects on moisture availability. The technique should be valuable for plant-moisture studies as well as soil studies.

Because most of the water in sandy soils is held at lower suctions, it is more easily removed by plants than is the water in clay soils. This property of sandy soils is important in semiarid dry-farming areas as well as in rangelands. Rapid absorption and easy release of the limited rainfall by sandy soils contrasts with the slow absorption and release of water by clay soils. Under irrigation, where water application can be controlled, the greater water-holding capacity of fine-textured soils is of more significance than ease of absorption or release. Under dry-farming and range conditions, the reverse generally is true.

Water moves from a wet to a dry soil more slowly than it moves into a moist soil. In uniform soils, movement into a dry soil occurs as a sharply defined front, unless the soil is very coarse-textured (8). Among the more interesting results from studies of water movement in the stratified soils that commonly occur in recent alluvium is the finding that coarse-textured layers obstruct water penetration (9), as is shown in Fig. 1. At first glance, it would appear that a sandy layer beneath a clay layer should permit ready downward movement of water. Instead, water accumulates above the sand until there is enough to fill the sand pores. This phenomenon seems to stop root penetration where there is a sharp boundary between a fine-textured layer and an underlying coarse-textured layer. Illustrated in Fig. 2 is the termination of growth of a cotton taproot when it reaches a sand layer. This may also account for some of the hard, iron oxide layers just above gravel layers in humid areas, as well as for hardened lime accumulations in similar soils in the arid regions. If the transition from fine to coarse soil is gradual, water movement does not stop.

An electric analog that simulates conditions in wet soils was designed by James N. Luthin (10) in California in 1952 to facilitate drainage studies. His approach also has been applied to studies of seepage from canals and of ground-water movement in aquifers. It

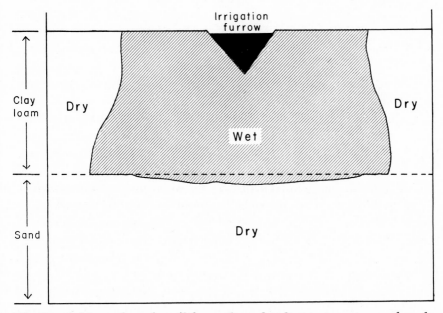

Fig. 1.   A layer of sandy soil beneath a clay layer presents an obstacle to the penetration of water from an irrigation furrow. Water accumulates above until there is enough to fill the sand pores.

permits a large number of soil and moisture factors to be varied under controlled conditions in the laboratory.

Salinity

Excessive soluble salts in the soil and high percentages of adsorbed (exchangeable) sodium are of prime concern. Leadership in solving these problems has been taken by the U.S. Salinity Laboratory at Riverside, California, a federal agency, in cooperation with state agricultural experiment stations. Although reliable figures are elusive, as much as 25 percent of the irrigated land in the West may be adversely affected by salt.

In places, such as Hudspeth County in extreme southwestern Texas, where surface waters are high in salts because of drainage from soils farther up the Rio Grande, practically all the soils are saline. Coupled with salty well waters, this makes for a hazardous irrigation agriculture. Millions of acres (hectares) of nonirrigated land in the West are similarly affected.

Since the days of Hilgard, much reclamation work has been done on salt-affected soils. Where salt is excessive, leaching is required to remove it. Where there is adsorbed sodium on the soil particles, with or without excess salt in the soil solution, leaching plus removal of the adsorbed sodium is vital. Leaching with good-quality water, adequate drainage, well-leveled land, the growing of adapted crops, and good soil management are essential for successful reclamation. In addition, some material that will supply calcium directly or indirectly to replace adsorbed sodium usually is necessary for reclamation of sodium soils.

An experiment conducted by Louis C. Boawn and others (9) on saline-sodium, fine, sandy loam soil in the Yakima Valley of Washington illustrates such methods. The soil was unusually high in adsorbed sodium, soluble salts, and pH. Leaching reduced the salt concentrations, but gypsum was needed to remove adsorbed sodium, the effects of which constituted the major limitation to the growth of sugar beets. Beet yields were negligible with leaching alone but showed a large increase with leaching plus gypsum.

When reduced soil permeability is an advantage, in irrigation canals or ponds, for instance, the reverse of the principles of reclamation of sodium soils can be employed. An example was the development of a pond on Treasure Island, near San Francisco, for the World's Fair there in the 1930's. To reduce water losses from the pond, a clay lining was spread over the bottom and sides and the pond was filled with sea water, which produced a saline-sodium clay. When the salts were washed out with fresh water, soil permeability decreased markedly and water losses dropped to one-tenth of what they had been previously. Similar techniques may someday become

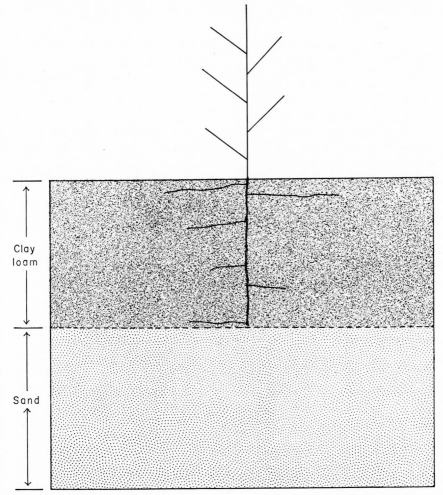

Fig. 2. The growth of a cotton taproot terminates when it reaches a sharp boundary between fine-textured soil and an underlying coarse-textured layer.

feasible for increasing runoff from watersheds in arid regions, if erosion losses can be minimized.

Where elimination of excess salt and adsorbed sodium is impossible because the irrigation water is of poor quality, or complete reclamation is uneconomic, some way to minimize their effect must be devised. For sodium soils, little progress has been made; but for saline soils, several methods have been found to reduce their severity. Among them are choosing salt-tolerant crops; planting on the side of the row instead of on the top where salts accumulate; planting in the bottom of the irrigation furrow where the salt concentration will be the lowest; irrigating more frequently than usual in order to keep the salts diluted; stopping irrigation when salt levels in the water are high, which usually occurs at the time of low streamflow; and using border irrigation, rather than furrow irrigation, to keep salts moving downward over the entire field.

These may be extreme, but they have meant the difference between success and failure in some places in Arizona, California, New Mexico, and Texas. Other measures, including the careful use of fertilizers to increase plant vigor, offer further hope. When the known difference in salt tolerance among varieties of the same crop can be put to use in plant breeding, a long step forward will have been made.

The history of salinity in western irrigated areas frequently follows a pattern. When irrigation is begun, salts usually are not a problem; little thought is given to drainage. Later, salinity increases with inadequate drainage or the use of salty water. A drainage system is installed and provision is made for periodic leaching. After salinity levels have been reduced on all but the most intractable soils, they may vary from year to year but generally remain within manageable limits as long as regular leaching is accomplished. During drought years, when water supplies are insufficient for leaching, salt levels continue to rise until water supplies improve enough to permit renewed leaching.

Water Quality for Irrigation

If he is to cope with them, a farmer must have some knowledge of the salts in irrigation water. Total salinity, relative proportions of sodium to calcium and magnesium, amount of carbonates and bicarbonates in relation to calcium and magnesium, and concentration of boron are the characteristics most commonly needed to evaluate the quality of water.

Numerous criterions have been established by various specialists for evaluating the potential salinity or sodium hazard of irrigation water. Most people would agree that water containing less than 200 parts per million of salt, or less than 50 percent sodium of the cations, is safe for use under nearly all conditions. Similarly, a water having more than 2000 parts per million of salt or more than 90 percent sodium usually would be expected to lead to trouble, sooner or later. Disagreement arises in the evaluation of waters that have intermediate salt and sodium levels. In this case, the suitability of water for continued irrigation depends on soil permeability, amount of water applied, gypsum content of the soil, tolerance of plants to high salinity or adsorbed sodium, and the kind of salts. A salt-tolerant crop like barley may give satisfactory yields when the water contains as much as 3000 parts per million of salt, if the soil is freely permeable, if large amounts of water are applied, and if the soil is leached periodically. On the other hand, the same crop probably would be a failure on an impermeable soil, even though the water had only 1000 parts per million of salt. The controlling factor is the quantity of salt in the soil rather than that in the water. Likewise, it is the sodium adsorbed on the soil particles, rather than the relative amount of sodium in the irrigation water, that is important.

Among the attempts that have been made to increase the reliability of prediction of the sodium hazard is the sodium-adsorption-ratio prepared by the U.S. Salinity Laboratory (6) and the concept of "residual sodium carbonate" by Frank Eaton (11). Neither is completely satisfactory, but both have proved to be useful.

The amount of leaching required for a given level of salinity in the drainage water has been termed the *leaching requirement* (6). It refers to the percentage of the applied water that must pass beyond the root zone to maintain the desired salinity level in the soil.

Use of the leaching requirement can provide a guide for the design of irrigation and drainage systems in order to reduce salt build-up in the soil. Also, it serves to emphasize that the use of salty water calls for regular leaching of the soil, and the saltier the water, the more the leaching to be done.

The changes in water quality that occur along a river where irrigation is practiced are illustrated in Table I. Salinity and sodium hazard, as shown by electric conductivity and SAR (sodium-adsorption-ratio), increase as water is diverted for irrigation and as drainage water returns to the river. Conditions vary from year to year with the volume of flow, but the general relationships shown in Table I tend to hold (12). The distance between Otowi Bridge and Fort Quitman is nearly 400 miles. Wells drawing water from the same ground-water basin show a similar relationship between salinity and sodium hazard (13).

Another major difficulty associated with irrigation water, particularly in the Southwest, is the presence of boron, which is beneficial to plants in small amounts but toxic in large amounts. Toxic concentrations, although infrequent in river waters, are not uncommon in well waters, and some soils are naturally high in boron. There is no practical way to remove this element from irrigation waters or to make it harmless in the soil. Boron-tolerant crops, such as alfalfa and sugar beets, must be grown if the water is to be used. When boron is a soil problem, it can be leached out, but large quantities of good-quality water must be applied. More leaching is required to remove boron than to make a soil nonsaline, apparently because boron is adsorbed by soils and released only slowly (14).

Water Quality for Other Uses

Domestic and industrial water users are primarily concerned with biologic pollution and hardness. In the West, hard waters (high in calcium and magnesium) are usual wherever salt concentrations approach or exceed the 500-parts-per-million maximum recommended by the U.S. Public Health Service for drinking purposes.

Hardness refers to the amount of calcium and magnesium salts that are dissolved in the water. Calcium and magnesium salts precipitate soap, thus causing economic loss to the laundry and similar industries. Calcium carbonates can cause scale formation in pipes and containers. Synthetic detergents have come to be used extensively in homes and factories to lower the surface tension of water in a manner similar to the action of soap but without the disadvantage of precipitation with calcium and magnesium. These synthetic detergents, however, are more resistant to biologic decomposition

Table I.   Quality of Rio Grande water at six gaging stations, 1961.

Gaging station	Electric conductivity (reciprocal $\mu\Omega$)	SAR[a]	Dissolved solids (ppm)
Otowi Bridge, N.Mex.	339	0.7	210
San Marcial, N.Mex.	650	1.7	420
Elephant Butte, N.Mex.	701	2.0	456
Leasburg Dam, N.Mex.	886	4.1	630
El Paso, Texas	1316	4.1	867
Fort Quitman, Texas	6031	12.0	4108

[a] Sodium-adsorption-ratio.
Source: Wilcox (12).

than soap is, and this has led to the unusual spectacle of rivers and irrigation canals covered with detergent foam. The foam is harmless, apparently, at the low concentrations that usually occur.

Some western well waters contain considerable amounts of nitrates and fluorides. In humid regions, the presence of nitrates in water ordinarily indicates pollution by sewage, but in arid regions the source may be nitrate minerals or nitrogen fixation by organisms. Well waters in Arizona and New Mexico have been known to contain more than 300 parts per million of nitrates, and surface deposits of nitrate salts have been observed in Colorado and elsewhere. An excess of nitrates in drinking water may be harmful to children under 6 months of age.

Fluorides, in concentrations less than 1.5 parts per million in drinking water, are believed to help make teeth resistant to decay. Higher concentrations, on the other hand, can darken the teeth of children. Although surface waters generally are low in fluorides, some well waters of the West contain excessive quantities.

The seriousness of the threat to the health of human beings and wildlife of pesticides and radioactive wastes in water is under investigation. The fact that they represent a potential hazard is widely recognized.

Fertilizers

General principles of soil fertility and management in the humid regions have proved to be helpful guides in the arid regions. Equally applicable are the need for a balanced ionic environment in the soil solution, the principles of cation exchange, the values of organic matter and crop rotations in maintaining desirable physical and nutrient conditions, and the control of wind and water erosion. Differences exist in their relative importance under the climatic, soil, and plant conditions of the West. Potassium, for example, occurs in water-soluble, exchangeable, and nonexchangeable forms in both humid and arid regions.

Although the proportion of potassium in these different forms is of major concern in humid regions, it is of minor interest in arid regions. In the latter, the soil solution usually contains enough potassium to satisfy crop requirements, even though exchangeable potassium is low. For this reason, and sometimes mistakenly, potassium frequently is relegated to a secondary position in soil-fertility studies in the West, except in the Pacific Coast region.

Research on fertilizers in the western United States has been centered on nitrogen and phosphorus. Iron, zinc, and manganese, in this order, probably are of next importance on calcareous soils. Sulfur is deficient, for legumes, in many upland soils on the Pacific Coast and in the Palouse section of Washington, Idaho, and Oregon. Some benefit has been found from molybdenum applied to legumes in the Pacific Northwest. Primary attention, however, has been directed toward the relationship between nitrogen and phosphorus.

The common nitrogen fertilizers in use are ammonium sulfate (20-percent nitrogen), ammonium nitrate (33-percent nitrogen), urea (45-percent nitrogen), anhydrous ammonia (82-percent nitrogen), and solutions of varying nitrogen content, such as aqua ammonia, and mixtures of ammonium nitrate and urea. All of these increase soil acidity, either in their original form or on oxidation of the ammonium ion to nitrate. In calcareous soils, this usually is an advantage. By and large, research indicates that the major sources of fertilizer nitrogen are equally effective.

Investigations of phosphorus have demonstrated that water-soluble fertilizers generally are superior to citrate-soluble fertilizers on calcareous soils. The one apparent exception, on which research is limited thus far, is Rhenania phosphate. In this fertilizer, most of the phosphorus is not water-soluble, but crop response seems to be about as good as with water-soluble superphosphates. Rock phosphates and other slowly soluble calcium phosphates are less effective than superphosphates, either single or concentrated. Ammonium phosphates are good sources of phosphorus as well as of nitrogen.

One of the significant contributions on phosphorus relationships in soils in arid regions has been the discovery that phosphorus fixation or reversion in calcareous soils is much less serious than it was believed to be (15). Residual effects of applications of phosphorus have been detected as late as 7 years after the last application. Changes in chemical composition of added phosphorus to a less soluble form occur rather soon in calcareous soils, but the precipitated calcium phosphates that result still supply significant amounts of phosphorus to plants.

The factors that control the availability of iron, manganese, and zinc in calcareous soils remain obscure. Iron deficiency, which is frequently called *lime-induced chlorosis* when it occurs on calcareous soils, is the third most important nutrient deficiency in arid-regions soils. Although high levels of soil lime usually are associated with iron deficiency, its occurrence is variable and is influenced by soil aeration, high bicarbonate ion levels in the soil solution, and the kind of plant. Ornamental shrubs, berries, fruit trees, beans, and sorghum are among the most susceptible plants.

Manganese deficiency is largely restricted to fruit trees. Zinc deficiency has been recognized as a problem on fruit trees, such as pecans and pears, but recently it has been observed in many field crops, particularly where lime layers have been exposed when land was leveled for irrigation.

The use of chelates to control deficiencies of iron, zinc, and manganese in calcareous soils holds considerable promise (16), but no ready solution is at hand. Reducing the pH of calcareous soils to make these elements available has not been practical on a field scale because of the tremendous amounts of acidifying materials required.

Dry Farming

In dry-farming areas, more effort has been aimed at the conservation of moisture and organic matter and the prevention of wind erosion than has been devoted to study of fertilizers. Crops have responded to nitrogen and phosphorus, however, in many areas, particularly in the wetter part of the dry-farming sections.

Soil moisture has been conserved by summer fallowing, by controlling weed growth, by minimizing runoff of water, and by keeping crop residues on the surface (*17*).

Although summer fallowing is recommended throughout the drier part of the dry-farming region, the water stored in the soil at the end of the fallow period usually totals only about 20 to 25 percent of the precipitation during that time. Furthermore, because many of the rains are light and of short duration, the relationship between moisture storage and precipitation is not close in summer-rainfall areas, such as the Great Plains. It is closer in the winter-rainfall areas.

In the Great Plains, which are the major dry-farming area in the United States, the best indicator of yields is the amount of moisture in the soil at seeding time. For winter wheat, average or better production can be anticipated most of the time if the soil is wet to at least 3 feet (0.91 meter) deep. The chances of obtaining good yields decrease as the depth of wetted soil becomes less. The importance of deep soils capable of holding adequate quantities of water is apparent.

An effective step in conservation of moisture has been the use of herbicides to kill weeds in both fallow and crop land. Transpiration by weeds can be a major source of water loss from subsoil, adding to the largely unavoidable (at present) losses by evaporation. Because of the wide plant spacings used in dry farming, more soil is exposed than in humid or irrigated areas, with a consequent increase in the evaporation potential. In view of the extent of evaporation, which amounts to perhaps 60 to 75 percent of the total precipitation, reduction of this loss is a principal challenge.

Crop residues left on the surface protect soil from the beating action of rain and slow the movement of water, thus reducing runoff and water erosion. Other methods are terracing and the use of contour tillage with strip cropping. In general, runoff problems are similar in humid and arid regions, but the intense storms that are common in the drier sections of the West may deposit an entire year's supply of rain in a few minutes or hours. Runoff-control structures must be designed with this in mind.

Wind-erosion control takes three forms: maintenance or development of a vegetative cover, reduction of wind force near the soil surface, and tillage to avoid a loose, finely divided soil surface (*17*).

A gradual improvement in understanding the physics of wind erosion and the principles of soil stabilization has aided all control measures. A good vegetative cover is the best solution but usually is difficult to achieve in the arid regions, once the original native cover has been disturbed. On rangelands that are subject to wind erosion, no better solution has been found than revegetation, and this is ordinarily a very slow process. Where plant cover is not complete, surface roughness and soil cloddiness become important. A rough surface and a well-aggregated soil are less susceptible to wind forces than a smooth surface and a poorly aggregated soil.

Wind-tunnel studies in Kansas have indicated that soil particles about 0.1 millimeter in diameter are the most erodible and those more than 1 millimeter in diameter are the least erodible. Under dry-farming conditions, stubble mulching (leaving crop residues on the surface) probably has done more to reduce wind erosion than any other single process. It has been made possible by specialized tillage implements, along with tractors powerful enough to pull them. Standing stubble helps to break the force of the wind, and the crop residues on the surface help to protect the soil. Strip cropping across the direction of the wind now is a standard erosion-control procedure that provides some protection to fallow strips between the cropped strips.

Fallowing to conserve moisture, when it is done well, automatically encourages wind erosion, because it leaves a bare soil surface. Use of herbicides, rather than tillage, to control weeds reduces the number of times the surface is disturbed. Continuous cropping, although it is preferable to fallowing in erosion control, also increases the chances of crop failure. In practice, a farmer must often compromise between conserving moisture and minimizing wind erosion.

Emergency tillage to roughen the soil surface by turning up clods from the subsoil, a desperation practice, sometimes is effective. On most soils, it can be done only a few times in a single season, because the number of clods turned up becomes less and less. Since a soil survey identifies soils that have fine-textured, compact subsoils, it plays a key role in determining which soils will respond to emergency tillage.

Nitrogen is the critical fertilizer element for dry farming and on rangelands. Responses to phosphorus have been observed, particularly in the eastern and northern Great Plains, but these frequently are erratic. Potassium deficiencies are rare and are confined to very sandy soils. Iron deficiency is sometimes noted on sorghum.

Wheat generally responds more than row crops to applications of nitrogen, but production decreases are common if the moisture supply is limited. In years of average or above-average rainfall, if it is well distributed throughout the growing season at rates of about 10 to 60 pounds per acre (5 to 27 kilograms per 0.4047 hectare), nitrogen usually increases yields. In dry years, however, yields are frequently lowered, because the growth stimulation depletes the soil moisture to the point where few plants have enough to mature normally. By and large, moisture limits crop production more than does soil fertility.

Fertilization of arid rangelands is a moot matter. Prospects for an economic response decline where there is less effective annual precipitation. The chances that response will occur, sooner or later, are good; the question is whether the chances are good enough to justify the expenditure.

Soil Testing

The testing of soil to arrive at recommendations for the use of fertilizer and for soil management is less widely undertaken in arid regions than in humid regions. Frequently, good crops are obtained in the West without fertilizers, and this has led to the generally lower consumption of fertilizers, even though there is considerable room for improvement in yields practically everywhere. A second reason has been the unreliable results obtained on calcareous soils with soil-fertility testing methods that were developed for acid soils. The arid regions have lagged behind in soil-testing research.

An understanding of the forms in which essential plant elements occur in soils of the arid regions is needed in order to devise chemical tests that will permit the making of predictions of their availability to plants. Development of reliable tests is not always easy, even when this information is known. For example, much information on nitrogen is available, but, to date, no satisfactory test for predicting the nitrogen status of a soil during the growing season has been found. The closest approximation has been to incubate the soil for a certain time and then to measure the amount of nitrate produced. A rapid and reliable chemical test is needed.

The picture is somewhat better with respect to phosphorus, the second most important fertilizer element in the arid regions. Recent work by Sterling Olson and his colleagues in the U.S. Department of Agriculture in Colorado has done much to identify the forms in which phosphorus occurs in alkaline and calcareous soils and has led to a chemical test for available phosphorus that uses sodium bicarbonate as the extracting reagent. This process is more reliable than some others that have been used, but it presents problems when it is used in routine soil-testing laboratories, where analytic procedures are not as closely controlled as they are in research. The extent of the disagreement among soil chemists about the best phosphorus test is shown by a recent survey made by Frank Bingham (18). Several western states use sodium bicarbonate, and others use water, fluorides, or carbonic acid in the extracting solution.

Chemical tests for determining the availability to plants of iron, manganese, and zinc in soils have not been successful, apparently because of the many factors that control their availability, such as the reduction-oxidation potential of the soil, pH, the effect of other elements, and differences in plant metabolism.

Mineralogic analyses of western soils have shown that the clay minerals are principally montmorillonite and illite. In addition, there is a growing recognition that amorphous minerals, such as allophane, are an important constituent of many soils, particularly strongly alkaline soils and those developed from volcanic ash. Volcanic ash is widespread in the western United States and Hawaii. Identification of amorphous constituents in soils is difficult by standard methods because of their noncrystalline character. The significance of allophane arises from its low bulk density, high water-holding capacity, strong aggregating effect, high phosphate-fixing capacity, and the indication that its adsorption of organic compounds reduces nitrogen availability to microorganisms and plants.

Classification

Recognition of the importance of soil characteristics in determining the land-use potential in the arid regions has come, all too frequently, from failures and near-failures experienced by new settlers. More emphasis has usually been placed on the physical conditions, such as depth, texture, and permeability, than on chemical properties. This is understandable where moisture relationships are more critical than fertility in limiting plant growth. The principal exception has been in irrigated areas where salinity is a problem.

Classification of upland soils in the West presents difficulties similar to those in the humid regions, and the soil-survey techniques are similar, with greater emphasis placed on factors that influence moisture relationships and the wind-erosion hazard. Numerous questions, many of them still unresolved, have been encountered in the classification of recent alluvial soils of the irrigated valleys. These arise from the stratified, highly variable condition that commonly exists in recent alluvium.

Soil-survey progress in the arid United States has been slow and largely restricted to irrigated areas. Published soil surveys cover only about 15 percent of the region, with about half of that in the three states of California, Nebraska, and Washington.

This shortage of published soil surveys seriously limits effective utilization of the West. Not only agricultural interests are served by soil surveys, but other users include such diverse interests as highway engineers, urban and suburban planners, pipeline companies, mining prospectors, tax assessors, and Army engineers.

The relationship of landform to soil formation is widely recognized by soil surveyors and others who use it to aid in soil mapping. Recently, a project was initiated by the Soil Conservation Service to investigate in detail the influence of landform, as well as geologic conditions, on soil development in an arid part of southern New Mexico. The project will be the most intensive of its kind in the United States. It promises to clarify many of the questions concerning effects of past and present climates, as well as landforms, on the kinds of soil that are now found.

Microbiology

Microbiologic research in the arid regions has been concentrated on nitrogen transformations, with less attention directed toward phosphorus relationships. Three aspects that have received special attention because of their significance in alkaline soils and arid climates are the effects of salts on microbial activity, effect of high pH on oxidation of ammonia to nitrate, and nitrogen fixation by algae.

J. E. Greaves and L. W. Jones (19) studied the salt problem as it affected ammonifying and nitrifying microorganisms in Utah. They concluded that the nitrite- and nitrate-producing bacteria are considerably more sensitive to high salt concentrations than are the ammonia-producing organisms, although the latter are also adversely affected. Saline soils that had been kept dry for 20 years were devoid of nitrifying organisms, whereas the ammonifying organisms survived. *Azotobacter*, the free-living nitrogen-fixers, are quite tolerant of high salinity. Greaves suggested that crop injury at low-to-moderate salt concentrations may be due more to the action of the salt on the nitrifying bacteria than on the crop itself.

A. B. Caster and his colleagues in Arizona (20) concluded that there was a pH threshold at about 7.7 for formation of nitrates from ammonium. Above this soil pH, nitrate formation rapidly decreased but nitrite formation continued. They noted that the pH of the soil mass probably is not the same as the pH of the soil in the immediate vicinity of the places where nitrification is proceeding. This would account for nitrification in soils that have a pH greater than the threshold value, since localized oxidation of ammonia causes a reduction in pH.

Evidence that algae, principally the blue-greens, added appreciable quantities of nitrogen to arid-regions soils was presented by Joel E. Fletcher and W. P. Martin (21). Since these algae live in the absence of free oxygen but require light, they may be active when the surface soil is saturated, a condition that can occur after rain or irrigation. Summer temperatures in the West favor rapid microbial activity if other conditions are conducive. After heavy irrigation, particularly in fields of alfalfa or other thick vegetation that reduces evaporation, an algal crust often appears within a few days. When the soil dries, the algae enter a resting stage and then are ready to become active again when the soil is wetted. The amount of nitrogen fixed by algae varies considerably with environmental conditions but probably reaches several pounds per acre (kilograms per hectare) under favorable conditions. This source undoubtedly helps to maintain nitrogen in arid-regions soils. It may add enough in irrigated soils to significantly reduce the fertilizer requirements of cultivated crops.

Prospects for the Future

If available knowledge is applied, the permanence of agriculture in the arid regions does not appear to be threatened by any soil problem now known. Reduced soil fertility limits yields on lands on which crops have been grown for many years without replacement of plant nutrients, but usually this deficiency can be corrected readily by proper fertilization. Salinity, waterlogging, and erosion remain the major problems, as they have been through the ages; and, although they are more difficult to control than low fertility, continued research on the fundamental properties of soils is leading to better solutions.

The only apparent restrictions on corrective measures are such nontechnical factors as economics, legal complications, and community cooperation. Economics should become less limiting as more effective measures are devised through continuing research.

Research should lead to increasing efficiency in the use of water through such things as automation of improved moisture-measuring devices, so that irrigation water will be supplied only when it is required by moisture conditions in the soil. Reduction of evaporation losses from the soil surface offers a major opportunity to save water. Sheets of plastic or other materials have been used successfully. Chemical treatment to reduce plant transpiration and soil evaporation are additional areas in which more research is needed.

One of the difficulties in the study of soils is that few procedures are available to determine their properties while they are in place in the field. Some progress has been made toward probes that will do this; they are quite limited at present. A benefit that may arise from the space-exploration program is the expediting of the construction of such devices, which would enable unmanned space vehicles to send back information on the environment of extraterrestrial bodies. The relatively harsh environment of deserts can serve as a laboratory in the design of appropriate instruments to explore the inhospitable moon and the other planets. In turn, these instruments would be useful on earth.

Undoubtedly, man will be less inclined in the future to accept without major change the soils that nature has given him. Soils that have undesirable layers of sand, silt, or clay are difficult to manage well. With the advent of powerful tractors and giant plows, some farmers in irrigated areas have plowed as deeply as 3 feet (0.91 meter) or more to break up such layers and mix them into the remaining soil. Others have added sand to tight clay soils and clay to porous sandy soils, with a resulting improvement in permeability and aeration in the first case and in retention of water and fertilizer in the second. These practices may become common.

Emphasis on soil-plant-water relationships has increased in the West. This should lead to improved methods of controlling trace-element deficiencies, to better soil tests for availability to plants of fertilizer materials, and to the ability to accurately predict soil conditions that will limit productivity.

Soil classification in the arid regions will become more of a science, and less of an art, as investigations in soil physics, chemistry, biology, and mineralogy continue. The classification system proposed by the Soil Conservation Service appears to represent an advance in this direction.

As people become aware that soil is a distinct entity among natural objects, the future nonagricultural use of soils-research data will probably show increased interest in the soil itself, whether or not it produces agricultural crops. Many persons, both scientists and non-scientists, have little knowledge of what soil scientists do or of the value of their accomplishments to other disciplines. A field as far removed from modern agriculture as archeology is using some of the techniques of soils research to date ancient settlements and to understand the changes that have occurred in what are now arid regions. Similar opportunities exist in other areas of study.

REFERENCES

1. H. Jenny and C. D. Leonard, "Functional relationships between soil properties and rainfall," *Soil Sci.* **38**, 363–381 (1934).
2. J. A. Widtsoe, *Dry Farming* (Macmillan, New York, 1911).
3. L. A. Richards and W. Gardner, "Tensiometer for measuring the capillary tension of soil water," *J. Am. Soc. Agron.* **28**, 352–358 (1936).

4. G. A. Bouyoucos and A. H. Mick, "An electrical resistance method for the continuous measurement of soil moisture under field conditions," *Mich. State Univ. Agr. Expt. Sta. Tech. Bull. 172* (1940).

5. W. Gardner and D. Kirkham, "Determination of soil moisture by neutron scattering," *Soil Sci.* **73**, 391–401 (1952).

6. L. A. Richards, Ed., "Diagnosis and improvement of saline and alkali soils," *U.S. Dept. Agr. Handbook 60* (1954).

7. L. A. Richards and G. Ogata, "Psychrometric measurements of soil samples equilibrated on pressure membranes," *Soil Sci. Soc. Am. Proc.* **25**, 456–459 (1961).

8. W. H. Gardner, "How water moves in the soil," *Crops and Soils* **15**, 7–9 (1962).

9. L. C. Boawn, F. Turner, Jr., C. D. Moodie, and C. A. Bower, "Reclamation of a saline-alkali soil by leaching and gypsum treatments using sugar beets as an indicator crop," *Proc. Am. Soc. Sugar Beet Technologists, 7th* (1952), pp. 138–145.

10. J. N. Luthin, "An electrical resistance network solving drainage problems," *Soil Sci.* **75**, 259–274 (1953).

11. F. M. Eaton, "Significance of carbonates in irrigation waters," *Soil Sci.* **69**, 123–133 (1950).

12. L. V. Wilcox, "Discharge and salt burden of the Rio Grande above Fort Quitman, Texas," *U.S. Salinity Lab. Res. Rept. 99* (1962).

13. H. E. Dregne and H. J. Maker, "Irrigation well waters of New Mexico," *New Mexico Agr. Expt. Sta. Bull. 386* (1954).

14. R. C. Reeve, A. F. Pillsbury, and L. V. Wilcox, "Reclamation of a saline and high boron soil in the Coachella Valley of California," *Hilgardia* **24**, 69–91 (1955).

15. H. B. Peterson, L. B. Nelson, and J. L. Paschal, "A review of phosphate fertilizer investigations in 15 western states through 1949," *U.S. Dept. Agr. Circ. 927* (1953).

16. A. Wallace, Ed., *A Decade of Synthetic Chelating Agents in Inorganic Plant Nutrition* (Arthur Wallace, Los Angeles, Calif., 1962).

17. R. V. Olson, Ed., "Agronomic trends and problems in the Great Plains," *Adv. Agron.* **10** (1958).

18. F. T. Bingham, "Chemical soil tests for available phosphorus," *Soil Sci.* **94**, 87–95 (1962).

19. J. E. Greaves and L. W. Jones, "The survival of microorganisms in alkali soils," *Soil Sci.* **52**, 359–364 (1941).

20. A. B. Caster, W. P. Martin, and T. F. Buehrer, "The microbiological oxidation of ammonia in desert soils: I, Threshold pH value for nitrification," *Ariz. Univ. Agr. Expt. Sta. Tech. Bull. 96* (1942).

21. J. E. Fletcher and W. P. Martin, "Some effects of algae and molds in the rain crusts of desert soils," *Ecology* **29**, 95–100 (1948).

9

Aridity and Agriculture

J. L. GARDNER

Settlement of the semiarid and arid sections of the United States by people from the more humid eastern areas of the country and by immigrants from northern Europe required adaptation of methods and concepts of food production. All of these settlers, in contrast to those of Spanish origin, were confronted with unfamiliar problems arising directly or indirectly from the aridity of the environment. Those who settled where water was available took up irrigation. Others resorted to dry farming or to raising livestock on the vast native ranges. Crops of the humid areas were poorly adapted to dry farming; problems of water supply developed, and irrigated soils became waterlogged or laden with injurious amounts of salts; native ranges deteriorated under heavy use, resulting in decreased production and in erosion by wind and water.

As the population increased, these and many other problems became acute. With the development of agricultural research by the state experiment stations and the U.S. Department of Agriculture, many of these problems have been alleviated, but many others remain to be investigated.

Perhaps in no other habitat is an organism subjected to such rigorous and fluctuating climatic conditions as in the arid regions. These extreme conditions make the management of arid ranges, for example, and the research needed for the sound use of them, a unique problem.

The contributors to this chapter were ARDEN A. BALTENSPERGER, THADIS W. BOX, C. W. LAURITZEN, and CARL B. ROUBICEK.

Range Management

Range management, a relatively new science, evolved primarily from the disciplines of ecology, animal production, and economics. Basically, it is a field of applied ecology. Much of the early research that led to the present basis for range management was done by plant ecologists. A recent trend considers the range site as an ecosystem, with study of the total environment and the interaction of organisms in the system; this is one of the greatest research needs on arid rangelands.

Succession, or the ecologic concept of the orderly process of community change, has become a major consideration in range management. In fact, the classification of ranges into condition classes is based on succession. The condition of the range, or its general health, ordinarily is measured by its departure from the stable vegetation of the region. The concept of succession is used to estimate carrying capacity, to set stocking rates, to select plants for reseeding, and in many other ways. In the more humid regions, such as the true prairie, the concept is very useful, but succession is extremely slow in arid zones if its exists at all. Although the concept is theoretically applicable to deserts, in practice the time required for an arid range to change from a poor range to a productive one through natural succession may be so great that it is not practical to rely totally on successional changes.

When a simple stand of desert vegetation is disturbed or destroyed, a young stand of the same species often replaces it. Thus, when a big sagebrush (*Artemisia tridentata*) stand is plowed and the site is reseeded to grass, the primary invader is the original sagebrush. Forrest Shreve (*1*) noted as long ago as 1925 that the concepts of succession developed on the prairie might not be directly applicable to deserts.

Several other workers have pointed out that the Clementsian concept of succession (developed by Frederic Clements) may not be useful under arid conditions. Indeed, there seems to be no orderly process of succession in deserts. Whether the dynamics of the desert community are called *succession* or *development and change,* however, the range manager must recognize and work with these changes to obtain the most productive plant communities.

The relative slowness, or complete lack, of succession in arid regions has caused many investigators to look for some sort of artificial establishment for the improvement of rangelands rather than use the management or manipulation of ecologic factors. Yet, much of the basic work on plant-animal-soil relationships contributed to knowledge that now allows broad-scale manipulation of the vegetation by artificial means.

Utilization of Vegetation

The arid regions of the United States may be classified in several ways. The discussion here is based on (i) the "cold" deserts, which are the northern desert-shrub and Great Basin areas; (ii) the "hot" deserts, which include the southern desert-shrub areas; and (iii) the semiarid grasslands, which include the steppe and short-grass Plains.

Winter precipitation, which comes mostly as snow, and a vegetation of cool-season habit characterize the cold deserts. The major growth of forage consists of such shrubs as big sagebrush (*Artemisia tridentata*), shadscale (*Atriplex confertifolia*), Nuttall saltbush (*Atriplex nuttallii*), and winterfat (*Eurotia lanata*). Herbaceous vegetation is almost totally cool-season in habit. Major forage plants on good-condition ranges in the foothills may be grasses such as bluebunch wheatgrass (*Agropyron spicatum*), bluegrass (*Poa* spp.), and fescues (*Festuca* spp.), and depleted ranges may have cheatgrass (*Bromus tectorum*) as the major forage species. In some valleys of the cold deserts, Indian ricegrass (*Oryzopsis hymenoides*) and squirreltail (*Sitanion hystrix*) may be virtually the only grass forage plants. The cold deserts make up most of the winter range for the cattle and sheep herds that summer in the mountains of the intermountain region. Livestock depends on shrubs for protein and vitamin A during the winter. Energy may come from the shrubs or from dry herbaceous plants.

In the southwestern United States, the hot deserts occur mostly south of the Grand Canyon. This is a region of low, unevenly distributed rainfall and extremely high evaporation rates. Moisture for plant growth often is not available during much of the year. The plants are mainly of warm-season habit. Most of the forage comes from grasses and herbaceous plants; shrubs are usually lowly palatable to livestock. Lowland areas of fine-textured soil support Tobosa grass (*Hilaria mutica*) in almost pure stands. On some of the lighter-textured soils there are gramas (*Bouteloua* spp.), three-awns (*Aristida* spp.), and other plants of hot, dry origins. Unpalatable shrubs such as creosotebush (*Larrea divaricata*) and mesquite (*Prosopis juliflora*) cover large areas. Animals usually graze the ranges at all seasons of the year.

The semiarid grasslands occur in a huge, almost treeless area that is bounded on the east by the true prairie, on the south by the Edwards Plateau of Texas, on the west by the Rocky Mountains, and on the north by the forests in Alberta and Saskatchewan. This vast area has a wide variation in climate.

The aspect of vegetation of the semiarid grasslands is one of steppe or short-grass plains. Species composition of plants varies from warm-season-dominated *Buchloe-Bouteloua-Hilaria* ranges in the south to cool-season-dominated *Stipa-Agropyron* ranges in the north. The extreme southern portions of the Plains are made up almost entirely of warm-season plants; fewer warm-season plants and more cool-season plants are found in the north. Therefore, management at any one point in the Plains may be complicated by the lack of a balance between the warm- and cool-season plants.

The arid regions of the United States are characterized by communities of drought-resistant plants. These xerophytes are usually able to survive in an arid environment, not because of their efficient use of moisture, but because of their ability to live under conditions of water deficiency and water stress. The range manager must meet the problem of efficient utilization of these types.

He is faced by a dilemma. His livestock must graze the native plants if the range is to be utilized, but removal of plant material during periods of moisture stress has been shown to reduce vigor of the plants. The major problems connected with grazing arid ranges are (i) determination of the basic ecology and potential productivity of ranges, (ii) the development of management systems for drought conditions, (iii) the utilization of low-value desert plants, and (iv) artificial improvement of desert ranges.

Ecotones—transition zones between plant communities—are sharp on arid and semiarid ranges. In general, large areas of vegetation can be correlated with climate and the general soil characteristics, but local communities are distinct from the larger vegetational zone. The sharp lines of demarcation between types of vegetation have stimulated several detailed plant-soil relationship studies in the

Great Basin. In most cases, plant communities were found to be controlled by soil conditions rather than by climate. Some site or soil conditions favor a more stable type of vegetation than others. Even small, local areas differ greatly in potential productivity.

The association of plants and soils continues to be one of the major areas of research in the arid regions of the West. Until the productive potential of the arid ranges is known, the ecologist or range manager is limited in his efforts to increase yield.

Grazing during Drought

Drought constantly threatens the livestockman who ranches in the arid zones. These drought periods may be seasonal during the year, or they may be cycles of several years' duration. The stockman must plan his grazing in such a way that desirable forage species persist during dry periods, but he must also harvest the excess forage during the wet periods if he is to make full economic use of the range.

All plants are affected by the removal of photosynthetic tissue, but perhaps the plants in arid zones are harmed more than those of humid regions. C. Wayne Cook reported that grazed wheatgrass that received adequate water was not damaged as much as the grass that grew under natural arid conditions. It is generally assumed that grazing during drought harms range plants more than grazing when there is adequate moisture. Despite this, the rancher must use desert plants during periods of moisture stress if he is to stay in the livestock business.

The effect of forage removal, either by clipping or by grazing, on the vigor and yield of pasture and range plants has been investigated throughout the United States. Generally, these experiments show that plant vigor and yield decrease as the frequency or intensity of clipping is increased.

One of the most intensive studies of clipping under arid conditions was made by Cook and his colleagues at Utah State University (2). They found that frequent clipping reduced vigor, yield, root size, stored root reserves, growth rate, and seed production in wheatgrass plants. Forage value of the frequently clipped plant was increased, however, because it contained smaller amounts of lignin, fiber, and other less digestible portions. Plants that were clipped early in the season produced more forage when they were clipped to a moderate height of 3 inches (7.5 centimeters). If the plants were not clipped until late in the season, the greatest yields were made by clipping at 1-inch (2.5-centimeter) heights. It can readily be seen that constant forage removal, or removal of forage early in the season, greatly reduces plant yield and harms the individual plant.

Animals must eat the year round, of course. Therefore, some system of deferment or temporary rest may be necessary for maximum production on arid rangelands. Simply changing the season of use may allow the more desirable plants on a range to improve. Heavy fall grazing of sagebrush-grass ranges in southern Idaho increased grass yield and reduced sagebrush.

Organized deferment and rotation may give even more dramatic results. Leo B. Merrill (3) reported that stocking rates near Sonora, Texas, declined from 125 animal units per section (259 hectares) in 1900 to 32 animal units per section in 1948. After 1948, stocking rates continued to decline under continuous heavy stocking, maintained the same level under moderate stocking, and rapidly improved under deferred-rotation management.

Not only do individual plants react, but entire plant communities change with grazing pressure. When animals are introduced on a range, they graze the most palatable plants. The plants lose vigor, store smaller amounts of root reserves, and produce fewer seeds. If they are continually grazed, they are forced out of the composition. These highly palatable plants have been called *decreasers*. When a plant is removed from the composition by grazing, its place is taken by a less palatable plant called an *increaser*.

When most of the decreasers are gone, animals turn to the increaser plants for food. Then, as the increasers are reduced in vigor and reproduction is slowed or stopped, plants from another community (*invaders*) fill the interspaces. Invaders usually are low-value plants or plants of seasonal importance.

Grazing on arid ranges must be planned to allow the more palatable, and generally more productive, decreaser plants to remain healthy. Since the decreaser plants are usually quite high on the successional scale, they do not have to be given a competitive advantage to improve and increase. However, the system must not

put them in a position of competitive disadvantage. Yearlong grazing tends to cause the animals to concentrate on the more palatable
plants; thus little or no improvement can be expected, unless the
stocking rates are kept extremely low.

Rotation Systems

Systems of grazing can be followed that will force animals to eat
the less palatable plants and give the more palatable ones an equal
competitive advantage. These have been called *rotation, deferred-
rotation,* and *rest-rotation* systems. Many different approaches have
been used since early workers suggested that a program of systematic
deferment might give higher yield from rangelands. Results from
deferred-rotation experiments on arid and semiarid ranges vary
greatly.

Most often, an improvement in forage yield follows deferment.
But when the yield is measured by animal gain, it may not differ
significantly from season-long grazing. Although some scientists have
concluded that deferment is not economically feasible on arid lands,
the theory of deferment is sound. Methods are needed for the many
different sets of environmental conditions that exist in arid regions.
A deferred-rotation system for arid regions must (i) be based on
the physiology of the individual plant species of the region, (ii) conform to the seasonal use of the range, and (iii) be compatible with
animal-husbandry practices. Research leading to the development
of systems of grazing that would allow the more desirable plant species to improve in vigor and condition during dry periods would be
one of the most important contributions to arid-range management.

Drought can completely wreck the financial structure of a ranch.
A recent drought in Texas caused ranchers to lose 37.5 percent of
their net worth in 3 years. Ranchers who stocked lightly lost only 15
percent of their net worth, but ranches that were grazed heavily by
livestock lost 73 percent of their net worth. Even with the best of
management, profits will be lowered during droughts, but sound
management can greatly reduce the hazards.

R. J. Hildreth and Gerald Thomas (4) analyzed rainfall records
at several locations in Texas and concluded that such records could
be used to set minimum stocking rates and predict drought hazards.

Recently, Forrest Sneva and Donald Hyder (5) found that production of grasses in the cold desert region of the United States can be predicted from precipitation that falls early in the year. Rainfall is highly variable in such an area, and there is no constant level of forage supply. Therefore, the ranch operation must remain flexible if maximum production is to be accomplished.

Several systems to attain flexibility have been presented. All of them include (i) a stocking rate that is in balance with the forage supply during adverse years, and (ii) a livestock-management system that maintains a herd that can be quickly and easily adjusted to short forage supplies but increased quickly during good years. One of the most common methods of obtaining flexibility is to maintain a base herd of cows that will go through most of the unfavorable periods with little additional feed. Excess feed is harvested either by keeping calves and selling them as yearlings or by buying feeder animals to harvest the feed during good periods.

Research has indicated that there are several precautions that a rancher may take to enable him to withstand drought periods. He should (i) keep the stocking rate in balance with the forage supply at all times; (ii) make livestock-management practices flexible by keeping the number of breeding animals below the carrying capacity of the range and utilizing excess grass with dry animals; (iii) cull the herd severely when feed is short, and keep calves when the forage supply is plentiful; (iv) develop a forage reserve in the form of deferred pasture, hay, or silage, (v) make conservative use of credit and protect credit rating; (vi) use two or more kinds of livestock.

Actually, the key to the management of ranges in arid lands centers around two major considerations: (i) a sound forage-management program based on the climatic and edaphic potential of each site; and (ii) a livestock-management system with maximum flexibility.

Utilization of Low-Value Plants

Some attempts have been made to convert low-value plants into emergency livestock feed. In Texas, ground mesquite pulp was fed to livestock during the drought of the 1950's with promising results (6). Spines from the pricklypear cactus (*Opuntia* spp.) are burned, and the plant is used as a common source of drought feed over much of the southwestern United States. Although low-value plants are popular during periods of feed shortage, the enthusiasm for research on them drops quickly when the rains come.

The utilization of cold, desert-shrub ranges has received considerable study in recent years. It has been discovered that forage from desert shrubs changes little in nutritive content during the critical winter grazing period. As the winter season progresses, protein and phosphorus generally decrease in all desert plants; whereas crude fiber, lignin, cellulose, and other carbohydrates increase. Forage from shrubs showed the least fluctuation during the season, and forage from grasses showed the greatest differences.

Because the diets of different classes of livestock vary, it is important to graze arid ranges with the class that will make the most efficient use of the native forage. In most foreign countries, goats, sheep, camels, and other animals use desert ranges, but in the United States, only sheep and cattle appear in any great numbers. In general, sheep make better use of desert ranges than do cattle. They eat more of the shrub vegetation, they have lower water requirements, and they can efficiently utilize rough ranges. Although little range research has been done with the lowly goat, it may well be the animal that will provide food for starving populations in many lands.

Many of the desert plants have high essential oil contents that lower their palatability and digestibility. One of the goals for research might well be the investigation of the problem of oil content of desert plants, with the goal of making them more digestible to livestock.

Not only should much research go into converting some of the unpalatable plants to livestock feed, but studies should be made on the possibility of using the by-products of such a process. For instance, if the essential oils in sagebrush (*Artemisia*) could be used in an industrial process that would pay for part of the cost of removing the oils, the West would have an almost untouched source of livestock feed.

The climax of much of our desert ranges is dominated by a desert shrub of some kind. Perhaps it would be more feasible to look toward utilization of these plants that apparently have reached the climax stage than to try to convert the range to some plant that is below the climax in the normal successional series and probably would remain only a short time.

Improvement of Arid Ranges

Many range technicians find it difficult to believe that ranges of the arid regions are actually such low-producing ecosystems. Many times the desert range is actually a result of abuse and overuse. Shrubs may have invaded natural grasslands. In such a case, improvement is indeed feasible. Other ecosystems may be climax deserts, and little improvement can be made.

Control of big sagebrush (*Artemisia tridentata*) has been a major item of concern for researchers in the cold desert region of the United States; many different techniques have been suggested. Control by fire is adequate in most situations on the nonsprouting sagebrush, but its use is restricted because of the fire danger involved. Both chemical and mechanical methods have proved to be successful in some situations. B. D. Gardner (7) studied the economics of sagebrush control in Colorado and suggested comparative cost figures. The choice of the control practice will depend on environmental conditions and the economic feasibility of the practice.

In the hot desert regions, most of the brush-control work has centered around the control of mesquite (*Prosopis* spp.) and juniper (*Juniperus* spp.). Several chemical and mechanical methods have been proposed, each with varying degrees of success. The choice of method will again be determined by the local ecologic conditions and the economics involved.

Perhaps no other range practice has received such widespread attention as range seeding. Seeding is hazardous on arid ranges, but it is usually possible to seed ranges if (i) seeds of adapted species are available, (ii) there is adequate seedbed preparation, (iii) the proper technique is used in seeding, and (iv) the seeding is followed by good management.

Range managers have long tried to utilize excess water from flash floods, which are common on arid lands. Various kinds of pits or small depressions have been tried with varying degrees of success. Range pitting and contour furrowing can be successful in some areas and almost useless in others. The success depends largely on the conditions of the soil and vegetation.

Efforts also have been made to spread the excess water over larger portions of the range. Water-spreading techniques vary from simple furrows to elaborate structures for capturing and diverting overland flow of water.

Needed Range Research

More economic research is needed on ranching in arid zones. Not only must the rancher have flexibility in his forage and livestock program, but he must have a system of credit that will allow him to achieve maximum freedom in his operation. Special credit programs for drought periods, techniques of buying and storing surplus feed during good years, and finance programs for range improvements are sorely needed.

New systems of raising livestock may change the use of arid ranges. Preliminary work at the Spur, Texas, Experiment Station indicates that cows and calves can be raised economically under drylot conditions on low-value agricultural feeds. Calves from penned cows could be used to utilize seasonal ranges.

Although much work has been done on the control of undesirable range plants, still more is needed. Methods and techniques should be developed for the economic control of such plants as *Larrea divaricata*, *Acacia* spp., and other resistant plants.

Concentrated efforts should be made to obtain the most efficient use of the small amount of water that falls on arid regions. More work is needed in the efficiency of water use by desert plants, methods and techniques of holding and storing water in the soil, and other watershed-management projects.

Arid regions have long been considered to be low-value ranges, and their potential has not been adequately explored. With the demands of a growing population for more food, more of the humid rangelands will be devoted to intensified agriculture, and the arid West will be the last haven of range-livestock production in the United States. A research program to meet this coming challenge must be planned now.

Research in the arid and semiarid lands of the United States not only can help the production of this nation's range industry but also may contribute important principles that are applicable to the less-developed arid countries of the world. Therefore, research projects on our own rangelands should be geared to an understanding of arid environments wherever they exist.

Climate and Livestock Production

Climate is the most important single factor that influences the distribution of domesticated animals. This is particularly true of environmental temperature and rainfall.

Productivity of animals is less in the hotter regions of the earth. Disease and parasitism, poor nutritive value of native feed, management practices, and breeds of animals, all contribute to this lessened productivity. When all possible factors are taken into account, however, the fact remains that weather alone, in some way, is the major one.

The problems of animal adaptation occur in both hot, humid regions and arid areas. Disease and nutritional problems differ, but in general, these problems have specific characteristics. Adaptability must include tolerance for high environmental temperature as well as for low nutritional status. Phosphorus deficiency is a general occurrence in the arid regions of the United States.

Research on the arid rangelands of Texas and New Mexico by the U.S. Department of Agriculture and the New Mexico Agricultural Experiment Station has demonstrated the value of supplying additional phosphorus to increase calf crops and improve the general health of range stock (8, 9). Under conditions of prolonged drought, vitamin-A deficiency can also become a factor in the animals' failure to reproduce.

The incidence of eye cancer is significantly higher for animals in hot, dry regions. Eyelid pigmentation and drooping eyelids become important, since they afford some protection against the effects of intense sunlight, insects, and natural irritants.

Attempts to increase production have indicated that the local breeds and types that are accustomed to local dietary and management regimes should be used as the basis for improvement of the stock. Apparently, in the field of infectious disease, nutrition of the host operates within a genetic framework, and the area of its operation may be defined as the area in which genetically heterogeneous hosts meet genetically heterogeneous pathogen populations.

Since there are fundamental breed differences in cattle in their reaction to environment and ability to adjust to various stress conditions, the introduction of European-type stock in arid or tropical countries has often had disastrous results (*10*). It is conceivable that, in the course of breeding animals in relatively kindly environments, some of the ability to adapt to a rise in body temperature, to relative dehydration, or to alkalosis may have been lost.

In all normal warm-blooded animals, the body temperature remains constant within relatively narrow limits. The ability to maintain a constant body temperature despite extreme variation in environmental conditions depends on the maintenance of an equilibrium between the heat produced by the animal together with heat it may absorb from the environment and the heat that is lost from the body. The precise range of the *comfort zone* of normal body temperature without physical or homothermic aids depends, in turn, on the productive level of the animal. The higher the productive level and the larger the individual, the greater the cold tolerance and the lower the heat tolerance.

The first step toward establishing and maintaining productive animals suitable to the climate of a region is to study the environmental conditions that are peculiar to the region and to determine the requirements for adaptability. Extreme ambient temperatures, amount and intensity of solar radiation, relative frequencies and duration of rainfall and drought, prevalent insects and parasites, accessibility of the terrain, and quantity of potable water are among the factors. Of these, high environmental temperature and intensity of solar radiation cause the most concern. It is the temperate (European) breeds of cattle that have difficulty adapting to high environmental temperatures. Environmental studies with cattle have, therefore, been chiefly concerned with the effect of high temperature.

Formulas for determining heat transfer by conduction, radiation, convection, and evaporation have been used to attain a better understanding of the physiology of heat tolerance. Newton's law of cooling indicates that the larger the surface area of a given body, the greater the rate of heat transfer. Since, from geometric considerations, the larger the body, the smaller the surface area per unit volume, heat dissipation becomes more difficult as the body size of the animal increases. The rate of heat loss (or gain) by radiation is proportional to the surface area of the animal but is modified by a "configuration

factor" (Lambert's law), since there is no heat loss by radiation
between surfaces that face each other. On a clear summer day, a
beef animal absorbs 20,000 kilocalories of heat by radiation alone.
With the heat of normal body processes being added at the rate of
800 to 1000 calories per hour, the animal is attempting to dispose
of this heat load in an environment with an ambient temperature
several degrees hotter than body temperature. It is no wonder that
the normal physiologic pattern is drastically altered, and the research
worker must consider this heat-stress animal as a biologic entity that
is entirely different from the same animal at moderate environmental
conditions.

Acclimatization Research

An impressive amount of research on acclimatization has been conducted at the University of Missouri and by the U.S. Department of
Agriculture at Beltsville, Maryland. The basic pattern for research
in the physiology of stress response of cattle was established at the
University of Missouri Agricultural Experiment Station; the procedures and findings have been published in an extensive series of
bulletins. These publications include data on detailed observations
of animals in the psychrometric chamber.

The normal body temperature of cattle is usually considered to
be a rectal temperature of 101° Fahrenheit (38.5° Celsius). An increase in body temperature has been used as a measure of heat stress.
Air temperature above 80° Fahrenheit (23.5° Celsius) will influence
the body temperature of cattle, but the degree of effect depends also
on the breed, age, stage of lactation, plane of nutrition, and previous
thermal state. The heat tolerance of an animal must be considered
not only in terms of the relative increase in body temperature but
also in terms of the ability of the animal to tolerate increased body
temperature without other body functions being affected.

More and more research emphasis is now being placed on sweating as a means of body temperature control in cattle. An important
factor in the heat-tolerance difference between zebu (Brahman)
and European cattle breeds is the additional sweat production of
the zebu. It has been determined that in acclimated cattle 50 to 60
percent of the body metabolic heat is dissipated by vaporization.

This Brahman (zebu) bull is typical of the breed that was imported from India. Because of their tolerance to high temperatures and resistance to ticks, the zebu cattle have proved to be notably adaptable to arid range-lands. (Courtesy University of Arizona)

The sweat-gland volume per area of skin has been used successfully to rank cattle types for heat tolerance. The ability of the cattle to withstand high temperature is considered to be in proportion to their capacity to vaporize water with its high specific heat of vaporization (11, 12). Respiration also serves as a means of body heat loss by vaporization.

Blood constituents of cattle that are subjected to temperature stress may be markedly different from those under normal conditions; yet, few, if any, of these constituents can serve as a measure of heat tolerance. Initial changes in blood volume or blood constituents are usually very different from the changes encountered in long-term stress. High temperature decreases thyroid activity (and, thereby, metabolic rate) as much as 30 percent below normal. The thyroid and adrenal glands are intimately concerned with various physiologic processes that enable an animal to withstand the stress of heat or cold.

There is not, at present, a satisfactory test or measure that can be used to predict or even to evaluate relative heat tolerance. A list of desirable characteristics for animals under hot, dry conditions includes (i) insulation against solar energy and hot winds, (ii) good evaporative mechanism, but with other means of conserving water, (iii) very high efficiency of converting food to useful products, (iv) ability to reduce heat production without reducing useful production, (v) ability to tolerate a rise of body temperature without loss of functional efficiency. A shiny, light-colored hair coat with lowered absorptivity to solar radiation is important in potential heat tolerance. Performance, in terms of growth, reproduction, milk production, and body development, is the best measure now available, but it certainly is not a predictive measure.

The principal difference between some adapted and nonadapted types of cattle appears to be heat production rather than heat loss. This suggests that the thyroid gland, as it affects metabolic rate, is basically concerned in adaptation. Heat production is also important in the safety mechanism—a critical level of body heat that determines the regulation of food intake.

Animals seem to adjust themselves to temperature changes by changing the proportions of different food nutrients that they ingest. High-protein and low-carbohydrate diets are preferred at high ambient temperatures. With a high level of feeding, the additional heat produced is not adequately lost by vaporization; the result is considerable cumulative heat storage and the effects that are associated with this condition.

Animals are best fitted to their environment when the caloric requirements are in harmony with the hemodynamic possibilities of oxygen transport. This harmony seems to be established when the logarithm of metabolism is proportional to the logarithm of body weight. If an animal is not in thermal equilibrium with its environment, its metabolism is not normal and, apparently, no amount of feeding will stimulate growth.

There is a lack of information concerning the effects of stress on specific nutrient requirements of domestic animals. Requirements for vitamin A are increased 4 or 5 times in hot weather. Vitamin-A deficient steers have a lowered resistance to heat stress.

Water Consumption

Food consumption is also a function of water consumption. The hypothalamic region is involved in both hunger and thirst. Water consumption of animals has generally been thought to be a direct function of environmental temperature, although there are enormous individual differences in the water-consumption response to increasing ambient temperature. Thus, the water consumption of range cows averages 2.6 gallons (9.85 liters) per day during the winter and 11.5 gallons (43.6 liters) per day during the summer. Even with the increased water consumption, a negative water balance is very common. This, in turn, causes physiologic symptoms associated with stress.

Howard Weeth, at the Nevada Agricultural Experiment Station, has been conducting research on the ability of cattle to tolerate high salt concentrations in drinking water. Since available water in arid areas often contains high salt concentrations, it is essential to know what effect this has on growth and reproductive performance.

One of the more important effects of high temperatures on cattle production is in reproductive performance. Spermatogenesis is adversely affected by high temperatures, but generally an extended exposure is required to produce serious damage. Recent evidence has pointed to high environmental temperatures as a causative factor in embryonic mortality.

The genetic aspects of heat tolerance in beef and dairy cattle are being studied in the humid gulf region of the southern United States by the U.S. Department of Agriculture and the Louisiana Agricultural Experiment Station. The general approach has been to introduce zebu adaptability in existing breeds and to develop new strains from a crossbred foundation. Crossing Brahman (zebu) cattle with existing beef-cattle breeds has consistently resulted in increased production. The animals have a faster growth rate, and the crossbreds are superior mothers. The Brahman crosses seem to be slower-maturing cattle, however, and produce lower-grading carcasses, judged by United States grading standards.

Zebu crossing for dairy production has not proved to be generally satisfactory. It now appears that systematic crossing of the existing dairy breeds is a more satisfactory approach to maintenance of production. Brown Swiss and Jersey are suitable for this purpose.

Several new breeds of beef cattle have been developed from the Brahman crosses with the Shorthorn, Angus, and Charolais. These include the Santa Gertrudis, Brangus, and Charbray. These breeds have good resistance to the high temperature and disease conditions of the South and Southwest but are generally lower in feedlot gain and carcass quality than existing beef breeds.

The development of adapted types of cattle for a particular environment must await more research on the genetic factors involved. Heritability studies and genetic correlations are very limited.

Unfortunately, there are only a limited number of aids that can be used in practical management to help cattle during the conditions of thermal stress. Adequate shade is by far the most important. Feeding a ration with a higher concentrate and lower fiber level to decrease the heat of digestion is usually worth while. Cool drinking water is expensive and not consistently beneficial. Sprinkling, or fogging, appears to add more to the discomfort of the animals than it helps in heat dissipation. Increased air movement by fans may help at temperatures below 100° Fahrenheit (38° Celsius), but above this temperature it has a heating effect rather than a cooling effect. It has been noted that weather fluctuations are actually beneficial to cattle. Because of their large thermal capacity (weight times specific heat), cattle can withstand very high day temperatures provided that the nights are cool. Methods for increasing the night cooling of cattle may be worthy of more consideration. These could include night feeding, air movement with fans, or combinations of several management procedures.

Cultivated Field Crops

Field crops in the arid areas must be highly productive and of high value to compete economically. In the irrigated sections of the western United States, the most important field crops are cotton, seed crops, feed grains, forages, and oilseeds. The average cotton yield in the Southwest is approximately 2 bales of lint per acre (0.4047 hectare), which is more than twice the national average. Alfalfa (*Medicago sativa*), clovers (*Trifolium* spp.), and grasses are the most important seed crops in the irrigated West. Sorghum (*Sorghum* spp.) and barley (*Hordeum*) are important feed grains in the Southwest, and more than half of the irrigated hay and pasture land in this area is devoted to alfalfa. Oilseed crops, such as safflower (*Carthamus tinctorium*) and castor bean (*Ricinus communis*), have been grown increasingly in recent years but are not yet highly important in terms of the total area cropped. The importance of the crops in an area changes rapidly because of economic, social, and technical factors.

Considerable crop-breeding and crop-management research has been conducted in the arid and semiarid regions. Not all of this research is peculiar to arid conditions, since the principles of inheritance and of plant growth do not vary with environmental changes. In the irrigated areas, crop-breeding and crop-management research has been directed mainly toward achieving maximum yields, and, at the same time, attempting to prevent the scarcity of water from becoming a limiting factor. Crop breeding in areas of low rainfall has provided improved varieties for both dry-land and irrigated farming. Breeding methods for all areas are the same, but selection criterions and selection pressures may vary because of local conditions.

Many of the early introductions of grain sorghum displayed a tall-plant type that was suitable for hand harvesting. Through the use of effective plant-breeding techniques, these tall types were converted to shorter plants that are suitable for machine harvesting. This achievement was as important to United States agriculture as the commercial use of hybrid vigor in sorghum. Although hybrid vigor in sorghum was described in 1927, it was not until the 1950's that J. C. Stephens, of the U.S. Department of Agriculture, and others working at Chillicothe, Texas, developed a commercial hybrid-sorghum-production method by the use of male sterility. The controlled evolution of sorghum during the last 50 years is a good example of successful crop breeding for both dry-land and irrigated agriculture.

Cotton improvement in the Southwest rivals the spectacular improvements made in sorghum. Large increases in lint production per acre (hectare) have been effected by the development of improved extra-long-staple cotton (*Gossypium barbadense*). Pima S-1, developed by Walker E. Bryan and his associates at the University of Arizona, was a considerable improvement over the older varieties in yield, plant type, and lint percentage. The extra-long-staple cotton industry is now an important, stable segment of agriculture in the Southwest. In the United States, this American-Egyptian cotton is grown primarily in Arizona, New Mexico, and Texas.

Lint quality of American Upland Acala cotton has been improved by careful evaluation of breeding material for fiber length, strength, and fineness. An instrument for accurate measurement of the tensile strength of cotton fiber was devised by Elias H. Pressley, at the University of Arizona, and has greatly aided in the breeding for, and evaluation of, the strength-quality factor. The Acala cottons developed in the Southwest by Pressley, of Arizona, and Glen Staten, of New Mexico State University, are well known for their high quality.

Crop adaptation in relation to the economic use of water has been reviewed by K. H. W. Klages (13), of the University of Idaho. He states that little can be done to reduce transpiration losses; therefore, the greatest effort has been directed toward increasing the yield. One management practice for increasing the yield that has been successful in semiarid regions is summer fallowing (see Chapter 8).

Salinity problems in relation to crop response have received much attention in the irrigated arid regions. L. Bernstein and H. E. Hayward, of the U.S. Salinity Laboratory at Riverside, California, have reviewed the physiology of salt tolerance (14). These authors divide the effect of salinity on plant growth into osmotic and ion effects.

D. R. Dewey, of the U.S. Agricultural Research Service, working at Utah State University, has recently shown that salt tolerance during germination varies within and among species of wheatgrass (Agropyron spp.) (15). He, therefore, concluded that selection within Agropyron species might isolate strains with greater salt tolerance. A similar investigation concerning bermudagrass (Cynodon spp.) and blue panicgrass (Panicum antidotale) is underway at the University of Arizona.

Drought Tolerance

Investigations of drought tolerance with particular emphasis on grass improvement have been reviewed by Neal Wright and L. J. Streetman, of the Agricultural Research Service at Tucson, Arizona (16), who point out that relative drought tolerance of some

Walker E. Bryan was photographed as he took notes in a field of Pima S-1 extra-long-staple cotton (*Gossypium barbadense*), which he and his associates developed. (Courtesy University of Arizona)

genera and some species within a genus is known; however, drought tolerance within species has not been determined. Wright and Streetman further reported that the development of plant material within a species that has strains with high and low drought tolerance would allow further research on why one strain exhibits high tolerance and another low tolerance. Perhaps the physiologic processes or morphologic characteristics that condition drought tolerance could then be isolated and described for each species.

Phreatophytes have received increasing attention in arid lands. Satisfactory forage replacement crops for phreatophytes in parts of the Gila River floodway in Arizona are bermudagrass (*Cynodon dactylon*) and blue panicgrass (*Panicum antidotale*), according to B. Powers and Keith C. Hamilton, of the University of Arizona (*17*). Cool-season forage crops that are also adapted to the same area are tall fescue (*Festuca arundinacea*), harding grass (*Phalaris tuberosa*), and alfalfa (*Medicago sativa*). The competitive effect of these crops against the invading phreatophytes has not been critically determined, but observations indicate that considerable phreatophyte control may be effected by good stands of adapted forage species. Experiments are in progress in Arizona to evaluate more critically the effect of these crops on phreatophyte control.

The use of plastic and petroleum mulch to conserve the moisture and increase the soil temperature around germinating seeds appears to be promising. Both private companies and colleges are working on mulch materials. Results in Arizona indicate that the use of petroleum mulch gives faster emergence and seedling development of field and vegetable crops; in many cases, this resulted in higher yields or more timely harvesting. Future studies will determine the extent to which these mulches can be advantageously used in the arid and semiarid zones.

With the increasing demands on water, more knowledge is needed concerning the efficiency with which plants use water. This has been called *water-use, or water-utilization, efficiency.* Both terms refer to the amount of water that is transpired from the plant and evaporated from the soil per unit of product produced. The lower elevations of the Southwest would provide excellent field laboratories for studies on this subject. Application of water could be closely controlled in field experiments. Some diseases would be less troublesome because of low humidity. Because there are few cloudy days in this area, daily variations in light would be low.

The deliberate breeding of crops for water-use efficiency has generally been neglected in the irrigated sections. In dry-land areas, the pressure for selecting the most efficient use of water is large because rainfall is so scanty. Varieties of crops developed for dry-land regions would presumably be highly efficient in water use within the range of prevailing moisture levels.

Water-Use Efficiency

Crops vary in the amount of water required to produce dry matter. Homer L. Shantz and L. N. Piemeisel (*18*), working in Colorado, determined the amount of water required by various crops to produce 1 pound (0.454 kilogram) of dry matter in the aboveground parts. The requirement ranged from 271 pounds (123 kilograms) of water for sorghum to 858 pounds (390 kilograms) of water for alfalfa.

It is more important to breed for the characteristic of water-use efficiency within a crop or a species than to breed for it among different crops. The possibility of changing a crop or populations of plants is predicted by the existence of genetic variability within a species for a given characteristic. Although differences among plants within a species for efficiency of growth at a specific moisture level have been noted by plant scientists and others, little such published information is available. However, W. Keller (*19*), at Utah State University, found that selected genotypes of orchardgrass (*Dactylis glomerata*) showed differences in water requirement, forage production, and total water used.

Since the breeding of crops for maximum productivity with minimum water use is only one goal, less than maximum production may be desirable if water is limited. Cleared floodways and abandoned lands are potentially productive, even if they are supplied with only limited amounts of irrigation water. Therefore, strains should be developed that will result in the largest amounts of quality product at low and intermediate levels of irrigation.

The following plan was developed by Arden A. Baltensperger for a sod-forming, cross-fertilized forage grass. First, estimate the genotypic diversity for water-use efficiency within the species selected for study. Data on the amount of water actually consumed by plants in relation to the productivity of strains within the species will be necessary. To estimate genotypic (gene-controlled) effects, some environmental effects can be measured and removed from the total phenotypic (physical or external) variation by the use of root stock from several clones.

If genotypic variation for water-use efficiency appears to be great and if selection on the basis of what can be seen is effective, genetic advance might be achieved by a simple breeding method such as mass selection. If, on the other hand, genotypic variation is small, progeny tests may be necessary. If it is assumed that there are hereditary differences in water-use efficiency within a species, repeated selection by the use of progeny tests should bring about improvement, even if the gene frequency for the characteristic is low or if it is conditioned by a large number of genes.

A study of water-use efficiency should involve several irrigation levels. If such a procedure is followed, germ-plasm pools (restricted plant populations) that are high in water-use efficiency may be developed for high, intermediate, low, or no irrigation. Since soil fertility, soil and water salinity, and the time and method of application of water affect water-use efficiency, these factors must be changed and be studied simultaneously with strain evaluation and improvement. If strains or varieties that differ greatly in their water-use efficiency are developed, physiologic and morphologic studies should help to elucidate the plant characteristics that contribute to it.

Irrigation Research in the United States

Control of water from the time it falls to the earth until it is placed in the root zone of the crop is the ultimate goal in irrigation procedures. This goal points to the need for closed storage and conveyance systems, increased attention to landforming, automatic regulatory structures, and better water management. Each succeeding year some progress is made.

Although soil-water-plant relationships constitute a large part of the investigational work in the United States, the following presentation is limited to investigations in the mechanics of irrigation and drainage. Irrigation research is conducted chiefly by federal agencies, universities, and state experiment stations. The federal agencies with major responsibility are the Bureau of Reclamation and the Agricultural Research Service. Although there is no sharp line that limits the activities of these two agencies, the work of the Bureau of Reclamation is related largely to problems associated with the design, construction, and operation of large dams, reservoirs, main distribution systems, and drainage. The Agricultural Research Service is concerned with farm water storage, farm water-distribution systems, water application, irrigation-water requirements, and drainage of agricultural lands.

The research done by the Agricultural Research Service and the universities has been important mainly in the establishment and application of principles. These have included mathematical developments that aid in the evaluation of energy relationships and flow patterns and the behavior of earthen materials in foundations and structures.

Since runoff takes place in short periods and, in most of the irrigated areas, early in the irrigation season, storage is required to allow full use of the available water. In order that water may be delivered to the land, provision must be made for conveyance and application, which, in turn, necessitate reservoirs, diversion works, canals, flumes, and pipelines. The efficiency with which water is provided and delivered to the land is governed by the performance and durability of these structures. Research has been focused on materials, site evaluation, construction techniques, and design.

An important aspect of this research is the evaluation and development of structural materials. Investigations have included conventional materials—concrete, steel, earth, and asphalt—as well as new materials (20). Better structures have resulted through improvements in standard construction components, and the new materials—resins, plastics, and rubber—have been used to supplement and, at times, replace materials with long-established uses. These advances have not been the product of any one organization but rather have resulted from the combined efforts of federal and state agencies working closely with industry and trade associations.

Although earth is the oldest and probably the most used of building materials, it is only recently that the structural properties of soil have become well understood and applied in construction. Among the properties that influence performance are size and distribution of particles, permeability, unit weight, shearing strength, and compressibility. A comprehensive summary of present knowledge and its application to the construction of, and use of new materials in, irrigation works is published in the *Earth Manual* (21) of the U.S. Bureau of Reclamation.

An example of a new material is epoxy resin, which, as a primer, helps to produce a bond strength between new and old concrete that is stronger than the concrete itself. It also has proved to be useful as a protective coating and for the bonding of other materials, including metals.

The use of air-entraining agents in concrete is another example of improvement in construction. There are several materials that, when they are added to concrete mixes, produce small, well-dispersed air bubbles in concrete. Two of these are a triethanolamine salt of a sulfonated hydrocarbon and a coal-tar hydrocarbon extract of pinewood. The entrainment of small, highly dispersed air bubbles greatly improves the weatherability of concrete. Many persons who represented numerous and varied interests, including industry, federal, and state agencies, contributed to this development. The Bureau of Reclamation estimates that it has resulted in a saving on bureau projects of $10 million during the past 10 years.

Model and Field Studies

Design is as important as material in the performance of a structure. The principles of classic mechanics are the bases of all design. Frequently, however, performance cannot be fully predicted on the basis of design principles alone. To compensate for this limitation, hydrodynamically similar models are made of nearly all major structures. Tests on models have resulted in money savings and better performance. In the Glen Canyon and Flaming Gorge dams, modifications in design that resulted from model testing of the spillway structures by the Bureau of Reclamation in Denver led to savings of $1,627,000.

Model testing is not confined to large structures but is used also for such devices as headgates, flumes, weirs, and sprinkler nozzles. Much of the testing on this class of structures is done by the Agricultural Research Service at its field stations, where the work is done in cooperation with agricultural experiment stations and other state and federal agencies. Among the stations that have been active in such studies are those at Minneapolis, Minnesota; Fort Collins, Colorado; Tempe, Arizona; Stillwater, Oklahoma; and Logan, Utah. Not only has model testing been useful in checking design, but it has provided basic information on the hydraulics of irrigation structures, application of fluid mechanics to such problems as water measurement, and the design of spillway and conveyance structures.

Although model testing is a useful supplement to the application of engineering principles, it is not always adequate in itself. This is particularly true of the problems of seepage, drainage, scouring, and sediment handling. To fill this gap, field studies have been instigated. The primary reason for the deficiency in model studies on these problems is the difficulty of identifying and simulating site conditions.

Because soil-profile characteristics are controlling factors, undisturbed soil samples are frequently used in studies of water transport. Land areas, as well as soil profiles, are heterogeneous; and undisturbed samples, even when they are taken in large numbers, may not be highly indicative of area performance. For this reason, field measurements, such as the pumping-well methods, for estimating water yield and tile size have distinct advantages over laboratory methods in the design of drainage systems.

The existence of lenses and other nonconformities makes successful drainage possible in many areas. These same textural and structural discontinuities frequently are primarily responsible for seepage in canals. However, seepage can be controlled in some canals merely by overexcavation and replacement of the material removed, if this is accompanied by compaction.

In the West, the most important source of irrigation water is the melting snowpack in the mountains. An electronic analog computer has been developed by the U.S. Agricultural Research Service and the University of Idaho at Moscow, Idaho, to calculate estimates of streamflow from snowmelt on source areas of the Pacific Northwest. Involved in the computations are snow storage and melting as they are related to climatic, topographic, and vegetational characters; losses from evapotranspiration as it varies with climatic factors; amount of rainfall; soil-moisture storage; ground-water storage and discharge; and observed streamflow. At present, the analog computer is used primarily as a research tool for the refinement of weather-forecasting techniques. It speeds up calculation processes, however, and has great potential for the handling of large amounts of data in connection with water-supply forecasts.

Large quantities of water are lost by evaporation from storage reservoirs. The extent of these losses is governed by the area of the water surface in relation to the reservoir capacity and the evaporation potential at the site. Reductions can be attained by diking to reduce the water surface and increase the average depth of the stored water. When alternate sites are available, consideration should be given to climatic factors that influence the evaporation potential.

The life and effectiveness of a reservoir are limited by silting, and the measurement of silt depositions has been the subject of much investigation. An instrument that permits a precise measurement of the density of silt in a reservoir has been perfected at the Agricultural Research Service's U.S. Sedimentation Laboratory at Oxford, Mississippi. This instrument measures the density of sediments as a linear (logarithmic) function of the attenuation of gamma rays from radium-226. Measurements of depths or thicknesses of silt are relatively simple with traditional models, but the necessary measurements of densities, or weight per unit volume, have long been a laborious problem, sometimes almost impossible to solve. Since silt-density measurements are necessary to forecast the useful life of reservoir storage and to relate the silting problem back to the source of the silt in the watershed, the instrument will be helpful in the evaluation of silting problems in reservoirs.

Although surface water constitutes the chief source of water for irrigation, ground water is being used increasingly. The 1959 U.S. Census of Agriculture lists a total of 72,997,259 acre feet (90,042 million cubic meters) of water as entering conveyance systems. Of this, 4,300,470 acre feet (5305 million cubic meters) had its source in ground water. An extreme example is the Santa Cruz Valley in Arizona. Pumpage from this basin was about 420,000 acre feet (518 million cubic meters) of water in 1941; 730,000 acre feet (900 million cubic meters) in 1945; and 1,250,000 acre feet (1542 million cubic meters) in 1949.

Excessive pumpage has caused a lowering of the ground-water tables in many areas. In some parts of the Santa Cruz Basin, ground-water levels dropped as much as 50 feet (15.25 meters) between 1940 and 1949 owing to overdraft. To relieve this situation, the artificial recharge of ground-water aquifers by spreading flood water on relatively permeable areas is being investigated at the University of Arizona and by the Agricultural Research Service in the San Joaquin Valley of California and in the High Plains of Texas. Intake or infiltration of water in the recharge areas is the most limiting factor to this approach. General information on the soil profile is helpful in the selection of promising sites for water spreading in the artificial recharge of ground-water aquifers, but field evaluation remains the most reliable criterion. In effect, a ground-water aquifer is a reservoir and has some advantages over surface reservoirs. Water stored underground is not subject to evaporation and frequently is available in the area of use without the necessity of conveyance systems.

Evaporation Control

Evaporation control is a much discussed problem and is the subject of extensive investigation. It has been estimated by the U.S. Geological Survey that 30 million acre feet (37,000 million cubic meters) of water per year is lost by evaporation and transpiration along watercourses in the 17 western states. Evaporation alone was estimated at 24 million acre feet (29,600 million cubic meters). The annual evaporation from Lake Mead in Arizona and Nevada has averaged 849,000 acre feet (1047 million cubic meters) during the past 10 years.

One approach to evaporation control has been the use of hexa-decanol [$CH_3(CH_2)_{15}OH$], which is a waxy, white solid at ordinary temperatures. When it is applied to water surfaces, it forms a monomolecular layer over the surface and impedes evaporation. Several factors limit the effectiveness of hexadecanol. The most important of these is the maintenance of the film in a fully compressed state on the water surface. The major difficulty appears to be blow-off, although there is some evidence of molecular breakdown through biologic processes and ultraviolet light.

The Bureau of Reclamation reports a 64-percent decrease in evaporation with the use of hexadecanol on a 4-foot (1.22-meter) sheet-metal evaporation pan during a 4-week period. Evaporation control in the order of 45 percent for commercial grade and 30 percent for chemically pure hexadecanol was obtained by the Agricultural Research Service under laboratory conditions at Logan, Utah. This apparently indicates that, if the film can be kept intact, more control is possible than has been indicated by field experiments. It seems to show also that the purity of the hexadecanol is a factor.

The most comprehensive study made to date was on Lake Hefner in Oklahoma in 1958 (22). This report states: "The over-all evaporation savings of 9 percent, as determined by the U.S. Geological Survey, were for an 86-day period, during which treatments were made on only 55 days. High winds and other conditions made it unfeasible to make applications on the other 31 days. For several shorter periods within the 55 days, savings of from 10 to 14 percent were achieved." More recently, reductions in evaporation as high as 22 percent for short periods are reported; these reports are based on tests made by the Bureau of Reclamation on Saguaro Lake near Phoenix, Arizona, and Lake Cachuma near Santa Barbara, California, and on other studies in California and Arizona. Costs ranged from $28 to $58 per acre foot (1233.5 cubic meters) of water saved.

Interest continues in other methods of collecting and saving water. Watertight bags with a capacity up to 40,000 gallons (151 cubic meters) have been prepared by the Agricultural Research Service at Logan, Utah (23), for storing small volumes of water, such as those needed for livestock and domestic purposes. At present, these bags are fabricated from butyl-coated nylon or unsupported butyl sheeting, depending on stress requirements. The butyl bags control evaporation effectively and, at the same time, eliminate vegetative growth and provide protection against contamination. It is doubtful, however, that this approach is a practical solution to the control of evaporation from large bodies of water, such as irrigation reservoirs.

Water Measurement

The Parshall flume (24) is a specially constructed Venturi flume, so designed that the water for unsubmerged conditions is forced to pass through the critical depth within the structure. Discharge is determined from a calibration table and the depth of water. A correction must be applied for submerged conditions. The Parshall flume has proved to be an excellent device for the measurement of irrigation water. Constructed of wood, metal, or concrete, it has advantages over other water measuring devices—such as weirs and orifices—in that it is less sensitive to upstream conditions and debris problems.

Agricultural Research Service investigators at Fort Collins, Colorado, found recently that accurate flow measurements can be made with a Parshall or Venturi-type flume section without a drop at the outlet if the depth of water is measured at specified points in both the outlet and inlet sections. The ratio of these two depths is known as *submergence*. The amount of submergence determines a correction factor that is applied to the depth-flow relationship without submergence for the correct flow measurement with submergence. A simplified procedure was developed for making these determinations.

Investigations have also shown that the angle of the converging section in Parshall flumes can be changed considerably with only small variations in the head-discharge relationship. Thus, measuring devices of this type can be altered within limits to accommodate canals that range widely in cross section without materially changing the rating curve. This allows savings in the construction cost of canal-measuring sections.

A watertight bag of synthetic cloth stores water in a small reservoir. Water fills the bag, which can contain up to 40,000 gallons (151 cubic meters), to about the ground line, and the top is held up by air pressure. (Courtesy U.S. Department of Agriculture, Agricultural Research Service)

Nearly all irrigation water is conveyed by, and applied to the land from, unlined canals and ditches. Records from 46 operating projects of the Bureau of Reclamation showed that, of 15,650,000 acre feet (19,304 million cubic meters) of water supplied for irrigation, approximately 3.9 million acre feet (4810 million cubic meters) of water was lost in seepage from conveyance channels.

Seepage losses can be greatly reduced by lining the canals. Many materials are used for lining, but probably the most satisfactory one in new construction is portland cement concrete. Linings of this material are relatively durable and, along with other hard-surfaced linings, usually have a great capacity. They tolerate high velocities and are resistant to mechanical damage. The chief objection to concrete as a lining material is the high cost, although long service and the smaller cross-section requirement tend to offset this cost when it is compared with other types of lining.

Much research has been directed to the development of lower-cost linings. Most of this work has been done by the Bureau of Reclamation under the guidance of its Lower-Cost Canal Lining Committee (25) and by the Agricultural Research Service at Logan, Utah, and Tempe, Arizona. Among the linings that have proved to be useful is thick, compacted earth. Buried asphaltic membrane, buried polyethylene and vinyl film, and buried butyl linings give better seepage control than concrete but have the disadvantages that are associated with buried linings. They are easily damaged in cleaning operations; larger cross sections are required to deliver the same water; permissible velocities are lower; and at times weeds are troublesome (26).

These buried linings generally are best adapted to earth canals that have been in operation for some time and to places where seepage control is the primary reason for lining. They can be installed rapidly and under conditions where concrete could not be applied. Satisfactory installations of plastic film and butyl sheeting have been made on very soft subgrades and in places where some water was actually in the canal.

Because of the short time that many farm laterals and ditches are in actual use, lining can seldom be justified on the basis of the cost of the water saved. Linings supplemented by checks and diversion structures, however, greatly reduce the labor of managing and applying water to the land; for this reason, most farm ditches are lined. Lining, in addition, is a good weed-control measure.

Practical research has resulted in the development of the subgrade-guided slipform and has greatly facilitated the construction of concrete-lined farm ditches. A slipform is a device for placing concrete linings in a continuous operation. The front section of the form is shaped to fit the ditch and rides on the subgrade. Immediately behind the front section is the hopper. Fresh concrete is placed in the hopper, and, as the form is pulled forward, the concrete is distributed on the subgrade and smoothed by the tail section. The thickness of the lining is determined by the vertical displacement of the tail section in relation to the front section.

Slipforms have reduced the cost of lining and have made possible the rapid construction of linings. Trencher-type ditch openers are now being developed. As these come into general use, concrete-lined ditches with less deviation from line and grade can be expected.

The most efficient way to convey and distribute water is in pipe or tubing. Until recently, most of the water was conveyed in steel, con-

A subgrade-guided slipform is used to line a farm ditch with concrete. Such a device greatly facilitates modern irrigation development. (Courtesy U.S. Department of Agriculture, Agricultural Research Service)

crete, asbestos cement, or aluminum pipe. Most of the pipe used is still prefabricated, but a device for casting concrete pipe in place has been developed by a California company. This cast-in-place pipe is being used extensively for low-pressure lines 36 to 60 inches (0.9 to 1.5 meters) in diameter. Plastic pipe up to 12 inches (30 centimeters) in diameter has recently become available and is being used to some extent. Another development is lay-flat tubing, which has many practical advantages.

Landforming

Landforming, or *leveling* as it is sometimes called, has contributed as much to irrigation efficiency as any practice that has been adopted in recent years. Large-scale landforming has been made practical by the availability of heavy earth-moving equipment. The trend is toward lower gradients and basin irrigation in some areas. Where topography is restricting, a type of landforming known as *bench leveling* has been employed. But, because of costs and problems presented to the operation of farm machinery, bench leveling may not be widely adopted on the steeper areas, for sprinkler irrigation can be used satisfactorily without the benching.

One of the most outstanding contributions of research in the last decade is the development and use of sprinkler irrigation. Since 1946, sprinkler irrigation has spread from a few isolated areas in the United States to every section of the country. Between 1949 and 1954, 200,000 acres (81,000 hectares) of land were brought into production by sprinkler irrigation. Although less than 12 percent of the irrigated land in the United States is sprinkled, sprinkling has made production possible on much land in the semiarid West that otherwise could not have been efficiently irrigated, and it has increased production of land in humid regions. Sprinkling is useful as an irrigation procedure in places where only supplemental irrigation or irrigations at infrequent intervals is required. With some crops, such as potatoes and sugar beets, the application of water by sprinkling increases production even in areas that are well adapted to irrigation from ditches.

The success of sprinkler irrigation can be credited to aluminum-pipe laterals, quick couplers, and sprinkler heads that are capable of reasonably good water distribution. A sprinkling system, if it is to operate satisfactorily, must be properly designed. Basic to any design is a knowledge of soil characteristics and of the crop to be irrigated. This information, along with engineering principles and other factors in design, is the subject of a book by the Sprinkler Irrigation Association (27).

The necessity for the hand moving of sprinkler laterals remains a problem. Mechanical moving devices are not entirely satisfactory and remain impractical in many places. All major sprinkler-equipment manufacturers, as well as many researchers in public agencies, are actively engaged in improving the efficiency and reducing the labor requirement of sprinkler irrigation.

Drainage

Methods for removing excess water from agricultural lands have been the subject of much research (28). When land is irrigated, drainage problems almost always follow. Hence, provision for drainage is an essential feature in all large-scale irrigation developments. The practice in the past has been to wait until high ground water and salinity threatened continued production before relief measures were undertaken. At present, there are two lines of thought: (i) wait until the problem develops and then take steps to correct the situation; (ii) assess conditions and provide preventive measures. The first is more prevalent and can be defended on the grounds that evaluation studies seldom provide a reliable guide to requirements. Consequently, when advance measures have been taken, they have often been faulty or inadequate.

Research is showing that drainage requirements could be practically eliminated in some areas, if conveyance losses were controlled and if water were applied to the land in accordance with soil and plant requirements. There are few, if any, areas where this idealized situation has been achieved; and, except in places where good natural drainage exists, provision for controlling ground-water elevation is still necessary.

Of primary importance in the design of a drainage system are the hydraulic conductivity of the soil profile and the quantity of water that must be removed to hold the water table at a satisfactory level. These two considerations determine the size, spacing, and depth of drains. Although soil-profile characteristics, as determined from soil samples, provide a guide to drainage design, they have their limitations. Field measurements, such as those that involve water-level recovery rate in an auger hole, provide more reliable data on which to base construction specifications.

Clay and concrete draintiles are used widely for subsurface drainage. Efficient operation and continuing effectiveness require that the soil be kept out of the lines. Of the several materials tested, Fiberglas mats were found to be the most effective for filtering out the soil and preventing clogging. To prevent breaking and tearing of the mat in backfilling, 2 to 4 inches (5 to 10 centimeters) of soil should be manually placed over the filter before backfilling. Ohio State University tests showed that water entering bare tile lines contained 7 times as much silt as lines that had Fiberglas filters covering 75 percent of the joint. Where the filter was wrapped entirely around the joints, protection against silting was almost complete.

Sometimes stabilizing materials of polyethylene, vinyl, and bitumen-coated Fiberglas are placed on the top of the joints. The stabilizing material reduces the amount of soil that moves into tile liners and is helpful in unstable soils. These materials may be used under the tile and, at times, are used in combination with Fiberglas filters.

A bituminous-impregnated fiber pipe is used in some areas in place of clay or concrete tile. The bituminous fiber pipe has some advantages over concrete and tile pipe, in that it is lightweight and comes in longer lengths—usually 8 feet (2.44 meters)—and is perforated to allow entry of water, the joints being watertight. Spacing and size of perforations can be selected to meet the requirements of the job. A limitation is that most tile-laying machines are not adapted to use these long lengths of pipe. This problem can be solved, as it was by a contractor in the Imperial Valley of California, who modified a conventional tile-laying machine to handle lengths of pipe up to 8 feet.

Mole drainage has never been very effective in the United States. The principal advantage of mole drainage is the low cost. The problem is to keep the drains open. In an attempt to do this, a machine has been developed for lining the drain with plastic. This is done by feeding a continuous roll of plastic into a guide attached to the shank of the mole plow. As the plastic sheet enters the opening behind the opener, it is formed into a tube that lines the opening left by the plow.

Few, if any, commercial installations have been made, but there are test installations in New York, Georgia, Florida, Louisiana, Colorado, Utah, Nevada, and California. This work has been a cooperative undertaking by the Agricultural Research Service, private companies, and several of the state experiment stations.

Although some progress has been made, plastic-lined mole drains have not performed satisfactorily. One of the most serious problems has been the tendency of the linings to collapse and the capacity to decrease. Before drainage with plastic-lined mole drains is practical, a liner must be devised that will have greater resistance to collapse, and equipment must be developed to install the tile at greater depths and to maintain a more uniform grade.

Thick-walled polyethylene tubing can be installed with a mole plow in much the same way as the plastic sheet. This tubing is 2 inches (5.08 centimeters) in diameter and has a wall thickness of 0.125 inch (3.2 millimeters). Before installation, it is perforated to permit the entrance of drainage water.

REFERENCES

1. F. Shreve, "Ecological aspects of the deserts of California," *Ecology* 6, 93–103 (1925).
2. C. W. Cook, L. A. Stoddart, and F. Kinsinger, "Responses of crested wheatgrass to various clipping treatments," *Ecol. Monographs* 28, 237–272 (1958).
3. L. B. Merrill, "Heavy grazing lowers range carrying capacity," *Texas Agr. Progr.* 5, 18–19 (1959).
4. R. J. Hildreth and C. W. Thomas, "Farming and ranching risk as influenced by rainfall," *Texas Agr. Expt. Sta. Misc. Publ. 154* (1956).
5. F. A. Sneva and D. N. Hyder, "Estimating herbage production on semiarid ranges in the intermountain region," *J. Range Management* 15, 88–93 (1962).
6. P. T. Marion, C. E. Fisher, and E. D. Robinsin, "Ground mesquite wood as a roughage in rations for yearling steers," *Texas Agr. Expt. Sta. Progr. Rept. 1962* (1957).
7. B. D. Gardner, "Costs and returns from sagebrush range improvement in Colorado," *Colo. Agr. Expt. Sta. Bull. 511-S* (1961).
8. W. H. Black, L. H. Tash, J. M. Jones, and R. J. Kleberg, Jr., "Effects of phosphorus supplements on cattle grazing on range deficient in this mineral," *U.S. Dept. Agr. Tech. Bull. 856* (1944).
9. J. H. Knox and W. E. Watkins, "The use of phosphorus and calcium supplements for range livestock in New Mexico," *New Mexico Agr. Expt. Sta. Bull. 287* (1942).
10. W. J. A. Payne and J. Hancock, "The direct effect of tropical climate in the performance of European-type cattle," *Empire J. Exptl. Agr.* 25, 321–338 (1957).
11. R. E. McDowell, B. T. McDaniel, M. S. Barrada, and D. H. K. Lee, "Rate of surface evaporation from the normal body surface and with sweat glands inactivated under hot conditions," *J. Animal Sci.* 20, 380–385 (1961).
12. R. G. Yeck and H. H. Kibler, "Moisture vaporization by Jersey and Holstein cows during diurnal temperature cycles as measured with hygrometric tent," *Missouri Univ. Agr. Expt. Sta. Res. Bull. 600* (1956).
13. K. H. W. Klages, "Crop adaptation in relation to the economic use of water," *Wyoming Agr. Expt. Sta. Bull. 367* (1960), pp. 11–32.
14. L. Bernstein and H. E. Hayward, "Physiology of salt tolerance," *Ann. Rev. Plant Physiol.* 9, 25–46 (1958).
15. D. R. Dewey, "Salt tolerance of twenty-five strains of *Agropyron*," *Agron. J.* 52, 631–635 (1960).
16. N. Wright and L. J. Streetman, "Grass improvement for the Southwest relative to drought evaluation," *Ariz. Univ. Agr. Expt. Sta. Tech. Bull. 143* (1960), pp. 1–16.

17. B. Powers and K. C. Hamilton, "Revegetation of a cleared section of a floodway," *Ariz. Univ. Agr. Expt. Sta. Rept. 198* (1961), pp. 1–23.

18. H. L. Shantz and L. N. Piemeisel, "The water requirements of plants at Akron, Colorado," *J. Agr. Res.* 34, 1093–1190 (1927).

19. W. Keller, "Water requirement of selected genotypes of orchard-grass, *Dactylis glomerata* L." *Agron. J.* 45, 622–625 (1953).

20. U.S. Senate, *Study and Investigation of the Use of Materials and New Designs and Methods in Public Works,* 87th Congr., Comm. on Public Works, Comm. Prints 1–7 (Washington, D.C., 1961).

21. U.S. Bureau of Reclamation, *Earth Manual* (U.S. Dept. of the Interior, Washington, D.C., 1960).

22. City of Oklahoma City, Oklahoma State Department of Health, U.S. Public Health Service, U.S. Weather Bureau, U.S. Geological Survey, U.S. Bureau of Reclamation, "Water-loss investigations, Lake Hefner 1958," *Evaporation Reduction Investigations* (1959).

23. C. W. Lauritzen, "Capturing precipitation," *Intern. Comm. on Irrigation and Drainage Ann. Bull.* (1962), pp. 52–53.

24. R. L. Parshall, "The Parshall measuring flume," *Colo. Agr. Expt. Sta. Bull. 423* (1936).

25. U.S. Bureau of Reclamation, "Progress report on the lower-cost canal lining program," *Linings for Irrigation Canals* (U.S. Govt. Printing Office, Washington, D.C., 1963).

26. C. W. Lauritzen, "Linings for irrigation canals," *Irrigation Eng. and Maintenance* 9, 10–11 (1959); 10, 12, 13, 21 (1960).

27. Sprinkler Irrigation Association, *Sprinkler Irrigation* (Washington, D.C., ed. 2, 1959).

28. J. N. Luthin, *Drainage of Agricultural Lands* (Am. Soc. of Agronomy, Madison, Wis., 1957).

10

Role of Watersheds and Forests in the Arid West

William G. McGinnies

Andrew L. McComb

Joel E. Fletcher

In the western United States, there is widespread interest in the possibility of increasing streamflow from watersheds. Greater streamflow is needed because water is used in large quantities (especially for irrigation agriculture), because population growth in the West is very rapid, and because per-capita consumption of water increases with increasing standards of living.

According to Edward A. Ackerman and George O. Löf (1), the total annual water yield in 17 western states—440 million acre feet (542,740,000,000 cubic meters)—is only 25 percent of the precipitation. In several areas—Arizona, for example—the present water use exceeds supply, and ground water is being mined. If the region is to continue to grow in population, the present supplies of water must be used more efficiently, and new supplies must be found. Other important water problems are distribution from areas of abundance to areas of scarcity, availability at the time most needed, and quality.

At intermediate and lower elevations, most or all of the precipitation occurs as rainfall, often of a torrential nature that results in silt-laden streamflow. At higher elevations, however, most of the precipitation falls as snow. The economic life of the western United States depends on the humid mountains, which, although they occupy only 10 to 20 percent of the total area, contribute up to 90 percent of the usable water.

A map of the major forest types, Fig. 1, shows the relationship of the more humid forested areas and the separating matrix. The matrix area varies in annual water yields from less than 0.01 inch

(0.03 centimeter) to about 2 inches (5 centimeters); the humid "islands" from about 2 inches (5 centimeters) to more than 40 inches (about 100 centimeters).

The vegetation of the matrix area can be divided into sagebrush (*Artemisia* spp.) and associated species north of the Grand Canyon of the Colorado River, and creosotebush (*Larrea divaricata*) south of the canyon, although it grades into gramagrasses (*Bouteloua* spp.) at the upper edges of the zone. A third area, which lies west of the Sierra Nevada, varies from bur-sages (*Franseria* spp.), saltbushes (*Atriplex* spp.), and big galletagrass (*Hilaria rigida*) to wild oat grasses (*Avena* spp.) at the upper areas.

Forest vegetation of the humid "islands" consists of pinyon pines (*Pinus* spp.) and junipers (*Juniperus* spp.) at low elevations; ponderosa pine (*P. ponderosa*), Douglas-fir (*Pseudotsuga menziesii*), firs (*Abies* spp.), larches (*Larix* spp.), hemlocks (*Tsuga* spp.), and incense cedar (*Libocedrus* spp.) at intermediate elevations; and spruce (*Picea* spp.), firs, and white pines (*P. flexilis*) at high elevations.

Although most of the water in the Northwest flows from the high-elevation humid islands, significant amounts come from the sagebrush zone, mostly as spring snowmelt. Water yields by months from a small watershed in southwestern Idaho that is typical of the sagebrush zone are compared in Table I with those from a similar watershed in the mixed shrub-desert grassland of Arizona.

Management practices aimed at improvement of water supplies must decrease losses from evapotranspiration at the higher elevations, retard floods, control sedimentation, and reduce evapotranspiration losses at the lower elevations.

The average evaporation loss for the world is approximately 70 percent, leaving 30 percent of the total precipitation for runoff or streamflow. Compared with this, the average evaporation in Arizona is 96 percent, but in the humid state of Oregon it is only 44 percent.

Snow as a Streamflow Source

Because so much of the streamflow comes from melting snow in the humid "islands," snow management is a challenge to watershed managers. Foliage and the stems of vegetation intercept snow, just as they do rain. Some of this intercepted snow sublimes, and the

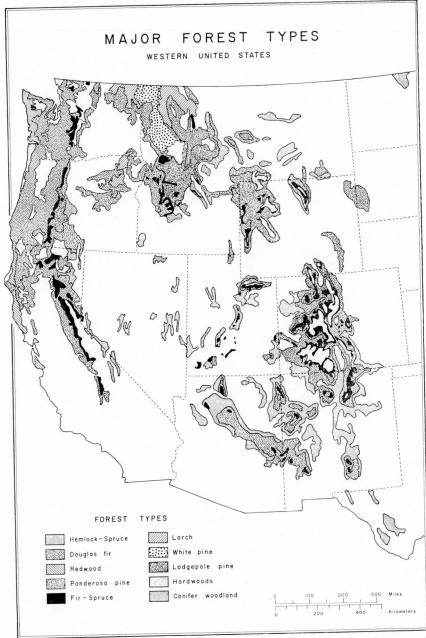

Fig. 1. Major forest types in the West are shown as they are delineated by the U.S. Forest Service, with some modifications made necessary by the reduction of the original map.

vapor becomes a part of the circulating atmosphere. Interception loss usually amounts to from 5 to 20 percent of the precipitation, depending on density, height, and other characteristics of the vegetation, the action of wind, the dryness of the atmosphere, and the quality of the snow. Water yields can be moderately changed by control of these factors.

Snow lying on the ground, like snow intercepted by tree canopies, evaporates. J. E. Church, one of the pioneers in watershed studies in the United States, states that "forests catch the falling snow directly in proportion to their openness, but conserve it, after it has fallen, directly in proportion to their density" (2). The tree crowns, which catch the snow and expose it to rapid evaporation, also intercept sun and wind and conserve the snow that has accumulated on the ground.

Evaporation from snow in the Northern Hemisphere takes place mostly on open, south-facing ridges or on slopes where wind movement is great. It is less in large forest openings, and the least where trees completely cover the ground. Studies in central Colorado showed that evaporation during the winter was 2.24 inches (5.7 centimeters) in the open and only 0.8 inch (2 centimeters) under a full stand of lodgepole pine (*P. contorta*). Condensation at night almost equaled evaporation during the day. There are undoubtedly places where condensation gains exceed sublimation losses, and watershed managers should beware of generalization not based on close study of individual watersheds.

To maximize water yields, rapid snowmelt should be encouraged, but if floods are to be minimized and streamflow maintained into dry periods of summer, melting should be retarded. In Colorado, Mario Martinelli, of the U.S. Forest Service, is investigating the control of water yielded from snow, with the object of maintaining summer streamflow at higher levels (3). Methods include artificially induced drifting on north-facing slopes and accumulation of snow in ravines. Snow fences have been used to deepen drifts and encourage snowbanks. Changing the absorption of radiation by the addition of colored materials, such as carbon black, has been suggested as a means of promoting more rapid melting.

Other Forest Service researchers in Idaho, Colorado, and California have found that by cutting timber, with variations in size and orientation of cut areas, they can manipulate the rate of melting.

Table I.   Percentage by month of annual water yield in arid areas.

Month	Arizona[a]	Idaho
January	0	5.8
February	0	4.3
March	0	10.0
April	0	38.2
May	tr[b]	27.4
June	tr	10.0
July	52.4	1.6
August	43.7	0.3
September	tr	tr
October	3.6	0.4
November	0	0.7
December	0	1.2
Annual yield	0.3937 inch (1 centimeter)	0.7874 inch (2 centimeters)

[a] Data from R. V. Keppel.
[b] tr means trace (less than 0.5 percent).

Maximum snow accumulation usually is found in forest openings no larger across than 2 to 10 times the heights of the trees. Maximum water yield is favored by narrow strips of forest surrounding openings about 2 to 5 times as wide as the tree heights. Late-season water yields and retarded melting are helped by openings 1 to 1.5 times the tree heights, so that the openings are shaded.

In contrast to the high-elevation forests, the more arid snow catchments that are inhabited by sagebrush and scattered woodland types of vegetation are subject to high winds during and following snowfalls. The snow, therefore, accumulates on the downwind side of ridges as cornice drifts and in low places. Snow on level ground and in areas that are subject to wind action collects to a depth proportional to the height of the vegetation. Interception loss in such areas is negligible.

Interception of Rain

Research shows that interception of rainfall equals, or slightly exceeds, that of snow. Andrew L. McComb states that he has stood under long-crowned hemlock trees during a downpour and never received a drop of rain. Rain starts to fall through forest foliage after the storage capacity of 0.01 to 0.02 inch (0.025 to 0.05 centimeter) of water has been reached, but it moves toward the crown periphery. Because of high storage capacity, showers up to 0.04 inch (0.1 centimeter) may be completely intercepted. As the amount of rain per shower increases, the percentage of rain intercepted decreases. Annual net interception losses in forests range from 5 to 25 percent of the rainfall. Water running down tree stems varies from 5 to more than 30 percent of the precipitation.

When throughfall and stemflow water reaches the soil, it wets the surface organic layers, which may vary from about 1 to more than 130 tons per acre (0.91 to 118 metric tons per 0.4047 hectare), and accumulates at rates of 0.5 to 3 tons per acre (0.45 to 2.72 metric tons per 0.4047 hectare) per year. Most of this water evaporates, since roots often do not ramify these layers. Water in excess of that required to saturate the litter, duff, and humus passes to the inorganic soil layers. Springs and seeps are supplied by water that percolates beyond the root zone.

The structure and porosity of a soil and its capacity to take in water are markedly affected by land and vegetation treatment, particularly fire, grazing, logging, and cultivation. Percy B. Rowe and others found that the infiltration capacity for California grass and sagebrush under heavy grazing was 0.19 inch (0.48 centimeter) per hour and under light grazing 0.94 inch (2.39 centimeters) per hour. In a chaparral type, infiltration was 0.36 inch (0.9 centimeter) per hour up to 3 years after burning, and 1.96 inches (5.0 centimeters) per hour 6 or more years after burning (4). It is paradoxical that in arid lands, where forage production is limited by insufficient water, moderate to heavy grazing by livestock decreases water infiltration and forage production.

Evaporation and Transpiration Losses

Water infiltrating the soil is subject to two types of vaporization losses: (i) direct evaporation, and (ii) absorption and transpiration by plants.

Watershed managers must understand the marked effect that vegetation has on the evaporation of soil moisture. Forest canopies intercept 70 to 99 percent of incoming solar radiation, causing daytime temperatures in summer to be lower than those in the open by as much as 7° Fahrenheit (4° Celsius). Surface soil temperatures in the open may be as much as 63° Fahrenheit (35° Celsius) higher than those in forests; the differences are much smaller at greater depths. Furthermore, wind speed in forests rarely is more than 1 to 2 miles (1.61 to 3.22 kilometers) per hour, and the soil is covered with an organic mulch. The net effect is a small vapor-pressure deficit and greatly reduced evaporation. Joseph Kittredge, an early forest hydrologist at the University of California, found that evaporation in a forest plantation soil to a depth of 20 inches (50.8 centimeters) was 0.59 inch (1.5 centimeters) in 30 days, in contrast to 1.34 inches (3.4 centimeters) in the open (5). Thus, the foliage and canopy, which cause interception losses, also reduce evaporation losses from soil, and it must be determined how nearly one offsets the other.

To increase water yields, evaporation of all kinds must be reduced. This is usually done by the thinning of watershed vegetation and the change from a high to a low moisture-using kind. A decrease in vegetation density generally lowers interception and transpiration losses more than it increases soil-moisture evaporation, and the result is increased water yields. A change in vegetation from deep-rooted oaks to shallow-rooted grasses resulted in material increases in water yield in California. In Arizona, John Decker, of the Forest Service, learned that bermudagrass (Cynodon dactylon), because of shallower rooting, consumed much less water than saltcedar (Tamarix pentandra) (6). Much of the difference among plants results from differences in depth and density of rooting and the efficiency of water movement into and within the plants.

Considerable effort now is being made to determine transpiration accurately and to separate it from direct evaporation of soil moisture. Much promise is shown by the vapor-production experiments of Decker, who places a transparent plastic tent over vegetation and measures the moisture content of the entering and leaving air. In New Mexico, the Forest Service is trying a method that involves detecting and measuring with thermocouples the rate of movement of a heated water impulse in the plant xylem. An older method is to grow plants in weighing lysimeters, with the soil covered with plastic to prevent soil-moisture evaporation. Much basic work on the energy budget is in progress.

Phreatophyte Problem

Throughout the arid western United States, about 16 million acres (6,475,200 hectares) of waterways are lined with trees and shrubs, such as cottonwoods (*Populus* spp.) and willows (*Salix* spp.), salt-cedar (*Tamarix pentandra*), and mesquites (*Prosopis* spp.). These water-wasting plants, which grow with their roots in the porous channel materials, are known as *phreatophytes*. They consume nearly 25 million acre feet (30.8 billion cubic meters) of water annually. Harry Blaney (7) estimates that a heavy growth of *Tamarix* may use water equivalent to a depth of 8 feet (2.6 meters) per unit surface area per year, when its roots are in contact with free water at shallow levels.

Where streamflow is ephemeral, runoff may occur in perhaps 10 to 15 events during a season, and the total time that water flows in the channel may be 200 hours. Thus, with phreatophytes using all the water stored in the channel materials between events, losses may be of the order of 10 acre feet per mile (12,335 cubic meters per 1.61 kilometer). Removal, then, of such plants, or their replacement with shallow-rooted species, would mean a considerable saving in water. For example, Blaney estimated that a saving of 50 percent, or about 32,600 acre feet (40,216,600 cubic meters) of water per year, could be obtained by replacing *Tamarix* with bermudagrass in the Pecos River channel between Artesia and Carlsbad, New Mexico, a distance of 36 miles (57 kilometers).

Phreatophytes also may clog channels with sediments until the channels no longer carry floodflows, and serious damage results to riparian farms and settlements. Control of most of the common phreatophytes has not been economically solved.

Vegetation and Floods

Streamflow consists of surface runoff and subsurface (deep seepage) flow. As surface runoff increases, floods and erosion are accentuated, water quality decreases, and problems related to stream and reservoir sedimentation are made more serious. There is less surface runoff and more infiltration on level topography with deep, sandy, porous soils that are well covered with large vegetation. On such areas, serious floods are uncommon; and streamflow is maintained during dry seasons. An example is the Sand Hills area of central Nebraska, which is drained by the Loup and Niobrara rivers. Conversely, the southwestern United States is known for flash floods, which develop from surface runoff from summer thunderstorms of short duration and moderate intensity. During August 1961, such a storm caused 22 automobiles to be washed down arroyos within the city of Tucson, Arizona, and the death by drowning of three persons. The high intensity of runoff from small watersheds is contrasted in Fig. 2 with the flow from large watersheds.

Vegetation management markedly affects the quantity of surface runoff. On the Northfork River in California, Percy Rowe and Ted Colman (8) found that there was no surface runoff from undisturbed natural vegetation, even though 61 percent of the 41.5 inches (105.4 centimeters) of precipitation was yielded to streams. On a similar but burned plot, 66 percent of the total runoff was surface runoff. Most research shows that dense vegetation effectively decreases surface runoff and erosion and gives greater yields of tree and forage products, but it usually does this at the cost of lower water yields.

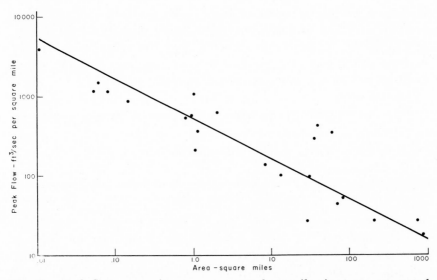

Fig. 2. Peak flow per unit area versus total contributing area expressed in cubic feet per second per square mile (cubic meters per second per square kilometer). This is much greater on small watersheds than on large ones. (Courtesy J. E. Fletcher and R. V. Keppel)

A complex task is the increase and regulation of water yields and, at the same time, the maximization of all products of the watersheds. Since the yields of water and vegetation are controlled by climate, geology and soils, vegetation, and topography, the first job of a watershed manager who wishes to alter water yields is to survey and inventory the watershed and then to measure and describe the conditions that affect evapotranspiration and water yields. With such an inventory at hand, and with research on how environment affects water and vegetation, it will be possible to predict the effect of land and vegetation practices and to develop management plans.

If more than one product comes from the same tract of land, there usually is competition for the factors that control production. Watershed managers must choose which product, if any, to favor. Water is a separate product of the land and yet is an ingredient of the timber, forage, animal life, and recreation. Forage for livestock and wildlife can be increased markedly in arid lands if all the water possible is used by the vegetation. Conversely, heavy cutting of timber to secure more water will decrease timber yields. The removal of phreatophytes from streambanks multiplies water yields but also raises the temperature of the water and changes the fish and game-bird habitats and the recreational environment.

Management to Increase Yields

Watershed investigations in the West have been sufficient to allow rough predictions of the effects of management on water yields. They have not, however, progressed to the point of making possible the fine quantitative predictions that are their goal. This research shows that by changing vegetation density, streamflow yields can be increased by as much as 50 percent. For instance, in Colorado, commercial clear-cutting of lodgepole pine increased the water content of the snowpack by 30 percent over that in the uncut forest. On an adjacent watershed, a 40-percent timber cut brought 25 percent more streamflow.

The drier the site is, of course, the less is the probability of a large increase in water yield with an induced change in vegetation. Yield increases of between 5 and 10 percent are estimated for the drier ponderosa pine forest of the Southwest.

According to a report to the U.S. Senate Select Committee on

National Water Resources, the possibilities of increasing yields vary greatly among the various vegetation types (9). Humid Pacific Coast forests, covering 25.5 million acres (10.3 million hectares), have an average water yield of 45 inches (114.3 centimeters), which is 60 percent of the precipitation. This probably is near the maximum for this type. The humid Rocky Mountain forests, which include spruce, fir, larch, white pine, and aspen (*Populus tremuloides*), with a total area of more than 47 million acres (19 million hectares), have an average water yield of 20 inches (50.8 centimeters), or 47 percent of the precipitation. It is estimated that yields can be increased on an average of 4 inches (10.2 centimeters) over about two-thirds of the area.

The Rocky Mountain ponderosa pine-Douglas-fir forests, with an area of 33 million acres (17.4 million hectares), have a water yield of 5.5 inches (14 centimeters), which is about one-fifth of the annual precipitation, and have a potential only for an increase of less than 1 inch (2.54 centimeters). Pinyon-juniper forests with an area of more than 61 million acres (24.7 million hectares) have a yield of 0.5 inch (1.27 centimeters), with a potential increase of 0.25 inch (0.6 centimeter). The most extensive type of all, the semiarid grass and shrub area, has a yield of less than 0.5 inch (1.27 centimeters) and practically no potential for increase.

Flood Control

When water yields are increased by a decrease in vegetation density, flood runoff, especially in low-elevation areas, is increased. The annual precipitation and the percentage that falls in the summer in the sagebrush zone are shown on the isohyetal map in Fig. 3. Thunderstorm activity is manifest in the rise in water yield during May and June at low elevations. These storms cause very high flood peaks for the watersheds. The time of rise to the peak is short. Since the runoff water traverses either dry or depleting channels, the precipitous high peak flows carry downstream until they are depleted. Where no cultivation is involved, essentially all of the sediment movement takes place from such storms.

In the Southwest, John H. Dorroh (10), of the U.S. Soil Conservation Service, estimated that the water yield of the arid matrix is about 6 percent of the total of all runoff for the Southwest; the other 94 percent comes from the humid "islands." This 6 percent is essentially the result of intense convective rainfall. Practically all water yielded from this arid area occurs as surface runoff in ephemeral streams. Vegetative cover is sparse, and much of the soil surface is exposed to the violent beating of the torrential convective rainfall. A typical histogram, Fig. 4, shows the short-duration, highly intense nature of these storms. When such intensity is contrasted

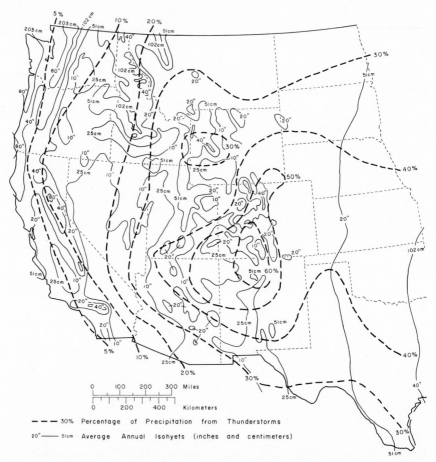

Fig. 3. The percentage of average annual precipitation from thunderstorms is mapped. Solid lines show average annual rainfall in inches and centimeters, and the broken lines show the percentage of the total that occurs as thunderstorms. (Courtesy U.S. Department of Commerce, Weather Bureau)

with the characteristically low infiltration capacities, it can be readily imagined that large amounts of runoff occur. It is not uncommon to have storm runoff for areas smaller than 1 acre (0.4047 hectare) exceed 80 percent of the rainfall.

As man crowds the flood plains of rivers and reduces the infiltration, storage, and detention capacity of watersheds, floods are becoming more serious. They may be controlled by watershed management and by man-made structures. Watersheds and structures op-

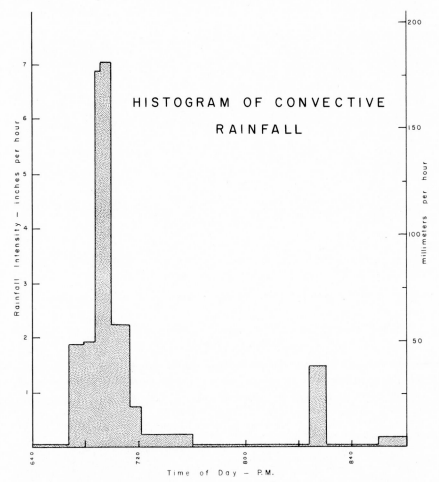

Fig. 4. This histogram of convective rainfall indicates the short duration and high intensity of summer thunderstorms in the southwestern United States. (Courtesy J. E. Fletcher and R. V. Keppel)

erate similarily in flood control: they receive water, hold it in storage, and then release it for flow to lower levels. Water stored in a structure is released as seepage, by controlled flow in streams or through valves and spillways, and by evaporation. Water leaves a watershed as streamflow or flow below the ground surface and through evaporation and transpiration. Some floods may be controlled by land and vegetation management; many require both structures and management.

Flood-control structures include levees and dikes to confine high flows, floodways and bypasses outside of natural channels, reservoirs on both small and large streams, retarding basins, trenches, terraces, and contour plowing and cultivation. In the Wasatch Mountains of Utah, contour trenching effectively controlled surface flows from heavily overgrazed mountain grasslands. Small dams built across arroyos in arid New Mexico have decreased floodflows by detaining runoff and allowing it to be led to adjacent level land for spreading and infiltration.

Convective thunderstorms pose peculiar problems. Although sediment movement can be reduced by making vegetation denser, the high intensity of the rainfall precludes large reductions in runoff. Thus, proper control of both floods and sediment requires a dual program—revegetation and engineering structures to detain volumes of water temporarily. In certain areas where geologic conditions permit, water from the detention basins may be recharged into ground water. Floods in the Northwest result from rain on snow or on frozen ground; major reservoirs may be required there to control the water adequately.

Erosion is a serious problem in arid lands, because (i) the low density of protective vegetation causes the geologic "normal" erosion to be greater than on humid lands, and (ii) vegetation once destroyed is often very difficult to reestablish, and the land may lie relatively unprotected for long periods.

Wind Erosion and Shelterbelts

Both wind and water bring about erosion. According to J. H. Stallings (*11*), soil particles are moved by *saltation, suspension,* and *surface creep* in wind erosion. One storm of 7 February 1939, originating in the Texas-Oklahoma Panhandle, deposited 200 pounds

A prerated flume for measuring ephemeral streamflow has been set up on the Walnut Gulch Experimental Watershed near Tombstone, Arizona. Most of the scant rainfall in the watershed falls in convective summer storms. (Courtesy U.S. Department of Agriculture, Agricultural Research Service)

per acre (224 kilograms per hectare) of soil particles on snow in Iowa, some 500 miles (800 kilometers) away. Soil moved by surface creep and saltation usually remains within or near the eroding area.

The ability of wind to transport soil is enormous. Stallings reports that winds blowing over the Mississippi River Basin can transport 1000 times as much soil as the Mississippi River itself. One cubic foot (0.02832 cubic meter) of air agitated to an average velocity of 5 miles (8 kilometers) per hour is capable of sustaining 0.057 gram of particles 0.04 millimeter in diameter. A windstorm in Kansas in 1950 removed 0.85 inch (2.16 centimeters) of topsoil.

Much of the basic work on wind erosion and its control has been done by W. S. Chepil (12) and his associates in Kansas. Control is effected by decreasing wind speed at the soil surface. A vegetative cover works well and does not have to cover all the land. An organic mulch, or the stubble of a crop left on the surface after crop harvest, creates an effective surface roughness. Listing or cultivating at right angles to prevailing winds also is effective. One of the purposes of the shelterbelt project of the 1930's in the Great Plains was the control of wind erosion.

Many shelterbelts have been planted in the semiarid plains to protect crops and lands from soil erosion and other damage. They hold snow, thus increasing soil moisture, temper hot, dry winds, and furnish habitat for wildlife. They may sometimes provide posts, poles, and fuel-wood as by-products; but, to preserve windbreaks for their original purpose, cutting should be restricted.

The experience gained from the shelterbelts planted in the mid-1930's has been a good basis for their evaluation. The area in which they have been established lies between the Rocky Mountains and the tall-grass prairies, with major concentration on the east side, which is an area of limited precipitation and high rates of evaporation and transpiration. Although some shelterbelts have been taken out or abandoned, there has been a renewed interest in recent years. Where they were not considered successful, failure could be traced to poor establishment practices, to improper care (especially during the early years before the trees overcame the competition), or to fine-textured soils with little available water.

In the United States, shelterbelts have generally been more successful where an appreciable amount of the total precipitation occurs as snow. Snow may accumulate to depths of 3 to 6 feet (0.9 to 1.8 meters). As an example of the importance of snow, Ernest George, a scientist with the U.S. Department of Agriculture, found in one instance that a snowdrift 4 feet (1.22 meters) deep had 10 inches (25.4 centimeters) of water, or the equivalent of 65 percent of the annual rainfall (13). He noted also that, under conditions where the soil moisture was at field capacity at the beginning of the season, trees exhausted all moisture to 6.5 feet (2 meters) by the middle or the end of the growing season. J. H. Stoeckeler, one of the pioneer shelterbelt researchers with the U.S. Forest Service, reported similar observations and said that "comparatively narrow shelterbelts occupy little space, are easier to keep free of weeds, and, in areas of considerable snowfall, tend to deposit more snow on adjoining agricultural fields than do wide belts with a dense shrub row on the windward side" (14).

The same extremes of climate that have excluded the extension of forests into the semiarid area also make it necessary that species be

Magnification dramatizes the splatter of a single raindrop, 5.7 milli-meters in diameter. The drop had fallen 7 feet (2.13 meters) onto sat-urated soil. (Courtesy U.S. Naval Research Laboratory)

carefully selected for shelterbelt plantings and that cultural opera-tions be strictly programed.

Water Erosion and Sedimentation

Water erosion consists of two steps: soil-particle detachment and particle transportation. Raindrop splash and flowing water are the two principal erosive agents. The energy imparted by raindrop splash detaches the particles and sometimes throws them up and out for distances of 5 feet (1.52 meters). On some terrains, splash is the principal soil-moving agent, and on others, particles loosened by splash are transported by surface flow. On most lands, both agents are active in transportation. Stallings reports that the kinetic energy of falling raindrops ranges from 1000 to 100,000 times that of sur-face flow. This pounding compacts the soil surface, greatly decreas-ing its infiltration capacity. Surface runoff is thereby facilitated, but splash also adds to the transportation capacity of flowing water by increasing its turbulence and soil-suspending capacity. When surface-flowing water becomes channelized, it can carry more soil.

Erosion is minimized and controlled by intercepting and deenergizing raindrops, by decreasing surface flow, and by increasing soil stability. The foliage of vegetation, the organic material on the surface soil, and stones are all effective absorbers of raindrop energy. Surface flow is decreased by interception and infiltration. The stability of soil aggregates is affected by vegetation, soil microorganisms, and chemical and physical soil properties.

Vegetation has an effect on all of these factors and is the principal means of controlling erosion on the wild lands of the western United States. On subalpine rangeland in Utah, Reed Bailey and Otis L. Copeland discovered that soil loss from plots with good ground cover was 0.05 ton per acre (0.045 metric ton per 0.4047 hectare) and from poor ground cover, 5.55 tons (5.08 metric tons), or 111 times as great (15).

Although the arid and semiarid areas of the West yield less than 10 percent of the water available, it has been estimated by Dorroh (16) that they yield more than 80 percent of the sediment. Sediment production seems to follow the frequency of convective activity, decreasing toward the north and west (Fig. 5). Joel Fletcher (17) emphasized this point by noting that erodibility was inversely proportional to the extent of weathering in the clays, which in turn indicated the moistness and warmness involved. He observed that soils high in lime and low in free iron oxides are among those that contribute to the silt load of ephemeral streams in arid areas.

The method of harvesting timber, especially the location and construction of logging roads, has a marked effect on erosion and stream sedimentation. Differences in the rate of silting of reservoirs also are associated with the density of undisturbed vegetation and the vegetation changes caused by land use. Lake Mead on the Colorado River, in the arid, poorly vegetated section of Arizona and Nevada, is filling at the rate of 42 to 63 million cubic yards (31,113,200 to 48,169,800 cubic meters) per year. The Colorado River carries 40 to 60 million tons (32,114,000 to 48,172,000 metric tons) of sediment each year.

Where past poor management has resulted in destruction of vegetation and erosion, frequently it is necessary to control surface runoff by mechanical structures, such as dams, terraces, contour furrows, and diversion ditches, until vegetation can be restored. At Sierra Ancha in Arizona, the removal of native shrubs and reseeding with lovegrasses (*Eragrostis* spp.) on depleted rangeland reduced erosion on small watersheds from 1220 and 6100 tons per square mile (1107 and 5534 metric tons per square kilometer) to 60 tons (54.43 metric tons). Many studies are seeking the species and methods best suited to revegetation of deteriorated range and forest lands.

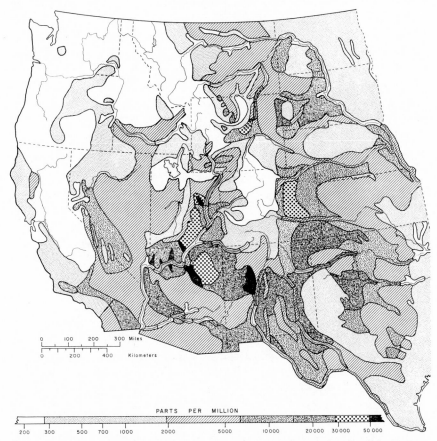

Fig. 5.   The sediment concentration of rivers is heavy in the Rio Puerco portion of the Rio Grande but is the heaviest in the West in the Arizona areas that are drained by the Colorado River.   (Courtesy U.S. Department of the Interior, Geological Survey)

Forest Types in the West

Its forested humid "islands" not only are the principal source of water for the arid West but also provide many other important items, such as timber, forage, and recreation.

One-third of the western United States is forest land, about evenly divided between commercial and noncommercial forests. The greatest acreage of forest land is in the Pacific Coast states. Washington, Oregon, and California have a total of 96,670,000 acres (39,122,000 hectares) of forest land, of which 62,682,000 acres (25,367,000 hectares) are classified as commercial. The Rocky Mountain and intermountain regions and the Black Hills of South Dakota have a combined forest acreage of 144,891,000 acres (58,637,000 hectares), of which 54,329,000 acres (21,987,000 hectares) are classified as commercial.

The U.S. Forest Service has classified commercial forest land on the basis of the species that make up most of the timber volume and has designated the major western timber types as they are shown in Table II and Fig. 1. In this same area, 124,550,000 acres (50,405,000 hectares) are classified as noncommercial forest, making a total of 241,561,000 acres (97,760,000 hectares) of forest land in the western United States.

The Douglas-fir (*Pseudotsuga menziesii*) grows to great size on the humid west coast and to medium size in the Rocky Mountains. The coastal Douglas-fir forests are some of the most productive in the West. Of less value for timber, the Rocky Mountain Douglas-fir forests, nonetheless, are important as watersheds. The forests that are dominated by hemlock (*Tsuga heterophylla*) and spruce (*Picea* spp.) belong in the humid group but have smaller trees than either the coastal Douglas-fir or the redwood forests, the latter being dominated by *Sequoia sempervirens*. The ponderosa pine type, which is found under less humid conditions, is characterized by pure stands of ponderosa pine (*Pinus ponderosa*) merging with other coniferous species at its upper and lower boundaries. It is the most extensive commercial timber type in the western United States, since it occurs from central California, eastern Oregon and Washington, throughout the Rocky Mountains, and eastward to the Black Hills. Although it is not as high yielding as the more humid forests, it is important for watershed purposes.

The western white pine (*Pinus monticola*) is the most valuable timber species in northern Idaho, northeastern Washington, and west of the continental divide in Montana. Lodgepole pine (*Pinus contorta*) occurs in extensive pure stands and in association with other species between the upper portion of the ponderosa pine range and the lower part of the spruce-fir zone. The forest types that are dominated by white pine and lodgepole pine have high watershed values.

Western larch (*Larix occidentalis*), Engelmann spruce (*Picea engelmannii*), and several species of fir (*Abies* spp.) occur mostly east of the Cascade Mountains in the Pacific Northwest and in the northern Rocky Mountains. They are characteristic of forests that have high watershed and recreation uses and moderate timber values.

Of the western hardwoods, quaking aspen (*Populus tremuloides*) has the widest range. It is generally low in timber value, but has high wildlife, recreation, and watershed values. Other hardwood types include broadleaf sclerophyll woodlands and chaparral. They have little value as timber and are difficult to manage as watersheds because of great fire hazard.

The pinyon-juniper type is dominated by pinyon pines (*Pinus edulis* and others) and junipers (*Juniperus osteosperma, J. monosperma,* and others). It is largely a noncommercial timber type with

Table II. Commercial forest land by major types in the western United States, as of 1 January 1953.

Forest type	Acres	Hectares
Douglas-fir	31,731,000	12,841,536
Hemlock-spruce	3,551,000	1,437,090
Redwood	1,590,000	643,473
Ponderosa pine	37,462,000	15,160,871
White pine	5,379,000	2,176,881
Lodgepole pine	4,422,000	1,789,583
Larch	14,467,000	5,854,795
Fir-spruce	13,619,000	5,511,609
Hardwoods	3,935,000	1,592,495
Pinyon-juniper	855,000	346,019
Total	117,011,000	47,354,352

Source: *"Timber resources for America's future,"* U.S. Dept. Agr., Forest Serv., Forest Resource Rept. 14 (1958), p. 713.

about 1 million acres (404,700 hectares) out of a total of 61 million acres (24,686,700 hectares) classed as commercial forest. Its greatest values are for watershed and grazing uses, in each of which the trees may not be an asset. Its timber values are exceeded by its forage values, and under certain conditions—especially when the trees have spread and thickened in density—the trees are a liability as far as grazing use is concerned and are of doubtful watershed value. This is a semiarid woodland type with low water yields but with high flood and erosion hazards.

A great deal has been learned about the management of these western forests for timber, water, forage, wildlife production, and recreation. Much of this knowledge is the result of research in many fields.

Forest Regeneration

One of the chief forest problems has been regeneration by both natural and artificial means. Planting with nursery stock is both expensive and time consuming. Therefore direct seeding has appealed to foresters and landowners as an inexpensive way to reforest cutover and denuded lands. A major difficulty in direct seeding has been the protection of seeds and seedlings from rodents. Recently, there have been encouraging results at the Pacific Southwest Forest and Range Experiment Station in northwestern California, where a formulation of endrin, arasan, aluminum dust, and asphalt was used to protect Douglas-fir seeds from rodents. The treatments gave good protection, and, at the same time, did not retard seed germination and seedling growth.

Shallow, dry soils and steep terrain in Idaho have not been conducive to successful plantations, but stripping with a bulldozer and trenching with a plow will increase survival up to 95 percent. This Forest Service study under the leadership of James D. Curtis has encouraged a similar approach in other areas in the intermountain region where planting has been unsuccessful in the ponderosa pine type (18).

Infrequent seed crops and poor-quality seeds have deterred natural regeneration of Douglas-fir in northwestern California. Even in the one good seed crop during a 7-year period, only about 25 percent of the seeds contained fully developed endosperms and embryos. Seed dispersal is limited to a maximum of 100 yards (91 meters) from the source; however, it was found that in a good year, a residium of two seed trees per acre (5 seed trees per hectare) was sufficient to provide adequate stocking under average conditions.

The impairment of the water-absorbing capacity of the soil during harvesting and slash treatment of virgin western larch-Douglas-fir can lead to high runoff and soil erosion. In one test, the infiltration capacity of skid roads, scarified areas, and broadcast-burned areas averaged 4.1, 15.4, and 62.5 percent, respectively, of capacity of undisturbed soil 1 year after harvest. Scarification and burning aided in the establishment of Douglas-fir.

Forest Management

In the early history of forestry in the United States, two leaders in forest management developed divergent recommendations for the management of ponderosa pine. In the Northwest, Thornton Munger proposed the "maturity selection" method; in the Southwest, G. A. Pearson advocated "improved selection" or "group" silviculture.

According to T. W. Daniel, the difference between the two programs was the result partly of inherent physiologic differences between the Northwest and Southwest and partly of Munger's greater emphasis on the economics of tree harvesting (19). Munger assumed that the silvicultural requirements would be fulfilled by a cut that averaged 50 percent over the working circle. Only trees that would show a net profit were cut, and rough, limby trees on poor sites were left (20). On the other hand, Pearson's method tried to correct deficiencies in the stand, such as deficient stocking and occasional overstocking, low productivity because of slow growth and high mortality, and the predominance of older-age classes (21).

The objective of improvement selection is to build up the stand of growing stock to the potential maximum. This may mean sacrifice of profits during the first cutting cycle in order to increase profits from future cycles. Each tree is considered from the viewpoint not only of its potential but also of how its retention or removal may affect the growth of the tree community. In recent years, the management of ponderosa pine in even-aged stands has received growing emphasis.

Because of ponderosa pine's intolerance to shade, canopy openings of 0.25 acre (0.1 hectare) or more are essential for establishment of seedlings. Reproduction depends on seed supply, seedbed, weather, and protection. Grass is the main cause of poor seedbed conditions. Heavy litter is also unfavorable. A covering of mineral soil is needed for good germination. Light slash may be beneficial. Conditions are the most favorable where logging has torn up the grass and stirred the soil. Frost heaving may occur, especially in the north. Grazing may favor the establishment of seedlings but may also damage reproduction. Time, intensity of grazing, and class of livestock must be watched.

Insects and Diseases

Insects and diseases have taken a heavy toll in the western forests. Beetles have been particularly destructive.

The populations of most of the native forest insects are held to subeconomic levels by their natural enemies, such as parasites, predators, and disease pathogens. Even where outbreaks occur, populations sooner or later return to normal levels, even though no direct control is taken. Introduced insect pests may become extremely destructive because of the absence of natural enemies. Under such conditions, it is often possible to introduce natural enemies from the native homes of these pests. For example, the spruce budworm (*Choristoneura fumiferana*) in the Pacific Northwest is susceptible to several species of hymenopterous parasites, and studies promise some control by the encouragement of parasitism. In the Southwest, it has been found that nematodes reduce the vigor of bark beetles (*Ips* spp.), and investigations are being made to develop ways to infest female beetles with nematodes.

Other insects may be kept in check through interference with their reproductive capacities. Because of the success with some nonforest insects, this is a field of active research. Biologic-control factors—for example, viruses and bacteria—can be made into sprays and used to control active infestations of certain insects. Generally speaking, biologic control is cheaper, safer, and longer lasting than conventional chemical methods.

Diseases caused by a wide variety of agents—including flowering plants, fungi, bacteria, nematodes, viruses, temperature and mois-

A typical stand of pinyon pine (*Pinus edulis*) and juniper (*Juniperus* spp.) near Window Rock, Arizona, on the Navaho Indian Reservation. This is a low-value mixture that is the most common forest type in the western United States. The type spreads with man's misuse of the land. (Courtesy Navaho Indian Tribe)

ture extremes, and nutritional excesses and deficiencies—may result in death, loss of growth, deformity, lowered quality, or destruction of wood. They cause greater loss than all other destructive agents combined, including fire, insects, and other animals.

Of the forest diseases, white-pine blister rust has been locally the most destructive; heart rots and dwarfmistletoe have caused the most widespread losses. Every timber species is subject to attack by one or more species of fungi, but a large amount of loss can be prevented through good forest management.

Much of the research has been studies of disease organisms and the forest conditions that favor losses. The greatest promise for economic control appears to be in harvesting and management practices that decrease injury and maintain a healthy, growing tree crop.

Forest pathologists are convinced that major losses from heart rot can be prevented. Some decay is sure to occur in any timber stand, but losses can be kept at low levels by adjustment downward of the cutting age, elimination of fire, reduction in felling and skidding injuries, removal of defective trees, control of dwarfmistletoes, and prompt salvage in stands that have been heavily damaged by fire, wind, or ice.

Dwarfmistletoes (*Arcuthobium* spp.) have been the most serious of the external parasites that reduce the volume and quality of growth in the forests of the western United States. Practically all western conifers are attacked by these parasites, and dwarfmistletoes rank second to heart rots as the cause of loss by disease. It is estimated that they reduce over-all production by nearly one-tenth over the entire area, and the growth rate may be reduced by as much as one-half in heavily infested areas.

Lake S. Gill, formerly a forest pathologist with the U.S. Forest Service, now retired, spent a large part of his professional career in the southwestern United States and Rocky Mountain regions working on mistletoe problems and, with Frank G. Hawksworth, has summarized existing knowledge in a literature review published in 1961 (22).

Control of dwarfmistletoe can be brought about by (i) the removal of infected trees or their parts by pruning, poisoning, or burning, or (ii) chemical treatment designed to kill the parasite. There has been some hope for the latter; but, so far, an effective treatment has not been found. Control, therefore, is a matter of forest management, such as harvest of timber in blocks or strips and removal of all infected material in the harvested area and, possibly, removal of infected material from the uncut portion to insure better growth before the next harvest. Economics and other forest uses may determine what should and can be done.

Forest-Fire Research

Fires have been a major threat to economic management of forest lands. They not only have seriously reduced timber production but also have caused serious loss of life and property, especially in the more heavily populated area of California. For example, the October 1959 fire on the Angeles National Forest cost the lives of two firefighters, and more than 50 people were seriously injured. The cost of controlling that fire was $1.4 million, and a 14,000-acre (5700-hectare) watershed valued at $21 million was laid waste. Floods and erosion after fires such as this cause additional damage.

A mountain stream dissects this mixed coniferous forest in western Montana, typical of the high, humid "islands" of the West. It is from such higher elevations that most water needs for the semiarid and arid areas are yielded. (Courtesy A. L. McComb)

Both prevention and suppression have received research attention, and there is an ever-growing knowledge to assist in the reduction of fire damage. There is still much to be done, however, in identifying potential runaway fires, controlling the more aggressive fires, and stabilizing the ever-increasing fire costs. At the same time, there is a need to develop safe and effective techniques for the use of fire as a tool in land management.

The fuels that may support forest fires have been classified by their susceptibility for starting fires and their characteristics in supporting combustion. Recently, it has been learned that small amounts of inorganic material may make a great deal of difference in the combustion characteristics of fuel. Reduction of the ash content has an important effect on the heat-sensitivity of materials.

In the chaparral areas of California, where fire is a major threat to watersheds and to human occupancy, the moisture content of chamise (*Adenostoma fascilatum*) offers a good index of fire conditions. When moisture content is low, fires burn more intensely and are more difficult to control.

Various aspects of fire prevention are receiving research attention. These include sociologic and psychologic efforts to determine why there are so many man-caused fires, and what can be done to reduce the number. Another field hopes to reduce fire hazards through land treatments, including the judicious use of fire.

Lightning, especially in the northern Rocky Mountains, has caused many disastrous fires, and various means have been sought to reduce the damage. One approach has been the seeding of lightning storms, but so far variable results have been obtained. In Montana and Idaho, the Forest Service reported reductions in cloud-to-ground lightning up to 38 percent. Yet, in the Santa Catalina Mountains of southern Arizona, experiments conducted by the Institute of Atmospheric Physics at the University of Arizona showed no significant reduction from seeding with silver iodide.

Speeding up the detection of, and the arrival time in getting to, fires has undergone many advances in recent years through the use of improved airborne equipment, including the development of infrared scanning devices to detect small heat sources. Even greater contributions have been made in the transportation of men and equipment to fires and, recently, in the use of various airborne fire retardants, such as borate, bentonite, and ammonium phosphate. Viscous water and algin gel have shown promise in California in a wide variety of retardants. Airborne tankers, large transport planes, and helicopters have become important parts of the firefighting organization.

The use of prescribed fire in land management is becoming more prevalent but is still regarded by foresters as a tool to be used with caution. Because a 14,000-acre (5700-hectare) wildfire in a pinyon-juniper forest on the Hualapai Indian Reservation in northwestern Arizona resulted in increased forage, burning has been adopted there as a range-improvement practice. The release from tree competition resulted in a significant increase of native grasses, but the greatest gain followed seeding with various grass mixtures.

Because of the generally open stands, it has been found that burning is successful only when the fire hazard is high. The humidity must be low, the stands must exceed 200 trees per acre (500 per hectare), and the winds must be fairly strong and steady. Pure juniper stands did not burn well; some pinyons were necessary to carry the fire.

Genetics and Tree Breeding

The Institute of Forest Genetics at Placerville, California, is the center for research in tree breeding in the western United States. This institution, which is now a branch of the Pacific Southwest Forest and Range Experiment Station, was founded as the Eddy Tree Breeding Station in 1925 by James G. Eddy, who recognized the possibilities of tree breeding long before it became a field for active research.

Originally, 70 to 80 species were planted. Now there are some 72 species, 35 varieties, and 90 hybrids, with a total of about 16,000 planted trees on a 55-acre (22.26-hectare) tract.

At first the genetics program was largely concerned with pines, but recently it has been extended to true firs, with particular attention to the development of better characteristics for Christmas trees. The objectives of the pine research are to obtain faster growth, improved form and wood properties, and resistance to diseases, insects, and climatic hazards.

The principal efforts toward improvement are through selection and hybridization. Hybrids and other pedigreed pine seedlings are propagated in a nursery and tested for early performance. Then they are moved to hybrid plantations where later development is studied and pedigreed seeds are produced for large-scale reforestation. Some of the early progenies are more than 25 years old and have developed to a point where their mature characteristics can be judged.

Recreation Research

Research on recreation in forests has developed rapidly in response to the growing demands for recreation facilities. The investigations have been concerned largely with (i) the biologic and physical aspects of management of forest recreation resources and (ii) the economics and social aspects of recreation as related to forests and forest use.

The impact of recreation on timber production has been of great concern to foresters and has been the subject for studies in various parts of the United States. One such study was made in California by Elliot L. Amidon and Ernest M. Gould, Forest Service economists. They made detailed analyses of three selected national forests in California to measure how much of the productive forest land would be involved if all suitable recreation sites and areas were used, and how much would remain for timber use (23).

For their study, they chose forests that would span the range of physiographic and recreation conditions in the state. In one, the present use was about one-fourth of the capacity of the established recreation complex; in another, the use was about one-third greater than the estimated capacity of the established recreation complex. They found that competition for land affected 10 to 12 percent of the total land on the more lightly used forests and, at most, only one-third of the more heavily used (and less timber productive) forest, even if every suitable area was diverted to recreational use. They concluded that the conflicting needs of recreation and timber can be resolved by compromise without serious impact on either use.

REFERENCES

1. E. A. Ackerman and G. O. G. Löf, *Technology of American Water Development* (Johns Hopkins Press, Baltimore, Md., 1959), p. 710.
2. J. E. Church, Jr., "The progress of Mount Rose Observatory, 1906–1912," *Science*, N.S. **36**, 796–800 (1912), quoted in W. U. Garstka *et al.*, "Factors affecting snowmelt and streamflow," *U.S. Bur. Reclamation* and *U.S. Dept. Agr., Forest Serv. Publ.* (1958), pp. 5–6.
3. M. Martinelli, "Alpine snow research," *J. Forestry* **58**, 278 (1960).
4. P. B. Rowe, H. C. Storey, and E. L. Hamilton, "Some results of hydrologic research," in "Some aspects of watershed management in southern California," *U.S. Dept. Agr., Forest Serv., Calif. Forest Range Expt. Sta. Misc. Paper 1* (1951).
5. J. Kittredge, "The influence of shade and litter of pine on evaporation from a clay loam soil at Berkeley, California," *Ecology* **35**, 397 (1954).
6. J. P. Decker, "Water relations of plant communities as a management factor for western watersheds," *Science* **138**, 532 (1962).
7. H. F. Blaney, "Consumptive use and water waste by phreatophytes," *Am. Soc. Civil Engrs.*, Irrigation and Drainage Div., *Rept. IR-3* (1961), p. 37.

8. P. B. Rowe and E. A. Colman, "Disposition of rainfall in two mountain areas of California," *U.S. Dept. Agr. Tech. Bull. 1048* (1951).

9. U.S. Senate, *Report of the Select Committee on National Water Resources,* 87th Congr., 1st sess., Comm. Print 29 (Washington, D.C., 1961).

10. J. H. Dorroh, Jr., "Water yield and sediment maps," *U.S. Dept. Agr., Soil Conserv. Serv. Publ.* (1951).

11. J. H. Stallings, *Soil Conservation* (Prentice-Hall, Englewood Cliffs, N.J., 1957), p. 575.

12. W. S. Chepil, "Dynamics of wind erosion," *Soil Sci.* **60**, 305, 397, 475 (1945).

13. E. J. George, "Effects of cultivation and number of rows on survival and growth of trees in farm windbreaks on the northern Great Plains," *J. Forestry* **41**, 820 (1943).

14. J. H. Stoeckeler, "Shelterbelt influence on Great Plains field environment and crops," *U.S. Dept. Agr. Prod. Res. Rept. 62* (1962).

15. R. W. Bailey and O. L. Copeland, "Vegetation and engineers structures in flood and erosion control," *U.S. Dept. Agr., Forest Serv., Intermountain Forest Range Expt. Sta. Publ.* (1961).

16. J. H. Dorroh, Jr., "Sources of water-transported sediment," *U.S. Dept. Agr., Soil Conserv. Serv., Southwestern Reg. Publ.* (1951).

17. J. E. Fletcher and E. L. Beutner, "Erodibility investigation on some soils of the upper Gila watershed," *U.S. Dept. Agr. Circ. 79A* (1941).

18. J. D. Curtis, "Silvicultural limitations of shallow soils," *U.S. Dept. Agr., Forest Serv., Intermountain Forest Range Expt. Sta. Misc. Publ. 24* (1961).

19. T. W. Daniel, "The middle and southern Rocky Mountain region," in *Regional Silviculture of the United States,* J. W. Barrett, Ed. (Ronald, New York, 1962).

20. T. T. Munger *et al.,* "Maturity selection system applied to ponderosa pine," *West Coast Lumberman* **63**, 33 (1936).

21. G. A. Pearson, "1950 management of ponderosa pine in the Southwest," *U.S. Dept. Agr., Forest Serv., Agr. Monograph 6* (1950).

22. L. S. Gill and F. G. Hawksworth, "The mistletoes: a literature review," *U.S. Dept. Agr. Tech. Bull. 1242* (1961).

23. E. L. Amidon and E. M. Gould, "The possible impact of recreation development on timber production in three California national forests," *U.S. Dept. Agr., Forest Serv., Pacific Southwest Forest Range Expt. Sta. Tech. Paper 68* (1962).

Native Animals and Plants as Resources

Gordon L. Bender

Persons who visit arid areas of the southwestern United States for the first time frequently are astonished at the number and variety of plants growing there. If they investigate further, they are even more surprised by the number and variety of animals. Somehow, a distorted image has been projected of the plant and animal life that inhabits arid regions.

It is true that, if organisms are to survive there, they must meet the demands of the major climatic factors. These factors are extreme heat and a scarcity of water. The existing balance between incoming and outgoing fluxes of heat and moisture determines the climate of an area and profoundly influences both plants and animals.

Arid regions may receive as much as 85 to 89 percent of the total amount of radiation that it would be possible for them to receive. This is because limited cloud cover permits most of the radiation to penetrate our atmosphere and reach the earth. Some of this radiant energy is used up in evaporating water from lakes and streams, from the soil, from the surfaces of plants, and even from animals. Most of it, however, remains to heat the air, the soil, and living things. Temperatures as high as 134° Fahrenheit (56.7° Celsius) have been recorded in Death Valley, California, and summer temperatures of 115° to 120° Fahrenheit (46° to 49° Celsius) are not uncommon in Arizona. These temperatures exceed the optimum for the existence of life. How, then, do so many different kinds of organisms successfully cope with such an extreme heat load?

The contributors to this chapter were Howard S. Gentry, Norris W. Gilbert, Quentin A. Jones, James A. McCleary, and Gale Monson.

The scarcity of water complicates the matter even more. Water, in some form, is absolutely essential for living things. The living substance itself is composed largely of water. If an organism loses too much water without adequate means for replacement, the normal body functions are impaired, chemical changes may occur, and death may result. To survive, then, it must either minimize, or have adequate means of replacing, the water lost.

Animal Adaptations

It might be assumed that desert animals are able to tolerate a body temperature much higher than animals elsewhere. This does not appear to be true. The temperature at which an animal dies does not seem to differ significantly for desert animals. This means that they survive because they are able to prevent their body temperatures from rising to the point at which they would die. There are a number of ways in which this may be accomplished.

Perhaps the most obvious way is to avoid contact with the large heat load. This may be done by seeking shade during the day; by burrowing into the soil where it is relatively cool; by coming out only at night when the heat load is at a minimum; or by remaining inactive during the hot periods of the year and emerging only when the temperatures have ameliorated somewhat.

If an animal cannot avoid daytime heat, it must in some way regulate its body temperature so that it does not rise to the thermal death point. One way is by heat transfer to the cool walls of a burrow. Another is by the evaporation of water; as the water evaporates, the body is cooled. By the latter method, however, the animal, in solving the problem of heat, has created an equally serious one, a deficiency of water. The expenditure of water for cooling purposes is particularly extensive in animals, such as man, that try to maintain a constant body temperature even when they are under a very heavy heat load.

Some animals do not attempt to maintain a constant body temperature but allow it to rise a few degrees when they are subjected to severe heat. Each degree of rise in body temperature effects a considerable saving in water to the animal.

If it is to exist in an arid environment, each animal must somehow effect a balance between the amount of water it expends in normal activities and the water available to replace that being lost. Perhaps this best can be explained in the form of a balance sheet, showing the sources of water loss and the sources of water gain.

An animal normally loses water (i) in the fecal material; (ii) in the urine, the watery nitrogenous wastes excreted; (iii) from the lung surfaces during breathing; (iv) by insensible water loss through the skin; (v) by perspiration or panting.

An animal has the following sources of water: (i) free water, that is, liquid water suitable for drinking; (ii) water contained in food; (iii) metabolic water, which is formed in the body as the result of normal life-processes.

Desert Rat

The kangaroo rat (*Dipodomys* spp.), which was studied in Arizona by Knut and Bodil Schmidt-Nielsen in a truly classic work (*1*), loses some water in the rather dry feces, very small amounts from the skin, some from the respiratory surfaces, and some in the urine. Structural modifications in the kidney, though, permit the excretion of urea with the expenditure of only one-fourth as much water as would be used by a human kidney in disposing of the same amount of urea.

The kangaroo rat obtains small quantities of water from the seeds and other dry foods that it eats; and metabolic water, formed by the body during the oxidation of foods, provides much of the water required. Nonetheless, on a hot, dry day, the rodent would experience a water deficit if it were exposed to extreme heat and desiccation. The water lost under these conditions would be greater than the amount it could replace from available sources.

So the animal compensates for this by moving around on the surface of the ground only at night; by day, it remains underground in its burrow, where the air is moist and cool. Under these conditions, the kangaroo rat is able to achieve and maintain a positive water balance.

Squirrels, Birds, and Invertebrates

George Bartholomew and Jack W. Hudson, of the University of California at Los Angeles, investigated the adaptations of two species

of ground squirrels that inhabit almost the same ecologic niche (2).
The antelope ground squirrel (*Citellus* spp.) and the Mohave
ground squirrel (*Citellus mohavensis*) live in the hot, dry regions
in the Southwest. They are able to exist successfully in this environment because of their ability to allow body temperatures to
vary within rather broad limits and to balance water losses and water
gains by means of physiologic and behavioral adaptations.

Desert birds can tolerate elevated body temperatures and, thus,
lessen their water losses; and because they are highly mobile, they
can fly to free water sources. Their ability to cool their bodies by
panting and the insulating properties of their feathers also are factors.

Large numbers and many kinds of invertebrates are found in
arid regions and, of course, are subjected to much the same environmental stress. As is the case with other animals, their adaptations
appear to be behavioral, morphologic, and physiologic. The picture is much less clear for invertebrates, however. Research now
underway at Arizona State University in Tempe on scorpions and
various species of desert insects may add to an understanding of
adaptations in these forms.

Plant Adaptations

For years there has been much discussion about how such a wide
variety of plants can exist in a harsh, arid environment. It was assumed that these plants must make economical use of water, and
papers were written elaborating on the functions of decreased leaf
size, thick waxy cuticles, and surface-volume ratios in the reduction
of water loss.

In recent years, however, more accurate methods of measuring
transpiration have shown that desert plants may actually lose large
quantities of water to the atmosphere through transpiration. The
infrared gas analyzer has been a helpful instrument to measure water
loss.

Lora M. Shields (3) has reviewed the literature that relates leaf
xeromorphy (structure of plant leaves) to physiologic and structural influences. She suggests that anatomic modifications of plants
in arid regions apparently are expressions of a changed metabolism
that enables the plants to withstand water shortage, but that these
modifications may have no value in themselves. Most xerophytic

(drought-resistant) plants do not seem to be structurally modified for reducing water loss. Rather, their effective adaptation to water shortage is the ability of their protoplasm to endure desiccation without permanent injury.

Desert annuals are good examples of this. The adaptation that enables them to withstand drought apparently is in the seed. Frits Went (4) reports that such seeds are slow to germinate except under conditions favorable for survival. A light rain may not result in germination, but a soaking rain not only produces good germination but also enhances the chances for survival. The rain leaches through the soil and dissolves the water-soluble inhibitors of germination that are present in the seed coverings.

Although much attention has been focused on water losses by plants under arid conditions, the effects of other environmental stress factors—high temperatures, for example—have been largely overlooked. The evidence is that there may be a basic chemical adaptation of plants that provides resistance to high temperatures. The literature concerning this has been briefly reviewed by Edwin B. Kurtz (5).

The earliest demonstration of a specific chemical effect of high temperature on plants was made by A. W. Galston and M. E. Hand in their work with pea plants (6). Optimum growth temperature for a pea plant is near 68° Fahrenheit (20° Celsius), but it will grow at temperatures up to 86° Fahrenheit (30° Celsius). If a plant is exposed to 95° Fahrenheit (35° Celsius) for a few days, it turns yellow and dies. Death, it would seem, is not caused by lack of water, excessive light energy, or insufficient mineral nutrients, since these factors were supplied at optimum levels. Thus, the possibility remains that the high temperature adversely affects some metabolic reaction or reactions. In the case of the pea plant, the essential metabolite affected was found to be the acid adenine ($C_5H_5N_5$). Early or premature yellowing and death of the plants can be prevented by supplying adenine. Similar relationships between temperature and metabolites have been shown in other plants. This chemical control of *climate illness* was suggested by J. Bonner (7) and was briefly reviewed by Frits Went (8).

Similar studies have not been carried on to any extent with native arid-lands plants, however. What the specific metabolic effects of high temperatures are on this group of desert inhabitants remains

to be determined. Are some plants excluded from arid regions because of temperature control of certain metabolites? If so, and if
it can be determined which metabolites are affected, then the possibilities of increased agricultural utilization become very promising.

The question of plant survival in arid environments is now seen
to be a very complex one, involving not only plant structure and
metabolism but also interrelationships between the plant and the
other biotic and physical factors. Yet, a study of these various factors for a particular species of desert plants has only recently been
undertaken—on the saguaro cactus (*Carnegiea gigantea*).

Saguaro Cactus

In 1958, the University of Arizona launched its arid-lands program, a cooperative effort among various departments and disciplines. One of the projects was a study of the saguaro cactus, the
giant cactus that is so characteristic of the Sonoran Desert. Earlier
research on the species, whose fruit has long been a delicacy to the
Indians, had been done about 1910 by Forrest Shreve, of the Car-
negie Institution's now defunct Desert Laboratory.

Using photographs of specimens of saguaro taken at intervals of
several years and height measurements of individuals, Shreve plotted
the relationship between height and annual apical growth (9).
From this, he defined height as a function of age. He then plotted
numbers of individuals against age (that is, their height) for two
populations. In each, he found the greatest number in an older
group and a steady decline in numbers for younger plants. The
saguaro clearly was failing to repopulate at these locations.

One of the study areas was at the edge of Tucson on Tumamoc
Hill, then the site of the Desert Laboratory but now the site of
the Geochronology Laboratories of the University of Arizona. For
the second population, the nearby Santa Catalina Mountains were
chosen. With these 50-year-old observations as a stimulus, investigators of the arid-lands program began their study of the saguaro.

The saguaro flowerbuds open at night and usually close by the
following afternoon, thereby leaving less than 24 hours during
which the flower must be cross-pollinated. Thus, some consideration was given to the possibility that reduced saguaro population
might be related to lack of pollination and, therefore, poor seed

A Papago Indian woman in southern Arizona harvests the sweet fruit of the saguaro cactus (*Carnegiea gigantea*), as her tribe has done for many generations. In the cliffside, in the background, is a southwestern archeologic landmark, Ventana Cave. Carbon-14 dating has confirmed that the site was occupied as early as 10,000 years ago. (Courtesy Arizona State Museum)

crops. Although honey bees are known to be effective pollinators, they were not introduced into Arizona until late in the 19th century. It seemed obvious that other pollinators must be involved, since the saguaro pollen is believed to be too large to be effectively carried by wind.

The recent studies showed that at least one species of birds and another of bats are about as capable of pollinating saguaro as are honey bees (*10*). Therefore, it seems probable that the lack of pollination is not a limiting factor to repopulation. But it was observed that a variety of birds, insects, and rodents disperse, or sometimes destroy, the seeds.

Germination for the seeds that remain requires rather specific conditions in specific sequence. These conditions include exposure to daylight (a visible spectrum of 3800 to 8000 angstrom units) or at least the red-light portion of the spectrum (approximately 6550 angstrom units). The seeds must be distributed on the soil surface or be shallowly buried in very translucent soil; and, before light can start the germination processes, the seed must have been sufficiently exposed to free water. Germination occurs then only within a limited temperature range of 68° to 95° Fahrenheit (20° to 35° Celsius) (11).

Insects and rodents are major dangers to the emerging seedlings. The larvae of the *Gerstaekeria* weevil feed within the seedlings and in some experimental plots destroyed as much as 13 percent of them, but the pack rat (*Neotoma albigula*) may be the main offender. Laboratory tests showed that pack rats can survive on an exclusive diet of saguaro seedlings and water; some other species of rodents were unable to do so.

Temperature, moisture, shade, and soil also affect the survival of seedlings. Charles H. Lowe, Jr., concluded that distribution of the plant in northern and upper elevations is controlled by extremely low temperatures over a 24-hour period, and that moisture stress plays a vital role in limiting the westward distribution. In addition, salinity, alkalinity, and nitrogen level of the soil are important to its survival.

It may take 125 to 130 years for a seedling to grow to a mature height of 30 feet (9 meters); meanwhile, the developing saguaro is subjected to many perils. Bacterial necrosis is caused by a bacillus, *Erwinia carnegieana,* that is related to the organism that causes *fire blight* in pears and apples and to other organisms that can cause *soft rot* in various vegetable and fruit crops. The bacilli are carried from one saguaro to another by the *Cactobrosis* moth. Alice M. Boyle isolated the bacilli from the adult moth, from the surface of the eggs, and from both the surface and the intestinal tracts of larvae. When the disease has run its course, the softer tissues have been destroyed, and only the harder, gaunt skeleton remains.

At Saguaro National Monument, Stanley M. Alcorn, of the U.S.

A long-nosed bat (*Leptonycteris sanborni*) thrusts its head into the flower of a saguaro (*Carnegiea gigantea*). University of Arizona zoologists found that bats are an important factor in the pollination of the giant cactus. (Courtesy Bruce Hayward, New Mexico Western College)

Agricultural Research Service, and his coworkers measured the height of 150 saguaros annually between 1951 and 1959, for a total of about 1100 measurements. From these studies, Alcorn and Hastings determined that the rate of growth varies, apparently depending in part on the size of the plant.

The relationship of climatic factors to growth of the giant cactus has been investigated by James Rodney Hastings, of the University of Arizona Institute of Atmospheric Physics. Saguaros seem to be unable to pick up water from rains of less than 0.20 inch (5 millimeters). Apical growth apparently is confined to the summer rainy season; the amount of this growth depends on when the summer rains begin, how much moisture is received, and the interval between rains.

These recent studies further document a decline in the Saguaro National Monument population of giant cactuses; Shreve had estimated that the decline began between 1850 and 1870, but Alcorn's height-age data indicate that it orginated in the 1880's. This was the period when people migrated heavily into southeastern Arizona. Large-scale cattle raising became common; there were other changes in vegetation, and arroyos were cut. Perhaps the decrease in *Carnegiea gigantea* can be blamed on these factors, for some saguaro populations that have been protected from both man and overgrazing are still successfully repopulating.

Of the vast variety of plants in the arid and semiarid lands, many are known to contain substances that are of potential value. Yet only a few have been developed. An examination of one plant, canaigre, illustrates the problems and possibilities.

Canaigre

Before the coming of the white man to the Southwest, canaigre (*Rumex hymenosepalus*) served many purposes in the lives of the Indians. Its long, tapering leaf blades and succulent petioles were cooked and eaten as a green vegetable, and the tender, white, new roots were eaten raw like radishes (*12*). The mature roots, which are rich in vegetable tannin, strongly pigmented, and highly astringent, were used to tan hides, dye fabrics, and treat various physical ailments, such as diarrhea, sore throat, and open sores and wounds (*13*). There is evidence that the Indians carried planting stock from place to place. In rural areas of northern Mexico, itinerant herb peddlers still sell canaigre roots.

The word *canaigre* is thought to be a corruption of the Spanish for sour cane, *cana agria*, the name by which the species is known in parts of Mexico. Its natural distribution is limited to the arid and semiarid portions of the Southwest and ranges from central Texas and western Oklahoma to the Pacific Coast and from southern Wyoming to northern Mexico. In some areas it has completely disappeared because of the disturbance of its natural environment by man. Oldtimers claim that canaigre, along with cottonwood trees,

Mature canaigre (*Rumex hymenosepalus*) has been used commercially as a source for tannin. Although other sources for tannin and synthetic leather have lessened interest in the desert plant, its medicinal and cosmetic potentials are being investigated. (Courtesy U.S. Department of Agriculture, Agricultural Research Service)

once was common along the Gila River in Arizona. Since the building of the water-storage dams, normal flow of water in the lower reaches of the Gila has stopped, and both the canaigre and the cottonwood trees have largely disappeared.

The possibility of the plant as a source of tannin for commercial leather manufacture was suggested as early as 1876. Nine years later, an exhibit of roots at the New Orleans Exposition further aroused interest (*14*). Freshly harvested roots had been shipped to New York and Europe in 1882, but these roots fermented and spoiled in transit.

Later attempts with sliced, dried roots were successful, however, and a thriving industry sprang up. The growing demand for tannin led to the exploitation of wild stands of canaigre all the way across its habitat. Hundreds of acres of *Rumex hymenosepalus* were dug by hand, and the roots were hauled by wagon to the nearest railroad loading point. In 1891 and 1892, the Southern Pacific Railway alone is reported to have transported 370 carloads of dried roots *(15)*. Factories for extracting the tannin were established at San Antonio, Texas; Deming, New Mexico; Tucson, Arizona; Rialto, California; and Cananea, Sonora, Mexico. The extraction plants at Deming and Cananea operated for many years.

After several years, the wild stands were depleted within reasonable hauling distance of railroad loading points. Attempts were made in several states during the 1890's to develop canaigre as a cultivated crop, with the University of Arizona taking the lead in experimental work. One planting near Phoenix, Arizona, totaled nearly 2000 acres (800 hectares). At the same time, other sources of vegetable tannin were being developed, both at home and abroad. Tanners were reluctant to buy canaigre extract, since there was no assurance that it would continue to be available in adequate quantities at competitive prices. Thus, interest in canaigre died out after the turn of the century.

Recent Research in Canaigre

An impending shortage of domestic tanning materials in the United States just before World War II, however, resulted in a revival of interest. The U.S. Department of Agriculture, after surveying all possible domestic sources of tanning materials, embarked on a research project, in cooperation with state experiment stations, to develop canaigre as a cultivated crop and canaigre extract as a tanning agent.

Strains high in tannin content and root yield and well adapted to cultivation were isolated and increased. Test plantings were made in many states to determine the regional adaptability of the plant as a cultivated crop. Cultural practices and production methods and machinery were developed.

In the laboratory, samples of roots were analyzed for tannin content. Problems of extraction were studied, and quantities of extract were produced for experimental tanning of hides. Leather tanned with canaigre extract was made into shoes and tested for wearing quality.

Canaigre as a cultivated crop and the factors that affect its production have been discussed (16, 17). Although cultural practices do not appear to affect the percentage of tannin in canaigre roots, the genetic constitution of the plant has a profound effect not only on chemical constitution but also on yield. Material collected at Whitewater, Colorado, for instance, contained less than 6 percent tannin and grew poorly in the nursery at Mesa, Arizona. Material collected along the Salt River at Mesa, on the other hand, included several highly productive strains that were well adapted to cultivation and contained 35 to 38 percent tannin and showed a high degree of purity.

Tannin has been recovered from canaigre roots and tested for leather manufacture by the Eastern Utilization Research and Development Division of the U.S. Department of Agriculture (18). Processes used in the tanning of hides with canaigre extract and tests of the wearing quality of the leather after fabrication into shoes also have been reported (19).

E. L. Griffin, Jr., and his colleagues concluded in 1959 that the estimated costs of production of canaigre tannin were too high for competition with other sources of tannin. A price war among tannin producers abroad, beginning in 1960, further reduced the competitive position of canaigre. At the same time, the success of leather substitutes greatly reduced the demand for leather. In a national emergency, when costs would be less of a factor, canaigre might be grown as an annual crop, and the acreage could be expanded rapidly, to supply domestic needs for tannin.

There has been some interest in the plant as a source of pharmaceutic and cosmetic components. Several physicians and dentists in the Phoenix area and at least two research laboratories are exploring its medicinal possibilities, and several cosmetic preparations now are marketed locally. A very small acreage of the crop is being grown to supply material for this development.

A major recommendation of the international conference on the future of arid lands, which was held in New Mexico in 1955, was that further studies of the pharmaceutic and industrial potentials of desert plants would be justified. The Agricultural Research Service of the U.S. Department of Agriculture has investigated these possibilities for a number of years.

Possible New Uses for Plants

Since about 1950, the New Crops Research Branch (formerly Plant Exploration and Introduction Branch) of the U.S. Department of Agriculture has supplied more than 20,000 plant samples to various laboratories for assay. Although these samples went to a number of institutions, most of them are represented in Table I, which shows the laboratories concerned, the number of samples referred to each, and the properties investigated.

Plants included in the study were selected because they are either native to, or cultivated in, lands where there is 20 inches (508 millimeters) or less of annual average precipitation. Plants that are cultivated by irrigation also were included. The investigations help to answer, in part at least, the question of the new-crop prospects for arid lands.

The discussion here is confined to some of the work on seed oils and proteins. References to results of investigations on other aspects are indicated at the end of this chapter (20, 21, 22).

Table I.   Screening of plant samples.

Laboratory	Samples referred (No.)	Properties investigated
Northern Utilization Research and Development Division, USDA	4500	Oils, proteins, seed germs, fibers for paper
Eastern Utilization Research and Development Division, USDA	7000	Steroids, flavarols, alkaloids, tannins, sterols
Heart Institute, National Institutes of Health	3600	Alkaloids and other drugs that affect the circulatory system
Cancer Institute, National Institutes of Health	4500	Tumor inhibitors

Source: New Crops Research Branch, Agricultural Research Service, U.S. Department of Agriculture.

Because fatty oils and proteins are among the major constituents of seeds, representatives of 113 different plant families were analyzed for their seed protein and oil content. The range of variability, particularly the high extreme, often is of more interest than the average value for the family (see Figs. 1 and 2). The family Leguminosae, for example, has a very low average oil content but occasional species of the family have seeds that are sufficiently high in oil content to recommend continued screening. On the other hand, the Gramineae, with about the same average oil content as the Leguminosae, do not offer the promise of an occasional species with an interestingly high seed oil content.

Of the 56 families that are the highest in average oil content, 40 also are among the 56 highest in average protein content. This does not mean that protein content is positively correlated with oil content in a given oilseed, but families that provide good hunting for oil-rich seeds are also likely to provide protein-rich seeds.

How do species of the arid regions measure up as potential sources of seed oils and proteins? Of the 2600 species screened, 304, or about 12 percent, were found to contain 30 percent or more oil in their seeds. Of these, 50 percent are plants of the arid regions. A similar ratio prevails in protein content: species of arid regions, constituting 27 percent of the total species tested, made up 40 percent of those with protein content of 30 percent and more. These trends definitely suggest a higher level of oil and protein deposition in seeds of the arid-lands species than exists in the species of more humid regions.

Not only are many arid-lands plants rich in seed oils, but many contain seed oils of unusual fatty acid composition. That is, these oils differ significantly from the common edible oils, either in kinds of constituent fatty acids or in relative proportions of given fatty acids, or both. Many species of wild plants equal or excel our present commercial oilseeds in desirable components.

Water-soluble, carbohydrate gums—often called *mucilages*—are used extensively in foods, pharmaceuticals, adhesives, explosives, and many other applications. Of the natural plant gums available, the United States imports about 40 million pounds annually. Seeds that contain minimal amounts of oil and protein and no starch are likely places to look for mucilages. Therefore, the legumes of the arid regions appear to be promising as potential seed gum sources.

Underdeveloped Plant Resources

The individual nature of all the plants mentioned in this chapter
varies enormously; they include herbs, shrubs, and trees with widely

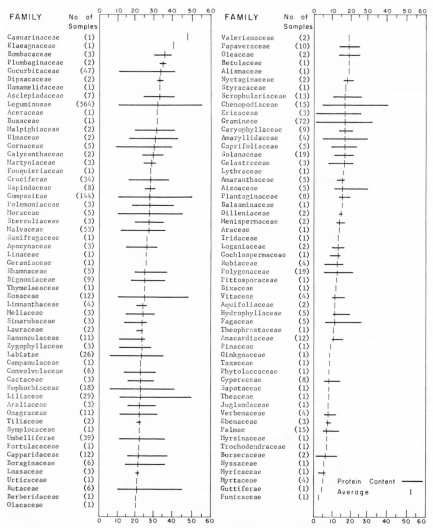

Fig. 1. The range of variability in the protein content of seeds of plant
families is indicated on the graph. The horizontal lines show the percentage of protein content, and the vertical lines show the average for
each family. (Courtesy U.S. Department of Agriculture, Agricultural
Research Service)

divergent adaptations to respective environments. Although it is beyond the limit of space to annotate all of them here, some of the prospective resources are presented.

Agave sisalana, A. atrovirens, and numerous other *Agave* species

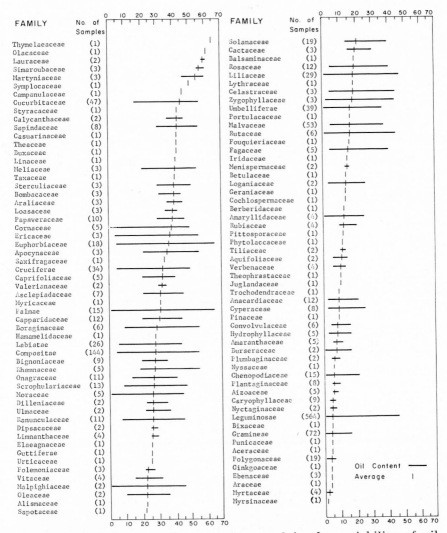

Fig. 2. Researchers may be more interested in the variability of oil content in various plant families, as is shown here, than in the average value for a family. This chart was prepared by the New Crops Research Branch. (Courtesy U.S. Department of Agriculture, Agricultural Research Service)

are sources of fiber, food, drink, and many other products, new among which are steroids. Steroids have had a spectacular development in medicine as precursors of cortisone, sex hormones, and related drugs. It is estimated that the nonfibrous *Agave vilmoriniana* would produce a gross value of $6000 to $7000 per acre (0.4047 hectare), with smilagenin at $10 per pound, when it is carried through the indicated 8-year generation period.

The important commercial fiber *ixtle* is obtained from *Agave lechuguilla,* which grows wild on limestone mesas and hillsides in west Texas and southern New Mexico. The fiber, which is obtained from the leaves, is used in the United States in the manufacture of brushes and in upholstery tow. In Mexico, ixtle fiber is woven into 2- and 3-ply rope and sacking. Each year, the United States imports about 6000 tons (5440 metric tons) of lechuguilla, worth about $1 million.

Cassia leptadenia and *C. leptocarpa* are excellent seeders with relatively high percentages of seed mucilages. Both are erect, colonial, annual herbs. The former is limited to the northern Sierra Madre region of Mexico and the adjacent United States; the latter has a much wider distribution, occurring in semiarid to tropical regions from the southwestern United States to South America. Apparently neither has been cultivated, but their seed productivity, their annual habits and local aggressiveness on disturbed soils, and their seed constituents recommend them for critical study and evaluation.

Lesquerella fendleri and relatives are indigenous to semiarid North America. They seed abundantly and, in seasons with favorable rains, form extensive, showy colonies on the open, sandy, and calcareous plains. The seeds have 20 to 40 percent oils with high amounts of hydroxy acids (C_{18} and C_{20}), a structure with versatile industrial potentials (23).

Sesbania sonorae and *S. exaltata* are tall, stemmy summer annuals that grow along flooded lands of the semiarid West. They have been grown as a soil-improvement crop, and the Indians employed the best of the fibers for fishing nets and lines. Recently, the stems have been tested with good results as a source for paper pulp. As a crop, they require irrigation.

Yucca whipplei is a xerophyte of the Californian climate with a rosette habit and a maturation period of 5 to 8 years. The dry, flowering stalks have been used as splints for surgical dressings on fractures. The fully mature leaves were found to contain about 1 percent sapogenin (mainly tigogenin), which is a potential source of pharmaceutic steroids. This constituent, combined with a high oil and protein content in the seeds and abundant cellulose in the fibers, indicates a considerable composite resource.

Various other species of yucca give promise of becoming important fiber plants. During World War I, *Yucca glauca* was turned into 80 million pounds (36 million kilograms) of fiber for burlap and bagging; during World War II, *Yucca schidigera* was utilized as a fiber source. Flower stalks of yucca are part of the fire-by-friction kits for the Boy Scouts.

Euphorbia antisyphilitica is the source of candelilla wax, which forms a surface coating over the stems of the plants. Because of its comparatively high melting point, it has been used in the making of shoe polishes, floor waxes, phonograph records, sealing wax, candles, electric insulators, and waterproofing materials, and as a finishing material in textiles.

Creosotebush (*Larrea divaricata*), which dominates about 20 million acres (8 million hectares) in the Southwest, contains a number of products of commercial interest. Nordihydroguiaretic acid, which is useful in very low concentrations for retarding rancidity in fats, oils, and carotene, may be extracted from the leaves. Certain resins also can be obtained from the leaves and be polymerized into varnishes. An edible livestock feed has been prepared from creosotebush (*24*).

Parthenium argentatum, a small, gray desert shrub, is a source of guayule rubber. Careful selection has produced strains that yield as much as 23 percent rubber, as compared with 15 percent in wild strains. As late as 1952, plans were made to cultivate this plant extensively, but competition from synthetic- and other natural-rubber sources forced the abandonment of the guayule project.

Jojoba, or goat nut (*Simmondsia chinensis*), is a relatively large desert shrub that is usually found on gravelly, well-drained slopes. The seeds contain up to 50 percent of a yellowish liquid wax, which has been used in furniture and floor waxes, in carbon paper, in paper impregnation, and in smokeless candles. Competition of imported and synthetic waxes has repressed further research.

Beargrass (*Nolina microcarpa*) leaves include fibers that have been sold as a substitute for broom straw, although the tensile strength of the fiber is rather low.

Introduced Plants

Several new crops are undergoing successful development in the United States, among them safflower (*Carthamus tinctorium*), sesame (*Sesamum indicum*), and castor bean (*Ricinus communis*). However, these are Old World cultivates and are new only to American agriculture. The tailoring of these plants for use in the United States consisted mainly in the genetic selection of varieties with superior oil content and with proper growth form and seeding characteristics for machine harvest.

Most of the native species have not been cultivated. Preliminary screening indicates that they are more or less promising. Although each has its own disadvantages, none has ever appeared impossible as a research problem. All of these could be grown in the arid West; yet they remain incompletely evaluated resources. The economic uncertainty discourages capital, restricts funds, and depresses applied research.

An obvious deterrent to new-crop development in the United States is our lack of real need for additional products and industries. Even as replacements for surplus crops, many new crops would have to meet domestic and foreign competition, or might impair foreign exchange markets. Few countries, of course, have the problem of farm surpluses. In arid regions that are deficient in productive land but are endowed with a surplus of labor, agriculture might gain much by the appraisal of the prospects that appear in these screening programs.

Animals as Resources

Although desert animals are interesting examples of adaptations to harsh environments, their economic potential as a resource lies mainly in their esthetic value, in their use as a tourist attraction, and, in some cases, in their use as a crop to be harvested by sport hunting.

People always have been interested in seeing animals in their habitats, and the arid regions of the United States have more than their share. Nature study groups, the Audubon Society, entomology clubs, hiking clubs, and others have worked hard to acquaint people with the esthetic values of these creatures and of the importance of preserving them for posterity.

The present protected status in Arizona of the horned lizard (*Phrynosoma* spp.) and the Gila monster (*Heloderma suspectum*) is largely the result of the actions of these conservationists. A few years ago, the populations of both of these reptiles in Arizona were being severely depleted. Horned lizards were being captured and sold to tourists as souvenirs; Gila monsters were killed, and their colorful skins were used to make purses and handbags. Through the efforts of professional biologists, educational institutions, various clubs, and interested citizens, state laws were passed to prohibit these practices.

The Arizona-Sonora Desert Museum, near Tucson, Arizona, provides outstanding evidence of the general interest in native animals. This museum features interpretive displays of living animals and plants native to Arizona and the adjacent state of Sonora, Mexico. A nonprofit, educational institution, it was visited in 1962 by about 185,000 persons. The value of such a museum perhaps cannot be calculated simply in terms of money; the esthetic rewards defy economic description.

Game Species Research

Sport hunting—the harvesting of game animals as a crop—probably is the most direct use of animals as a resource. Game research in the United States is a relatively new field; until the 1930's, technical studies were primarily of a taxonomic nature.

Game research received its first real impetus with the passage in 1937 of the Pittman-Robertson Federal Aid to Wildlife Restoration Act, which diverts into a special fund all money derived from a federal excise tax on sporting arms and ammunition. The money is apportioned to the state game and fish departments on the basis of their land area and number of paid hunting-license holders. There is a 25-cent state matching contribution for each 75 cents of excise tax revenue received.

Although a large share of the funds has been spent for developmental purposes, such as dam, dike, and water-diversion constructions, tree and shrub plantings, and various food- and cover-crop seedings, a good deal of the money has been channeled into research projects. Essentially, these have consisted of general regional or statewide surveys and inventories, the devising of new management methods, the gathering of facts and figures for sound harvest recommendations, and the evaluation of exotic species that might be used to broaden hunting opportunities.

Almost every species of game that occurs in the arid regions has been the object, in one way or another, of field investigations. The result has been that there is now a great body of published knowledge on nearly every aspect of the management of game species, separately and as an ecologic whole.

A comparatively new note has been introduced in recent years, with examinations of the economic value of game species. Each state in the region has randomly sampled hunters and fishermen to ascertain how much time and money are spent. These polls have shown a surprisingly large expenditure of both time and money by sportsmen.

Another considerable body of research has been conducted on game species by the cooperative wildlife research units, which are administered by local coordinating committees with representation from the state fish and game departments, the state land-grant colleges, and the U.S. Bureau of Sport Fisheries and Wildlife. The Wildlife Management Institute, a fourth contributor to each of the units, designated the Bureau of Sport Fisheries and Wildlife as its agent.

The units have embraced a wide variety of subjects. The Arizona unit has tended to concentrate on the collared peccary (*Pecari angulatus sonoriensis*) and Gambel's quail (*Lophortyx gambelii*), but almost every game species has been studied in one way or another. Similarly, the Texas A & M College unit has investigated a wide variety of game species and habitat problems throughout that state.

During recent years, research in the field of sport fishing has also come into its own. After the success of the Pittman-Robertson wildlife restoration program, the Dingell-Johnson Act was enacted in 1950; it reserves federal excise taxes on fishing tackle for use in the restoration and management of sport fish. In the few years that

Collared peccaries (*Pecari angulatus sonoriensis*) were photographed from behind a blind as they crowded around a waterhole. The peccary (javelina) is protected under Arizona law. (Courtesy Lewis Wayne Walker, Arizona-Sonora Desert Museum)

this program has been in effect, some funds have gone into research on sport-fishery problems. These projects are concerned mainly with basic inventories of the fishery resources but include a little work on diseases of sport fishes.

Although the arid regions may be generally considered a desert—with little sport fishing—large reservoirs along the Colorado, Gila, and Salt rivers, as well as on the Rio Grande and the Pecos River, provide a considerable amount of fishing water. Besides the reservoirs, there are numerous small impoundments, some of which have been constructed with combination Pittman-Robertson and Dingell-Johnson funds to provide fishing and create waterfowl habitats.

A few studies in the arid regions also have been made by other agencies. These include the early research on desert bighorn sheep

(*Ovis canadensis*) that was sponsored by the National Audubon Society and, in the years since 1940, investigation of desert bighorn sheep by the Bureau of Sport Fisheries and Wildlife at the desert game range in Nevada and on the Kofa and Cabeza Prieta game ranges in Arizona, and by the National Park Service at Death Valley National Monument in California. The Bureau of Sport Fisheries and Wildlife has conducted limited investigations on migratory-bird depredation-control techniques in the Southwest. A few selected examples of the work with individual species of game animals may illustrate the values of scientific management of animals.

Desert Bighorn Sheep

Early settlers reported that the desert bighorn sheep (*Ovis canadensis*) were numerous in mountain ranges of the Colorado River Basin, but, by 1840, they began to decline. By 1900, the sheep had decreased to only a fraction of the original numbers, principally because of poaching, market hunting, indiscriminate killing, competition with domestic livestock for water and forage, change in the kinds of forage plants, and diseases introduced by domestic livestock.

In 1950, the Arizona Game and Fish Department initiated an intensive cooperative study of the desert bighorn. The initial phases included research on climate, vegetation, taxonomy, census methods, life-history, mating behavior and reproduction, food habits and forage, competition and association with other species, and disease and parasites.

Management recommendations, as reported by John Russo, the project leader, were (i) development of present water sources; (ii) construction of additional small tanks or impoundments; (iii) stringent control of grazing; (iv) trapping and transplanting sheep to new locations; (v) limited hunts to remove surplus mature rams; (vi) continued research (25).

Arizona now has a limited hunt for mature rams. In 1962, 85 permits to hunt them were issued, and 26 rams were taken. Thus, through careful research and management, the bighorn sheep again is an increasingly important game animal. An interesting account of its life-history is given by Ralph and Florence Welles, who spent more than 6 years examining the animal in Death Valley, the hottest and driest of habitats (26).

This desert bighorn sheep (*Ovis canadensis*) band, led by the old ewe in the center, was photographed below sea level in Death Valley, California. The crimped, notched horn and other distinguishing features of the ewe, believed to be about 10 years old, made it possible for biologists to keep track of the band. (Courtesy Ralph E. and Florence B. Welles)

Collared Peccary

Once considered a pest, the collared peccary, or javelina (*Pecari angulatus sonoriensis*), has become a recognized game animal. Largely as a result of pressure from stockmen, who claimed that it damaged stock ranges, the javelina was ruthlessly slaughtered. In 1929, it was declared a game animal in Arizona and placed on the protected list, where it remained until an open season was permitted in 1939. As late as 1946, though, cattle interests were attempting to have the javelina declared a predator and removed from the list of game animals. The Arizona Game and Fish Department began in 1950 a federal-aid research study designed to determine (i) the distribution and number of javelinas; (ii) whether javelinas are detrimental to the range; (iii) whether they pollute waterholes; and (iv) rancher attitudes toward the species. The results were reported by Theodore Knipe, a department biologist (27).

Because of the controversy, considerable public attention has been focused on the javelina as a characteristic animal of the Southwest. Probably more popular articles have been written about the javelina than about any other big-game animal of the Southwest. Unfortunately, many of these articles are somewhat sensational and present a distorted image. More and more people now are recognizing the animal as a unique renewable resource, which should be retained and managed. Although the javelina is an attraction for tourists, it is in sport hunting that the animal holds the greatest interest. In 1941, fewer than 2000 hunters took to the desert in search of javelinas. In 1961, 21,958 resident hunters and 955 nonresident hunters bought tags to hunt them.

A number of other animals now classified as predators as a result of deep-seated but outmoded biases and prejudices could be reclassified as game animals, managed as a renewable resource, and converted into an economically and esthetically important component of the local scene.

Sage Grouse in Wyoming

The discovery of the sage grouse (*Centrocercus urophasianus*) by white men is credited to the Lewis and Clark expedition, although it had been known to Indian tribes, of course, for many years. Its original range conformed closely to the distribution of sagebrush (*Artemisia* spp.). Its present habitat still is closely tied to the sagebrush climax, but probably as much as 50 percent of its original habitat has been eliminated.

In British Columbia, the species was totally exterminated. Many states closed hunting seasons in order to give some protection to the bird, and Wyoming discontinued hunting seasons on the sage grouse between 1937 and 1948. By 1950, high grouse populations resulted in the reestablishment of general open seasons. A detailed history of the bird, its life-history, biology, and management are presented by Robert L. Patterson, of the Wyoming Game and Fish Commission (28).

The sage grouse story is important because it strikingly illustrates that, as human populations increase and as suitable habitat disappears under the pressure of housing, agriculture, reclamation activities, or industry, wildlife populations must decline. Overgrazing, poorly conceived irrigation projects, and piecemeal planning of resources have all taken their toll of grouse populations.

Problems and Prospects

Despite the scope and variety of game research that has been conducted in the arid regions, particularly in the last 15 years, much remains to be done. Increasing attention must be given to the relationship of the human population's expansion to hunter opportunity. This involves the fundamental philosophy and psychology of hunting. To what extent is there an esthetic devaluation of the sport arising from too many guns in the field? Should the number of hunters be curtailed, and, if such curtailment is necessary, how should it be handled? Will the human population and its modern appurtenances expand to the point that, no matter how thinly the hunting opportunity is spread, there still will not be enough left to give satisfaction? Will the strictly nonconsumptive uses of game become more important than the consumptive uses, and, if this becomes the case, how then will management and perpetuation of game species be financially supported? Should there be an enlarged effort to set aside and develop lands and water for the benefit of game, before the pressure of other uses becomes so great, and land values so high, that uses connected with game animals and birds will be ruled out?

Another area of research that demands attention would deal with game animals, like the desert bighorn sheep and the Sonora antelope (*Antilocapra* spp.), and with such migratory birds as the white-winged dove (*Zenaida asiatica*) and various waterfowl whose continued existence depends on international action. The minimum habitat required for bighorn sheep and antelope survival is not known, yet these animals are practically without protection in Mexico and may be receiving all too little attention on the United States side of the border. Almost the entire population of white-winged doves nesting in Arizona and southern California is dependent on Mexico for its wintering range. The same is true to a lesser extent of several species of waterfowl, chief among them the cinnamon teal (*Anas cyanoptera*). Research must determine the scope of the problem and then develop an effective solution.

It is evident that the rapid expansion of the human population in the arid Southwest, which probably will not slacken in the foreseeable future, provides game administrators and researchers with problems that must be considered at once and on a large scale.

REFERENCES

1. K. and B. Schmidt-Nielsen, "The desert rat," *Sci. Am.* **189**, 73–78 (1953).
2. G. A. Bartholomew and J. W. Hudson, "Desert ground squirrels," *Sci. Am.* **205**, 107–112 (1961).
3. L. M. Shields, "Morphology in relation to xerophytism," in *Bioecology of the Arid and Semiarid Lands of the Southwest*, L. M. Shields and J. L. Gardner, Eds. *New Mexico Highlands Univ. Bull. 212* (1961).
4. F. W. Went, "The ecology of desert plants," *Sci. Am.* **192**, 68–76 (1955).
5. E. B. Kurtz, "A chemical basis for the adoption of plants," in *Bioecology of the Arid and Semiarid Lands of the Southwest*, L. M. Shields and J. L. Gardner, Eds. *New Mexico Highlands Univ. Bull. 212* (1961).
6. A. W. Galston and M. E. Hand, "Adenine as a growth factor for etiolated peas and its relation to the thermal inactivation of growth," *Arch. Biochem.* **22**, 434–443 (1949).
7. J. Bonner, "The chemical cure of climatic lesions," *Eng. and Sci.* **20**, 28–30 (1957).
8. F. W. Went, "The experimental control of plant growth," *Chron. Botan.* **17**, 313–317 (1957).
9. F. Shreve, "The rate of establishment of the giant cactus," *Plant World* (now *Ecology*) **10**, 235–240 (1910).
10. S. E. McGregor, S. M. Alcorn, and G. Olin, "Pollination and pollinating agents of the saguaro," *Ecology* **43**, 259–267 (1962).
11. S. M. Alcorn, "Natural history of the saguaro," *Arid Lands Colloquia for 1955–1960, 1960–1961* (Univ. of Arizona, Tucson, 1962), pp. 23–29.
12. F. Russell, "Report on the Pima Indians," *Bur. Am. Ethnol., 26th Ann. Rept., 1904–1905* (1908), pp. 77, 80.
13. R. Gilmore, "Uses of plants by the Indians of the Missouri River region," *Bur. Am. Ethnol., 33rd Ann. Rept. 1911–1912* (1919), p. 77.
14. H. Trimble, "Canaigre," *Am. J. Pharm.* **61**, 395 (1889).
15. G. E. Colby, "Analyses of canaigre or tanners' dock," *Calif. Univ. Agr. Expt. Sta. Rept.* (1897), p. 186.
16. N. W. Gilbert, "Canaigre, a tannin-bearing plant," *U.S. Dept. Agr. Mimeographed Publ. T & SC-21* (1957).
17. ——— and D. S. Black, "Canaigre, a potential domestic source of tanning," *U.S. Dept. Agr. Prod. Res. Rept. 28* (1959).

18. E. L. Griffin, Jr., N. F. Roger, C. S. Redfield, J. B. Claffey, and R. K. Eskew, "Tannin extracts from canaigre roots," *U.S. Dept. Agr. Publ. ARS-73-22* (1959).

19. L. Seligsberger, C. Mann, and J. Naghski, "A field test of canaigre-tanned heavy leather in low quarter shoes," *Footwear and Leather Ser. Rept. 15* (U.S. Army Quartermaster Res. and Eng. Command, 1959).

20. J. J. Willaman and B. G. Schubert, "Alkaloid-bearing plants," *U.S. Dept. Agr. Tech. Bull. 1234* (1961).

21. J. Leiter, "Cancer chemotherapy screening data IX," *Cancer Res.* **21** (3) (1961), pt. 2.

22. M. E. Wall *et al.*, "Steroidal sapogenins," *J. Am. Pharm. Assoc., Sci. Ed.* **43**, 1–7, 503–505 (1954); **44**, 438–440 (1955); **46**, 653–686 (1957); **47**, 695–722 (1959); **50**, 1001–1034 (1961).

23. H. S. Gentry and A. S. Barclay, "The search for new industrial crops," *Econ. Botany* **16**, 206–211 (1962).

24. P. C. Duisberg, "Development of a feed from the creosotebush and the determination of its nutritive value," *J. Animal Sci.* **2**, 174–180 (1952).

25. J. P. Russo, *The Desert Bighorn Sheep in Arizona* (Arizona Game and Fish Dept., Phoenix, 1956).

26. R. E. and F. B. Welles, "The bighorn of Death Valley," *U.S. Natl. Park Serv., Fauna Ser. 6* (1961).

27. T. Knipe, "The javelina in Arizona," *Wildlife Bull. 2* (Arizona Game and Fish Dept., Phoenix, 1956).

28. R. L. Patterson, *The Sage Grouse in Wyoming* (Wyoming Game and Fish Comm., Sage Books, Denver, Colo., 1952).

12

Human Factors in
Desert Development

Douglas H. K. Lee

The capabilities and limitations that man faces in arid regions to-day, and particularly technologic man, differ radically from those that confronted the aborigines, and quite markedly also from those that our pioneer fathers faced. Modern man enjoys much greater control of infectious disease and understanding of conditions that provoke or favor disease development. On the other hand, by the very act of protecting its members from the more devastating or demanding stresses of the environment, the population accumulates a greater proportion of individuals who are unfitted to meet such stresses and, thereby, increases the necessity for continuing and guaranteeing the protection.

In similar fashion, society allows the individual a greater freedom of choice of the conditions under which he desires to work or live and, thus, does somewhat less to force his adaptation to arduous conditions. Under the shield of an increasingly protective technology, the adaptive mean, so to speak, has been shifted to a lower position in the range of environmental stress.

This is a truly evolutionary shift for the population as a whole, since in general the shield can probably be regarded as permanent. But the few people who, for any reason, have to operate outside the shield find themselves correspondingly handicapped in comparison with their less civilized forebears and, so, deserve a greater degree of consideration than might be realized. Both groups of persons—the less rugged, but protected, majority and the poorly adapted, but exposed, few—will be involved in any sort of development that takes place in the arid lands, and both groups must receive due consideration.

In the course of measuring man's physiologic reactions to arid, and particularly hot desert, conditions, and of applying environmental physiology to the problems of desert development, I have been led to a definite set of beliefs. My thesis must be stated clearly here, since much of this chapter is either the evidence that prompted this stand or the applications to practical activities that stem logically from it. It can be summarized as follows.

1) Unhealthy persons and those at extremes of age may show a reduced ability to maintain equilibrium and productivity in hot desert, as compared with temperate, conditions.

2) Persons who are not completely acclimatized, or are still undergoing training for unaccustomed activity, can expect to find their capacities reduced.

3) A healthy, acclimatized person, however, can carry on normal activities, with normal productivity, in all but exceptional naturally occurring desert environments.

4) The desire for activity, on the other hand, may be reduced by hot desert conditions, even though the capacity for activity is unaffected. Motivation is correspondingly more important than in temperate conditions.

5) Certain conditions of desert living—barrenness, isolation, dust —are unattractive to many people and act as a deterrent.

6) To be successful, desert development must provide a strong incentive to secure the desired individuals and, then, continued stimuli to motivation beyond the stimuli that operate in competing temperate developments.

7) If only for the aforementioned reasons, desert development is likely to call for greater investment, to be slower, and to show less over-all efficiency of human effort than equivalent activities in temperate environments, particularly before the point at which a self-sustaining population is reached.

8) The thoughtful application of existing knowledge on man's reactions to desert conditions, on methods of modifying these reactions, and on ways of protecting him from environmental stresses can do much to optimize his efficiency, reduce costs, and facilitate social growth. It can be done, it is being done; but it takes resolution, know-how, and resources.

Historical Background

The basis of modern thermal physiology was ushered in by J. S. Haldane's report in 1904 on the Cornish tin miners (1). His work was concerned with very humid environments but emphasized for the first time the importance of quantitative expressions of heat loss. This was followed by J. Lefèvre's monumental text (2) in 1911, Leonard Hill's work with the katathermometer (3), the revolutionary development of the effective temperature scheme by the research group of the American Society of Heating and Ventilating Engineers at Pittsburgh (4), and the British studies with the globe thermometer.

These studies, and many others to follow, were concerned with the thermal environment in general, and particularly with the environments that were to be found in industry or in the home. The desert, as such, received no more than casual mention, even though major catastrophes occurred in military operations in the desert phases of World War I.

It should be pointed out that practically all of the studies made on man's reactions to desert conditions concern the hot, dry months. Such problems as he may encounter in winter are either accepted as within his normal capabilities or included in cold-climate studies in which the desert areas are not distinguished as such.

Systematic Studies

Except for the studies by Dill (see next paragraph), American accounts of man's reactions to desert conditions before World War II were similar to those published elsewhere in that they were largely travelogs. These include J. S. Chase's *California Desert Trails* (5), D. C. Hogner's *Westward, High, Low, and Dry* (6), and W. L. Manly's *Death Valley in '49* (7). Here and there appeared a clinical, and perhaps an approach to a physiologic, account by an observer who happened to have an interest in that direction. Possibly the best example is the account by J. H. King, in 1878, of the sufferings of a detachment of cavalry lost in the Llano Estacado of Texas and deprived of water for 86 hours (8). W. J. McGee's article in 1906, "Desert thirst as a disease" (9), sought an underlying unity in such phenomenons.

During the summers of 1931 and 1932, D. B. Dill and his colleagues at the Harvard Fatigue Laboratory made an extensive and
systematic study (*10, 11*) of men working on the construction of
Hoover (Boulder) Dam in the valley of the Colorado River. There,
the high valley walls not only increase the reflection of solar radiation but also narrow the arc of sky through which heat may be lost
to outer space. The configuration tends, too, to promote strong
winds, which, at air temperatures above skin temperature, add heat
to the worker without materially assisting the already high rate of
evaporation.

Using themselves, as well as the workers, as test subjects, the investigators demonstrated quite clearly the way in which the electrolyte and water equilibriums between body cells and extracellular
fluids, such as blood and lymph, are affected by the high water turnover; the close association between salt and water in these exchanges;
the tendency of the kidney, when the normal balance is upset, to
maintain osmotic pressures at the expense, if necessary, of hydration;
the existence of a critical level of chloride in the blood below which
heat cramps are likely to develop; and the marked decrease in salt
content of the sweat with acclimatization.

Studies in controlled-atmosphere rooms at the Harvard Fatigue
Laboratory, both before and after these field observations, served
to confirm the findings and to lay down, for the first time, a scientific
basis on which to build an understanding of the strains that are
likely to be developed in the human body by the stresses of work in
hot, dry environments, and to point out the way in which a principal strain—deficiency of chloride—is reduced by acclimatization.
(The timeliness of these studies was not foreseen. When I visited
the Fatigue Laboratory in 1936, one resolve stood out from the con-
fusion of postdepression adjustments: the United States was not
going to be involved in any further military excursions! But 6 years
later, these studies were being hurriedly extended in the face of a
clear probability of just that.)

Wartime Research

When the United States entered the war in 1941, it was faced with
the problem of organizing and training forces for effective combat

in any part of the world, and particularly in deserts. Its allies were already fighting in North Africa, but the reports that came back on such aspects as water requirements and the endurance of the human body were, to say the least, confused. Estimates of water required for daily drinking varied from 1 gallon to 1 quart imperial measure (4.5 to 1.136 liters), but the conditions under which the estimates were made were not clearly stated. The old notion persisted that men could be trained to get along on minimum amounts of water; but physiologists were highly skeptical.

It was this situation that prompted the Office of Scientific Research and Development to support an investigation by Edward F. Adolph, University of Rochester physiologist, the results of which were published in his classic monograph on the physiology of man in the desert (12). As is pointed out in the introduction to this work, deserts were, even at that time, being increasingly used for various purposes, ranging from travel and vacation to mineral exploitation and even agriculture. On the other hand, it seemed certain that desert, and particularly hot desert, conditions impose a heavy burden on the body's economy. The margin of safety is small, and the consequences of overtaxation are great. Water is lost by evaporation of sweat almost as fast as it is formed, at a rate that may not be fully appreciated by those who see only a relatively dry skin. The central problem to man's survival is the supply of adequate water or, where water is scarce, its most efficient use.

As Adolph pointed out, the results reported in his monograph were obtained by a number of scientists who made hundreds of tests in the Colorado Desert of California and in the climatic chamber of the Desert Laboratory Unit at the University of Rochester. They removed the question of man's tolerance from the realm of speculation to that of demonstrable and repeatable scientific data.

On clothing and shelter, the following points emerged: (i) on most occasions during the hot hours in the open desert, clothing serves to protect the man, retarding heat gain from solar radiation and hot air more than it interferes with evaporation; (ii) one function of clothing in this connection is to give incident heat back to the environment by reradiation and convection without letting it reach the skin; (iii) men who lie on the sand gain more heat and need to sweat more than those who sit or stand; (iv) aside from clothing, shade of any kind is the most important protection from heat; (v) it is obvious that nighttime has advantages as a working period.

With regard to water requirements, Adolph found that the average intake on maneuvers in vehicles was 6.3 U.S. quarts (6 liters) in 24 hours, when the maximum air temperature was 102° Fahrenheit (39° Celsius) ; that the maximal intake was 12.6 quarts (12 liters) in 24 hours; that restrictions of drinking water did not result in any over-all saving of water; and that a few hours of carelessness in the hottest season may lead to death. The studies revealed no practical method for relieving the sensation of thirst or the deterioration that results from lack of body water (Figs. 1 and 2). The map reproduced as Fig. 3 is one of a set prepared for the world's arid areas to show the daily water requirements for a man at rest in the hottest month. This section of Adolph's report concludes with practical suggestions for carrying and dispensing water in adequate amounts.

The monograph does not stop at a description of man's reactions but goes deeper into the physiologic mechanisms involved. It extended prior knowledge by demonstrating conclusively the high rates of water turnover, the magnitude of the heat load on the exposed person, the signs and symptoms of water deprivation, the unequal way in which the various tissues part with water, the mechanisms involved in the sensation of thirst, the consequences of dehydration for both cellular and systemic body functions, and the processes of restoration that follow rehydration.

Adolph sees the relevance of these findings to a perennial problem in applied physiology, that of equating the significance to the body of different kinds of strain. Using the pulse-rate response as a criterion—a method with which not everyone agrees—he expresses graphically the equivalence of various degrees of body dehydration, air temperature, and work load. Adolph found that the body will try to preserve heat regulation through continued sweating, even though it produces dehydration. But the absoluteness of this sacrifice is open to some question, as is shown later.

Prompted by wartime requirements, a number of other systematic studies on man's reactions to heat and cold were organized in different parts of the country. Hot, dry environments were naturally included and provided further information related to desert prob-

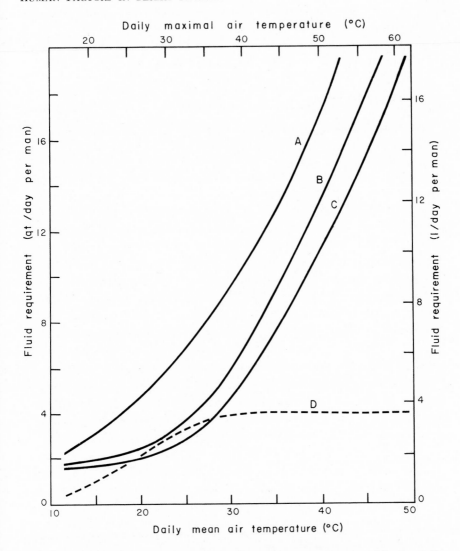

Fig. 1. This graph shows correlations of air temperatures with the daily fluid requirements in arid regions of men who work hard in the sun for 8 hours a day (*A*), men who work hard for 8 hours each night but rest in the shade by day (*B*), and men who rest in the shade all the time (*C*). Broken curve (*D*) shows the saving in water that results from working at night instead of in the sun during the day. (Reprinted with permission from E. F. Adolph, *Physiology of Man in the Desert*, p. 121, John Wiley & Sons, New York, 1947)

lems, although the studies were not specifically designed for this purpose. Warm, humid environments probably received relatively more attention in view of the military commitments in tropical areas.

Lessons from the Field

Military operations, of course, did not await answers from scientists but went ahead on the best judgment of those in charge. As was only to be expected, in the absence of adequate guidance, errors were made and men suffered. Probably the most dramatic and

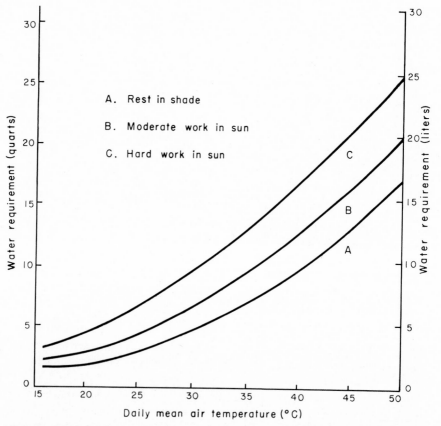

Fig. 2. Recommendations by the U.S. Army Quartermaster Corps for daily water supply for men at rest in the shade all the time (*A*), men performing moderate work in the sun during the day (*B*), and men performing hard work in the sun all day (*C*).

unfortunate result of such unavoidable haste was the death of at least 190 soldiers from heat stroke in the course of their training.

Malamud, Haymaker, and Custer (*13*) published a detailed report from the Army Institute of Pathology on 125 fatal cases, by far the most extensive and exhaustive account to date. Of these 125

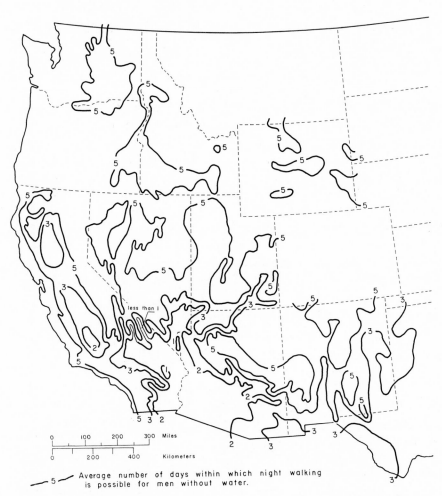

Fig. 3. Survival time without water in July in the Southwest is suggested in this map. If men rest in the shade by day and walk only at night, they should be able to continue walking for the number of days indicated by the lines. Not walking at all greatly increases survival time. (Reprinted with permission from E. F. Adolph, *Physiology of Man in the Desert*, p. 275, John Wiley & Sons, New York, 1947)

deaths, 92 occurred in Texas, Georgia, Mississippi, Florida, Virginia, and Louisiana. The relative proportion of deaths compared with the number of troops in the area was 4.7 in the California-Arizona maneuver area, 2.8 to 2.0 in Georgia, Virginia, Mississippi, and Louisiana, and less than 2.0 in all other states. It must be remembered, however, that physical exertion could have been greater in the first-named area. All deaths occurred in the warm months of May through September, with the maximum of 59 cases in July.

With respect to length of continuous duty in the south, the cases clustered around two categories: 1 to 2 weeks and 2 to 6 months. No information is given on whether the latter were winter inductees facing their first summer. In 118 cases, there was a history of exposure to sun under conditions of high environmental temperature, and the great majority were engaged in some form of military exercise, such as long marches, drill, or target practice. There was a history of previous intolerance to heat in only five cases. Most of the patients were somewhat overweight or actually obese.

Elizabeth Schickele (14), from the U.S. Army Quartermaster Corps, analyzed the environmental conditions under which heat stroke developed, with the results shown in Fig. 4. For the classification, etiology, and treatment of heat effects, see W. S. S. Ladell (15), D. H. K. Lee (16), or C. S. Wyndham (17). I do not have any relevant data, but I gather that heat stroke was quite a rare occurrence in troops serving overseas in the desert or tropics. My own experience leads me to believe that it occurs only rarely in healthy, acclimatized persons, and then under quite unusual circumstances.

Perhaps the most important effect of wartime demands was a growing realization that, for the study of man in a given environment, a number of approaches involving different disciplines must be followed and their results integrated. Data are necessary on the environment itself, and in a form that is meaningful for the biophysicists, physiologists, and engineers who must use them. Frequencies, as well as mean values, and spatial distribution of conditions, both vertical and lateral, must be available. Meteorologists must provide most of the data, but they will have to be informed of the nature of the data and the form of presentation that will be most useful.

Biophysicists must study in some detail the processes by which heat—conductive and convective, sensible and evaporative, radiative

—is transferred between the body and its environment through the quite complex structures of clothing (Fig. 5). Transient, as well as equilibrium, conditions need elucidation, and the considerable variations in physical circumstances at different parts of the body must be taken into consideration. Physiologists are concerned with the body's reactions to changes in heat balance through transfer and

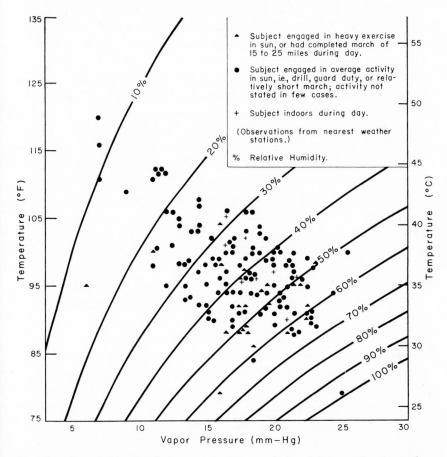

Fig. 4. Humidity, maximum temperature, and activity on the days when soldiers suffered fatal heat stroke during World War II are summarized in this chart. Trained, acclimatized persons seldom develop heat stroke under conditions reported for cases at the lower left half of the group. (Reprinted with permission from E. Schickele, "Environment and fatal heat stroke," *Military Surgeon*, now *Military Medicine*, vol. 100, p. 240, 1947)

production and with the significance of these changes for human efficiency and welfare.

Engineers and architects must relate their design of environmental control systems, shelter, and housing to the physical and physiologic needs of the occupant on the one hand and to the actual environment on the other, thus closing the circle of interrelated considerations. The major American wartime contributions were brought together in L. H. Newburgh's *Physiology of Heat Regulation and the Science of Clothing* (*18*), which includes a chapter on hot desert environments.

Through the cooperative efforts of the Office of Scientific Research and Development and the U.S. Army, the basis for cooperation among disciplines and integration of results was firmly laid. All elements could be seen clearly cooperating, for example, in the Office of the Quartermaster General, which had the tremendous responsibility for developing and supplying each soldier with the food, clothing, and equipment that he needed for the environmental conditions. Both the compound approaches and their integration will be more clearly seen in the discussion of postwar developments, but the need and the method were established while hostilities were in progress.

Postwar Investigations

Tabulation of relevant environmental conditions has proceeded apace, especially in the United States. Of the four meteorologic factors most concerned, temperature remains the best documented. A network of some 51 stations in the arid western states of Texas, New Mexico, Arizona, Utah, Nevada, and California report hourly temperatures. From these the annual, diurnal, and macroclimatologic distribution can be obtained. The same stations report such measures of humidity as wet-bulb temperature, relative humidity, or dew point with same frequency.

It is a matter of some concern to physiologists, however, that much emphasis is still given to relative humidity instead of to the directly operative factor of vapor pressure or its near counterpart, dew point. Wind-speed records are also less useful in that man is only on occasion exposed to environments in which wind dominates the rate of

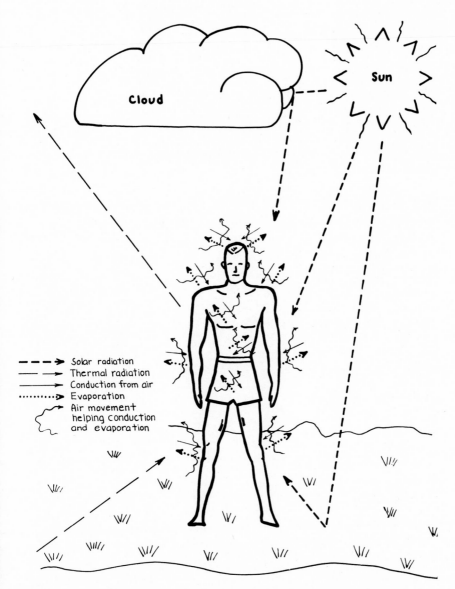

Fig. 5. Diagramed are the major factors that enter into the exchange of heat between the human body and hot, dry environments. The considerable gains of heat can be offset only by a small loss by radiation to the sky, and by evaporation of sweat. For any set of conditions there is an optimum air movement; more than this simply adds heat from the air.

air movement over his person. The data on radiative conditions are the least satisfactory, but great improvement has taken place since World War II; 17 stations in the arid western states now report hourly rates of solar-radiation incidence, and most of the 51 stations that report general meteorologic conditions also include data on hours of sunshine or cloud cover, from which estimations of probable incidence can be approximately determined.

From such data and a knowledge of the reflectivity (albedo) of the terrain, the incidence of solar radiation on an exposed person can be calculated. More uncertain is an estimate of the infrared heat exchange that may be taking place between a person and his surroundings, such as the ground and sky. Approximate estimations may be made of ground temperature, but there have been very few measurements of "sky" temperature to serve as a guide. For a description of methods for calculating the radiative heat load on an exposed man, see Lee (19).

Anyone who wishes to relate climatic data to human reactions or needs must necessarily have recourse to the data that are tabulated by the U.S. Weather Bureau or to statistical abstracts. Attempts to present this type of information in the form of maps have so far not succeeded in giving more than a superficial view of the situation, since the simultaneous presentation of time-dependent data on four or more variables is beyond the potentialities of conventional mapping.

If the simultaneous effect of all the variables on human function could be reduced to a single quantitative expression, a solution might be found; but no one so far has devised a scheme of doing this that wins even token acceptance. Special aspects of climatic patterns that prevail in the arid western states, and of their significance for human activities, can be found in reports prepared by the U.S. Army Quartermaster Corps, as can descriptions of variability in conditions with terrain type. In the absence of more comprehensive presentations, these can be very useful; it is a pity that they have not appeared in the literature that is read by more of the scientific community.

The biophysics of heat transfer between man and his environment has not been greatly advanced beyond that described in Newburgh's text (18). Careful measurements of heat absorption in sunlight, made with the "copper man" (a copper replica of man on which the heat load is measured electrically) at the Yuma Test Station in Arizona, have shown that color makes very little difference, at least with the relatively thin clothing usually worn in summer. The heat absorbed under black clothing was less than 5 percent greater than that under identical white clothing, owing, probably, to the fact that white fibers reflect sunlight inward as well as outward. Although a smaller fraction of the heat was absorbed by the white clothing, the absorption took place deeper in the layers, where it was closer to the skin and protected from removal by ambient air. A. H. Woodcock has shown (20), by elegant analysis of the physical processes involved, that, when air temperature exceeds skin temperature, there is an optimum air movement, below which sweat accumulates on the underventilated skin, and above which a further requirement is placed on the already burdened sweat mechanism for more water to take care of the heat added from the air.

Under these conditions, forced air movement, such as fans produce, may be worse than useless. In a series of studies using the reactions of test subjects as criterions, I have shown, by experiments in a climatic chamber with transparent plastic walls, that exposure to the full radiation load of the open desert in summer is equivalent to a rise of air temperature of 12° to 17° Fahrenheit (7° to 9° Celsius), depending on the clothing and air movement at the time.

On healthy, acclimatized, and trained soldiers, I obtained the relationships between temperature and sweating shown in Fig. 6. For activities up to the maximum used in these studies—level walking, without a pack, at 3.5 miles (5.6 kilometers) per hour—pulse rates were found to be little affected by temperature in the better-motivated subjects but were responsive in the less cooperative subjects. With this level of exercise, there also was very little rise of rectal temperature unless the air temperature exceeded 115° Fahrenheit (46° Celsius). These studies were made at vapor pressures that are characteristic of deserts not exposed to moisture-laden winds.

A long series of service reports from the Quartermaster Corps give the effect and effectiveness of various methods of load-carrying under desert conditions. Studies on Negro and white soldiers who possessed equivalent degrees of acclimatization, nutrition, and training gave the following results: " (i) Under hot-wet conditions, with both Negroes and whites clothed and walking, the Negroes had a higher physiological tolerance. (ii) Under hot-dry conditions, with both groups clothed, walking or sitting, they had about equal tolerance. (iii) Under hot-dry conditions, with both groups nude and exposed to the sun, sun-tanned whites had the higher tolerance" (21).

Effects of Dehydration

The question of the extent to which varying degrees of dehydration affect body functions has been repeatedly examined, with somewhat conflicting results. Some investigators find no reduction of sweating, for example, when water intake is restricted, but others report significant reductions.

F. Grande (22) studied subjects who were living in a temperate environment. They walked for 2 hours each day at 3.5 miles (5.6 kilometers) per hour on a 10-percent grade, with food intake restricted to 1000 kilocalories a day and with three levels of water intake—as much as they wanted whenever they wished it, 1800 cubic centimeters, or 900 cubic centimeters per day. He found that the increase of rectal temperature during exercise was twice as large in the low-water group as in the controls, but very little greater in the medium-water group. The rate of weight loss was somewhat greater in the medium-water group in the first few days than among those who drank freely, but it was approximately the same after that. It did not diminish when they were permitted unlimited water intake.

The rate of weight loss was much greater in the low-water group, was changed into a rapid weight gain when unlimited drinking water was permitted, and then settled down to a rate similar to that in the other two groups. Sweat loss during exercise was reduced in both the low- and the medium-water groups and did not return to the initial values when rehydration was permitted. It would seem, from these experiments, that readjustments can occur that permit the body to operate at somewhat lower levels of hydration than those to which it is accustomed. P. F. Iampietro found a voluntary lowering of body water content of about 1.05 U.S. quarts (1 liter) in soldiers stationed at Yuma, during the summer, without any apparent ill effects.

The findings of Dill (10, 11) and of J. W. Conn (23) that a marked reduction of chloride in the sweat is a feature of acclimatization has been extended by R. L. Dobson's (24) careful studies of sweat-gland cytology. The reduction in chloride concentration, which is so important to desert adaptation, appears to be associated with reduction in a specific cell type ("large pale cell"). Both the reduction of chloride and the degeneration of cells of this type are postponed by high-salt diets.

Of 12 subjects camped for several weeks in Death Valley during the summer of 1950 and subsisting on army field rations, I found only one who showed a low urinary chloride output, and then only temporarily. Persons who are acclimatized and are carrying out work for which they are trained appear not to need the addition of extra salt to a normal diet, even under severe outdoor desert conditions. D. E. Bass and colleagues (25), working at the Yuma Test Station, found that during the first 4 days of exposure the volume of extracellular or tissue fluid was increased, and that salt was retained

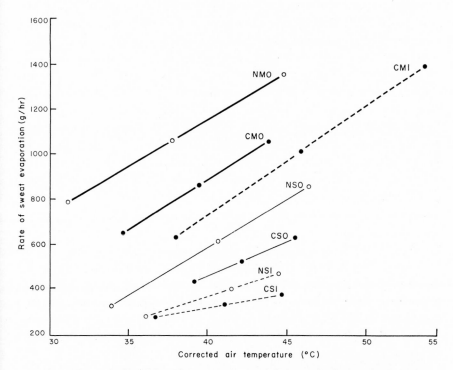

Fig. 6. The relationship of sweat evaporation and air temperature to various activities and attire are shown here. NMO indicates the rate for persons walking in the sun without any clothing; CMO, clothed and marching in the sun; CMI, clothed and marching in the shade; NSO, nude and sitting in the sun; CSO, clothed and sitting in the sun; NSI, nude and sitting in the shade; CSI, clothed and sitting in the shade.

by the kidney to compensate for this. The increase reached 16 percent on the fourth day and was unchanged on the fifteenth day. The volume of fluid circulating in the blood, on the other hand, returned to normal by the fourteenth day.

These investigators also found that the disappearance of symptoms of heat exhaustion on the third day was accompanied by constriction of both veins and small arteries in the limbs, but that these changes later disappeared. Complete acclimatization appears to depend on changes that are rather slow in developing, but a set of temporary adjustments can be seen helping to tide the person over until the permanent ones are established. The fact of acclimatization is very clear and some of its constituents are known, but its basic mechanism is still obscure.

Once we get away from the general statement that a healthy, acclimatized person can carry on normal activities, with normal productivity, in all but exceptional naturally occurring desert environments, we find ourselves in difficulty. A great deal of thought and effort has been given, especially in the United States, to devising a scheme for predicting the response of an individual to given environmental conditions, but so far no one proposal has been satisfactory.

The "effective temperature" scheme of the American Society of Heating and Ventilating Engineers workers (4) is not applicable very far outside of the "comfort zone." H. S. Belding and T. F. Hatch's "heat-stress index" (26) really is applicable only to nude subjects, and such corrections for clothing as have been suggested are not entirely satisfactory. We cannot answer, with any degree of confidence at the present time, such questions as these: What rest periods should be included in a work plan? What should be the maximum work rate for 30 minutes? What increase in productivity could be expected if shade were provided? Those who are experienced in working or supervising work will develop empirical answers, but objective guides are few.

Desert Clothing and Housing

The basic work on desert clothing, carried on during World War II and reported in Newburgh's text (18), has been extended by design studies, chamber tests, and field trials conducted by the Quartermaster Corps. In addition to making systematic measurements of the

A climatic chamber for studying the reactions of subjects to solar-radiation loads in the desert was devised by Lee and others at the Yuma Test Station. Transparent, plastic walls permit entry of 90 percent of the solar radiation, while air temperature and humidity are kept constant by machinery in an adjoining trailer. The subject walks on a treadmill. Body tapes keep the thermocouples in place on the skin.

subjects' reactions while they were wearing various items of clothing and equipment and performing set military tasks, one group of investigators also studied their own reactions while they were camped for several weeks in Death Valley.

These studies served to confirm Adolph's findings (*12*) that clothing can provide a significant degree of protection against environmental heat gain. The problem of the designer is to maximize this protection and at the same time avoid interference with evaporation. Translated into actual design, these requirements call for fairly complete coverage of the body, with a lightweight but moderately insulating ensemble, permeable to water vapor, loosely fitting, and compatible with the individual's task so that unnecessary work is eliminated. Neck, cuff, and waist openings should be adjustable, so that ambient air can be admitted during active periods or excluded when the air temperature is high and the wind is strong.

The most effective headgear provides a light, floating shade to the neck and shoulders, as does the conventional Arabian headcloth. Next best is a broad-brimmed felt hat, preferably with a head suspension separated from the headband so that the space above the crown is ventilated. The ubiquitous cap is one of the least satisfactory forms of headgear for hot desert use.

Although the interest in, and progress of, architecture have been tremendous in this country, consideration of housing design as a specific factor in protecting man from the stress of hot, dry environments has been almost peripheral. In an affluent society, it is easier to add sufficient heating in winter and cooling in summer than to compromise a design that gives pleasure, stability, functional satisfaction, or economic use of space; or at least it would seem so. Yet, here and there, evidence of thought for the less affluent or less easily impressed can be found.

A basis for climatic consideration of housing was offered by the American Institute of Architects, in conjunction with the magazine *House Beautiful,* in the form of a series of regional climatic analyses, replete with information on the frequencies of temperature, humidity, wind, precipitation, and so forth, month by month, and illustrated with maps of geographic distribution. Part IV of the series relates to the southwest arid areas with Phoenix, Arizona, as the center. Detailed analyses of the thermal load to be expected, the influence of design on the total thermal load, heat transfer through materials and structures, methods of returning the imposed heat to the environment, and the significance of these procedures for the human occupant have been given by V. G. Olgyay (*27*), J. E. Aronin (*28*), the Building Research Advisory Board (*29*), and me.

At the Conference on Solar Energy held in 1955 at Tucson, Arizona, and the World Symposium on Applied Solar Energy immediately afterward at Phoenix, housing came in for its fair share of comment. Attention was mainly directed, however, to the effective collection and use of solar energy for house heating or, in one instance, as the energy source for cooling. The devices recommended seem not to have made much economic impact. Two conferences held in 1959, one called by the University of California at Los Angeles on Designing the Indoor Environment and one by the American Institute of Architects on Research for Architecture, did little more than focus attention on the need for taking environment into account.

It is perhaps appropriate here to mention studies made in the United States on the significance of desert conditions elsewhere. The most extensive work of this character, as one might expect, has been done by the U.S. Army, and particularly by the Quartermaster Corps. In a series of service reports, climatic conditions in various desert areas of the world are compared in some detail with those prevailing at Yuma, and, in another report, the prevalence of several environmental conditions in southwest Asia are mapped in some detail, as is also the significance of these conditions for human operations. It is again a matter of regret that this type of information has not appeared in a more readily available form.

Studies in Other Countries

Of course, the studies in the United States just described, far from taking place in isolation, were based on pioneer work done elsewhere, with full knowledge of what was being studied in other countries, and sometimes in active collaboration with scientists abroad. Only the aspects of work elsewhere that are directly related to arid conditions are reviewed here, although again it must be remembered that important information and ideas emerge from more basic physiologic work, and that much of the intensive study of humid tropical conditions has relevance to hot, arid environments.

The experience of the British Army in India, and of the French legionnaires in North Africa, led to empirical rules and practices, which, in the light of present-day knowledge, show an interesting mixture of the very good and the very bad. The floating headcloth so often seen in pictures of the times was an excellent idea that has been rather perversely discarded, but the spine pads and cummerbunds, which were based on mistaken notions, have passed into well-deserved oblivion. The pith helmet, or topee, when fitted with a head suspension separated from the headband, has a certain use and charm in quiet urban or garrison life but is not well adapted to field activities.

A pernicious item in the code, however, was the belief that a man could "learn" to get along on a fixed low ration of water—usually

1 British quart (1.136 liters) per day. In spite of disasters, such as those encountered in the Mesopotamian campaign of World War I, it was still firmly entrenched in much military thinking at the beginning of World War II.

In Africa south of the Sahara, a network of stations, with a compilation center in the Union of South Africa, has been set up to record various aspects of solar radiation on a uniform basis. C. H. Wyndham, working out of the Applied Physiology Laboratory of the Transvaal and Orange Free State Chamber of Mines, investigated the reactions of a number of ethnic groups to a hot, humid atmosphere. His results were rather complex; but, in general, it appears that the Caucasians, Bantus, Arabs, and aborigines showed very similar reactions, in spite of marked anthropometric differences.

At what is now the University of Dakar, R. R. Lemaire made a study of water and electrolyte balance responses to the high evaporative demands of hot desert environments, the results of which confirm and extend those of Adolph and others in this country. PRO-HUZA (Centre d'Etudes et d'Informations des Problemes Humains dans les Zones Arides), in collaboration with B. Metz from the University of Strasbourg, has initiated an excellent series of field studies in the Sahara, in spite of the very unsettled state of that region.

Their most interesting findings concern the importance of psychologic and social factors. A battery of tests included psychomotor, general intelligence, practical intelligence, and certain nonquantitative tests. The general conclusions are interesting: (i) when a group lives without protection against a particularly severe environment, the degree of adaptation depends closely on its degree of internal organization; (ii) when a group is well protected against the stressful environment in which it operates, its adaptation as a whole is related to the degree of comfort provided and, far from being tied to the structural organization of the group, varies with individual initiative and attitude; (iii) each group of indigenes has a level of psychologic performance fashioned by its general mode of life, showing variations within the group as a result of individual education, but apparently not related in any way to the severity of the physical environment.

There is, naturally, much interest in Israel in man's adaptation to arid and semiarid conditions. Organizations, such as the Hebrew

University, the Negev Institute for Arid Zone Research, the Building Research Institute, and the Israel Institute of Technology, are engaged in studies that range from measurement of solar radiation, through detailed physiologic responses of the water and electrolyte balance, to the development of climatic indexes and details of optimizing water consumption at work.

UNESCO, through its arid-zones project, has done a great deal to foster a worldwide approach to these problems. Man's reactions naturally find a place in this approach, as is evidenced by papers in such volumes as *Human and Animal Ecology—Reviews of Research* (*30*). More recently, and more specifically, UNESCO has arranged for a series of papers on the physiology and psychology under arid conditions.

Problems of Present Research

The environmental factors that affect man are the same as those that operate for agricultural, industrial, livestock, or any other human endeavors; but the mode in which the information is presented and the emphasis to be placed on the individual items are different; hence, somewhat special systems of compilation are necessary. Climatic classifications for other purposes are seldom applicable to man. Temperature, vapor pressure, air movement, and radiant-heat exchange must be considered conjointly, and methods for estimating the combined stress are available. Gross meteorologic data are generally available in the United States but are often less readily obtained elsewhere. Factors that control micrometeorologic variations are only partially known, and estimation for a given situation is a matter of judgment. Solar-radiation data are less extensive than those on other elements, but estimations can be made from records of hours of sunshine or cloud cover.

The incidence of infectious disease in arid areas, in sharp contrast with that in the humid tropics, is not spectacularly affected by arid-zones conditions. Existing technology can do much to reduce the incidence of stress and relieve much of the resultant strain. The psychologic and sociologic effects of arid-zones conditions have been very poorly studied.

In spite of nearly 60 years of study, there is still no satisfactory way to estimate the net effect or strain of given environmental conditions on a given group of individuals. Very little attempt has been made to integrate rates of heat transfer that differ with parts of the body or with time. Although estimates can be made of the stress imposed by "average" conditions, estimates of strain are based on one or a few easily measured body responses, which give no more than a glimpse of the total strain. In instances of mild stress where sensations of discomfort are relevant, techniques for eliciting responses are far from standardized. Such indexes as have been developed have been based on responses to relatively simple and stable laboratory environments, which leaves their applicability to natural environments or the use of meteorologic data open to question.

The turnover, distribution, and internal adjustment of water and electrolytes, particularly those involving sodium, potassium, and chloride ions, bear the brunt of adjustment to hot, dry conditions. The detailed physiology is being worked out, but several uncertainties still exist. The hormone aldosterone is believed to play a major role. A critical feature of acclimatization is reduction of sweat chloride loss to a level that is compatible with a normal diet. Heat cramps ensue when the chloride concentration of the blood falls below a critical level, but the detailed mechanism is not understood. It is not known to what extent the addition of unnecessary salt to the diet of a healthy man may be harmful.

It is doubtful that arid environments make any particular dietary demands beyond those of an adequate supply of water and sufficient salt for people who are unacclimatized or are undertaking unusually hard physical work in very hot weather. Food increases the amount of water required for renal excretion and, thus, imposes an extra demand when water supply is severely limited. The significance of the "voluntary dehydration" practiced by many is still disputed. It is safer to encourage free water drinking, provided that the salt balance is maintained, but not to the point that the individual has gastric distress or nausea.

Discussion of permissible percentage of weight loss is vitiated by lack of definition of the original effective water content of the body. Dehydration is accompanied by a reduction of sweating in some, but not in all, cases. When it occurs, the rise of body temperature may more than offset any benefits to be gained from conservation of body water.

The thermoregulatory hierarchy is more complex than was once thought. It is becoming customary to apply cybernetic arguments to the operation of the heat-regulating mechanism. In the argument about the relative roles of peripheral and central thermosensitive receptors, the sensible middle ground seems to be developing that both sets cooperate, the former as far as skin heat exchanges and external stresses are concerned, the latter when metabolic heat production and oscillations in actual blood temperature are involved. The electroencephalographic changes in newcomers to the desert reported by the French workers should be pursued.

Possibilities in Psychology

Psychology provides the exciting pioneer fringe, even though the tools may still be primitive. The present position may be summarized: (i) a single exposure to a hot environment may induce a feeling of lassitude and result in a sense of increased work cost, increased errors or frustration, and excitement; (ii) with repeated exposures, two contrary processes are seen, one tending to diminish the effects through a species of "acclimatization," the other being a cumulative effect that lowers the threshold for the appearance of psychologic peculiarities; (iii) motivation and directed activity raise the threshold for untoward developments; (iv) actual performance is determined by the interplay of the aforementioned effects; (v) resultant psychologic effects badly need definition and quantitation; (vi) the term *tropical* may be prefaced to the term *neurasthenia* only as an indicator of the circumstances under which the condition developed, and not as the label of a distinct entity. (The adjectives *industrial, rural,* or even *academic* may be equally admissible, each in its own place.)

Present opinion tends to deemphasize the importance of morphology as a determinant of heat tolerance, as long as heat transfer or any component of it, such as sweat rate, is expressed per unit of surface area. Where water or food is in chronic short supply, there may be a certain selection pressure in favor of the small individual who puts fewer demands on the available resources. Race, in general, seems to be of less importance to adaptation than the experience and training of the individual, although certain generalizations can be drawn, such as the increased tolerance (low body temperature in spite of low sweat rate) of Australian aborigines and perhaps American Negroes.

It is not clear to what extent the customs of indigenes apparently well adapted to arid conditions really owe their origin to climatic conditions, or to what extent they are accidental accompaniments stemming from isolation and meager resources. Determination of the part that metabolic differences may play in the adaptation of ethnic groups waits upon development of satisfactory methods of investigating energy-transfer processes in human tissues.

Many opportunities now available for observing the effect of cultural change on reactions to desert environments are likely to disappear in the next couple of decades as primitive and isolated groups are overtaken by the rapid march of "civilization."

The principles of design for shelter and housing are also well determined but are largely ignored in the architectural practice of the United States, where design deficiencies are offset by artificial heating and cooling. The economic advantage of cooling in hot weather is apparently becoming established. For people who are journeying in waterless areas, three basic rules are paramount: do not set out without adequate water; rest in the shade if you do get caught; and stay near objects that can be seen from the air. Death is the probable punishment for violation.

Organizations for Research

There is a plethora of organizations but very little organization. In the United States, World War II gave an urgency to the consolidation of knowledge during actual hostilities, so much so that information was passed along at the premanuscript stage, and physiologists worked in close association with meteorologists and geographers on the one hand, and with suppliers of clothing and equipment on the other. This association was crystallized in the organization of research activities in the Quartermaster Corps and continued until 1960 with an effectiveness to be judged from the more than 500 research and technical reports that were issued. With the breaking up of this close association as a result of reorganization, liaison at the moment rests almost entirely on personal initiative.

A study group on bioclimatology, set up by the National Science

Foundation and the American Meteorological Society, provides a forum for expression of national requirements but in no way meets the need for an active group of representative scientists working full time and in close association in the development, compilation, and dissemination of integrated information.

On the international plane, UNESCO has provided both the stimulus and the opportunity for the presentation of knowledge, with a fair degree of cooperation, if not coordination, among the various disciplines involved. This, however, was not intended to be more than temporary. Further association now returns to the realm of individual initiative, which, of course, has been the traditional method of scientific cooperation. But there does seem to be some need, in this increasingly complicated world, for a focal organization where collaborative application of knowledge to a major practical problem can be carried on in continuous fashion.

REFERENCES

1. J. S. Haldane, *Report to the Secretary of State for Health on the Health of Cornish Tin Miners* (H.M. Stat. Office, London, 1904); "Influence of high air temperatures," *J. Hyg.* **5**, 494–513 (1905).
2. J. Lefèvre, *Chaleur animale et bioénergétique* (Masson, Paris, 1911).
3. D. Hargood-Ash, L. Hill, *et al.*, "The katathermometer in studies of body heat and efficiency, *Med. Res. Council Spec. Rept. Ser. 73* (H.M. Stat. Office, London, 1923).
4. F. C. Houghton and C. P. Yagloglou, "Determining lines of human comfort," *Trans. Am. Soc. Heating and Ventilating Engrs.* **29**, 163–176, 361–384; **30**, 193–212 (1923–1924).
5. J. S. Chase, *California Desert Trails* (Houghton Mifflin, Boston, 1919).
6. D. C. Hogner, *Westward, High, Low, and Dry* (Dutton, New York, 1938).
7. W. L. Manly, *Death Valley in '49* (Pacific Tree and Vine Co., San Jose, Calif., 1894).
8. J. H. King, "Brief account of sufferings of a detachment of U.S. Cavalry from deprivation of water, during a period of 86 hours, while scouting on the 'Llano Estacado' or 'Staked Plains' of Texas," *Am. J. Med. Sci.* **75**, 404–408 (1878).
9. W. J. McGee, "Desert thirst as a disease," *Interstate Med. J.* **13**, 279–300 (1906).

10. D. B. Dill, F. C. Hall, and H. T. Edwards, "Changes in composition of sweat during acclimatization to heat," *Am. J. Physiol.* **123**, 412–419 (1938).

11. D. B. Dill, B. F. Jones, H. T. Edwards, and S. A. Oberg, "Salt economy in extreme dry heat," *J. Biol. Chem.* **100**, 755–767 (1933).

12. E. F. Adolph and Associates, *Physiology of Man in the Desert* (Wiley, Interscience Div., New York, 1947), especially pp. 5, 16, 345.

13. N. Malamud, W. Haymaker, and R. P. Custer, "Heat stroke—a clinicopathologic study of 125 fatal cases," *Military Surgeon* (now *Military Med.*) **99**, 397–449 (1946).

14. E. Schickele, "Environment and fatal heat stroke, an analysis of 157 cases occurring in the Army in the U.S. during World War II," *Military Surgeon* (now *Military Med.*) **100**, 235–256 (1947).

15. W. S. S. Ladell, J. C. Waterlow, and M. F. Hudson, "Desert climate —physiological and clinical observations," *Lancet* **1944-II**, 491–497, 527–531 (1944).

16. D. H. K. Lee, "Human organism and hot environments," *Trans. Roy. Soc. Trop. Med. Hyg.* **29**, 7–20 (1935).

17. C. S. Wyndham *et al.*, "Methods of cooling subjects with hyperpyrexia," *J. Appl. Physiol.* **14**, 771–776 (1959).

18. L. H. Newburgh, *Physiology of Heat Regulation and the Science of Clothing* (Saunders, Philadelphia, Pa., 1949).

19. D. H. K. Lee, "Proprioclimates of man and domestic animals," *Arid Zone Research* (*UNESCO*) **10**, 102–125 (1958).

20. A. H. Woodcock, R. L. Pratt, J. R. Breckenridge, *Heat Exchange in Hot Environments* (U.S. Army Office of the Quartermaster General, E. P. Branch, Rept. 183, 1952).

21. P. Baker, "American Negro-white differences in heat tolerance," *U.S. Army Quartermaster Res. and Eng. Center Tech. Rept. EP-75* (1958).

22. F. Grande, "Nitrogen metabolism and body temperature in man under combined restriction of food and water," paper 35, *Symp. Environ. Physiol. and Psychol. in Arid Conditions*, Lucknow, India, 1962, *Arid Zone Research* (*UNESCO*), in press.

23. J. W. Conn, M. W. Johnston, and L. H. Louis, "Acclimatization to humid heat: a function of adreno-cortical activity," *J. Clin. Invest.* **25**, 912–913 (1946).

24. R. L. Dobson, "The effect of repeated episodes of profuse sweating on the human eccrine glands," *J. Invest. Dermatol.* **35**, 195–198 (1960).

25. D. E. Bass, E. R. Buskirk, P. F. Iampietro, and M. Mager, "Comparison of blood volume during physical conditioning, heat acclimatization and sedentary living," *J. Appl. Physiol.* **12**, 186–188 (1958).

26. H. S. Belding and T. F. Hatch, "Index for evaluating heat stress in terms of resulting physiological strains," *Heating, Piping, Airconditioning* **27**, 129–136 (1955).

27. V. G. Olgyay, "The temperate house; how to do something about the weather by natural means," *Architectural Forum* **94**, 179–191 (1951).
28. J. E. Aronin, *Climate and Architecture* (Reinhold, New York, 1953).
29. Building Research Advisory Board, "Housing and building in hot-humid and hot-dry climates, *Natl. Acad. Sci.–Natl. Res. Council (U.S.) Conf. Rept. 5* (1953).
30. UNESCO, *Human and Animal Ecology—Reviews of Research, Arid Zone Research (UNESCO)* **8** (1957).

13

Economic Development of Arid Regions

Morris E. Garnsey

Nathaniel Wollman

The economic analysis of the arid regions of the United States begins with a paradox—the paradox of plenty in the midst of poverty. On the one hand, these regions are poverty-stricken in rainfall and water by comparison with the humid regions and, as a result, they are poor in population and total income. On the other hand, they have grown steadily in population and income since 1900 and rapidly since 1940. Moreover, the future rise is likely to be more rapid even than that of the last 20 years.

The key to this economic riddle is to be found in the distinction between physical scarcity and economic scarcity. Economic scarcity is determined by demand, by cost, and by substitution possibilities— all of which are derived from decisions made by men. In contrast, physical scarcity arises from natural phenomenons that are largely beyond man's control and independent of his wants, desires, and values. The rain may fall equally on the just and the unjust; but it rewards those on whom it falls as a regularly spaced, annual average of 30 inches (760 millimeters) and punishes those on whom it falls irregularly from season to season and year to year in average amounts of 20 inches (500 millimeters) or less.

Yet within the limits of these conditions, man has had, and still has, a wide freedom of maneuver. The extent of his success in achieving growth in population and income within the physical limits of aridity is determined by his ability to manipulate the environment in ways that will overcome the limits of physical scarcity. There are several ways to do this.

369

The first has been to extend control to unappropriated surface and ground water wherever and whenever the rising demand is sufficient to cover the higher costs of appropriation. Two striking recent examples of this reaching out for "free" water in the face of higher costs are the California project, which will transport water 585 miles (941 kilometers) from the northern part of the state to the south, and the upper Colorado River storage project. These projects will cost at least $13 billion to $15 billion.

Second, in the various subareas of the region, the costs of scarce water have been kept down successfully by technologic improvement. Also, economies of scale have been realized—mainly through multiple-purpose, river-basin developments. Often where increased costs of storage and distribution have been encountered, a successful effort has been made to shift these costs to others than the direct consumer-beneficiaries. The federal government has granted large subsidies to water-development projects and, at the same time, has kept its user-charges low. In southern California, in Colorado, and elsewhere, water has been sold to consumers at prices below cost, and local taxpayers have shouldered the deficit.

Third, since these activities are expensive, they are accompanied by attempts to economize water in the strict sense—to use less for any given purpose. There are many examples of this, of which the most common is the reduction of so-called "waste." That is, irrigation ditches can be lined to prevent losses, reservoirs can be covered, and leaky faucets can be repaired. Finally, substitution among uses can take place: water once used in low-return activities, such as agriculture, can be shifted to higher-return uses in industry and domestic consumption.

Alternate Uses of Water

These shifts in uses are a matter of primary concern to economists. Here the economic problem of the allocation of resources appears in its purest form, uncomplicated by considerations of technology and politics. It is not surprising, therefore, that economists have begun to analyze this problem intensively. One of the first publications on the subject compared the effects on the economy in two subregions of New Mexico (12 counties in the Rio Grande and San Juan basins) of various patterns of water use based on the anticipated technology of water use in 1975 (*1*).

The New Mexico study dealt with irrigated agriculture and specified manufacturing industries, including related municipal use, mining, and "recreation" (sport fishing, camping, and picnicking). Manufacturing and related municipal uses and mining uses were combined into a single category called *municipal and industry*. The engineering costs of water were subtracted from the gross product to yield an adjusted gross product per acre foot (1233.5 cubic meters). Since the different models involved different product mixes within a given category of use, the adjusted gross product per acre foot (1233.5 cubic meters) varied by model. Models also varied in size of transbasin diversion from the San Juan to the Rio Grande. Only the smaller-sized diversion is shown in Table I. Thus, taking the product mix for which value added (or gross product) per unit of water is highest for agriculture and lowest for industry and municipal uses, the value-added ratios, based on agriculture, are as follows: agriculture, 1; municipal and industry, 73; recreation, 17.

In these estimates, gross product was computed as being derived from the primary transactions. That is, the production and first sale of agricultural, manufactured, and mined product plus the value added by purchases of firms engaged in primary production. Since there is no "primary product" attributable to recreation, value added for the latter was based wholly on "value added by purchases" of those engaged in recreation. This results in an obvious understatement of recreational value added in relation to the other two categories. Yet even with this understatement, recreational uses added substantially more to the region's economy than did agriculture.

Table I. Gross dollar product per acre foot (1233.5 cubic meters) of water used[a].

Model	Agriculture ($)	Mining and industry ($)	Recreation ($)
High irrigation-low industrial	17	1237	293
Low irrigation-high industrial	14	2154	291

[a] After adjustment for costs of water.

A much more ambitious study now in preparation projects water use in the river basins of the southwestern United States to the year 2000 (2). This study indicates that the following ratios of value added per unit of water hold, all expressed in relation to unity for agriculture: manufacture of food, 12; of pulp and paper, 10; of chemicals, 179; and petroleum refining, 47.

These ratios not only reflect the industrial uses of water but also take into account the fact that manufacturing workers are usually urban residents, that manufacturing employment gives rise to other urban-related employment, and that both the manufacturing workers and the nonmanufacturing workers will have families who must be supplied with water. The agriculture figure is limited to water use per dollar's worth of value added. The manufacturing figure is equal to the total water used in the designated manufacturing industry, the water required as waste dilution after maximum treatment, and the water required for the municipal uses of the manufacturing employee and his family, in addition to the domestic water used by one additional urban worker and his family plus the waste dilution after maximum treatment of waste by the municipal sewage-disposal plant. The waste dilution is designed to provide a stream quality of approximately 4 parts per million (4 milligrams per liter) of dissolved oxygen.

Substitution possibilities also may be studied in terms of employment per unit of water rather than value added. For the arid parts of the United States, direct employment per 1 million gallons (3747 kiloliters) daily in agriculture ranges between 5 and 10 persons, depending on the regional patterns of product. In manufacturing, even when the industry is a heavy water user, and after the flows required for waste dilution after treatment have been taken into account, employment per 1 million gallons daily is as follows for the southwestern part of the United States: food, 46 persons; pulp and paper, 19 persons; chemicals, 178 persons; petroleum refining, 158 persons. Employment per 1 million gallons daily in other manufacturing industries is much higher, since not only is process water used in smaller quantities but also there is less pollution per unit of product that requires dilution. Thus, the difference in employment per unit of water between agriculture and manufacturing is on the order of from 2 to 35 times. The employment capacity of water will become increasingly important as population grows.

Population Trends

This brings us to an examination of some of the details of population trends. As a preliminary to any analysis in detail, it should be held in mind firmly that, in a general sense, population changes in the arid West are primarily a function of the population growth and economic expansion of the nation as a whole. Much of this expansion has been a function of the westward movement—the "filling up" of the continent as the population of the humid East grew rapidly from natural increase and immigration. Here the true substance of the paradox is now revealed, for the westward movement encountered a real barrier in the physical hostility of the arid, mountainous West. The genuine effectiveness of this hostility is reflected by population density. In 1960, the population density of the continental United States was 59.9 persons per square mile (23.1 persons per square kilometer). In the entire mountain West, by contrast, this density, as is shown in Table II and Fig. 1, was only 8.8 persons per square mile (3.4 persons per square kilometer), and in the Great Plains, the average was approximately 6.8 persons per square mile (2.6 persons per square kilometer).

It is true, of course, that much of the terrain of the region is rugged and mountainous and unsuited for human habitation by present standards. Yet the rugged areas are small in relation to the total area of arid and semiarid lands. In this over-all sense, the physical scarcity of rainfall and the resulting high cost of using surface and ground water in relation to the humid areas are the primary cause of low population density in the region—a density only one-tenth of that of the United States, one-fortieth of the density of the Middle Atlantic States, and one-twentieth of the population density of relatively inhospitable New England. This is not to say that aridity has been the only factor that inhibited population expansion in the Great Plains and mountain West. There are few independent variables in economic analysis. Causation is complex, and the growth of population and income exhibits strong feedbacks and multiplier effects.

Cumulative effects that were inimical to settlement in the arid regions also resulted in the westward movement's "leaping over" the barrier of aridity to the comparatively favorable environment of the Pacific Coast. There the stimulating effects of settlement on eco-

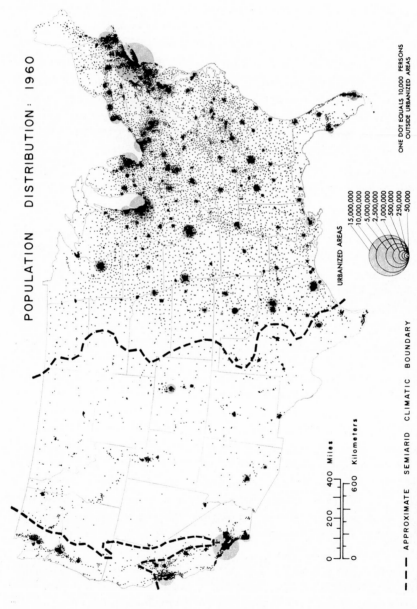

Fig. 1. Population of the arid West remains sparse compared with the rest of the nation.

nomic production provoked further migration. Thus, in 1960 the density of population in California had risen to 100.4 persons per square mile (38.8 per square kilometer). In the coastal areas of Washington and Oregon also, population density had exceeded the national average by 1960. In the last two decades, however, the population of the interior, arid West has been growing rapidly— apparently under the twin pressures of the "filling-up" process from

Table II.   Population density.

Region	Persons per square mile[a]			Percentage increase 1940–1960
	1940	1950	1960	
United States	*44.2*	*50.6*	*59.9*	*36*
Great Plains[b]	5.4	6.0	6.8	26
North Dakota	6.3	6.0	6.1	−3
South Dakota	4.1	4.2	4.9	20
Montana	2.7	2.8	3.3	22
Wyoming	3.5	3.9	4.4	26
Nebraska	6.0	5.8	5.6	−7
Kansas	6.7	7.2	7.2	7
Colorado	5.3	5.2	4.6	−15
New Mexico	4.5	5.4	6.4	42
Oklahoma	3.9	4.6	4.5	15
Texas	10.6	15.0	20.7	95
Mountain West	5.2	6.8	8.8	69.2
Wyoming	2.6	3.0	3.4	31
Idaho	6.3	7.1	8.1	29
Montana	3.8	4.1	4.6	21
Washington[c]	10.4	15.9	19.1	83.6
Oregon[c]	2.3	3.0	3.3	43.5
Utah	6.7	8.4	10.8	61
Colorado	10.8	12.8	16.9	56
New Mexico	4.4	5.6	7.8	77
Arizona	4.4	6.6	11.5	161
Nevada	1.0	1.5	2.6	160
California	44.1	67.5	100.4	128
Arid counties	14.7	24.4	33.6	129
Southern third	67.6	104.4	165.4	145

[a] One square mile equals 2.59 square kilometers.
[b] Great Plains portion only of these states. See map of the natural regions in Chapter 2.
[c] Arid counties only.
Source: U.S. Bureau of the Census.

Table III. Population.

Region	Total population 1940	% of U.S. population 1940	Total population 1960	% of U.S. population 1960	Increase 1940–1960 (%)
United States	131,669,275		178,464,236		35.5
Great Plains[a]	2,126,918	1.61	2,898,086	1.61	36.3
North Dakota	211,132	0.15	205,499	0.11	2.6
South Dakota	233,146	0.17	257,005	0.14	10.2
Montana	220,516	0.17	264,652	0.15	20.0
Wyoming	99,181	0.07	125,151	0.07	26.2
Nebraska	230,336	0.17	215,659	0.12	6.3
Kansas	162,310	0.12	181,031	0.10	11.5
Colorado	163,164	0.12	140,824	0.08	15.9
New Mexico	197,713	0.15	282,874	0.16	43.1
Oklahoma	22,198	0.01	25,623	0.01	15.4
Texas	587,222	0.44	1,199,768	0.67	104.1
Mountain West	4,456,416	3.38	7,374,687	4.13	65.4
Wyoming	250,741	0.18	330,066	0.18	31.6
Idaho	524,873	0.39	667,191	0.37	27.1
Montana	559,456	0.42	674,767	0.37	20.6
Washington[b]	200,172	0.15	368,389	0.20	76.4
Oregon[b]	106,241	0.08	151,269	0.08	42.3
Utah	550,310	0.41	890,627	0.49	61.8
Colorado	1,123,296	0.85	1,753,947	0.98	56.1
New Mexico	531,818	0.40	951,023	0.53	78.8
Arizona	499,261	0.37	1,302,121	0.72	160.8
Nevada	110,247	0.08	285,278	0.15	158.7
California	6,907,387	5.24	15,717,204	8.76	127.5
Arid counties	1,195,322	0.90	2,741,202	1.52	129.3
Southern third	3,840,733	2.91	9,398,722	5.24	144.7

[a] Great Plains portion only of these states.
[b] Arid counties only.
Source: U.S. Bureau of the Census.

the East and a "backwash" from the Pacific Coast. This tendency can be seen by a closer examination of population data for the region (Table III and Fig. 2).

An inspection of the economic indicators that are used here—population, employment, and income—leads to the conclusion that the entire arid and semiarid West can be divided into three broad economic subregions: (i) the Great Plains, (ii) the mountain West, which here includes the arid parts of Washington and Oregon, and (iii) California.

Great Plains

Population in all three of the subregions of the arid West has now increased more rapidly than that of the United States as a whole since 1940. However, the growth in the Great Plains has been concentrated almost entirely in west Texas, where a substantial petrochemical industry developed after World War II. In the rest of the Great Plains, where agriculture predominates, the absolute growth of population has been much below the national average. As a result, the Great Plains, excluding west Texas, by 1960 provided habitation and employment for only 0.48 of 1 percent of the population of the United States, whereas in 1940, 0.62 of 1 percent of the national population lived in the region.

These observations apply equally well to the plains sections of

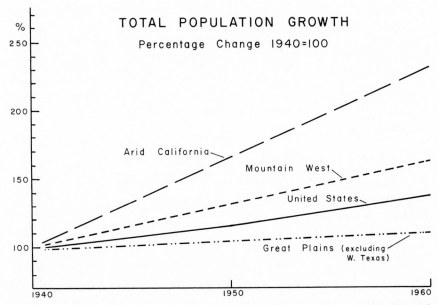

Fig. 2. The filling-up process in the western United States is indicated by percentage population growth during the two decades that ended in 1960. In the arid and semiarid regions, only the Great Plains did not see a notable rise in population.

Montana, Colorado, Wyoming, and New Mexico. Total population changes there have been dominated by the changes in their mountain areas where population is concentrated. In general, the plains areas of the four states have lost population—in some cases absolutely, in all cases relatively—to the rest of the state and to the United States.

Thus, the "filling-up" process has given way over vast areas of land surface to an "emptying-out" process. The migration from the Plains has been accelerated by great technologic improvements in agriculture, which simultaneously increase income per farm unit and reduce sharply both the number of farm units and the total employment in agriculture. Add to this the rapid trend toward urbanization in the Plains region, as elsewhere, and we truly see the phenomenon of an empty land stretching from Oklahoma to the Canadian border and beyond. Here the hostile character of aridity and the failure of man to cope with it fully are sharply revealed. A limit to this "emptying-out" process may be expected. The *Denver Post,* on 28 January 1963, for example, described Baca County in southeastern Colorado as having reached economic stability as a result of better adaptation of agriculture to the conditions of the area—that is, more in grass, improved methods of dry-land farming, and the introduction of irrigation from ground water. At present the population of the county is 4310, having been reduced from 10,570 in 1930.

Mountain West

The story is quite different in the mountain West. In the two decades from 1940 to 1960, its population has grown relatively much faster than that of the United States as a whole—65.4 percent for the region, as compared with 35.5 percent nationally. By 1960, the mountain West accounted for 4.13 percent of the total United States population, as compared with 3.38 percent in 1940.

Within the region, population growth has shown a marked variation from north to south, being slowest in Montana, Idaho, and Wyoming, where natural increase has been partially offset by a net emigration from these states since 1930. In Utah, Colorado, and New Mexico, growth rates have been nearly double the national rate for the last 20 years. Colorado is still the largest state in the mountain West, although Arizona is now the second largest state and has grown more rapidly than any state in the region. In the case of Nevada, the very small population base in 1940 causes an overstatement of its growth when percentages are used.

These figures suggest that aridity has been a factor in the growth pattern. When low humidity is combined with relatively mild or warm winters, an environment exists that is attractive to many persons (3), and low humidity plus air-conditioning makes summer climate acceptable, if not positively attractive, even when temperatures are relatively high. The regional pattern thus indicates that the southern half of the mountain West is responding to the "population explosion" through both the "filling-up" and the "backwash" effects.

California

What is there left to say about California? A few years ago Carey McWilliams devoted a whole book to the thesis that California is the exception to all ordinary rules of economic, social, and political behavior (4). The expansion of the state, and particularly of the arid southern third, has been phenomenal. Broadly speaking, this has been based, first, on climatic attractions, including low humidity, then on the motion pictures, then on the aircraft and shipbuilding industries, then on outer-space technology and defense (5). Somewhere in this chain of events the cumulative effects of growth interaction began to operate, exerting their multiplier effect in such a way that the rate of growth was compounded by the expansion of most types of manufacturing and services employment.

Within the context of this process, the scarcity of water always has been a factor but never a serious obstacle. Astute economic and political management has permitted the reaching out for water supplies to farther and farther limits. Usually the costs of such extensions of supply have been met in large part by federal or state subsidy. Thus, their limiting effects to the water user have been minimized.

Today California is our largest state in population, and nearly 10 percent of the total population of the United States resides there (8.76 percent in 1960, more than 9 percent in 1963). The bulk of this population is concentrated in the arid and semiarid southern third of the state. This area long ago transcended the limits of a

Table IV.   Total employment.

Region	Labor force 1940	% of U.S. employed 1940	Unemployed (%) 1940	Labor force 1960	% of U.S. employed 1960	Unemployed (%) 1960	Increase 1940–1960 (%)
United States	52,789,499		9.6	68,144,079		5.1	29.1
Great Plainsª	565,480	1.07	7.3	616,623	0.90	3.9	9.0
Mountain States	1,647,569	3.12	10.0	2,668,382	3.91	5.2	61.9
Arid California	469,659	0.88	12.1	990,744	1.45	7.4	110.9

ª Excluding west Texas.
Source: U.S. Bureau of the Census.

resource-based economy and appears to have developed enough economic momentum and strength to overcome any potential limits of the effect of a scarce supply of rainfall or water. As early as 1938, McLaughlin marveled over the growth of the Los Angeles core of southern California: despite inadequate rainfall or nearby water source and despite the lack of coal, he pointed out, Los Angeles had become a large and industrialized city (6). Led by the aggressive enterprise and opportunism of southern California, the Pacific and southwestern areas were able to turn "desert" and sunshine into assets and obtain a relatively high percentage of the military installations and defense-oriented industries during World War II and the postwar period.

Labor Force and Employment

It is to be expected that the over-all growth of the labor force and of employment should follow closely the growth of population. Thus, in the Great Plains, excluding west Texas, the total labor force has grown at a slower rate than that of the United States, and the percentage of the total national labor force residing in the Great Plains has declined (Table IV and Fig. 3). In contrast, the southern Mountain States have experienced a rapid rise in the size of the labor force and in total employment, as well as a rising share of the nationwide labor force. This relative change has not been as great as the relative increase in population, since for this region the percentage of the total population in the labor force is below the United

States average. This is explained by the fact that high birth rates and net immigration make for a younger population and a larger percentage of persons who are unable to participate in the labor force.

In California, we again see the effects of a major shift in the geographic distribution of the United States economy. The share of southern California in the total national labor force has more than doubled in the last 20 years. The percentage of unemployment also has been well above the average. In the mountain and plains regions, again by contrast, unemployment has tended to be a smaller percentage of the labor force than in the United States as a whole.

The growth of employment in the arid regions has been accompanied by a significant reorganization of the patterns of employment in many parts of the area. The Great Plains, outside of west Texas, have shown the smallest change. In 1940, more than half of the labor force in the Great Plains was in agriculture. By 1960, this percentage had fallen to about one-third—still far above the 6.7 percent of the total United States employment in agriculture, forests, and fish-

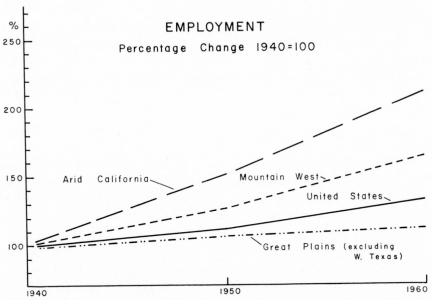

Fig. 3. Except in the Great Plains, where there was a decline, the percentage of persons employed rose rapidly between 1940 and 1960. The employment increase reflects growth of population.

eries. Only in west Texas had a new pattern emerged in the Great Plains.

In the southern half of the mountain West, a decided shift away from agriculture has been accompanied by a strong shift to government and manufacturing—all this in relative percentages of total employment. The shift away from agriculture has been largely the effect of nationwide forces, such as technologic advance. The result, however, has been to deemphasize agriculture as a source of regional employment and income, almost to the extent of conforming with the national pattern; that is, 6.7 percent of the nation's labor force was in agriculture, forests, and fisheries in 1960, and employment in these occupations in Colorado was 7.8 percent; in Utah, 6.0 percent; in New Mexico, 7.3 percent; and in Arizona, 8.1 percent. In these states, the concomitant shift to manufacturing as a percentage of all employment has been significant, but the importance of manufacturing still lies far below that for the United States as a whole. A substantial proportion of the new employment in manufacturing has been in industries concerned with the outer-space program and with defense. In several specific instances, the low density of population and the wide sweep of uninhabited terrain have been major location factors for these industries.

In Colorado, personal income derived from manufacturing was 8.8 percent of the total state personal income in 1940. This rose to 12.3 percent in 1960. As a percentage of United States manufacturing income, this was an increase from 0.33 to 0.53 of 1 percent. In dollars, personal income from manufacturing was $200 million in 1950 and $501 million in 1960. Major defense-oriented manufacturers accounted for 33 percent of this increase. This defense manufacturing payroll was $120 million in 1960, which was 18 percent of all manufacturing employment in Colorado in 1960, whereas defense manufacturing furnished only 7.3 percent of all manufacturing employment in the United States as a whole. In addition, it is also estimated that military construction in Colorado increased 5 to 10 times between 1950 and 1960 and accounted for 17 percent of all construction income in the state in 1960. These are only direct employment figures. The amount of employment arising from the respending of this income on other goods and services—such as utilities, materials, business services, and fuels—has contributed substantially to the high-level prosperity in Colorado in recent years.

Growth of Manufacturing

The aircraft-missile-electric industry hardly existed in Arizona before 1948. In 1957, the manufacturing of electric machinery and transportation equipment (other than automobiles) accounted for more than 40 percent of all wages and salaries paid in manufacturing in the state. When manufacturing in primary metals and machinery other than electric is considered, this figure rises to more than 60 percent. These four categories (electric machinery, transport equipment, primary metal manufacturing, and nonelectric machinery) paid $12 million in wages in 1948, $61 million in 1953, and $122 million in 1957. This represents more than 70 percent of the gain in manufacturing wage payments in Arizona during this period. Yet, interestingly, a poll of new migrants into Arizona taken in 1960 showed that 28 percent of them moved there for health reasons, 23 percent for the climate, and only 17.5 percent as a result of company transfers and 16 percent to take advantage of economic opportunities there. The largest number of these new people were professional and highly skilled workers.

Employment figures list no missile-industry workers in Utah in 1956. Starting in 1957, there were 1200 people employed in this industry, and, by 1961, there were 14,000 so employed, and a further increase of 30 percent in employment in this industry was projected for 1962. Employment in the missile industry was roughly 5 percent of the total nonagricultural employment in Utah in 1961. A comparison of the increases in employment in this industry with the change in total nonagricultural employment indicates that the increase in missile employment produced approximately 50 percent of the total increase in nonagricultural employment in 1958, 33 percent in 1959, 25 percent in 1960, and 50 percent in 1961.

In New Mexico as well, the most important stimulus to growth has been the expansion of federal activity, most of which has been associated with national defense. In 1959, one-sixth of New Mexico's labor force was employed by the federal government and 80 percent in activities directly associated with national defense. One-third of these people were employed in research and development work. In 1961, 17 to 20 percent of the total wages paid in New Mexico was in activities directly related to defense and space.

Activity related to the development of nuclear energy has been especially important in New Mexico, notably the work at Los Alamos and at Sandia Base in Albuquerque. This increased government work in defense has, to a large extent, determined the direction in which private industry has developed—ordnance, electronics, aircraft, and scientific and engineering services—as well as stimulated a significant increase in construction.

The general importance of federal government activity in the economics of these arid states is illustrated by a comparison of federal civilian employment as a proportion of total population in each state. The highest proportion in the nation is in Utah, followed in order by New Mexico, Nevada, Washington, Colorado, Oklahoma, and California. In addition, the federal government still owns or controls much of the land area in the arid and semiarid Mountain States—just under 50 percent of the total land of New Mexico, for example.

Although this large proportion of employment in defense-oriented activities has acted as an insulator against economic recession in these areas in recent years, it may not be an unmixed blessing. The likelihood of abrupt cutbacks in defense is remote, yet many leaders in the growing urban centers feel that there is a danger of overdependence on defense spending and are attempting to broaden their economic base.

In most of the states, the rise in manufacturing employment has been conditioned to some extent by the aridity factor. Before 1940, the small population of the mountain West was insufficient to provide an adequate regional market for many types of manufactured goods. The influx of new defense enterprises in the late 1940's and 1950's attracted a substantial migration and encouraged the establishment of manufacturing plants to serve the regional market. Thus the cumulative growth effect that has dominated California's modern economic history is now being repeated in the Mountain States, only on a much smaller scale. Although the extent of this growth in the future is difficult to predict, it is reasonably certain that it will not be inhibited by a lack of water—at least not for many decades.

By 1960, California had become an industrial state. The tremendous growth in employment during and after World War II resulted in an employment pattern in which resource-based employment continued to fall faster than the average national trend and manufacturing employment continued to rise faster. At the same time, the

Table V. Disposable income.

Region	Income (billions of $) 1940	% of U.S. income 1940	Income (billions of $) 1960	% of U.S. income 1960	Increase 1940–1960 (%)
United States	*71.7*		*358.1*		*399*
Great Plains[a]	0.6	0.92	2.8	0.82	342
Mountain West	2.2	3.08	13.7	3.82	520
Arid California	0.8	1.11	5.7	1.60	720

[a] Excluding west Texas.
Source: Compiled from basic data as reported in "Survey of buying power," *Sales Management* **48**, 166–278 (1941); **86**, 55–342 (1961).

balance of the distribution of employment showed a wider, or more even, distribution among the several categories than that of the United States as a whole. Much of the total growth for the state has been concentrated in its arid southern third. Clearly, aridity has been a secondary, or even minimal, factor in this growth.

Income in the West

The per-capita income of a state or region is the most comprehensive and the most complex indicator of the economic status of the population. And changes in the regional income over time represent one way to express the absolute and relative improvement in the well-being of the people (Tables V and VI and Figs. 4 and 5). Unfortunately the complexity of causation that underlies variations of

Table VI. Disposable per-capita income.

Region	Per-capita income ($) 1940	% of the national average 1940	Per-capita income ($) 1960	% of the national average 1960
United States	*546*	*100*	*1974*	*100*
Great Plains	439	80	1708	87
Mountain West	535	98	1828	93
Arid California	669	122	2057	105

Source: Compiled from basic data as reported in "Survey of buying power," *Sales Management* **48**, 166–278 (1941); **86**, 55–342 (1961).

income makes it nearly impossible to assign relative weights to even
the most easily discernible causes. It is even more difficult to probe
beyond the purely economic causes to such underlying factors as
aridity. However, in the foregoing discussion, we have advanced the
hypothesis that in the semiarid, agricultural Great Plains population
growth has been slowed, and per-capita income from manufacturing
and trade has been discouraged, even though *per-capita* agricultural
income may be rising; California, on the other hand, has created an
industrial economy, largely unhampered by aridity and characterized
by a relatively high per-capita income.

This hypothesis may be tested by a comparison of per-capita income
changes in North Dakota and California since 1940. Table VII shows
plainly why a North Dakotan might have been motivated to emi-
grate to California in 1940, for in North Dakota, per-capita income

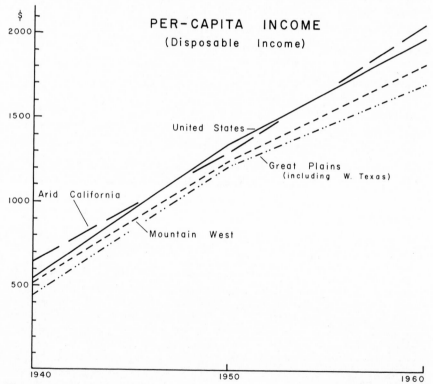

Fig. 4. Per-capita income in some areas of the western United States
increased almost fourfold during 20 years and converged toward the
national average.

Table VII. Per-capita income for North Dakota and California.

State	Per-capita income ($) 1940	% of the national average 1940	Per-capita income ($) 1960	% of the national average 1960
North Dakota	350	59	1741	78
California	840	141	2741	123

was only about 40 percent of that in California. This attraction remained in 1960, even though per-capita income in both states has converged toward the national average during the last 20 years. Here can be seen also a probable reason why population growth through the "filling-up" process will continue to be slow in the

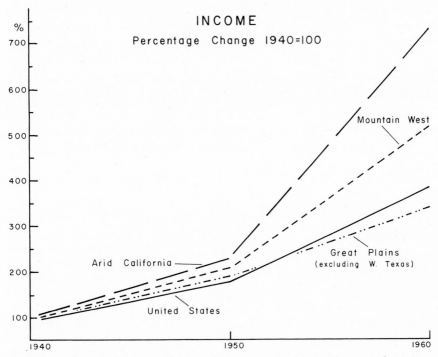

Fig. 5. The percentage increase in total disposable income between 1940 and 1960 reflected the rapid rise in population in California and the mountain West.

Great Plains, even though total United States population rises rapidly.

In the mountain West, the California pattern of employment is being repeated, in miniature, in the states that show the largest relative rise in per-capita incomes. In Colorado, Arizona, and Utah, a growing population has been turning to manufacturing and away from agriculture and mining. In these states, however, the growth process has caused per-capita incomes to rise steadily toward the national average, but in California the economy has been unable to absorb the very large numbers of migrants, except at the cost of a relatively falling per-capita income.

These illustrations, which show the effects of some of the major factors that have been producing income changes in the various parts of the arid West, also demonstrate the difficulty of separately assessing aridity as a factor that influences economic change.

The preceding analysis may be summarized by the observation that, since 1940, population and employment have grown very rapidly in California and rapidly in the southern half of the mountain West, but in the northern Mountain States and in the Great Plains there has been slow absolute growth and relative decline (except in west Texas). Further, the forces that make for growth in the Southwest have so far encountered little hindrance from aridity or scarcity of water. Indeed, it has been observed frequently that little hindrance is to be expected from the adverse aspects of aridity in the short-run future in the entire Southwest. On the other hand, climatic features probably are a handicap to the northern Mountain States and help to prevent their approaching the breakthrough to sustained growth. As for the Great Plains, aridity and climate seem to have been significant factors in inhibiting growth since 1940, an effect that probably will continue for the foreseeable future.

These generalities are projected in quantitative terms in a recent study published by the National Planning Association (7). Some of the most significant results of this analysis are reproduced in Table VIII. The major categories of employment are described as "increasing or decreasing" in the various states of the arid West, compared with total national employment in that particular type of employment. This tabular arrangement permits one to see at a glance which western states will continue to "fill up" in response to national population growth, and which will be unable to respond to this pressure.

The projected trends in per-capita income of the states are more diverse than the trend in employment and income, and not so pessimistic in outlook for the slow-growth states. However, the explanations for these various projections involve a detailed analysis, industry by industry.

Economic Research

If aridity is regarded as a factor that limits the productivity of these regions in relation to the humid regions, then it is apparent that the range of research required to seek out ways to increase productivity in arid lands is very wide indeed. Much—probably most—of such research, moreover, belongs in the domain of the natural sciences and technology, not in the field of economics. From the economic point of view, however, research effort might be seen as directed toward (i) increasing the supply of water, (ii) reducing the cost of controlling the existing supplies, (iii) increasing the efficiency of the use of available water, and (iv) increasing the efficiency of the allocation of water among competing demands.

Table VIII. Expected change in the share of national employment by industry by state.

State	Trend	Agriculture	Mining	Construction	Manufacturing	Transportation, communications, utilities	Wholesale and retail trade	Finance, insurance, real estate	Services	Government
Wyoming	Decline	—	—	—	—	—	—	—	+	—
Idaho	Decline	—	+	—	+	—	—	—	+	—
Montana	Decline	+	+	—	0	—	—	—	0	—
Utah	No change	+	+	—	—	—	—	—	—	—
Colorado	Increase	—	+	+	+	+	+	+	+	+
New Mexico	Increase	+	—	—	+	+	+	+	+	—
Arizona	Increase	+	+	—	+	+	0	—	+	—
Nevada	Increase	+	+	+	+	+	+	+	+	+
North Dakota[a]	Decline	+	+	—	—	—	—	0	—	—
South Dakota[a]	Decline	+	0	—	0	—	—	—	—	—
California	Increase	+	—	+	+	+	+	+	+	+

[a] Representative of the Great Plains.
Symbols: + means increase expected; — means decrease expected; 0 means no change.
Source: National Planning Association (7).

A major research effort now underway in the desalinization of water might also result in an effective increase in the supply of water, depending on the ultimate costs achieved. The problem of pollution is common to both arid and humid parts of the United States. A difference between the two regions is the kind of pollution that is experienced. In the humid East, much water is used as a waste carrier of organic matter and chemicals. In the West, where industry and population are sparse in relation to eastern density measures, the main pollution problem is salinity. The economic characteristics of the two forms of pollution—organic matter versus salinity—are quite different. Organic matter can be removed from water by the usual biologic sewage-treatment plants and can be further removed by the action of sunlight, aeration, and biologic processes in natural bodies of water. Salinity, on the other hand, undergoes no natural amelioration and can be removed from water only by the relatively expensive process of desalinization.

At the moment there are only two feasible methods of handling salinity on a large scale. One is to eliminate the source of the salts; the other is to dilute the saline water to an acceptable strength. Since the projected levels of water use in the arid West for 1980 and 2000 exceed available supplies without taking into account any water required for dilution, this is not considered a feasible solution. There will be, therefore, increasing necessity to eliminate the sources of salinity, which means, of course, that irrigation of soils that contribute to salinity will have to be reduced. Considerations of water quality, as well as quantity, will, therefore, bring about a reduction in irrigated agriculture.

The Colorado River Basin project of the U.S. Public Health Service was launched in 1961 to develop a long-range quality-control program for the entire Colorado River Basin. The project will require alternative economic projections for the basin, to which will be tied the studies of water quality and the degree to which projected uses are compatible with designated water-quality specifications.

Integrated Water Studies

In the second and third categories of research, a major effort to unite economics, engineering, and hydrology into a basic research program has been made in recent years by the Harvard water-research program, the results of which appeared in 1962 (*8*). This is a fundamental and general research effort, aimed at dealing with the problem of a multipurpose water-resource development in terms of economic efficiency. Economic efficiency means that the design of the project with relation to the number and size of reservoirs, power plants, and so on, should be such that amounts of water that will yield the maximum benefits can be supplied to alternative uses (that is, irrigation, hydroelectric power, flood control). This can be done either by the increase of benefits from any or all uses, or by the reduction of costs of any or all facilities, or by both methods simultaneously. Participants in the Harvard project contend that the optimum in design rarely has been achieved in the past, because of the lack of sufficiently accurate economic and engineering analyses. The purpose of the project was to develop such techniques, and in 1963 experimentation in the application of the techniques still was being carried on in a cooperative effort by the Harvard group and the Army Corps of Engineers.

In addition to generalized projects of the Harvard type, many more specific research projects have been, and are being, carried on by engineers and hydrologists in the various land-grant colleges and federal research agencies. These seek to improve the efficiency of methods for increasing the utility of existing supplies of surface and ground water.

The fourth type of research falls directly within the scope of economics as a science. Here the problem is to discover the optimum allocation of scarce water resources among competing uses of different marginal productivities. Economists, in dealing with this problem for many years, have developed the cost-benefit analysis as a primary tool. Recently, this entire approach and its methodology have been subjected to intensive scrutiny by economists, and a number of books and many technical articles have been published on the subject. The results of this examination have been salutary. At the same time, it has become clear that cost-benefit analysis is not a sufficient guide to the optimum allocation or reallocation of water resources over time (*9*).

Economic analysis should be extended beyond the project or list of projects to consider a wider range of alternatives. A significant effort of this kind is to be found in the recent work of a University of New Mexico committee, whose results have already been mentioned (*1*). A group at Utah State University also is studying the marginal values of water in alternative uses, using the Wasatch front region of Utah as the "laboratory." Similarly, economists at Colorado State University are assessing the problems involved in the transfer of water from agricultural to industrial-urban use.

Finally, a fifth type of economic analysis that has been undertaken recently is the attempt to project water supply and demand into the future. In 1959 the U.S. Senate established a Select Committee on National Water Resources to undertake studies of "the extent and character of water-resource activities, both governmental and non-governmental, that can be expected to be required to provide the quantity and quality of water by use for population, agriculture, and industry between the present time and 1980 . . . ." This committee issued a final report in 1961 (*10*), together with 32 committee prints covering a variety of detailed subjects.

One contribution to research in water projections is contained in Committee Print 32, prepared by Nathaniel Wollman (*11*), in which are developed projections of the amounts of water that will be required for given levels of population and economic activity that may be expected in the future. His projections for water losses and sustained flows in five western regions for 1980 to 2000, using medium projections, are shown in Table IX. It is assumed in Table IX that the per-capita use of water for irrigation, fish, and wildlife will remain constant as population increases. The result is that, by 1980, maximum streamflows in the arid regions will not provide enough water to meet the demands.

Table IX. Projections for water losses and sustained flows, 1980.

Region	Sustained flow (m.g.d.[a]) [b]	Losses by 1980 (m.g.d.[a])				Flow as a % of estd. loss	Deficiency (%)
		Irrigation	Fish and wildlife	All other	Total		
Upper Missouri	27,000	15,000	13,000	1,000	29,000	93	7
Rio Grande	1,000	5,000	1,100	200	6,300	16	84
Colorado	10,000	14,000	2,000	1,100	17,100	58	42
Great Basin	9,000	6,700	4,000	200	10,900	83	17
South Pacific[c]	300	3,300		700	4,000	8	92

[a] Millions of gallons per day. One million gallons equals 3747 kiloliters.
[b] After adjustment to reservoir losses.
[c] Requirements now largely met by importation of water.

Here, for the first time, a framework has been established within which to assess the degree of urgency or lack of urgency that should be attached to research and solution of various water-related problems. Senator Clinton P. Anderson, of New Mexico, a believer in the urgency of the water problem, has introduced legislation to establish water-research laboratories in each of the 50 states (*12*). To aid further in coordinating water-research activities, the Committee on Interior and Insular Affairs, of which Anderson is a member, has compiled an inventory of water-research projects that are being carried on in the federal departments and the universities of this country (*13*). These proposals grow directly out of the work of the Senate Select Committee.

This brief sampling of economic research that is relevant to the problems of aridity is intended to illustrate the development of activity in the field. It is by no means a complete catalog of all the research now underway. It does indicate, however, the increasing scope and volume of research.

A Look at the Future

There is need for a last word. The major conclusion of this chapter is that, although aridity has strongly repressed the growth of population, employment, and income in the western United States since 1900, it has not been, nor will it be, a barrier to substantial future growth within the broad framework of existing supplies of rainfall and surface and ground water. Thus, the growth of employment and income in the next decade is projected at rates consistent with the recent rapid economic growth of much of the region.

If we look farther ahead, say, to the year 2000, then the picture may change radically. If the United States population rises at a very rapid rate for the next 50 years, as many believe it will, there are certain to be repercussions on the arid West. If the aridity barrier continues to be overcome as effectively as it has been since 1940, national population growth will accelerate the "filling-up" process, and population density in the western states may move closer to the national average. If, on the other hand, the physical limits of water supply are reached, the contrast between the arid West and the rest of the country will become very striking indeed.

According to Table X, the Senate Select Committee in its popu-

Table X.   Projected United States and regional population, A.D. 2000.

Region	Total population (millions of persons)		Population per square mile[a]		Percentage of U.S. population	
	Committee pro- jection	Filling- up hypoth- esis	Committee pro- jection	Filling- up hypoth- esis	Committee pro- jection	Filling- up hypoth- esis
United States	*430.8*		*145.0*	*145.0*	*100*	*100*
Great Plains	7.2	12.8	16.8	30.0	1.66	3.0
Mountain West	23.2	46.2	25.1	50.0	5.36	10.7
California	51.0		325.4		11.81	

[a] One square mile equals 2.59 square kilometers.
Source: U.S. Senate Select Committee on National Water Resources, Comm. Print 5, p. 6, for columns 1, 3, and 5.

lation projections for the year 2000 apparently assumes little "filling up" for the arid West. Population density is assumed to increase at just about the same rate as that of the United States as a whole with little change in the percentage of the total population residing in this region.

By contrast, if we assume a "filling-up" trend, we see density of population in the West increasing at a faster rate than in the rest of the country, and the arid West becoming the home of a more important portion of the population.

Which way do the greater probabilities lie? The answer to this question is urgent, not only in the United States, but in every country of the world that is witnessing a "population explosion." The pressure to find the capital, the technology, and the will to make the arid lands fruitful and habitable is everywhere increasing. This chapter and this book demonstrate that there is substantial evidence to support each side of the question. Economists are likely to conclude that, as the ogre of economic scarcity of water is held in bounds by improved technology and, to an even greater extent, by the reallocation of water to more productive uses, the burden of economic evidence points to a continued rapid growth of population, employment, and income in the arid West of the United States.

Acknowledgment: The authors thank Karl Starch, University of Colorado, without whose research assistance this chapter could not have been written.

REFERENCES

1. N. Wollman, *The Value of Water in Alternative Uses* (Univ. of New Mexico Press, Albuquerque, 1962).

2. ———, *The Supply and Demand for Water*, in preparation under a grant from Resources for the Future, Inc. This is a study of the Rio Grande and Colorado River basins, the Great Basin, and southern California.

3. V. Fuchs, "Statistical explanations of the relative shift of manufacturing among regions of the United States," *Reg. Sci. Assoc. Papers* **8**, 103–125 (1962).

4. C. McWilliams, *California: the Great Exception* (Wyn, New York, 1949), p. 377.

5. M. Gordon, *Employment Expansion and Population Growth; the California Experience 1900–1950* (Univ. of California Press, Berkeley, 1954).

6. G. McLaughlin, *Growth of American Manufacturing Areas* (Univ. of Pittsburgh Press, Pittsburgh, Pa., 1938), p. 213.

7. National Planning Association, *State Employment Trends to 1976*, "Regional Economic Projections Series," Rept. 1, 1962 ser. (National Planning Assoc., Washington, D.C., 1962).

8. A. Maas, M. Hufschmidt, *et al.*, *Design of Water Resource Systems; New Techniques for Relating Economic Objectives, Engineering Analysis, and Government Planning* (Harvard Univ. Press, Cambridge, Mass., 1962).

9. M. E. Garnsey, "Welfare economics and resource development," *Western Resources Papers 1961, Land and Water: Planning for Economic Growth* (Univ. of Colorado Press, Boulder, 1962), vol. 3, pp. 191–204.

10. U.S. Senate, Select Committee on National Water Resources, *Report of the Select Committee on National Water Resources* (Washington, D.C., 1961).

11. ———, *Water Supply and Demand*, Comm. Print 32 (Washington, D.C., 1960).

12. U.S. Senate, S. 3579, 87th Congr., 2nd sess., a bill to establish state water-resources research institutes (Washington, D.C., 1962). This bill was passed by the Senate on 23 April 1963 and is now in committee in the House.

13. U.S. Senate, Committee on Interior and Insular Affairs, *Water-Resources Research*, memorandum of the chairman to the committee (Washington, D.C., 1962).

14

Political and Social
Institutions in Arid Regions

DEAN E. MANN

In an examination of the political institutions, social organization, and attitudes found in the arid West, it must be recognized that most of the institutions and attitudes are part of a much larger and pervasive culture, which has spread to the West after maturation in a humid eastern setting. Centuries of experience, especially in England and in the eastern United States, have resulted in fervent acceptance of political processes and social attitudes. The extent to which these attitudes and institutions have been modified by the exigencies of life in an arid region is of primary interest here, but it must be recognized that these modifications follow a basic pattern that prevails throughout the United States.

An examination of the values that pervade the American culture will be helpful to a discussion of the processes and attitudes that are peculiarly western. Unquestionably, the most important of these factors is the preference for private decision-making in the management of the economy. Although both the national government and the states have been willing to foster development of the economy through the chartering of corporations, public subsidies, and even construction of major public works to facilitate and encourage the economy, the primary goal has been to allow private corporations or individuals to determine its character. The history of the disposal of public lands by the United States shows a penchant for private ownership and management of one kind of property that constitutes one of our most valuable natural resources *(1)*.

Complementing the preference for private ownership was an earlier tendency to view the nation's resources as inexhaustible, both in quantity and in quality. The continuing presence of new land on the frontier, the obvious abundance with which the country had been endowed in both renewable and nonrenewable resources, and remarkable advances in technology, all tended to convince the typical American that relatively little concern needed to be paid to husbanding these resources. Moreover, the remarkable advances that continue to be made in such fields as the desalinization of ocean water and the development of solar energy contribute to an optimism that any resources shortages in the future will be avoided by scientific ingenuity (2).

A third important value that affects policy-making and administration in the United States is the preference for local management and control when public intrusion in the economy is required. The original concept of the federal system presumed primary emphasis on local institutions to meet public needs, with the federal government restricting itself to relatively limited activities that pertained to internal order and defense.

In the West, the ideologic preference for local control is as popular as elsewhere but has had less practical impact on the management of natural resources. The national government long has been involved in the support of state and local activities, one of the most important of which was the support of land-grant institutions and agricultural experiment stations. The national government, independently and in cooperation with the states, has made extensive surveys of the water supplies of the country. The Reclamation Act of 1902 established the national government as a partner in the development of water supplies for irrigation districts that were established under state law.

Until well into the 20th century, the population of the United States was overwhelmingly rural and economically active in, or dependent on, agriculture for its livelihood. During the long period of agricultural predominance, there developed a dogma of the intrinsic superiority of the agricultural life as against life in the urban centers. The agricultural subsidy program, which is operated to restrain economic forces from driving the small marginal farmer from his land, can be justified primarily on this basis. The persistence of the limitation of 160 acres (65 hectares) as the basis for a family-sized farm, even in the arid West, is evidence of the deep-seated attachment to this doctrine, and the 160-acre land limitation in the Reclamation Act is a modern reminder. But when 90 percent of the population is occupied in nonfarm pursuits and where the great bulk of the population is located in large metropolitan areas, it is inevitable that serious questions will arise regarding a conception of life so far removed from existing circumstances.

In spite of their strong value preferences, Americans are remarkably adaptable people. Practical solutions to pressing problems have met with more favor than undying attachment to seemingly outworn principles. The recognition, for example, that a multiplicity of interests have a stake in the management of natural resources has brought the adoption of the principle of multiple use under federal management, which, with regard to forested lands, has now become enshrined in statute. Vague as this definition is as a guide to management, it does purport to reflect the existing public attitudes toward resources use and to buttress support for continued public management. The demands on forested lands as sources of lumber, as recreational areas, as grazing land, and as producers of a large amount of the water supplies in the West, all make such an approach necessary. But even such an unchallengeable principle is violated in practice and questioned in principle. National Park Service land is held inviolable by commercial interests, and the establishment of new parks and each expansion of the wilderness system raises the issue again.

Interaction of Institutions

At least since the days of Frederick Jackson Turner, students of political and social institutions of the West have sought to explain their development in terms of the unique conditions that existed on the frontier. A supreme environmentalist, Turner concluded that men and their institutions were forced to submit themselves to a transformation that virtually destroyed the traditional cultural ties with western Europe and created a new product in each man's experience (3). Beyond that, the western frontier taught men in a republic to solve their large-scale problems through their attachment to the nation rather than to section. And because of the unlimited opportunities that the frontier offered to men, they became idealists who struggled for a higher type of society. Although the frontier closed in 1890, these forces had permeated the individual thinking and the social institutions that men developed in America.

Walter Prescott Webb made an impressive case for the imposition of new institutions and patterns of life on men who settled on the "great American desert" (4). Eastern land law and water law no longer applied to conditions that required the establishment of the ranch for cattle raising. Only with the development of certain technologic innovations—the Colt .45, barbed wire, the windmill, and the adaptation of certain laws and policies developed in the humid lands —was it possible to cross the boundary of the Great Plains and settle the arid lands proper. Only haltingly did the eastern ways yield to the new environment, but yield they did. The resulting pattern of life created the image of the romantic life of the cowboys, their great cattle drives, lawlessness, and political radicalism.

As persuasive as these analyses appear, some reservations must be made. As Webb himself suggests, the industrial revolution as exemplified by the coming of the railroads welded the western economy to the eastern market, and the widespread use of the barbed-wire fence tended to limit the use of the open range. Persistent encouragement by Congress for settlement by farmers through the various land acts made the domination by the ranching patterns less than it might have been. The development of new and competing forms of economic activity and their integration with eastern financial interests, such as in the mining industry, and the development of an indigenous class of wealth in the oil industry made the radical influence less than Webb divined. Moreover, settlers who came to the Great Plains brought with them a strong attachment to the institutions they had inherited or had had a role in fashioning in the eastern humid lands. Carl Kraenzel suggests that the failure to modify humid-land institutions early has made it difficult to adapt them now (5).

The extremes to which Turner and Webb went in attempting to explain American institutional development in terms of the experiences of settlers on the frontier have led many critics virtually to disregard their theses as tenable explanations of American political institutions even on the frontier itself (6). If the environment of the western region determined institutions, as Turner believed, it seems unquestionable that these influences would have been felt strongly in the development of attitudes, practices, and institutions for the development and management of natural resources in the West. Often western developments are reflections of broad national developments with variations in the West that may have little or nothing to do with the physiographic conditions that exist there.

Water Law

Perhaps the best evidence of the impact of topographic and hydrologic conditions on social institutions is found in the water law of the West. When American settlers crossed the 100th meridian and began to settle in a land far less well watered than the land they had left, they found that their legal doctrines derived from English and early American experience were totally unsuitable. Utterly dependent on the streamflow to irrigate their crops, they were forced to construct works to divert the water from the stream to land, and often some distance removed from the banks of the stream. The riparian doctrine (derived from humid-land experience) permitted only the owner of land adjacent to a stream to make reasonable use of its waters and then only on his riparian lands. All riparian owners were entitled to share equitably in the use of water, and each was entitled to a continued natural flow of the stream. The right of the riparian owner was not affected by use or disuse.

The appropriation, or arid-regions, doctrine was derived from the experience and custom of miners who diverted water for panning and sluicing of precious minerals. It was also based on the experience of the early Spanish settlers who constructed *acequias* to convey water from the natural streambed to their arable lands. The basis for appropriation of water is beneficial use. The earliest appropriator has the prior right, and the rights of all subsequent appropriators are subject to those with prior rights. Actual application of the water is required to perfect an appropriation, and disuse of the water usually results in loss of the right. Water is not tied to riparian lands but may be transported away from the land that is immediately adjacent to the stream (7, 8).

The advantages of the appropriation system over the riparian system for arid-lands conditions are generally recognized. Water presumably will be used where it is the most beneficial to both the individual user and the general public. Second, the establishment of priorities allows a much greater degree of certainty of rights. Third, emphasis is placed on actual beneficial use, thus reducing wastage or claims of unused rights that may threaten existing uses. Finally, administrative procedures are established or are available for establishing and adjudicating rights and for determining distribution of the water (9).

Although it is not without its imperfections, this doctrine has been flexible enough to meet modern needs. On the other hand, there are limitations to the precision with which the priorities of rights may be established and the degree to which the allocation of the water may reflect these priorities. Moreover, it is not entirely clear that an appropriation system necessarily results in the application of the water to the most beneficial purpose. Finally, considerable waste has resulted from excessive applications of irrigation water, simply because farmers had the right to so much water.

In spite of the generally agreed-upon superiority of the appropriation doctrine, the riparian doctrine for surface water and the common-law doctrine for ground water persist in many of the western states. Several states, including California, Washington, North Dakota, and Texas, utilize both the riparian and the appropriation systems. Conflicting application of these two doctrines results in considerable litigation and, as in the case of California, has led to the imposition of the standard of reasonable use on those who claim rights under either doctrine.

Early settlers in the West found little use for ground water except for domestic consumption and stock watering and, therefore, saw little reason to alter the English rule that gave to the overlying landowner absolute control over the subsurface waters, with the exception of underground streams, which in some places were made subject to the prior-appropriation doctrine. With the development of more efficient pumps, however, these waters became of great economic importance, even surpassing surface waters as the chief source of irrigation water. There appears to be a trend toward adoption of the statutory appropriation system for ground waters.

Hydrologists are discontented with existing conflicts between the statutory appropriation system and the common-law doctrines that are applied to a hydrologic unity. The U.S. Geological Survey stated: "For successful formulation of law, there is a great need, in all but a few of the States, for recognition of the fundamental facts that water in the underground reservoirs all follows the same physical laws and cannot be subdivided successfully; and that ground water and surface water are interconnected and cannot be treated separately" (10).

The degree to which water law, as well as other important institutions of the West, responded to existing conditions in an arid region is significant, not only in the relatively primitive state on the frontier, but also in a modern industrialized society where the needs of society have changed. The legal systems designed to insure the security of water rights in a predominantly agricultural community may now impede the transfer of the use of this water to other purposes, such as domestic consumption and industrial use. It may be expected, therefore, that water law of the West will be significantly changed in the next few decades.

Irrigation Districts

As one would expect, some of the unique institutions of the West are related to the development and use of water resources. The earliest settlers in the West, except for the Mormons (Latter-Day Saints) and a few other isolated communities, diverted their water for mining and agriculture on an individual basis. Very quickly it was recognized, however, that more efficient utilization of water on which an entire community depended would be accomplished by a community organization. These water organizations adopted three different forms: cooperative irrigation companies, commercial irrigation companies, and irrigation districts (11, 12). Cooperative irrigation companies are essentially private corporations operating on a nonprofit basis under the corporation laws of the state. These companies are governed by stockholders who elect a board of directors to operate the district. Because of a very limited market for their bonds, their most serious problems are related to financing.

Irrigation districts are public or quasi-municipal corporations organized under state laws and constitute political subdivisions of a state with the power to issue bonds and secure revenue from tax assessments on land. Formation of such districts depends on approval of a specified percentage of the landholders that own a certain percentage of the land in a given area. With most irrigation development now being carried on by the federal government and the formation of an irrigation district required by the Bureau of Reclamation, this has become the most common type of local irrigation organization in the West. Both the mutual companies and the irrigation districts are likely to respond to local interests, but the latter organization is more likely to be better financed and capable of providing the expert management required by a demanding operation. Moreover, the relationship between the irrigation districts and the Bureau of Reclamation makes the availability of trained technicians in all fields considerably greater.

Under the terms of the Reclamation Act, the national government established a revolving fund from which monies were to be drawn to develop irrigation projects; these monies would be repaid by the beneficiaries in 10-year periods. For numerous reasons, the irrigation districts were unable to meet their obligations, and the result has been a series of acts extending the repayment time over longer periods—some as long as 50 years. No attempt has been made to depend exclusively on the reclamation revolving fund; instead, funds are now appropriated directly by Congress.

The policies of the national government under the reclamation laws have been designated deliberately to stimulate family-sized farms and to avoid land monopolies. To become eligible for a share of water from a federal reclamation project, a beneficiary must dispose of all land in excess of 160 acres (65 hectares), or 320 acres for a married couple. This provision in reclamation law has been under almost constant attack from larger landowners who resist its operation. The most recent attack on the 160-acre limitation has occurred in California, where the state supreme court has declared invalid contracts with the Bureau of Reclamation that required the disposal of the excess land.

Communal Organization

John Wesley Powell, in 1878, stressed the desirability of maintaining the greatest possible grouping of residences in order to provide for communal benefits (13). Seldom, however, was Powell's advice followed; and, where such communal arrangements existed, they were the result of forces far removed from physiographic conditions.

There is a tendency to see in social organization the impact of particular geographic conditions. This is exemplified by the inferences drawn about the compact village communities established by the

Mormons in Utah and the other Mountain States in which they settled. But, as Lowry Nelson suggests (14), such settlements were not the result of the western environment but rather of peculiar Mormon doctrines, which emphasized community life under the direction of a powerful priesthood—a doctrine the Mormons brought with them from the East. The fact that Mormon doctrines were particularly suited for the physical characteristics of the area in which they located helped to assure their success. For one thing, the Mormons held a socially conscious outlook toward the land. But their experience was unique and was in sharp contrast with the scattered, specialized, and exploitative frontiers in other localities.

Certain trends, however, reveal the changing characteristics of the arid regions and the institutional adjustments that are required. The marginal nature of farming operations in some areas of the West—for example, in the northern High Plains country—has resulted in practices known as *sidewalk farming* and *suitcase farming*. Sidewalk farmers live in nucleated settlements but within 30 miles (48.3 kilometers) of the farming operation. The tendency toward absentee ownership and tenant farming, combined with a desire for the amenities of urban living, led farm operators to seek urban residences, traveling the necessary distance to the farm operation each day. There appears to be some increase also in the number of suitcase farmers who live long distances from their farms and must make periodic trips to them.

In much of the arid West, space is a very real social cost. Distance increases the costs for all of the services that the rural community requires—medical care, electricity, education—and decreases the extent to which the rural dweller can participate in community life (15, 16). As economic conditions change, greater attention must be paid to community organization to increase the efficiency of the services.

Kraenzel has pointed out the high social costs that resulted from failure to adopt John Wesley Powell's plan for social organization on the frontier (5). Township forms of government were adopted that were totally unsuited for conditions on the Plains, where great distances and sparse population resulted in high costs of maintaining such government. Extremely small school districts constituted a serious burden. Smaller units of local government also resulted in unequal distribution of services and in unequal burdens of the tax levy. The "yonland," or hinterland, communities often had the least capacity to bear the costs of governmental services but at the same time had the greatest need. The factor of distance made the burden on them even greater.

Kraenzel expresses great faith in the capacity of the people of the Great Plains to develop cooperative organizations to provide a regional solution to their problems, such as more flexible credit and taxes and provision for such vital services as medical care and educational programs. Unfortunately, the evidence to support the optimistic view that such a program would ameliorate the problems of the Great Plains farmer is scanty indeed.

Cultural Groups

The persistence of dominant cultural values and their significance for the chances of success in the arid regions are indicated by a study of modern pioneers in New Mexico. A "homestead" community was settled by migrants from the southern Plains, who brought with them their strong value preferences (17). In an inhospitable environment where they could expect only 3 good farming years in each 10, their emphasis on independence created factionalism that impeded attention to communal activities. Their practice of loafing led to shifts from cotton and wheat farming to bean farming, because the latter provided greater opportunity for off-season loafing. Their emphasis on mastery over nature in the face of continued failure resulted in a boasting or gambling psychology accompanied by a constant emphasis on future success.

Gradually the size of the homesteading colony has been reduced as the younger people leave and the older people sell out to the ranchers.

The problems associated with cultural adaptation to arid-lands conditions under changing economic and social patterns are indicated also by the fate of the descendants of early Spanish-American settlers in New Mexico. The early settlers held reasonably large, irrigated farms and grazed their livestock on vast acreages on surrounding mesas. In contrast with the Anglo-puritanical emphasis on hard work, the Hispanos viewed work as a means of achieving leisure and independence.

Because of large population increases and elimination of "free" grazing lands, the land that once supported 10 families in comfort today supports 100 families in poverty. The practice of dividing land equally among heirs has resulted in reduced size of holdings, particularly in view of the inability of the Hispanos to leave their homes to enter a hostile community. In many ways their form of social organization, which emphasizes social cooperation in village life, appears to be propitious for arid-lands living; and yet under present circumstances, without massive help from the United States government, their prospects as communities seem relatively dim.

Local Government

When John Wesley Powell discussed political organization, he suggested that new states draw their county boundaries along the dividing lines between hydrographic basins rather than on arbitrary political lines on a map (*13*). Such natural geographic and topographic units would become natural political and economic units as well and would be particularly effective in governing the allocation of water and the uses of land. Seldom did the architects of state and local institutions pay any attention to such natural unities; they apportioned out political responsibility on the basis of immediate advantage for the politicians themselves or the interests they represented, or on some arbitrary lines drawn on a map.

Since Powell's time, students of rural local government have suggested several reforms, including the consolidation of school districts and counties, the abolition of townships, the election of fewer local officials, and the provision for alternative forms of county government. In spite of the excessive costs of administration and inefficiency, except in the area of school-district consolidation and in the atrophy of the township as a useful unit of government, these recommendations have been virtually unheeded in the western states. Even the reduction in the number of local school districts has not been followed to as significant an extent in the West as in the nonwestern states.

One instrument of local government of great importance to cities in the West has been the metropolitan water district. This is an area-wide organization, authorized by state statutes, that pools the financial resources and the needs of adjoining communities to provide an adequate water supply for an entire region. Organizations

of this type have been particularly important in the Los Angeles
and San Francisco Bay areas of California and have provided locally
a means of solving a crucial local problem (18).

Economic and Demographic Change

One of the most striking facts about modern western life is its
rapid urbanization. This is a phenomenon that is not peculiar to
the western states, but it has gone on there at a more rapid pace than
elsewhere. This rapid urbanization has been the result not only of
farm-to-city migration but also of migration from other parts of the
country to the West, particularly California and Arizona. The availability of economic opportunity is a basic factor in this movement,
but the search for amenities associated with a favorable climate appears to play a considerable role. The urban areas in the Mountain
States increased 65 percent in population from 1950 to 1960, the
highest over-all rate in the nation.

This rapid urbanization has raised serious questions concerning
the direction that the economy should take in the West, particularly
with regard to the role of agriculture. Extensive areas of the prime
agricultural land are being absorbed as cities expand in what has
come to be known as an *urban sprawl*. Land speculation and local
taxation policies have played a part, but the basic factor appears to
be rapid population growth accompanied by a demand for individual
dwellings at a low price. Under such circumstances, the value of
land for agriculture is seldom as high as that of land for the construction of dwellings, and such land quickly passes into the hands
of the subdivider.

The issues raised by such changes in the economic pattern of life
are numerous, and only a few are discussed here. One involves the
necessity of using less productive lands; this results in higher costs,
and, with the tendency toward mechanization in agriculture, short-
run profit considerations suppress questions of social cost. A more
serious question arises over the rationality of large-scale projects
that call for reclamation of additional land or the salvaging of existing land, both of which require heavy subsidies from power users,
urban water users, and the general taxpayer. Both of these questions
are relevant to the decisions regarding construction of the Feather

River project in California, the central Arizona project, and the upper Colorado River storage project.

Even with the resources economy there are powerful forces working for reallocation of resources uses. Lands that were formerly the most valuable for grazing or forestry may find their highest use in providing recreational outlets for the expanding urban population. With increased mobility and reductions in the cost of travel, the western states potentially can provide important recreational resources for the entire country. In the Great Plains region, the primary change necessary is the transfer to grazing of land unsuited for crops.

Changes in the nature of the economy and in the allocation of resources bring with them important social and political consequences, few of which have been systematically investigated. New interests develop and aline themselves with other interests in the community to challenge the dominance of groups that controlled the community during its earlier period. The problems that arise are associated with both the intelligent control of growth and the compassionate amelioration of the ills that are associated with decline. Suggestive of the political and social consequences of economic change are studies made of the Williston area of North Dakota, which experienced an oil boom, and the experiences of Eloy, Arizona, which has fallen into economic decline as a result of the increased costs of ground water (*19, 20*).

State Administration

The American preference for local political control has not resulted in an awareness of the need to provide political and administrative machinery that responds to the environment to be controlled. Few states in the West or in other parts of the United States have paid adequate attention to their resources responsibilities in administration. The increasing recognition that the management of natural resources requires an integrated approach has seldom resulted in integration of resources agencies. It is, unfortunately, true that the arid-lands states have not led the way in administrative reorganization, in spite of the fact that in the field of natural resources they operate under more severe pressures.

Where primary responsibility for resources development has resided in the national government, with the states performing only an advisory or ancillary role, there has been little encouragement for an integrated resources program. Often state agencies have been created to cooperate with federal agencies on specific programs or to receive federal money in a cooperative federal-state endeavor. These rather narrow federal-state programs have been supported by vigorous interest groups within the states that have seen advantages in the relative independence of these units.

This leads to a second important consideration: the unwillingness of powerful interest groups to permit an integrated approach to resources management (*21, 22*). Farmers jealously guard their agricultural extension programs and even their colleges of agriculture against attempts at administrative reorganization. State fish and wildlife agencies, partly because of their unique financial dependence on sportsmen for their support, vigorously oppose integration. Similar attitudes can be found among the grazers, lumber interests, and mineral interests.

A third important factor in explaining the cluttered administrative situation in most of the western states is the fact that the basic administrative patterns for these states—their constitutions—were written during a period when distrust of concentrated power had reached its apotheosis. The Populist movement saw remedies in the breaking up of concentration of power, both in the private economy and in governmental administration.

Finally, the states have lagged far behind in the provision of personnel and research facilities. Only 5 of the western states have a merit system that covers most of the state employees. Salaries are frequently low; hence, competent managers and researchers are tempted by alluring offers from national agencies or private groups. Partisan and interest-group intrusions into personnel decisions have had a deleterious effect on state administration. As a result, most students of the subject have found state administrations (including those of the western states) "outmoded, cumbersome, and creaking at the joints" (*23*).

Several western states have created independent water agencies that integrate a major part of the water-resources functions in the state. California and Idaho have created such agencies. Some states, such as Colorado and Nevada (but not many in the West), have established departments of natural resources that include divisions of water resources. In addition, a number of other states—again not necessarily in the West—have established independent administrative boards or commissions that are responsible for large segments of water-resources programs.

But the chief failing of the states lies not in their reluctance to rationalize administrative structure but in their unwillingness to undertake responsibility for important public programs. When the states eliminated their state planning boards in the 1930's, they threw away excellent chances to guide both the national government and the states in the development of their resources. By the very fact that resources are an integrated whole, crossing state boundaries, primary responsibility may have to be lodged in the national government for effective and comprehensive planning and development. But the states have an important role in exercising their police, taxing, and educational powers to improve private and local resources use.

Even in outdoor recreation, the western states have not uniformly led the way, despite their advantages in terms of space and low density of population. Arizona, Colorado, Utah, and Wyoming have only incipient state park systems. Arizona's state park system was established only over the determined resistance of those who believed that "the hoofed animal was still the state's greatest heritage" (24). Too often these groups have stood back and waited for the national government, with its greater tax resources, to undertake responsibilities that they later complain about.

Vincent Ostrom concluded that the states "seem best organized to serve the purposes of groups of users relating to a particular resource utilization" (25). In another place, Ostrom writes concerning the role of states in the management of water resources. Instead of regulating watercourses, he says, the states have sought to regulate "the conduct of persons," and their policies seldom consider both consumptive and nonconsumptive water uses (26).

Only slightly more favorable was the U.S. Senate Select Committee on National Water Resources, which concluded in 1961 that all of the states of the West are aware of their failings in the area of planning water-resources development and administration (27). It noted, however, that many states at present have poor organization for long-range planning; their water-resources agencies lack financial support, and some even lack administrative agencies to undertake the over-all planning job. The Senate Select Committee found exceptional examples of basin planning in California and Kansas and a few other states.

Western Politics

In the folklore of the United States, there is a tendency to believe that westerners are basically independent in their outlook, generous in their motivation, and gregarious in their relationships with others. Some have also professed to see the West as a citadel of liberalism in contrast with eastern conservatism, a liberalism that makes them more willing to countenance new patterns of activity and new methods of doing things. But Alfred DeGrazia, after studying popular attitudes in the West in the 1952 election, concluded "that no temperamental differences of great consequence separate the Western population from the rest of the United States population" (28).

Some differences do exist, however, and they are worthy of some consideration. Perhaps the most salient differences between western politics and the politics of the eastern states is the independence of the western voter. Party identification is comparatively weak, and there are strong tendencies to vote for personalities rather than for political parties. The reason for this independence and lack of devotion to party principles is not self-evident. An explanation would appear to be founded on the clear facts of geographic dispersion, diversity of interests, and rapid population movement.

The rapid influx of population into the western states in the past 20 years has brought large numbers of people who raised questions about their basic party affiliation in their new setting. Only in the West, for example, is the proportion of Democrats in the rural areas greater than the proportion of Democrats in the urban areas. Some people have brought their Republican traditions with them to the urban centers of the West, but others, particularly those from southern Democratic backgrounds, have tended to change their party affiliation upon arrival in the western cities.

The result of the relative independence of the voters in the western states has been frequent alterations in power of the two major political parties. In national elections, the western states have established no clear preference for either of the major political parties.

State Legislative Politics

The converse of the fact that governors of most western states lack the tools with which to establish political and administrative leadership is the fact of legislative domination of the policy-making processes. Lacking strong party machinery, lacking control of the executive branch, and often without such elementary devices for leadership as an executive budget, western governors find themselves in a situation of having to accept legislative leadership even in areas that are usually the preserve of the highest executive official. Although this situation resulted partly from Populist distrust of executive authority and lack of faith in elective officers, it also reflects the basic pattern of interest-group efforts to control the political machinery in states that traditionally have been dependent on the development of natural resources for their economic sustenance.

The rural areas in the western states, as in most states throughout the country, are greatly overrepresented in the state legislatures. The bias in favor of rural areas in chambers of the western state legislatures is indicated by the ratios of largest to smallest districts in terms of population per member. In the lower houses, Nevada shows the highest ratio, 31.4 to 1; in the upper chambers, California shows the greater disparity, 422.5 to 1. But even greater biases can be found in other states throughout the United States, so the situation is hardly unique. It may be expected that the U.S. Supreme Court decision in 1962 (*Baker v. Carr*), making apportionment of representation subject to judicial control under the equal-protection clause of the Fourteenth Amendment of the United States Constitution, will have a powerful impact on the allocation of political power in these states.

The converse of relatively weak party organization and discipline is relatively strong interest-group organization and activity. Since the parties are unable to develop broad programs that unify their members and dispose them to vote for the party program, members of state legislatures are likely to be receptive to other influences, among the most potent of which are interest groups. In her study of state legislatures, Belle Zeller found that in 6 of the western states, pressure politics was strong, and in 4, party organization was weak. Only in 2 states were the parties considered strong and pressure politics weak (*29*).

Among the most powerful interest groups in the western states are those that are concerned with the management and development of natural resources. In nearly every state, they play a crucial role in the legislative process. Often these groups work in alliance with one another in order to promote a common goal, which as frequently as not involves the prevention of some action desired by the urban areas. In particular, these resources-minded groups are concerned about state taxes, and they tend to look at all increases for state spending with a jaundiced eye.

The result of interest-group domination of the legislature is a strong tendency for the users of a state's resources to have a somewhat free hand in the determination of the manner in which the resources will be used. Grazers, who want a minimum of regulation of a state's public lands, are able to keep the appropriations for state land departments relatively low, in order to guarantee less effective administration. Mining interests, which are particularly concerned about valuation of their land and properties, often are able to prevent statewide valuation, which puts rural land on a par with other areas of the state.

The rapid growth of the population in urbanized places in the western states threatens to break the control of the rural interests, with or without legislative reapportionment under judicial restraint. The traditional primary users of natural resources must reconcile or compromise their interests with those of the urban areas, whose votes will no longer be so heavily discounted. The farmers' desire for increased irrigation water will have to be balanced with the demands of the urban areas for the same water supplies for domestic and industrial purposes. In addition, the farmers will have to justify any form of subsidy required of the urban taxpayers to reduce the price that the farmers pay for irrigation water.

In other areas the urban interests in improved education and in social welfare measures will force upon rural interests taxation, which they have heretofore successfully opposed. It is clear that in most western states, and particularly in those that have the greatest amount of urbanization and industrialization, this process has already gone a considerable way. The most notable example is in California. Manufacturing and other forms of industry have supplanted the resources-based industry as the largest employers and most important generators of economic activity, and these interests have tended to impose a broader mandate on the resources users. Although the gigantic project of bringing Feather River water from northern California to the southern part of California may be questioned on economic grounds, it seems apparent that this project recognizes the demands of urban interests for increased water supplies in an increasingly water-short area.

National Resources Administration

The United States government has played, and continues to play, a crucial role in the development and management of resources in the western United States. In part, this national involvement is traceable to the long periods of territorial status of most of the states, during which time the national government ultimately controlled every aspect of policy-making and administration. But of greater importance were the nature of the resources themselves and the spirit of the times during which the new states of the West were created and the disposition of their resources had to be decided.

In spite of the wholesale disposition of public land to private ownership, the national government still retains ownership, or the responsibility for management, of approximately 450 million acres (182,115,000 hectares), 90 percent of which are located in 11 western states. The United States owns or manages from as little as 36 percent of the rural land in the state of Washington to as much as 84 percent of the rural land in Nevada (Fig. 1). Nearly one-half of this land in public ownership is in the public domain and is managed by the Bureau of Land Management in the Department of the Interior. Lacking water for irrigation and often physically unsuited for agriculture, this land was unclaimed by settlers and for many decades remained open range, used almost exclusively by grazers and subject to no regulation or management. Only with the passage of the Taylor Grazing Act in 1934 did this land come under some form of positive administration. In the foreseeable future this land is expected to remain in public ownership.

In addition to the land that is of little potential value in private ownership, there are large tracts of public land in the West that are of great economic value but have been retained in public ownership in order to protect them against despoliation. The reservation of these lands was made primarily during the late 19th and early 20th centuries, the period in American history when the conservation movement emerged. Deep concern was registered over misuse of the land that passed into private ownership and the unsuitable uses to which much of the land was being put.

The policy of the national government in mineral development has been similar to that in farming—to dispose of land that is valuable chiefly for its minerals under general mining laws. Lands created out of the original public domain, whether forested or grazing lands, are still subject to mineral entry. Remarkable increases have occurred in the number of mineral leases during the past 20 years, putting much of the public land that might produce oil and gas under lease. Nearly all of the crude oil produced from the public domain came from four western states—Wyoming, California, Colorado, and New Mexico—and constituted a large percentage of the total production of these states. Only a small percentage of the leased lands are producing oil and gas; much of the land is being held for speculative purposes or carried as reserves by oil developers because of the low rental fees. Oil and gas leases constitute the most important forms of mineral development on the public lands, but other forms of leases are also important, such as those for potash, coal, phosphate, and sodium. Much of the land that is leased for mineral development is also used for grazing, although there are occasional conflicts in their dual uses.

As with entry on the public lands for homesteading purposes, numerous fraudulent claims occurred under the mineral-leasing laws. Under the pretext of mineral development, large tracts of forested land were entered for the purposes of lumbering with only the minimum of developmental work accomplished. In recent years, even more serious has been a failure to develop a consistent approach to mineral exploration and development on the public lands that would provide for maximum development. Other problems have resulted from the fact that the mineral laws were framed to prevent individuals from claiming large sections of mineral land and creating

---

Fig. 1. This pattern of landownership indicates that much of the western United States is either owned by, or, as is true of Indian reservations, administered by, the national government. Almost half of this federal land is public domain and is used mainly for grazing.

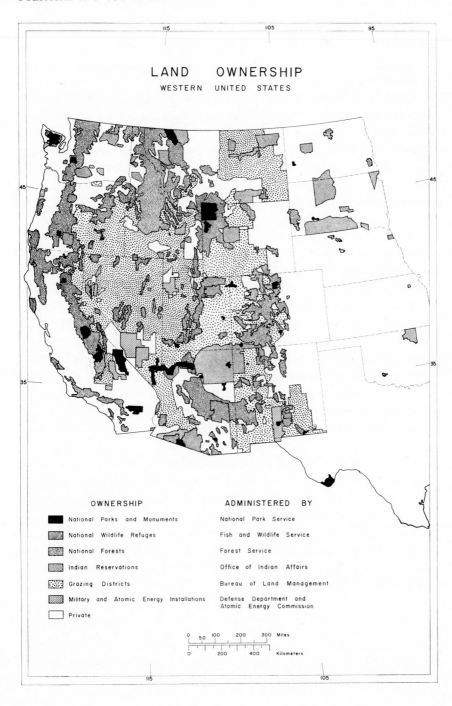

LAND OWNERSHIP
WESTERN UNITED STATES

OWNERSHIP

ADMINISTERED BY

National Parks and Monuments — National Park Service

National Wildlife Refuges — Fish and Wildlife Service

National Forests — Forest Service

Indian Reservations — Office of Indian Affairs

Grazing Districts — Bureau of Land Management

Military and Atomic Energy Installations — Defense Department and Atomic Energy Commission

Private

monopolies. When the high-grade ore played out, however, these laws obstructed efficient development. Recent mineral production has depended on extensive tracts of low-grade ores, for which the filings under the mining laws were inadequate.

National responsibility in the development of water resources in the West has been a natural consequence of federal ownership of public lands and also of certain delegated powers under the United States Constitution. The U.S. Supreme Court has disposed of water controversies between states on the basis of an equitable apportionment formula, and Congress has participated in interstate compacts, many of which are designed to apportion waters among states in a single river basin.

The role of the national government in the development of western resources is understandable, not only because of its responsibility for management of its lands, but also because of the fact that the resources themselves know no state boundaries. The major river basins of the West—the Columbia, the Colorado, the Missouri, and the Rio Grande—all are interstate basins, and the approach to their maximum development must be on a basis broader than a single state. A second important factor leading to national involvement is the cost of development of these resources. Projects the size of Grand Coulee, Hoover (Boulder), and, more recently, Glen Canyon dams require the enormous resources of the national government. Moreover, national construction was a necessity because of the fact that the benefits from the projects transcended state boundaries.

In spite of the positive benefits to the West through national development and management of these resources, some interests in the West aggressively support the transfer of the responsibility for ownership and management of these properties to the states or to private interests. This is particularly true with regard to the lands now under the administration of the Bureau of Land Management and the Forest Service. The most popular argument is based on the notion that national management of these lands constitutes an unwarranted invasion of the rights of states to manage their own affairs, but behind this argument is the basic antipathy of western grazers, in particular, toward positive and restrictive management programs. Periodically, major efforts are made in Congress to transfer jurisdiction to the states or to sell these public lands, but seldom have these movements received serious consideration.

Legislative Organization

Part of the explanation for the success of the western states in getting national investment in resources development lies in the basis of representation in the United States Congress. The 17 western states in which reclamation projects have been constructed send 34 senators to the United States Senate, slightly more than one-third of the total membership. The West is much weaker in the House of Representatives, however, sending 66 representatives, or only 15 percent of the total membership.

Representation in the Senate especially overweights the influence of the West when it is measured in terms of population, giving the western states a bargaining position through which they can seek the assistance of senators from the other states. On many issues, of course, such as those concerning the development and maintenance of recreation areas and scenic parks, the western states find allies and even leadership in conservation groups that are influential in the other states. The influence of western congressmen and senators is further enhanced by the decentralization of power in both houses of Congress.

Leadership on specific legislative matters generally is lodged in the committees. Western congressmen and senators, especially in the Senate, make up the bulk of the membership of the committees on interior and insular affairs, which are the committees that handle most of the resources legislation that affects the West. The members of these committees become specialists on legislation presented to their full membership and are in a position to influence favorably the full House and Senate in voting on their legislation.

But just as the administrative machinery is decentralized among a great many agencies, so is the responsibility for policy-making divided among several committees in each legislative chamber. Legislation concerning agriculture and forested land is under the jurisdiction of the committees on agriculture, and legislation concerning public works—particularly flood control—and pollution is under the jurisdiction of the committees on public works.

Depending on their analysis of the advantages and disadvantages that this committee system affords, interest groups develop their strategy in formulating legislative proposals. Although it may appear to be incongruous that the committees on agriculture should be responsible for the legislation that affects the forested lands of the West, certain advantages are found in the fact that the chief opponents of federal management—grazing, mining, and lumbering interests—have less influence on the agriculture committees, whereas if the national forests were under the jurisdiction of the interior committees, the national forests would be in a much more vulnerable position.

It must be recognized, however, that the western states do not occupy such a favored position in the committees that concern themselves with appropriations for the support of federal programs. The subcommittees of the appropriations committees that deal with western resources programs seldom are dominated by western interests to the same extent as the legislative committees. Thus, programs may be adopted by Congress but given niggardly support.

One of the most serious problems in congressional consideration of resources policy is the practice of *logrolling,* in which members of Congress vote for one another's local projects on a reciprocal basis; without serious examination of the economic justification of these projects, the legislative committees concerned with public works, often working with the administrative bureaus that develop the plans for these projects, biennially steer these bills through each chamber of Congress with hardly any threat of a veto by the President that cannot be overridden. Whether Congress will be willing to accept unified executive leadership in the development of water-resources planning and project authorization, and whether it will control its constituent parts—its committees—remains to be seen. The past argues against it.

Administrative Organization

The executive instruments of policy development and administration at the national level are no more integrated than at the state level. Partly for historical reasons, but also for reasons of interest-group control of the policy processes, the executive branch is characterized by scattered authority and divided responsibility. In view of the remarkable technologic advances, the confused administrative picture has been called a "cultural lag" in the development of water resources (*30*).

In spite of innumerable recommendations that the natural-resources responsibilities of the national government be concentrated in a single executive agency, the pattern of administrative decentralization prevails. This decentralized administrative process, combined with the corresponding divisions of functions within Congress, has resulted in conflicting policies and goals and inadequately coordinated programs. Moreover, the lack of coordination has had its effect on the states in inducing them to adopt parallel administrative structures within state governments. It has operated to the benefit of particular interest groups that have sought maximum benefits from federal agencies that were competing for their patronage.

The primary resources agencies at the national level are found in the Department of the Interior and the Department of Agriculture. The mandate of the Department of the Interior cuts broadly across the natural-resources field, including responsibility for water-resources development, management of the public lands, parks and outdoor recreation, fish and wildlife, minerals, and the development of hydroelectric power. The resources-management responsibilities in the Department of Agriculture are found in the Forest and Soil Conservation services. Each department supports major research units, such as the U.S. Geological Survey and the Agricultural Research Service. In addition to these two departments with broad responsibilities in the soil- and water-conservation field, there are other agencies, particularly in the field of water resources, that share in the responsibility for resources. Among them are the Army Corps of Engineers, the Federal Power Commission, and the Public Health Service.

The effectiveness of federal programs varies widely from agency to agency, depending on a number of factors, including financial support by Congress, which in turn reflects the degree of political support given to the agencies by their chief clientele groups and the method of organizing their affairs. The vitality of the programs of the Bureau of Reclamation can be explained by the overwhelming support these programs have received from virtually all interests in the western area. Only in the instances where a reclamation project has threatened to invade a hallowed scenic area, such as the Dinosaur National Monument or the Grand Canyon National Park, have serious controversies arisen.

The ethic of the conservation movement and its particular emphasis on the national forests as a lasting national heritage, plus the effective inculcation of traditional conservation values in the forest rangers, have made the Forest Service an organization powerful both in its capacity to obtain funds to sustain its developmental programs and to avoid domination by the users of the forests. In contrast, the Bureau of Land Management, having no powerful supporting interest groups and not serving a variety of clientele groups as does the Forest Service, has been subjected to powerful political pressures, both national and local, and has, therefore, been only a moderate success.

Existing administrative structure at the national level has been criticized severely for its failure to provide a coordinated program of resources development in the West comparable to that which has been accomplished in the Tennessee Valley through the Tennessee Valley Authority. In the water-resources field, the authority for development is spread out among the Bureau of Reclamation, the Army Corps of Engineers, and the Federal Power Commission. The result frequently has been highly dramatized in political controversies among these agencies, with various interest groups lining up on the side most favorable to their interests. Not untypical of these conflicts has been the controversy between the Corps of Engineers and the Bureau of Reclamation over the developmental program for the Kings River in California, the controversy over the Missouri River, and the conflict between the plans of the Bureau of Reclamation and the Corps of Engineers, and later the Bureau of Reclamation and the Federal Power Commission, over the construction of dams on the Snake River in Idaho.

Because a department of natural resources is politically infeasible at the present time, some have suggested the establishment of a council of natural resources—an interagency consultative body at the national level to coordinate the programs of the various agencies and to advise the President on programs in the resources field. Another recommendation has been made for the creation of independent valley authorities along the lines of the Tennessee Valley Authority. This approach has little support today in the western region, partly because of the opposition of local interests, partly because of the opposition of established agencies, but also because of serious questions about the authority device in terms of its relationships with the Chief Executive, with other established agencies, and with local interests.

It should be recognized that national responsibility for resources management or development does not necessarily imply centralized control. Some federal agencies, notably the Forest Service, have been able to establish a strong regional organization, which nevertheless adheres to the core values of the Forest Service. Other agencies, such as the Fish and Wildlife Service, operate to a considerable extent through state fish and game agencies. The Bureau of Reclamation and the Army Corps of Engineers have made notable strides toward decentralization of their planning and project-development programs. The advantages of decentralization are important, but at the same time they emphasize the necessity of field coordination.

Efforts to solve the problems of regional planning and coordination generally have taken the form of interagency or interdepartmental coordinating committees. These coordinating agencies have been established on a regional basis and have brought together technicians from many services to discuss common resources problems. Lacking any pressure to develop a consensus or a common viewpoint for the management and development of resources, they have had only slight success in overcoming the limitations inherent in a decentralized administrative system. More recently, efforts have been made to integrate the planning of resources development through study commissions, such as the Texas Water Commission. The result of this appeared to be a program that would maximize the interests of each agency represented on the commission, but little provision was made for an integrated plan with a scale of priorities.

Interagency basin committees in the West have been established in the Columbia, Missouri, and Pacific basins. They generally have included state representation as well as representatives from the major resources agencies. Ernest A. Englebert concludes that they have not become integrated, intergovernmental planning bodies, although they have been the means of fostering an awareness of basin-wide problems, of facilitating some research in administrative cooperation, and of solving some minor issues (31). The states often represented on these bodies seldom have played an important role in their activities.

An alternative to federal responsibility in resources management, often preferred by state and local interests, is the interstate compact. In the western states, however, it has proved to be of very limited utility, and, in the case of the Colorado River compact, it has been the basis for a dispute that has lasted more than a quarter of a century. Although the interstate compact allows regional interests to solve their problems on a regional basis, there are serious limitations on its capacity permanently to resolve conflicting interests. Unanimity may be obtained on the original compact; but it is frequently difficult to obtain any modification of that compact, since unanimity remains a primary requisite of all compact decision-making. Seldom is an administrative agency created to plan for, or carry out, an integrated basin-wide program. The opportunities for obstruction by local and state units and the pressures for state and local preferences tend to defeat the regional goals.

Policy Issues

The foregoing discussion suggests numerous policy issues that require the attention of legislators, administrators, and the general public. Some of these issues raise basic questions about the allocation of resources in our society. Others raise questions about the distribution of responsibility for policy decisions. In most instances these matters are inseparable.

1) *Development versus protection.* The rapid increase in population and its urban character will require a careful assessment of conflicting resources values. Current debate over the protection of wilderness areas is indicative of this kind of issue. Those who are concerned about the development of resources for economic use tend to look upon the conservationists as unrealistic dreamers who are unconcerned about the indefinable term *progress.* The conservationists, on the other hand, see little progress in efforts to invade Grand Canyon National Park through a high-power dam at Bridge Canyon or the intrusion of cattle on national parks. In an affluent society, what price do we place on space, primitive nature, scenic beauty, and solitude?

2) *Community values.* To alleviate the strains that earlier policies have imposed, national and state policy-makers must be concerned increasingly about the long-range impact of their decisions on local communities. Continued subsidization of marginal farms may create more, rather than less, distress in areas where farming itself is marginal. Subsidization may change its form to help families adjust to a new life. Where adequate water supplies do not exist,

disposal of public lands either to speculators or to homesteaders who impose additional burdens on water supplies must be avoided. Cutting practices on the forests must be adjusted carefully to avoid "boom-and-bust" effects on small communities in a forested region. Resources-development programs for the Indians must be accompanied by an awareness of the spiritual and social impact on the Indians of the change from tribal to modern life.

3) *Rural versus urban values.* The urbanization of the West continues to challenge allocations of resources that favor rural areas directly through demands for water and indirectly through taxation and subsidies. Unless irrigation uses are substantially subsidized, economic pressures appear to favor reallocation toward urban uses of water. Political changes appear to run strongly against the rural areas and are likely to result in a very real modification of the dominant positions of the farmers, the miners, and the grazers. Continued subsidization of agriculture at high rates—amounting to several billion dollars a year nationally—will be called into question.

4) *Single versus multiple use.* A more careful evaluation of the multiple-use concept may result in the adoption of a single-use principle in areas that are characterized by a single dominant interest. Where the dominant interest is water, some uses, such as the growing of trees, may be modified if not totally eliminated. The practice of block cutting of forests is an indication of the adoption of a single-use principle in a system that espouses the multiple-use concept. Recreational use may reduce the use for grazing. It is necessary to insure that the decisions with regard to these principles are community decisions reflecting long-range public values and are not reflections of immediate economic interest.

5) *Private versus public decision-making.* In the West a fundamental issue has been raised over decision-making by private groups or public agencies, with the interests arraigned on each side in terms of their particular values, whether they be economic, political, or esthetic. Movements to shift ownership of the western public lands from federal to state or from federal to private ownership meet with passionate opposition from conservationists, because of their fear of inadequate state administration and private irresponsibility. Nevertheless, it seems reasonable to examine the advantages of private versus public ownership in its variable contexts rather than in terms of an immutable principle. In some instances, outright sale of some

grazing lands would provide more effective management than continued public ownership would. In deciding whether public or private institutions shall produce and distribute hydroelectric energy, a decision may be made in terms of particular economic consequences and needs, as in the transmission of power from Glen Canyon Dam, rather than in terms of a rigid application of an article of faith.

6) *Federal versus state responsibilities and rights.* Periodically, efforts are made to shift the responsibility for management of the western resources from the national government to the states. This generally involves the national forests and the rangelands. Usually these movements are thinly veiled disguises for efforts by private interests to gain control of these lands. The interrelationship of resources, greater financial capacity, and a history of more effective management of these lands at the national level seem to preclude any great enlargement of state responsibility beyond that which the states already have. Increased responsibility at the state level would appear to depend primarily on the states' demonstration of a capacity and a willingness to undertake the responsibilities. But with an increasing sense of responsibility, their role in the planning and operational stages may expand.

7) *Legislative and administrative reorganization.* Existing organization and procedures for decision-making in the field of natural resources, both at the state and at the national level, must be measured by their capacity to promote examination of values in terms of objective criterions. The influence of interest groups cannot be exorcised, nor should it be; but the means must be created by which particular resources programs are examined in terms of a set of economic or other criterions and in a framework of reasonable alternatives. Thus, Congress should be encouraged to examine reclamation projects in relation to national standards, which force evaluation of each project in objective terms rather than in local interest terms. Competition among administrative agencies should be reduced by adoption of similar sets of design and economic criterions.

REFERENCES

1. B. H. Hibbard, *A History of Public Land Policies* (Macmillan, New York, 1924).

2. T. B. Nolan, "The inexhaustible resource of technology," in *Perspectives on Conservation,* H. Jarrett, Ed. (Johns Hopkins Press, Baltimore, Md., 1958), pt. 2.
3. F. J. Turner, *The Frontier in American History* (Holt, New York, 1920).
4. W. P. Webb, *The Great Plains* (Ginn, Boston, 1931).
5. C. F. Kraenzel, *The Great Plains in Transition* (Univ. of Oklahoma Press, Norman, 1955).
6. B. F. Wright, Jr., "Political institutions and the frontier"; L. M. Hacker, "Sections—or classes?"; and G. W. Pierson, "The frontier and American institutions: a criticism of the Turner theory," in *The Turner Thesis concerning the Role of the Frontier in American History,* "Problems in American Civilization Series," Amherst College (Heath, Boston, 1949).
7. S. C. Wiel, *Water Rights in the Western States* (Bancroft-Whitney, San Francisco, 1912).
8. C. S. Kinney, *A Treatise on the Law of Irrigation* (Becker-Moss, San Francisco, 1912).
9. F. J. Trelease, "A model state water code for river basin development," *Law and Contemp. Probl.* **22**, 303 (1957).
10. U.S. Geological Survey, "Water law with special reference to ground water," *U.S. Geol. Surv. Circ. 117* (1951), p. 5.
11. R. E. Huffman, *Irrigation Development and Public Water Policy* (Ronald, New York, 1953).
12. F. Adams, "Community organization for irrigation in the United States," *Food Agr. Organ. U.N., FAO Agr. Develop. Paper 19* (Rome, Italy, 1952).
13. J. W. Powell, *Report on the Lands of the Arid Regions of the United States,* W. Stegner, Ed. (Harvard Univ. Press, Belknap Div., Cambridge, Mass., 1962).
14. L. Nelson, *The Mormon Village* (Univ. of Utah Press, Salt Lake City, 1952).
15. A. H. Anderson, "Space as a social cost," *J. Farm Econ.* **32**, 411 (1950).
16. M. M. Kelso, "Costs of space in the West," in *Land and Water Use,* W. Thorne, Ed. (Am. Assoc. for the Advancement of Science, Washington, D.C., 1963).
17. E. Z. Vogt, *Modern Homesteaders* (Harvard Univ. Press, Belknap Div., Cambridge, Mass., 1955), p. 188.
18. V. Ostrom, *Water and Politics* (Haynes Found., Los Angeles, Calif., 1953).
19. R. B. Campbell, S. C. Kelley, R. B. Talbot, and B. L. Wills, *The Williston Report: the Impact of Oil on the Williston Area of North Dakota* (Univ. of North Dakota, Grand Forks, 1958).
20. D. A. Bingham, R. Stone, and H. Morgan, "Eloy, a cotton town in transition," *Arizona Rev.* **9** (July–December 1960).

21. D. E. Mann, *The Politics of Water in Arizona* (Univ. of Arizona Press, Tucson, 1963).
22. Council of State Governments, *State Administration of Water Resources* (Council of State Governments, Chicago, 1957), p. 23.
23. M. E. Garnsey, *America's New Frontier: the Mountain West* (Knopf, New York, 1950), p. 284.
24. F. Tilden, *The State Parks: Their Meaning in American Life* (Knopf, New York, 1962), p. 486.
25. V. Ostrom, "The state administration of natural resources in the West," *Am. Political Sci. Rev.* **47**, 493 (1953).
26. ———, "The water economy and its organization," *Nat. Resources J.* **2**, 55–73 (1962).
27. U.S. Senate, *Report of the Select Committee on National Water Resources,* 87th Congr., 1st sess., Comm. Print 29 (Washington, D.C., 1961), p. 49.
28. A DeGrazia, *The Western Public: 1952 and Beyond* (Stanford Univ. Press, Stanford, Calif., 1954), p. 176.
29. B. Zeller, *American State Legislatures* (T. Y. Crowell, New York, 1954), pp. 190–191.
30. E. A. Ackerman and G. O. G. Löf, *Technology in American Water Development* (Johns Hopkins Press, Baltimore, Md., 1959), p. 463.
31. E. A. Englebert, "Federalism and water resources development," *Law and Contemp. Probl.* **22**, 342–344 (1957).

15

Critical Review of Man's History in Arid Regions

MARION CLAWSON

Man has damaged the otherwise natural environment of the arid and semiarid United States. He has changed it in various ways in which neither damage nor improvement is clear, and he has improved it in some respects. The details of some of the major changes are supplied later in this chapter, but a few general comments are appropriate here. Words such as *damage* and *improvement,* obviously, must include value judgments and are not merely the results of impartial research.

Synoptic or synthesizing research, which combines into an integrated whole the results of much specialized and analytic research, is basic to this chapter. The division of human knowledge into specialized fields and the greater manageability of clearly, but narrowly, defined research topics have led to a far greater output of analytic research than of synoptic research. The latter requires the summation of frequently unlike variables. How, for instance, does one balance the elimination or drastic reduction of some species of wildlife against the gain in food output for human consumption that results from plowing the prairies? With all of its difficulties and pitfalls, however, a look at man's actions as a whole and in total, in relation to his environment, is essential at intervals.

Perhaps in arid regions generally, but certainly in the arid United States, it is possible to distinguish two broadly contrasting relationships of man to his environment. On the one hand, there is the self-sufficient or relatively closed economy, which is likely to be produced by the slow infiltration of a people into a new and unfamiliar environment from which they must draw their sustenance on pain of death if they fail. Indian penetration of the arid United States was of this type; to a lesser degree, so was that of the Spaniard and the Mexican. Each brought some artifacts and technology with him, but transportation techniques severely limited original importation and virtually precluded any further importation of major items of food, shelter, clothing, or large tools.

As geographer R. J. Russell (1) pointed out long ago in connection with distribution of vegetative types, such cultures are probably "more closely related to the occurrence of an occasional extreme drought than to the normal climatic boundary itself." The same may well be true for adverse relationships other than drought. This type of culture is likely to develop into a traditional one, with emphasis on custom and experience, and with resistance to change.

By contrast, there is the present-day arid-lands economy, which is an integral part of a larger national economy, with relatively large-scale importation of necessary production and consumption goods, and with export of specialized products to the larger economy. In the case of the United States, this relationship has a further distinguishing characteristic: the new economy was associated with an overwhelming influx of population, its culture, and its goods. Such a culture can draw—and, in the case of the western United States, repeatedly has drawn—upon the assets of the humid regions of the nation whenever disaster or unfavorable conditions strike. Crop failure in modern South Dakota does not mean starvation, there or elsewhere.

This type of culture may change rapidly. It has done so in the western United States; and the forces of change that any innovation sets in motion may have failed to work themselves out before another major innovation sets in motion a wholly new set of forces. Many wheat farms in the Great Plains, for instance, have "graveyards" of obsolete farm machinery, which was abandoned for newer and more efficient models before the old ones were completely worn out.

The physical consequences of resources use are often slow in reaching full realization in an arid region; overgrazing in one decade may set in motion a train of ecologic change that will not work out fully to a new equilibrium until several decades later. Rapidity of social change may wholly obscure the slower, but perhaps more inexorable, forces of physical process, leading modern man to assume that he has somehow escaped the consequences that his forefathers would inevitably have suffered.

Knowledge of Arid Regions

Man's knowledge of his environment is never perfect, and this certainly has been true of the arid regions of the United States. Indian cultures had accumulated a great deal of knowledge through long experience but, lacking a modern scientific base, they often were mistaken about causation. A traditional or custom-bound society changes slowly; this is both its strength and its weakness. When Europeans began to invade the arid regions, they brought knowledge and experience with them, mostly from a more humid environment. As they lived in the arid region, they acquired experience and tended to generalize or draw conclusions from it. Because of climatic variability, they often were seriously misled by their short-term experience. Settlers sometimes went into dry-land farming districts of the Great Plains and intermountain regions in periods of favorable rainfall; a few favorable crop years seriously confused them with regard to the long-run hazards of drought, hail, and other adverse events.

It is easy to be highly critical of this kind of pragmatic, narrow-focus "knowledge." Many pioneers were severely limited in formal education and in experience in different geographic regions. They had personal experience, true enough, but not necessarily common experience. They tended to generalize much too easily and broadly from personal experience. But we must also recognize that "scientific" men of the day often were as mistaken about the true resource characteristics of the arid West. The myth of the "great American desert," as applied to the Great Plains, came from men with at least some pretensions to professional knowledge. The rainmaker was only a little more mistaken than those who proclaimed that rain followed the plow. It is not enough that today we are able to identify men (John Wesley Powell, perhaps) whose advice at the time was sound even by modern standards. In their time, however, their voices were among many with different messages, each claiming to be authoritative.

Given the speed of settlement already noted, and given the highly dynamic culture, technology, and economy that have prevailed in the past 100 years or so, forces tending toward equilibrium have never achieved it. For instance, the plowing of prairie soils may set in motion a cycle of erosion, but different methods of crop production or reversion to grass may arise out of new technology or out of a reduced demand for wheat from such lands, thus greatly modifying the original erosion forces. This has happened in numerous localities in the Great Plains that were too dry or had soils unsuited for continuous crop production. Irrigated croplands may be subjected to serious salt accumulations; but before this reaches its inevitable end, the whole area may shift to urban or defense use.

With longer experience and with accumulated scientific inquiry, our knowledge of the arid lands has increased substantially. But important segments of the total population either never have been informed of major basic facts or have tried to disregard them. We must agree that we simply do not know the long-run consequences of many resources uses in the arid West, and that many groups have attempted resources use about which the gravest of questions must be raised. As an example, what possibly can be the long-run future of an area that mines its ground water, where natural replacement is virtually zero?

Whatever his impact on the resources may be, man's spatial relationship to other men in arid lands falls into two broad patterns: oasis settlement and either nomadic or fixed, diffused settlement. Indian and Anglo-American experience in the western United States has been of both types; Spanish and Mexican experience was nearly all oasis or group settlement.

Those who settle in the oasis try to capture the advantages of group living, to create an essentially humid man-land pattern within a small area where unusual desert or dry-land conditions prevail. Within the oasis, they try to shut out the desert. As geographer Alonzo W. Pond suggests (2), they are *in* but not *of* the desert. Most present-day settlement in the western United States is, in this sense, oasis in type. More than most other peoples in arid climates, Americans have made their own oases, often conducting the necessary water long distances by elaborate engineering works. Towns and cities within oases include groups of people living as nearly like their counterparts in humid zones as they can, benefiting from the peculiar conditions of arid and semiarid climate as much as they can. They have not come to terms with aridity in that their lives depend on an arid environment.

In contrast, other groups in arid lands, completely or wholly dependent on a relatively localized environment, have lived necessarily in a much more diffused pattern of settlement. Indian and other seasonally shifting people, although often grouped into small bands, nevertheless, were highly dispersed geographically. The rancher and the dry-land farmer particularly, in present-day times, are scattered over the landscape. Even some of their service population lives in extremely small settlements or in genuine open country. The more diffuse the pattern of settlement, the more must people live directly in the arid environment, and the less can they modify it by import from other economies and climates.

Man's History in the Arid Regions

Man has been in the arid and semiarid parts of the United States for several thousand years. Nearly the whole of this long experience was by Indians. Europeans have been here only a few centuries, although man's impact on his environment during the past century may have been as great as that of all his forebears combined. After the Civil War, the transcontinental railroads were the forerunners of vast and swiftly accelerating change. Ranchers, dry farmers, and irrigators each appropriated land and water to their use, with material modification of the natural environment. The earliest irrigation was comparatively simple diversion of natural streamflow, especially from the smaller streams that were easy to control. But, by the beginning of the present century, major irrigation developments, such as that in the Imperial Valley of California, had begun.

More recent times, in the memory of us still alive, have seen equally dramatic changes. The Plains were homesteaded mainly around 1900 and plowed shortly thereafter, to be abandoned in time of drought and duststorm. Depopulation of the Plains and other western areas has been general and widespread in the rural areas since 1920. But in oases within the arid region, and even more along its western fringes, cities grew greatly during and after World War II, in large part as a result of war and defense spending.

This capsule review of arid-lands history is suggestive only to those reasonably familiar with it, or with some of its parts. The history of arid lands in the western United States is dealt with more fully in Chapter 4 of this book, and in still more detail in the references cited there. It is tempting to discuss this chapter primarily in historical terms. Since time is one dimension, this would at least give an unequivocal frame to the discussion. In spite of this temptation, it seems wiser to use a somewhat different approach for the remainder of the chapter. I turn, therefore, to a topical treatment, but with the topics in a more or less historical order, and with some suggestion of the main historical period into which each resources use mostly fell.

Fire as an Influence

Fire is one of man's most ancient tools, and with it he has affected his environment materially in many parts of the world. Fire has been of negligible influence in desert areas, for these lack sufficient fuel to carry a wildfire. However, in the semiarid grasslands of the Plains, especially in the northern Plains, in the woodland (juniper) areas of the Southwest, and in drier forest areas in the foothills and lower mountains throughout the West, fire has been one of several influences. Under most circumstances, frequent fires favor grasses rather than trees and shrubs.

The Indians, apparently, regularly burned old dried grass on the Plains. Lewis and Clark reported extensive smokes and fires on the Plains for many days at a time in 1805, especially in the early spring. The Indians burned certain areas in the California foothills more or less regularly; the floor of Yosemite Valley was treeless when white men first saw it, whereas today it is heavily forested. Although the record of regular burning is less clear in the juniper woodlands of the Southwest, the large extension and thickening up of tree stands in these areas since fires have been kept out are indirect evidence of the role of fire at an earlier time. In addition to fires set deliberately, there have always been some fires started accidentally by man or by lightning.

With the coming of more widespread settlement and travel into all parts of the West, since perhaps 1875, the fire hazard has increased enormously. One might have expected much greater acreages to be burned each year. In fact, this did happen for a time, but for the past 40 or 50 years, efforts at fire prevention and control have been so effective that the areas burned each year have decreased.

This control over fire has often been hailed as a major conservation accomplishment, and so it is. But forester Charles F. Cooper (3) has shown that elimination of fire from forests that had evolved in its presence has seriously downgraded the quality and productivity of these forests. Fire in forests serves as a pruning and thinning agent. In its absence, young trees compete for available moisture without, however, eliminating the less successful ones. A stagnated, dwarfed forest results, at least in the Arizona watersheds studied by Cooper.

The conservationist's and the forester's horror of the ravages of uncontrolled wildfires led to propaganda programs for eliminating fire from areas subject to burning, greatly hindering its use as a deliberate tool of management. However, in very recent years, fire has come to be considered useful in certain types of land-management programs. In California, for instance, carefully planned and managed fires have been used to reduce or eliminate brush on rangelands. When controlled fire was followed by artificial reseeding of grasses and careful management, productive rangelands resulted on favorable sites. Prescribed burning, under favorable conditions, may eliminate the fuel that otherwise might be the basis of destructive fires at other seasons. This is the situation along the California foothills, especially around the towns and cities.

Irrigation and Its Effects

Irrigation has been practiced in the arid Southwest for at least 1000 years, and elsewhere in the arid United States on a more modest scale and for shorter time periods. Some Indian groups were capable, both technologically and organizationally, of building canals that extended for some miles from diversion point to irrigated area. In many cases, the diversions were important both at the time and in their long-term effects, the latter arising out of salt accumulations in the soil that resulted from leaky canals and poor drainage. But in total area, they were relatively small.

Much of modern irrigation development was begun and carried out with little thought or knowledge about long-run consequences. Water often was carried to land without consideration of the soil characteristics, which in some cases precluded successful crop production even with ample water. Large parts of the federal Umatilla reclamation project, for instance, proved to be too sandy for irrigation and had to be abandoned, even though canals had been constructed to them. No thought was given to possible drainage problems, and, in many areas, these arose shortly, sometimes to be solved by open or tile drains and sometimes not (4).

Salt accumulation in the soil has already become serious in some localities in almost every irrigated area and will surely continue to be a problem in many others (5). Although salt control is possible if sufficient flushing water is available and if adequate drainage exists, a mere listing of the conditions necessary for its control shows that adequate control is difficult or impossible in some areas.

Water is almost universally diverted to irrigated land in larger quantities than careful experimentation has shown to be the optimum amounts. This not only wastes a scarce resource; it often does positive damage to land as well. Massive subsidization of irrigation water in the West certainly contributes to such waste, for it removes financial incentives to farmers to conserve water by better land preparation and better water control when they are irrigating.

One feature of irrigation, especially early irrigation by white men, deserving emphasis is the erosion that it caused. Diversion dams in small streams often were washed out, with consequent destruction of the previously stable streambanks, and an erosion cycle started. Several streams or small rivers, particularly in the Southwest, shortly gutted their alluvial valleys as a result of this type of erosion. Alluvial bottom lands along the Virgin and other rivers in southern Utah and along the upper Gila River in Arizona have been washed away in this fashion. Canal breaks occurred also in some instances. Application of water to fields also led to accelerated erosion, sometimes very serious. Those responsible for the early irrigation often did not understand the erosive forces with which they were dealing. Later irrigation, notably the larger projects, ordinarily was free of these difficulties, although farmers sometimes continued to use water unwisely on their own fields.

A matter of special concern in the arid West is the general overuse of ground-water resources. Ground-water basins exist in all major regions of the United States and have been exploited to a greater or lesser extent everywhere; as a result, cones of depression have developed in wells in many areas (6, 7). Ground-water reservoirs with perennial overdraft, however, are heavily concentrated in the arid West, especially in the Southwest. In some localities, measures have

Man's impact on the land is dramatically demonstrated in these two photographs. When the top picture was made, runoff from about 45,000 acres (18,211 hectares) had cut a gully 35 feet (11 meters) deep. At that time, in 1937, an earthen dam was being built (in background) to plug the arroyo. By 1940, deposition of sediment had filled the dam-blocked arroyo. Both photographs were made from the same point on Figuerido Creek on the Navaho Indian Reservation in northwestern New Mexico. (Courtesy U.S. Department of Agriculture, Soil Conservation Service)

been taken to balance draft and replenishment, but in others over-draft continues to deplete stored water.

This type of water exploitation is closely akin to the mining of minerals, and in time the deposit will be exhausted or so depleted that it will have little value or be wholly worthless. The long-run economic future of areas, such as the High Plains of Texas, where natural recharge is extremely small, is questionable. An institutional or legal structure that permits each landowner to use water without regard to his effect on the total balance of draft and recharge in the ground-water basin as a whole almost forces each landowner to use whatever water he can get, and all he can get, before someone else uses it.

The construction of dams for storage of irrigation water and other purposes has provided entrapment for sediments in streamflows in many parts of the West. In some cases, as in the Elephant Butte reservoir on the Rio Grande in New Mexico, siltation has seriously reduced the original storage capacity of the reservoir. Lake Mead on the Colorado River has accumulated immense quantities of sediments, but the capacity of this reservoir is so large that they occupy a very small part of the total capacity. This entrapment of stream sediments at least keeps them from deposition on irrigated fields or along lower reaches of the same rivers, but it is a symptom of serious erosion, often of seriously accelerated erosion, in the upper watersheds.

But it would be less than accurate to disregard the great benefits of irrigation. More than half of the value of all agricultural output in the West is from irrigated land (8), and the secondary income and employment effects of this type of agriculture are very great. It is also a fact that in many irrigated areas, true soils (with humus, microbiologic life, and developed horizons) have been built out of raw desert-soil materials. Although these soils would revert to raw soil materials if irrigation were permanently abandoned, they do represent a new productive resource created by man's action. Future maintenance and development of productivity in irrigated lands will constitute a continuing challenge to man's ingenuity in the West, but for most of the irrigated area it is not an unsolvable problem. The larger irrigated areas represent oasis settlement at its fullest.

Results of Hunting

Hunting is one of the oldest exploitative techniques, vastly older than irrigation. Most Indians were hunters to some degree; some depended on hunting for food almost exclusively. Given the numbers of Indians, their techniques, and the other restraints on both the hunted animals and the Indians, it seems probable that their hunting, prior to the white man's arrival, was not a major ecologic force. With the coming of the white men, who provided the Indians with important new tools (the horse and the gun, particularly) and with a market for furs, this situation changed markedly. One may speculate that in another century or so the increased hunting pressures so created would have led to severe resources problems for the Plains Indians in the absence of any other changes; but, in fact, other and more damaging effects on the ecologic balances arose almost concurrently.

The white man himself hunted on a massive scale, primarily for furs. There is little evidence that the precontact Indian trapped beavers extensively, but the development of a beaver-fur market and the direct trapping by white men virtually eliminated this animal from much of its original habitat. Thousands of small streams throughout the intermountain and plains regions once provided a habitat for beavers; the latter were limited in numbers primarily by their food supply. As far as I know, no one has attempted a quantitative measurement of the erosion effects of the reduction or elimination of beavers from these small streams, but it may have been considerable, especially along stream valleys with deep alluvial fill that was easily removed, once grass and dam protection were destroyed.

White men hunted down the buffalo, especially in the first years after the Civil War, solely for hides. More than 1 million hides were shipped to the East in the 3 years from 1872 to 1874. The drastic reduction in buffalo numbers was perhaps the most important factor in depriving the Plains Indians of their chief food source and, thus, largely in breaking their military power.

The activities of the white man, including his influence on the Indian, greatly reduced the abundance of certain species of wildlife and even reduced its variety by eliminating some species. Buffaloes, grizzly bears, wolves, antelopes, and many others have been reduced greatly in range. The low point for many species, and for wildlife management in general, perhaps was reached about 1920. Game laws were conspicuous by their looseness up to that time. Since then, management of wildlife has gradually become more scientifically based, more generally accepted, and more adequately implemented by public action.

Today, wildlife (other than predators) is valued for its esthetic and recreation value and only incidentally as a source of food and furs. Deer numbers have increased greatly in areas where deer were once scarce—so much so that deer are a problem in many places. Beavers have been planted again in streams from which they had once been eliminated; and other local reintroductions of native species have taken place. For the most part, wildlife in the United States today is an amenity consumption good or resource, not a significant part of the productive machine.

We must recognize also that beef cattle, which have largely replaced the buffalo, are able to produce vastly more and tastier meat from the same grassland resource; they are able to use the help of man in producing feed supply for winter, in control of their use of grazing land, in breeding, and in other ways. Moreover, under proper management, beef cattle are no more destructive to grass and other vegetative cover than were the buffalo and other wild animals.

Mining and the Environment

The discovery of gold in California had a tremendous effect on western development. The myth of gold is difficult to understand. It seems clear that the early gold miners in California suffered great hardships and on the average made little gain, but the hope of a rich strike continually spurred them on. The actual value of the gold from California, and later of the gold and silver from other western states, was not negligible. Vastly more important, however, was the impetus given to transportation and to settlement. The early mineral discoveries opened up local markets for agricultural produce, and the failure to find gold turned some men to agriculture, especially in California.

Mineral development in the West has led to many ghost towns, and it may well produce more in the decades ahead. Mining unavoidably exhausts its own basic resource. When the mines can no longer be operated profitably, the economic base for a community disappears. Thus far, we have not been very successful in devising alternative sources of employment and income for such towns.

Mining, especially placer mining and dredging for gold, has led to extensive stream pollution in many western areas. Strip mining for coal and other minerals in the arid West, as elsewhere, has destroyed the original soil cover. The long-run economic future of oil- and gas-producing districts is in doubt, too, as their reserves are ultimately used up.

These are some of the adverse aspects of mining; offsetting them have been the extensive wealth produced and the importance of the minerals for national industrial development. The wealth produced from mining often has not been reinvested locally, but elsewhere in the nation. Although this often has led to local resentment, it reflects differences in investment opportunity.

Livestock Grazing

Grazing began as a major use of natural resources in the arid and semiarid West in the years immediately after the Civil War and continues to this day as a major land use. Range-livestock grazing frequently has been charged with causing much adverse resources change. Although there has been some exaggeration of the evils of overgrazing, it must be acknowledged that considerable damage has been done. Domestic animals managed by man put much greater pressure on grazing lands than do wild animals. Climatic hazards, especially an unusually severe winter or unusually severe drought, often hold wild animals to numbers that do not strain the normal grazing capacity of native ranges.

Man is able to provide cultivated crops or harvested wild hay for winter feed, and to import feed or provide water during drought, thus greatly reducing the adverse effects of these natural hazards. By his control over animal movements, by means of fencing and herding, he can and usually does secure a more nearly complete utilization of all available feed each year. Wild animals presumably harvested forage less completely, at least in some years for each area, thus allowing some measure of recuperation to the native vegetation. By drilling wells, building small reservoirs, improving natural springs, and in other ways, man provides water for livestock, thus enabling them to graze fully areas that were used more lightly by game animals.

All of this was complicated by the misconceptions the white man brought to the arid grazing lands about their true grazing capacity (9). He almost always overestimated that capacity; he tended to regard an unusually favorable year as normal and to stock accordingly. This tendency to overuse was further complicated by the land-tenure situation in which the grazing-livestock industry grew up. Much of the land was federally owned; ranchers used it without specific legal right and without control. It was a matter of first come, first served. Unofficial and usually illegal controls developed in many local areas, but these sometimes broke down and frequently were forced to give way to the landowning settler.

The situation was bad enough on the Great Plains, which mostly passed from public to private ownership roughly within the 30 years from 1870 to 1900. It was much worse in the intermountain region and in some of the more rugged plains, where land remained in federal ownership but was not brought under definite management until after the passage of the Taylor Grazing Act in 1934. This experience demonstrated, if demonstration is needed to drive home the obvious, that public landownership unmatched by competent administration is at least as bad as, and probably a good deal worse than, private landownership, even when the latter is misguided or shortsighted.

Significant changes in species composition and plant vigor resulted in many parts of the grazing region as a result of this early, usually uncontrolled, and frequently excessive grazing. Unseasonal use was perhaps as destructive a force as any other, especially for some species. Overgrazing undoubtedly contributed to accelerated runoff and to accelerated erosion in many areas. However, one should be very cautious in identifying overgrazing as the sole, or even the chief, cause of the presently evident severe erosion. For one thing, much of the arid regions had naturally severe erosion long before any domestic animals were introduced; one characteristic of arid regions around the world is relatively rapid natural erosion. It is not always easy, even for the expert, to distinguish between normal and accelerated erosion. Irrigation development contributed materially to accelerated erosion in some localities; so did road and other transportation development. The precise role of overgrazing is by no means clear in this general picture.

The low point in conservation use of natural-forage resources seems to have been reached about 30 to 40 years ago, although this varies considerably from locality to locality. There has been some recovery since, although one must avoid overstating this, too. Above all, knowledge of plant growth, of range management, and of livestock management has increased greatly in the past generation. Research by federal agencies and by universities has contributed to this increased knowledge. Effective educational means have aided by carrying the results of the research to the ranchers. Specific improvements have been made on grazing lands. Extensive areas have been reseeded, mostly to introduced species. Water has been developed to permit more uniform utilization of available forage and to reduce trailing over the range. Fencing has brought more positive control over livestock.

Range conservationist Fred G. Renner said, in 1954, that range conditions had improved markedly over the previous quarter-century, and that the livestock population had increased 41 percent (10). But extensive areas of public land are still on the downgrade, larger areas are producing below their present potential level, and the productivity of some has been reduced permanently as a result of past mistreatment (11).

The range-livestock industry is an integral part of the total economy of the arid West. It, irrigation, and dry-land grain production are the major divisions of arid-regions agriculture. In most semiarid regions of the world, extensive use of native forage plants is made by domestic livestock, because the total forage production is so low that the only practical means of harvest is by livestock. The grazing industry in the United States is unique only in the fact that there is a large, high-income, urban market for its products within the same nation and within economical shipping distance.

One cannot leave the range-livestock industry of the western United States without commenting on its cultural, as well as its economic, aspects. Someone has said that the cowboy is America's sole contribution to man's folklore. Perhaps this is too sweeping, but surely cowboys, Indians, range wars, six-shooters, and all the rest are known around the world today. I have suggested that more range wars are fought out annually on television than ever occurred in the whole history of the West. Almost the only cowboy who carries a gun today is the one on television, but the legend dies hard.

Crop Production

Cultivated crop production from unirrigated land is a relative newcomer to the natural-resources utilization scene in the arid western United States. It is impossible in highly arid areas, except along streambeds or channels where water naturally accumulates. But in the extensive semiarid lands of the Great Plains and in more localized spots throughout the mountain and intermountain regions, cultivated crops, particularly wheat, can be grown under dry-land conditions.

An annual rainfall of perhaps 14 to 16 inches (350 to 400 millimeters) in northeastern Montana, and its equivalent (allowing for higher evaporation rates) elsewhere, is about the lower limit for continued successful production of crops that grow during the summer. Along the Pacific Coast, where the Mediterranean climate brings winter moisture and temperatures high enough for cool-season crops, some crops can be grown in the winter in some areas of less precipitation. Given the great climatic variability of the arid West, many localities offer physical conditions that allow the production of good crops in some years, but the average over a long period is too low for successful farming.

The plowing of native sod or other vegetative cover types anywhere in the semiarid regions in order to grow dry-land crops was an ecologic change comparable in microcosm to a volcanic eruption. A natural equilibrium of water penetration, microbiologic activity, nitrogen cycle, and other relationships was suddenly and severely disrupted. In numerous cases, there followed severe erosion by wind or water or both. This situation was aggravated by the usually high wind speed in much of the Great Plains, especially during winter and early spring.

The combination of extended drought or subnormal annual precipitation, unwise plowing of soils that were too sandy or otherwise unsuited for continuous crop production, low incomes to wheat farmers, which made soil conservation measures more costly than they could finance, and a general ignorance of the hazards of wind erosion and of measures to control it, all combined to produce a Dust Bowl in much of the Great Plains in the early 1930's *(12–14)*. Unusually severe windstorms carried some of the finest soil material in the air as far as the Atlantic seaboard, and even out to sea, and attracted nationwide attention. The extent of the soil damage from wind erosion was variable each year from locality to locality, and even from field to field. Nearly 15 million acres (6 million hectares) were seriously damaged in some years, and the total area suffering serious wind damage at any time was surely much higher.

Under the adverse economic conditions of the early 1930's, a substantial proportion of all farmers in most of the Great Plains received some form of public financial assistance or charity. With the return of normal or unusually favorable weather, with higher wheat prices, and with new methods of crop production, which minimize wind damage, soil erosion from wind was brought under much better control during the 1940's. In the 1950's, severe wind damage, though less spectacular than that of the 1930's, occurred again, as drought struck anew.

The basic problem of trying to grow crops on land unsuited for this purpose on a long-term basis is still unsolved. The U.S. Soil Conservation Service *(15)* estimates that nearly 15 million acres (6 million hectares) in cultivated crops on the Great Plains are on land physically unsuited for continued crop production; and M. H. Saunderson *(16)* has estimated that 10 million acres (4 million hectares) in the same region have long-range moisture prospects too poor to justify continuous farming. These estimates compare with a total area of cropland of about 150 million acres (61 million hectares) in this region. Although the greatest attention has been directed at the Great Plains, the problem in many other areas is equally serious but not on as large a scale. In addition to losses of soil materials through actual erosion, this type of farming often has led to serious loss of soil fertility.

A great deal of the plowing of grasslands and other natural areas was a serious mistake, from the point of view of the settler who ultimately failed, as well as from the point of view of society, which saw some valuable resources destroyed or downgraded in this way. Such plowing often was done under a serious misconception about the crop-production possibilities of the area. The institutional framework contributed to this error; land was available typically in 160-acre (65-hectare) and other units that were economic, if at all, only for crop production.

Some historians have blamed the Homestead Act for its too-small unit, but railroad-grant land was sold typically in similar units, even when no legal limitation prevented larger units. Settlers simply expected to transplant to the semiarid zones the farm types and sizes that had proved to be successful in the humid areas to the east. In this, they were no more mistaken than the political scientists and businessmen who attempted a similar transplant of government and business structure. The planting of dry-land areas was undertaken in a time of horse-drawn machinery, moldboard plows, binders, and stationary threshers. A technologic revolution in farm energy and machinery has drastically changed the whole man-resources relationship, further complicating the maladjustment begun by inappropriate-sized units on poorly adapted land.

Although these deficiencies in the use of dry-land crop areas are now obvious in the wisdom of hindsight, the picture is not complete without a description of the productivity and output so obtained. Wheat is the predominant crop on these dry lands. There is no major crop in the United States for which labor inputs have declined more than wheat, or for which the competitive market price would be lower, compared with conditions some decades ago. This excess itself has resulted in a tremendous expense to the federal government.

The American embarrassment is crop surplus, not crop scarcity, and wheat is one of the major surplus crops. We have in storage vast quantities of wheat that we do not want, cannot sell abroad at free market prices, and cannot even sell or give away at heavily subsidized prices. It is often pointed out, accurately, that many countries in the world would be delighted to have such generous wheat-production capacity and that, if we must choose, it is better to have a wheat surplus than a wheat deficit. But these are unreal alternatives; our real choices are different. Our problem is to reduce wheat production to a level that is more in line with domestic and commercial export needs, and to achieve this reduction in a manner politically and economically acceptable to wheatgrowers and to the nation.

Plant Introductions

Plant introductions, purposeful or unintentional, of new species have been a factor in man's use of the arid West. Many of the common cultivated farm crops in the West today are importations from other countries, most of them from other arid regions of the world. Even these original importations have undergone significant changes —by crop breeding—to become better adapted to commercial agriculture in this region. Corn was native to North America, but it has been modified materially by breeding. Both pasture and range grasses have been introduced.

These deliberate introductions of cultivated and grass crops have been beneficial. At the same time, various undesirable plants often were introduced, usually unintentionally and often without realization of the fact at the time. Russian thistle (*Salsola kali*), halogeton (*Halogeton glomeratus*), and many other weeds now compete with the desired crops and grasses. The introduction of such plants often is lost in obscurity, but they have spread in numerous ways as man, especially the white man, extended his activities. Yet these introduced weeds of the arid West are, in general, no more serious than introduced weeds in the humid areas.

Transportation in the West

Transportation facilities are absolutely critical in an arid-region culture and economy that is part of a larger national culture and economy. Perhaps the most productive of all conceivable uses of land and other natural resources is for transportation purposes, at least up to a level where a minimum adequacy of transportation is provided.

But transportation facilities have not been without their price in real resources terms. A major factor leading to accelerated water erosion in many localities of the arid and semiarid zones has been the road; hooves and wheels broke sod or soil material crust that had been highly resistant to erosion, provided a local collecting trough for runoff, and in time led to serious gullying. This has been especially serious in many valleys that are filled with soft erodible alluvium, as well as on rolling plains and in mountain meadows. In

many parts of New Mexico, Colorado, Utah, and Nevada, I have
found traces of old roads, each moved higher up the valley to escape
the encroaching deep gully that was largely started by the first such
road. As recently as 1950, seismograph exploration crews exploring
for oil and gas were creating serious erosion problems with their
trucks and other vehicles on the public lands in New Mexico,
Wyoming, and Montana.

Forestry Practices

Timber harvest cannot be a major activity in truly arid areas, because commercial timber does not grow there. However, in the
mountain "islands" of the arid West and along the Pacific Coast, extensive natural forest areas are found, and they have been harvested
(in considerable part) in ways that are generally similar to timber
harvest in the eastern humid areas. The West escaped the worst
kind of forest exploitation, such as had been prevalent in the East
and South, largely because lumbering occurred later when techniques
for better forestry were further developed, and old-growth timber
was coming to have greater value and, hence, could be conserved
more profitably.

Still, it is not difficult to be critical of much of the forestry practiced in the West, especially on private lands. But one should not
leave the forestry field without recognizing the many advances that
have occurred. In the past generation, forest landowners have developed new attitudes and new skills for sustained-yield forest management. Professional foresters, particularly those in the U.S. Forest
Service, long decried the wasteful and destructive management practices of the forest industry. But in the most recent appraisal of the
forest situation in the United States, the Forest Service concluded
that, by and large, the larger private forest operations were conducted
as well, with as much attention to conservation and to sustained-yield
management, as were the federal forests. All is not perfection, but
improvement has been great, especially since World War II.

Cities in Arid Areas

Oasis living has always involved relatively large groups of people
within short distances. City-building is one of man's oldest activities

in the arid western United States, but it has been accelerated enormously in the past generation.

Extensive cities constitute a major change in the microenvironment, in both humid and arid regions. The extensive impervious surfaces resulting from paved streets and tight roofs greatly accelerate the runoff of rain water, which may mean destructive floods and sometimes in arid regions means a reduction in total infiltration to ground-water levels. The same impervious surfaces, often heat-reflecting to a major degree, along with some actual heat dissipation from houses, are likely to result in higher air temperatures in and around cities than in the surrounding environs. Above all, cities mean extensive air pollution. In these and other ways, they tend to damage to a greater or lesser degree their own microclimates and microenvironments.

In arid regions, the greatest impact of concentrated population on the total environment may be in the water demands that the city and its activities set up. Some of this water is for direct consumption, more is often process water of various kinds, and usually still more is waste-disposal water. For example, arid areas, with few exceptions, use water to dilute and to carry waste. In this respect, as in so many others, technology and culture from humid areas have been carried unmodified into the arid areas. But arid regions in the Southwest may well be limited in their total economic growth unless they can find drastically different water-use technologies or can import truly massive quantities of water from distant regions that have a surplus.

In another generation, all available water and all the most suitable land areas near the present larger cities of the West will be taken over completely by these cities, to the exclusion of agriculture. Agriculture will disappear largely or completely from Arizona's Salt River Valley, and around Tucson, along the middle Rio Grande in New Mexico, along most of the Rocky Mountain front north of Denver, from the Salt Lake Valley, from all of southern California south of the Tehachapis (except in the Imperial Valley), and from the Santa Clara Valley (17).

These massive conversions from agriculture to urban land and water use will have major social, as well as economic, consequences. In the past, cities in the arid regions of the United States have sought to capitalize on their attractive climate, as well as to be efficient loci for economic activity, but serious question well may be raised regarding their future attractiveness if recent trends continue much further. Cities in arid zones can get as traffic-congested, as inefficient, and as smelly as cities in humid zones.

Amenity Resources

Amenity resources, particularly climate and outdoor environment, have long been among the major assets of the arid West. People wish to live where they find life enjoyable, as well as where they can make a living. As national income standards have risen, more and more people reside where they wish, and industrial and economic activity has increasingly followed a labor supply. The amenity resources account mainly for the relatively large population growth of Florida, California, and Arizona since World War II. Much modern industry is not as closely bound to sources of raw materials as was industry a generation ago; a skilled labor force is now more of an attraction than it once was.

Such resources have always had, and will have in the future, two additional effects. They have attracted and will attract retired and semiretired people. As average per-capita income rises, and as retirement arrangements of many kinds provide modest, but adequate, incomes for retired people, a proportionately much larger population will be able and willing to go where conditions of life are the most pleasant. Too, the amenity resources have always attracted large numbers of people for seasonal recreation. The national parks and other scenic wonders of the West have drawn them in ever-increasing numbers. Their economic impact is great.

One can only wonder about the future attractiveness of these natural assets. On the one hand, the national social and economic trends toward more population, higher real incomes per capita, more leisure, and more ability and willingness to travel will almost certainly dispose vastly more people to enjoy these resources—for year-round living, for retirement, or for seasonal recreation. On the other hand, increasing exploitation of these resources may destroy the very qualities that made them attractive in the first place.

Hordes of people congregated in small congested parts of the national parks may well reduce these to something no more attractive than a more mediocre, but less crowded, local park back home.

Many friends of national parks have become increasingly disturbed over the effect on the environment of the constantly increasing number of visitors to national parks, and over national park administration that encourages this type of mass-recreation activity. Some segments of the arid-zone business and political life have been as intent on short-run exploitation of the amenity resources as the gold miners ever were on the finding and exhausting of placer gold deposits. How far can, must, or should a region look to its longer-run future, even at the possible expense of short-run profit?

Pollution

Pollution of water, air, and soil is a universal problem of societies with large populations and intense modern economic activity. But it may have peculiar features in the arid zones. Man has always used running water to carry away his wastes, and this is one of the most important economic functions of water. He has always burned fuel to provide for his own comfort and to generate energy, letting unburned wastes be discharged into the atmosphere. And he has always dumped his wastes on the ground, letting them be decomposed or leached away as natural processes dictated. Until perhaps a generation ago, a really serious pollution problem seldom arose, partly because the volumes concerned were not large.

The general pollution problem has special aspects in arid zones. In some respects, water pollution is less serious. Beautiful, free-flowing, pure streams have never been a major part of their assets, as they have been in humid zones. Consequently, however, the arid zones simply cannot "solve" their problem by floating pollution downstream to other areas; they lack the water supply required to do so. People in the arid zones will be forced by the very scarcity of water to seek solutions that consume less water. This may be achieved by actually using less water or by reusing it more generally.

Air pollution also may be more serious in arid zones, in part because the pure clear air has been a traditional resource of the arid West. The Los Angeles smog has attracted international comment, perhaps more than the facts warrant, but it surely is a serious irritant to pleasant living.

Chemical pollution of the soil in arid regions thus far has been confined largely to irrigated areas. The spraying of fruit trees to control codling moth and other pests has long been a source of chemical pollution in localized areas. The irrigated areas, in common with crop areas in humid regions, have experienced a more diversified and larger pollution in recent years. As yet, however, man-applied pollutants have probably been less serious than the chemical accumulations from the irrigation water itself. Use of insecticides and herbicides is spreading into dry-land agricultural areas in the Great Plains and elsewhere. In time, soil pollution there may become even more serious than in irrigated areas, because limited rainfall cannot provide a means of leaching chemicals to the lower-lying soil strata or into streams.

As one attempts to survey the use of resources in the arid zones, the pollution problem is the one where it is the hardest to relieve gloom by pointing to offsetting gains. Pollution may have been a necessary side effect of desirable change, although one is certainly justified in challenging its necessity. The evils and the dangers of pollution somehow must be coped with, in ways that are not now employed or are not yet clearly evident, if future large-scale adverse effects are to be avoided or decreased. This is perhaps the most challenging problem that faces the arid West today.

Resources Ownership and Tenure

Some of the most enduring and important changes that Europeans brought to the arid United States lie in resources ownership and tenure. The right to own land or other resources, including the right to sell, bequeath, use as one chooses, and the like, is essentially a relationship of man to man. It is true that ownership and tenure involve a relationship of man to the resource concerned; but this relationship takes meaning and force chiefly as it enables one person to exclude or limit use of the same resource by others. Fee simple ownership is so universal in the United States that we sometimes overlook the fact that many other man-to-man relationships exist for land, both in other countries today and in our own country at an earlier time.

The American Indian had a concept of landownership and tenure that was drastically different from ours. The individual rarely, if ever, had exclusive permanent possession of specific tracts of land, with the power to keep all others off his property. Where agriculture was practiced, tracts were assigned to individuals, but only for as long as they were used.

The explorers, trappers, miners, and early stockmen simply moved across the land, taking from it such of its products as they wanted or were able to use economically, without specific legal authority, usually without concern on their part about the need for such legal authority. Existing laws often did not forbid their actions but simply were silent about them, because the possibility of such use was not recognized. In the first half of the 19th century, for instance, there was no law that regulated hunting and trapping on the lands west of the Mississippi River. When the gold miners first began to take gold where they could find it, there was no legislation to preclude such action.

Conflict was almost constant among the various user-groups. Fur-trading companies had their own trappers and were in the severest rivalry among themselves. One outcome was the development of local law, or extra-law, by the users concerned. Gold miners in California instituted local mining laws 20 years before a federal mining law was passed. Cattlemen in the northern Plains established their own rules for roundups and the like. This system may be criticized because it was instituted by the strongest and enforced by them for their own benefit; but it may well have been better than the absence of any semblance of law. It arose in large part out of the delays and lack of understanding of more remote, but more legal, lawmakers. And it was transitory; either it was swept away by major changes in landownership and use under federal law, or else it was embodied in federal or state legislation. The latter was largely the case with both mining and water rights.

Disposal of Public Lands

The story of acquisition, disposal, reservation, and management of the federal lands of the United States, and of the West in particular, has been told well many times (18–25). When this nation acquired the first of these areas in the West, the federal government had already begun disposition of its earlier holdings east of the Mississippi River. The dominant philosophy in the first half of the 19th century, and for some time thereafter, was the rapid disposal of public land to private ownership.

The process was headlong, even heedless. No real attempt ever was made to classify the land or to determine whether it was suitable for the purposes sought and in the units available. Through it, about two-thirds of the federal land was disposed of, directly to individuals or first to grantees who mostly sold it to individuals. In the arid zones, the percentage disposed of was lower, half or less. Much of the arid region was not attractive for private ownership even under the relatively generous terms available. Ranchers and others could often use public lands without the investment in, and cost of owning, them.

This land-disposal process has been criticized widely by historians and land economists. There was considerable fraud and nearly universal speculation. Yet the lands had been surveyed so that land identification was firm and clear in nearly all instances. Land records were such that each owner had, or could establish, a clear legal title to his land, and the result was widespread landownership, in units roughly appropriate to the technologic farming possibilities of the day. By these rough tests, the United States experience with land colonization and settlement was one that a major part of the world today would be delighted to have. In many localities, and even states, the average size of land-disposal units was too small for good farm operation. Substantial consolidation of landholdings was necessary.

The federal land-disposal system was designed to provide land for farming, though it had deficiencies even for this purpose. The deficiencies were greater for land for mineral production and for land for forestry. I have noted that no method existed for acquisition of federal land for mining at the time of the California gold rush and for many years thereafter, and that the miners themselves devised a system of local law, which was taken almost unmodified into federal law some years later. This law has proved to be notably inflexible, with severe resistance to any change, in spite of wholesale misuse. Modest reforms were made in 1955.

The land-disposal system was ill-adapted to making land available for commercial sustained-yield forestry. It is true that there was little desire for this kind of forestry and little economic incentive for it during the period of wholesale land disposal. Much timber was cut in trespass from the public lands, more in the Great Lakes states than in the arid West. The timber operators who sought ownership of the land from which they expected to harvest trees often had to resort to subterfuge—and even fraud—to acquire land in the acreage and at the prices they considered necessary.

Dissatisfaction with this indiscriminate disposal of land began to arise, first among the intellectuals of the day, later in a substantial segment of the electorate. The ultimate result was permanent reservation of some land in public ownership for public use. National parks, national monuments, national forests, national grasslands, grazing districts, wildlife refuges, and other miscellaneous types of permanent federal land reservations, each for defined purposes, have been established in the intervening years. At present, nearly half of all the land within the arid zones, as they are defined in this book, remains in federal ownership.

Although the American economy and culture are an intricate mixture of public and private effort in nearly every sphere, nowhere is this more evident than in the use of the federal lands. Their management in the early years consisted of little more than fire and trespass control. As the demand for use of the land and its products has risen, the intensity of management has increased greatly. Today, about $300 million is expended annually on these lands, with gross revenues of equal or greater size.

Diverse social trends were manifested in this century and a half of land history in the arid West. In this span of time, relatively brief by the measure of human history, half of the land area of the nation came into possession, in a proprietary sense, of a national government; half of that was disposed of to a few million individual claimants, and the necessary foundation was laid for a great economic growth based on natural resources. Few other historical processes possess the same drama, at least to me. There was a century of wholesale appropriation to private ownership of public property; this was the era of "get yours while the getting is good."

Although land disposal reached a large number of people, a larger number were not its beneficiaries because they lacked even the minimum capital required, because they were unable or unwilling to take the risks and hardships involved, or simply because they were in the wrong part of the country. One might well have expected this kind of disposal of natural resources to create a privileged class and a disadvantaged one, to widen greatly the spread between the "haves" and the "have-nots," and to work against political and social equality.

It can well be argued that a different land-disposal process in Latin America had these very effects. There is widespread dissatisfaction in Latin America itself with a relatively few large *haciendas* on the one hand, and with multitudinous very small *minifundia* on the other, and with the whole political, social, and economic structure based on this landownership pattern. The differences in present-day owner-ship patterns between the United States and Latin America trace directly back to their policies in land disposal.

But the land-disposal process of the United States must be seen and evaluated in the context of the total economic growth of the nation during the same era. The national economy was growing and industrializing, the nation was urbanizing rapidly, and out of this came economic opportunity not associated with landownership and occupancy. Neither economic nor social nor political opportunity or position depended on landownership. On the contrary, during this whole era, the city-dwellers generally advanced more rapidly than did the farmers, and there was a steady stream of migration from farm to city. Had the nonfarm economy developed more slowly, or been stagnant, the ownership of land would have assumed greater significance, and conceivably an undesirable concentration of landownership might have arisen.

The rise of federal landownership and management during this same era actually increased resources availability to those who could not own or preferred not to own land. This has been very important with regard to recreation use of federal lands; millions of people have the opportunity each year to enjoy one or more of the federal areas. It also is of some importance to the rancher whose livestock graze on public land and to the small timber operator who depends on federal timber for his operations.

A Verdict?

Where does the balance lie? I have explored briefly, and with a broad treatment, some of the specific relationships of man to his environment in the arid western United States. What is the final verdict on his record? At the beginning of this chapter, I stressed the need and the difficulty of summing or aggregating dissimilar facts into some kind of a net balance. After this exploration of some of the specifics, it is apparent that the problem is, if anything, more difficult than I suggested then. But it is also true that the rendering of a net balance or net judgment is an unavoidable matter, at least for the population as a whole. Man, as a responsible animal, simply cannot escape consideration of his own future.

The arid West is like a well-lived-in house. Such a house exhibits many signs of wear and tear; the paint may be chipped in places; the rug and furniture are worn. Such signs often are more evident to the stranger than to the resident. But such a house is also full of memories of all the events that go to make up a family history; it has performed a real function over the years; and the family it has housed is a social unit of great strength and value.

The arid West clearly shows some signs of wear and tear. Its soils have been eroded, severely in some places. Its ground-water resources have been depleted in many areas; its forests have been cut in part, not always under the best of practices; its air has been polluted, especially over its larger cities; and other evidences of wear and tear exist. As in the case of the house, these signs perhaps are more apparent to the stranger than to the resident who has come to take them for granted. But modern man also has built in the arid West a large and highly productive economy, with high material well-being for its members and a complex but powerful social structure.

More important than the physical wealth is the social structure, with its families, schools, research institutions, churches, business organizations, and government. In these are the real strength of the society. No one can argue seriously that the individuals in the arid West today are less well off than were its inhabitants 50, 100, or more years ago; or that the social structure existing today is less capable of carrying out group activities than was that of the earlier times. We have obviously created great economic strength, and this would not be possible without a social organization to match it. The hazard, if hazard there be, lies in the future; have we planted the seeds for our own destruction? Have we set in motion processes that, carried to their inevitable conclusion, will destroy the very things we have built?

A judgment on such broad but necessarily imprecise questions must be as much a statement of faith, an exercise of personal beliefs and standards, as an objective and scientific evaluation. But, throwing all scholarly restraints to the wind, let me summarize in a single sentence: Problems, *Yes*; disaster, *No*, if we exercise reasonable thought and care. This assumes that man in the arid West can and will exercise intelligence and diligence to meet emerging problems. He does not have to be perfect in his foresight and ingenuity to meet them.

Acknowledgments: In the preparation of this chapter, helpful suggestions were received from Homer Aschmann, University of California, Riverside; Blair Bolles, Fairbanks, Morse and Company, Washington, D.C.; Wesley Calef, University of Chicago; Carl F. Kraenzel, University of Montana; Donald W. Meinig, Syracuse University; Donald M. Powell, University of Arizona; Carl O. Sauer, University of California, Berkeley; C. L. Sonnichsen, Texas Western College; Andrew W. Wilson, University of Arizona; and Richard B. Woodbury, University of Arizona.

REFERENCES

1. R. J. Russell, "Dry climates of the United States, II, Frequency of dry and desert years, 1901–1920," *Univ. Calif. (Berkeley) Publ. Geography 5* (5) (1932).
2. A. W. Pond, *The Desert World* (Nelson, New York, 1962), p. 201.
3. C. F. Cooper, "Changes in vegetation structure and growth of southwestern pine forests since white settlement," *Ecol. Monographs 30,* 129–164 (1960).
4. R. E. Huffman, *Irrigation Development and Public Water Policy* (Ronald, New York, 1953).
5. E. A. Ackerman and G. O. G. Löf, *Technology in American Water Development* (Johns Hopkins Press, Baltimore, Md., 1959).
6. H. E. Thomas, "Underground sources of water," in *Yearbook Agr., U.S. Dept. Agr.* **1955** (1955).
7. ———, *The Conservation of Ground Water* (McGraw-Hill, New York, 1951).
8. M. Clawson and W. Calhoun, *Long-term Outlook for Western Agriculture—General Trends in Agricultural Land Use, Production and Demand* (U.S. Dept. of Agriculture, Bur. of Agricultural Economics, and U.S. Dept. of the Interior, Bur. of Reclamation, Berkeley, Calif., 1946).
9. U.S. Congress, *The Western Range,* S. Doc. 199, 74th Congr. 2nd sess. (Washington, D.C., 1936).
10. F. G. Renner, "The future of our range resources," *J. Range Management 7,* 55–56 (1954).
11. K. S. Landstrom, *Annual Report of the Bureau of Land Management 1961* (U.S. Dept. of the Interior, Washington, D.C., 1961).

12. J. Muehlbeier, "Land-use problems in the Great Plains," in *Year-book Agr., U.S. Dept. Agr.* **1958** (1958).

13. H. H. Bennett, *Soil Conservation* (McGraw-Hill, New York, 1939), pp. 726–770.

14. Special Presidential Committee, *The Future of the Great Plains* (U.S. Govt. Printing Office, Washington, D.C., 1936).

15. Soil Conservation Service, "Facts about wind erosion and duststorms on the Great Plains," *U.S. Dept. Agr. Leaflet 394* (1955).

16. M. H. Saunderson, "Range problems of marginal farmlands," *J. Range Management* **5**, 13–15 (1952).

17. M. Clawson, "Changing patterns of land use in the West," in *Resource Development: Frontiers for Research*, F. S. Pollak, Ed. (Univ. of Colorado Press, Boulder, 1960).

18. ———, *Uncle Sam's Acres* (Dodd, Mead, New York, 1951).

19. ——— and B. Held, *The Federal Lands: Their Use and Management* (Johns Hopkins Press, Baltimore, Md., 1957).

20. S. T. Dana, *Forest and Range Policy—Its Development in the United States* (McGraw-Hill, New York, 1956).

21. ——— and M. Krueger, *California Lands—Ownership, Use, and Management* (American Forestry Assoc., Washington, D.C., 1958).

22. B. H. Hibbard, *A History of Public Land Policies* (Macmillan, New York, 1924).

23. J. Ise, *The United States Forest Policy* (Yale Univ. Press, New Haven, Conn., 1920).

24. ———, *Our National Park Policy—a Critical History* (Johns Hopkins Press, Baltimore, Md., 1961).

25. E. L. Peffer, *The Closing of the Public Domain* (Stanford Univ. Press, Stanford, Calif., 1951).

16

Challenge of the Future

Peter C. Duisberg

Any attempt to forecast the development of the arid and semiarid regions of the United States is very difficult. Some of the regions are in the midst of a period of fundamental and rapid change. Such vital resources as water are in limited supply; much depends on how they are managed and controlled and on the impact of advances in technology. Finally, the arid regions are the least-developed part of the nation and will be greatly affected by national trends.

Nevertheless, forecasts such as those cited in Chapter 13 have been made for the remainder of the century. They are based largely on assumptions that population and economic growth trends of the past 20 years will continue—that the arid regions, which now contain only one-eighth of the national population, will continue to grow at a more rapid rate than the nation as a whole. These are reasonable assumptions, except that they do not sufficiently take into account the possible limiting effect of scarce resources or the loss of some of the recent artificial stimuli, such as defense expenditures. They assume that the trend toward urbanization and industrialization will accelerate and that the large regional centers (for example, the metropolitan areas of southern California; Phoenix and Tucson, Arizona; Albuquerque, New Mexico; El Paso, Texas; and Denver, Colorado) will have the economic and political power to go to great extremes and expense to acquire sufficient resources. In some instances, the result will be an inhibiting of the potential of the less-developed hinterland.

According to the predictions, progress will be extremely irregular. Some areas may become depressed, and others may experience spectacular expansion. Half of the total population growth is expected to be concentrated in about 2 percent of the area—in southern California. On the other hand, only about 7 percent of the growth is foreseen for the two-fifths of the total area in the northern mountain and plains states.

Many people believe that even the urban areas will not achieve the predicted growth. They point out that ground water and minerals are being depleted rapidly and that soil erosion is increasing. These events may result in economic loss and abandonment in many localities, with a consequent adverse effect on the urban centers that depend, to a large extent, on trade conditions in the surrounding areas. They also suggest that the present period of prosperity has been relatively short and depends, to a considerable extent, on defense installations and defense industry. Authors like Paul Sears (1) and Fairfield Osborn (2) have shown that in the long run man has created much more desert than he has reclaimed.

Some people think that science and technology will, in time, provide solutions to all problems that pertain to resources. Others believe that the need is not so much for increased scientific and technical knowledge as for better social management, control of resources, and use of present knowledge.

Obviously, the future of the arid regions cannot be predicted with any certainty. It might vary within wide limits, depending on the extent of national growth, on national policies, and on the vision shown within the region in planning for the future and in meeting resources problems.

Impact of the Nation

Typical predictions of national and regional growth are illustrated in Fig. 1. Nationally, it is considered reasonable to expect population to double, national income to increase fivefold, and the use of, or demand for, water to triple during the remainder of this century. The index of industrial activity is expected to increase at least 5 times by the year 2000. Research and development expenditures increased 2.5 times between 1953 and 1960 and are expected to triple during the 1960's.

Agricultural production is expected to keep pace through technologic advances and shifts in land use (3). If the anticipated national growth occurs, and if people in the arid regions show wisdom in developing the resulting opportunities, the West may reach economic and cultural equality with the humid areas.

The Southwest and the mountain West seem to have been strongly influenced by national decisions to locate defense installations there. Aridity itself has become an asset. The dry climate, cloudless skies, and vast, uninhabited spaces are valuable for military bases. The profound impact of this on the regions is described in Chapter 13 in some detail. States like Arizona and New Mexico have gained an

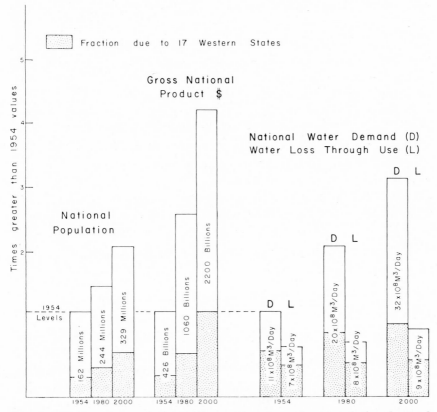

Fig. 1. National population, gross national product, and the demand for, and use of, water are projected to the year 2000, with the fraction expected for the 17 western states indicated by the stippled portions. Predictions are based on studies published in 1960 by the U.S. Senate Select Committee on National Water Resources, *Population Projections and Economic Assumptions,* Comm. Print 5, and *Water Supply and Demand,* Comm. Print 32 (Washington, D.C., 1960).

entirely new outlook. The balance of political power and leadership in such states is rapidly shifting to the growing urban areas and away from the traditional farm, ranch, and mining interests.

On the other hand, too much of this prosperity is still based on the fragile foundation of defense spending. Even southern California, the one western area that has become highly industrialized, remains heavily dependent on its industrial defense contracts, which amount to more than $5 billion annually. These contracts are double those of any other state in the nation and are worth more than the total value of all California agricultural and mineral production (4).

There is little likelihood that cutbacks in defense spending will be abrupt. The challenge for the rapidly growing regions is to achieve economic alternatives. The problem is more easily recognized than resolved. However, the approach of El Paso, Texas, is typical. In recent years, seven organizations have been formed there to promote industrial and economic development. Gradually, with experience, they are having increasing success.

Fortunately the recent defense program has within it the seeds of some alternatives. It has been the chief sponsor of the aerospace, nuclear-energy, and electronics industries, all of which have become strongly established in the arid areas. These are among the most promising nonmilitary pursuits for the future. In addition, many intelligent and articulate scientists and technicians have found employment in the arid regions and have helped to formulate more progressive and receptive public attitudes toward science and technologic change. They also provide trained talent for new industries. Another related advance has been the improvement of many of the regional universities and the expansion of their research programs. Perhaps, as Carl Kraenzel has pointed out, one of the most discouraging aspects for the future of the Great Plains is the deficiency in universities and cultural centers (5).

A careful study of the unplanned but crucial effect of the defense program on parts of the arid regions should be made. If factors involved in regional change are identified, it may be possible to devise ways to obtain considerably more benefit from this program.

Among the most important challenges to the arid regions for the future are (i) the assurance of an adequate water supply; (ii) the development of means for overcoming the problem of water and air pollution, and (iii) the prevention of deterioration of the natural setting and ethnic distinctiveness of the region. Besides these, the northern Mountain States and the semiarid Great Plains present unique problems.

Water Supply

A great fear in any locality is that the water supply will be inadequate to support future growth. Information and opinions are so contradictory and confused that undoubtedly many potential new industries have already been discouraged from locating in the arid regions. This is understandable in view of the publicity that is given to conflicts, such as the Colorado River dispute between Arizona and California, which was recently decided in the U.S. Supreme Court after about 40 years of controversy. In addition, periodic water shortages occur in most of the rivers of the West, and groundwater reserves are being depleted in many places.

It is seldom realized that the amount of water withdrawn from streams and wells in the arid and semiarid regions to support 25 million people is approximately the same as the amount that supports more than 150 million people in the remainder of the nation. The difference is that the humid areas depend on rain for agriculture, and the water is used primarily for domestic and industrial purposes. In the arid areas, more than 90 percent of the water is used for irrigation agriculture.

Studies by Nathaniel Wollman (6) and Allan Kneese (7) indicate that the value of water in industry in the West may average 70 times its value in agriculture and provide 10 times the employment. This is explained in more detail in Chapter 13. As early as 1955, Louis Koenig made the then dramatic statement that "the use of irrigation in the arid lands [of the United States] of the 20th century is not an appropriate use of that valuable resource, water . . . ." (8, p. 328). It is certainly true that the concept of irrigation as the most logical use of water in arid areas has been universally accepted and, until recently, rarely questioned.

Although the people engaged in agriculture might strongly oppose systematic conversion of any part of their water rights to industrial and other nonagricultural uses, such conversion has occurred as cities have encroached on farmlands, giving farmers large profits for their land and, sometimes, for their water rights. Theoretically, the economic advantage that favors industry is so great that water could be leased on an annual basis for more than most farmers earn from their crops.

Numerous serious difficulties, which vary with local and regional conditions, remain to be overcome, but they are almost all social rather than physical. The whole concept of water law will have to be reexamined in the light of higher economic uses of water. Surface and ground waters will have to be regulated as a unit.

Nevertheless, the potential advantages of developing practical means for reallocation of some of the water now being used in irrigation are so great that this may be the most important possibility for resolving the western water problems of the next generation. If only 1 million acre feet (1.2 billion cubic meters) of the approximately 90 million acre feet (111 billion cubic meters) of water now being used for irrigation in the West could be transferred to industrial uses, the value of the increased production would almost equal the present $3-billion total value of irrigated crops. Thus, only a small portion of agriculture would have to be replaced, and the individual farmers who would retire land and transfer water rights would be well compensated. The remaining farmers would have increased markets and services as new population and industry entered the area.

In places where many farmers now face eventual ruin because of declining water tables, such reallocation of water could be a salvation. Sufficient farmland might be taken out of production to reestablish a satisfactory balance between water use and recharge.

Although the reallocation of water offers hope of a rather general solution to many problems of water supply, there is little reason to believe that the public understands the importance of this opportunity or that it is yet willing to insist on adequate water law or on policies to decrease water waste.

Scientific and Engineering Alternatives

Strangely enough, one of the chief obstacles to facing the social, political, and legal aspects of water supply is the common belief that science and technology will provide dramatic solutions. Technology alone has not produced stability in the arid regions in the past; in fact, failure to understand and control the social implications of change often has led to much human and physical waste and actual ruin. The most recent instance is the deep-well pump. At first, it appeared to be a tremendous blessing because it permitted the expansion of irrigation agriculture. It soon developed into a Pandora's box and, in many areas, seems to be leading toward depletion of ground water and eventual abandonment of towns and farms. Nevertheless, if present scientific and engineering knowledge were combined with an adequate policy of management, control, and distribution, most of the problems of water supply could be solved.

In 1963, Secretary of the Interior Stewart L. Udall pointed out the inefficiency of the present use of Colorado River water in Arizona, California, New Mexico, and Mexico. He proposed that the large water projects in this area be integrated with new saline-water conversion plants on a regional basis. In Udall's words, the plan envisions erasure of "the outmoded concept limited by state lines and concentrates on meeting the total water needs of a region" (9) .

Opportunities to Save Water

In an analysis of the water situation in southern California, Jack Hirschliefer and his colleagues have concluded that an increase of 60 percent in urban population (more than 5 million) would be possible merely through changes in pricing policy, limited conservation measures, and some reallocation of the present supply (10) .

In the future, much more attention may be given to efficient use of water in cities. Urban per-capita consumption is generally high, averaging from about 150 gallons (568 liters) per day in most arid urban centers to 250 gallons (946 liters) per day in cities like Salt Lake City and Phoenix. Most of the cities actually encourage wasteful consumption through lower unit rates for high levels of use and, during the summer, for lawn watering. The watering of vegetation represents as much as 40 percent of the annual consumption in some cities, for example, El Paso.

Concepts about lawns in arid areas may undergo drastic revision. Arrangements of low-water–consuming native plants and colored gravel and stones are already in use, and plastic lawns are a possibility. The trend in the more affluent areas toward private swimming pools and artificial lakes in the desert is expected to continue.

With strict regulation, however, water losses could be cut drastically by recirculation and plastic covers.

There are promising possibilities for reuse of industrial and municipal water and for substitution of brackish or sea water for industrial and urban uses. For instance, one of the steel companies established a mill at Fontana, California, by an engineering design that made it possible to recycle water many times; water demand was cut to about 2 percent of the amount considered normal for the industry. The city of Amarillo, Texas, obtained a new oil refinery by offering its treated sewage waters for this purpose (11). Corrosion-resistant alloys, cathodic protection through the use of renewable magnesium metal anodes, strong polyethylene and polyvinyl chloride pipes, and bituminous coatings for large steel pipes have increased the possibilities for the direct use of sea and other salty waters. These waters already are being consumed extensively in industry for cooling and where quality is of less importance; their use may be required in many areas in the future (12).

Irrigation Prospects

Losses of water in irrigation agriculture are great. They include about 20 million acre feet (25 billion cubic meters) of water from canal-conveyance losses and 30 million acre feet (37 billion cubic meters) from inefficiencies. Many of these losses result from insufficient economic incentives. The price is too low to encourage efficient distribution and application, and the water is not always accurately measured.

It now seems to be clear that, no matter how efficient irrigation agriculture becomes, it will never be able to approach the values that are attainable through use of the same water for industry. However, there will be many technologic improvements, some of which may lessen water requirements appreciably. Soil evaporation and transpiration losses may be cut sharply.

Black polyethylene plastic strips and sheets, which are already being tested or applied to crops, probably can reduce soil evaporation and control weeds and soil temperature (13). Chemicals that retard evaporation, such as hexadecanol, and bituminous and other types of soil sealants also may prove to be practical in the reduction of evaporation. Open ditches will be replaced increasingly by sub-

A high-capacity spray boom has been devised by the U.S. Water Conservation Laboratory, Tempe, Arizona, to spread low-cost waterproofing material on soil. Runoff from each square yard (0.836 square meter) of treated soil amounts to 56 gallons (212 liters) for each 10 inches (254 millimeters) of rainfall. (Courtesy U.S. Department of Agriculture)

surface pipes, and methods will be devised for applying water from below the surface. Experiments are now in progress in this field at Texas Technological College, at the U.S. Water Conservation Laboratory in Tempe, Arizona, and at the University of Arizona Institute of Water Utilization. Plants that use water efficiently will be bred, and the search for crops, such as canaigre (*Rumex hymenosepalus*), with low irrigation requirements will continue.

Other research is concerned with cutting transpiration loss. Work along these lines is being conducted at the University of Illinois. Chemicals that retard evaporation are applied to the soil, from which they may be absorbed by plants, with a resulting reduction of transpiration. Possibilities for expanded use and development of the techniques of artificial recharge and for the increase of runoff through the management of the plant and snow cover of watersheds are in prospect. A more limited possibility would be the use of sea water for the irrigation of relatively salt-tolerant plants. Salt concentrations on sand can be kept to moderate levels by frequent irrigation, and soluble fertilizers might be used. Studies in this field have been described by Hugo and Elizabeth Boyko (14).

Lloyd Myers, of the U.S. Water Conservation Laboratory, has estimated that, of the losses connected with the collection and management of water for irrigation (owing to useless water-wasting plants, evaporation on lakes and reservoirs, and losses in conveyance in canals and on the farm), 10 million acre feet (12.3 billion cubic meters) of water may eventually be recoverable through research and technology (13). The overdraft in pumping for irrigation in the High Plains of Texas, Arizona, and the San Joaquin Valley of California, to mention only three areas, equals this total.

New Sources

Among the possible new sources of water, weather modification may yet offer limited possibilities. It does not appear to be promising in strictly arid areas, although in some of the high-mountain humid "islands," which provide much of the water supply for parts of the region, favorable conditions exist. Unfortunately, there would be many legal and technical difficulties, and these areas are not those with the greatest need.

The costs of desalinization have been too high thus far for any but very specialized high-valued types of irrigation. In many areas, desalinization may be a practical solution for municipal and industrial water. The best possibilities for large-scale desalinization exist in the coastal areas of Texas and southern California. If integrated regional approaches to the problem of water supply, such as those suggested by Udall, eventually are adopted, some water now being used on the coasts may be released for areas of greater need.

Southern California, however, already is moving to solve its water problem for the remainder of the century through the California water plan. The expectation is that 22 million acre feet (27.1 billion cubic meters) of water per year would ultimately be delivered by aqueduct from comparatively humid northern California to the drier areas in the south (15).

The possibilities for even larger-scale diversions are considerable. These, however, will raise difficult political, as well as technical and economic, questions. Past experience leads to the belief that 30 years or more may pass before projects of major regional significance become operational. A major domestic source of water for diversion might be the Pacific Northwest, which has an estimated surplus of 240 million acre feet (296 billion cubic meters) of water. In addition, the adjacent Canadian provinces have large surpluses. One unusual suggestion for diversion has been to transport the water in resistant plastic pipelines under the ocean surface near the Pacific shore.

A major disadvantage of large diversion projects is the necessity of building in terms of estimated long-term demands, even though initial need may be much less. Because future requirements may not occur as estimated, the costs for water delivered during the early years of the venture may be high. J. M. Milliman (*16*) reported that, during the first 15 years of the Colorado River aqueduct, metropolitan Los Angeles, where most of the taxes were collected but comparatively little of the water was used, actually paid about $1200 per acre foot ($1 per cubic meter).

Water for Limited Groups

Technologists probably will devise ways to provide water for small groups of people or to supply small permanent towns in almost any part of the arid or semiarid United States. This accomplishment will permit the planned dispersal of people with fixed incomes, such as pensioners, and of small industries or the maintenance of limited groups with scientific or military assignments.

Variations of the old method of water harvesting by collection of runoff from rooftops, concreted or otherwise artificially sealed rocky slopes, and small watershed areas could have important applicability. Artificial catchment structures already are collecting and storing rainfall for wildlife and livestock. Recent efforts by the U.S. Water Conservation Laboratory have lowered installation costs of such catchments from about $1 to $3 per square yard ($1.10 to $3.30 per square meter) for concrete to about 10 cents per square yard (12 cents per square meter) for polyethylene and cationic asphalt emulsions. Lloyd Myers (*17*) suggests that annual maintenance expenses of 1 cent per square yard (less than 1 cent per square meter) are within reach and that soon it should be possible to collect water in

10-inch (254-millimeter) rainfall areas for 36 cents per 1000 gallons (3785 liters) and for 75 cents where rainfall averages 5 inches (127 millimeters). These prices are lower than many achieved so far by desalinization and, in conjunction with concerted reduction of water waste, could be feasible even now for domestic or industrial use.

There are several unusual possibilities for obtaining water for very small groups of people. Some of these may be by-products of the national space program. For instance, the principle of closed ecologic systems in spaceships, in which fluid losses would be kept to the absolute minimum, could be applied to housing in very dry areas (18). Even the possibility of extracting water with solar heat from volcanic rocks and from hydrated minerals containing hydrogen and oxygen, such as serpentine, might work under special conditions in extremely dry, isolated, and inaccessible places.

Although concern over water shortages is justified, the supply available to the arid areas could support many times the present population if existing knowledge were properly applied on a regional basis.

Organic Water Pollution

The problem of water pollution from wastes as a potential limiting factor in economic growth is directly related to water supply. If the supply is sufficient to permit more industrialization and population, such pollution could become very serious.

The solution appears to be the reduction of the quantity of waste materials. In arid areas, waste water should be considered an asset, and maximum reuse before final disposal should be required. The case of the aforementioned steel company illustrates what can be done.

Nathaniel Wollman has stated that factories can be designed to remove 90 percent of the oxygen-demanding organic pollutants and that efficiencies may approach 97.5 percent by 1980 (19). There is no scientific reason why such treated waters could not be reused for domestic supply, but there is the all-important psychologic reason. Industries that can achieve high values added per unit of water used should be required to practice maximum reuse of waste waters and to dispose of the most harmful pollutants separately. The National

Technical Task Committee on Industrial Wastes reports that many large plants are installing multimillion-dollar treatment systems for separate disposal.

In arid regions, treated waste water also can be an asset to nearby irrigators. The phosphorus and nitrogen content and some of the organic components of the water may supply fertilizing nutrients. Thus, the water does not necessarily have to be diluted and carried to the sea by rivers.

Disposal of the final concentrated wastes after maximum reuse may be the major problem. Louis Koenig has made a study for the U.S. Public Health Service of the possibilities of ultimate disposal of these concentrates. The possibilities include wet oxidation of the concentrates at elevated temperatures, incineration, placement in underground cavities, spreading on the soil, injection to underground formations, pipelining to the ocean, and recovery of salable products.

The importance of concentration of wastes and their ultimate disposal has been recognized only in recent years and is a major subject in the research program of the U.S. Public Health Service. There is considerable reason to believe that new methods will become more generally practical for the arid regions as the work of this research program progresses.

The problem of water pollution could become a serious limiting factor to growth in parts of the arid United States. If it does, it probably will be the result more of the lack of application of technical knowledge than of the lack of such knowledge.

Natural Setting

Perhaps the resources that will be the most important to the regional growth of the western states by the 21st century will be the scenery, potential for outdoor recreation, and the colorful ethnic and cultural groups. All of these will be powerful attractions to increasingly mobile industries, to retired people seeking new homes, and to tourists from all over the world.

The question is, How many of these resources will remain unimpaired? Many who marvel at the spectacular economic growth of southern California deplore the cost of this growth in natural charm. W. H. Whyte partly sums up this feeling when he writes, "flying from Los Angeles to San Bernardino—an unnerving lesson in man's infinite capacity to mess up his environment—the travelers can see a legion of bulldozers gnawing into the last remaining tract of green between the two cities" (*20*, p. 133).

A relatively few poorly planned or poorly located developments can destroy the natural appeal of an arid area. Developers already have discovered that desert land, aridity, sunshine, and spaciousness are very salable items. Whole new cities have been promoted in the southwestern dry lands of California, Nevada, Arizona, New Mexico, and west Texas, some of them complete with swimming pools, golf courses, and artificial lakes. In the Mohave Desert of California alone, more than 300 active subdivisions were selling land in 1963. The customers were disenchanted metropolitanites and the growing army of retired citizens. If only 2 million of this latter group were to transfer their fixed incomes to the arid West, the added income would total more than the present value of all irrigated crops. Moreover, the number of pensioners in the United States is expected to grow from 15.5 million in 1963 to 24 million by 1980.

State and federal governments have taken some mild steps to curb overzealous and misleading advertising, but whether they see the opportunity to direct and channel this remarkable demand for space into better-balanced growth remains to be seen. The current private land development is reminiscent of that of ground water just before the recent period of overdevelopment and depletion. Will the same kinds of mistakes be repeated?

Thanks in part to a bygone generation of visionaries and conservationists, the 11 westernmost continental states contain 75 percent of the land designated as outdoor recreation areas, including 75 percent of the national capacity for winter sports and 55 percent of the capacity for camping.

Marion Clawson and his colleagues have estimated that the demand for outdoor recreation by the year 2000 will be 40 times the present levels (*21*). Although this is considerably more than the projections of the Outdoor Recreation Resources Review Commission (*22*), both groups agree that such things as the use of national parks will sharply increase.

Indian and other cultural groups constitute unique and colorful assets. Many Indian tribes may elect, or be forced by economic necessity, to become fully assimilated into the national population. Others may find a middle way that will enable them to adopt some aspects of the national culture, achieve relative economic equality, and still maintain a high degree of distinctiveness and cohesion.

The Spanish-American communities of the Southwest, which have maintained much of their traditional way of life, seem almost certain to become overwhelmed by the national culture. The experiment described in the Embudo case history in this book indicates that more perceptive and intensive efforts will be necessary if the Spanish-American group is to share the rewards of modern society without being submerged (23).

Long-term policies for the development of the remaining public and private lands and for the encouragement of ethnic and cultural groups to retain their distinctiveness should have a high priority. There is little indication that these needs have been recognized, even though they appear to be keys to balanced regional growth.

Slowly Developing Regions

One of the great challenges for the future will be the development of the colder arid regions. These areas in such northern mountain states as Idaho, Wyoming, and Montana have magnificent scenery, superior summers, and all manner of winter and summer sports possibilities, especially in their mountainous watersheds, abundant energy resources, large areas of undeveloped space, and plentiful sun. If a few environmental disadvantages can be overcome, these areas might easily repeat the phenomenal growth record of the Southwest during the remainder of this century. These disadvantages are no more formidable than the problems presented by heat in the hot, dry deserts before the development of practical methods of air-conditioning and cooling.

Perhaps the greatest barrier to the development of the arid northern mountain states for year-round living is the idea that the winters are cold and unpleasant. This idea is somewhat exaggerated and, from a technologic point of view, many of the actual problems could already be solved. Technology has made indoor housing completely pleasant. The problem of winter snow and ice can be managed through the use of many types of improved machines for disposal. In fact, in the arid regions, the disposal of snow and ice could be turned into an opportunity to collect water for subsequent use.

Experience in arctic, antarctic, and alpine areas and in the national space program has resulted in new possibilities to maintain a comfortable environment while a person is out of doors. The selection ranges all the way to space suits and plastic helmets with various kinds of insulation, chemical or electric heating, and thermostatic control. Thus, an individual in the colder, arid areas of the United States in the future should be able to control his outdoor environment as effectively as he now controls his indoor environment.

A number of experts consider the decline in farm population and the tendency for the rural social structure to break down to be one of the greatest challenges for the arid and semiarid areas. This problem is especially acute in the Great Plains, where the possibilities of attracting new population and of developing recreation and industry do not appear nearly as bright as elsewhere.

One significant fact is that per-capita productivity in agriculture on the Plains has been increased enough to make the average income higher than the national average. This situation has resulted partly from price supports on commodities, such as wheat, but the present surpluses may disappear in the future. It has been predicted that, by 1980, the increased national population may need 60 to 185 million additional acres (24.3 to 74.9 million hectares) of farmland (6). The present high productivity also is the result of widespread farm mechanization and the consolidation of smaller farms into larger, more efficient units.

Further gains may be possible through marked increase in the efficiency of livestock feeding, the demand for agricultural products, and the development of fish, wildlife, and recreation. For instance, the Plains contain the most important duck-breeding areas of the nation.

Thus, there is a good chance that the region can maintain relatively high per-capita incomes. This offers an interesting possibility to other parts of the world: the use of science and technology to provide a sparsely populated, arid, agricultural hinterland with social, cultural, and economic opportunities equal to, or superior to, those of urbanized industrialized areas. With improved ground and air transportation, distances are no longer formidable. Major services, such as hospitals, churches, schools, professional services, and shopping centers, are close, at least in terms of the time required to reach them.

Arrangements might be made to include the rural people in the

Beside the Salton Sea (background) in the hot, dry Imperial Valley of California, promoters have laid out a desert city for the future, complete with paved streets, yacht club, and marinas. The development is far from metropolitan areas. (Courtesy *Life Magazine* © 1962 Time, Inc.)

social and cultural life of the regional centers, and to have the social cost of dispersion shared by the urban and rural areas. As the national trend toward urbanization continues, the value of the remaining farms for providing weekend retreats and interesting restful vacations may greatly increase. If a highly dispersed, arid-agricultural population can enjoy the benefits of both rural and urban life and support itself at high levels, it may demonstrate a real alternative to the increase of urbanization for all developing areas.

Trends in Research

Some general opinions can be given on the recent trends in arid-zones research and the needs for the future. There is, of course, more and more support for research connected with water, whether it be basic or applied. This is manifest, to cite one example, in the move in Congress by Senator Clinton P. Anderson, of New Mexico, and 19 other senators to create a water-resources research center in each of the 50 states. Another indication of this support is the ten-fold increase in funds voted for the federal desalinization program for the period ending in 1967.

There has also been a renaissance in arid-zones research during recent years. The University of Arizona has had an arid-lands program since 1958, and the University of Nevada recently established a Desert Research Institute. The 20 Associated Rocky Mountain Universities propose to concentrate on arid-zones research. In addition, institutes, conferences, and symposiums have been organized to deal with specialized arid-zones fields. It has been recognized that fundamental research in the physical and natural sciences in arid zones—for example, in such fields as atmospheric physics and hydrology—is fully as important as applied research. Expenditures for the arid-zones sciences are expected to expand at a much more rapid rate than regional income.

Many fields, however, are neglected. This is particularly true in the social sciences, with the exception of economics. It has not yet been understood that perhaps the most critical need in the arid and semiarid regions of the United States is for research aimed at understanding the rapid changes in the regions and the consequent changing relationships among man, environment, resources, and technology. Expanded research in sociology, psychology, and political science is crucial. There is need for an interdisciplinary research center to sharpen the focus on the over-all aspects of what is happening in the arid and semiarid United States, and what alternatives remain.

Need for Regional Approach

The physical barriers of aridity and scarcity of resources seem less formidable when one views the possibilities of more rational management and of technologic advance. The likelihood is not great that these can be accomplished, however, under the current conditions of competition between a few expanding metropolitan areas and a varied set of state policies and attitudes. The basic problems are of human organization rather than of aridity itself.

Udall (9) has said: "In the parched Pacific Southwest, we can prosper together or slowly shrivel separately. Only regional action—coordinated at every level—will suffice." If this statement were broadened to mean total development of the arid and semiarid regions of the United States, it would describe the course of action that is the most likely to benefit the entire region. One of the urgent needs is for a regional sense of purpose and an "arid-zone mentality," which could create a mental shift in public attitudes of the order of that recently made by the people of western Europe in their development of institutions such as the Common Market for cooperative effort.

Some small steps have been taken toward coordination by the 11 westernmost continental states, in association with Alaska and Hawaii. Since almost all of these states are arid or semiarid, aridity affects their philosophy. The links between them include a governors' council, the Western States Council for Economic Development, and the Western Interstate Commission for Higher Education.

Although these trends are promising, they are not likely to bring effective answers to the foreseeable problems, unless they are greatly accelerated and broadened in the direction of a regional agency with power to operate in such fields as joint planning, public and private land development, and integrated water policies.

Many federal agencies, among them the U.S. Forest Service, operate partially on a regional basis. They could be closely attached to any regional agency. In the Great Plains, efforts have been made to obtain legislation for a federal Great Plains administration with broad functions that might extend to regional development. These efforts have been unsuccessful but undoubtedly will be revived at the next drought or economic crisis.

The arid regions have now grown to the point where they could maintain, and benefit by, a regional planning and coordinating agency, perhaps with technical and financial assistance from the federal government. What seems to be lacking is sufficient vision to see the mutual advantages of their joining to solve their resources and economic development problems. The rapid development in southern California and the other urban centers of the Southwest and Mountain States is impressive but may not have enough momentum, if large hinterland areas remain depressed, or if there is a sharp decline in the national economy or abrupt changes in the defense program. These urban areas are especially well supplied with leadership and economic reserves, which would enable them to take a leading role in a regional approach.

Previous experience indicates that a sparsely populated, arid region needs both a strong economic stimulus, such as was given by the defense program, and progressive, technologically oriented people to provide leadership. It indicates also that the traditional fields of agriculture, mining, and ranching, to which most other countries with arid lands must devote their initial efforts, do not offer a long-term basis for support of developed societies with rising economic standards. These fields undoubtedly are essential opening wedges. However, to judge by the United States experience, care must be taken to avoid entanglement of the resources in a maze of legal, political, and private property-right problems from which they cannot easily be extricated for eventual uses of higher value.

REFERENCES

1. P. B. Sears, *Deserts on the March* (Univ. of Oklahoma Press, Norman, rev. ed., 1947).
2. F. Osborn, *Our Plundered Planet* (Little, Brown, Boston, 1948).
3. U.S. Senate, Select Committee on National Water Resources, *Land and Water Potentials and Future Requirements for Water*, Comm. Print 12 (Washington, D.C., 1960).
4. H. Humphrey, "Economic impact of arms control agreements— study by Senate Committee on Disarmament," *Congressional Record*, 5 Oct. 1962.
5. C. F. Kraenzel, *The Great Plains in Transition* (Univ. of Oklahoma Press, Norman, 1955).
6. N. Wollman, Ed., *The Value of Water in Alternative Uses* (Univ. of New Mexico Press, Albuquerque, 1962).
7. A. Kneese, *Water Resources Development and Use* (Federal Reserve Bank, Kansas City, Mo., 1959).
8. L. Koenig, "The economics of water sources," in *The Future of Arid Lands,* G. F. White, Ed. (Am. Assoc. for the Advancement of Science, Washington, D.C., 1956).
9. U.S. Department of the Interior, press release, 22 Jan. 1963.
10. J. Hirschliefer, J. de Haven, and J. Milliman, *Water Supply* (Univ. of Chicago Press, Chicago, 1960).
11. H. Jordan, "The increasing use of water in industry," in *Water, Yearbook Agr., U.S. Dept. Agr.* **1955** (1955), pp. 653–655.
12. E. A. Ackerman and G. O. G. Löf, *Technology in American Water Development* (Johns Hopkins Press, Baltimore, Md., 1959).

13. L. E. Myers, Jr., "Conservation of irrigation water supplies in arid climates," in *Agricultural Problems in Arid and Semiarid Environment,* A. A. Beetle, Ed., *Wyoming Univ. Agr. Expt. Sta. Bull. 367* (1960).
14. H. Boyko and E. Boyko, "Seawater irrigation," *Intern. J. Bioclimatol. Biometeorol.* 2 (11), sect. B1 (1959).
15. California Department of Water Resources, *The California Water Plan,* Bull. 3 (Sacramento, Calif., 1957).
16. J. M. Milliman, "Problems of water districts," *Calif. Agr.* 12, 2–16 (1958).
17. L. E. Myers, Jr., "Water harvesting," *Proc. Nevada Water Conf., 16th* (Department of Conservation and Natural Resources and Nevada State Reclamation Assoc., Carson City, 1963).
18. M. Del Duca, R. Huebscher, and A. Robertson, "Regenerative environmental control systems for manned earth lunar spacecraft," in *Man's Progress in the Conquest of Space* (Institute of Aeronautical Sciences, New York, 1962).
19. U.S. Senate, Select Committee on National Water Resources, *Water Supply and Demand,* Comm. Print 32 (Washington, D.C., 1960).
20. W. H. Whyte, Jr., "Urban sprawl," in *Exploding Metropolis, Fortune* Eds. (Doubleday, Garden City, N.Y., 1958).
21. M. Clawson, R. Held, and C. Stoddard, *Land for the Future* (Johns Hopkins Press, Baltimore, Md., 1963).
22. Outdoor Recreation Resources Review Commission, *Outdoor Recreation for America* (Govt. Printing Office, Washington, D.C., 1962).
23. P. van Dresser, "Development potentials of the northern New Mexico uplands," *Reg. Develop. Assoc. Northern New Mexico Rept.* (1962).

Tucson: A Problem in Uses of Water

ANDREW W. WILSON

At the beginning of 1962, the urban population of Tucson, Arizona, was estimated to be more than 260,000 inhabitants and growing at a net increase of about 15,000 a year. Since many people like to live in this sunny, arid area, with only 10 inches (254 millimeters) of average annual rainfall, there seems to be no reason to believe that there will be much change in this rate of growth, an almost constant 80 to 90 percent each decade for the past 60 years (*1*). But a key to the growth of large cities in an arid environment is the supply of water.

The industrial and municipal water consumption of the Tucson urban area and the three copper mines south of the city during the 5 years from 1956 to 1960 was believed to average about 49,500 acre feet (61 million cubic meters). All of this water was pumped from underground water supplies (*2*).

Since the recharge of the underground reservoir, all by natural processes, was calculated during the same years at about 50,400 acre feet (62.2 million cubic meters), the water situation might seem to be in reasonable balance. This is before consideration of the water used to irrigate the agricultural products being grown on 15,200 acres (6151 hectares). The net withdrawal from the underground reserves for this purpose was estimated for the 5 years to average an additional 45,600 acre feet (56.2 million cubic meters). Phreatophytes used another 3800 acre feet (4.7 million cubic meters). When these figures are summed, we find that the annual overdraft of water from the underground reserves, deposited there by nature over past millenniums, is about 48,500 acre feet (60 million cubic meters).

According to estimates in 1951, there were some 6.6 million acre feet (8141 million cubic meters) of stored water in the alluvial deposits of the Tucson basin down to 300 feet (91.4 meters) (3). More recent knowledge of the water-holding characteristics of these deposits indicates that this figure may be too high, since many strata seem to be more or less dry. On the other hand, it is now known that water exists in varying amounts to below 2000 feet (609.6 meters). Comparing only the supplies down to 300 feet with the recent annual overdraft of 48,500 acre feet (60 million cubic meters) per year, we find that Tucson (assuming constant consumption) will not run out of water down to 300 feet for about 135 years. Even allowing for greatly increased usage and overly optimistic estimates of reserves, it is apparent that there is no immediate crisis in water supplies in the area.

Nevertheless, it is also apparent that this overuse of water cannot go on indefinitely, that the water table will be deepening (except perhaps in unusually wet years), that the energy expended to raise water to the surface will increase constantly, and that sooner or later consumption of water must be restricted or the annual available supply must be supplemented from other sources. A decision on a course or courses of action cannot be postponed indefinitely without serious consequences.

Water Once Was Plentiful

But this concern about water scarcity was not always true. When historical records were started for the area, the Indians of three villages raised crops on the fertile, nearly level flood plain of the Santa Cruz River, near which the community of Tucson was founded. In those years before 1700, and for many years afterward, the Santa Cruz was a nearly perennial stream; and the area to the northwest of the present center of Tucson was swampy, with many beaver dams, and the pools reflected the trees of an extensive streamside forest. Tall grasslands generally extended to the hills from the edge of the forest, although some mesquite scrub forest apparently did exist. Until 1880, no pumps lifted ground water to the surface, nor had the modern trenching of the recent alluvium begun. Ground water, in many places, was within reach of crop- and tree-root systems.

In 1700, the first mission was built at the large village (800 inhabitants) called San Xavier del Bac, and a canal was dug to bring water from the Santa Cruz River to the mission. European crops and domestic animals were introduced.

With the building, in 1776, of the walled presidio of Tucson, more farmers were attracted. They built canals to irrigate their fields of wheat and other crops, the water coming from the slow-flowing river or from El Ojito (Little Eye) Spring, south of the presidio a few hundred feet. At the first sign of the approach of an Apache war party, the farmers fled to the safety of the town walls. Water consumption still was far below the annual recharge of the river basin (4).

After the purchase of the area from Mexico in 1853 and occupation by the United States, water from El Ojito was peddled from door to door in the growing village at 5 cents per gallon (3.785 liters). Water for bathing, laundry, and gardens was carried from the river, a "free" source.

In the 1870's Simpson's Public Baths were built at the spring to simplify the bathing-water problem, and these soon became a local institution, a place of pleasant social gatherings on Saturday nights.

Even before the time of the public baths, however, the beaver dams on the Santa Cruz, which might have survived the depredations of trappers, were joined by a man-made dam built for water-power purposes. This dam, which formed Silver Lake about 1 mile (1.6 kilometers) south of town, was built in 1857. By 1860, the dam had been harnessed for flour milling with milling stones bought in San Francisco. It was in use for such industrial purposes, off and on, for some 30 years.

The end of Silver Lake began with the coming of the railroad and other events of the early 1880's. In September of 1882, the Tucson Water Company began to pump water from its new wells through newly laid mains. This put El Ojito Spring out of business as a source of domestic supply. The water pumps were steam-powered, using wood for fuel, as were the railroad and several flour mills other than the one at Silver Lake. The fuel wood came from the forest along the river. At about the same time, other portions of the forest were removed to create farmland, for the danger from the Apache tribe was waning. The grasslands, reportedly tall enough to brush a horse's belly, which carpeted the valley beyond the forest zone,

were being destroyed concurrently by large herds of horses and cattle. From 1883 to 1890 the number of cattle in southeastern Arizona
quadrupled.

Vegetation Destroyed

Destruction of the vegetative cover allowed the heavy summer
rains to start entrenching the recent alluvium, as the water rushed
pell-mell toward the Gila River. The dam at Silver Lake was damaged by floods in 1886, rebuilt, and again destroyed in 1890. The
floods of 1891 were even worse and threatened to destroy completely
the primitive irrigation system that was based on ditches.

As a result, presumably, of the increased pumping of water, the
deterioration of natural vegetation, and the continued erosion and
trenching of the channel, the flow of the Santa Cruz disappeared
underground (4). Perhaps the only advantage from all this was the
dramatic decrease in the prevalence of malaria after the disappearance of swamps and the extinction of the beavers and their ponds.
The numerous disadvantages included the termination of all irrigation or other uses of water from surface supplies. Automatically,
then, water became more expensive, even though it was purer and
more conveniently available than formerly. More capital was needed
now to develop a supply of water.

Improved transportation and increased population in the 20th
century further strained the water resources. Irrigation increased
until a maximum of 60,000 acres (24,282 hectares) was reached in
1953, much of it north of, or downstream from, the city of Tucson.
There has been a slight decline since as a result of acreage allotments, lower support prices, and loss of export markets for cotton
and other major products. Meanwhile, nonagricultural uses of water
have increased rapidly.

Although a large part of the population of Tucson was engaged
in farming in the early years, the area's exploding population has become overwhelmingly urban. It would be interesting to know how
much the consumption of water jumped when the Tucson Water
Company began to pipe water into homes and businesses. Modern
use in Tucson has seen consumption climb to about 180 gallons (681
liters) per capita per day in 1961. This figure includes all types of
use from the mains of the city water utility.

In the early stages of human use of the Santa Cruz Valley, there was little need to worry about the adequacy of water. For more than 60 years, however, it has been a growing problem, until in 1963, it was apparent that the future of man's use of this area is dependent on his adjustment to the limitations set by this most scarce of the essential resources. He cannot escape the consequences of this limitation by refusing to face it. But by making an attempt to reach a rational decision in regard to the possible alternatives in the use of water, he may be able to decrease to a minimum the deleterious effect of the scarcity of water (*1*).

If we assume that the decision is to be based on the well-known conservation principle of providing for the greatest good for the greatest number over the long run, it is possible to indicate which uses of water should be encouraged and which discouraged. One way to approach this problem is to ascertain the sources of *basic* employment and income in the community—the elements that result from selling goods or services to buyers who live outside the community. Since no advanced, modern economy is self-sufficient at the local level, its growth and health are dependent on its ability to purchase goods and services from the outside. Basic income makes this possible and is an essential part of every nonsubsistence local economy.

Varying Values of Water

Once basic employment and income have been determined, the water consumption per unit of basic income or employment provided by each major industry in the community can be determined or estimated. The industries that provide the greatest basic income (or employment) per unit of water consumed are the ones that contribute the most to the economic welfare of the area and should be encouraged as much as possible without subsidies, which would tend to reduce the economic benefits in another way.

A rough example of this method of approach is shown in Table I. Agriculture produces $212 of basic income per acre foot (17 cents per cubic meter) of water used, but manufacturing, for example, returns $3205 per acre foot ($2.61 per cubic meter). Total nonagricultural use of water produces about $1670 in earned basic income per acre foot ($1.36 per cubic meter) of water consumed. Only if some noneconomic reason prevails, such as a cultural bias in favor

Table I. Basic employment and income payments to individuals for Tucson, 1952, with water consumption for combined Tucson metropolitan and Sahuarita districts, Arizona, 1956–1960, inclusive.

Industrial category	Percentage of total basic employment	Percentage of total basic income	Water consumption (millions of cubic meters)	Percentage of water used in Tucson	Basic income per cubic meter ($)
Agriculture	9.6	7.2	56.3	46.1	0.171
Mining	5.4	5.0	2.2	1.8	3.042
Manufacturing	19.4	13.7	7.0	5.8	2.610
Contract construction	2.7	3.5			
Transportation and utilities	10.3	7.5	52.1[a]	42.7[a]	0.573
Trade	4.5	3.9			
Finance	0.3	0.3			
Services	12.4	7.3			
Government	35.4	25.7	4.4	3.6	8.004

[a] Includes all other uses and losses, including contract construction and natural losses.
Sources: Wilson (1) based on Schwalen and Shaw (2).

of agricultural work as an essential part of a way of life, can irrigated agriculture logically be permitted to continue in this area.

Nevertheless, such a radical change in water-consumption practices as the elimination of irrigated agriculture is not consummated overnight in a democratic society. Public opinion must be informed of the problem, and political action must be initiated. If this is not done, however, the present rapid drop in the level of the water table will continue, in the pattern that is common throughout the basin in this century. Water levels in many wells in Tucson have dropped through the years. Drops of 40 feet (12 meters) in 15 years are not uncommon, and in some areas the fall in the water table is greater. Generally, the rate of drop is accelerating. In any case, it has several ramifications.

Willard C. Lacy, geologist at the University of Arizona, has pointed out that the bleeding of water deposits under the city, and in other basins of southern Arizona, has caused a subsidence of the surface, which may approach 10 inches (254 millimeters) in the Tucson area. Along the edge of the valley pediment (which is stable itself) the differential change in elevation has resulted in serious damage to buildings, causing slowly the type of cracking and settling that one might expect to find produced quickly along an earthquake shatter belt. It may be that this consequence is augmented by the desiccation of clay beds beneath the most seriously damaged areas. At any rate, the more rapidly the water table drops, the more quickly and extensively buildings will be damaged.

A more widely recognized result of the falling water table is the increased cost of pumping water from greater and greater depths. Eventually this is expected to price agriculture out of the area, and so end the accelerating effects of the drain from that source. But by that time, the cost of water for the economically more productive urban uses will be much higher.

In any case, major costs are going to occur in an attempt to solve the problem of an adequate water supply for the Tucson metropolis of the future. In 1963, the city government was proposing the second raise in water rates in 5 years. It seems to be appropriate to evaluate carefully the possibilities of restricting and guiding present uses of water in order to keep the long-run costs of water as reasonable as possible (5). In contrast, the more familiar pattern of the past—to look always for new sources of water at almost any cost rather than to conserve already available supplies—is still in effect. Although additional supplies from more distant sources may be possible, it is quite certain that these will be increasingly expensive, too.

REFERENCES

1. A. W. Wilson, "Economic aspects of decision-making in water use in semiarid and arid lands," *Colloq. Intern. Geograph. Union, Comm. on the Arid Zone,* Heraklion, Crete, Greece, September 1962 (UNESCO, in press).
2. H. C. Schwalen and R. J. Shaw, "Progress report on the study of water in the Santa Cruz Valley, Arizona," *Univ. Ariz. Agr. Expt. Sta. Rept. 205* (1961).
3. L. C. Halpenny *et al., Ground Water in the Gila River Basin and Adjacent Areas, Arizona—a Summary,* prepared in financial cooperation with the Underground Water Commission of Arizona (U.S. Geological Survey, U.S. Dept. of the Interior, Tucson, Ariz., 1952).
4. J. R. Hastings, "Vegetation change and arroyo cutting in southeastern Arizona," *J. Ariz. Acad. Sci.* 1, 60–67 (1959).
5. G. F. White, *The Changing Role of Water in Arid Lands,* Riecker lecture 6, November 1960 (Univ. of Arizona Press, Tucson, 1962).

Upper Rio Grande:
Embattled River

JOHN HAY

Some of the most complex water problems known to man are compressed into the narrow, parched valley of the upper Rio Grande. They are compounded by delicate relationships between cities and farmers, between and within states, and even between nations.

About 34,000 square miles (88,000 square kilometers) of land are drained by the upper river (Fig. 1), and its watershed contains a population of almost 1 million people, largely concentrated in the expanding urban centers of Albuquerque, New Mexico; El Paso, Texas; and Ciudad Juarez, Mexico. More than 99 percent of the water supply comes from Colorado and New Mexico, mostly as runoff from melting snow in the high mountains. The arid lower reaches have average annual rainfalls of only about 8 inches (200 millimeters).

There are three natural divisions. The San Luis section in Colorado, bordered on three sides by mountains, includes an irrigated area of about 650,000 acres (260,000 hectares) and is known for its potatoes. The middle section, the main stem of the river through the northern two-thirds of New Mexico, is largely confined in canyons or in narrow subvalleys. Thus, the total irrigated acreage is small. The southern section extends from Elephant Butte Reservoir in south-central New Mexico to Fort Quitman, Texas, about 80 miles (130 kilometers) southeast of El Paso. In the Rincon and Mesilla valleys of New Mexico, the El Paso Valley in Texas, and its Mexican counterpart, the Juarez Valley, about 175,000 acres (70,000 hectares), mostly in cotton (*Gossypium*) and alfalfa (*Medicago sativa*), are irrigated.

491

In the early 16th century, the Spanish conquistadores found 20,000 to 30,000 peaceful agricultural Indians well established in pueblos along the main stream (1). Even after the Spanish conquest, the pressure of grazing on the land was not excessive; the way of life changed little for many generations.

Not until the 1880's, which were marked by unusual drought, was there tremendous overgrazing of the limited pasture. This helped to initiate a disastrous cycle of severe soil erosion. These same years also saw the beginning of extensive irrigated agriculture in the San Luis Valley of Colorado. With the rapid influx of colonists from the eastern United States, each individual claiming a share of the already scarce water, disputes inevitably arose.

The ranchers blocked off streams in the upper reaches to supply their increasing herds, and the farmers took what water they needed without regard for the people below them on the river, and the constant buildup of population added new demands on the already overtaxed water resources. The disputes became more and more serious until, inevitably, the more responsible parties met to discuss what might be done to alleviate the situation.

Elephant Butte Dam

The meetings and discussions led to the formation of a compact in 1906 that attempted to spell out the various needs of farmers and ranchers in the valley and, more particularly, the needs of those in its lower sections. A direct result was the construction in 1914 of Elephant Butte Dam and reservoir, which, it was believed, would resolve the problems.

Although much thinking went into the formation of the 1906 compact, it soon became apparent that the situation was much more complicated than had been realized. Although the creation of the dam and the series of canals and ditches that were constructed below it under the auspices of the U.S. Bureau of Reclamation alleviated water shortages immediately below the dam, grave problems were created above it. Accelerated erosion continued in the unprotected, overgrazed uplands. Great amounts of sediments were deposited in the new lake and along the channel of the river, and the water table under the irrigated lands of the middle valley began to rise. The aggradation of the streambed caused increased flood

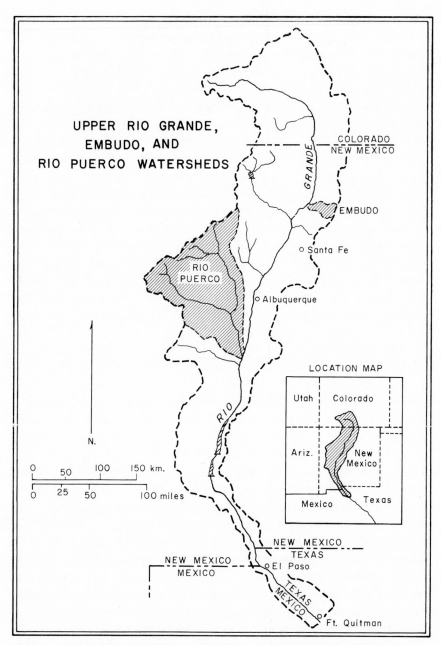

Fig. 1.   More than 34,000 square miles (88,000 square kilometers) of land are drained by the upper Rio Grande. (Adapted from map by New Mexico State Engineer Office, 1956)

hazard upstream and necessitated the construction of expensive dikes and other works and later large flood-control dams.

The rising water tables resulted in aggravated problems of water-logging, and of salinity, as the water drawn to the surface by capillarity evaporated and left dissolved salts on the surface of the soil. Various specialized governmental agencies found themselves at odds regarding a solution. Irrigators in the downstream areas had grievances against those upstream. Misunderstandings between ranching and irrigation interests increased, and both had problems with the growing cities.

The differences in understanding of the problems were so far apart that another series of meetings was held. These meetings led to the realization that further study was needed by representatives of the three states involved. The need for more definitive planning was felt to be so urgent that a fund of $100,000 was set up and allocated to the National Resources Planning Board to make a study of the total estimated amount of water available in the basin and the amount that could safely be allocated to the states. As a result, a Rio Grande compact was drawn up and ratified by the three states in 1941. The United States government, through its ownership of national forests and various other federal lands within the basin, was a fourth interested party to the compact, which was hailed as the answer to all of the valley's problems.

One provision was the establishment of what might be termed a "water bank." Under the compact terms, a certain number of acre feet (1 acre foot equals 1233.5 cubic meters) of water was to be delivered to each state in normal years. In dry years, states would be allowed to build up deficits to the states lower on the watershed and then pay back the deficits in years of excess water. In actual practice, this has not worked, partly because the need for control of the pumping of ground-water was not foreseen and included in the compact. In times of drought, ground water was lowered through excessive pumping to maintain normal irrigation water. In wet years, much of the excess runoff served to build up the depleted ground-water supply in the northern projects; hence, important benefits of increased runoff were lost to the lower reaches.

Beginning in 1943, the frequency of drier years increased, thus aggravating the situation (2). Structures that had been built earlier at higher elevations were allowed to fall into disrepair. Denudation

When this photograph was made in 1951, the reservoir behind Elephant Butte Dam in New Mexico was virtually dry; high-water marks can be seen. Farther down the Rio Grande, severe salinity resulted, and farms were abandoned. (Courtesy *El Paso Times*)

of the natural grass cover increased on the already badly overgrazed upland ranges, and more silt and soil were carried into the main river channel through floods. As a consequence, the aggradation of the river itself began. This brought about the waterlogging of numerous farms along the riverbank, and they had to be abandoned to swampy bosques. These conditions and events encouraged the growth of saltcedars (*Tamarix pentandra*) and other phreatophytes along, and in, the dry river channels and drainage ditches, further depleting the scarce water supply.

Social Stress of Water Shortage

The upper Rio Grande is an example of the strains on man of severe water shortage. These strains were apparent during the extremely dry period from 1951 through 1956, when Elephant Butte Lake went dry for the first time in its history. Man is relatively unconcerned during times of abundant water, and this attitude makes intergroup planning difficult. Few people recognize the need for cooperation and planning until the competitions engendered by critical shortages make cooperative group action on a broad basis difficult or impossible.

When the threat of water shortage loomed in the projects south of Elephant Butte, for instance, a few farsighted individuals suggested the possibility of cooperative wells to supplement the surface water in the river. But as soon as shortage became probable, some people drilled private wells and became opposed to any group solution for which they might be taxed. Thus began the expensive trend that led to more than 1000 uncontrolled wells in a few years.

Before a serious study could be made of the economic feasibility of constructing a lined canal, the ground-water level declined to a point where some upriver farmers felt that they were obtaining special recharge benefits, and they were not inclined to eliminate this supposed personal advantage. In reality, benefits were lost to all, for by 1956, the water table had declined so much that 75 percent of the riverflow was being lost as seepage. The city of El Paso abandoned its practice of pumping water from well fields into the river channel for delivery to the treatment plant a few miles (kilometers) downstream, because the water often did not reach the treatment plant (3).

As the water table declined, dissolved salts remained in the soil or contaminated the ground water. Salinity levels increased especially in wells in the downstream areas, where the reused river water became progressively saltier.

This was especially true of Hudspeth County, Texas, where irrigation farming expanded after the construction of Elephant Butte Dam and depended on the unused water that was discharged by the irrigation districts upstream. Water was so plentiful in the early decades that the unused and drain waters of the project constituted a free and dependable source, and the Hudspeth County farmers saw little need to join the Elephant Butte project. During the drought years, however, the upstream districts began to manage their water supplies more carefully. Little water was permitted to enter Hudspeth County, and the area became dependent on wells. These grew saltier each year until, by 1956, they averaged more than 5.5 tons of salt per acre foot (2 metric tons per 1233.5 cubic meters).

About two-thirds of the irrigated area, including many elaborate homes, was abandoned.

Another example of strain during the period was the increased antagonism between cities and rural sections. Even though the farmers were steadfastly against any restriction of their rights of uncontrolled pumping, for instance, they resented the city's having the same right. Their justification was that the degree of pumpage by the city was greater per acre (hectare) owned or leased.

The Juarez Valley in Mexico suffered severely. During the period of water shortage, its quota of 60,000 acre feet (74 million cubic meters) of water was cut in proportion to the reduction in allotments on the United States side, and in 1955 and 1956 it averaged less than 8000 acre feet (10 million cubic meters). About half of its acreage, or about 25,000 acres (10,000 hectares), was abandoned or retired from production.

Legal Controversy

Actually, the most bitter controversy was the interstate argument between the state of Texas, acting for the water districts south of Elephant Butte Dam in Texas and New Mexico, and the state of New Mexico, acting for the middle section. By 1951, the middle section owed, under the compact, more than 330,000 acre feet (407 million cubic meters) of water, and the southern water users ordered the total draining of El Vado Dam in northern New Mexico. This was especially resented in the middle section, because even the relatively small amounts of water needed to maintain its fish were ordered released. Resentment had already been caused in the southern area, because it was felt that water was sometimes released so slowly that reduced amounts actually reached Elephant Butte Reservoir.

The next step was a legal suit to force New Mexico to pay its water debt under the Rio Grande compact. After 6 years, this expensive suit was dismissed by the U.S. Supreme Court on a technicality. After the court decision made certain that New Mexico could not be compelled to pay its water debt, the southern areas adopted a more compromising attitude. Formulas were devised that have resulted in the desired upriver projects, in more water for the south, and in improved relations.

Relations with Colorado are deteriorating rapidly, though. Its water debt, according to the compact, was more than 700,000 acre feet (850 million cubic meters) in 1963, and it is probable that the problem cannot be resolved until the interdependent ground- and surface-water supplies are jointly regulated and water waste is controlled.

It is obvious that the combination of aridity and man is the cause of the increasing number of water-short years in the upper Rio Grande—and that a serious situation, such as prevailed in the 1950's, will recur. There is little evidence that much has been learned from experience.

REFERENCES

1. E. J. Dortignac, "Watershed resources and problems of the upper Rio Grande Basin," *U.S. Dept. Agr., Forest Serv., Rocky Mt. Forest Range Expt. Sta. Paper* (1956).
2. H. E. Thomas, "Effects of drought in the upper Rio Grande Basin," *U.S. Geol. Surv. Profess. Paper 372-D* (1963).
3. P. C. Duisberg, Ed., "Problems of the upper Rio Grande, an arid zone river," *U.S. Comm. Arid Resource Improve. Develop. Publ. 1* (1957).

Embudo: Rise and Decline of a Program

EDGAR A. IMHOFF

The oft-presented picture of the poor but happy Spanish-American—peacefully following an idyllic pastoral life in a sunny mountain village—is as fictional as the writings in which it appears. The rural Spanish-American in the underdeveloped areas of northern New Mexico, and surely elsewhere, finds himself in an environment of considerable complexity.

His fields and pastures provide less and less subsistence, as the Spanish custom of dividing the land equally among children produces small, noncommercial plots, and as poor usage practices, including overgrazing, contribute to the declining productivity. He experiences, too, the discrimination of the modern market when he attempts to exchange his sheep, cabbages, or apples for cash. The lack of any organization to collect, standardize, advertise, and hold his farm products for favorable market conditions results in a low cash income from the land.

In the 18th and 19th centuries, there were villages that thrived despite their difficult environment, but today's depressed Spanish-American communities, inefficient in the application of the resources, put their limited supply of water to poor use. They lack capital, engineering know-how, and, sometimes, incentive. Their croplands are sporadically nourished by ingenious but primitive irrigation systems, often are improperly drained, and sometimes are unprotected from floods (*1*).

Under these conditions, the villager must have additional income. Two alternatives are open to him: (i) remain in his community and attempt to supplement the land and forest income, or (ii) mi-

499

grate from his father's land in search of a way of life outside his beloved uplands, away from familiar customs, but in a more bountiful economy. The vigor of the villages is being sapped as an increasing number of the 25- to 54-year age group choose the latter alternative. Too, this alternative is not always the solution, for the Spanish-speaking migrant may find that his educational and occupational background has not equipped him for a desirable job in the city. The majority of those who find it easier, or more pleasant, to stay in the community may supplement their incomes with such seasonal work as firefighting, trail-cutting, sheepherding, and road repair—and with welfare. The residents of certain rural communities in northern New Mexico obtain nearly 20 percent of their income from direct welfare donations from state and federal funds.

Why are more jobs not available, and why is a certain amount of welfare necessary? There is no large-scale industry in these areas, and certain bountiful resources have not been exploited by the villagers. Despite nearness to excellent fishing, hunting, and camping areas of unusual natural beauty, the villages offer few accommodations or services to recreation-minded America. In addition, annual growths of timber are not harvested. The extraordinary native crafts of weaving, wood-carving, and pottery-making are not marketed to the extent possible. Many of the villages are replete with unique art forms and architectural styles representative of early Indian, Spanish, and Mexican cultures. Unpaved roads, poor tourist facilities, and lack of publicity have kept them from profiting materially from these unusual cultural resources.

Governmental Interests

Fortunately, the Spanish-American in the underdeveloped communities has not been abandoned to fend entirely for himself. Because of landownership, jurisdiction, and function, many private, state, and federal organizations have strong interests and obligations in the communities. Most of the forest and grazing land in New Mexico is owned by the state or federal governments, but the citizen is allowed considerable use of its products. In addition to the natural-resources agencies, many government organizations are functioning to improve the human resources. State and national health units, for example, provide financial and technical aid in water supply, medical care, and sewerage. From 20 to 30 organizations, perhaps more, have an interest in each of the underdeveloped areas.

Although each functions for a particular purpose—for instance, soil conservation—many of the agencies have long felt the need for cooperative effort in treating the entire environment, to raise the standard of living and accelerate economic development. In 1959, about 30 agencies were voluntarily organized into an Interagency Council for Area Development Planning, for the purpose of joint research and planning toward these goals.

The group elected to concentrate its efforts on one unit of communities that was typical of the underdeveloped rural areas in New Mexico and wanted assistance. Chosen was the Embudo watershed (see map on p. 493), an area populated by about 5000 indigenous Spanish-Americans and Indians occupying 12 villages.

There, the same families have tilled the same soil for more than two centuries, and "to a reasonable degree the culture of 18th-century Spain has been retained in the form of an Old World agricultural village pattern and a social structure built around the extended family and the church" (2).

Most of the stream runoff flows to the Rio Grande from snowmelt higher in the mountains, although most of the settlement is in the brushland and woodland below 8000 feet (2400 meters). Of the some 300 square miles (777 square kilometers) in the watershed, only 8457 acres (3422 hectares) are arable, and they are badly eroded.

To my knowledge, the attempted project was unprecedented in terms of the great number and many kinds of organizations that were pledged to do research and planning for the eventual improvement of all the resources in the ecologic watershed unit. But problems of coordination among agencies became apparent immediately, for many of the individuals were committed to other work and had only a limited time for Embudo. There was a natural tendency for an agency to approach the unified problem as if each phase were the whole problem.

Problems of the Project

Problems of purpose also arose early in the project. The cooperating agencies were, perhaps, unanimous only in wanting to help the people in Embudo; they were not in agreement on how this should be done. Many participants felt that immediate technical and financial action should be taken to assist the villagers in such activities as improving irrigation systems, preserving unique architecture, and experimenting with new crops. Others believed that a program of combined research and action, with the cooperation of the villagers, was the answer. This philosophy was indicated by the statement of one council member: "Let's not encourage the expenditure of a great deal of energy or capital in improving irrigation systems until we know that this is the most beneficial use of water and land to these people."

Still a third group held that the function of the Interagency Council was only research, to develop planning techniques and ideas about how social and economic improvement might be effected—by the local citizenry. There was no formal organization of the holders of these various philosophies, but the beliefs were apparent in the workings of the council.

Whatever the merits of the particular philosophy, the problem of financing caused the selection of the method of doing something about Embudo. Although many of the participants were contributing free time, the project was still costly. Therefore, the New Mexico State Planning Office made a contract with the federal government for financial assistance. The contract stipulated that the Embudo project would be a study to develop planning techniques for a small-village rural community, and that the information would be published. The techniques so developed were to be applied to statewide planning. Embudo, to the dismay of some of the idealistic founders of the project, became an experiment directed primarily at development of planning techniques and the means of coordinating a horde of participants.

Many unpaid, busy individuals with varying backgrounds and beliefs were in the council, work roles and responsibilities were difficult to define, and deadlines were hard to enforce. Delays and interruptions in the project also were caused by a turnover in key personnel in the State Planning Office. A final delay came in writing and publishing the results of the study. The original planning grant period of 7 months grew to 24 months before the report *Embudo* (2) was published.

Erosion has gnawed away at the hillside that slopes up behind tiny Tres Ritos, a typical adobe village in the Embudo watershed. Annual precipitation here averages about 24 inches (609 millimeters), twice the amount that is received lower in the watershed. (Courtesy New Mexico State Tourist Bureau)

Project Results

With the publication of *Embudo* and the satisfaction of a few contracts, the core of the financial and technical support was removed from the Interagency Council for Area Development Planning. Officially, 30-odd organizations still belonged to the council in 1963, but only a handful of individuals were active. What have been the measurable results of the effort, often unpaid, by scores of contributors? The most evident result is, of course, the report—142 well-written, excellently illustrated pages. It presents (i) a fairly comprehensive study of the existing human and natural resources, (ii) techniques to be used in planning for Embudo and similar areas, and (iii) a few specific recommendations on needed improvements and developments in land, water, recreation, and so on.

It was, nearly everyone agrees, a good report—especially good for the State Planning Office, which fulfilled an overdue contract and developed and nurtured agency and personal avenues for obtaining and analyzing information. Many individuals feel, however, that the publication, although an accomplishment, was a poor substitute for the original intent of the Interagency Council to move Embudo people closer to economic development and improved standards of living.

A common complaint of the Spanish-Americans of Embudo was that (i) the report explained an existing situation with which one was already familiar, or (ii) it was published in English, and one could not understand it.

The activities of the remnant Interagency Council and the report have stimulated some of the Embudo citizens to action. A local group has formed the Embudo Watershed Development Committee to study and carry out some of the suggestions offered in *Embudo* and other sources. This development committee has made application to the federal government for financial and technical assistance to create a watershed project, under Public Law 566, that would solve some of the flood and sedimentation problems in the narrow valley and denuding uplands. It also is seeking federal aid to establish a U.S. Forest Service experimental forest in Embudo and to improve road conditions and access to the scenic recreational areas. All of these worth-while projects are in the preliminary stage. Before the flood-protection project is approved, the people of Embudo will be called on to display a high degree of local initiative, cooperation, and ability to pay part of the costs, which may amount to several million dollars. Public Law 566 and the experimental forest are excellent investments, but they will not produce any immediately dramatic benefits.

In appraising the results of the Embudo project, we must recognize that, given more time and funds, the Interagency Council and the State Planning Office might have been able to prepare a comprehensive plan for Embudo. There would still, however, have been the action or development stage, and this is where the purpose of the Interagency Council was not realized. As an illustration of this, a key figure in the Embudo project, when he was asked about the possible abortive termination of the project, answered: "[We] supported this project *not* primarily to assist the . . . area, but to develop methods and techniques that could be used to prepare comprehensive, long-term plans for the development of similar or larger regions." One cannot help but sympathize with the native of the watershed, who, on hearing of another organization that would study the area, is reported to have replied: "So, they are coming to examine us again. A lot of looking but no more *pesos*! If I charged only a few *centavos* to the *federales* who have looked at my small field and my cows, I would be *rico!*"

REFERENCES

1. O. Leonard and C. P. Loomis, "Culture of a contemporary rural community, El Cerrito, New Mexico," *U.S. Dept. Agr., Bur. Agr. Econ., Rural Life Ser. 1* (1941).
2. Interagency Council for Area Development Planning and New Mexico State Planning Office, *Embudo: a Pilot Planning Project for the Embudo Watershed of New Mexico* (Santa Fe, N. Mex., 1962).

Rio Puerco: Abused Basin

EDWARD J. DORTIGNAC

Soil out of place—the major land-resources problem of the southwestern United States—is epitomized in the history of the Rio Puerco, which is an example of man's failure to live in harmony with the soil, topography, vegetation, and climate.

Today the Rio Puerco Basin is riddled with huge gullies. Since 1885, an estimated 600,000 to 800,000 acre feet (740 million to 987 million cubic meters) of soil has washed from it into the Rio Grande. Even now, the Rio Puerco, which comprises 23 percent of the contributing basin in the upper Rio Grande above Elephant Butte Dam, produces 45 percent of the measured sediment in the main channel but only about 3 percent of the basin runoff. This sedimentation threatens the future occupancy of downstream areas—just as siltation menaced, and eventually contributed to the decline of, earlier civilizations in arid regions.

Situated in northwestern New Mexico, the Rio Puerco watershed covers 3.9 million acres (1.6 million hectares), as is shown in Fig. 1 and the map on page 493. It is a permanent stream only through the upper few miles of its channel. The remaining part and all of its tributaries have ephemeral or intermittent flow. The main tributaries from the west, the Rio San Jose and Arroyo Chico, are ephemeral, although they originate near the continental divide. Average annual precipitation varies from 8 inches (203 millimeters) near its mouth at 5000-feet (1520-meters) elevation to about 25 inches (635 millimeters) near its headwaters above 10,000 feet (3050 meters). Yet, 75 percent of the basin receives less than 14 inches (406 millimeters) of precipitation annually.

The resultant annual runoff averages less than 60,000 acre feet

(75 million cubic meters) of water. How can such an arid region with so little waterflow contribute so much sediment? The answer may lie in the relationship of the watershed characteristics to the history of settlement and use.

Erodible Soils

Most of the soils are derived from highly erodible Cretaceous sandstones and shales that are subject to *piping,* a form of subterranean erosion. Cracks develop in the soil or parent material because of the expansion and contraction that accompany alternate wetting and drying. Water enters and concentrates in these cracks, as well as in holes formed by burrowing animals, and forms underground conduits or tunnels called *pipes.* Runoff enters the pipe openings at the surface of the soil mass and travels as far as 100 feet (30.5 meters) underground before it reaches the arroyo wall. This waterflow erosion eventually results in the collapse of the overlying soil and the extension and widening of the gullies.

Vegetation, which is about evenly divided between pinyon-juniper (*Pinus edulis-Juniperus* spp.) woodland and grassland, is in delicate balance with the droughty climate and saline soils. Historical records and reconnaissance surveys indicate that a good cover of grass, mostly alkali sacaton (*Sporobolus airoides*), galleta (*Hilaria jamesii*), and blue grama (*Bouteloua gracilis*), was once present over much of the watershed. Dead root crowns of alkali sacaton can now be found on uplands and steep slopes as well as in the valleys—mute evidence that the vegetation was once in harmony with the erosive soils under this semiarid climate, with its recurrent, protracted droughts. The steep slopes and pointed hilltops on which grass formerly grew are of Cretaceous shale origin. Sagebrush (*Artemisia* spp.) still occupies from 3 to 4 percent of the watershed.

Archeologists and dendrochronologists claim that the Pueblo Indians were forced out of Mesa Verde in southwestern Colorado into the less severe conditions in Arizona and northern New Mexico during an extended drought from 1276 to 1299. About seven or eight major dry cycles of varying length and severity have since occurred in the Rio Puerco. The most severe and extensive one began about 1560 and ended about 1593 (*1*). The present drought, which started in 1942, and the one between 1871 and 1904 were the severest since the measurement of precipitation was started.

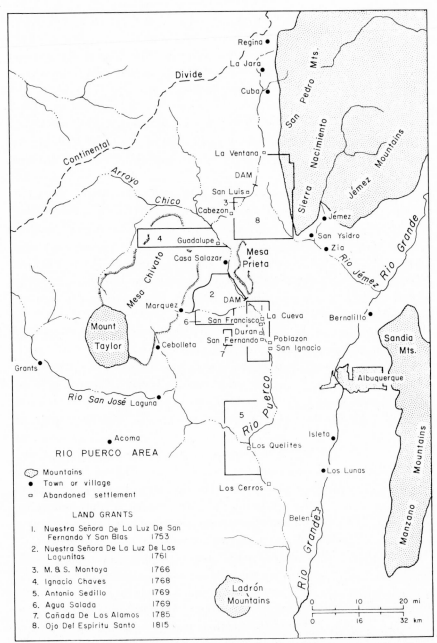

Fig. 1. Rio Puerco watershed, including land grants made when New Mexico was Spanish territory. (Adapted from "Historical geography of the middle Rio Puerco Valley," by J. G. Widdison, unpublished University of Colorado thesis, 1958)

History of Settlement and Grazing

Many Indian ruins on both sides of the Rio Puerco and on the adjacent mesas indicate that a rather large Indian population once existed there. But these early occupants did little to upset the balance of nature. In contrast, the arrival of the Spaniards with their grazing animals may have quickly upset the soil-vegetation equilibrium. These Spanish settlers were the first of two groups who have occupied the middle Rio Puerco Valley within the past 200 years (2).

The first period of occupancy began in the mid-18th century and ended in the first part of the 19th century, when the inhabitants of the Rio Puerco north of Cabezon were ordered to retire with their 10,000 head of cattle to the Rio Grande Valley for military protection from Navaho raiders. Yet this abandonment may not have been entirely due to the danger of marauding Indians. There is strong indication that the land resources had begun to fall apart.

In the beginning of this first period of settlement, thousands of sheep grazed out from the villages on the Rio Puerco and wintered in the main valley, where grass and brush afforded feed and protection. But later, because of Indian depredations, grazing was restricted to the vicinity of the towns and villages. Accordingly, deterioration of vegetation in these locales, which is now quite marked, may have started the cycle of accelerated erosion and the system of gullies.

Between the end of the first period of occupancy and 1848, when the United States acquired the region from Mexico, few settlers and grazing animals remained in the basin. The arrival of Anglo-Americans with capital and the lessening danger of marauding Indians provided an impetus to resettlement and the resumption of grazing. Extension of the transcontinental railroad to the middle Rio Grande Valley in 1880 created a means for marketing livestock. As a result, an enormous increase in livestock began about 1860 and continued until a maximum was reached in 1900, when 533,000 animal-units were grazing in the upper Rio Grande Basin in New Mexico. Today there are fewer than 150,000 animal-units. Since the period of maximum stocking occurred almost concurrently with the drought of 1871 to 1904, it is unlikely that the soils were given any protection during the violent summer rainstorms that occurred each year in the growing season. Existing arroyos were cut wider and deeper, and many new ones were formed by the excessive runoff that followed each torrential rain.

Cutting of the Main Channel

Old records do not mention that the Rio Puerco channel was wide or deep. Moreover, most of the early land surveys of section lines and grant boundaries, beginning about 1855, recorded the width, but not the depth, of the Puerco channel.

The first important documents are the diaries and reports of army explorers in the middle of the 19th century. These sources indicate that the Rio Puerco was mostly uninhabited and that the channel was already entrenched at several locations. Vertical banks 10 to 12 feet (3 to 3.5 meters) high in the Puerco west of Atrisco (Albuquerque's west mesa) and some 30 feet (9 meters) high in the vicinity of the deserted settlement of Poblazon were reported in 1846 (3). Upstream from the now deserted village of Cabezon, 20- and 30-foot (6- and 9-meter) vertical streambanks had to be graded down to allow passage of artillery and pack animals in 1849 (4). In 1853, the bed of the Rio Puerco was 18 feet (5.5 meters) below the alluvial valley where it joins the Rio San Jose. But later, in 1870, the flood plain was without a deep channel at Cabezon, where a small bridge was used to cross the river. That same year, upstream at La Ventana, the channel was 8 feet (2.5 meters) deep; now it is approximately 50 feet (15 meters) deep.

Thus, accounts indicate that Rio Puerco was already entrenched at several places by the middle of the 19th century and that at other places the banks were low or inconspicuous. The main discontinuous channel probably had a volume of about 17,000 acre feet (21 million cubic meters) in 1885. A survey in 1939 showed that the volume was 267,000 acre feet (330 million cubic meters) from below Cuba to the channel's mouth (5). The volume of tributary arroyos was estimated at 276,000 acre feet (341 million cubic meters) in 1927. It is considerably more today.

But how did this cycle of gully erosion start? Some scientists have explained it in terms of geologic erosion, admitting that misuse of plants and soil by man and his animals started the breakdown of a once stable balance of nature. However, early maps and recent aerial photographs, used in exploring field conditions, show that a sequence of events led to the breakdown in the climate-soil-vegetation equilibrium. Perhaps compaction of soil in animal and foot paths, then in wagon roads, and finally in motorways started and later accelerated this arroyo cutting. These lanes of travel paralleled the watercourses and provided ruts and channels for runoff water to cut downward into the deep alluvium. Once this carving of the landscape began, piping in the adjacent soil mass accelerated the extension of the gullies headward. But the runoff produced on compacted travel lanes alone could hardly account for the present destruction of these lands. The breaking of the sod and clean cultivation of the fertile valley bottoms, combined with removal of vegetation cover and compaction of soil by grazing animals on the adjacent rangelands, permitted the damaging runoff that dissected the alluvium.

Decline and Abandonment

In the 1870's, small farms and villages were again established along the main Rio Puerco channel and on some of its tributaries. Most of the new villages were at the same locations as the old ones, probably because the new settlers were heirs of the first inhabitants. Once the Indian danger no longer existed, resettlement of the valley was rapid.

During this decade, the Rio Puerco was an ephemeral stream with numerous brief, but occasionally severe, floods. It flowed in a flood plain that was subject to overflow and had a discontinuous channel. The small flow in the Puerco could be diverted to irrigate adjacent fields merely by placing a small amount of brush and rocks in the narrow stream. In years of flood, most of the valley floor was inundated, and good crops of corn, wheat, and beans were raised. Farming prospered at Cabezon and in the valley between San Luis and Casa Salazar. The Puerco Valley reportedly became known as the "breadbasket of New Mexico."

Irrigated areas existed along the main Rio Puerco Valley from Los Cerros to the headwaters; these areas were watered from small diversions in the discontinuous channel. But in time a new, deep channel formed from the mouth headward and destroyed the diversion dams. Los Cerros, 34 miles (55 kilometers) upstream, was

This gully-dissected alluvium in a tributary typifies the erosion that has riddled the Rio Puerco watershed, once a productive rangeland. (Courtesy U.S. Department of Agriculture, Forest Service)

abandoned about 1888, and San Ignacio and San Francisco, 62 and 73 miles (100 and 117 kilometers), respectively, upstream from the mouth, were abandoned by 1896. Casa Salazar was abandoned in the late 1920's, and the last family recently moved out of Cabezon.

The main cutting of the arroyo took place between 1885 and 1910 (6), and, as it proceeded headward, settlements were abandoned. Of 16 villages and settlements along the main Puerco Valley, only Cuba, Regina, La Jara, San Luis, and La Ventana remain populated. La Ventana has a single family, and San Luis has two families.

Abandonment followed the destruction of irrigated land—the basis of the village economy and sustenance. Irrigated acreage from Casa Salazar to Cuba declined from 10,000 acres (4047 hectares) to 3000 acres (1214 hectares) between 1880 and 1925. Irrigation below Cuba ended with the destruction of the San Luis diversion dam by a large flood on 25 July 1951, more than half a century after the failure of the masonry diversion dam between the Lagunitas and Montaño grants. As late as 1939, more than 5500 acres (2226 hectares) in the upper valley (above Cuba) were irrigated by 17 ditch systems. Much of this acreage and most of these ditches have been abandoned.

And now, what once was good, deep, fertile, irrigated alluvium has been largely replaced by deep, fingering arroyos. This network of gullies, aided by soil piping, has extended upstream into formerly good, productive rangeland. These adverse conditions are further aggravated over most of the rougher uplands, breaks, and mesas, where the deteriorated vegetation cover is absent or too sparse to provide effective protection against torrential rains or even minor storms. As a result, runoff water produced from rainstorms rushes down the existing arroyos, cutting them deeper and wider and extending them headward. The washed silt is added to the vast quantities of sediment already deposited at one point or another in the Rio Grande Valley.

Recovery of these lands will require many years of prodigious effort; the full cost may appear to be prohibitive today. Nonetheless, there have been recent efforts to revegetate them, to release runoff under control, and to hold the soil in place. Whether or not this rehabilitation takes place, the fundamental question remains: Could this deterioration have been prevented? The answer here as elsewhere lies in the fundamental behavior of man. Will man benefit from past mistakes? The future holds this answer.

Acknowledgment: I thank Eastburn Smith and Harry Pearson, who have devoted many years of work toward the solution of the vegetation-soil-water problems of the Rio Puerco and whose efforts have contributed knowledge and inspiration to me.

REFERENCES

1. T. L. Smiley, S. A. Stubbs, and B. Bannister, "A foundation for the dating of some late archaeological sites in the Rio Grande area, New Mexico; based on studies in tree-ring methods and pottery analysis," *Univ. of Ariz. Lab. Tree-Ring Res. Bull. 6* (1953).

2. J. G. Widdison, "Geography of middle Rio Puerco Valley," *New Mexico Hist. Rev.* **34**, 248–284 (1959).

3. J. W. Abert, *Report of Lieut. J. W. Abert of His Examination of New Mexico in the Years 1846–1847,* House Ex. Doc. 41, 30th Congr., 1st sess. (1848), pp. 417–548.

4. J. H. Simpson, *Journal of a Military Reconnaissance from Santa Fe, New Mexico, to the Navajo Country Made with the Troops under Command of Brevet Lt. Col. John M. Washington, Chief, 9th Military Dept., and Governor of New Mexico, in 1849 (James H. Simpson, First Lt. Corps of Topographical Engineers)* (Lippincott, Grambo, Philadelphia, Pa., 1852).
5. U.S. Department of Agriculture, *Rio Puerco Watershed Flood Control Survey Report, New Mexico* (Albuquerque, New Mex., 1941).
6. K. Bryan, "Historic evidence on changes in the channel of Rio Puerco, a tributary of the Rio Grande in New Mexico," *J. Geol.* **36**, 265–282 (1928).

Los Angeles: Growing Pains of a Metropolis

WARREN A. HALL

"The land was of a clayey consistency and, as far as the eye could reach, entirely bare of trees and even shrubs; and there was no sign of a town, not even a house to be seen. What had brought us into such a place we could not conceive" (1).

Thus, Richard Henry Dana recorded his first impression of the Los Angeles basin. Although his later visits proved this description to be somewhat harsh, his first and subsequent views were in marked contrast to the view that greets today's visitor: the lush subtropic vegetation in the basin provides a sharp contrast with the barren deserts beyond the encircling mountains.

Indeed, the visitor's first hint that the climate may have some disadvantages comes with the first smoggy day. He is not fully appreciative of the relationship of his headache to the unseen aridity. Oldtimers assure him that automobiles and industry are responsible. He may hear an occasional reference to a mysterious *inversion* and sooner or later adopts the word into his vocabulary as he "explains" the problem to the next arrival. In the meantime, he brags of the climate and wonders when "they" are going to do something about the smog.

But, before "they" can solve the problem of smog, "they" must conquer two stubborn enemies—an arid climate and the irrepressible desire of millions of people to migrate to the subtropic paradise whose virtues have been extolled, perhaps with some unwarranted embellishments, from coast to coast.

"They" have accomplished great works for southern California by conquering one and accommodating the other. Despite these impressive accomplishments, it is apparent today that the ingenuity of man has kept him less than a decade ahead of his problems. Perhaps this is a basic law of economic development. On the other hand, it may have been only a fortuitous sequence of events that has generated a megalopolis across the coastal plains of southern California, spilling over into its interior desert valleys.

The climate of Los Angeles is at once its greatest resource and its greatest problem. Unlike many arid areas, it does not suffer from extremes of temperature, either high or low. Thunderstorms are rare, and, except for the occasional Santa Ana winds that blow hot and unpredictably from the desert, there is little in the way of air movement beyond a welcome summer sea breeze. Subsiding air from the mid-latitude highs acts both as a barrier to divert cyclonic storms and as a trap to create a low ceiling, an inversion trap from which the airborne refuse discharged by an industrial, automobile-minded community can escape only with difficulty.

The annual precipitation near Los Angeles varies considerably, averaging about 15 inches (380 millimeters). As is usual in arid climates, averages mean little. During the 157 years of Los Angeles history, 94 years have had less than average rainfall. Less than average runoff has occurred in two-thirds of these years (2).

With such a record for dry years, it is inevitable that a history of violent floods exists. These floods are accentuated by the geography of the region. The surrounding mountains are characterized by steep canyons and precipitous slopes that rise near the city. At the foot of the mountains, the slope changes abruptly, and an alluvial plain is formed by intersecting fans from the major canyons. The debris from the erosion of the steep mountainsides tends to deposit at this break in slope, clogging both natural and man-made channels and making extensive flooding of the entire plain quite possible.

Concepts such as flood-plain zoning are not generally applicable under these conditions. Flood-control measures in the form of lined channels, dams, and debris basins have been extensively undertaken by the Los Angeles County flood-control district, particularly after the disastrous floods of 1938. Since that time, control measures have been reasonably effective and are being steadily improved.

In 1781, a charter was granted by the King of Spain to a tiny village with the improbable name of El Pueblo de Nuestra Señora La Reina de Los Angeles de Porciuncula. By 1850, its population was only 1610. During this period, the pueblo was the mercantile center of a vast empire of cattle ranches. Thoroughly dominated by the *vacquero* and the hides and tallow economy that had brought Dana and his compatriots around Cape Horn, it had developed a distinctive culture, which was only slightly affected by the change from the Mexican to the American flag.

Results of Drought

Interestingly enough, a bitter 45-year drought was primarily responsible for the population explosion that saw the number of inhabitants in Los Angeles grow from 1610 in 1850 to approximately 100,000 at the end of the 19th century and to 2 million midway through the 20th century. From 1862 to 1864, virtually no rain fell. Grass failed throughout the vast cattle ranches. The great herds of cattle were decimated. This calamity was the end of the road for the cattle barons, and the interminable process of subdivision was begun.

The drought continued with only minor relief until 1890. Ground water was available from flowing artesian wells, but hides and tallow could not pay for irrigated grass. More intensive, high-value, irrigated agriculture, however, lacked only a means of transportation to eastern markets to exploit the hidden resource. By the time the Southern Pacific (1877) and Santa Fe (1885) railroads arrived from the East, the south coastal basin of California was over-ripe for the greatest land boom in the history of the United States.

The little city with the long name moved rapidly toward its destiny as the big city with a short name. By the mid-1860's, a population of 5000 made the open-ditch and water-wagon system inadequate, and the city council turned the city's water rights to the Los Angeles River over to a private concern on a 30-year lease.

This experiment ended in 1902, when the lessees returned the rights to the city for $2 million. In return for the $2 million, the city received a headache and a bargain. The headache was a water system quite incapable of serving a mushrooming city. The bargain came in the person of William Mulholland, self-educated *zanjero* who had by that time shoveled himself out of the mud of the *zanja madre* into the position of superintendent of the Los Angeles City Water Company. If there had not been men of vision, such as Fred Eaton, and men of action, such as William Mulholland, the southern

California citrus economy would have followed the cattle barons into oblivion, and Los Angeles might yet be a sleepy pueblo waiting for *mañana*.

Fred Eaton was well acquainted with the vicious vagaries of flood and drought. By 1900, he was convinced that the only hope for Los Angeles lay in the importation of water from the Sierra Nevada, 250 mountainous miles (400 kilometers) to the north. Going over the ground from the Owens Valley to Los Angeles foot by foot, he convinced Mulholland of the feasibility of a gravity aqueduct to convey this water to Los Angeles. Both felt that this supply would meet the needs of Los Angeles forever.

Mulholland was a dedicated public servant who believed fervently in the principle that no man has the right to profit excessively at the expense of the taxpayers. For him, secrecy in the preliminary steps was essential if the ever-present land speculators were to be prevented from gouging the city. Indeed, one might say that William Mulholland made only three serious mistakes during his life and, in each case, he invoked his cherished principle.

Eaton purchased an option on the Long Valley ranch and its crucial reservoir site, paying $100 to bind a $450,000 option. Directly, and through agents, he quietly cornered land options in the lower valley.

The Owens Valley was a bustling, prosperous community in 1905. Even better prospects were in sight, for the U.S. Bureau of Reclamation had begun investigations for water development that would have brought an additional 100,000 acres (40,000 hectares) of land under cultivation. But when he was privately approached, J. B. Lippincott, head engineer for the regional office of the bureau, agreed that the government should step aside for Los Angeles—provided that the project was entirely publicly owned.

It was a difficult decision for Eaton to make when he was asked to give up his plans and turn over his options in the lower valley to the city. To his credit, he was unselfish enough to do so. Since the reservoir would not be immediately required, however, he reserved Long Valley ranch.

The consternation that reigned in Owens Valley when the story came out can well be imagined. Consternation turned to despair when the U.S. Department of the Interior officially stepped aside in favor of Los Angeles.

Los Angeles voters responded in a manner that has been characteristic whenever and wherever water-supply problems are concerned. By a vote of 14 to 1, they approved $1.5 million in bonds for engineering studies, then backed these 10 to 1 with an additional $23 million for construction. Bids received from private contractors were, in Mulholland's opinion, exorbitant. In keeping with his principle, he recommended rejection of all the bids. The aqueduct could be built complete for $25 million, according to his estimates, and in 5 years' time. Given permission by the city, Mulholland proceeded to build the longest aqueduct in the world, well within both estimates (3).

By November 1913, the water was delivered, but the problem was far from solved. In Owens Valley were the embittered residents, abandoned by the federal government and apparently without recourse to prevent economic ruin of the valley. Most of the water brought to the southland would be used for irrigation of the San Fernando Valley. Thus, their loss was a gain for the land speculators of Los Angeles, and huge profits were taken in a few years' time. It would be hard to convince any rancher under these circumstances that it was all for the best. When it was accomplished under the banner of "the greatest good for the greatest number," the valley folk could hardly be blamed for their fears of the next move on the part of the city.

Attempts were made to resolve the conflict of interests that would certainly develop. An agreement was drawn by which the city would guarantee water to the remaining ranch properties, but it was never ratified. To be able to give such an assurance, a large dam would be required in Long Valley to regulate the seasonally variable flow. Fred Eaton held the reservoir site and, in an attempt to salvage something from his master plans, set the price at $1 million.

Owens Valley War

In defense of Eaton's price, it must be remembered that had he chosen to invest in San Fernando Valley land, his profit would have been close to $4 million. To his credit, he chose to invest in the system itself until he was forced out by public policy. To Mulholland, nonetheless, a profit of $550,000 was simply an attempt to gouge the city, and he would have none of it. By invoking his moral principles, he made the second mistake of his life, inadvertently provoking the "Owens Valley war."

Faced with another drought and no reservoir, the city secretly resumed purchase, through agents, of land options, which culminated in payment of $1 million for 100 cubic feet (2.84 cubic meters) per second of water from the owners of the McNally ditch. It is interesting that the price paid to start the "war" was almost exactly the price that could have been paid to prevent it. This second clandestine purchase left little doubt in the minds of the ranchers that the city intended to break the valley, piecemeal.

The trouble began quietly enough. Under the leadership of the Watterson brothers, owners of five banks and other businesses in the valley, the ranchers above the aqueduct headgate simply diverted the entire flow of the river, leaving the aqueduct dry.

Los Angeles retaliated by indiscriminate land purchases. When any person on a ditch sold to the city, his share of the ditch-maintenance costs necessarily was passed on to the remaining owners. Thus, purchase of a relatively few options could force panic selling of the remainder.

Yet the owners on the lowest ditch, Big Pine, presented both well-organized resistance and a diversion capacity sufficient to keep the aqueduct dry. From this position of strength, they forced the city to buy the entire block at a price that again exceeded both the price of the reservoir site and the potential economic value of the land (4).

Although Los Angeles had now paid twice for the water, only a fraction of it reached the aqueduct. Led by the Wattersons, the upper valley was prepared to use the same tactics that won victory at Big Pine. The water would be withheld until the city purchased the entire valley for $8 million, including "reparations" to valley merchants (the Wattersons among others). Visions of wealth now stood beside righteous indignation, and it is doubtful that even Long Valley reservoir would have been accepted at this point.

In late May 1924, the war entered its violent phase (4). The aqueduct was dynamited near Lone Pine. Newspapers in the valley openly called the dynamiting a "protest of an outraged people." In November, a cavalcade led by Mark Watterson took possession of the Alabama Gates and spilled the entire flow of the aqueduct back into the Owens River. The arrival of the sheriff changed the situation not a bit. A temporary restraining order from the superior court had even less effect. More than 700 persons took part in the demonstrations. By then, Watterson had raised the price to $12 million.

Four days later, the purpose having been admirably fulfilled, the gates were closed. One last gigantic barbecue, attended by 1500 persons, celebrated the success of the seizure. From coast to coast, newspapers broadcasted the story of the embattled farmers, sometimes factually, sometimes sensationally. California newspapers also severely condemned the actions of the city. Even the governor refused to intercede (5), and the citizens of Los Angeles, for the first time, were fully aware that interbasin transport of a water supply is not a simple matter of physics and engineering.

Early in 1925, Los Angeles announced that it was ready to purchase all lands that were being served water from the Owens River, leaving no isolated pieces. No reparations would be paid to merchants. At this point, the Watterson brothers broke the valley unity by selling their 1200-acre (485-hectare) ranch and 22 others on the Bishop Creek ditch to the city.

Although water could no longer be prevented from reaching the aqueduct, the remaining ranchers were not yet beaten. In quick succession, two city-owned wells were dynamited. A month later, the aqueduct was dynamited near the Alabama Gates, and on 27 May, the giant No Name siphon was dynamited and demolished. The next night, a pipe section near Big Pine Creek was destroyed.

Los Angeles dispatched detectives and armed guards to the scene with orders to "shoot to kill" anyone loitering near the aqueduct (4). This precaution proved to be insufficient; a week later 150 feet (46 meters) of aqueduct was blown up opposite Owens Lake. The next night, another blast hit near Lone Pine, and additional guards were ordered.

Meanwhile, Watterson's hardware store ordered 60 Winchester carbines and delivered them to willing hands. By this time, "shooting the duct" had become a weekly pastime. The newspapers were still solidly behind the "defenders of the valley." The city was beaten. The only alternative to bloodshed was to meet the Wattersons' demands. But before this action could be taken, the valley was figuratively rocked by an explosion many times greater than all the dynamitings combined.

At the suggestion of a suspicious city official, the state corporation commission sent an examiner to look over the books of the Watterson banks. By noon the next day, all five banks were closed.

The Wattersons immediately denounced the action as a part of the machinations of the city scoundrels. So great was their reputation for honesty and leadership that the entire valley flocked to their support. Very quickly, however, the examiners announced their findings; $2.3 million was missing. It was discovered that securities placed in safekeeping by friends had been sold. Mortgages paid off by farmers were still on the books. Lifetime savings were lost, including a substantial portion of the payments the city had made to the ranchers for their property. Ranchers and businesses alike were ruined. The Owens Valley war was over.

Unfortunately, the price to be paid for Mulholland's principles was not yet reckoned. During the drought and struggle for water, Mulholland fully understood the need for a reservoir for additional storage. The Long Valley site was not available as long as Eaton held to his demand. A site in Big Tujunga Canyon was also rejected on principle when the owners asked speculative prices. Under emergency conditions, Mulholland turned to a reservoir site in San Franciscito Canyon and constructed the St. Francis Dam, after a somewhat overhasty assessment of the foundation.

Failure of St. Francis Dam

The critical material of the dam was a conglomerate under the west side of the concrete gravity structure. When it was bone-dry, this conglomerate had all the appearances of a hard, well-cemented rock. Apparently, Mulholland's engineers found it in this condition and approved it without further tests. When it was placed in water, however, the apparently hard rock rapidly underwent slaking, disintegrating into a muck within a few minutes (6).

About midnight on 12 March 1928, with the reservoir filled to capacity, the slaking caused by seepage had reached the point where the foundation failed. Within moments, the entire structure collapsed, sending a wall of water 125 feet (38 meters) high down the valley. In a construction camp below the dam, 140 workers were picked up by the flood, including a heroic nightwatchman who scorned certain safety in an attempt to warn the others. On down the Santa Clara River, the torrent rushed, at times 100 feet (30.5 meters) in depth. Piru, Filmore, and Santa Paula were swept over with little or no warning. In all, 385 lives were lost and 1250 homes were destroyed, in addition to millions of dollars' worth of other property damage (6), an unhappy monument to man's inability to resolve the human side of his water problems.

Following the tradition of the civil-engineering profession, Mulholland accepted full responsibility for the tragedy. Such was his prestige and fame that, at the inquest, it was suggested, as a way out, that he often left engineering details to subordinates. As is characteristic of truly great men, he refused to accept the suggestion (4).

Civil-engineering schools still cite the St. Francis Dam failure as a lesson, both in physics and in professional responsibility. But nowhere is there a school of human engineering to teach and emphasize the lessons of the Owens Valley war. There is no curriculum to impress those in the professional public service that there are two sides to every coin; that there are many admirable principles on which men can rightfully stand, yet be on opposite sides of that coin.

For a brief time, the eyes of the city were opened to the realization that there was more to its water problems than engineering, legal technicalities, and hardheaded business. Two years after the St. Francis Dam disaster, the city voted $12 million in bonds to acquire Owens Valley. Not only were the remaining ranch properties purchased at a price favorable to the ranchers, but the city also moved to buy the town properties. Despite the fact that the nation had entered the Great Depression, peak 1923 prices were paid.

Almost ironically, the city now moved to build Long Valley dam. Fred Eaton had lost heavily in the crash of the Watterson banks. Long Valley had to be sold at any price. In December 1932, the city paid an appraisal price of $650,000 for the property. The dam, completed in 1941, was about the same size as had been demanded by the farmers 20 years before. To save $350,000, the city expended tens of millions of dollars for lands, for repairs to the aqueduct, for a dam that failed, and for the damages caused by the ensuing flood. Such is the nature of human relations.

Use of the Colorado River

Owens Valley proved to be only one of a series of battles for water for Los Angeles and its southern California neighbors. The Colorado River had a greater reputation for devastating floods than for peaceful farms along its banks. But if Mulholland expected that his action in filing for 1500 cubic feet (55 cubic meters) per second of water would be relatively unopposed, he was badly mistaken.

The Boulder Canyon Act, passed in 1928, authorized construction of the mighty Hoover (Boulder) Dam, a masterpiece of engineering and art. It cleared the way for construction of the Colorado River aqueduct by the Metropolitan Water District of Southern California, to which Los Angeles tied its water fortunes in 1928.

The story of the political struggle for the river need not be told in detail. Like a western movie, the locale and characters often changed, but the plot always remained the same. It could not be otherwise, for the stakes in the game for water are high in an arid land. Neither sentiment nor equity is given consideration when, as in Owens Valley, the economic future of an entire region may depend on a political decision. Suffice it to say that California considered it had emerged a "victor," only to be confounded by a difference between the language of the Boulder Canyon Act and the Colorado River compact, which cast an uncertainty on the rights obtained. Arizona made effective use of this difference to reassert its claims before the U.S. Supreme Court, substantially reducing the entitlement of the metropolitan water district to Colorado River water. Although the full effect of this decision has not yet been assessed, history may yet repeat itself, if agents of thirsty cities attempt to purchase water rights from ranchers in the Imperial Valley or on the Colorado Plateau.

The phenomenal growth of the sleepy pueblo into a megalopolis covering the entire coastal plain exceeded the wildest of predictions. By 1950, many cities of the metropolitan complex were living on borrowed time and mined ground water. All around the periphery of the basin, sea-water intrusion was threatening pollution of the vast underground reservoirs, a vital resource in a state with a highly variable water supply and a record of many prolonged droughts. Obviously, another water project was urgently needed.

Experienced by now at the business of importing water, southern

California organized itself to appropriate the unused waters of the Feather River, 500 miles (800 kilometers) to the north. Here there were no problems of sovereign states or existing legal water rights. With the center of population of the entire state well within the city limits of Los Angeles, there was little question of the power of southland voters to bring the water south. But the battlelines drawn were once again appropriative doctrine versus reservations for the areas of origin. Despite the valiant efforts of state senators from the north to safeguard the right to develop the most readily available water for local use at such time in the future as it might be required, the inevitable approval of the Feather River project and the necessary $1750 million in bonds were given by popular referendum in November 1960.

As water planners look even farther northward toward the day when a second California aqueduct will be required, the question invariably is asked: "Why not desalt the oceans at Los Angeles's front door rather than fight interminable water wars?" Perhaps someday this may be feasible, but water demands do not wait patiently for a scientific breakthrough. The best technology yet demonstrated gives a cost for each unit of water that is nearly 4 times the cost of natural fresh water carried from northern California.

Some hope exists if very inexpensive atomic or nuclear energy could be made available. Even here, there is question concerning competitive costs for very large quantities of water. The same inexpensive energy can pump water and produce cement and the other materials required for aqueducts perhaps as inexpensively as it could produce fresh water from the oceans. This does not mean that sea-water conversion will never be a major source of fresh water. There are many arid areas on the earth where adequate natural fresh water supplies are simply not available. Furthermore, there is the very real possibility that research may produce a new and different process that gives a much more efficient technology with reduced capital and operating costs. In the meantime, water planners must look both ways if water needs are to be met on time.

REFERENCES

1. R. H. Dana, *Two Years Before the Mast* (Houghton Mifflin, Boston, 1840).

2. Metropolitan Water District of Southern California, *History and First Annual Report* (Los Angeles, 1939).
3. Los Angeles Board of Public Service Commissioners, *Final Report, Construction of the Los Angeles Aqueduct* (Los Angeles, 1916).
4. R. A. Nadeau, *The Water Seekers* (Doubleday, Garden City, N.Y., 1950).
5. W. F. McClure, *Owens Valley-Los Angeles Controversy* (Calif. State Printing Office, Sacramento, 1925).
6. Report of the Commission, *Causes Leading to the Failure of the St. Francis Dam* (Calif. State Printing Office, Sacramento, 1928).

Central Valley: Water Use at Its Maximum

HAROLD E. THOMAS

Man has developed and utilized the water resources of the Central Valley of California for more than a century and has increasingly controlled these resources for more effective use. In this century, he has also learned much about the hydrology of the valley, including the natural flow system and the effects of modifications by man.

The Central Valley is a gigantic trough whose floor is a gently sloping plain about 400 miles (650 kilometers) long, paralleling the California coast, and averaging 40 miles (65 kilometers) in width. Mountains surround the valley, except for a gap along the central part of its western margin; through this gap the combined waters of the Sacramento River (draining the northern part of the Central Valley) and the San Joaquin River (from the south) flow into San Francisco Bay.

The valley's drainage basin occupies more than one-third of the total area of the state and contains 60 percent of its irrigable land. Irrigation agriculture and associated industries are the chief basis of the economy of the valley, which has a present population of about 3 million. The 5 million irrigated acres (2 million hectares) produce a greater variety of crops than any other state in the Union and yield an annual revenue that exceeds $700 million.

Yet, early visitors saw chiefly barren plains, little better than a desert, with little water or vegetation other than that along the flood plains of the rivers.

Gold brought the first big migration to California, starting in 1849, and the earliest extensive use of water was for placer mining along the eastern slopes of the Central Valley. As the washing method progressed from miner's pan to sluice and eventually to hydraulic mining, the use of water increased and developments included pipe-lines, flumes, numerous reservoirs, and ditches. The influx of miners also caused a boom in agriculture and service industries. Steamships plied the Sacramento River, carrying passengers and supplies from San Francisco to Sacramento.

After a long conflict between agricultural and mining interests, hydraulic mining along tributaries of the Sacramento River was vir-tually terminated by court injunction in 1884, chiefly on the grounds of the damage to navigation that resulted from mining debris in the navigable channels. Thereafter, the dominant use of water in the Central Valley was for irrigation.

Nevertheless, regulation of streamflow by storage came slowly. Agriculturists became the beneficiaries of some of the reservoirs and ditches that had been constructed in the gold-mining country. Con-trol structures were built at some natural reservoirs. But the first big dams for storage of water for irrigation were constructed in the 1920's, several years after major reservoirs had been created in other western states.

Part of this delay in storage development may be traced back to 1850, when the California legislature adopted the English common law and, thus, inadvertently subscribed to the doctrine that the nat-ural flow of the stream belongs to the riparian landowner—whether he uses the water or not—and that he has no right to store the water; the nonriparian landowner is ignored. It took a constitutional amendment, in 1928, to limit these riparian rights to the quantities that the riparian owners could use reasonably and beneficially.

Start of Pumping

For those to whom surface water was unavailable for irrigation—whether legally or geographically—ground water was the alternative source. Flowing wells in the bottom lands, which had initial yields during the 1880's sufficient to irrigate several acres (hectares), grad-ually diminished in flow, although more than 500 still were flowing in 1905. As electricity became generally available, starting in 1900, pumped irrigation wells became more numerous.

Many wells were fortunately situated: the water pumped out was fully replenished, either from streams or from lands irrigated by sur-face water. In some, the replenishment from surface irrigation was great enough to cause waterlogging, a condition that was corrected by using the pumped water for irrigation farther down the canal. Thus some irrigation districts, although they are dependent on an unregulated stream as their ultimate source, utilize ground-water storage to achieve a regulated supply.

Many other wells have received little or no replenishment of the water pumped; hence, pumping lifts have increased, or the yields have decreased progressively, as water has been withdrawn from storage. In widespread localities that include those where flowing wells once existed, water was found in deep sandy zones, with thick overlying layers of clay and silt and the artesian head drawn down. The total decline in the water table, as of 1962, exceeded 100 feet (30 meters) in extensive sections of the San Joaquin Valley and reached a maximum of 460 feet (140 meters) in one locality.

Subsidence

Land subsidence has been noted for the past three decades. In two parts of the San Joaquin Valley, the rate of subsidence has approached 1 foot (30 centimeters) per year and has been correlated with the reduction in the artesian head caused by pumping.

Subsidence has occurred, too, in two areas 6 to 9 miles (10 to 15 kilometers) wide and 22 miles (35 kilometers) long along the western edge of the San Joaquin Valley, owing to irrigation and the subsequent compaction of soil and near-surface sediments that evidently had not been saturated previously. This subsidence created local problems in land use and maintenance of irrigation facilities and led to the use of sprinkler irrigation on many farms.

The differentiation between places where pumped ground water is replenished by surface water and others where it is not is for the purpose of classifying the problems. But such situations are not separate or independent, and the problems have coalesced in some places. A case in point is the Los Banos-Kettleman City area, west of the axis of the valley but adjacent to the lower parts of the San Joaquin and Kings River fans. The intensive west-side pumping has created a hydraulic gradient and, therefore, has induced ground-water movement across the axis of the valley from these fans. This movement is far too slow to permit full replenishment of the water pumped on the west side but is of sufficient strength and quantity to be a significant drain on the east side. In recent years, water levels have declined in wells in several parts of the Kings River fan, which may be attributed in part to drought, but the west-side pumping certainly is a contributing factor.

Surplus Water

The early visitors who saw "little better than a desert" also reported swamp and overflow lands totaling about 2 million acres (800,000 hectares), which were rendered undesirable by too much water. About one-fourth of this area is at the confluence of the Sacramento and San Joaquin rivers—the delta—where the original land surface was approximately at sea level.

Croplands there are irrigated by diversion of water from the adjacent waterways, or are drained by the pumping out of excess water. In periods of minimum flow, particularly during dry years, sea water intrudes into the delta channels. Upstream, the bottom lands are naturally places of rising ground water, high water table, high rate of evapotranspiration, and accumulation of saline residues. With increasing use of water upstream, there has been less water for the bottom lands, and this supply has included an increasing amount of irrigation return flows. Thus, with increasing inflow of salines and decreasing quantities of water to carry the salines, the salt balance has become a problem.

The southern part of San Joaquin Valley includes several closed basins, which are occupied by Tulare, Goose, Buena Vista, and Kern lakes. These lakes seldom fill to overflowing, and Tulare Lake last discharged to the San Joaquin River in 1878. With more use of the tributary streams for irrigation, the beds of the lakes have been generally dry except during major flood years. In large part, they have been converted to croplands that are protected by levees and irrigated from canals or deep wells. As long as there is no outflow from these basins, the accumulation of salts is inevitable.

An aggravating factor is the leaching action that results from irrigation of previously undeveloped lands that have accumulated salts in typical arid-regions fashion. The excess irrigation water in some places has created a high water table, with water too saline for reuse. The alternative—high irrigation efficiency with negligible percolation through the root zone—has caused higher and higher concentrations of salts near the soil surface.

Need for Valley-Wide Planning

For the first three-quarters of a century, it is evident that developments in the Central Valley were chiefly the separate and independent efforts of individuals or irrigation districts or other local groups. They were approaching the point of diminishing returns in utilization of the water resources. These developments had also set the stage for several problems that would become critical.

But there were still unused surpluses at certain times, and at all times in some parts of the valley. And there were still people with inadequate water supplies, and irrigable lands that were not being used. Two obvious needs were for storage during periods of water surplus for use during periods of natural deficiency, and the transport of water from regions of abundance to places of scarcity. Comprehensive planning, construction, and financing were required to meet these needs. The California legislature in 1921 directed the state engineer to develop a general plan, and this was presented in 1930.

Federal funds were made available in 1935 for construction by the Bureau of Reclamation of the Central Valley project, of which the principal units include major reservoirs on the Sacramento and San Joaquin rivers; the Delta-Mendota canal, carrying Sacramento River water from the delta southward 115 miles (185 kilometers) chiefly as an exchange for San Joaquin River water; and the Friant-Kern canal, carrying water of the San Joaquin River southward 150 miles (240 kilometers) into the Kern River Basin.

Then in 1947, the legislature called for a comprehensive plan for the development and use of all water resources of the state. The resulting California water plan, published in 1957, includes separate local developments and a general aqueduct system to convey water from areas of surplus to areas of deficiency. This plan transcends basin boundaries and makes it possible to use surpluses from the north end of the state to relieve shortages near the Mexican border; thus, the water passes through the entire length of the Central Valley and southern California.

Hydrology

Pacific storms are prevalent in winter, and more than 80 percent of the average annual precipitation on the drainage basin occurs in the 5 months from November to March. Pacific storms are more numerous and larger in the north than in the south, and the average precipitation on the valley floor diminishes from 32 inches (800 millimeters) at the north end to 6 inches (150 millimeters) at the south. Average precipitation increases with altitude; thus, the valley floor is a semiarid region rimmed on all sides by wetter areas. The flat "valley and mesa" lands, which make up about 40 percent of the drainage basin, receive an average of about 17 million acre feet (21 billion cubic meters) of precipitation annually. The mountains and foothills receive 4 times as much.

Average annual runoff from the Sierra-Cascade mountain chain to the valley is about 29 million acre feet (36 billion cubic meters), and streams entering Sacramento Valley from the west side—draining the Coast Ranges—discharge nearly 3 million acre feet (3.7 billion cubic meters) of water annually. Precipitation in the Sacramento Valley has been sufficient to add another 1 million acre feet (1.2 billion cubic meters) to the runoff; hence, the natural outflow from the valley should be nearly 33 million acre feet (41 billion cubic meters). By 1960, however, the average annual outflow had been reduced to about 15.5 million acre feet (19 billion cubic meters) because of man's use of the water on the valley and mesa lands.

Both precipitation and runoff deviate markedly from the average, which is based generally on records for half a century. The annual precipitation has ranged from 50 to 150 percent of the mean for the drainage basin, and the runoff has varied even more widely.

These variations underline a need for storage of water. In most of the valley, irrigation is essential to agriculture, and some storage of floodflows is required for use in the late summer, when natural runoff is minimum. As of 1960, dams had been completed on all major streams entering the valley, and natural lakes had been regulated, to provide an aggregate storage capacity of nearly 15 million acre feet (18.5 billion cubic meters). Additional reservoirs authorized, or proposed in the California plan, will add 8-million-acre-feet (10-billion-cubic-meters) capacity each in the San Joaquin and

Sacramento valleys; hence, the ultimate surface-reservoir capacity will approach the average annual runoff from the mountains.

Ground water has been an essential element in the valley's development for half a century. In recent years, the annual pumpage for irrigation has been approximately 11 million acre feet (13.6 billion cubic meters) from about 55,000 wells, or more than one-fourth of the total pumpage from wells in the United States. About 90 percent of this pumping is in the San Joaquin Valley.

The Central Valley ground-water reservoir—or reservoir complex —under natural conditions received substantial quantities of water by seepage from streams, especially into the permeable sand and gravel of the east-side streams and during floods. The ground water then moved gradually toward the axis of the valley and subsequently along that axis toward the delta. En route, a substantial amount moved into strata where it was confined under artesian pressure by overlying clays; some of the natural discharge from the artesian reservoir has doubtless been by slow upward movement through those clays.

Man has made major modifications in this cycle, although there is still some ground-water recharge from the natural channels of the tributaries, and ground-water discharge by evapotranspiration or seepage into sloughs in the valley bottoms. Probably more than 80 percent of the ground water pumped is now replenished from surface water. Coming from streams as it does, this replenishment accounts for nearly half of the reduction in average outflow from the valley in recent years.

However, some of the water pumped out—from 800,000 to 1.5 million acre feet (1 billion to 2 billion cubic meters) per year—is not replenished. Investigations indicate that in one area, at least, about half the water permanently withdrawn has been squeezed out of the aquifer system by compaction of the deposits, causing a permanent reduction in storage volume.

Ground-Water Capacity

The capacity of the ground-water reservoir in Central Valley has been computed in the zone between 10 and 200 feet (3 to 60 meters) below the land surface. Assumptions are that the use of shallower zones would be undesirable, because of evapotranspiration loss and danger of local waterlogging, and that general pumping lifts greater than 200 feet (60 meters) would be frowned on by present-day economists, even though fresh water occurs at far greater depths and is tapped by numerous wells. According to these calculations, the ground-water reservoir has a storage capacity of 120 million acre feet (148 billion cubic meters). This storage capacity is not reduced significantly by the compaction of sediments that cause land subsidence, because the compaction and reduction in pore space occur chiefly in the fine-grained silt and clay.

Just as storage capacity is required for collection of water in times of surplus and use in times of deficiency, redistribution facilities are required for collection of water in areas of surplus and transport to areas of deficiency. Major canals already are moving surplus waters southward, and the California plan proposes that this be done on a really grand scale. But, as Joseph found in Egypt, the surpluses of several years must be stored up for the famine years that are sure to come. Cyclic storage is thus a key feature in the plans. Fortunately, there is a large natural storage capacity, particularly in the southern part of the valley where precipitation and runoff are the least. So far, artificial recharge has been outstandingly successful in a few areas and slightly so in some others; but it remains a major unsolved problem in a good many places, particularly where the natural supplies have been confined under artesian pressure.

Unsolved Problems

The principal value of the record of progress of the Central Valley in water matters is its usefulness as a guide to what can, and should be, accomplished. The present generation has a great advantage over the pioneers, whose actions often seemed dictated by unenlightened self-interest; today self-interest is probably not greatly diminished, but people feel enlightened.

The California water plan will require manipulation of the natural flow system of the Central Valley—sufficiently complex in itself— on a scale grander than has been attempted anywhere else. Aside from questions of economic justification, financial feasibility, and social implications of specific projects, the master plan brings forth many physical problems that must be solved as a prerequisite to success of certain stages of the plan.

1) Assuming that the storage space lost by compaction is permanently gone, can means be found to recharge during the wet periods the sand and gravel aquifers from which the water is pumped, or is this water also nonreplenishable?

2) Land subsidence poses many problems. Planning for the aqueducts or canals necessary in the California plan requires long-range predictions of areas and rates of subsidence in many parts of the Central Valley.

3) To avoid deterioration of the soil or the underlying ground water—in other words, to insure that these natural resources shall continue to benefit mankind—the salts in the soils must be disposed of where they can do no harm. This will require adequate and effective drainage and allocation of a sufficient amount of the total water supply to the specific purpose of disposal of saline residues and other wastes.

4) Under natural conditions, soluble salts were carried from the valley. If, as is contemplated under ultimate development, this outflow is reduced, some of the salts that would have been disposed of naturally to the ocean must remain in the valley; or else the outflowing water must be far more mineralized, to the detriment, for instance, of farmers in the delta, who now use this water for irrigation.

Most of the water problems are actually people problems and arise, in part, from competing and conflicting special interests in water and, in part, from deep-rooted convictions that are part of the North American culture.

As might be expected in our security-minded age, some of the people in water-deficient areas that will receive increased water supplies under the California plan are demanding guarantees of specific quantities to meet their "requirements." The wise politician should be wary of any contracts that include such guarantees. He cannot be sure that the deficiencies incurred during an exceptional drought will be entirely offset by exceptional rainfall during his term of office, or even during his lifetime.

It is hoped and expected that the vast ground-water reservoir of the Central Valley will serve as a cushion against the sharp bumps of periodic natural excesses and deficiencies. But here, aside from the physical problem of getting water into the reservoir, there will be a spate of problems that involve owners of the overlying land

and their property rights in the water. It is likely that effective water management will be achieved only by some regimentation and loss of individual prerogatives.

The people of the Central Valley have made mistakes in the past, but they have the advantage of a natural resource that is a true wealth of water: one can squander and survive more successfully in wealth than in poverty. On the other hand, the people, after learning just where and when this wealth exists, have improved on nature —which in this valley was truly a wastrel—and have reaped benefits in the process.

Acknowledgment: In the preparation of this summary, I am grateful for the information, suggestions, and critical review provided by Joseph F. Poland, of the U.S. Geological Survey.

Great Plains: A Region Basically Vulnerable

CARL F. KRAENZEL

Caught between the humid, industrial East and the oases-based industrial and metropolitan complexes of the arid West, the semi-arid Great Plains of the United States have always been a high risk area. From the earliest days of settlement, the Plains were a region to be crossed hurriedly, and not without suffering. But the "dust blows" of the 1930's and later and the fact that agricultural depression preceded the great national depression of the same decade put the problems of the Plains in bold relief.

The U.S. Department of Agriculture, the experiment stations, the federal Extension Service, and Congress, all rallied to the cause of helping agriculturists to change the Dust Bowl of the 1930's—controlling insects, conserving the limited moisture that did fall, and raising the income of the Plains people. Some new ways were found to control soil blowing; but rains, too, came again and, perhaps, did as much as technology and soil management to control the dust. This is said because, in the early 1950's, drought came again to the southern Plains, perhaps as severe as in the 1930's; and to the northern Plains also, a little later. President Dwight D. Eisenhower met with farm leaders and officials of the region, and the older program of soil and resources management was speeded up, extended, and implemented. It became known as the Great Plains program.

To understand the vulnerability of this region, one must realize that the complex industrial and urban society of the United States places great value on stability. There are perhaps three props that undergird this esteemed stability (1). These are (i) certainty and stability of income in agriculture as well as in industry, (ii) certainty and stability of contract performance, and (iii) certainty and predictability of future income-cost relationships.

The arid West is capable of accomplishing these stability objectives, in large part, by virtue of the oasis nature of the settlement—irrigation to make wet that which is dry (2), thus limiting settlement and, therefore, all institutional services to the oases areas. Space is, therefore, less of a cost, economies can be accomplished, and the resources base of the oases is made richer by the periodic exploitation of adjacent nonirrigated areas. There are only limited exceptions to this, such as the lumbering, mining, or recreational areas and an occasional favored dry-land area, such as the Palouse Hills.

Because they do not have this esteemed stability, the Great Plains are deeply vulnerable. The fluctuations between wet and dry years, singly or in series, make for instability. Also, some years are half wet and half dry, with the wet part at the wrong time. The Great Plains have been "next-year" country, the epitome of instability.

A second reason for instability in the Plains is that this region lacks the oasis character of settlement that is typical of the arid West. Instead, settlement is all over the land, as it is in the humid East. People live everywhere. This means that schools and school districts are located all over, as they are in the humid area. Local government is spread out, as are public-health and medical-care services, religious organization, and other services.

There are occasional irrigated areas in the Plains, but, compared with the total settled areas, these serve only a very limited population. Often these irrigated sections, called *Sutland* areas (3), are favored with railroad, air, and bus transportation, with public utilities, and with the more important wholesale and retail services; and often they contain the seat of special services, such as public health, medical care, and county government. The industrial urban-humid area ways of life become established in these isolated Sutland settlements and are passed on unadapted to the dispersed settlers and dry-land communities of the Great Plains. The Sutland areas can be, in fact, a burden to the dry-land farming and ranching of the region, unless they purposefully integrate themselves.

Thus, instability in the Plains is the result of sparse population that is spread out all over the land; of the concentration of most of the facilities in the Sutland areas, which are often far away from *Yonland* (hinterland) settlers; and of the high social cost of space. More of the problems in the Great Plains are created by the imported, unsuitable, unadapted humid-area ways than by the semi-arid climate.

Certain technology and management practices have been adapted to the agriculture of the Plains and have reduced the hardships and damages of recurrent and unpredictable drought. Greater stability, the prop for an advanced civilization, has been partly achieved by these adaptations. But the recurrence of drought in the 1950's indicates that technology and management alone cannot, for long, give the necessary stability required for a high level of living in the region. Furthermore, the drought of the late 1950's in the Plains was different in one important respect from the drought of the 1930's.

In the 1930's, drought and depression came at the same time. In the 1950's, the prosperity in the rest of the nation and the high cost of mechanized operations meant that a low yield in crop and livestock income, coupled with depressed agricultural prices, resulted in starvation income. Only population exodus and industrial employment in the oil-extraction industry, at missile sites, and in other national defense activity located in the Plains helped to ease the low-income situation of this period. Another part of the low-income problem was solved by reduction of taxes and curtailment of expansion in education and other public services—steps that were taken by the 1961 Montana legislature. But further insecurity and instability resulted.

Evidence of Adaptation

It is difficult for people to recognize their problems and then do something about them if they do not have the help of institutions, cities, and social organization. The humid-area way of life was thrust on the Great Plains and rejected all that might have encouraged adaptation. Historians, economists, sociologists, and political scientists have shown how, in the trek westward, the settlers from the humid East brought with them into the Plains many unadapted ways.

And humid-area man did not look for models that he might have followed. The American Indians had adapted ways, as did the Spaniards and the Texans when they were a nation. The early cattlemen and sheepmen, too, had adapted ways. And as early as 1878 John Wesley Powell had made some specific recommendations for successful living in the arid regions (4). But humid-area man was highly ethnocentric and, therefore, could not readily learn from others.

It took repeated drought, frequent bankruptcy of farmers, ranchers, and merchants, repeated influx and exodus of population, extensive human misery and suffering, bankruptcy of local governments and local school districts, and duststorms to teach settlers that certain adjustments had to be made. These lessons were learned slowly and have not been effectively meshed into the traditions of the region. Even now some of these lessons are rejected, as is indicated by the slight margin by which the production-control program for wheat (*Triticum*) won out in the fall of 1962, and lost in 1963. Plains agriculturists, afraid of an uninformed but vocal urban and humid-area press, like *Time Magazine,* for example, are once again, as they were after World War I, willing to take the road to anarchism and poverty—a road that humid-area industrialists, businessmen, and laborers are not willing to take (5).

Through a process of evolution, the Plains farmers, with the help of the experiment stations and the U.S. Department of Agriculture, developed dry-land farming, an ingenious, many-faceted system that might serve as a model for adaptations in other areas of living. Ranchers, too, developed adapted techniques, which were more suitable than some of the former ways. Feed reserves were emphasized, first, as "black-top" haystacks and, later, as ensilage and feed supplements that were deliverable as concentrates. Rotation pastures helped to preserve the soil and the sod; dikes, dams, and well development distributed the livestock in an effort to slow down the erosion of pasture and rangelands.

Progress has been made in the establishment of adapted practices through the U.S. Soil Conservation Service program and through the agricultural conservation program. Some of these measures were unknown before the Dust Bowl days, and others evolved still more recently. Some of them have been possible only because of group-organized, as contrasted with individual, efforts.

In this way it has been possible to halt the threat of unwise competition, which has led, in the past, to overgrazing on the range and to exhaustion of the cropland by overuse. The federal government has cooperated by paying, out of taxes, a portion of the cost of installing these improvements, because the competitive market price would not pay the farmers and ranchers enough income to make these conservation investments in the land resources. The Plains, located far from markets, are in an especially vulnerable position for economic reasons, as well as for reasons of recurring drought; therefore a special program has been necessary for them.

One of the adapted farm and ranch practices for the Plains has been farm storage—a practice of building reserves to enhance stability. But it has not been developed to its maximum, since acreage allotments have been preferred over bushel (liter) or yield allotments. Periodically, this farm storage program has deteriorated or has been subjected to severe criticism.

Farmers and ranchers are still deceiving themselves into thinking that they have an absolute right in landownership and control of resources, and city people conspire with or against farmers and ranchers in dealing with these serious situations. The farmers and ranchers, who are voiceless for lack of cities and communication facilities, are seldom able to take a long-range view, because they find it difficult to communicate with each other, not to say anything of the difficulty of communication with the urban people, both in and out of the region. For example, both farmers and ranchers in the Plains need extensive credit for their operations. The Spokane branch of the Federal Land Bank has experimented with a future-repayments program. By this means, the regular principal and interest payments are accompanied by additional payments during high-yield years. These additional payments go into a reserve fund to apply on regular principal and interest installments in years of low or no income. However, the urban residents inside and outside the region do not encourage and foster this adapted financing procedure; rather, they insist on pushing the unadapted humid-area techniques on the region.

Adapted Farming Practices

The adapted agricultural practices that lend greater stability to the Great Plains can be summarized under three principles. The first is the development of reserves—a truly adapted technique. A second is the development of flexibility in farm and ranch operations. Farmers have sought to store the crop of high-yield years for a carry-over into low-yield years and, thus, develop reserves and also flexibility; income is available through deferred sales when there is no yield. Shifts from wheat to cattle production, and back again, and mixed-crop and livestock farming under conditions of area diversification are other illustrations of flexibility. For ranchers, the supplementing of the basic cowherd and baby beeves by purchase of range feeder cattle in "good grass years" introduces a form of flexibility.

A third principle for more adapted living in the Plains is the introduction of mobility in farm and ranch operations. In addition to the fact that farms are now larger, many operators cultivate acreages in several areas, miles apart, so that drought and hail in one area will not necessarily affect the other parts of the unit, and, therefore, the total production of the farm does not fluctuate violently. More crop farmers now live in town the year around and, thus, are more mobile in matters of farm operations; at the same time, they reduce the costs of mobility and living by bringing the family within easier reach of medical care and education. Ranchers bring public-domain land and large blocks of private, nonresident-owned land together and manage the whole as grazing districts. By this means, home-based ranching lands and public or private grazing lands are brought together, into manageable operating units, even though they are miles apart.

These three traits—reserves, flexibility, and mobility—are major keys to the survival of agriculture in the Plains. They enhance the aforementioned three props to stability.

Continued Unadapted Ways

The adaptations in ranching and farming cannot, and have not, solved all the problems of the region. There may well be an increasing number of facets of living in the Plains today that are basically unsuited for semiarid conditions.

First of all, the increased mechanization, both in ranching and farming, and its greater efficiency have resulted in sparser population on the land and in the smaller towns. There has not been an accompanying concentration of population in oasis-like fashion, except accidentally as agricultural and small-town youths and adults, on their way out of the region, make a first stop at the smaller towns and cities before they or their children finally leave the region. The remaining population has continued to live everywhere, throughout the region, and so it has been necessary to take the services to them

—free rural mail delivery, rural electrification, schools, and hospitals. The 1960 census shows that the population has become sparser, especially in the rural areas, yet the cost of the services per capita or per unit of service has increased. This means that the cost of space is now higher—a cost paid not by the individual but by the society in taxes.

A second consequence is that the level of living today includes many added or new services. Education has been extended to include more years and has become more specialized; for Plains youth, education is not only for living in the region and for agriculture but also for living outside the region, usually in industrial surroundings. This widens the range of educational requirements demanded of a community, enlarges its cost, and introduces new standards. The increased costs and the impinging of standards are not accepted quickly or gracefully, but eventually they are adopted, because farmers and ranchers see only limited opportunity in the region for their sons and daughters.

Public-health and medical-care facilities are in great demand today, not only because people require them as a part of the level of living, but also because the span of life has been lengthened. Hence, more services than formerly are required in public health and medical care. To these must be added old-age assistance and social-work services, old-age and survivors pensions, unemployment compensation and reemployment office services, rehabilitation, and job retraining services.

In addition to enlarging the costs, these services introduce standards and procedures that are new to the region. Often they are based on intensely urban and industrial situations, not on the facts of the high cost of space, the need for reserves, the need for flexibility, and the need for mobility, all of which characterize the Plains. Furthermore, these new services do not necessarily enhance but may detract from certainty and stability of income in the Plains. They may introduce added risks. They do not enhance certainty and predictability of future income-cost relationships, and they may cause this relationship to become more unpredictable. The Plains society should, of course, have these advantages, but the services must be achieved by different techniques. This is the significant point.

Other services rendered by the groups and associations today— among them modernized mental-health services, modernized prison and reformatory care, governmental services of all kinds, taxation procedures, church and religious organization—are more costly today compared with former times. They are considered to be an essential part of social living, but often they are patterned after urban and industrial standards, and the chances that they will be suited for the semiarid conditions of the Plains are small. Today there is great dependence on the "boughten" aspect of these services, especially those that are produced outside the region, and, hence, their unsuitability for the situation in the region would appear to be ever greater.

It is clear, then, that many of the new services are not adapted to the Plains conditions, and their final adaptation is dependent on the cooperation of "Mainstreet" people. The adapted agricultural programs and practices have been instigated by farmers and ranchers as individuals or, at best, by them as groups. Mainstreet people appear not to have developed or applied the adapted practices—reserves, flexibility, and mobility techniques—to their operations. And the entire institutional structure of local and state governments and other institutional organizations have not faced up to these requirements. What school districts and what county governments have set aside reserves during high-income years to operate during years of low income, so that taxes can be reduced in low-income years? What urban business has introduced the principle of reserves, so that operating costs can be lowered or credit extended during years of little or no income to ranchers and farmers? What church program has such reserves, and what prepaid medical- and hospital-care program has such provisions?

These are only a few illustrations to indicate that the Mainstreet people have largely failed to understand the problem of living in the region and have failed to do anything about meeting the problem in an organized and concerted manner on their side of the street. At the same time, they have failed to encourage the farmers and the ranchers in their attempt to cope with this situation. There are instances where city and village people have eventually made some adjustments and have cooperated with the farmers and ranchers, but these instances only point up the importance of the adaptations.

The result is a great schism between farmers and ranchers on the one hand and Mainstreet people on the other. And the tragedy is that this schism is accompanied by another handicap: there are too few people to support the essential group and institutional services. It appears that the social cost of space may yet destroy the residents of the region, unless adaptations are introduced into all aspects of living in the Plains. Whether this can be accomplished will be tested in the immediate future—unless another war postpones this test.

REFERENCES

1. C. F. Kraenzel, *The Great Plains in Transition* (Univ. of Oklahoma Press, Norman, 1954), chaps. 16–21.
2. R. E. Huffman, *Irrigation Development and Public Water Policy* (Ronald, New York, 1953), chap. 14.
3. C. F. Kraenzel, "Sutland and Yonland setting for community organization in the Plains," *J. Rural Sociol.* **18**, 344–358 (1953).
4. J. W. Powell, *Report on the Lands of the Arid Regions of the United States,* W. Stegner, Ed. (Harvard Univ. Press, Belknap Div., Cambridge, Mass., 1962). Originally published by U.S. Geographical and Geological Survey, 1878; 1879.
5. *Time,* 9 Feb. 1962, pp. 14–15.

Sandstone Creek: How a Watershed Was Saved

HAROLD M. KAUTZ

Sandstone Creek, a 69,000-acre (28,000-hectare) tributary of the Washita River in western Oklahoma, lies in the Rolling Red Plains Land Resource Area. Because the shallow soils and steep topography of most of the upland make it suitable only for grazing, livestock provides the major source of income to the landowners.

Ownership of the 4700 acres (1900 hectares) of bottom land in the watershed is closely associated with ownership of the ranch lands that surround the valley. Consequently, slightly more than 90 percent of the cultivated bottom land is used for forage crops, small grains, grain sorghums (*Sorghum*), and alfalfa (*Medicago sativa*).

Sandstone Creek lies in the 25-inch (635-millimeter) rainfall belt and has periods of drought as well as intense rainstorms. During droughts the watershed cover becomes depleted unless the range is carefully managed. Poor cover conditions cause greater runoff and increased flooding of the bottom lands. Loss of supplemental feed crops owing to flooding often leads to heavier grazing of the uplands, and the circle of events is repeated.

Such were the conditions when the U.S. Soil Conservation Service was asked to help the local people to solve their problem. First, flood problems and damages were investigated to determine the types of structures and practices needed to make farming and ranching operations safe. The 20-year period from 1920 through 1939 was selected for study as being representative of normal rainfall in the area. During the period, 184 storms had caused floods; 59 of them brought serious damage. The great drought of the early 1930's occurred during these same two decades.

Sediment damages were found to be severe, and improper land use and management had increased surface runoff, which caused the main channels to deepen at the headwaters and numerous gullies to develop. Deposits of sediment were found on 4115 acres (1665 hectares) of the 4700-acre (1900-hectare) flood plain. Approximately 3700 acres (1500 hectares) were covered to depths of 1 to 8 feet (0.3048 to 2.44 meters). As the loss of topsoil by erosion increased, the deposited material became more sandy and less fertile. Costs of crop production went up as a result, and productivity of the valley land went down.

Information was obtained from more than three-fourths of the landowners or operators in the flood-plain area to determine the extent of flood damage to crops, land, and other agricultural property caused by floods within their memory. They provided data also on land use, acreages of cultivated crops, and the value of the flood-plain land. Damages to roads and to bridges were reported by the county commissioners.

All this basic information was used to determine the damage from floods and sediment. The average annual damages were as follows: crop and pasture damage, $40,100; flood-plain scour, $400; streambank cutting, $2200; other agricultural damages, such as loss of livestock, fences, and equipment, $3900; road and bridge damage, $1000; deposition of sediment on valley lands, $5700; and indirect damages, $5300.

Project Plan

A watershed plan was developed by the soil-conservation-district supervisors, landowners, interested organizations, and agencies of the government. This called for the conservation treatment of the farmland as a means of protecting it against excessive soil loss and runoff. It also called for such measures as detention dams to retard floodwater, sediment-control dams, and channel improvement.

The total needs of the watershed included more than 400 miles (645 kilometers) of terraces and 50 acres (20 hectares) of vegetated waterways to help control erosion on 6200 acres (2500 hectares) of cultivated land; seeding 5800 acres (2350 hectares) of idle or severely eroded cropland to native grasses; 125 farm ponds to promote proper distribution of grazing on rangeland and pasture land; improved

Good range management was a key part of the Sandstone Creek water-shed project. Here, a rancher admires the tall bluestem grass (*Andropogon gerardi*) in one of his pastures near Cheyenne, Oklahoma. (Courtesy U.S. Department of Agriculture, Soil Conservation Service)

crop rotations on 6200 acres (2500 hectares) of cropland; and improved range and pasture management on 58,500 acres (23,800 hectares). Supplemental measures included 24 floodwater-retarding dams, 13 sediment-control dams, and 1 mile (1.61 kilometers) of channel improvement.

The 24 detention dams were planned to control the runoff from 70 percent of the total watershed and to protect 95 percent of the flood plain. A typical detention dam in this locality has an average drainage area of 5 square miles (12.45 square kilometers). The floodwater-detention pool is designed to hold the maximum runoff to be expected once in 25 years. Floodwaters temporarily stored behind the dam are released slowly through an ungated drawdown tube; hence, the water is carried by the stream channel without overflowing the bottom lands below. The lower part of the storage basin is reserved for the deposition of sediment. The storage allotted for this purpose is enough to hold the sediment that will be delivered to the structure during the 50-year period following construction.

The dam has a vegetation-covered spillway that can pass the runoff from a storm that occurs when the detention basin is full; such a situation might occur once in 100 years. A dam of this type is an economical structure that can control the runoff from extremely large storms. Its economy lies in the simplicity and range of design. Because approximately 95 percent of the total flood damage in an agricultural watershed of this type is caused by the smaller storms that occur more frequently than once in 25 years, no attempt is made to store the runoff from major storms.

In the larger, more active gullies that could not be healed by vegetation alone, 13 grade-stabilization or sediment-control dams of the drop-inlet type were planned. Total benefits from the recommended program on Sandstone Creek were calculated to be approximately $3 for each $1 of cost.

Farmers and ranchers cooperated wholeheartedly. By the time the plan was completed and approved by the local people, soil- and water-conservation plans had been prepared on 87 percent of the watershed through cooperative agreements between the landowners and the soil-conservation districts.

Late in 1948, after 60 percent of the needed land-treatment practices had been applied on the land, the supervisors of the soil-conservation district and others started to obtain land rights for all the proposed dams. Construction was completed in November 1952.

Evaluation of the Project

A cooperative evaluation program was developed by the U.S. Soil Conservation Service and the U.S. Geological Survey to determine the effects of land treatment and structures on rainfall-runoff relationships, ground-water recharge, streamflow, and sediment production, and to get information of importance to all groups interested in the conservation, use, and management of water. Fourteen recording and 25 standard rain gages were installed over the watershed.

Water-stage recorders were located on 11 of the 24 retarding dams, and sedimentation ranges were established for future use in measuring sediment deposition in the pool areas. The 11 structures were selected to provide a range in shape and size of drainage areas, land-use pattern, soil types, and cover conditions. Arrangements were made to inventory the condition of the drainage areas annually in order to provide a basis for evaluating the effect of land use and management on sediment production and runoff into the structures.

Three automatic stream-gaging stations were located on the major tributaries and main stem of Sandstone Creek to measure monthly and annual streamflow, peak discharges from storms, and return flow to the stream by water that had been infiltrated into the soil. In addition, four wells were selected for observation of changes in ground-water level. The studies described here will be continued until adequate basic data are obtained.

Sedimentation ranges were surveyed on the 11 structure pools about 5 years after construction, and four of these pools were surveyed again 9 years after construction. It is estimated that the planned treatment was increased from 80 to 90 percent during this 4-year period, with the result that sediment yield was reduced, on the average, about 0.25 acre foot (308 cubic meters) per square mile (2.59 square kilometers).

Between 1953 and 1960, there were 17 storms, or about two per year, that would have caused damage prior to the project. An average of only 90 acres (36.42 hectares) of flood plain was flooded by runoff from these storms. Without the installations and procedures of the project, the average area flooded would have been 870 acres (352 hectares) per storm.

Reductions in flood damage brought about by the project during this 8-year period amount to $182,390, which represents an average saving of $22,800 per year to the flood-plain landowners, but the reductions make up only part of the total benefits from the watershed project.

Through the safe and more intensive use of the productive flood-plain lands, the owners profit also from reduced upland erosion and the ability to manage their ranges properly for higher beef production. All the sediment pools and the water in the stream channels provide needed watering places for livestock.

Fifteen landowners have purchased irrigation equipment, and five regularly irrigate about 200 acres (81 hectares) of land. The yield of cotton (Gossypium) has tripled, and the yields of wheat (Triticum) and alfalfa (Medicago sativa) are more than double the nonirrigated yields. With the application of irrigation water and the more intensive use of the protected flood-plain lands, the net increase in income to the flood-plain landowners has greatly exceeded the $11,000 annual enhancement benefit that was originally estimated in the plan.

Sediment pools of the 24 floodwater-retarding dams provide a total of 660 acres (267 hectares) of water surface and are being used to a considerable extent in an area where there previously had been no suitable facilities for boating, water skiing, swimming, or fishing. Several of the larger pools have been opened to the public for these purposes. Camping areas are being developed; and there are numerous duckblinds in nearly every pool. These incidental recreational and wildlife benefits and the secondary benefits to merchants from sales of boats, motors, trailers, fuel, ammunition, skis, and other sporting equipment were not evaluated in the original plan.

With their uplands protected from erosion and their bottom lands protected from flooding, and with water for livestock and recreation, the people in the watershed community are proud of their cooperative effort. But, if possible, they seem to take more pride in the fact that they have changed Sandstone Creek from a normally dry watercourse to a perennial stream.

Selected Bibliography

The following list of publications was compiled to provide source and reference materials in addition to those cited in the various chapters of this book.

General Publications

B. T. Dickson, "Guide book to research data for arid zone development," *Arid Zone Research (UNESCO)* **9** (1957).

J. W. Krutch, *The Voice of the Desert* (Sloane, New York, 1954).

L. M. Shields and J. L. Gardner, Eds., "Bioecology of the arid and semi-arid lands of the Southwest," *New Mexico Highlands Univ. Bull. 212* (1961).

W. B. Smythe, *The Conquest of Arid America* (Macmillan, New York, 1899).

L. D. Stamp, "A history of land use in arid regions," *Arid Zone Research (UNESCO)* **17** (1961).

C. W. Thornthwaite, "Atlas of climatic types in the United States, 1900–1939," *U.S. Dept. Agr. Misc. Publ. 421* (1941).

G. F. White, *Science and the Future of Arid Lands* (UNESCO, Paris, 1960).

Indian Adaptations

E. E. Dale, *The Indians of the Southwest: A Century of Development under the United States* (Univ. of Oklahoma Press, Norman, 1949).

J. D. Jennings, Ed., "The American Southwest: a problem in cultural isolation," in "Seminars in archaeology," R. Wauchope, Ed., *Mem. Soc. Am. Archaeol.* **11**, 59–127 (1956).

P. Kirchhoff, "Gatherers and farmers in the greater Southwest: a problem in classification," *Am. Anthropol.* **56**, 529–550 (1954).

W. R. Wedel, *Prehistoric Man on the Great Plains* (Univ. of Oklahoma Press, Norman, 1961).

History

R. G. Athearn, *High Country Empire: The High Plains and Rockies* (McGraw-Hill, New York, 1960).

B. A. DeVoto, *The Course of Empire* (Houghton Mifflin, Boston, 1952).

O. W. Freeman and H. H. Martin, Eds., *The Pacific Northwest: A Regional, Human, and Economic Survey of Resources and Development* (Wiley, New York, 1942).

W. J. Ghent, *The Early Far West: A Narrative Outline, 1540–1850* (Tudor, New York, 1936).

L. R. Hafen and C. C. Rister, *Western America: The Exploration, Settlement, and Development of the Region beyond the Mississippi* (Prentice-Hall, Englewood Cliffs, N.J., 1941).

W. E. Hollon, *The Southwest: Old and New* (Knopf, New York, 1961).

T. A. Rickard, *A History of American Mining* (McGraw-Hill, New York, 1932).

R. E. Riegel, *The Story of the Western Railroads* (Macmillan, New York, 1926).

Meteorology

H. E. Landsberg, "Trends in climatology," *Science* **128**, 749 (1958).

T. F. Malone, "Progress, purpose, and potential in the atmospheric sciences," *Bull. Am. Meteorol. Soc.* **43**, 229 (1962).

T. K. Sherwood and H. Wexler, "Desalination, evaporation reduction, artificial precipitation, and large-scale weather and climate modification," *U.S. Papers Prepared for U.N. Conf. Appl. Sci. and Technol. (Geneva)* (U.S. Dept. of State, Washington, D.C., 1963), vol. 1.

T. L. Smiley, Ed., *Climate and Man in the Southwest* (Univ. of Arizona Press, Tucson, 1958)

P. D. Thompson, *Numerical Weather Analysis and Prediction* (Macmillan, New York, 1960).

G. T. Trewartha, *An Introduction to Climate* (McGraw-Hill, New York, 1954).

UNESCO, "Climatology and microclimatology," Canberra Symp., *Arid Zone Research (UNESCO)* **11** (1958).

UNESCO, "Climatology—Reviews of Research," *Arid Zone Research (UNESCO)* **10** (1958).

Water

C. S. Conover, "Ground-water conditions in the Rincon and Mesilla valleys and adjacent areas in New Mexico," *U.S. Geol. Surv. Water Supply Paper 1230* (1953).

W. B. Langbein, "Annual runoff in the United States," *U.S. Geol. Surv. Circ. 52* (1949).

R. L. Nace, "Water management, agriculture, and ground-water supplies," *U.S. Geol. Surv. Circ. 415* (1960).

T. W. Robinson, "Phreatophytes," *U.S. Geol. Surv. Water Supply Paper 1432* (1958).

J. A. Schufle and J. E. Fletcher, Eds., *Symposium on Water Improvement (Denver, Colo.)* (Comm. on Desert and Arid Zones Research, Am. Assoc. for the Advancement of Science, Tucson, Ariz., 1963).

S. A. Schumm, "Effect of sediment characteristics on erosion and deposition in ephemeral stream channels," *U.S. Geol. Surv. Profess. Paper 352-C* (1961).

H. E. Skibitzke *et al.*, "The history of development of water supply in an arid area in the southwestern United States, Salt River Valley, Arizona," *Ground Water in Arid Zones, Intern. Assoc. Sci. Hydrol. (Athens) 57,* **2,** 706–742 (1961).

C. V. Theis, "The source of water derived from wells," *Civil Eng. (N.Y.)* **10,** 277–280 (1940).

W. C. Walton, "Selected analytical methods for well and aquifer evaluation," *Illinois State Water Surv. Bull. 49* (1962).

Minerals

A. J. Eardley, *Structural Geology of North America* (Harper & Row, New York, 1963).

A. F. Taggert, *Handbook of Mineral Dressing* (Wiley, New York, 1945).

U.S. Bureau of Mines, "Mineral facts and problems," *U.S. Bur. Mines Educ. Bull. 585* (1960).

Soils

G. V. Jacks and R. O. Whyte, *Vanishing Lands* (Doubleday, Garden City, N.Y., 1939).

C. E. Kellogg, *The Soils That Support Us* (Macmillan, New York, 1941).

G. W. Robinson, *Mother Earth* (Murby, London, 1937).

U.S. Department of Agriculture, *Soil, Yearbook Agr., U.S. Dept. Agr.* **1957** (1957).

Agriculture

A. A. Beetle, Ed., "Agricultural problems in arid and semiarid environments," *Wyoming Agr. Expt. Sta. Bull. 367* (1960).

F. E. Clements, *Plant Succession and Indicators* (Wilson, New York, 1928).

D. S. Hubbell and J. L. Gardner, "Effects of diverting sediment-laden runoff from arroyos to range and crop lands, *U.S. Dept. Agr. Tech. Bull. 1012* (1950).

R. R. Humphrey, *Range Ecology* (Ronald, New York, 1962).

K. H. W. Klages, *Ecological Crop Geography* (Macmillan, New York, 1942).

L. A. Stoddart and A. D. Smith, *Range Management* (McGraw-Hill, New York, 1942).

D. W. Thorne and H. B. Peterson, *Irrigated Soils: Their Fertility and Management* (McGraw-Hill, Blakiston Div., New York, 1954).

J. E. Weaver and F. W. Albertson, *Grasslands of the Great Plains* (Johnsen, Lincoln, Nebr., 1956).

Watersheds and Forests

J. W. Barett, Ed., *Regional Silviculture of the United States* (Ronald, New York, 1962).

E. A. Colman, *Vegetation and Watershed Management* (Ronald, New York, 1953).

S. Haden-Guest, J. K. Wright, and E. M. Teclaff, *A World Geography of Forest Resources* (Ronald, New York, 1956).

J. Kittredge, *Forest Influences* (McGraw-Hill, New York, 1948).

Society of American Foresters, *Forestry Handbook* (Ronald, New York, 1955).

U.S. Department of Agriculture, *Trees, Yearbook Agr., U.S. Dept. Agr. 1949* (1949).

————, *Water, Yearbook Agr., U.S. Dept. Agr. 1955* (1955).

U.S. Forest Service, "Timber resources for America's future," *U.S. Dept. Agr., Forest Serv., Forest Resource Rept. 14* (1958).

Native Plants and Animals

L. Benson and R. A. Darrow, *The Trees and Shrubs of the Southwestern Deserts* (Univ. of Arizona Press, Tucson, 1954).

E. L. Cockrum, *The Recent Mammals of Arizona: Their Taxonomy and Distribution* (Univ. of Arizona Press, Tucson, 1960).

E. C. Jaeger, *The North American Deserts* (Stanford Univ. Press, Stanford, Calif., 1957).

T. H. Kearney and R. H. Peebles, *Arizona Flora* (Univ. of California Press, Berkeley, 1960).

P. A. Munz, *A California Flora* (Univ. of California Press, Berkeley, 1959).

P. Train, J. R. Henrichs, and W. A. Archer, "Medicinal uses of plants by Indian tribes of Nevada," *Contributions toward a Flora of Nevada 45* (U.S. Dept. of Agriculture, Agricultural Research Service, Beltsville, Md., 1957).

Human Factors

J. Chapelle, *Nomades noirs du Sahara* (Librairie Plon, Paris, 1957).
M. Croce-Spinelli and G. Lambert, *S.O.S. Sahara* (Flammarion, Paris, 1961).
D. B. Dill, *Life, Health, and Altitude: Physiological Effects of Hot Climates and Great Heights* (Harvard Univ. Press, Cambridge, Mass., 1938).
D. H. K. Lee, *Physiological Objectives in Hot Weather Housing* (U.S. Housing and Home Finance Agency, Washington, D.C., 1953).
———, *Climate and Economic Development in the Tropics* (Harper & Row, New York, 1957).
PROHUZA (Center d'Études et d'Informations des Problemes Humains dans les Zones Arides), *Journées d'Information Medico-sociales Sahariennes* (AMG ed., Paris, 1959).
UNESCO, "The problems of the arid zone," Paris Symp., *Arid Zone Research (UNESCO)* **18** (1962).

Economics

H. H. Landsberg, L. L. Fischman, and J. L. Fisher, *Resources in America's Future* (Johns Hopkins Press, Baltimore, Md., 1963).
K. C. Nobe and A. V. Kneese, "The role of economic evaluation in planning for water resource development," *Nat. Resources J.* **2** (1963).
H. S. Perloff, E. S. Dunn, Jr., E. E. Lampard, and R. F. Muth, *Regions, Resources, and Economic Growth* (Johns Hopkins Press, Baltimore, Md., 1960).

Political and Social Institutions

W. Calef, *Private Grazing and Public Lands* (Univ. of Chicago Press, Chicago, 1960).
I. K. Fox and L. C. Crane, "Organizational arrangements for water development," *Nat. Resources J.* **2**, 1–44 (1962).
H. Kaufman, *The Forest Ranger* (Johns Hopkins Press, Baltimore, Md., 1960).

J. V. Krutilla and O. Eckstein, *Multiple-Purpose River Development: Studies in Applied Economic Analysis* (Johns Hopkins Press, Baltimore, Md., 1958).

T. T. Sasaki, *Fruitland, New Mexico: A Navajo Community in Transition* (Cornell Univ. Press, Ithaca, N.Y., 1960).

Use by Man

M. Clawson, *The Western Range Livestock Industry* (McGraw-Hill, New York, 1950).

H. C. Hart, *The Dark Missouri* (Univ. of Wisconsin Press, Madison, 1957).

C. McKinley, *Uncle Sam in the Pacific Northwest* (Univ. of California Press, Berkeley, 1952).

M. H. Saunderson, *Western Land and Water Use* (Univ. of Oklahoma Press, Norman, 1950).

R. Terral, *The Missouri Valley: Land of Drouth, Flood, and Promise* (Yale Univ. Press, New Haven, Conn., 1947).

W. L. Thomas, Jr., Ed., *Man's Role in Changing the Face of the Earth* (Univ. of Chicago Press, Chicago, 1956).

Index

Abert, J. W., 95
Abies spp. *See* Fir
Acacia, control of, 249
Acclimatization, of human beings, 353–356, 362, 363; of livestock, 250–254
Acequia. *See* Irrigation
Ackerman, E. A., 277
Adaptation, of Americans, 399; of animals, 310–312; to arid lands, 5, 239, 541–544; of human beings, 16–18; of Indians, 55, 66, 80–84; of plants, 312–314. *See also* Acclimatization
Adenine, in plant growth, 313
Adenostoma fascilatum. See Chamise
Adolph, E. F., 343, 344, 357, 360
Africa, 127, 343, 359, 360
Agave *(Agave* spp.) , 42, 325–326
Agricultural experiment stations, 105, 216, 217, 218, 222, 239, 274, 320, 539, 542
Agriculture, Census of, 266; credit in, 406, 543; failures in, 2, 47, 50, 215, 430, 539; improvements in, 217, 239, 378, 408, 541, 542; income from, 50, 386, 405, 539; land for, 404, 415–416, 485, 499; and legislation, 419; in mountains, 46; and population, 377; prehistoric, 8, 55–66; production in, 389, 432, 444, 445–446, 462, 464, 476, 550; shift away from, 381, 382, 388, 449; and statehood, 103–106; subsidization of, 398, 425; value of water in, 17, 372, 487, 488; water use in, 258, 260, 262, 392, 403, 465. *See also* Farming
Agropyron spp. *See* Grass, wheat-
Air, compressed, 182; for mineral separation, 198; movement of, 351, 361; pollution of, 18, 133, 141, 449, 451, 457, 517; sources of, 23, 42, 45, 48; temperature of, 344, 353, 357. *See also* Atmosphere

Air-conditioning, 5, 16, 18, 134, 475
Aircraft industry, 112, 379, 383, 384
Alabama, water used in, 6
Alamo (Arizona) , 150
Alamogordo (New Mexico) , 26
Alaska, 56, 479
Albedo, of earth, 151, 352
Albuquerque (New Mexico) , 30, 121, 384, 461, 491, 493, 509, 511
Alcorn, S. M., 316, 318
Aldosterone hormone, 362
Alfalfa *(Medicago sativa)* , 30, 38, 50, 226, 235, 256, 257, 259, 260, 491, 549, 553
Algae, in arid soils, 235
Algin gel, as fire retardant, 304
Algodones Dunes (California) , 25
Alkali flats, 28, 153, 177
Alkalinity. *See* pH
All-American Canal, 13, 42
Allophane, in soil, 233
Alluvium, 24, 25, 27, 33, 42, 52, 152, 193, 195, 196, 221, 436, 484, 511, 513, 514, 518
Almond, 33
Altithermal, 122
Aluminum, 173, 298
Amarillo (Texas) , 121, 190, 468
Amenities, as resources, 45, 408, 450, 451, 473
American Association for the Advancement of Science, Committee on Desert and Arid Zones Research, 123, 178
American Institute of Architects, 358, 359
American Meteorological Society, 134, 365
American Society of Heating and Ventilating Engineers, 341, 356
Amidon, E. L., 306
Ammonium, 228, 229, 235, 304